AF478479

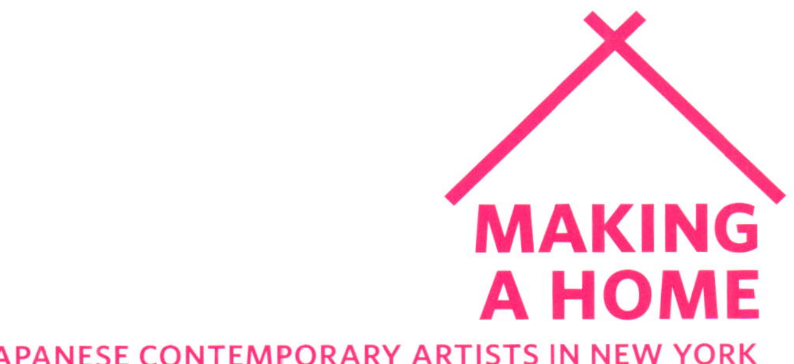
MAKING
A HOME
JAPANESE CONTEMPORARY ARTISTS IN NEW YORK

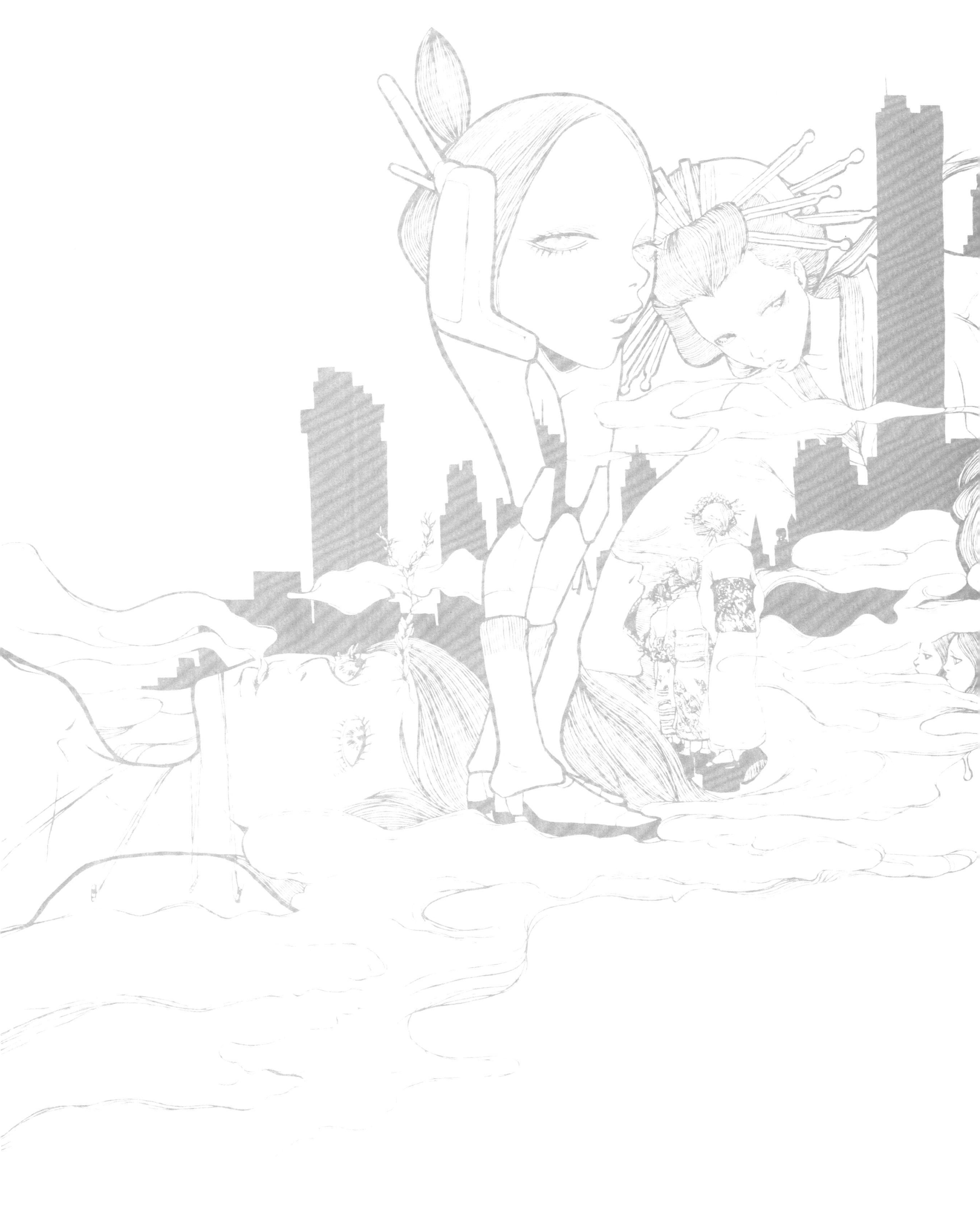

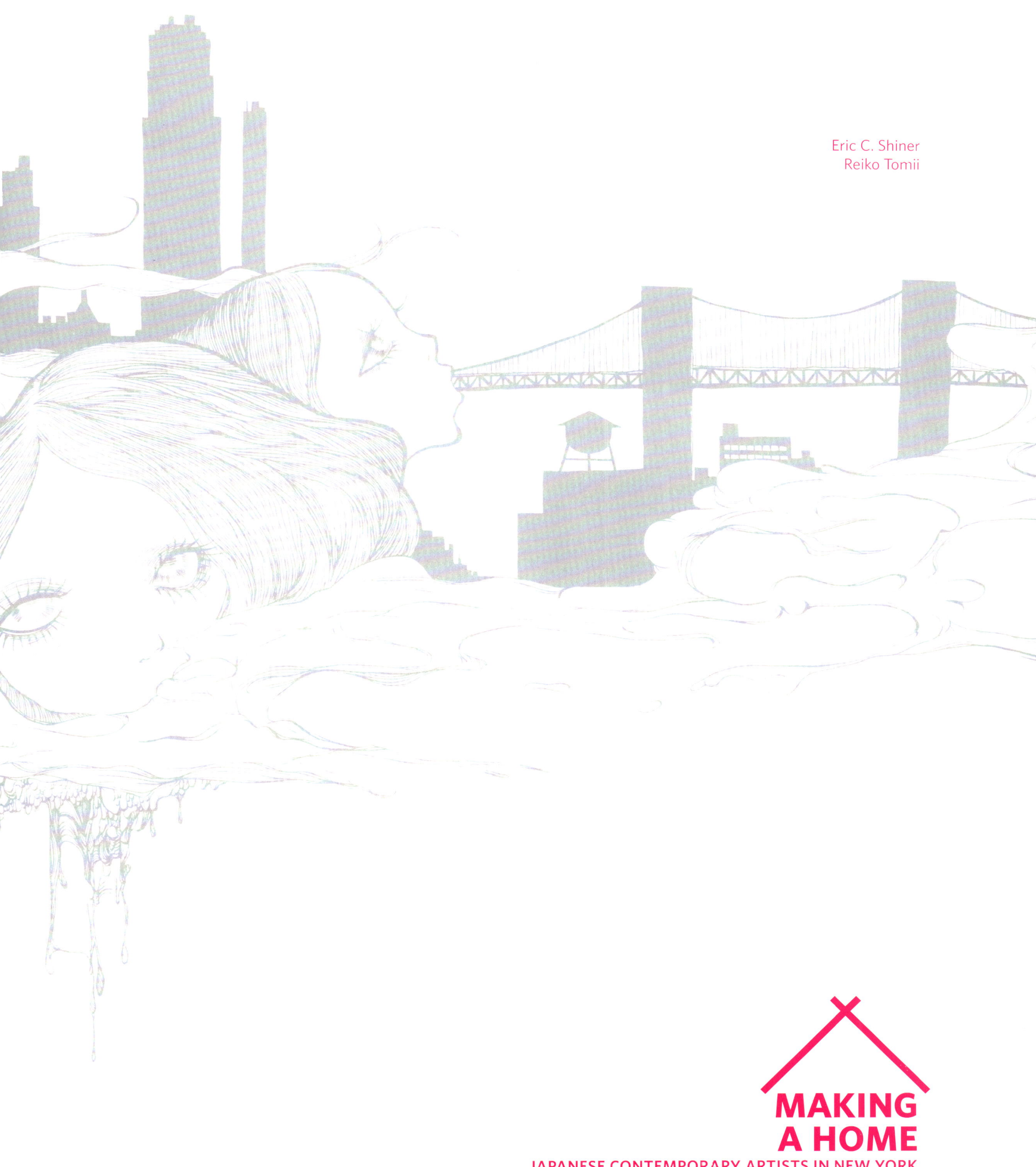

Eric C. Shiner
Reiko Tomii

MAKING A HOME
JAPANESE CONTEMPORARY ARTISTS IN NEW YORK

Published by Japan Society, New York
Distributed by Yale University Press, New Haven and London

This volume accompanies the exhibition *Making a Home: Japanese Contemporary Artists in New York*, presented at Japan Society Gallery, New York, from October 5, 2007, through January 13, 2008.

Making a Home: Japanese Contemporary Artists in New York is sponsored by

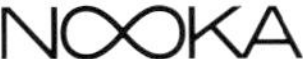

Additional support is provided by The Japan Foundation, the New York State Council on the Arts, Tug Studio, Jack and Susy Wadsworth, Chris A. Wachenheim, and the Leadership Committee for *Making a Home*.

Media sponsorship is provided by 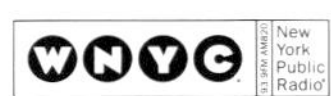

As part of the Millennium on View program, Millennium UN Plaza is the preferred hotel partner of Japan Society's Centennial.

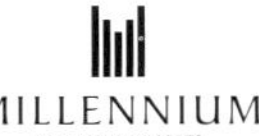

Transportation assistance is provided by 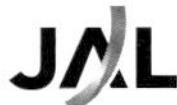

Exhibitions at Japan Society are also made possible in part by the Lila Wallace–Reader's Digest Endowment Fund and the Friends of the Gallery. Installations at Japan Society Gallery are supported by a generous gift from Henry Cornell.

Managing Editor: Reiko Tomii
Project Editor: Kathleen M. Friello
Photo Editor and Publication Liaison for Japan Society: Haruko Hoyle

Design by Berrymatch LLC.
Creative Direction: Matthew Waldman
Art Direction and Design: Yumi Asai
Assistant Design: Mieko Anekawa

Typeset in Whitney

Printed by Thames Printing Company, Norwich, CT
Bound by Acme Bookbinding, Charlestown, MA

Cover: Hiroki Ōtsuka, *Evening Calm Union*, 2007, *sumi* ink on paper, 15 x 21 ¼"
(38 x 54 cm), collection of the artist (Pl. 17.1)

ISBN: 978-0-300-12634-1 (hardbound; Yale University Press)
ISBN: 978-0-913304-60-0 (softbound; Japan Society)

Library of Congress Control Number: 2007928868
Distributed by Yale University Press for Japan Society

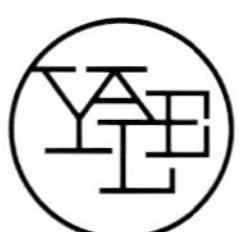

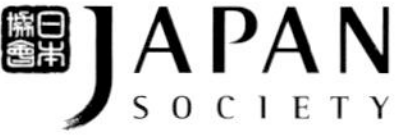

Yale University Press
302 Temple Street
P.O. Box 209040
New Haven, CT 06520-9040
www.yalebooks.com

Japan Society Gallery
333 East 47th Street
New York, NY 10017
www.japansociety.org

人

On the occasion of Japan Society's Centennial,
we dedicate this publication to
the past four directors of the Gallery:

Rand Castile (1971–1986)
Anthony Derham (1986–1989)
Gunhild Avitabile (1990–1998)
Alexandra Munroe (1998–2005)

whose service to the Gallery and
commitment to Japanese art and artists were exemplary.

It is also dedicated to
all Japanese artists in New York City, past, present, and future,
whose struggles and achievements are part of our history.

CONTENTS

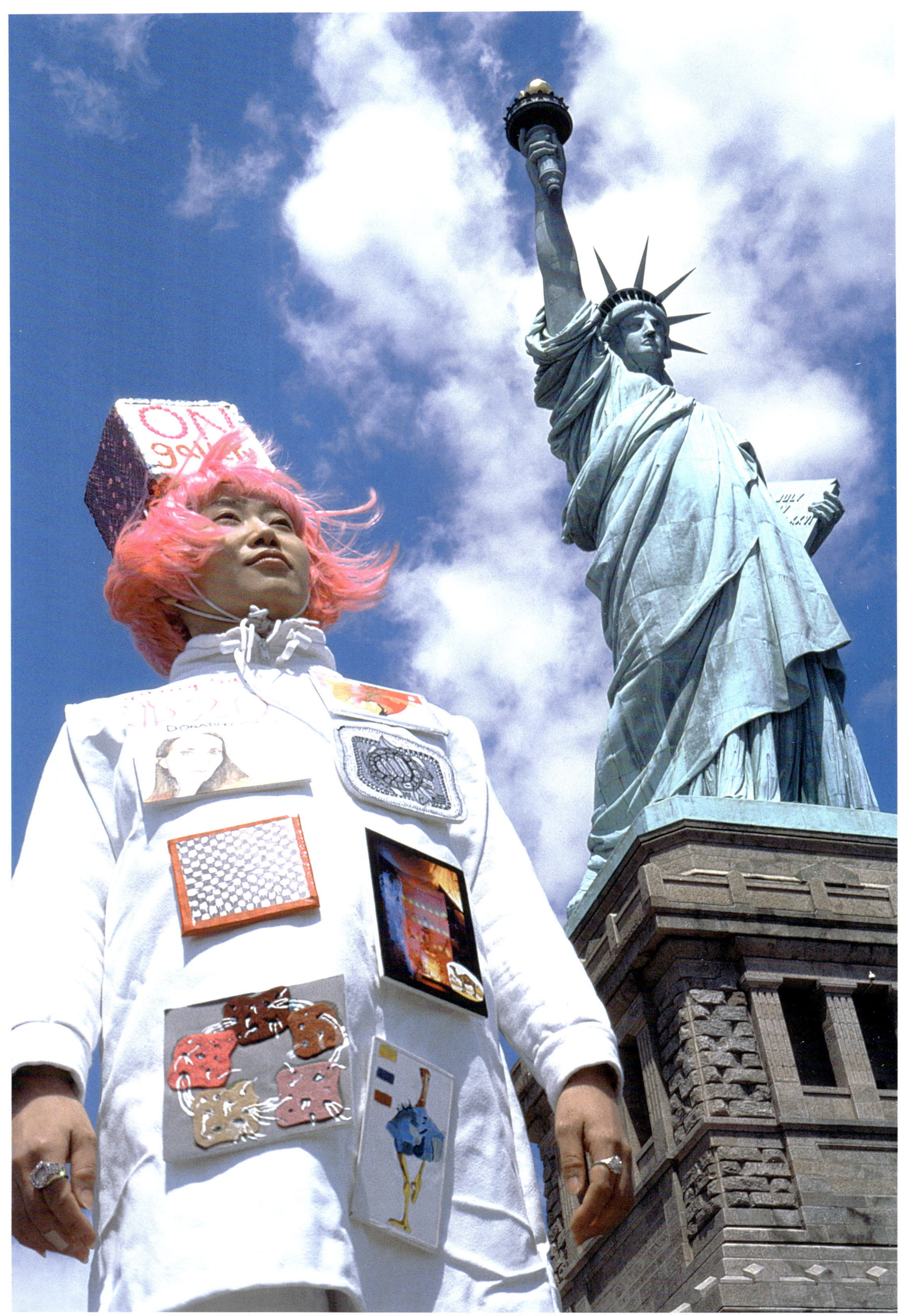
ONE
gallery

FOREWORD

RICHARD J. WOOD
President, Japan Society

Interpreting contemporary culture in Japan and the United States is a key dimension of Japan Society's mission to bring the peoples of both countries closer together. In art, as in politics, economics, science, and literature, ease of travel and communication, along with other trends in recent decades, have made that task ever more complex. Our two cultures are increasingly interpenetrated in the mix of multiple cultures that encompasses Korea, China, and Canada, among others.

Making a Home is a multi-sensory artistic exploration of the complexity of being a Japanese contemporary artist in New York City. Our guest curator, Eric C. Shiner, ruled out for this purpose Japanese Americans, Japanese who usually work in Japan but sometimes come here, or those who commute back and forth. All the featured artists have well and truly made their homes in our city.

Making a Home will be both challenging and rewarding to those who give it close attention. We hope the visitors to the Gallery enjoy this diverse and challenging aesthetic and emotional experience. Although it is "about" being Japanese artists in New York City, this presentation is not driven by a single narrative idea, as are many art exhibitions. However, a few distinctive tendencies run through the varied paintings, installations, sculptures, sound pieces, fashions, video works, photographs, and performances that have been brought together for display in Japan Society's building and elsewhere in New York. Several artists celebrate or meditate upon the physicality of the Manhattan cityscape. Others use the materials of our consumer society to create environments that allude to natural and manmade features of traditional Japan, or to interrogate the very system that brought those materials into being. Some focus on the experience of immigration and assimilation and the ways they have affected their own practice and that of fellow artists, while others document the process of making and living in a new home, creating art in it and sharing it with other Japanese artists. Some explore and parody American and European historical stereotypes; others, needless to say, triumphantly defy classification.

This ambitious project would not have been possible without the support and cooperation of its 33 participating artists. Our sincere thanks are extended to the corporate sponsors, foundations providing grants, and individuals who made the exhibition possible.

Japan Society is deeply indebted to guest curator Eric C. Shiner, whose dynamic ideas and inexhaustible energy proved incalculable assets in the realization of this exhibition. We are fortunate to have the independent scholar Reiko Tomii on the team, who not only co-authored this volume but also directed the whole conceptual and editorial process of bringing the publication to fruition.

Together with the guest curator, I would like to thank Executive Vice President and Interim Director of the Gallery Kendall Hubert, who tirelessly worked for the completion of this project and Joe Earle, Vice-President and Gallery Director designate, who provided valuable advice.

Last but not least, to the wisdom of my predecessor as President, Frank Ellsworth, we owe the selection of this exhibition celebrating the Centennial of Japan Society.

FIGURE 1.1

ON megumi Akiyoshi
ON gallery at The Statue of Liberty
2002
Performance by artist in costume
exhibiting a group show
Dimensions variable
Collection of the artist
PHOTO: OLIVER IRWIN

ACKNOWLEDGEMENTS

KENDALL HUBERT
Executive Vice President and Interim Director of the Gallery, Japan Society

It was in 1974 that Japan Society Gallery, then known as Japan House Gallery, presented its first exhibition of "new art" comprising the works of living artists, entitled *Ikeda & Ida: Two New Japanese Print Makers*. Since then, contemporary art has been one of the Gallery's main areas of investigation. The current exhibition, *Making a Home: Japanese Contemporary Artists in New York*, guest-curated by Eric C. Shiner, marks the Gallery's 94th exhibition and celebrates Japan Society's Centennial.

By far this exhibition is one of the Gallery's most ambitious undertakings, presenting 33 Japanese-born artists who have made the city of New York their home. We would like to express our utmost appreciation to all the artists in the exhibition, whose dedication and enthusiasm for this endeavor have made it a truly collaborative project. Lenders, separately listed on a following page, graciously agreed to loan their precious treasures, for which we are immensely thankful. Organizing an exhibition is an inexact science: this exhibition is a tribute to the art of the participating artists as much as to that of hundreds, perhaps thousands, of other Japanese artists who live and work in New York, whose achievements and struggles never left our mind throughout this project.

Japan Society is deeply indebted to the corporations, foundations, individuals, and government agencies whose generous support has been key to the realization of an exhibition of this scope and magnitude. *Making a Home* is sponsored by Nooka, with additional corporate support from participating sponsor Tug Studio. We are also indebted to Japan Airlines for their ongoing and critical transportation support of the Gallery. Japan Society would like to thank The Japan Foundation, the New York State Council on the Arts, Jack and Susy Wadsworth, and Chris A. Wachenheim for their very special support of the Centennial exhibition. The Society also wishes to thank the members of the *Making a Home* Leadership Committee for their commitment to this project; the devoted committee includes Susan Hancock, Aaron Nir and Satoko Miyake, Masako and Jim Shinn, Chris A. Wachenheim, Jack and Susy Wadsworth, Charles T. Danziger, Thomas Danziger and Laura B. Whitman, and an anonymous individual. Japan Society thanks WNYC New York Public Radio and LTB Media for their support as media sponsors of the 100th Anniversary, and Millennium Hotels and Resorts, in particular Diarmaid O'Sullivan, former Director of Cultural Programs, for support throughout the Centennial.

Exhibitions at Japan Society are made possible in part by the Lila Acheson Wallace–Reader's Digest Endowment Fund and the Friends of the Gallery. We would like to acknowledge Henry Cornell for his support of installations at Japan Society Gallery.

We express our profound gratitude to Yoko Ono for her enormous contribution to Japan Society and for lending her important work to the institution as part of *Making a Home*. The Ono family has a long history with the Society. Her grandfather Eijirō Ono was the first Treasurer of Japan Society in 1907; her father Yeisuke Ono served on the Japan Society Board of Directors from 1955 to 1958. Ms. Ono became involved with Japan Society in the 1960s as she was starting her career in New York, and later became the featured artist of the widely acclaimed Japan Society exhibition *YES YOKO ONO*, which opened in New York in 2000 and traveled to twelve venues worldwide over the following three years.

Japan Society's commitment to Japanese contemporary art has a long history. By definition, contemporary art renews itself constantly, especially so in this globalizing age. To be "in sync" with its quickly changing scenery, we need the fresh eye of a keen observer, which is provided by Eric C. Shiner, the guest curator of *Making a Home*. He has brought to this project his abiding interest in the contemporary art of Asia and beyond, his broad network of artists, curators, critics, collectors, and gallerists, and his dynamic personality, in order to successfully pull together this massive exhibition with 33 living artists.

He was joined by his senior colleague Reiko Tomii, who has closely consulted with him from the onset of this exhibition project. A leader of the field of post-1945 Japanese art history and *sensei* to many of us, Dr. Tomii co-authored this volume and served as managing editor. Japan Society is immensely indebted to her for her continuing support of this institution, her rigorous scholarship, and her unending dedication to Japanese contemporary art. Midori Yamamura's critical biography on Kusama Yayoi is an invaluable addition to this publication, helping us understand the contributions of this important Japanese artist to the history of 1960s art in New York. Co-authors Shiner and Tomii assembled an impressive panel of curators, scholars, and writers who contributed entry texts on the participating artists. They are Luis Camnitzer, Kevin Concannon, Jonathan Goodman, Ryan Holmberg, Hiroko Ikegami, Yukie Kamiya, Caleb Kelly, Barbara

London, Alexandra Munroe, Yasufumi Nakamori, Miwako Tezuka, Shinya Watanabe, and Midori Yoshimoto. Sachiko Hisajima capably created a massive compilation of the participating artists' data. Profiles of these contributors are included at the end of this volume. Together with the co-authors, they represent a small but growing community of specialists who are seriously engaged in the study of Japanese and Asian contemporary art.

The book's editorial team consisted of two veterans of past Japan Society Gallery projects, Dr. Tomii and Kathleen M. Friello, whose professional contribution dates back to the exhibition *Enlightenment Embodied: The Art of the Japanese Buddhist Sculptor (7th–14th Centuries)* organized by the third gallery director Gunhild Avitabile in 1997. While Dr. Tomii served as Managing Editor and directed the overall editorial operations, Ms. Friello, as Project Editor, expertly edited the volume, giving critical attention and steadfast care to the project and bringing a fine sense of language to her work. She also compiled the Index, assisted by Sachiko Hisajima. Haruko Hoyle, Gallery Officer, doubled as Photo Editor and Publication Liaison for Japan Society, competently attending to countless and complex administrative details.

The *Making a Home* catalogue continues the tradition of innovative scholarship in contemporary art long cultivated at Japan Society Gallery. We are honored to have Yale University Press as our publication partner, distributing this volume as the latest of our collaborations. We are grateful to Patricia J. Fidler, Publisher, Art and Architecture, and Carmel M. Lyons, Art Book Publishing Coordnator, for their enthusiastic and continuing support of the present volume. The book's inventive and contemporary design was created by Berrymatch LLC's Creative Director, Matthew Waldman, and Art Director, Yumi Asai, with assistance from designer Mieko Anekawa.

Curatorial vision always requires a team of professionals who know how to turn an idea into a physical reality. We thank Thomas Morbitzer and Goil Amornvivat of Tug Studio for their creative installation design, which changed a gallery space into an intimate home setting. Scott Hoefer and his staff at Insight Group masterfully fabricated the installation architecture. Chief art handler for this exhibition was Jon Newman. Miko McGinty and Christine Knorr, Manager, Graphic Design & Production at Japan Society, handled exhibition graphics. Casey Collier and Haruna Ōtsuka worked as Exhibition Interns.

︿

Studying and exhibiting contemporary art requires an ongoing engagement not only with individual artists but also with a larger community that supports them on many different levels. On behalf of Mr. Shiner, Japan Society would like to thank his curatorial colleagues for their advice and support given to him during the course of this project: Barbara London, Curator, Department of Film and Video,

The Museum of Modern Art, New York; Denise Markonish, Curator, Massachusetts Museum of Contemporary Art; Alexandra Munroe, Senior Curator of Asian Art, Guggenheim Museum; Christopher Phillips, Curator, International Center of Photography; Maura Reilly, Curator, Elizabeth A. Sackler Center for Feminist Art, Brooklyn Museum; and Elizabeth Thomas, Matrix Curator of Contemporary Art, University of California, Berkeley Art Museum & Pacific Film Archive. We also thank these colleagues for their friendship and advice: the artists Bingyi Huang, Susan Kleinberg, Naoto Nakagawa, and Jane Philbrick; and Katsuya Isnida, Naomi Koyama, and Tomio Koyama in Japan. He is also blessed with the generous support and advice of Sophie Crichton-Stuart, Susan Hancock, Dr. Michael Jacobs, Claire Montgomery, Kristine Russell, Nancy Seltzer, and Larry Warsh.

We thank the following galleries in New York and elsewhere for their assistance in securing works and assisting the *Making a Home* artists in many ways: Josée Bienvenu Gallery; Ethan Cohen Fine Arts; James Corcoran Gallery, Los Angeles, especially Tracy Lew Kawaguchi; Kravets/Wehby Gallery; Marlborough Gallery; Mehr Gallery; Robert Miller Gallery, especially Peter Miller and Royce Howes; M.Y. Art Prospects, especially Miyako Yoshinaga; SCAI The Bathhouse, Tokyo; Leslie Tonkonow Artworks + Projects; Zabriskie Gallery; and Zone: Chelsea Center for the Arts.

The collaboration with other institutions was vital to realizing the expansive vision embraced by this exhibition. We thank RoseLee Goldberg and her staff for their support of Ei Arakawa's project *BYOF (Bring Your Own Flowers)*, presented at *Performa 2007*; Claire Montgomery and the entire staff of Location One for their generous contribution of studio space for Yoshiaki Kaihatsu; the Getty Research Institute, Los Angeles and PoNJA-GenKon for their support of Ushio Shinohara's *Boxing Painting*; and the Absolut Vodka Art & Fashion Collection, especially Marion Kahan, Curator, for lending the mannequins for United Bamboo's installation.

Individual artists received in-kind support and other assistance in realizing their projects for the exhibition. The participating artists' individual acknowledgements are found at the end of this volume. In particular, we would like to thank AROMAC Co. Ltd. for the donation of optical fiber for Nobuho Nagasawa's *Bodywaves*; and Arnold Reception Desks, Inc. for the donation of the desk for Momoyo Torimitsu's *Willingly or Unwillingly, You Are Welcome*. The wall covering for the "painting salon" section is provided by Innovations.

︿

The accomplishments of Japan Society Gallery have been built through the vision, creativity, and hard work of its past directors and their staff. This dedication and passion have widened the understanding and study of Japan and its visual culture around the world. Japan Society is deeply grateful to those who have contributed to this heritage as Gallery Director—Rand Castile,

Anthony Derham, Gunhild Avitabile, and Alexandra Munroe—who together have built an extraordinary legacy.

During the course of this exhibition project, Japan Society was very pleased to appoint and announce Joe Earle as a new Vice President and Director of Japan Society Gallery. An exhibition of this size and magnitude is not uncomplicated at any institution; the Society is thankful for his insight and consultation on the final stages of this Centennial exhibition.

Japan Society is also grateful to the extraordinary guidance and support of the Art Advisory Committee chaired by Sam Sachs.

From the current gallery staff, we are grateful to Haruko Hoyle, Gallery Officer, for her continuous and immense hard work, dedication, and good cheer. She has tirelessly and capably managed the publications, press, operations, and general support of the Gallery. This exhibition would not be what it is without her. We are also grateful to Miho Fang, Gallery Assistant, for providing critical support to the Gallery's operations. Japan Society wishes to express its deep gratitude to Marion Kahan, Project Exhibition Manager, for her great expertise and professionalism in exhibitions management for this and other exhibitions at Japan Society during our Centennial year.

An exhibition with 33 living artists also requires extraordinary care in legal counsel. For this we would like to thank Danziger & Danziger, particularly Tom and Charles Danziger, for their excellent counsel for this and other Japan Society exhibitions.

I would also like to thank Blue Medium, our public relations firm for Japan Society's Centennial and this exhibition. In particular, I would like to thank John Melick, President, for his insight and creativity in approach to publicity and promotions, together with his excellent team, Antoine Vigne and Kellie Honeycutt, who have been dedicated advocates and excellent publicists for Japan Society and the Gallery.

Japan Society wishes to thank Dr. Frank Ellsworth, former President, for his contribution to Centennial planning and his foresight and support of this project from its inception, as well as current President Dr. Richard J. Wood for his enlightened and constant advocacy, together with that of the Board of Directors, in support of this exhibition. They were joined by the Japan Society Centennial Honorary Committee, co-chaired by David Rockefeller and Dr. Shōichirō Toyoda. We also thank Ray Cochran, Vice President of Finance and Administration and Treasurer; Juan Montes, Chief Information Officer; Ruri Kawashima, Tokyo Representative; Ann Niehoff, Director of Government and Foundation Relations; Jamie Brown, Director of Corporate Giving; Karen Sorensen, Director of Individual Giving; Yoko Suzuki, Director of Special Events and Assistant to the President for Community Relations; and other members of the Development staff, whose efforts have contributed greatly to the realization of this project.

Japan Society dedicates the second major exhibition of its anniversary year to the experiences of Japanese artists coming to and living in New York, further enhancing and expanding the scope of Japan Society's Centennial, which involves all of New York City, whether in the area of performing arts, film, or visual arts, in a city-wide celebration of Japan, the Society, and the Japanese arts across New York. This expansive exhibition programming will be accompanied by a wide variety of public and educational events, including public lectures, panels, performing art events, film screenings, and programs for teachers and students. For this we thank Daniel Rosenblum, Vice President and Director of Corporate and Policy Programs; Yoko Shioya, Artistic Director and Director of Performing Arts; Dr. Robert Fish, Director of Education; Shannon Jowett, Director of Communication; Jason Cremerius, Director of Digital Media; and Reiko Sassa, Director of the Language Center; as well as all staff and departments whose hard work has contributed to the successful planning of the integrated activities and communications related to this exhibition and Japan Society's Centennial.

LENDERS TO THE EXHIBITION

Dorothy and Martin Bandier

Robinson and Nancy Grover

Jeremy Kost

Dr. and Mrs. Thomas Loeb

Lewis and Diana Meyers

Craig Robins

Ann Schaffer

Whitney Museum of American Art, New York

Private collections

NOTES TO THE READER

1 Japanese Language

In transliterating the Japanese language, the modified Hepburn Romanization system has been employed. The notable deviation from the original Hepburn is the use of "n" before b, m, and p (e.g., *shinbun*).

Macrons are used to indicate long vowels in Japanese names and words, as a guide to pronunciation (e.g., Haryū Ichirō, *happō*). Commonly known names and words adopted into English are given without macrons (e.g., Tokyo, Yoko Ono).

Exceptions are made for the names of participating artists, where sanctioned by the Ministry of Foreign Affairs of Japan for passport use (e.g., Ambe, Ayakoh).

2 Name Order

Japanese and other East Asian names are given in the traditional order, surname first. Exceptions are made in the case of individuals who primarily reside outside their native countries *and* adopt the Western system; their names are listed in the Index as inverted (e.g., "Noriko Ambe" in text; "Ambe, Noriko" in Index). When in doubt, the reader is advised to consult the Index to confirm the name order.

3 Captions

All work titles are given in English. Unless otherwise noted, dimensions of works are given in order of height by width for two-dimensional objects, and height by width by depth for three-dimensional objects.

4 Works in the Exhibition

In the Plates section, captions accompanied by ⟨ are either in the exhibition or related to works in the exhibition (e.g., different versions or studies). The reader is advised to consult the checklist which may be found at www.japansociety.org for the final list of works in the exhibition.

5 Interviews with Participating Artists

The Plates section includes excerpts from interviews with the participating artists, accompanied by abbreviated questions. The full interview questions are as follows:

1 When did you first realize that you wanted to be an artist, and what motivated you to pursue that dream?

2 Why did you decide to leave Japan to pursue your career as an artist?

3 Why did you choose New York as your ultimate destination? Did you come directly, or did you live elsewhere before settling here?

4 Please discuss your first days in New York City. What was your initial impression?

5 How long did it take you to establish your art career here? What difficulties did you face? What were the highlights of your first interactions with the New York art world?

6 Did you have any interactions with other artists or supporters that were especially beneficial to you and your work?

7 How has your work changed since living in New York? Has your style changed significantly? Are you influenced more by Japanese aesthetics, or by global trends?

8 Please discuss the experience that gave you the most satisfaction as an artist in New York.

9 Do you ever regret leaving Japan? If so, why?

10 How has your experience as a New York–based Japanese artist influenced your thinking on globalism, migration and the international art world? Do you consider yourself to be a Japanese artist, an American artist, an international artist, or a hybrid of all three?

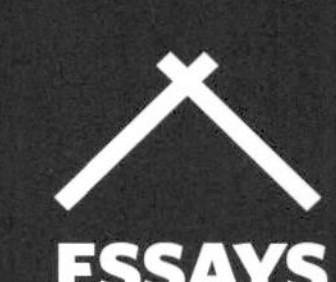
ESSAYS

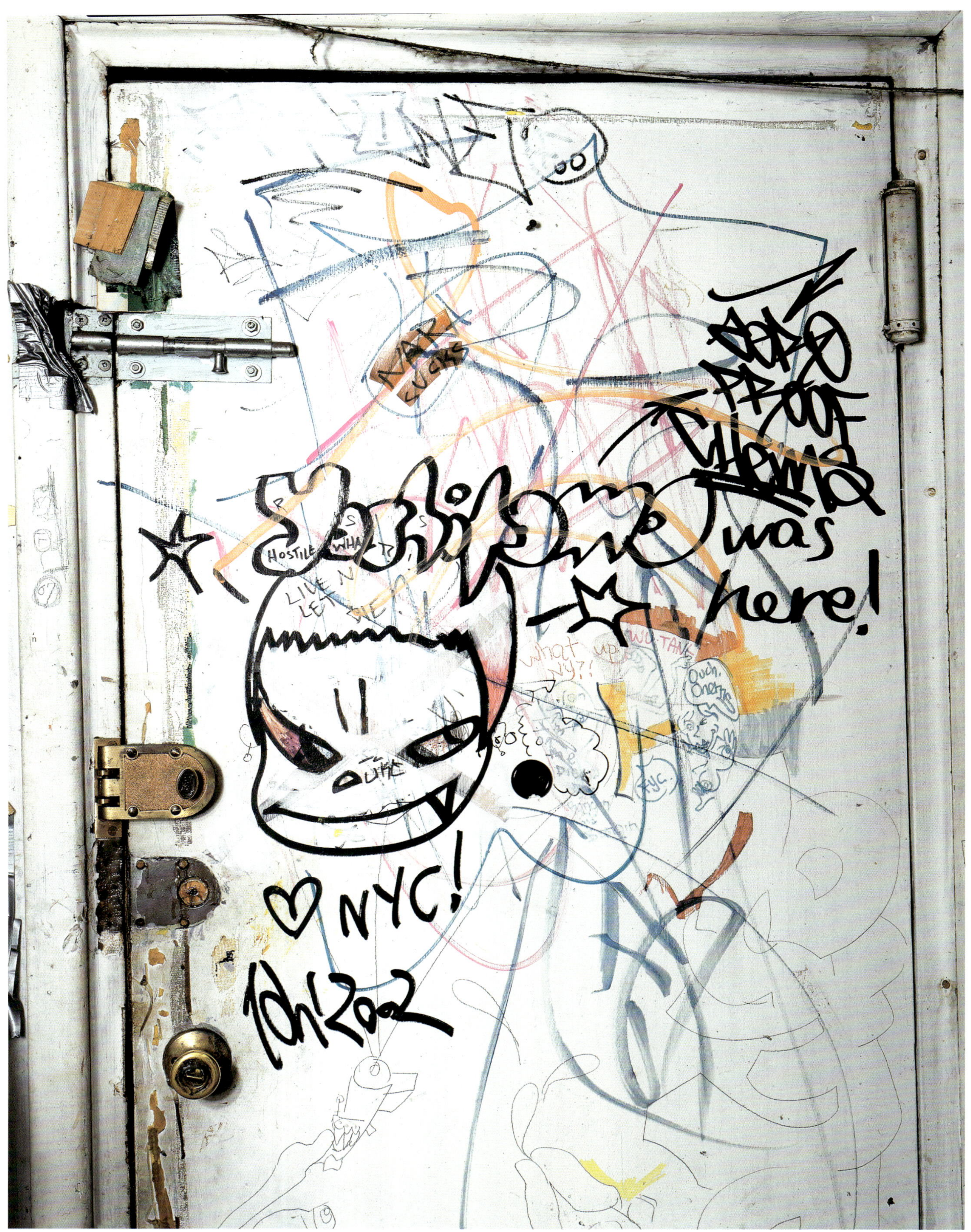

NAR SUCKS
HOSTILE WHAT IS
LIVE N
LET DIE
WU-TANG
what up NY?!
Ouch, Onette
NYC
was here!
NYC!
Ph 2002

BORDER-CROSSINGS
A Preface to the Exhibition

REIKO TOMII

In this age of globalism, an internationally minded artist has seemingly countless options when selecting a home base in which to live and work—Tokyo, Paris, Berlin, London, or New York; Mumbai, Johannesburg, Shanghai, Seoul, Sydney, Rio de Janeiro, or Mexico City. It may not be an overstatement to say that "migration itself is not an issue unless you are in a situation like political exile," as observed by the seasoned avant-garde musician Yasunao Tone, who is included in the current exhibition, *Making a Home: Japanese Contemporary Artists in New York*. Still, as some other artists in the exhibition recount their lives and careers, the location of one's home is determined as much by fate as choice. This feels especially true with New York.

New York has long held a special allure for artists and non-artists alike, even before the center of the international art world shifted across the Atlantic Ocean, from Paris to Gotham, in the 1950s.

> New York is the thing that seduced me.
> New York is the thing that formed me.
> New York is the thing that deformed me.
> New York is the thing that perverted me.
> New York is the thing that converted me.
> And New York is the thing that I love too.[1]

When musician-poet Patti Smith, a native of Chicago, composed this tender poem, she gave words to the sentiment of many transplanted New Yorkers, the *Making a Home* artists included. Featuring "New York" as an encompassing framework, this exhibition first and foremost pays tribute to the transformative power that permeates the city, which has been the home of the exhibition's organizing institution, Japan Society, for the past 100 years.

New York is the adopted home of the 33 Japanese-born contemporary artists represented in this exhibition. By coming to this metropolis, they have expanded their horizons to varying degrees. Among this diverse set of artists, Miwa Koizumi, who began her professional life outside Japan in Paris, evocatively explains what New York means to her:

> In France I was already *broken* (my identity was transformed). And in New York I have been broken again and again. There is so much variety and so much change that I can be broken every day. In France I could have a relationship with "French culture." In New York, there are no containers, there is no center or middle. Every day, I have to ask, Who am I? and Where am I? I have to ask, How do I relate to the rest? I always had trouble fitting into pigeonholes. Here there are no containers. I can be as complex and different as I like.[2]

Although individual experiences of New York differ from artist to artist, this sense of "stepping out of one's culture and seeing afresh what has been familiar"[3] is an undercurrent running through the interviews of the participating artists conducted for this publication, as much as the sense of freedom they embrace in New York away from the confines of Japanese society and culture they were born into. (Excerpts from these interviews, including Tone's above statement, are included in the Plates section.) In this sense, these artists have not only crossed the border that separates countries geographically; they have also crossed the border emotionally, an experience which no doubt feeds into their work. The more years one spends in this city, the more one loves (or hates or love-hates) it. When asked what New York meant to her, another *Making a Home* artist, Yoko Ono, gave a succinct yet poignant answer that could only be said with more than three decades of making the city her permanent home.

> It's where I gave my blood, sweat and tears. It's my home.

More importantly, what connects many of the artists in this exhibition, characterized by generational and artistic diversity, is the spirit of border-crossing in their art that manifests itself conceptually, aesthetically, strategically. This trait marks their practices as genuinely "contemporary," as does their critical engagement with the urgent issues of our contemporary life, which is examined by the exhibition's guest curator, Eric C. Shiner, in his walk-through introduction that follows this preface.

Yoko Ono exemplifies three strategic aspects of border-crossing present in the exhibition: interdisciplinary approaches, interactions with or interests in the public sphere, and collaborations with others. Throughout her career that began in New York in the late 1950s, Ono has "mov[ed] sometimes indistinguishably between art and music," as observed by Kevin Concannon. (See

---

FIGURE 2.1

Nara Yoshitomo
♡ *NYC!*
2002
Drawing on front door of Ushio and
Noriko Shinohara's residence in
Brooklyn. Drawings underneath are by
Alex Shinohara

his full discussion of her work accompanying Ono's Plates in this catalogue.) Fluidly traversing different disciplines, she managed to engage a broader audience by often operating outside the confines of art and advocating utopian social ideals. Significantly, just as she waged a campaign for peace with her husband John Lennon through her *Bed-Ins* and *War Is Over!* in the midst of the Vietnam War in the late 1960s, she has undertaken the campaign *Imagine Peace* since the onset of the current Iraqi War for the community of the whole world. *Wish Tree*, first realized in 1996 and included in this exhibition, has became a vital component of her peace campaign, soliciting active participation from the viewer and thus creating a site of collaboration, a mode of action conducive to peace (Pl. 16.3).

A bridge between vanguard art and experimental music was also made by Yasunao Tone, Ono's colleague of the Tokyo Fluxus group. With the novel rubric "sound art" frequently categorizing his work today, time has finally caught up with the pioneering and inventive exploration of new technology he began in the mid-1960s, when it was called "intermedia." He ingeniously combines imagery and sound in his performance of *Molecular Music* (his contrarian take on "electronic music"), as well as creating what can be called "portable installations"[4] through his CDs, such as *Yasunao Tone* (Asphodel 2011) from 2003 (Pls. 27.1–3; not in the exhibition).

Architecture and fashion are two creative disciplines attracting interdisciplinary interest in contemporary art today. On a modest scale, Katsuhiro Saiki reinterprets New York's skyscrapers through his photography-cum-sculpture, while another photographer, Mayumi Terada, functions as an architect of miniature structures (Pls. 18.1, 25.1–8). In contrast, Yumi Kōri, a licensed architect, contributes to visual art her inspired expertise of manipulating space and light (Pls. 13.1–5). A heightened fashion consciousness, pervasive to the global mix of contemporary art, is embodied by the designer duo United Bamboo, who frequently offer exhibition opportunities to visual artists through, most notably, their collaborative T-shirt design projects (Pl. 30.4). *Making a Home* artist Hiroshi Sunairi curated one such exhibition in 2003. (For individual artists' biographies and activities, see the Artists' Data section that follows the Plates section.)

The interaction with the public sphere also originated in 1960s art. One pioneer who led what was art-critically termed the "descent to the everyday" (*nichijōsei eno kakō*)[5] was Ushio Shinohara, the third avant-garde giant represented in *Making a Home* who emerged during that crucial decade of contemporary art. His *Boxing Painting*—which he has frequently performed before a live audience at museums and galleries for the past 10 years—was more than an original artistic expression (Pl. 21.2). In 1961, he chose to perform *Boxing Painting* before the eye of the mass media in his sober reckoning of the commercially "rewardless" (*mushō*)

nature of vanguard art; he sought his reward instead in the form of publicity in the public sphere.[6] It was a brilliant move by Shinohara at a time when contemporary art asserted its feisty existence at the periphery of mainstream culture.

Today, engagement with the public sphere by contemporary artists takes many different forms. Social, cultural, and historical references abound in the exhibition, as the artists typically confront pressing contemporary issues. In a more direct manner, Yōichirō Yoda and Nobuho Nagasawa act as a sociologist and an archaeologist conducting field research in local communities—be it Times Square or Sharjah, United Arab Emirates—and bring their researches back to the realm of art (Pls. 33.1.–7, 14.3). In a more whimsical vein, ON megumi Akiyoshi transforms herself into *ON gallery*, bringing an exhibition to the streets in critique of the commercial gallery system (Fig. 1.1). With her portable gallery, there is no art form that cannot be displayed; she even puts an engulfing room-size installation on her body (Pls. 1.2–3). While the street likewise becomes a site of performance for Momoyo Torimitsu, who takes her corporate-warrior robot for a crawl (Fig. 3.1), the city is a scavenging ground for Yoshiaki Kaihatsu, who builds a teahouse from discarded polystyrene foam packaging (Pls. 8.2–3). What makes his teahouse "Japanese" is not so much his appropriation of Japan's traditional culture as his reference to its advanced recycling culture.

Collaboration calls into question the modern notions of "solitary author" and "originality," opening up the act of making art as a shared experience. Collaboration and collectivism are indeed a strong suit of Japanese contemporary art, not because of the so-called "group conformity" mentality of the Japanese people, but in spite of it. Or, more precisely, contemporary artists in postwar Japan have learned from historical precedents of collectivism and have continued to reformulate it since the 1960s onward.[7]

Among the *Making a Home* artists, Ei Arakawa embraces a fluid conception of "group" in his attempt to destabilize the self and identity (Pls. 3.2–4). Working within various local communities, Nagasawa often practices a participatory collectivism to create a tangible vision for an invisible community, as she demonstrates in *her render: she gives back naturally what is true in her nature*. Emiko Kasahara's *SHEER*, premiered at Japan Society, presents her collaboration with volunteers who gave testimonies about their memories of loss (Pl. 10.1). For the volunteer, giving such a testimony in his or her native tongue in solitude can be a deeply unsettling yet cathartic experience; for each of us, listening to it through a nipple-shaped terminal will be an equally secretive and moving experience, even if we do not understand the particular language. An invisible community is thus created through giving and receiving the voices of sorrow.

Ultimately, the most salient feature of contemporary art is the ongoing redefinition and reinvention of the practice itself. The study of contemporary art accordingly has to expand itself. In recent critical discourse, "diaspora" is a keyword of global contemporary art that helps us comprehend a matrix of artistic communities formed outside a homeland by emigrants and their descendents. In Japanese art history, a diasporal perspective has just begun to emerge. Japanese contemporary art in New York is at once an extension of the Japanese art world and a significant part of the New York art world. The convergence of two locales in this diaspora will require a double vision, in fact a multiple vision, as New York is but one among many diasporas of Japanese contemporary art.

The 33 Japanese artists in *Making a Home* are already living the reality of diaspora, aware of a multifaceted community forming around them. In their interview responses, many have acknowledged the support of their artist-friends and others, often non-Japanese, in New York. (Another shared response was an emphatic "No!" almost across the board to the question, "Do you ever regret leaving Japan?") A diasporal formation is exemplified by Kunie Sugiura's photogram series, *The Artist Papers*, which memorialized her respect and kinship for fellow New York artists, Japanese-born or otherwise (Pls. 23.1, 23.3–4).

Also memorable is an impromptu drawing made by Nara Yoshitomo, an occasional New York visitor, on the front door of Ushio and Noriko Shinohara's residence-studio in Brooklyn in 2002 (Fig. 2.1). The graffiti-like drawing resulted from a chance meeting of Noriko, a *Making a Home* artist, with Nara at the opening reception of *Kazari: Decoration and Display in Japan, 15th–19th Centuries*, held at Japan Society in October 2002.[8] She struck up a conversation with him and found a kindred spirit in the younger artist. (Noriko's interest in German Expressionism resonated with Nara's long residency in Germany.) The following night, she attended his gallery opening in Chelsea and he in turn dropped by her home the next day, while making the rounds of the Dumbo Art Festival in her neighborhood.

It is notable that since the onset of the *Making a Home* project, this sense of community has further grown, as the participating artists have come to know each other, adding other participants into their networking and vice versa. The expansion of the diasporal community is another positive outcome of their border-crossings, indicating that we have surely reached a certain threshold in the history of Japanese contemporary art. This exhibition at once acknowledges this historic moment and plays a part in it.

Notes

1   Smith recited this poem during an interview by the BBC in 1971. This footage was recently incorporated in a documentary film directed by James Crump, *Black White + Gray* (2007), and quoted in Philip Gefter, "The Man Who Made Mapplethorpe: A Film Trains a Lens on the Photography Collector Sam Wagstaff," *New York Times*, April 24, 2007.

2   Miwa Koizumi, e-mail to author, May 25, 2007.

3   Koizumi, telephone interview with author, June 5, 2007.

4   Yasunao Tone, e-mail to Haruko Hoyle, June 13, 2007.

5   For the art critical discourse surrounding the public sphere in 1960s Japan, see Reiko Tomii, "*Geijutsu* on Their Minds: Memorable Words on Anti-Art," in *Art, Anti-Art, Non-Art: Experimentations in the Public Sphere in Postwar Japan, 1950–1970*, ed. Charles Merewether with Rika Iezumi Hiro, exh. cat. (Los Angeles: Getty Research Institute, 2007), especially, 39–41.

6   Ibid., 49–53. The video of *Boxing Painting* included in *Making a Home* was produced at the Getty Center in Los Angeles on April 27, 2007, as part of the "Day 1: Film Screenings and Live Performances" program of the three-day conference, ラジカル！ *(Rajikaru!) Experimentations in Japanese Art 1950–1975*, co-organized by the Getty Research Institute and PoNJA-GenKon, in conjunction with the exhibition *Art, Anti-Art, Non-Art*.

7   Tomii, "After the 'Descent to the Everyday': Japanese Collectivism from Hi Red Center to The Play, 1964–1973," in *Collectivism After Modernism*, ed. Blake Stimson and Gregory Sholette (Minneapolis: University of Minnesota Press, 2007), 44–75.

8   Noriko Shinohara, telephone interview with author, June 14, 2007.

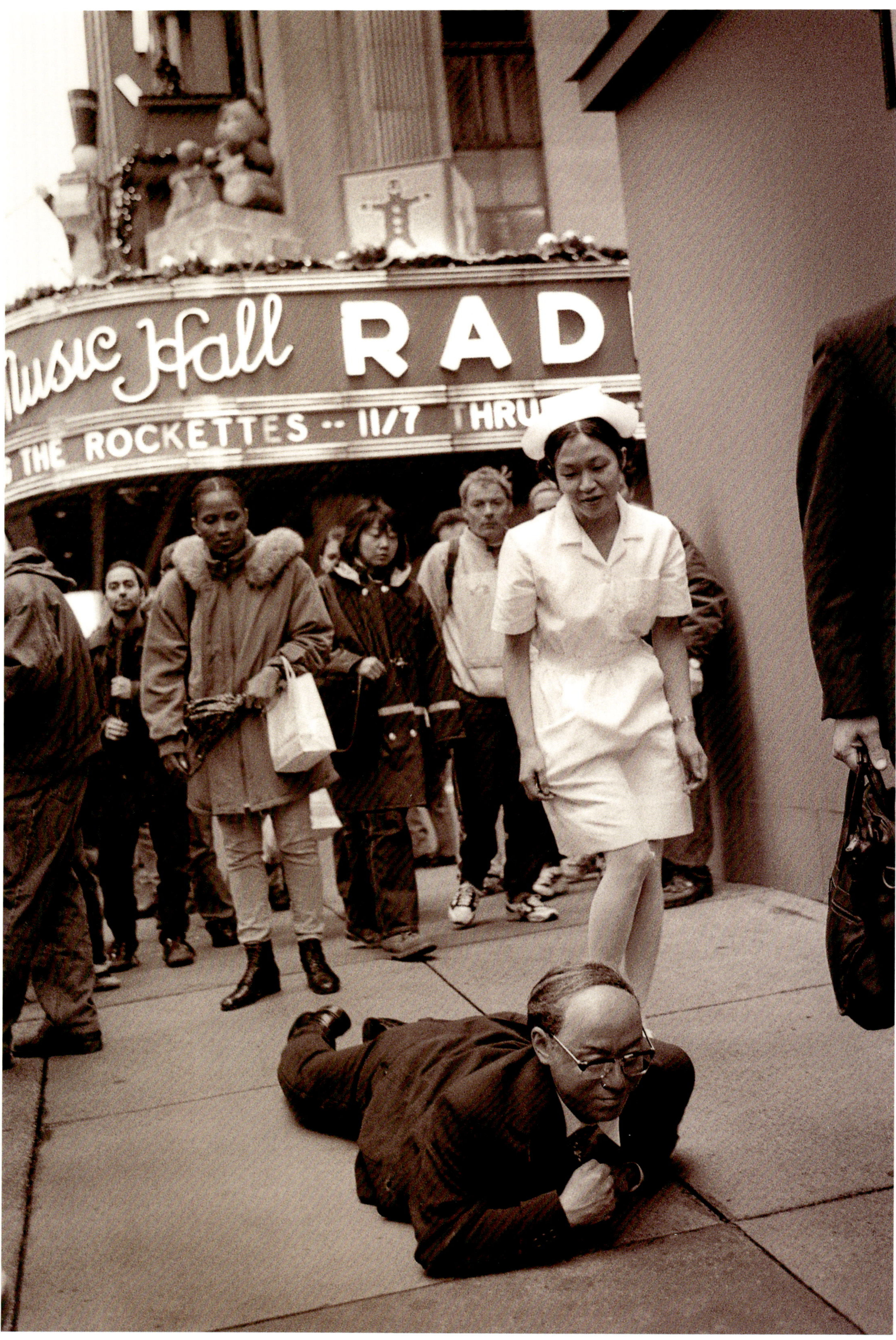
Music Hall RAD
THE ROCKETTES -- 11/7 THRU

MAKING A HOME FOR JAPANESE CONTEMPORARY ARTISTS IN NEW YORK

A Curatorial Walk-Through

ERIC C. SHINER

Presenting 33 artists living and working in New York, *Making a Home* aspires to expand the concept of "Japanese contemporary art" and establish the idea of a Japanese aesthetic diaspora in New York City. In doing so, it examines the contribution of Japanese contemporary art to global trends, identities, and outlooks. Today, it is no longer possible to speak about Japanese contemporary art as a purely *Japanese* phenomenon. The rapid flow and integration of information has made it necessary to view the production of Japanese artists both inside and outside Japan within a *global* framework.

The artists selected for this exhibition are all Japanese-born, actively working artists; all but one, the "accidental New Yorker" Yōichirō Yoda, decided to leave Japan and make their way to New York to establish a new home base. Beyond this commonality, they are as different from one another as possible in terms of generation, personality, and sexuality, as well as the media in which they choose to practice. This exhibition is premised upon the ideas surrounding a home, ranging from the comfort and safety found in a physical structure to the angst and loneliness felt from living in solitude. These emotions play out in *Making a Home*, often reflecting the artists' coping strategies with life in New York City. The exhibition is loosely grouped into six main areas, all deeply rooted in the idea of a home, both physical and conceptual: Building Environments, Intimacy and Identity, Coping with Loss, Meditative Space, The Process of Making, and Referencing the Landscape. What follows is a virtual walk-through of the exhibition, with each theme illuminated by the work of an artist or artists outside the exhibition, to extend the idea of *Making a Home* to a broader context.

Prologue: New York in the World

The exhibition begins inside Japan Society with a stack of postcards as Yoko Ono's conceptual work *Hole To See The Sky* (Pl. 16.2). Embodying the artist's optimistic hope for the future, the cards are offered for visitors to mail to friends around the globe, uniting the world via the blue sky we all share. Upstairs, Ono continues to engage us in a community of hope with another work that solicits active participation from visitors, her inspiring *Wish Tree* (Pl. 16.3). Visitors are asked to write a wish on a slip of paper and then to attach the wish to the tree. At the close of the exhibition, these individual and silent wishes will be collected to be enclosed in a new permanent installation, *Imagine Peace Tower*, that Ono will inaugurate in Iceland on October 9 this year. The work connects the viewers with their dreams, the world with New York City, and reminds us that to make a home safe, happy,

and prosperous, sustaining our optimism for the future is of the utmost necessity.

1. Building Environments

It is impossible to think about "home" without thinking about space. A number of the *Making a Home* artists are obsessed with creating environments. Informed by the politics of space, they build aesthetic microcosms reflective of the outside world or construct free-standing structures as safe havens in which to hide from it. Through site-specific installations, their medium of choice, they create private spaces, a reflex of the immigrant experience, of the artist who left a safety zone behind to venture forth into the great unknown. A prime example is Kawamata Tadashi's *Project on Roosevelt Island* of 1992 (Fig. 3.2). Kawamata, a former New York resident now based in Japan, added his signature exoskeleton of jutting timbers to an abandoned smallpox hospital on the southern tip of the island. Attaching a massive, seemingly erratic skein of architectural chaos to an extant building with its own unsettling history, Kawamata, like the artists in this exhibition, formed his own universe in the center of New York.

At Japan Society, the indoor pond and bamboo grove in the first floor lobby and the second floor atrium are transformed by several *Making a Home* artists. Some negate space, others populate it; their works suggest their relationships with New York distilled from years of navigating a city tinged with fantasy and replete with the hard reality of the quotidian world.

Indeed, the pulsing energy of New York provides endless source material for artists drawn from across the globe, who inject their own jolt of vivacity into the mix, forming a self-contained system that thrives on and produces boundless creative energy. Misaki Kawai plugs into this system, creating personal sanctuaries of fun-infused bedlam, containing dolls sporting photographs of her friends' faces, stuffed animals, cars, and ephemera culled from

FIGURE 3.1

Momoyo Torimitsu
Miyata Jirō Performance in NY
1996
Polyester resin, motor, business suit, nurse costume
24 x 67 x 27 ½" (60 x 170 x 70 cm)
Dikeou Collection, Peter Norton Family Foundation

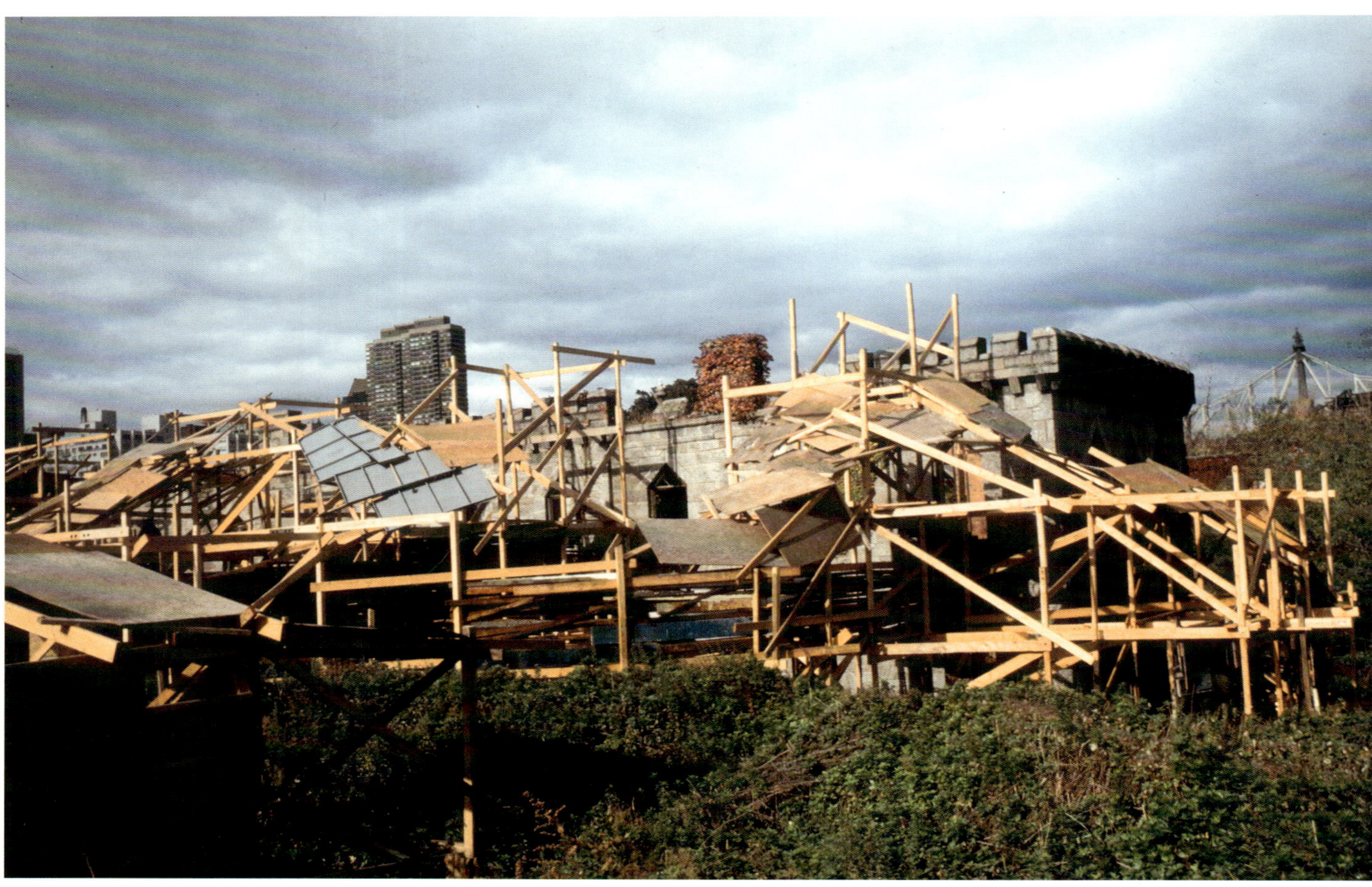

childhood recollections and hipster ideals. Her *Space House* is a multi-room living space with additional pods connected by a monorail (Pl. 11.1). Hovering over the Japan Society lobby pond, it draws the spirit into Kawai's realm of the hyper cute. This in turn lures the eye up to Hiroki Ōtsuka's equally whimsical wall mural, *Evening Calm Union*, that conflates cute with cunning in a world populated by vacant-eyed nymphs with transformed bodies that morph between human and machine (Pl. 17.1). Painted in black *sumi* ink, the former erotic comic-book artist's works reference the fantasy world of Japanese manga, just as they reflect his own desires and fears. The imaginary of corporeal transformation continues beyond in the bamboo grove with a group of mannequins strutting the dreamlike stream-cum-catwalk, wearing the latest fashions from design duo United Bamboo's Spring/Summer 2008 collection. These creations beckon the wearer to put on a fresh identity and take to the streets of the city of waking dreams and fantasies (Pls. 30.3, 30.5).

Yasunao Tone straddles the border between fantasy-based and everyday worlds in his lifelong pursuit: the deconstruction of sound. He uses the tools and theories of technology to mangle music, re-invent voices, and alter sounds, creating an alternate universe of aural chaos (Pls. 27.1–3). His proposed work for *Making a Home* would negate sound on the staircase floating over the pond, to produce an interstitial zone between the outside bustle of Manhattan and the realm of art that lies beyond.

So do artists take inspiration from the mundane, using the detritus of daily life as their material and subject matter. Yoshiaki Kaihatsu uses polystyrene foam packing material that he found in proximity to Japan Society to construct his *Happō-en Teahouse*, giving a contemporary spin to Japanese tradition and tying the work to the Society's neighborhood (Pls. 8.2–3). Set atop found plastic milk crates, this elegant structure made from the cast-offs of life reminds us that shelter from the outside world can come in many forms. Likewise, Yūken Teruya uses toilet paper tubes in his intricately cut work *Rain Forest* that mimics the natural bamboo surrounding it (Pl. 26.1). Like his signature works made from commercial bags (Pl. 26.2), their "faux nature" critiques the relationship between the natural realm and the constructed world of our contemporary consumer culture.

Momoyo Torimitsu picks up the idea of constructed worlds in her new site-specific installation *Willingly or Unwillingly, You Are Welcome* that mimics a pristine corporate environment, complete with reception desk. Known for her performances with salaryman robots (Fig. 3.1), Torimitsu turns the domain of corporate culture into a large-scale, interactive sculpture where guests buy their

FIGURE 3.2

Kawamata Tadashi
Roosevelt Island Project
1992
Site-specific installation
Courtesy of the artist

admission tickets to the exhibition and make the transition from public space to the rarefied sanctum of art.

2. Intimacy and Identity

Whether with a lover, a spouse, a roommate, or the noisy neighbor across the airshaft, New Yorkers constantly cohabitate with others in sometimes voluntary, sometimes inevitable, and always cramped proximity. This close contact with others might express itself in academic pursuits, group sublimation, cultural exchange, domestic upheaval, sexual abandon, familial bonding, or inner philosophizing to avoid the world beyond. These potential modes of interaction point to the fact that one's identity is at once intimate and political.

During her residency in New York from 1958 to 1973, Kusama Yayoi used all of these tropes in her artistic production. In her *Self-Obliteration Event* held on the Brooklyn Bridge, *the* symbol of New York, in 1967, Kusama orchestrated a Happening with male and female performers, fully naked except for the polka dots and dabs of paint that she applied to their bare flesh (Fig. 3.3). By advocating "self-obliteration," Kusama negated the self in the public realm; she and her performers become anonymous players engaged in conceptual intercourse with the city.

Noriko Shinohara analyzes life behind closed doors, stripping away veneers of perfection to expose the campy travail of life with husband Ushio through cartoon-like vignettes that depict his drinking and womanizing—and her empowered alter ego Cutie taking control, including a dominatrix scenario (Pl. 20.3). Noriko's paintings provide a comic escape from the burdens of her married life. Conversely, photographer Takahiro Kaneyama depicts family privacy in his work through regularly photographing his mother and her two sisters on trips to famous sites around Japan, at home, and in the hospital where his mother, who suffers from schizophrenia, is a regular patient (Pls. 9.1–2, 9.4). The photographs illustrate the sorrows and joys of his far-away family; they remind him of their love, just as they haunt him with their pain. Kaneyama freezes sickness and aging in time, allowing him to remember the past while avoiding an unknowable future. Painter Kyōko Sera undertakes an interior journey to the limits of the human mind, of memory, and indeed of history. Her complex painting installations with canvases hung high and low or at the corner of the gallery reference geometry and psychology and contort the medium to its absolute ends (Pl. 19.1).

Painters Hiroyuki Nakamura and Aya Uekawa create alternate identities in sublime works that might best be read as self-portraits of the artists at the epicenter of the cultural hybridity that is New York. Nakamura's work often includes sexually hazy cowboys focused on their morning ablutions or peering blankly into space (Pls. 15.1–3). They force the viewer to question gender norms and

the iconography of the American West, just as they disrupt racial stereotypes and the macho Marlboro man. Uekawa takes the sublimation of race as her subject, creating racially indefinite women in vague environments rich in texture and detail (Pls. 29.1–4). Her haunting characters seem trapped within their socially-inscribed facades, yearning to break free from the confines of the picture plane. The two painters' subjects engage in a silent conversation on gender, race, and identity here; they remind us that social constructions affect us and our relationships day in and day out. Noritoshi Hirakawa also analyzes the state of race relations in the United States in his video *Le Va et Vient*, an elegant diatribe veiled as an ethnographic film about "African" dance and dating/mating rituals (Pl. 7.3). He conflates the ideas of racism by laying them bare, using stereotypes to deconstruct the notion that identity is tied to the body, that our race defines who and what we are.

Identity formation and its reverse, obliteration, play a key role in Ei Arakawa's video work *Make Your Name Foreign* (Pl. 3.3). It is simultaneously an ode to and critical reading of renowned artist On Kawara, himself a longtime resident of New York. Arakawa picks up on Kawara's choice to paint his well-known *Date Paintings* in Esperanto when working in Japan, filming an assembly line of international art students painting faux Kawara works which are immediately sawed in two and piled in a heap. Statements such as "On Kawara can be located somewhere in between the hippies and Japanese tourists" turn Kawara into an itinerant soul

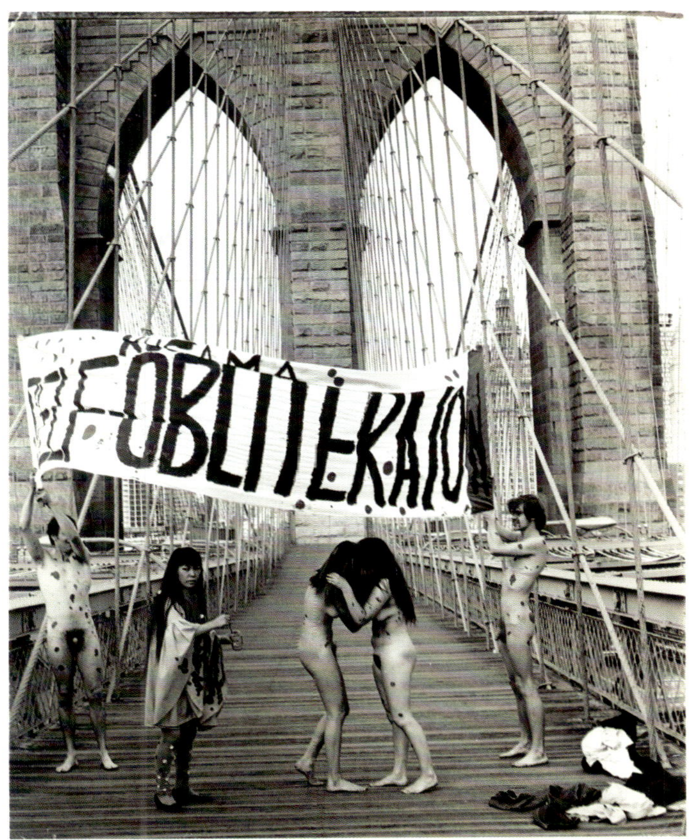

FIGURE 3.3

Kusama Yayoi
Self-Obliteration Event
1967
Performance on Brooklyn Bridge

unable to come to terms with his nationality or newfound home. Arakawa thus ties himself to Kawara in a smart, if unauthorized, dialogue between two generations of artists working in the milieu of globalism, albeit years and mindsets apart.

3. Coping with Loss

Along with the triumphs and celebrations we encounter in life, the subject of loss is a constant; historically, artists have taken up the theme to address the unfairness of the human condition, at times to celebrate it, at others denounce it. In New York today, the tragedy of 9/11 is at once a loss of personal and collective magnitude, and the secrets of mourning inhabit all of our souls.

Loss is a topic that part-time New Yorker Takashi Murakami often addresses with his idea of Superflat, or the pure surface essence of painting and the emptiness that lurks beneath. Murakami reckons that Japan, victimized by two atomic bombings at the end of World War II, has never recovered as a nation, that its citizens face life with empty shells that depend on the so-called underground subcultures of Hello Kitty, anime, and sexual perversions to survive. His character DOB encapsulates this theory in its hovering facade, a Disney-esque character with a mammoth grin and blank eyes (Fig. 3.4). It is pure surface that recalls childhood phobias and the

banality of life; it is void of emotions and indicative of Murakami's theoretical position. The artists included here, however, do not hide behind the blank face of an imaginary character, nor do they dwell on the *otaku* (geek) insecurities of Murakami and his followers. Instead, they instill their work with the very loss that informs it; they take the inequities of life and present them as they are. To avoid the topic of loss with a thin surface of happiness is, for them, missing the point.

Hiroshi Sunairi tackles the topic of 9/11 head on in his work *White Elephant* (Pl. 24.1), in which the body of a juvenile elephant in white ceramic is dispersed throughout the installation, a leg here, the head there. It references the collapse of bodies and spirits in times of national crisis, yet borrows on the Buddhist idea of benevolence that white elephants bring. It becomes a meditative space where all New Yorkers can reflect on their own losses and the healing that followed from an event of disastrous proportions that still floats in the forefronts of our minds.

Emiko Kasahara's new work *SHEER* also becomes a zone of contemplation where the voices of anonymous victims pour forth stories of heartbreak and failure, sadness and doubt (Pl. 10.1). A whispering sculpture, the work includes voices speaking in languages from around the world, all sharing instances of personal loss.

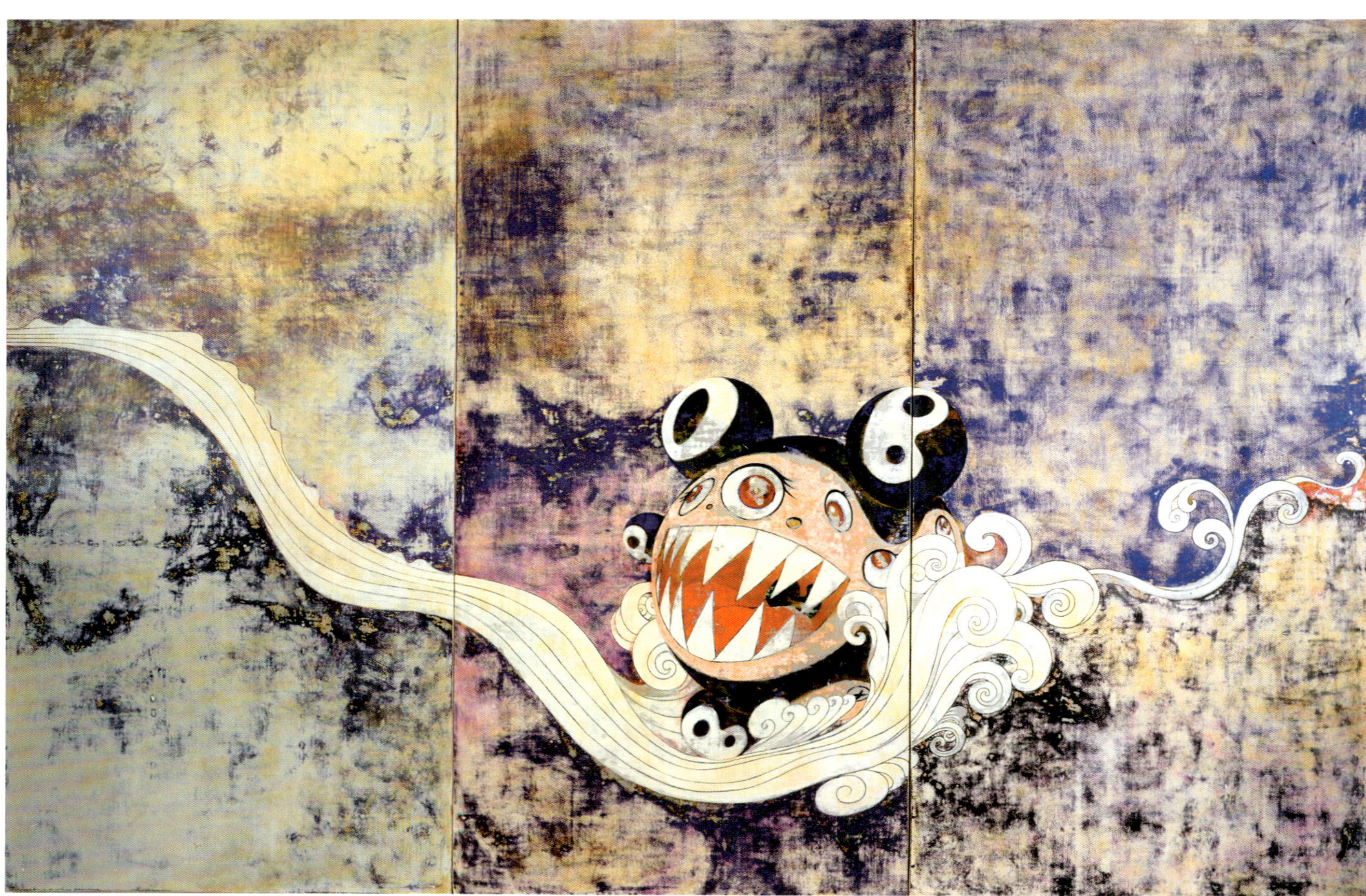

Figure 3.4

Takashi Murakami
727
1996
Synthetic polymer paint on canvas board (three panels)
9' 10" x 14' 9" (300 x 450 cm)
The Museum of Modern Art, New York
Fractional and promised gift of David Teiger, 251.2003.a-c

Kasahara weaves a narrative of sadness that elicits tears, just as it inspires hope. Ayakoh Furukawa also confronts personal loss in her drawings *100 Ways to Torture the Innocent* which reimagine the death of her pet hamster Wachacha, who unexpectedly died while Furukawa was visiting her family in Japan (Pls. 5.1, 5.3–4). The works are loving and intimate, just as they are murderous and bloody. For Furukawa, taking control of her dear pet's passing was the only way to conquer the void that came with it.

Nobuho Nagasawa's installation maps the artist's life, producing an environment of private memory and history connecting past and present. It comprises a rusted hourglass, signifying the repetition of time and containing sand from Japan and the United States; corporeal specimens (Nagasawa's umbilical cord and gray hair); and a rocking chair reflecting her heartbeat in light pulsations coursing through fiber-optic strands. This is the artist's place of rest, representing her new home, New York.

4. Meditative Space

Finding a sanctum for introspection in the hustle and bustle of New York City can itself be a trying endeavor. The creation of a dedicated space for meditation is as old as the practice itself. Artists have attempted to create zones steeped in tranquility, and Japanese artists from a strong Buddhist tradition might be even more aware of the importance of meditation.

Based in New York, Mariko Mori has increasingly focused on Eastern thought and the human need for contemplation. Her large-scale interactive sculpture *Wave UFO* was installed in the glass atrium of 590 Madison Avenue in New York City in 2003 (Fig. 3.5). A large pod in iridescent synthetic materials, the work invited three viewers at a time to enter the capsule and rest on soft reclining seats while viewing graphic imagery, derived in part from biofeedback, projected on the domed ceiling. The piece offers a physical zone within which the participants immerse themselves in a deeper consciousness and experience an interconnected universe.

The meditation chambers created by three artists for *Making a Home* also invite the viewer to enter, relax, and, at least for a moment, escape from the outside world.

Architect Yumi Kōri's *Shinkai* (literally "deep sea") is populated by mysterious transparent balloons, red lights, and a haunting electronic soundtrack that allows viewers to feel as though they are submerged in a Precambrian sea of solitude (Pl. 13.4). Intrigued with the potentiality of space and light in forming environments that rely on shadows and perspective to ground the viewer's perception of space, Kōri creates a zone for the viewer that seems to stretch into infinity.

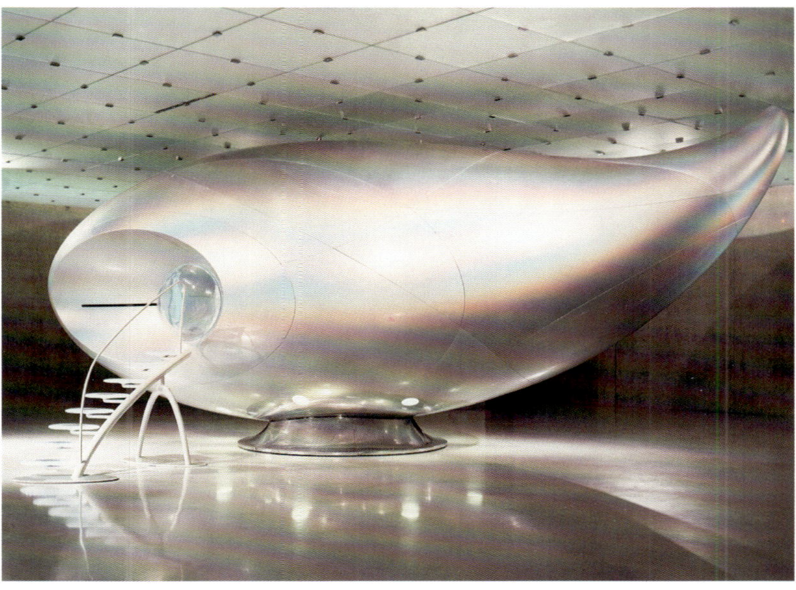

ON megumi Akiyoshi foregoes austere spaces, favoring bright environments of artificial happiness painted with larger-than-life flowers in pinks, oranges, and yellows (Pl. 1.3). She breaks these florid wonderlands with a single Rococo gilt frame, its interior completely blank. This void becomes a focal point for meditation where viewers can imagine any outcome they desire. Akiyoshi explodes the idea of painting and the framing of images, just as she relies on those very topics to actualize her energizing environments of pink-infused optimism.

Kunie Sugiura creates a mythical realm populated with the shadows of her colleagues—present and past residents of New York, Kusama Yayoi, Takashi Murakami, and Ushio Shinohara—cast by three massive photograms from her series *The Artist Papers* (Pls. 23. 3–4) reflected on mirrored floors and Mylar walls. The resultant environment is one of moving forms, shadows, and reflections steeped in the bodies of Japanese contemporary art, giving viewers the chance to ponder their forms and personae, what they gave to New York, and what they took away.

5. The Process of Making

The artist's mode of production and the processes that she or he undertakes to realize a work, from its conception to its presentation, are of the utmost importance in understanding how art is made. Sculptors are said to sculpt, painters are said to paint, and yet, the processes behind the materialization of artwork are not as simple as that. The way that an artist creates a work is many times as interesting as the finished piece itself. Artists are influenced by the world around them, and their experiences infect their thinking and their making, oftentimes a process that unfolds and changes over time.

Mariko Mori
Wave UFO
1999–2003
Brainwave interface, vision dome,
computer system, fiberglass, Technogel,
acrylic, carbon fiber, aluminum
Approx. 16 x 37 x 17' (4.9 x 11.3 x 5.3 m)
PHOTO: RICHARD LEAROYD; COURTESY MARIKO MORI
STUDIO, NEW YORK

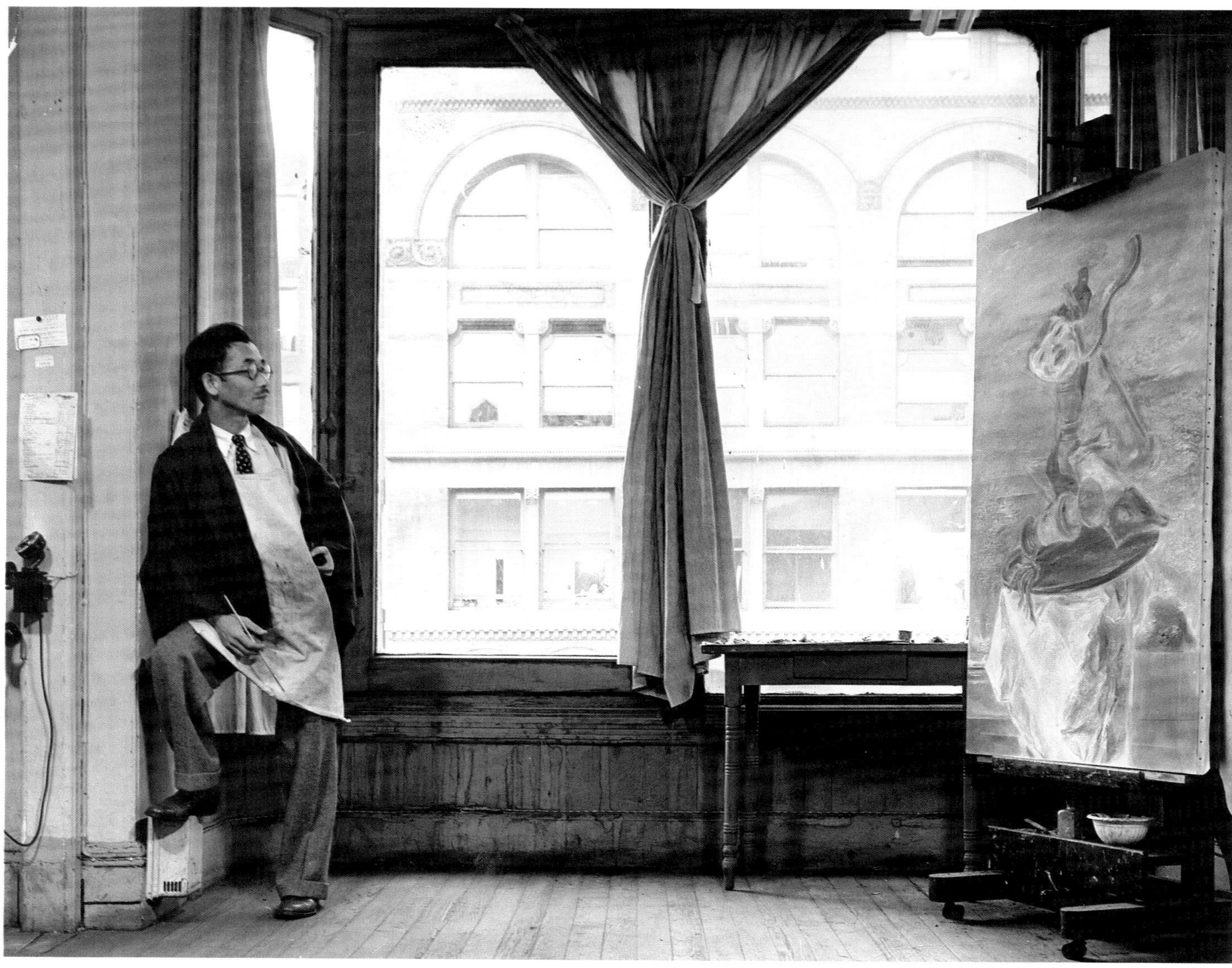

Renowned painter Yasuo Kuniyoshi was enthralled with his relationship with the canvas as a painting took form, as seen in an archival photograph of the artist in his studio from 1940 (Fig. 3.6). Kuniyoshi came to America in 1906, living and working in Seattle and Los Angeles before settling in New York in 1910. The canvas shown here was part of the Federal Art Project, a division of President Franklin Delano Roosevelt's Works Progress Administration (WPA) program that was formed to help lift America out of the Great Depression through the erection of buildings and the celebration of American art. Kuniyoshi was included in this project, clearly viewed as an American artist after his 30 years in New York, with his hand, his experiences, and his identity all informing the process of his work.

The same factors also inform the artists included in this section, obsessed as they are with the act of making things, of giving birth to objects through tactile intervention.

Indeed, Ushio Shinohara's making is forever bound to his corpus in terms of performativity and process. His *Boxing Painting* series begun in 1961 labeled him an action painter from the start (Pl. 21.2). In this work, the artist dons boxing gloves, dips them in paint or black ink, and engages with the canvas, punching it in an unscripted dance of emotional release. His works are equal parts traditional Japanese ink paintings and Pollock-esque drip paintings. The process of attacking the canvas with blunt blows allows Shinohara to leave behind an indexical interaction with the work; it is a momentary happening that, once the paint dries, is frozen in time forever.

Miwa Koizumi often uses food as an ingredient of her artwork. Her work *SuperSpa* consists of a humbly constructed boxing ring that surrounds two massage tables (Pls. 12.3–4) and a video that shows "clients" receiving beauty treatments while a female voice describes them in a soothing tone. The applications applied by "trainers" in the performance are not commercial products, but made by the artist herself from edible components, including cucumbers, honey, and rice bran.

FIGURE 3.6

Max Yavno
Yasuo Kuniyoshi, October 31, 1940
Black-and-white photographic print
7 ⅞ x 9 ⅚" (20 x 25 cm)
Courtesy of the Federal Art Project,
Photographic Division Collection,
1935–1942, Archives of American Art,
Smithsonian Institution

For certain, making things by hand is the primary urge of artists, whether it be a small object made from paper or a massive sculpture forged from steel. Three artists in *Making a Home* rely on paper as their main medium, shaping it, cutting it, or photographing it to create their works. Noriko Ambe becomes obsessively and tactilely close to her work through hours of creating lines through the subtractive process of cutting sheet after sheet of paper to create three-dimensional works that appear to be quarried mines or excavated landscapes (Pls. 2.1–2). She also cuts into books (Pl. 2.3) as though an archaeologist searching for secrets of the past. For her, process involves not only the physical interaction between hand, knife, and paper, but also the endurance needed to form her highly intricate works.

Mayumi Terada's black-and-white photographs appear at first glance to be modernist interiors or lovingly crafted pieces of furniture (Pls. 23.1–8). Yet, her beautiful scenes are in fact small maquettes she made by hand from photographs, cardboard, polystyrene foam, and fabric. Terada shoots these shoebox-sized models at close range, allowing the sensation of a life-size room to come across in the final print. She literally *makes a home* from scratch and presents it as the real thing, manipulating and mastering space as she goes.

Finally, Satoru Eguchi re-creates his Brooklyn studio in paper, cardboard, paint, and photographs, copying every last item, from a potted plant to his laptop, from his desk to his tubes of paint (Pl. 4.2). It is all handmade and becomes a simulacrum of an actual place, an ideal copy of the artist's lair. Eguchi worked for months to create each component of this installation, all to exact scale. He thus shares with his guests the painstaking process of deceit made possible through exacting craftsmanship and obsessive attention to detail.

6. Referencing the Landscape

The cityscape of New York has influenced untold numbers of artists, instilling in them a sense of awe inspired by majestic soaring skyscrapers, or compassion for the poverty-stricken homeless in the streets. The architectural and geographic fabric of New York provides countless opportunities for the artist. In recent years, Japanese architects have contributed much to the skyline of New York. Following in the footsteps of Yoshimura Junzō, who designed Japan Society's current home (1971), the first contemporary Japanese building in New York, and Taniguchi Yoshio, who gave the city the new MoMA, the Japanese architectural firm SANAA designed the New Museum of Contemporary Art building, which opens during the run of *Making a Home* and forever ties Japanese aesthetics to the realm of contemporary art, Gotham-style (Fig. 3.7).

Photography particularly is a potent medium that captures the physicality of the city. Japanese photographers have a long history of engaging with the city's landscape. From 1904 to 1919, photographer Kikuchi Toyo lived in New York, snapping the cityscape before returning home to Japan to found the Oriental Paper Industry Company, the leading supplier of photographic paper there for decades. Two photographs in the collection of New York photography collector and dealer Charles Schwartz afford us a glimpse into the mind of a Japanese photographer fascinated by the city. The products of Ōtake Studio, one image, circa 1930, is of two Caucasian men sitting in Central Park, a row of buildings visible in the background (Fig. 3.8). This photo in turn appears in the other which shows Ōtake Studio itself in the northern city of Sendai, years later (Fig. 3.9). The presumed Ōtake-san was so moved by his experience in New York that he decided to hang that image—and that image alone—in a place where he would see it every day. Among the countless other Japanese photographers who have shot the city is Hiroshi Sugimoto, who divides his time between New York and Tokyo. His phantasmic portrait *Guggenheim Museum (Frank Lloyd Wright)* of 1997 captures one of the city's most enduring monuments to art (Fig. 3.10).

Two photographers in *Making a Home* have also turned their cameras on the landscapes and structures of New York City to amazing ends. Gō Sugimoto walks the streets of the city in the middle of the night, relying only on the moon, street lamps, or other *in situ* lighting to illuminate his subject matter (Pls. 22.1–3). The trees and buildings he shoots using a long exposure become spectral forms that float and glow in the surrounding darkness. His work is

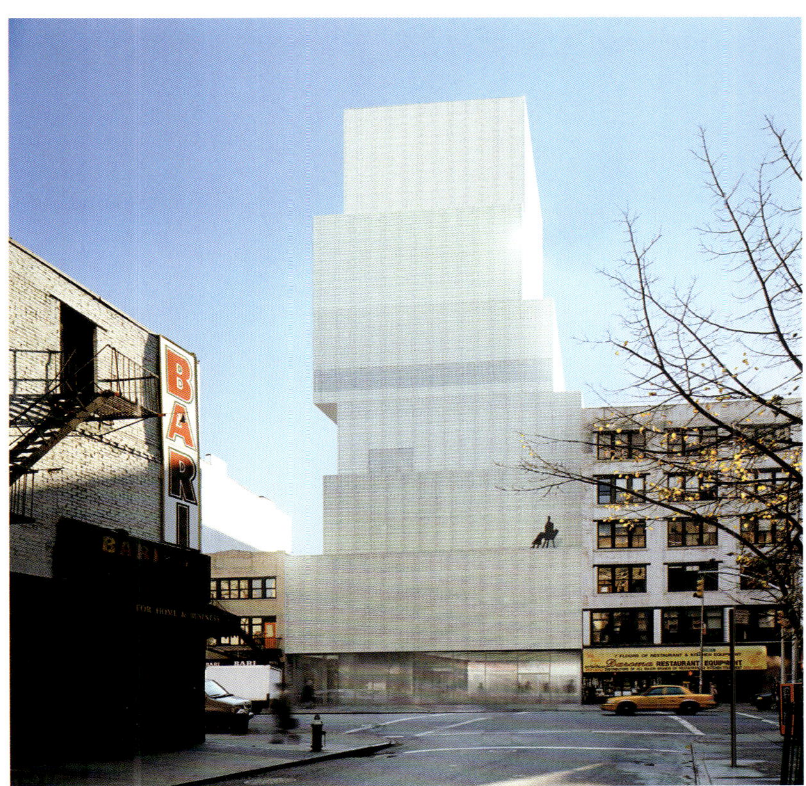

FIGURE 3.7

Design for New Museum of
Contemporary Art at 235 Bowery,
New York
Projected opening: late 2007
Design and visualization: Sejima +
Nishizawa/SANAA; site photography:
Christopher Dawson

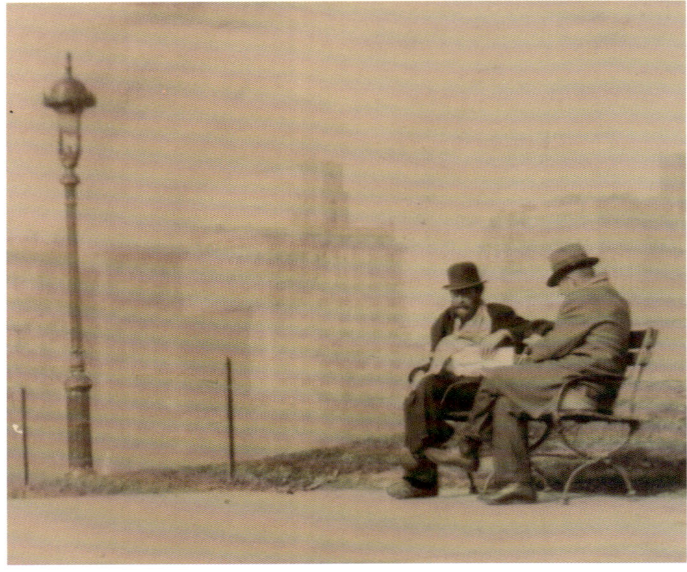

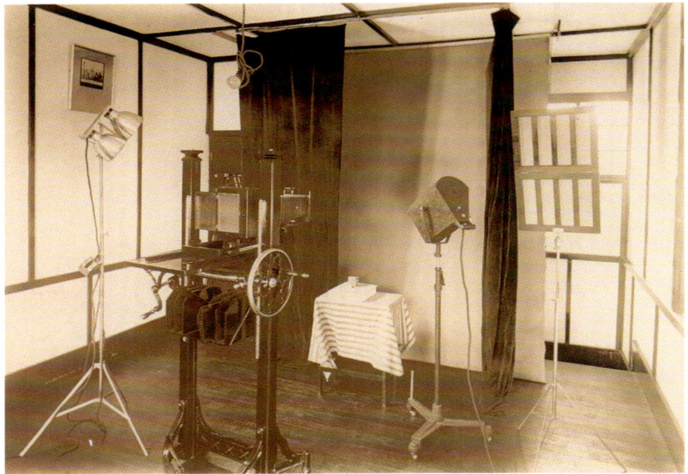

York's beloved waterway, the Hudson River, in her massive canvas, *The Hudson* (Pl. 31.2). Combining theories of satellite mapping technology with the traditional materials of paint and Japanese paper, Yoda depicts a vast landscape in the relatively small confines of an 8 x 12–foot painting, and shows that "New York" is much more than a cluster of buildings and millions of people—it is an entire system that was originally settled thanks to its benevolent proximity to life-giving water. Father and husband Toshihisa Yoda also creates worlds in paint, fantastical environments populated by geometric forms bound together in DNA-like strands that replicate architectural forms, just as they envision mathematical equations (Pls. 32.2–3). Yoda is intrigued by the inner workings of bodies and structures—and of the networks that fuel and sustain them—and has successfully captured these ideas in static paint and vivid color. For the entire Yoda family, the concept of landscape is a shared trope that takes on a variety of different guises, each referencing the physical and philosophical world around them.

Epilogue: New York in the World, Again

At the lower level of Japan Society, Tōru Hayashi's work encapsulates all six sections of *Making a Home*. His intimate drawings in ink on paper, called *Equivocal Landscape*, create miniature environments in a few well-drafted lines (Pls. 6.1, 6.4). They are intimate in scale and evocative of loss in their minimalism, yet meditative in their ephemerality. They capture the artist's process of daily drawing, and, in essence, become landscapes of the mind. Hayashi is as worldly as he is introspective, offering us a virtual journey to faraway cities both real and imagined. His works are informed by his own travels, whether a jaunt to Central Park or a residency in New Delhi (Pls. 6.2, 6.5).

Like all of the artists in *Making a Home*, Hayashi is a true citizen of the world. He and his peers have ventured beyond their homeland of Japan to enjoy the benefits that being an artist in New York brings, as well as the necessary uncertainty that comes with starting afresh. They have dedicated their lives and careers to the making of beautiful and thought-provoking works, and have established a true Japanese contemporary art diaspora in the very midst of New York City. For them, making a home and making art are one and the same.

a raw look at a sleeping city, a narrative epic played out in shadows. Katsuhiro Saiki also uses actual buildings as the foundation for his three-dimensional photography-based sculpture whose skin is made from photographs of modern architectural masterpieces in New York such as the 1958 Seagram Building designed by Mies van der Rohe with Phillip Johnson (Pl. 18.1). He borrows the designs of the world's greatest architects and restructures them to his own liking. For him, the cityscape of New York is a fluid notion that can be bent and abstracted at will.

Yōichirō Yoda has also been engaged in a long study of actual New York spaces in his series of works that portray the now extinct pleasure palaces of the Broadway Theater district. His paintings capture the interiors of several theaters that once stood where skyscrapers, movie theaters, and restaurants are now located, while his video shows the destruction of many of these structures, now the ghosts of the Great White Way (Pls. 33.1–5). His mother, Junko Yoda, uses paint and paper to record the entire system of New

FIGURE 3.8

Ōtake Studio
Two Men in Central Park
1930s
Gelatin silver print
7 ¼ x 6 ¼" (18.4 x 15.9 cm)
Charles Schwartz Collection

FIGURE 3.9

Ōtake Studio
Ōtake Studio (with Fig. 3.8 on the wall)
1930s
Gelatin silver print
6 x 4 ¼" (15.2 x 10.8 cm)
Charles Schwartz Collection

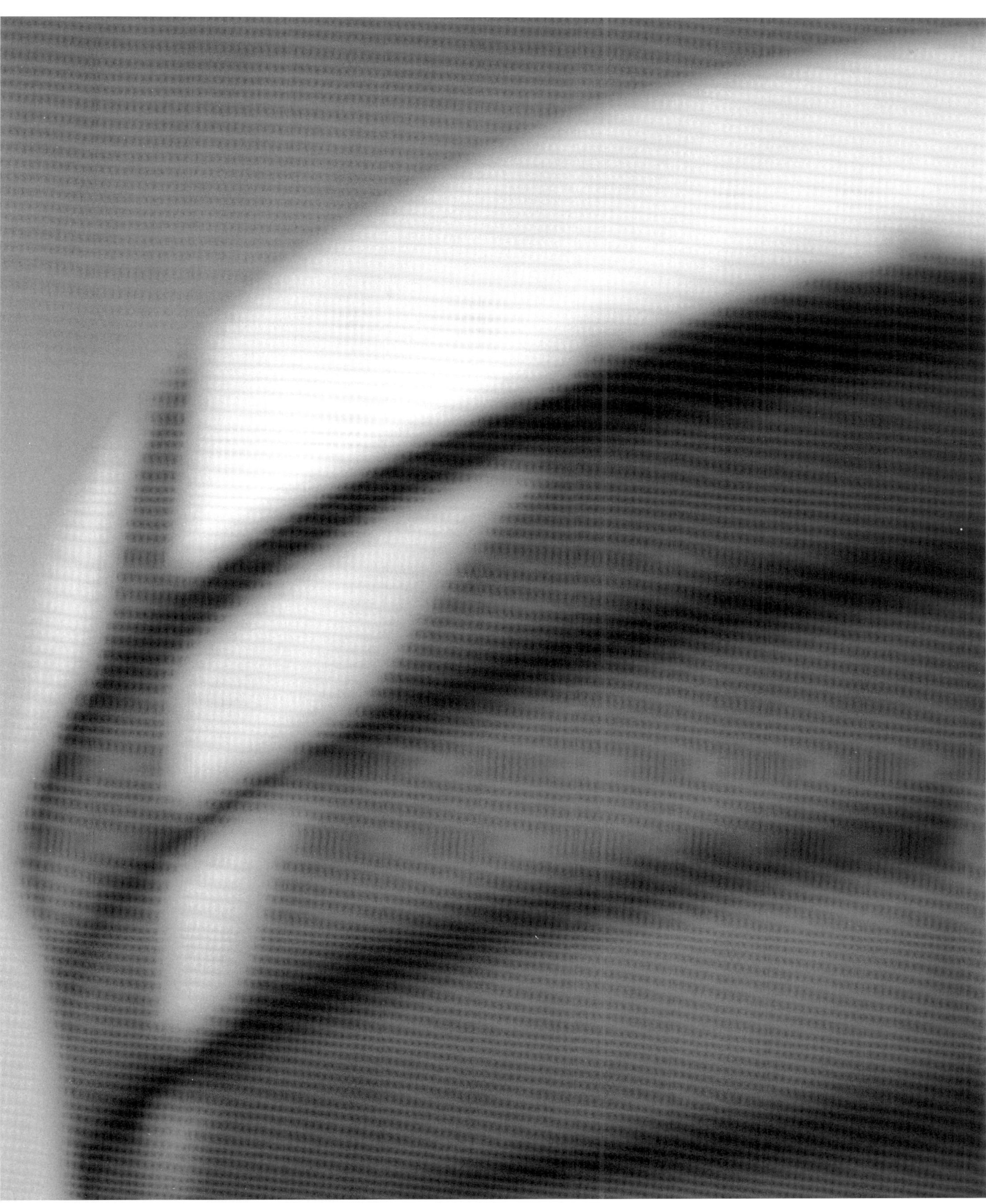

Hiroshi Sugimoto
Guggenheim Museum (Frank Lloyd Wright)
1997
58 ¾ x 47″ (150 x 120 cm)
Gelatin silver print
PHOTO COURTESY OF HIROSHI SUGIMOTO

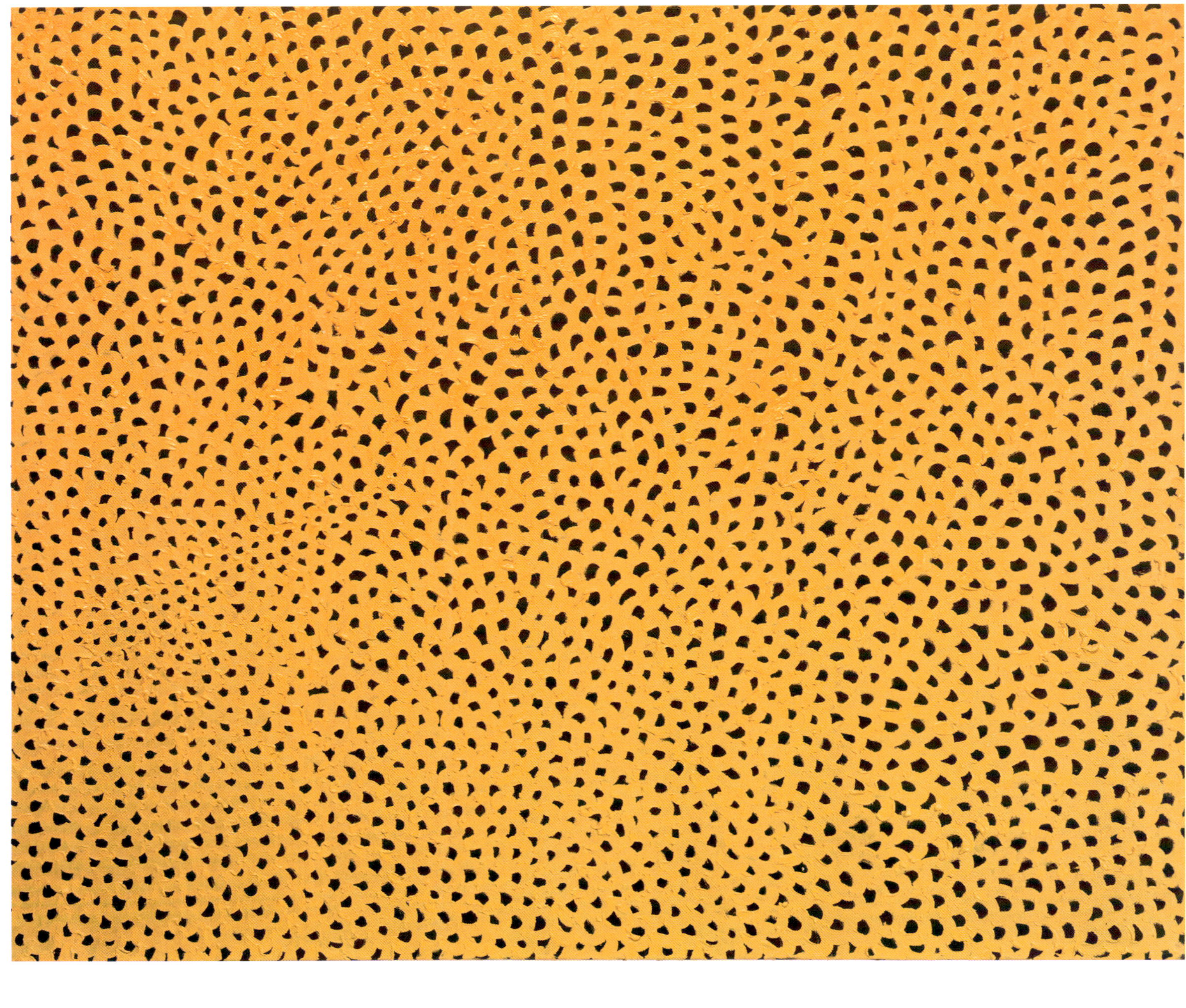

SNAPSHOTS FROM THE PAST

Japan Society and *Gendai Bijutsu*—From the Perspective of 1960s Art

REIKO TOMII

When we enter the lobby of Japan Society today, what we see is the same space of understated yet distinct aesthetics created by the architect Yoshimura Junzō more than 35 years ago. As in 1971, when the building was inaugurated, we climb the stairs to visit the Gallery on the second floor. The sudden release we feel from the impression of restraint—effected by the characteristically low ceiling and dim lighting—is further amplified by the four-story-high skylight added to the structure in the major renovation of 1997. The Manhattan sky soars over the water, filling a two-tiered indoor pond and a waterfall with the serene light from the skylight mediating heaven and earth.

For the past few years, an observant visitor to Japan Society may have also noticed a small yellow painting hanging near the stairs (Figs. 4.1–2). This is a work by Kusama Yayoi, a once New York–based Japanese artist, entitled *Net S.P.*, dating from 1961.[1] Measuring 30 x 36 inches, this canvas is relatively tiny for the artist, who frequently created an engulfing environment with huge canvases at that time (see Fig. 5.7). Still, it is a gem that reveals an unmistakable kinship to the larger works in her signature *Infinity Net* series. Its obsessive yellow-on-black net pattern in particular recalls a huge canvas from 1960 that was originally owned by Frank Stella, her contemporary and a leading Minimal painter, and is now in the collection of the National Gallery of Art in Washington, D.C. "Why is this here?" is an obvious question for Kusama enthusiasts and informed art lovers alike. Although the precise circumstances have yet to be researched, the artist presumably gave the work to Japan Society in the early 1960s as a token of appreciation when the institution most likely aided her visa application. For decades it lay forgotten in the Society's basement storage. Alexandra Munroe, a Kusama scholar and the fourth director of Japan Society Gallery (1998–2005), heard about a Kusama painting at the Society shortly after curating a pioneering retrospective of the artist in 1989 at the Center for International Contemporary Arts (CICA), a now-defunct organization in New York. Still, it was not until 2000 that the painting was literally excavated by the Gallery's Exhibitions Manager, Eleni Cocordas, who at Munroe's direction searched the art storage area to locate the legendary work. To everybody's delight, the painting, wrapped in brown paper and casually tucked away, was in almost pristine condition; in the following year, it was installed in the lobby, where it resided until April 2007.[2] *Net S.P.* will be re-installed in a publicly visible space in the Society for the duration of *Making A Home: Japanese Contemporary Artists in New York*, honoring Kusama as an important predecessor to many of the artists represented in the exhibition.

If Yoshimura's architecture embodies the stability of institutional history, Kusama's canvas speaks for the fleeting nature of historical memory—even recent events involving what is termed "contemporary art" are prone to oblivion. Still, the true lesson of this painting is that what may seemingly be lost *can* be recovered, by accident or design. On the occasion of Japan Society's Centennial, one may wonder what still remains in the metaphorical basement storage of institutional history. With this question in mind, I conducted a preliminary investigation at the Society's library. The result was intriguing. As a student of post-1945 Japanese art, I was pleasantly surprised to find that significant connections were made between the Japanese world of *gendai bijutsu* (literally, "contemporary art") and New York, thanks to Japan Society's programs. Writing an exhaustive history is the task of an institutional historian. What I offer here, instead, is a selection of "historical snapshots" from the institution's past, that provide us with an insight into Japan Society's relationship with Japanese contemporary artists and its larger contexts.

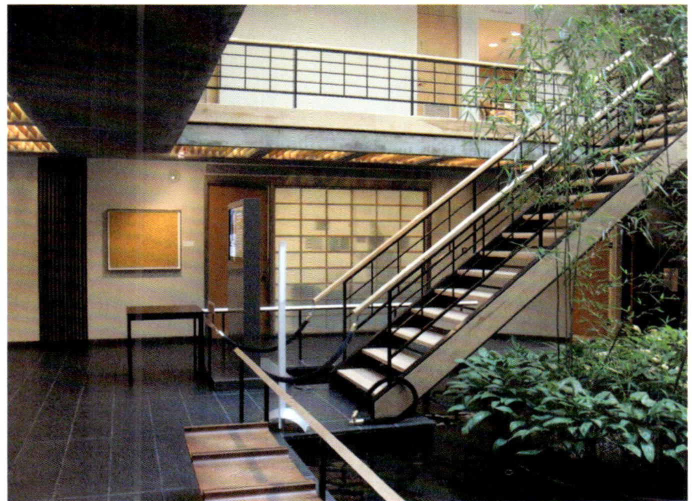

FIGURE 4.2

Kusama's *Net S.P.* installed in Japan Society's lobby, April 2007. Visible in the foreground is a bench from *Japan Art Festival*, 1966
PHOTO: REIKO TOMII

Speaking from a personal perspective, Kusama was the first Japanese contemporary artist I studied in a professional capacity; my research at CICA for her 1989 retrospective also put me in touch with Munroe, and this association led to a long working relationship with Japan Society Gallery. In launching my study of Japan Society's past, however, I had another, equally important motivation: the death of a Japanese artist by the name of Matsuzawa Yutaka (1922–2006) last October at age 84 (Fig. 4.3). A pioneering conceptualist and a major 1960s figure, Matsuzawa spent six months in New York in the late 1950s. Whenever I met with him, he would tell me, knowing I am based in New York, that he had been a "Japan Society Fellow" and he therefore wanted to return to the Society some day to exhibit his work. This piece of information had long been tucked away in my own basement storage of scholarship, although I never really forgot it. When I learned of his passing, I felt profound regret for my failure to pursue this lead. My initial inquiry at the library was thus primarily concerned with the "Japan Society Fellows" program in the 1950s, but my research quickly took on another life as I saw numerous names of other familiar figures from 1960s art in the Society's past publications. A few of these discoveries constitute the "archival snapshots" that provide the basis of this essay.

My selections here are informed by my interest in 1960s art. Coincidentally, the 1960s is a period immediately preceding the opening of Japan Society Gallery in 1971 (initially known as Japan House Gallery and renamed in 1987). There are few organized records of Japan Society's art-related programs prior to the

Gallery's existence. *Japan Society 1907–1982: 75 Years of Partnership Across the Pacific*, a commemorative publication authored by the noted historian Edwin O. Reischauer, includes a number of references to the Society's exhibitions and related programs, beginning with its first exhibition in 1911, which featured "Japanese Colour-Prints" and was accompanied by an illustrated publication by Frederick Gookin.[3] But in Reischauer's study, more focused on political and economic history, arts and culture are not a primary topic. A personal account by Rand Castile, the first Gallery Director (1971–86), recently published in the journal *Impressions*,[4] greatly adds to our understanding of the Gallery's exhibition program and its relationship with Japanese contemporary art, but in light of his tenure period, the 1960s have been understandably still little explored. In this respect, I hope my essay makes a small contribution to the compilation of the history of Japan Society's visual arts program.

In a larger context, New York was a site of international exchange in the 1960s, which was a crucial decade of innovations and experimentations in vanguard art worldwide. In particular, as seen from the other side of the Pacific Ocean, the 1960s was the time of "international contemporaneity" (*kokusaiteki dōjisei*),[5] marked by the awareness that new practices on the archipelago resonated with those in New York and other Euro-American locations. An imagined sense of camaraderie was often informed by the news carried by the print media of international art and fostered by the occasional physical presence of Euro-American artists and their work in Japan. For example, during the 1960s, the Japanese audience had an increased opportunity to see in person New York art, beginning with John Cage and David Tudor's tour in 1962, which was followed by exposure to Robert Rauschenberg, Merce Cunningham, Jasper Johns, and the exhibition *Two Decades of American Painting* organized by the Museum of Modern Art, New York.[6] An influx of Euro-American contemporary art in this decade culminated in the Tokyo Biennale of 1970. By 1970, the awareness of international contemporaneity in part prompted the formation of *gendai bijutsu* as an area of practice distinct from the more established domestic practices of *yōga* (Western-style painting) and *Nihonga* (Japanese-style painting), two cornerstones of the development of Japanese modern art since the late 19th century.

The perception in New York was vastly different. Since the 1950s, New York art had emerged as a dominant international force with the rise of Abstract Expressionism, with its central place symbolically confirmed by the grand prize in painting awarded to Rauschenberg at the Venice Biennale in 1964.[7] The presumed supremacy of New York art attracted an international set of artists, turning the city's art scene into a mosaic of races and ethnicities. In this environment, the individual experience of Japanese artists varied from short-term visits (for days or weeks at a time) to more extended stays or determinedly permanent residencies. At

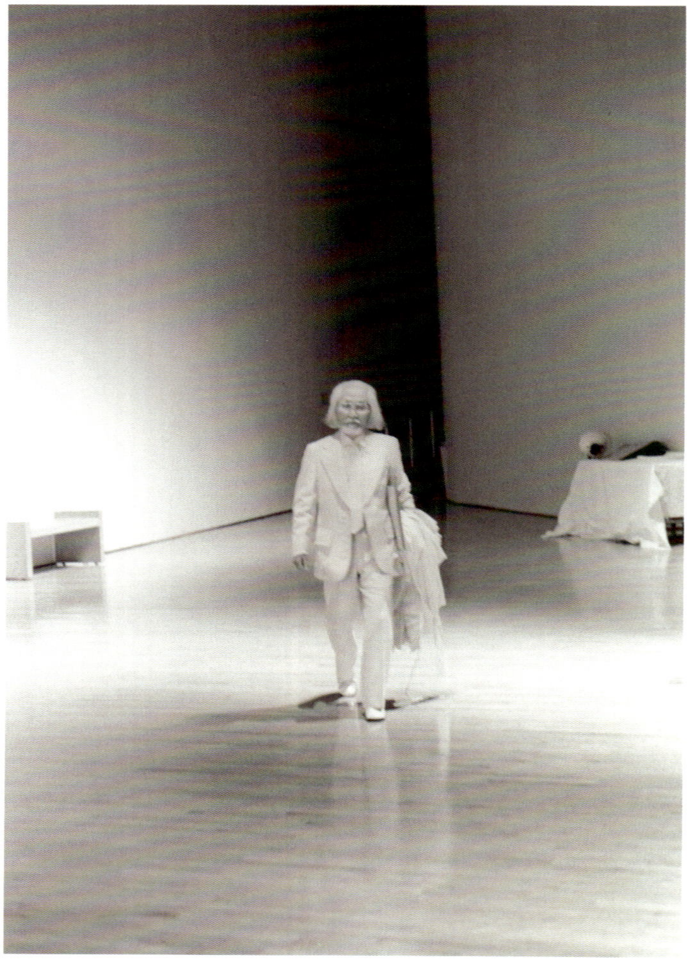

Figure 4.3

Matsuzawa Yutaka, after his performance at Queens Museum of Art, New York, 1999
PHOTO: TOYO TSUCHIYA

the same time, the works of *gendai bijutsu* themselves traveled from Japan to this shore via a variety of channels, museological, commercial, individual, and governmental. The intersection of Japan's *gendai bijutsu* and New York were not infrequent, but tended to be unnoticed or left out of Eurocentric art-historical accounts beyond a few names that became securely incorporated in postwar art history, such as Kusama, On Kawara, and Yoko Ono, a majority of whom were long-term residents of New York. My essay, therefore, attempts to uncover and recover some of the "interchange" episodes that took place in New York, and while doing so explore stories of *gendai bijutsu* behind them.

Snapshot 1
Matsuzawa Yutaka as a Japan Society Fellow
(Japan Society's Student Program in the 1950s)

In the institutional archives there are two types of publications in which official records of activities were compiled. Annual reports generally summarize the year's activities and newsletters announce recent developments and forthcoming events. On the open shelves of Japan Society's library I found postwar issues of its annual reports and newsletter, published under the title *Japan Society Forum*, from September 1953 through March 1971 (Fig. 4.4). (*Forum* was then renamed *Japan House Newsletter*, which was renamed *Japan Society Newsletter* in August 1977; in October 2000, the Society's website was formally launched to replace the printed newsletter.) In the bound volumes of *Forum*, I quickly noticed a program varyingly called "Japan Society Student Grants," "Japan Society Fellowships," and "Japan Society Fellows." In a nutshell, this program provided financial aid primarily to Japanese graduate students already studying in the U.S., assisting them to complete their goals (in most cases to obtain degrees).

The name of Matsuzawa Yutaka was among 27 grantees or "Japan Society Fellows, 1956–57," announced in the June 22, 1956 issue of *Forum*, which also included such now well-known cultural figures as Ichiyanagi Toshi (avant-garde composer), Kobayashi Kenji (violinist), and Minagawa Tatsuo (musicologist).[8] The brief description of Matsuzawa explains that he planned to:

> carry on his study of the fine arts at the Massachusetts Institute of Technology. He will return to his teaching position at the Suwa Vocational High School in Japan. He also has plans for establishing a new arts research center.[9]

This is the first archival snapshot in my essay. Two storylines intersect in this brief notice: Japan Society's student program that was a vital part of its operation in the 1950s; and grantee Matsuzawa Yutaka, who would become a pioneer conceptualist, as important and unique as Yoko Ono in the history of contemporary art, to a significant degree thanks to this program.

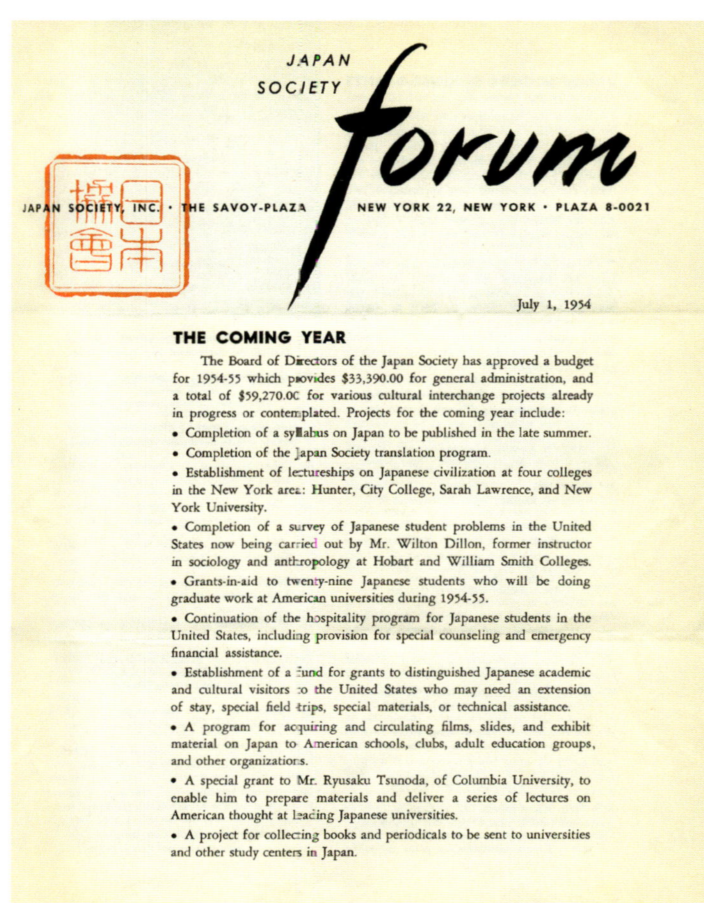

THE COMING YEAR

The Board of Directors of the Japan Society has approved a budget for 1954-55 which provides $33,390.00 for general administration, and a total of $59,270.00 for various cultural interchange projects already in progress or contemplated. Projects for the coming year include:

- Completion of a syllabus on Japan to be published in the late summer.
- Completion of the Japan Society translation program.
- Establishment of lectureships on Japanese civilization at four colleges in the New York area: Hunter, City College, Sarah Lawrence, and New York University.
- Completion of a survey of Japanese student problems in the United States now being carried out by Mr. Wilton Dillon, former instructor in sociology and anthropology at Hobart and William Smith Colleges.
- Grants-in-aid to twenty-nine Japanese students who will be doing graduate work at American universities during 1954-55.
- Continuation of the hospitality program for Japanese students in the United States, including provision for special counseling and emergency financial assistance.
- Establishment of a fund for grants to distinguished Japanese academic and cultural visitors to the United States who may need an extension of stay, special field trips, special materials, or technical assistance.
- A program for acquiring and circulating films, slides, and exhibit material on Japan to American schools, clubs, adult education groups, and other organizations.
- A special grant to Mr. Ryusaku Tsunoda, of Columbia University, to enable him to prepare materials and deliver a series of lectures on American thought at leading Japanese universities.
- A project for collecting books and periodicals to be sent to universities and other study centers in Japan.

For Japan Society, the 1950s was first and foremost a period of resumption following the decade of inactivity necessitated by the war between the U.S. and Japan in 1941. Since its founding in 1907, the Society's mandate was to further mutual exchange and understanding between the two countries. Japan's attack on Pearl Harbor in December 1941 inevitably forced the Society to cease its operation.[10] In 1951, with Japan's signing of the San Francisco Peace Treaty, which brought Japan back to the fold of the international community, the Society was ready to resume its function.

In this context, a vital task for Japan Society was to reintroduce Japan, a former enemy in World War II, to the American people and aid it to rebuild itself. One effective way was through "education," concentrating a good part of the Society's energy and resources on three areas: a) Japanese students in the U.S.; b) cultural exchange; and c) improving curricula on Japan in American schools.[11] For example, the front page of the July 1, 1954 issue of *Forum* announces 10 projects the Society would undertake in "The Coming Year" (Fig. 4.4),[12] which include "Establishment of lectureships on Japanese civilization" at Hunter College, City College, Sarah Lawrence College, and New York University; and "Completion of a survey of Japanese student problems" in the U.S. The "Japan Society Fellowships" program is among these projects,

FIGURE 4.4

Front page of *Japan Society Forum*
(July 1, 1954)

TABLE 1

Japan Society Fellows in the Arts, 1954–1959

. . . .

1954–55

Yuize Shin'ichi (composer/*koto* player), Columbia University

. . . .

1954–57, 1958–59 (3 consecutive grants plus 1)

Ichiyanagi Toshi (composer/pianist), Juilliard School

. . . .

1955–56

Nakaseko Kazu (musicologist), Yale University

Yokoi Teruko (artist), Art Students League

. . . .

1955–58 (3 consecutive grants)

Kobayashi Kenji (violinist), Juilliard School

. . . .

1956–57

Heima Tatsuhiko (painter), New School of Social Research

Matsuzawa Yutaka (fine artist), MIT

Toyama Michiko (orchestra conductor), Columbia University

Watanabe Shigeo (violinist), Juilliard School

. . . .

1956–58 (2 consecutive grants)

Minagawa Tatsuo (musicologist), Columbia University and NYU

. . . .

1957–58

Atsumi Takayori (cellist), New England Conservatory of Music

Azuma Norio (artist), Art Institute of Chicago

Urushihara Miyako (designer), Pratt Institute

. . . .

1957–59 (2 consecutive grants)

Kanda Masako (dancer/choreographer/teacher), Martha Graham School of Contemporary Dance

Yamamoto Yuri (musician), Juilliard School

. . . .

1958–59

Ishikawa Kohei (architect), Miami University

Notes

This list is compiled based on the Japan Society Fellows announced in *Japan Society Forum* issues, July 1, 1954; June 15, 1955; September 20, 1955; June 22, 1956; October 10, 1956; March 20, 1957; and June 15, 1958. Listed here are Fellows' name, vocation, and school proposed to attend (which may be different from the school the grantee actually attended). Multiple-year grants are so indicated after the year.

listed as "Grants-in-aid to twenty-nine Japanese students who will be doing graduate work at American universities during 1954–55."

The emphasis on Japanese students is evident in the annual reports. In *Japan Society Report 1955*, the executive director's report for the fiscal year 1954–55 begins with "Student Activities," wherein the first item mentioned is the fellowship program.[13] From 1953, when the fellowship program was instituted, through 1961–62, when the program was phased out, a total of 203 individuals received stipends averaging $1,000.[14] The Society's own resources were greatly augmented by funds received from the New York Community Trust and the Ford Foundation. In the late 1950s, $1,000 was a sizable sum,[15] if barely sufficient for Japanese students who often lacked second-year funding to complete their degree program. Typically, their study was funded just for the first year, their student-visa status restricted their work in the U.S. to obtain additional funds, and the Japanese government maintained tight currency control, limiting the maximum amount carried by an individual going abroad to $500.[16] The demand was high for this kind of stipend: for the 1954–55 grants, more than 300 students sent applications to the Society,[17] when the estimated number of Japanese students in the U.S. was about 1,300.[18]

Of these 203 Japan Society Fellows, 16 were in the arts (see Table 1). Most other grantees were academics, reflecting the priority the Society placed on future leaders and teachers.[19] Certainly, Matsuzawa is today lesser known outside Japan than Ichiyanagi Toshi, whose vanguard credentials as John Cage's student and one of Japan's most influential experimental composers distinguish him in this list. Matsuzawa nonetheless presents a compelling case that the Society's fellowship was well allocated, yielding an extraordinary result to advance vanguard art in Japan.

If Ichiyanagi received inspiration for new art from Cage's classes at the New School for Social Research, Matsuzawa received his from the most unlikely source: a late-night radio program specializing in UFOs.[20] Matsuzawa's story goes back to wartime Japan, where he studied architecture at Waseda University in Tokyo. Having witnessed the decimation of the Japanese capital, he graduated in 1946 with his thesis project "Plan for Fujimi Village Artists Colony," which was accompanied by a poetic essay entitled "On the Ruins." His key statement, "That which humans make will eventually perish, humans will eventually perish," was echoed in his speech at a graduation party: "I don't believe in the solidness of iron and concrete. I want to create an architecture of soul, formless architecture, invisible architecture." A few years later he gave up on architecture altogether and returned to his hometown of Shimo Suwa in central Japan. While teaching mathematics at night high school, he sought a new possibility of expression, first through poetry, then visual art. He was among the more progressive artists in the region, whose network included the young Kusama,

FIGURE 4.5

Matsuzawa Yutaka
On "Meaning of Psi" and "Psi Chamber"
1961
Flier
13 ¼ x 9 ½" (33.6 x 24.1 cm)

〈プサイの意味〉および〈プサイ函・Psi Chamber〉に就いて

— Nil novi sub sole

松 沢 宥

僕の考え方は新しいことでも奇妙なことでもない。僕の思想的祖先の名前をあげてみれば、ゾイセ、ヴェッセル・ガンスフォルト、ニコラス・クザヌス、サヴォナロラ、また善無畏、不空、さらにユーサピア・パラジノ、G・H・ラインその他である。また別の意味の先達にサッケーリ、ヤノス・ボーヤイ、クライン、N・ウィーナーがある。

さて、精神空間時間物質は、〈プサイ函〉より発生されると考えよう。〈プサイ函〉は〈プサイの意味〉の立体への発展であり、〈プサイの意味〉がマンダラの図像学的構成を借りて平面内において精神空間時間物質の関係を象徴的に表現しているのに対して、〈プサイ函〉ではこれをG・ガモフの四次元の超立体のモデルを借りて立体的に象徴しているのである。

故に、〈函・Y.M.〉の中に〈函・S.M.〉が抱かれていると考えるものである。即ち、〈函・Y.M.〉の八個の頂点が〈函・S.M.〉の八個の頂点と時間の中で連結されるのである。

而も、〈函・Y.M.〉と〈函・S.M.〉は個別的でなく自己同一的である。

次に〈プサイ函〉の構造について。

各面の表裏の計十個の画面は夫々一個づつ独立したものであり且また全体の部分である。

●振動型●により視点を移動させる場合は（II図参照）空間時間の中で陰陽、正反の間を視点は振動するものである。●回帰型●によれば（III図参照）内と外を順次に経験しつつ遂に永遠に回帰するものである。固来、宗教哲学科学の世界において、振動、回帰等の語のもつ意味は深甚である。ともに超位相的構造である。ニル。この構造を通してPsiが発生されるのである。そして上述の厳密な視点移動にしたがうために、〈函〉の周囲を巡り、腰を屈伸し、首を曲折する動作を壮厳に行うことが儀式・Ritualまたは秘術Occultである。

〈函・Y.M.〉と〈プサイの意味〉と〈函・S.M.〉が一つの軸上に等間隔に配置された全体は（I図参照）それ故に、祭壇Altarである。

〈プサイの意味〉の視点移動は1から順次9に至るもので夫々別の時間における空間を経験し、9から1へは多次元の時空を通過して回帰する（IV図参照）。時間の始めは終りであり終りは始めである。空間は有限にして無限である。尚1から9までの全てを同時に視ることは時間空間の始めから終りまでを一挙にして体験することである。

僕の作品中に用いられている記号は、今の段階では、意識的に科学の世界から借用しているものと、デッサン中無意識的に反復現れてくる僕の署名に等しい性質のものとの二種である。記号とコミュニケイションの問題は記号学Semiology、意味論Semantics、サイバネティックス、超心理学Parapsychology、その他の協力により、やがて明らかにされて来るだろう。

これは芸術のみでなく文明プロパーにとって重大なことである。

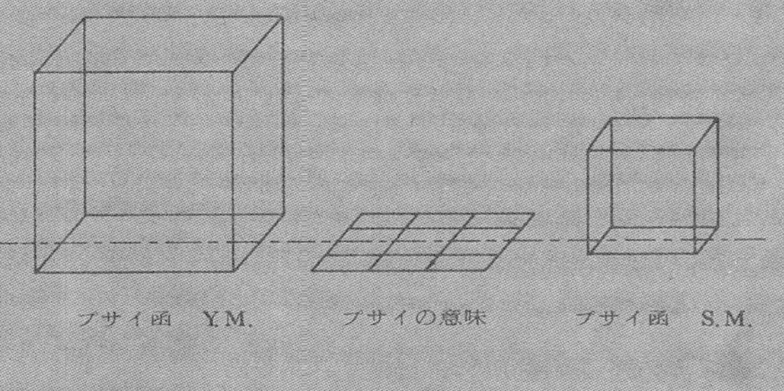

I 図

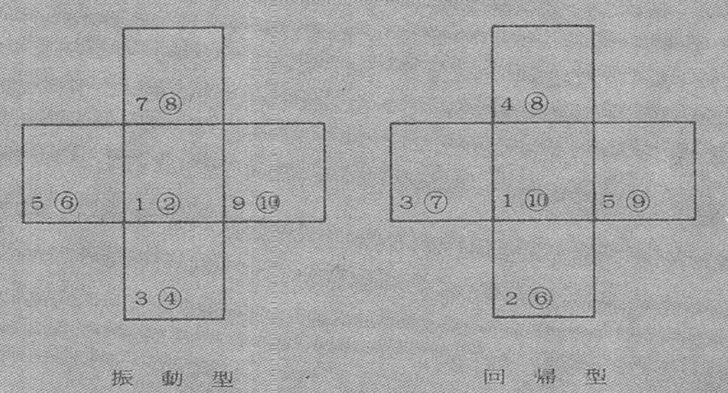

II 図　　　　　III 図

○印は裏面
数字順に視点を移動させる

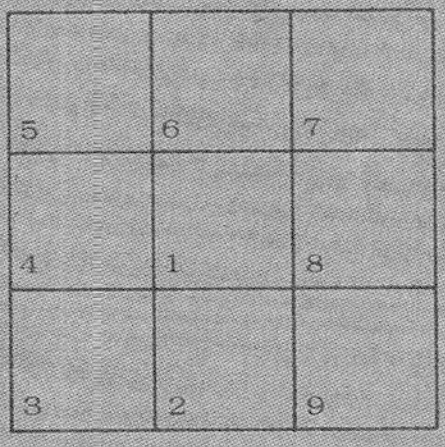

IV 図

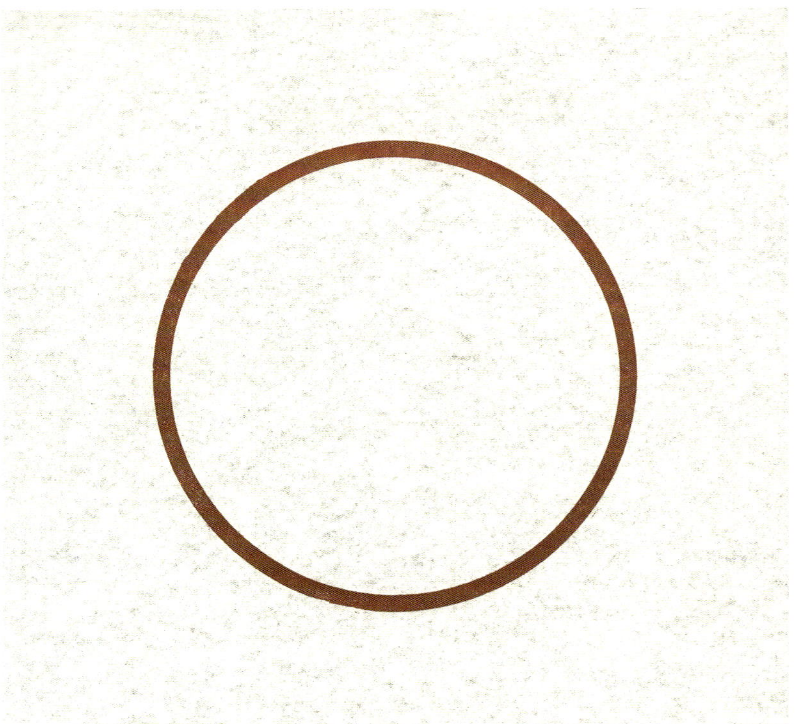

a resident of nearby Matsumoto, who would casually come by to talk shop, wearing a pair of *geta* clogs, as he fondly recalled. He contributed, in turn, a poetic homage to her in the brochure accompanying her solo exhibition in October 1952.

In 1956, Matsuzawa left for the U.S. on a Fulbright Fellowship. For a year, he was affiliated with Wisconsin State College-Superior (now University of Wisconsin-Superior), as a visiting scholar to conduct research on the "objective measurement of beauty." While there, he contacted Gyorgy Kepes, formerly at the New Bauhaus in Chicago and then teaching visual design at MIT, who invited him to Cambridge for the following year. As indicated by the *Forum* profile, Matsuzawa must at one point have entertained the offer from a like-minded teacher skeptical of the alienation of art from advanced sciences; however, he changed his mind, lest the school's "specialization in architecture should result in a decorative tendency" in his work. New York was more conducive to his research in contemporary art (he specifically remembered seeing the work of Rauschenberg). His study of religious philosophy and art history at Columbia University was however interrupted on February 2, 1957 (at 2 AM to be precise), when he happened to tune in to WOR's talk radio program that aired from 1 to 5 AM. The topics discussed by specialists and experts were often alternative in nature, including UFOs, outer space, hypnosis, astrology, psychic phenomena, and yoga philosophy, as well as psychology, mathematics, biology, medicine, engineering, and so forth. Every night since then until he suddenly left New York on March 5, he would listen to the program, absorbed in the discussions about afterlife, levitation, psychic phenomena, parapsychology, parascience, and parareligion, among other unusual subjects.

This window opened to alternative realities had a defining impact on the development of Matsuzawa's work. He was already conversant with mathematics and contemporary physics, which requires the visualization of the invisible; as a devout Buddhist, he was equipped with intimate knowledge of the mysticism of the Esoteric Shingon sect, which embraces cosmology that encourages visualization beyond human logic. With his late-night study in New York, he now had permission to "dematerialize painting" and actively explore the invisible in art. The first manifestation in this direction can be seen in the flier of 1961, *On "Meaning of Psi" and "Psi Chamber,"* his first language-only work, wherein he introduced his key concept "psi" (Ψ) that signified both "psyche" and the solution to Schrödinger's equation in quantum mechanics (Fig. 4.5). A litany of names he invoked to justify his enigmatic transformative theory of "psi" between different dimensionalities points to his awareness of different strains of mysticism: Heinrich Seuse (Christian mystic); Nicholas of Cusa (theologist); Girolamo Savonarola (Dominican reformer); Subhakarasmiba and Amoghavajra (Indian priests who translated the main Esoteric sutras into Chinese); Eusapia Palladino (spirit medium); J. B. Rhine (parapsychologist); Gerolamo Sacchari (geometer); Janos Bolyai (non-Euclidean geometry pioneer); Felix Klein (mathematician); and Norbert Wiener (cybernetics pioneer).[21]

Matsuzawa was thus spiritually and intellectually well prepared, when, as the legend has it, he heard a voice announce, "Vanish the objects!" while he was still in his futon at the dawn of June 1, 1964. By June 4, he knew he had to eschew material objects and turn to immaterial language to pursue an art that is "non-sensory." The rest is history: from then on, Matsuzawa rapidly developed a repertoire of cosmic conceptualism, even advocating the vanishing of humankind, to become the foremost conceptualist in 1960s Japan.[22] Among his work, *Anti-Civilization Exhibition* demonstrates his extraordinary faith in the human faculty to visualize void and nothingness, by exhorting us to mentally erase the clutter of an entire art exhibition (Fig. 4.6).[23] As for the "new arts research center" he had proposed to establish in his grant application, he kept his promise in his own terms: many of his mail-art works were sent out from "Void/Imaginary Space Exploration Center" (Kokūkan Jōkyō Tanchi Sentā), a conceptualist tag of his own invention.

Snapshot 2
Beate Sirota Gordon and Visual Art
(*Japan Art Festival* of 1966)

Were Japan Society to compile oral histories to chronicle its past activities through firsthand accounts, an interview with Beate Sirota Gordon would be essential. On the Society's staff from 1955 to 1981, she was instrumental in the establishment of the Society's Performing Arts Program in 1958 and its subsequent development. (From 1970 onward, she also headed the Performing Arts Program at Asia Society, New York.) Encouraged by the recurring advice to "talk to Beate" in the course of my research, I met with her to understand her role at the Society.[24]

The daughter of Leo Sirota, an internationally acclaimed Russian pianist, Gordon was born in 1923 in Vienna.[25] Her father left Kiev for Vienna in 1904 to study with the famed pianist-composer Ferruccio Busoni, and later became an Austrian citizen. The family subsequently traveled to Japan on a concert tour; they intended to stay only six months but her parents stayed for 17 years and Beate grew up to become "part Japanese." Today, she is best known for her contribution of the gender equality clause to the postwar Japanese constitution at the age of 22, while at the Government Section of GHQ (General Headquarters) under General Douglas MacArthur. However, she still had a full life ahead of her: she came to the U.S. in 1947 and married Joseph Gordon, a New Yorker and fellow-member of the Government Section in 1948. They have since lived in New York City, where her life was closely tied to the arts and culture of Japan.

At Japan Society, Gordon was initially assigned to the Student Activities Program, when the entire staff consisted of a mere six persons, in addition to the executive director, Douglas Overton.[26] One of her fondest memories from the 1950s concerns her inventive scheme to help cash-deprived Japanese music students (such as Ichiyanagi Toshi and Kobayashi Kenji), who were in her view "already professionals" but had to use their tools of trade, i.e., hands, to earn what little money they could by washing dishes. A small concert she organized to put those tools to proper use with proper pay eventually evolved into the school assembly program and college concerts, which functioned as an effective educational outreach strategy for the Society. It was also the beginning of the Performing Arts Program itself.[27]

An episode like this eloquently speaks of a tremendous degree of resourcefulness, imagination, and knack for generating positive attention that Gordon deployed to further the cause of Japanese culture in the U.S. As she managed the Performing Arts Program, she assisted visual artists as well as students. This was in part necessitated by the role the Society assumed in New York throughout the 1950s and 1960s, serving in effect as *the* clearinghouse of information about all things Japanese for its American constituents and all things New York and American for their Japanese counterparts. Generous and sympathetic by nature, Gordon took it upon herself to help those in need, at a loss, and with problems. For example, she placed the young artist Yoko Ono (who lived in New York since 1956 with her then husband Ichiyanagi), who was as conversant with traditional Japanese culture as with avant-garde art, to perform in many of the Society's cultural demonstration programs. She also became a confidant to Kusama Yayoi, who in her judgment needed little professional guidance, as the rapidly emerging talent seemed to know her way around the New York art world; but Gordon recalls helping her on a personal level with day-to-day problems. For the more established artists arriving in New York, she often gave introductions to galleries, such as Willard Gallery and Marlborough Gallery, which were seriously interested in new art from Japan.

It is no surprise, then, that when Japan Society launched the Print Artists Program in 1958, the task of assisting the invited Japanese printmakers fell to Gordon. In this program, which continued through 1961, the Society invited three artists, Sekino Jun'ichirō, Munakata Shikō, and Mori Yasu, from Japan. (Under this program, the Society also sent the American artist Arthur Flory to Japan in its final year.) Gordon grew especially close to Munakata, who was internationally established after winning prestigious print prizes at the São Paulo Biennale in 1955 and the Venice Biennale in 1956. She accompanied him on his travels in the U.S. as his interpreter and helped arrange his media appearances, exhibitions, and demonstrations. In a sense, she was his interpreter, personal manager, producer, and press officer all rolled into one. Her affinity to the free-spirited master was evident from several of his woodblock prints adorning the living-room walls of the apartment she and her husband share on the Upper West Side of Manhattan. Gordon's friendship with Munakata also helped her to raise money to fund a special student-aid program for emergency purposes, with Munakata donating a total of 135 prints of three small works, which she sold at $10 each. The sales notice for what she calls the "Munakata Fund" is published in the June 30, 1960 issue of *Japan Society Forum* (Fig. 4.7). It is also important to note that as a result of Gordon's close relationship with Munakata, Japan Society today holds the largest and finest collection of Munakata prints among American museums, including a complete set of *The Ten Great Disciples of Buddha* (1939 and 1948) and *Tokaidō Munakata Hanga* (1964). These were donated directly by the artist and by Mrs. Blanchette Hooker Rockefeller on the occasion of the opening of Japan House Gallery in 1971.

There are many great stories of Gordon's tenure at Japan Society. Some of them are recounted in her autobiography, *The Only Woman in the Room*, in which she admits her gift for public relations work.[28] Indeed, she was an inspired publicist who knew the pulse of the American media. A little-known episode in this vein is her involvement with *Japan Art Festival*, which opened at the Union Carbide Building in March 1966. This emerged in our conversation, when I pressed her to tell me more about her work in the area of visual art. "Yes, Tange's sculpture. I still have the model!" said Gordon, her eyes twinkling and voice animated. It was a tiny but beautifully crafted model, about 12 inches in length, made of wafer-thin wood, which lies on one of her decorative shelves (Fig. 4.8). Its units were sequentially numbered to indicate the order of assembly. The second archival snapshot in my essay is this model, which helps shed light on an understudied topic of Japanese art in New York in the 1960s.

The year 1966 saw two large-scale exhibitions of Japanese contemporary art held in New York, one better known than the other. The one that is already inscribed in art history is *The New Japanese Painting and Sculpture*. Organized by William S. Lieberman and Dorothy C. Miller of the Museum of Modern Art (MoMA), it presented the mostly modernist works of 47 artists, including one ceramicist. It toured eight venues in the U.S., beginning at the San Francisco Museum of Art in April 1965, reaching MoMA in October 1966, and ending at the Milwaukee Art Center in May 1967. Opening seven months earlier than the MoMA show, *Japan Art Festival*, which presented 33 painters, sculptors, and printmakers and more than 50 crafts artists, is an undertaking relatively unknown in postwar Japanese art history (and a blind spot in my own scholarship).

Japan Art Festival was a semi-governmental endeavor organized by the Japan Art Festival Association, Inc. Conceived by Asō Yoshikata, a member of the House of Representatives, the Association comprised influential politicians (such as Nakasone Yasuhiro, a

future Prime Minister) and corporate figures (such as Nagano Shigeo, President of Fuji Iron & Steel). An equally impressive roster of critics and curators, including Kawakita Michiaki, Deputy Chief of the National Museum of Modern Art, Tokyo, formed the selection committee.[29] The festival's goal was saliently expressed in the Association's Japanese name, Kokusai Geijutsu Mihon'ichi Kyōkai— literally, "Association for the International Trade Fair of Art." The promotion of Japanese contemporary art was closely tied to that of Japanese trade, as Asō believed that the reputation of Japanese export goods would be enhanced by demonstrating the high quality of contemporary artistic production in Japan.[30]

Japan Society was obviously not directly involved, but Eugene Langston, the Society's former deputy director, was the Association's "non-regular member" and Gordon Washburn, Gallery Director of Asia Society (Japan Society's sister institution established in 1956) was on the selection committee. It is not difficult to imagine that when the Association sought a capable and knowledgeable person to head its New York bureau, it found an ideal candidate in Gordon, who was duly "loaned" out from Japan Society.[31]

As Gordon recalls, when the architect Tange Kenzō, who was entrusted to design the exhibition, came to New York, he told her, "I want big publicity." Gordon immediately suggested that he should

FIGURE 4.7

Notice of Munakata Shikō's prints for sale, as printed in *Japan Society Forum* (June 30, 1960)

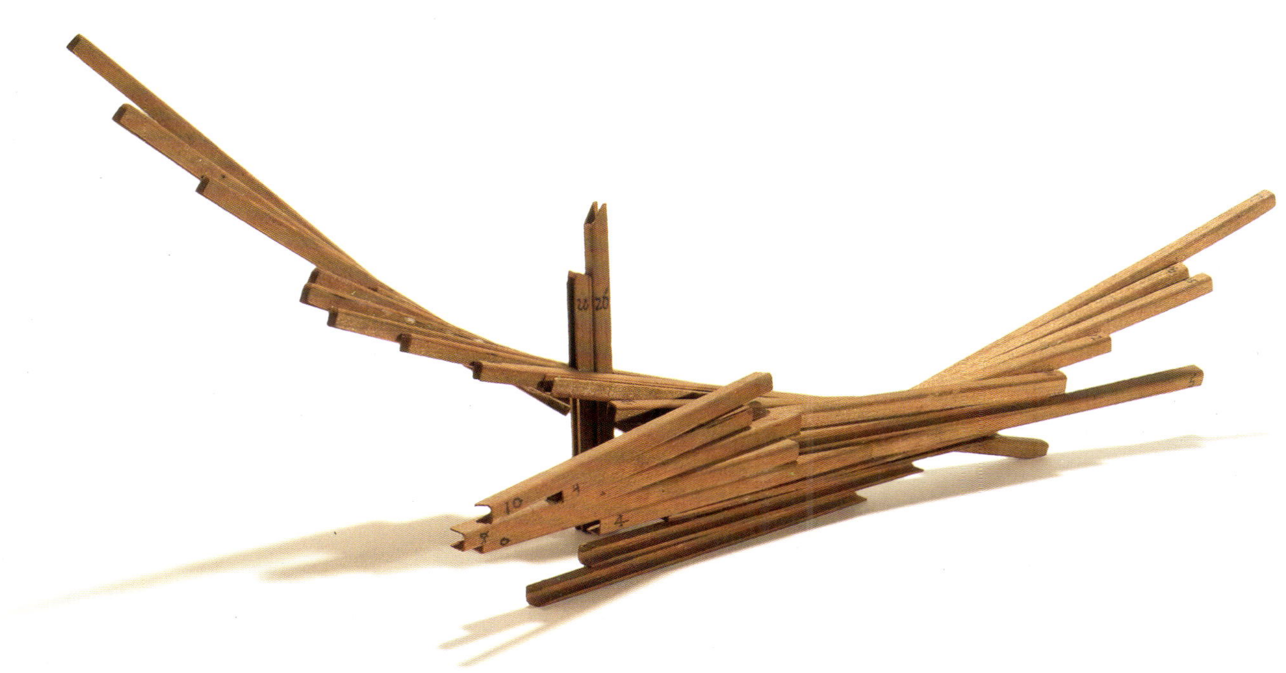

think of something big to install outside the Union Carbide Building (presently the Chase Building) at 270 Park Avenue, in Midtown Manhattan; otherwise, nobody would know there was an art exhibition going on inside the office building. Tange quickly set to work, conceiving a sweeping shape of bent, laminated plywood, as dynamic as the curved roof of the Yoyogi National Gymnasium he had designed for the Tokyo Olympic Games of 1964. A link between the interior and the exterior was created by using the same bent wood for pedestals and other displays. While the exhibition scheme represented a simple elegance and stately order, the sculptural *Theme Tower* installed outside on the sidewalk embodied a bursting energy and progressive movement. Thanks to Gordon's advice, Tange's dream for "big publicity" came true: on April 3, 1966, *Japan Art Festival* was given a sizable space in the New York Times, with a striking photo of Tange's tower accompanying a sarcastic review by the art critic John Canaday (Fig. 4.9).

After New York, *Japan Art Festival* traveled to Pittsburgh, Chicago, and San Francisco. It was followed by the second, third, and fourth Festivals in 1967–69, with the fifth coming back to New York in 1970. Notably, the fifth *Japan Art Festival*, co-organized with and presented at the Guggenheim Museum, included Matsuzawa Yutaka among six artists invited to participate, in addition to 53 artists selected through an open-call competition in Japan.[32] By then recognized as a leading practitioner of Japanese conceptualism, he sent a photostat of *My Death*, a work he created for the Tokyo Biennale of the same year.[33]

Japan Art Festival is a rich subject to study beyond the scope of this essay. Concluding this section, however, is a footnote pertinent to the history of Japan Society. A remnant of the 1966 festival may be found at the Society today: the benches made of laminated plywood placed in and around the lobby area were designed for *Japan Art Festival*, to offer a moment of rest to those visiting the Union Carbide Building to see Japanese contemporary art (see Fig. 4.2).

Snapshot 3
Okamoto Shinjirō as a Japan Society Fellow
(Japan Society's Art Grant Program in the 1960s)

Annual reports form an institution's autobiography. As "material objects," annual reports also speak for the state of the institution through their designs and other material properties. From the early years of Japan Society, for example, a small booklet of 1916, handsomely bound in a Japanese style, reveals a not-so-subtle intention to familiarize its membership with Japanese design tradition.[34]

Nice Try. Too Bad It Didn't Work

By JOHN CANADAY

THE Japan Art Festival, as it is called, which is an installation of painting, sculpture and crafts in the Union Carbide Building, 270 Park Avenue, is just about as puzzling an affair as has hit this city within my memory. Almost everything about it is recognizable as a good idea well carried through, yet almost nothing about it is successful. As a failure it is not even dramatic. You go to it with high hopes but you come out of it feeling that you have been through an unseasonal freeze during the cherry blossom season.

Kenzo Tange, described in the announcements as Japan's best - known architect, preplanned the installation as a unit for the space it occupies. The detailed calculation of his scheme is apparent in his scaled working model of the lobby of the building and its displays—which is on exhibition. Special photo murals some 45 feet high were originated for certain walls, and smaller ones for others; Mr. Tange designed a spectacular sculptural construction as a three-dimensional insignia and signboard. It stands on the sidewalk on Park Avenue. The U-shaped plywood beams from which it is executed are the modular unit for the interior installation, including some of the handsomest benches imaginable, the scheme as a whole and in details has a fine, elegant austerity, and electronic music was commissioned from Toshi Ichityangi and Toru Takemitsu as an accompaniment for the whole business.

Going Down

Perhaps the smallest but most damaging defects in the show are exemplified by the facts that Mr. Tange's sidewalk sculpture, designed to stand free in city space, is surrounded by unsightly stanchions and ropes ("Insurance problems," a spokesman explained), which were removed for purposes of the photograph reproduced on this page, and that the music coming through the pipes on my first visit was an anonymous mush best identifiable as Music to Ride in an Elevator By, and, on my second, a very pleasant but incongruous cocktail - piano rendition of "Oh, You Beautiful Doll, You Great Big Beautiful Doll."

Some very small, beautiful dolls of Japanese extraction serving as hostesses but hardly as sources of information back of the information desk were unable to tell me when, if ever, the special music would be played, and indeed, they hardly seemed to understand what I was talking about, which cannot be held against them since my mastery of Japanese is inferior to theirs of English. Their sweet, uncomprehending politeness, as they stood waiting for me to answer my own questions, with evident willingness to stand there thus until closing time, had its advantage, since it placed no time limit on the pleasure of staring at them, a pleasure great enough to make you wonder why, with such material at hand, the Japanese should worry about whipping up any other products for export.

You get here to a more than secondary trouble with the festival, which is that the art on display is exhibited as an export product. Basically conceived as a trade fair (the photo murals are montages studded with dramatic shots of transportation systems and skyscraper construction), the festival pays flattering tribute to art as a symbol of national vitality. But at the same time it seems less interested in the art as art than in propounding the idea that the Japanese artist, like the Japanese industrialist, is ready to compete with westerners on their own terms. The paintings and sculptures are hybrids that on one hand proclaim pride in Japanese esthetic traditions—from the painstaking technique of lacquerware to the free-est expression in calligraphy—but at the same time compromise traditional disciplines with concessions to the self-indulgent esthetics of contemporary Western art.

Three visits to the festival, over the period of a week (it opened Tuesday a week ago and closes April 23) were insufficient to modify my impression that while its hybrid art often rises above the European kindergarten exercises that we inflate and call serious abstract painting today, they do so at the expense of debasing a great native tradition.

Finally, there is no getting around the sad truth that the festival is installed not in a gallery but in a passageway. For all that the Union Carbide Building's first and second floors provide expanses of open, beautifully illuminated space; for all that it should be quite wonderful to have art installed virtually on the street for the enjoyment of passers-by; for all that the space has been so rationally studied and organized by Mr. Tange—in spite of all this, the art is still installed in an area planned first of all as a space you pass through in order to get somewhere else. The exhibition seems to be there by sufference, emphasizing the uneasy position of art today as a take-it-or-leave-it accessory to be grafted on, at best, to the really important business of practical affairs that keep the world turning.

Under such confusions, the quality of the paintings and sculptures becomes a little difficult to evaluate. The selection emphasizes large panels and screens that are adaptable as accessories (again that key word) to an installation where the architectural character is predominant. The art serves the scheme, not the scheme the art. Standing around in the lobby, the big paintings are like murals that have been detached from their walls; they have the uneasy, waiting look of people who have arrived early for an appointment. One is torn between admiration for the installation scheme as a scheme and recognition that it has been allowed to steal the show, but one wonders finally whether any scheme could have been devised that could contradict the area's function as a public passageway.

Now that these reservations have been stated, however, it should be emphasized that the selection includes some extraordinarily handsome paintings and sculptures. I found it impossible, even so, to rid them of a general air of impersonality. It will be interesting to see how some of the artists look in the hands of the Museum of Modern Art. Of the 42 artists and craftsmen in the festival, 22 are painters and six are sculptors. Of these, 18 overlap the museum's list in an exhibition now on tour and scheduled for New York next fall.

Getting back to the missing music: the press office of the festival advises that the two compositions, each lasting about half an hour, are scheduled to be piped at 10:30 A.M. and 2:00 P.M. daily but subject to change to accommodate other events. The hours in general are from **9:00 A.M. to 6:00 P.M.** Monday through Friday, and Saturdays from **10:00 P.M. to 5:00 P.M.** Admission is free.

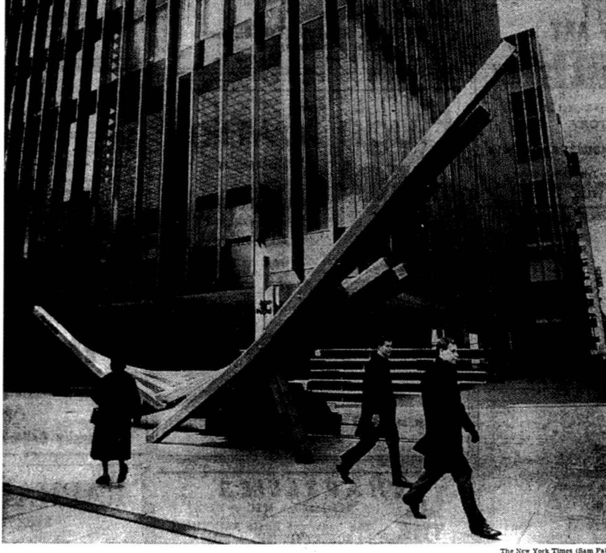

The New York Times (Sam Falk)

It Says "Japan" on Park Avenue
Kenzo Tange's plywood construction in front of the Union Carbide Building

FIGURE 4.9

New York Times article on *Japan Art Festival*, dated April 3, 1966
Copyright © 1966 by The New York Times Co. Reprinted with permission

In the initial postwar years, the earliest annual reports through 1954 are mimeographed, pointing to the stage of operational resumption after long inactivity. From 1955 through 1967, the format was fairly constant, at 8 ½ x 5 inches, with certain texts and phrases recurring year after year in the account of continuing projects. The 1967–68 report shows a sudden change. The format is reduced and made horizontal, the typeface is modernized, and text is interspersed with charming illustrations and some photographs. In the following year, the report becomes square, a format that continues until 1976–77; drawings and occasional calligraphy are included, but by 1973–74, the use of photographic reproductions becomes the norm.

The third archival snapshot of this essay is the delightful drawings in *Japan Society Report 1967–1968* (Fig. 4.10). They were created by the painter Okamoto Shinjirō, who was another Japan Society Fellow for a seven-month period in 1967–68/1968–69. Unlike the Japan Society Fellows program in the 1950s, in which grantees in the arts were a minority vis-à-vis close to 200 academic recipients, the fellowship program between 1965 and 1969 was specifically "designed to strengthen American-Japanese relations in the cultural, artistic, and intellectual fields."[35] The program was supported by the JDR 3rd Fund and the Ford Foundation, which financed a combined quarter-million-dollar project. By design, the program would offer traveling grants for "Japanese artists, writers, and other 'creative' individuals" to spend an average of eight months in the U.S. and other countries. The grants were awarded to 36 individuals, six being Americans. (One grant was given to the eminent art historian Meyer Schapiro to travel to Tokyo and attend a UNESCO conference, the other two were not in the arts). Among 30 Japanese recipients, 28 were practitioners in the arts (see Table 2).

Although this list by no means represents a who's who of contemporary art in Japan, it still provides us with a fairly good cross-section of *gendai bijutsu*. Aikō Kenji was an editor of *Bijutsu techō* (Art notebook), which is a leading contemporary art magazine; the critic Tōno Yoshiaki, a frequent contributor to *Bijutsu techō*, was a champion of *gendai bijutsu* and an astute observer of American contemporary art since the late 1950s. Between two curators on the list, while Sugahara Hisao specialized in traditional art, Tomiyama Hideo was a modern and contemporary specialist, who went on to become Director of the National Museum of Modern Art, Kyoto in the 1990s. Three artists represented a new generation of printmakers: among them, Ikeda Masuo won the grand prize in printmaking at the 1966 Venice Biennale, following Munakata's footsteps. A number of the Japan Society Fellows were included in the two landmark exhibitions of 1966 in New York, indicating their status in the Japanese art world: Motonaga Sadamasa (a Gutai member), Tomioka Sōichirō, Shinoda Morio, and Tsuji Shindō were shown at both the MoMA and *Japan Art Festival*; Ikeda was selected for the festival; and Kuno Shin, Minoru Niizuma, Okamoto Shinjirō, and Yoshimura Masunobu participated in the MoMA show. In the Fellows list, the inclusion of three vanguard artists who resided in New York at the time—Kusama, Yoshimura (a Neo Dada member), and Kosugi Takehisa (a Group Ongaku member)—points to the obvious fact that New York was fast becoming a diaspora of sorts for *gendai bijutsu*.

The career of Okamoto Shinjirō demonstrates what it meant to "make it" in the world of *gendai bijutsu* in the mid-1960s. Okamoto was born in Tokyo in 1933 (younger than Ushio Shinohara, represented in *Making a Home*, by one year). Having no formal training in art, he first attracted attention at the annual Yomiuri Independent Exhibition, in which he started participating in 1956. Embracing his firm belief in "imagery," he stopped his exhibition activity for three years when the Japanese painting world was swept by a dominant tendency of gestural abstraction, which was dubbed the "*Informel* whirlwind." When he resumed his activity around 1960, his painting shed a heavy materiality and a surrealistic imagery; instead, his canvas quickly assumed the style of what the critic Haryū Ichirō called "abstract manga" (*chūshō manga*) characterized by the simplified images, clearly delineated and flatly colored, that anticipated the anime- and manga-inflected sensitivity of recent Japanese painters, such as Nara Yoshitomo and Takashi Murakami (Figs. 2.1, 3.4).[36] Okamoto's visibility in the art world grew as he received two consecutive honorable mentions at the annual open-call competition of *Shell Prize Exhibition*, whose express purpose was to discover promising young artists, in 1962 and 1963. In 1964, his inclusion in *Young Seven*, curated by the critic Tōno for Minami Gallery in Tokyo, cemented his avant-garde standing, although his graphic style was closer to Tateishi Kōichi than to the junk aesthetics practiced by such luminaries of Anti-Art (*Han-geijutsu*) as Miki Tomio, Kudō Susumu, and Nakanishi Natsuyuki, among the selected artists.[37] The show at Minami in January was followed in November by a truly momentous event for any young contemporary artist in Japan: Okamoto was awarded the grand prize in the inaugural competition sponsored by the Museum of Contemporary Art, Nagaoka, the first ever contemporary art museum in Japan, which had opened its door just a few months earlier. His *Ten Little Indians*, whose "colorism, humor, and formal expression" impressed the jurors, not only won him 1,000,000 yen (approximately $2,800) but also turned him into an overnight star.[38] (In 1968, the Nagaoka contemporary museum's competition crowned yet another star, Sekine Nobuo, who spearheaded the movement of Mono-ha [Things School].)

Fast forwarding to 1968, we see Okamoto receive an unexpected invitation to New York as a Japan Society Fellow.[39] Although he was not so interested in American art, he "did not want to lose out to an import culture backed by the international market," as he had "pride as a postwar (*sengo*) artist"—by which he means an artist who experienced the arduous postwar years. So he accepted the invitation, taking a sabbatical from his day job as art director at a

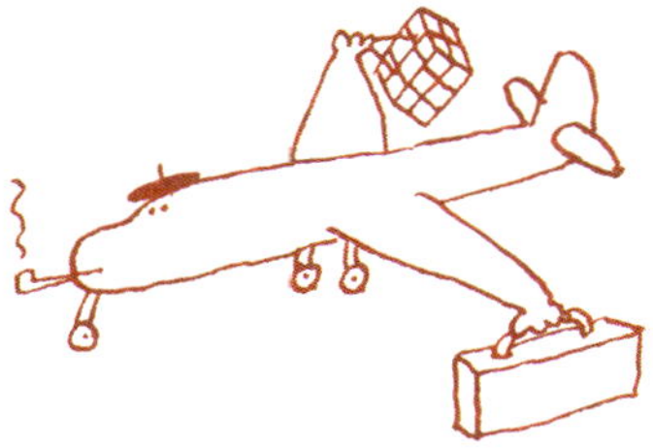

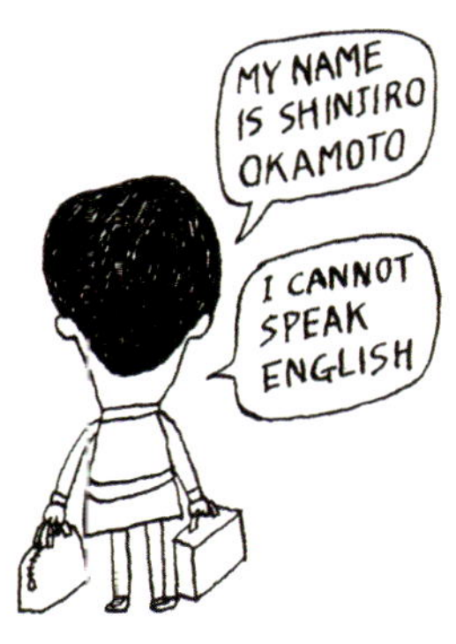

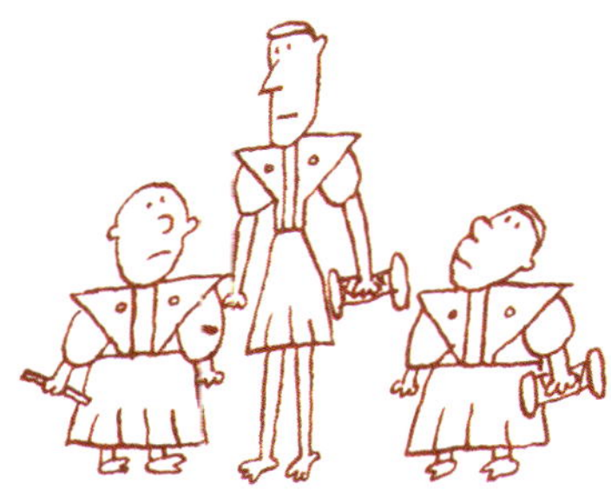

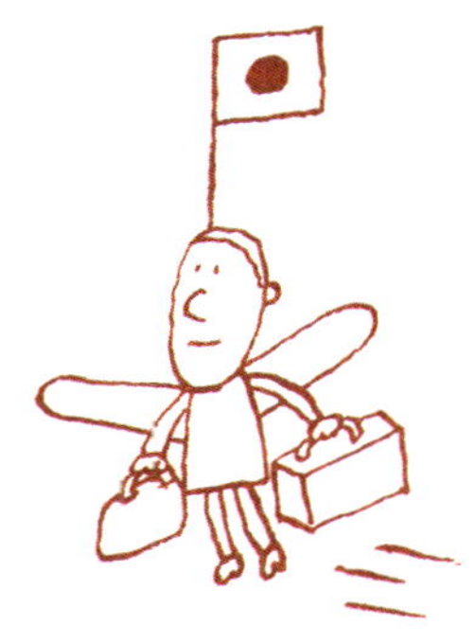

FIGURE 4.10

Okamoto Shinjirō
Illustrations reproduced in *Japan Society Report 1967–1968*

TABLE 2

Japan Society Fellowship, 1965–69: Arts-Related Japanese Recipients

Name	Occupation	Year	Duration	Project Description
Aikō Kenji	art editor	1966–67/ 1967–68	9 months	Visits museums and galleries in Europe and the U.S., observes the state of art publishing, and confers with professional colleagues
Hamaya Hiroshi	photographer	1966–67	3 months	Photographs in the U.S.
Hani Susumu	filmmaker	1966–67		First American trip; attends the Flaherty International Film Seminar and meets professional colleagues in the U.S.
Ichinohe Saeko	choreographer	1968–69		Assists in arranging the choreography of a ballet presented by the Boston Ballet Company
Ikeda Masuo	printmaker	1965–66/ 1966–67	6 months	Studies and practices printmaking in the New York area
Kanō Mitsuo	etcher, printmaker	1967–68	9 months	Observes, studies, practices, and demonstrates etching and printmaking in the U.S.
Kazuki Yasuo	painter	1966–67		Observes contemporary art in the U.S.
Kojiro Yūichirō	professor of architecture	1965–66	8 months	Surveys American architecture tradition and lectures on Japanese design
Kosugi Takehisa	avant-garde composer	1966–67		Supplemental living expenses and return travel to Japan
Kuno Shin	painter, metalist	1965–66/ 1966–67	8 months	Studies contemporary American art
Kusama Yayoi	painter, sculptor	1965–66	4 months	Exhibits her works, studies, and travels in the U.S.
Motonaga Sadamasa	painter	1966–67/ 1967–68	12 months	Observes the state of American painting and paints in the U.S.
Niizuma Minoru	sculptor	1966–67		Replaces lost tools
Nishi Daiyū	sculptor, caster	1965–66/ 1966–67	4 months	Attends the Sculpting and Casting Conference, University of Kansas (May 1966), and studies and travels in the U.S.
Okamoto Shinjirō	painter	1967–68 1968–69	7 months	Studies and observes contemporary American painting, paints, and travels in the U.S. and Europe
Shinoda Morio	sculptor, industrial designer	1965–66/ 1966–67	4 months	Attends the Sculpting and Casting Conference, University of Kansas (May 1966), and studies and travels in the U.S.
Shirai Akiko	etcher, printmaker	1965–66/ 1966–67	8 months	Observes, studies, practices, and demonstrates etching and printmaking in the U.S.
Sugahara Hisao	museum curator	1966–67/ 1967–68	6 months	Observes American and European museum curatorial practices
Tanaka Keisuke	mosaicist	1966–67/ 1967–68	9 months	Visits museums and sites of mosaics in the U.S., Mexico, Europe, and North Africa
Tanikawa Shuntarō	poet, playwright, social critic	1966–67		Observes American life and meets professional colleagues
Tomioka Sōichirō	painter	1965–66/ 1966–67	8 months	Studies and observes contemporary American painting and travels in "snow country" to gather materials for his landscape painting
Tomiyama Hideo	museum curator	1966–67		Observes American and European museum curatorial techniques and practices
Tōno Yoshiaki	art critic	1965–66	8 months	Surveys contemporary American art, makes contacts with museums, galleries, and artists
Tsuji Shindō	sculptor/ceramicist	1965–66	4 months	Travels in the Indian country of New Mexico, attends the Sculpting and Casting Conference, University of Kansas (May 1966)
Yamazaki Masakazu	playwright	1965–66	2 months	Supervises the production of the English version of his play *Zeami* in New York
Yoshimura Masunobu	sculptor	1965–66		Travel and incidental expenses
Yuasa Jōji	composer	1968–69		Studies avant-garde music (electronic music, computer music, and graphic musical scores) in the U.S. and meets composers

Notes

This list is based on *Japan Society 1966 Report*, *Japan Society 1967 Report*, *Japan Society Report: 1967–1968*, and *Japan Society Report: 1968–1969*. "Duration" of individual fellowships is given where provided in the above sources. "Occupation" is given based on the above sources. "Project Description" is edited from the above sources.

major printing company. The hotel recommended to him by the Society was Prince George Hotel at 14 West 28th Street, documented in his painting *Queenie the Mother*, which he created after coming back to Japan (Fig. 4.11). With a monthly stipend of $600, he had a surplus of $100 after paying for the hotel, food and other necessities, and art supplies. The critic and curator Miki Tamon, who happened to stay at the same hotel around that time, remembers the artist's room was set up as a studio, with newspapers spread on the floor to keep it from being stained by paint.[40] While in New York, Okamoto met with the painter Saul Steinberg at his home, but the most memorable person he encountered was Queenie, a friendly African-American maid at the Prince George, who took great care of a lonely Japanese away from his family. The painter saw a "Blues-like pathos in her chubby body," and later transformed her into a "folksy Holy Mother" with Child represented in the invitation card to her son's birthday party in *Queenie the Mother*. The maid's abstract likeness became part of the painting series and print portfolio, entitled *Betty Boop's Country* (1968–74), in which he portrayed his impressions of New York. His credo to "respect the real-life feelings of ordinary people,"[41] as much as his humorous observation, permeates the series. After *Betty Boop's Country*, Okamoto's painting shed cosmopolitanism and turned to more indigenous subject matter. This shift might not have been unrelated to an enigmatic vision he had on the flight from Tokyo: as he flew to New York, he felt his self split into "two halves, one heading to New York, the other turning back to the Tokyo of his boyhood, [not like urbane Shinjuku but like] the folksy *shitamachi* district of Asakusa."

Snapshot 4
Naoto Nakagawa as a New York Artist
(Japan Society Gallery and Contemporary Art Exhibitions)

Japan Society moved to the new headquarters called "Japan House" at its current location on East 47th Street, near the U.N., in 1971. Although the Society since the 1950s presented exhibitions of Japanese contemporary artists in collaboration with other institutions and galleries,[42] the opening of the namesake "Japan House Gallery" within its own building was a major development. From the outset, art and visual culture of modern and contemporary Japan were topics as integral to the exhibition programming as those of premodern Japan. Rand Castile, the founding director, who had joined the Society's education staff in 1967, recently observed that the Gallery filled a void in the U.S., where "no art museum … was systematically showing Japanese art."[43]

In particular, Castile's inclusion of Japanese contemporary art was a major innovation, as pointed out by Alexandra Munroe, Castile's protégé and the fourth gallery director, who started her professional career as Assistant to the Director and Editor under Castile in 1982–88.[44] Significantly, the inaugural exhibition that presented the traditional subject of Rinpa was followed by a solo exhibition of the 20th-century master of ceramic art, Kitaōji Rosanjin, which marked Castile's first curatorial endeavor at the Gallery. With his forward-looking programming, Castile not only articulated a key mission of Japan Society Gallery—the continuing engagement with Japanese contemporary art—but also took a prescient initiative in the field that was nonexistent at that time but thrives today: Asian contemporary art. It was not until 1994, for example, that Asia Society began its contemporary programming with *Asia/America: Identities in Contemporary Asian American*

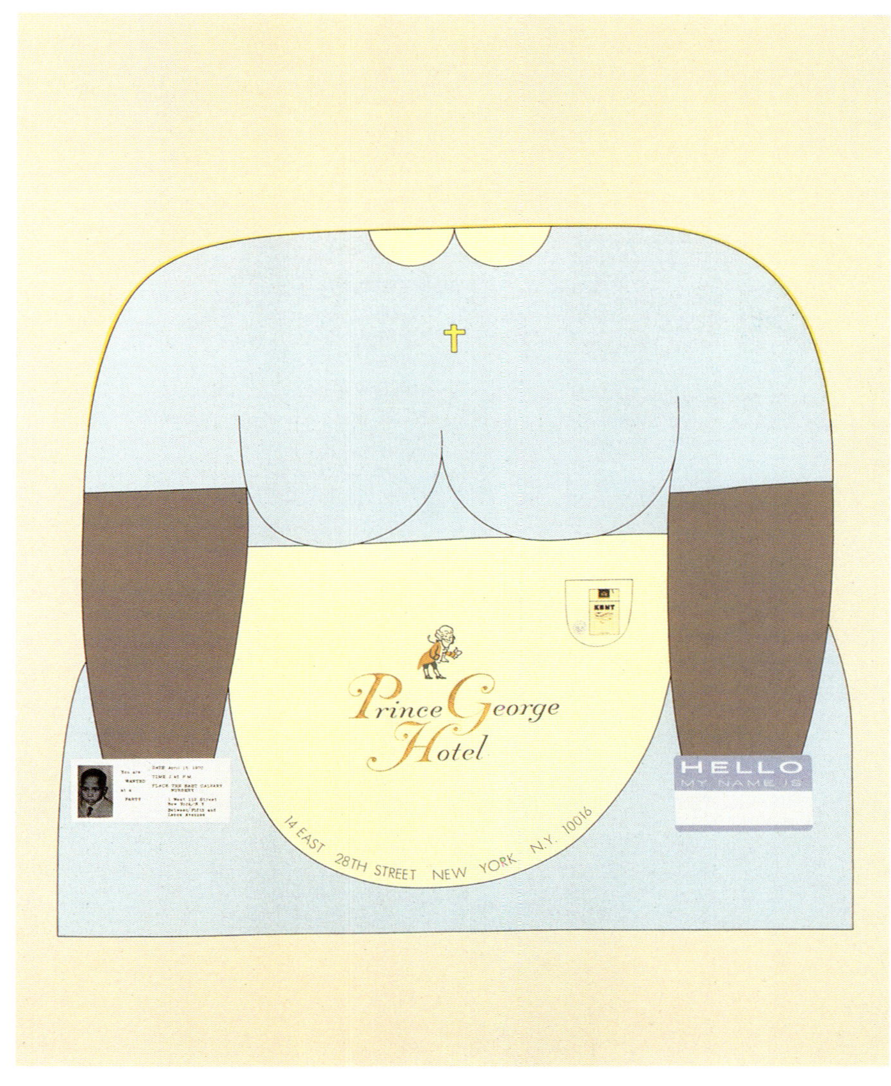

Figure 4.11

Okamoto Shinjirō
Queenie the Mother
1974
Silkscreen
22 ⅞ x 18 ⅛"(58.2 x 46.2 cm)
PHOTO COURTESY OF THE ARTIST

Art. The concerted effort Castile made to present contemporary art is amply demonstrated by the appointment of the Gallery's Art Advisory Committee, which included influential figures in American contemporary art. Its chairman was Porter McCray (chairman: 1978–90; member: 1976–91), who pioneered the postwar international exchange in modern and contemporary art, first as the director of circulating exhibitions at MoMA and then as the director of the JDR 3rd Fund. The committee members included William Lieberman (1974–90), curator of painting and sculpture at MoMA; Arthur Drexler (1974–86), director of architecture and design also at MoMA; and Martin Friedman (1980–90), director of the Walker Art Center.

With *Making a Home*, the Gallery's exhibition history marks the 94th presentation (see Table 3). Among 94, 32—or about one third of the past exhibitions—have featured modern or contemporary Japanese themes, including the current one. Among them, 12, again including this one, have thematized *gendai bijutsu* or Japanese "contemporary art" in the narrower sense (that is, vanguard practices of painting and sculpture as well as a range of non-painting/non-sculpture experimentations, including conceptualism, performance, and video art). The chronological distribution bears out the solid commitment to *gendai bijutsu* by two past directors, Castile and Munroe, whose tenures were 1971–1986 and 1998–2005, respectively.

The exhibition programming has expanded over time. The earlier contemporary exhibitions were one- or two-person exhibitions of living Japanese artists, many of whom were based in New York (e.g., Shigeko Kubota, Tadaaki Kuwayama, and Ushio Shinohara). Munroe introduced an art-historical perspective by presenting large-scale retrospectives (e.g., Yoko Ono, Moriyama Daidō, and Tōmatsu Shōmei), while continuing the inter- and multi-disciplinary vision exemplified by *Tokyo: Form and Spirit* (1987) and adding a dimension of popular culture (e.g., *Little Boy: The Arts of Japan's Exploding Subculture*). Collaboration with other institutions has also become more frequent.

On the archival front, looking through the exhibition catalogues produced by the Gallery, we notice a dramatic change over time, especially in contemporary catalogue design, which also echoes the general sea change in museum publications on contemporary subjects. In comparison with the Gallery's own lavishly produced, hefty tomes of the past few years, such as *YES YOKO ONO* and *Little Boy*, the slim volumes of *Ikeda & Ida* (1974) and *Shinohara* (1982) may feel minimalist. At the time, however, these publications were the most comprehensive studies on these artists published in the English language. In design, the starkest among them is no doubt *Contemporary Japanese Art in America (I): Arita, Nakagawa, Sugimoto* (1987), whose title adorns the otherwise white cover (Fig. 4.12). The 1987 catalogue signals a considerable departure from preceding contemporary catalogues both in terms of design (having a more substantial format) and content itself. Its title, "Contemporary Japanese Art in America," announces itself as a larger project than just another exhibition to show the work of individual artists. The curatorial ambition is substantiated by a researched art historical essay by Munroe entitled "Japanese Artists in the American Avant-Garde, 1945–1970." It spans 11 pages of solid text including endnotes, unlike the Society's previous contemporary catalogue essays which are generally short and art critical. Since Munroe returned to the Gallery as Director, the scholarly approach to contemporary art has been a hallmark of Gallery publications.

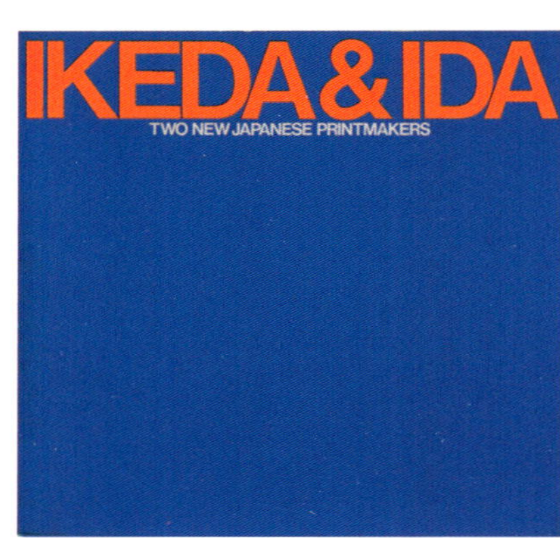

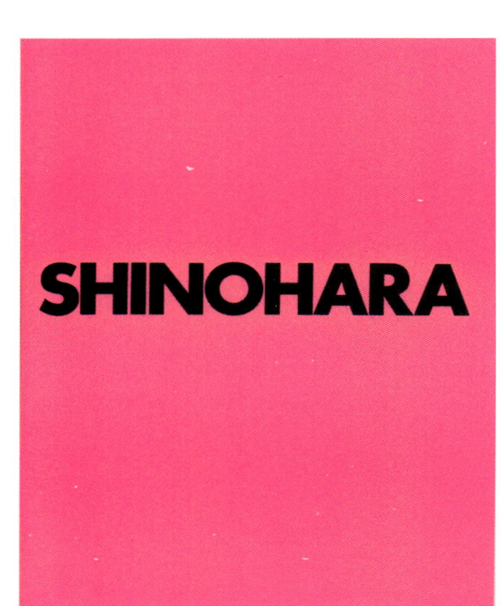

FIGURE 4.12

Three contemporary art catalogues from Japan Society Gallery: from left, *Ikeda & Ida* (1974), *Contemporary Japanese Art in America (I): Arita, Nakagawa, Sugimoto* (1987), and *Shinohara* (1982)

TABLE 3

Chronology of Exhibitions at Japan Society Gallery, 1971–2007
With Emphasis on Modern and Contemporary Visual Culture

1972	Rosanjin: 20th Century Master Potter of Japan (No. 2)
	Contemporary Japanese Posters (No. 3; held at K.B.S., presently The Japan Foundation)
1974	**Ikeda & Ida: Two New Japanese Print Makers** (No. 10)
1975	Japan Society Exhibition of Munakata Works in Honor of the Visit to Japan House of Their Majesties the Emperor and Empress of Japan (No. 14)
1978	**4 Video Sculptures by Shigeko Kubota** (No. 20)
1979	Japan: Photographs, 1854–1905 (No. 26; traveled)
1980	**Japanese Art Now: Tadaaki Kuwayama & Rikurō Okamoto** (No. 29)
1981	**Sound on Paper: Music Notation in Japan** (No. 32)
1982	Shikō Munakata (1903–1975): Works on Paper (No. 36)
	Shinohara (No. 37)
1985	New Public Architecture: Recent Projects by Fumihiko Maki and Arata Isozaki (No. 43; traveled)
1986	Tokyo: Form and Spirit (No. 46; organized by Walker Art Center)
1987	**Contemporary Japanese Art in America (I): Arita, Nakagawa, Sugimoto** (No. 47)
	Paris in Japan: The Japanese Encounter with European Painting (No. 48; traveled)
1988	Shikō Munakata and Kitaōji Rosanjin: Works from the Japan Society Collection (No. 49)
1991	Made in Japan: American Influence on Japanese Quilts (No. 58; traveled)
	The Nemunoki School: A Model of Education through Art for Physically and Mentally Handicapped Youth (No. 59)
1992	Souvenirs from Japan: Japanese Photography at the Turn of the Century (No. 61)
	The Dragon King of the Sea: Japanese Decorative Art of the Meiji Period from The John R. Young Collection (No. 63; traveled)
1993	Modern Japanese Ceramics in American Collections (No. 67; traveled)
1996	Rainbows and Shimmering Bridges: Contemporary Japanese Lacquerware (No. 73; traveled)
1998	Shikō Munakata: The Modern Master of Woodblock Prints (No. 76)
	The Art of Twentieth-Century Zen: Paintings and Calligraphy by Japanese Masters (No. 77)
1999	**Daidō Moriyama: Stray Dog** (No. 79; traveled)
2000	**YES YOKO ONO** (No. 81; traveled)
2001	Frank Lloyd Wright and the Art of Japan: The Architect's Other Passion (No. 82)
2002	The New Way of Tea (No. 84)
2003	Isamu Noguchi and Modern Japanese Ceramics (No. 87; organized by Arthur M. Sackler Gallery, Smithsonian Institution, Washington, D.C.)
2004	**Shōmei Tōmatsu: Skin of the Nation** (No. 89; organized by San Francisco Museum of Modern Art)
2005	**Little Boy: The Arts of Japan's Exploding Subculture** (No. 90)
	Hiroshi Sugimoto: History of History (No. 91; traveled)
2006	Contemporary Clay: Japanese Ceramics for the New Century (No. 92; organized by Museum of Fine Arts, Boston)
2007	**Making a Home: Japanese Contemporary Artists in New York** (No. 94)

Notes

This list includes exhibitions held at Japan House Gallery (1971–87) and Japan Society Gallery (1987–2007) that explored predominantly modern and contemporary themes. Surveys not exclusively devoted to modern and contemporary periods (e.g., *Japanese Theatre in the World*, 1997) are excluded. "Dates" indicate the year the exhibition opened at Japan House/Society Gallery. Titles are followed, in parentheses, by consecutive numbers assigned to the exhibitions, beginning with the first in 1971. Organizers are given only when Japan Society is not a primary organizer; co-organizers are not mentioned. Titles in bold denote exhibitions devoted to *gendai bijutsu*, or "contemporary art."

The catalogue of 1987 makes the fourth archival snapshot in this essay, as it simultaneously points to the future of the Gallery and guides us back into the 1960s, when one of the three artists, Naoto Nakagawa, emerged as a New York artist.

Born in Kōbe in 1944, Nakagawa came to New York at 18 in 1962, taking a freight ship across the Pacific Ocean.[45] Upon his arrival, his $500 was promptly stolen from beneath his pillow at his apartment (found by his fellow passengers), and he began the hard life of a would-be artist. From 1963 to 1965, he was enrolled at the Brooklyn Museum Art School, one of the few schools in New York which many young Japanese artists attended to maintain their visa status as students. His classmates included On Kawara and Shūsaku Arakawa, senior to him by about a decade, who had already achieved recognition in Japan and were making their crucial moves toward conceptualism. The younger Nakagawa was still in search of his own voice. While his two conceptually oriented classmates organized a number of discussion sessions, understandably paying no attention to painting at all, he devoted himself to painting *and* participated in these talks.

Three different inspirations converged in Nakagawa's early years. His grandfather was Murakami Kagaku, a reclusive yet revered *Nihonga* artist, whom he regarded as belonging in the long tradition of literati art in East Asia. He was also familiar with the radical experiment of the Osaka-based Gutai group.[46] And his admiration for Abstract Expressionism—which he saw at an exhibition in Osaka—brought him to New York, instead of Paris. Once in New York, however, he "embraced urban culture," avidly reading Marshall McLuhan among other authors, and aspired to create "metaphysical statements" about the state of the world by using everyday objects.

Nakagawa gradually built his network of contacts, which first resulted in two solo exhibitions in 1968 at MoMA's Lending Gallery (open only for its members) and Judson Gallery. His artist-friend Kate Millet was especially instrumental in the realization of the latter: she brought to his studio Jon Hendricks, who directed Judson's programs. This exhibition, entitled *Extended Objects & Their Images*, caught the attention of *Village Voice* critic John Perreault, whose short text published in the alternative paper became the first critical review in Nakagawa's career.[47] Aikō Kenji, who was in New York as a Japan Society Fellow, wrote an illustrated article on Nakagawa's MoMA show in *Bijutsu techō*, which was his first ever Japanese review.[48]

Nakagawa's loft building at 123 Chambers Street was a hub of activities. Tenants included Michael Snow, whose revolutionary experiment in film-making, *Wavelength* (1967), captured Nakagawa walking in and out of the loft. At loft parties held two or three times a week he met with Nam June Paik, David Tudor, and La Monte Young, among others. Through his close friendship with Kawara,

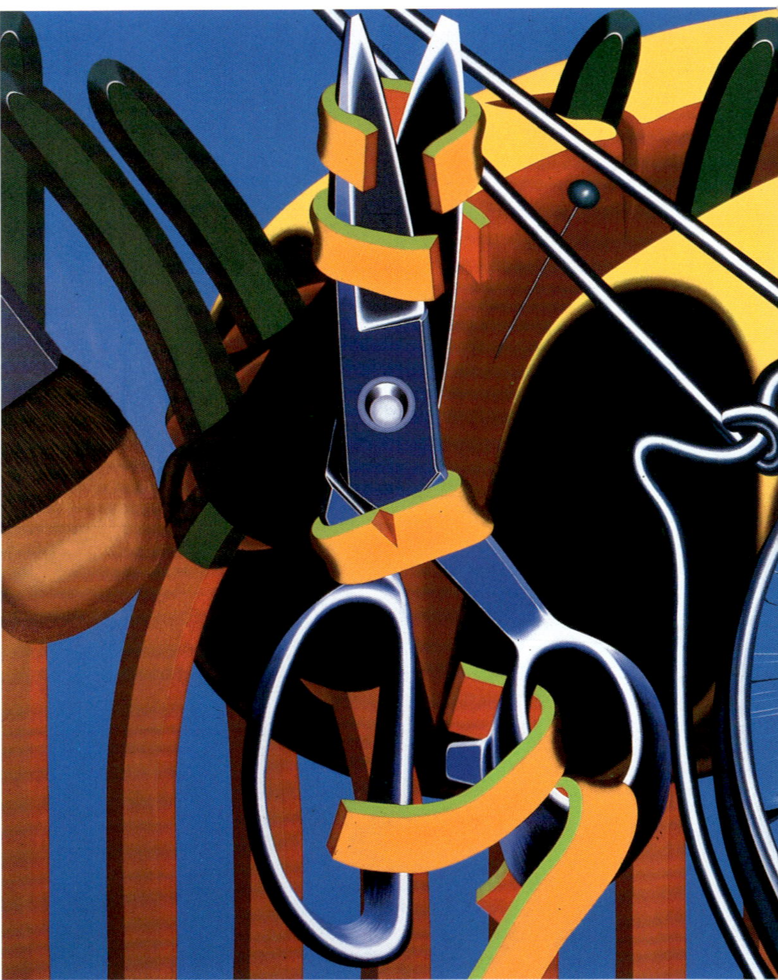

he also met with Ay-O, a Japanese Fluxus member, and witnessed many Fluxus events. After a couple of years of representation by Reese Paley Gallery, one of the galleries that first opened in SoHo, he was called by Ivan Karp. Weighing both Karp and the veteran gallerist Sidney Janis, who also approached him, he decided to join O.K. Harris, because Karp's galley was "coveted by everybody at the time." He showed with Karp five times between 1972 and 1979. One of the early works he showed was a mural-size *Echo II* (1972). This and other explosive yet luscious compositions received a rave review in 1972 from Perreault, who was at once attracted, repulsed, and frightened by the "objects [that] seem to have a malevolent life of their own" and form "a puzzle of images to which there are no discernible solutions"[49] (Fig. 4.13).

A New York artist who happened to be Japanese, Nakagawa was also part of an expatriate community. In 1973, when the painter Kondō Tatsuo (New York residency: 1961–2001) was contacted by the reporter Kōichi Saekawa to provide photographs for his article "Japanese Artists in SoHo" published in *Trends*, a cultural affairs magazine issued by the American Embassy in Tokyo, Nakagawa was among seven artists whose work and portraits Kondō photographed (Fig. 4.14).[50] The opening photo is evocative of the

FIGURE 4.13

Naoto Nakagawa
Echo II
1972
Acrylic on canvas
90 x 215 inches (228.6 x 546.1 cm)
Collection of the artist; courtesy Ethan Cohen Fine Arts, New York

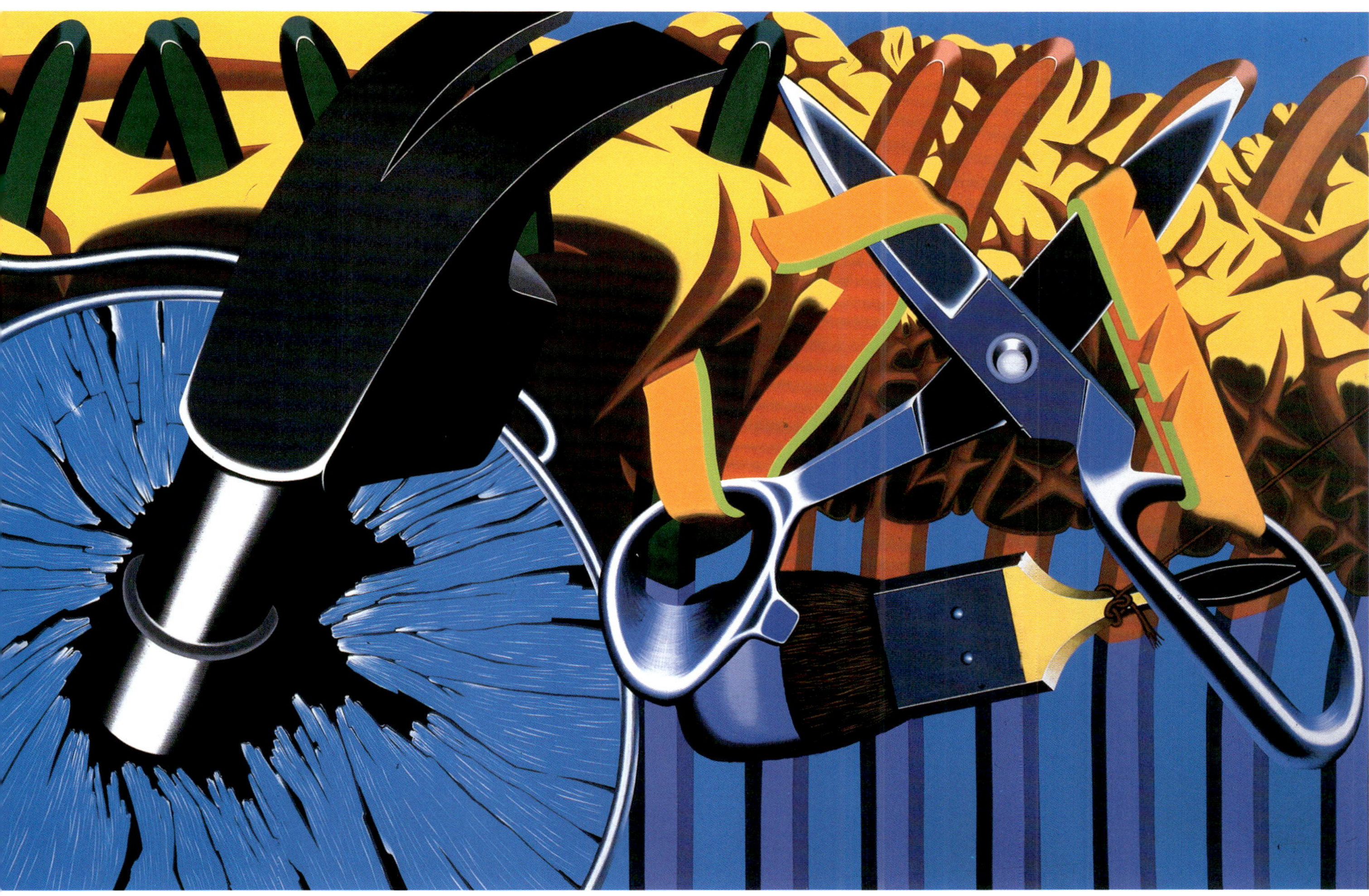

era: four bohemian-artists—Ushio Shinohara, Yoshida Minoru (now in Kyoto), Risaburō Kimura, and Kunio Iizuka—posed with their works in front of Shinohara's loft at 25 Howard Street (Fig. 4.15). The article estimates the number of Japanese artists in New York as high as 700.[51] To generate a supportive network among these artists, the Japanese Artists Association of New York (Jaany) was founded in 1972, with Iizuka as its first president, in order to "create a better community through our art."[52] (Ayakoh Furukawa, represented in *Making a Home*, is the current president of Jaany.)

Japanese artists residing in New York had a whole range of relationships with the Japanese art world. Some who had established track records in Japan, such as On Kawara and Shūsaku Arakawa, were able to maintain a presence in their homeland by sending over their new works or making occasional trips. For example Arakawa, who left Tokyo in 1961, sent his new "diagram painting" to the exhibition *Young Seven* at Minami Gallery in 1964; and Kawara's conceptualist works were duly noted in *Bijutsu techō* and other art press. Some artists doubled as "art reporters," filing the latest news of New York art to Japan and thus creating a steady flow of information from New York to Tokyo. They include Kunie Sugiura, Junko Yoda, and Toshihisa Yoda, among the roster

of *Making a Home*. Others are Ikuko Roth, Gen Hikage, and Kondō Tatsuo (now in Tokyo), the last of whom in particular made a great contribution of at once watching the development of new art and chronicling the ins and outs of Japanese artists in New York on the pages of *Bijutsu techō* and *Geijutsu Shinchō* (literally "New trends in the arts").[53]

Nakagawa, unlike his schoolmates Kawara and Arakawa, had little previous connection to the Japanese art world. In this sense, he was closer to Kusama, who had little luck in finding Japanese representation during the 1960s, although she was extremely active in New York as well as European cities. Nakagawa's first solo exhibition in Japan did not happen until 1983, when Fuji Television Gallery, a reputable modern and contemporary specialist in Tokyo, added him to its roster. (Kusama also joined Fuji Television Gallery in 1984). This time lag created a curious void of information. In Japan, he has been primarily known as a hyper-realist of surrealistically serene still lifes and landscapes—the style he developed after 1973, following his discovery of transcendental meditation. His edgy metaphysical experiments of his early years are, however, beginning to find their audience in his homeland after a selective retrospective presented by White Box in New York in 2007.

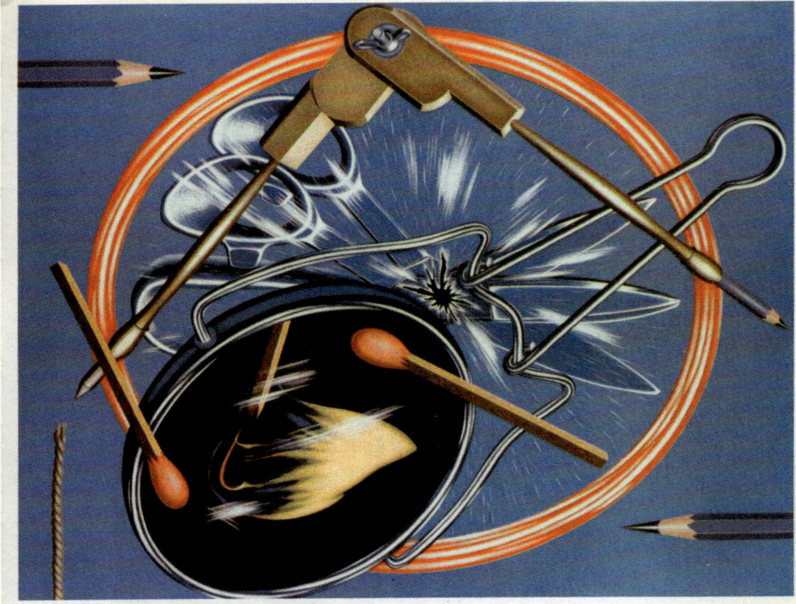
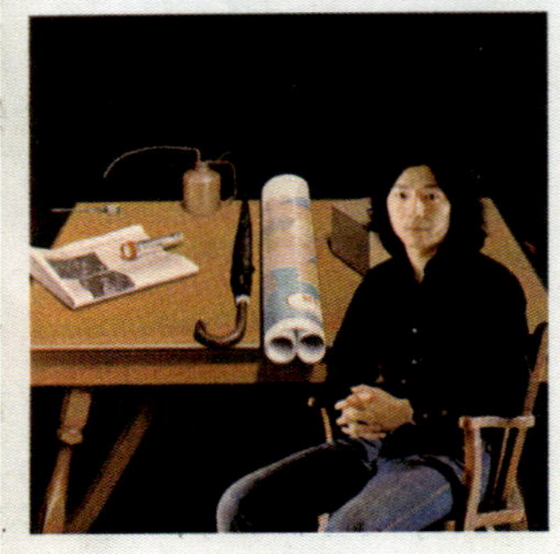

We study history because the past points to the future. Or, to paraphrase Confucius, one must learn from the old (the past) to know the new (the present). My study of Japan Society's relationship with contemporary Japanese artists is no more than a small slice of postwar art history. Nonetheless, the range of vanguard practices that illustrate it is rich and diverse, from Kusama Yayoi's abstraction to Matsuzawa Yutaka's conceptualism, from Munakata Shikō's printmaking to Tange Kenzō's public sculpture, from Okamoto Shinjirō's witty image-making to Naoto Nakagawa's vision of terrorizing objects. Such breadth is testament to the Society's dedicated engagement with *gendai bijutsu* from the 1950s onward. At the same time, what this essay uncovers is not just the development of *gendai bijutsu* in Japan or contemporary art in New York, but the formation of New York as a diaspora of Japanese contemporary art.

The vexing question of whether, say, Kusama's oeuvre from the 1960s belongs to Japanese art history or American art history may be solved once the all-inclusive notion of "world art history" gains currency. Still, the duality, or even multiplicity, of a New York–based Japanese artist's identity can never be absorbed into the convenient and generalized categories of "international" or "global." This problem confounds us much more today than in the 1960s, with the accelerating globalization that has made the earth once again "flat." Even the identity of a Japan-based Japanese artist cannot be assumed to be immutably monolithic. To look at contemporary art, be it in Tokyo or New York or elsewhere, we need a multiple and layered vision that is more fluid than the rigid region-by-region perspective, which has long dominated the discipline of art history. In this context, the role that Japan Society has played in contemporary art is at once transnational and diasporal, serving as a nexus of exchange in a vast matrix of global art as staged in New York. The current exhibition, *Making a Home*, is precisely situated in this tradition of Japan Society, extending it into the future by giving a cross-generational look at Japanese contemporary artists based in New York.

FIGURE 4.14

Naoto Nakagawa
Reproduced in "Japanese Artists in SoHo," *Trends*, no. 9 (1973?). *Four Corners* (1971), top, is reproduced sideways
PHOTOS: KONDŌ TATSUO; ORIGINALLY PUBLISHED BY AMERICAN EMBASSY, TOKYO

ソーホーの日本人アーティスト

枝川公一（文）　近藤竜男（写真）

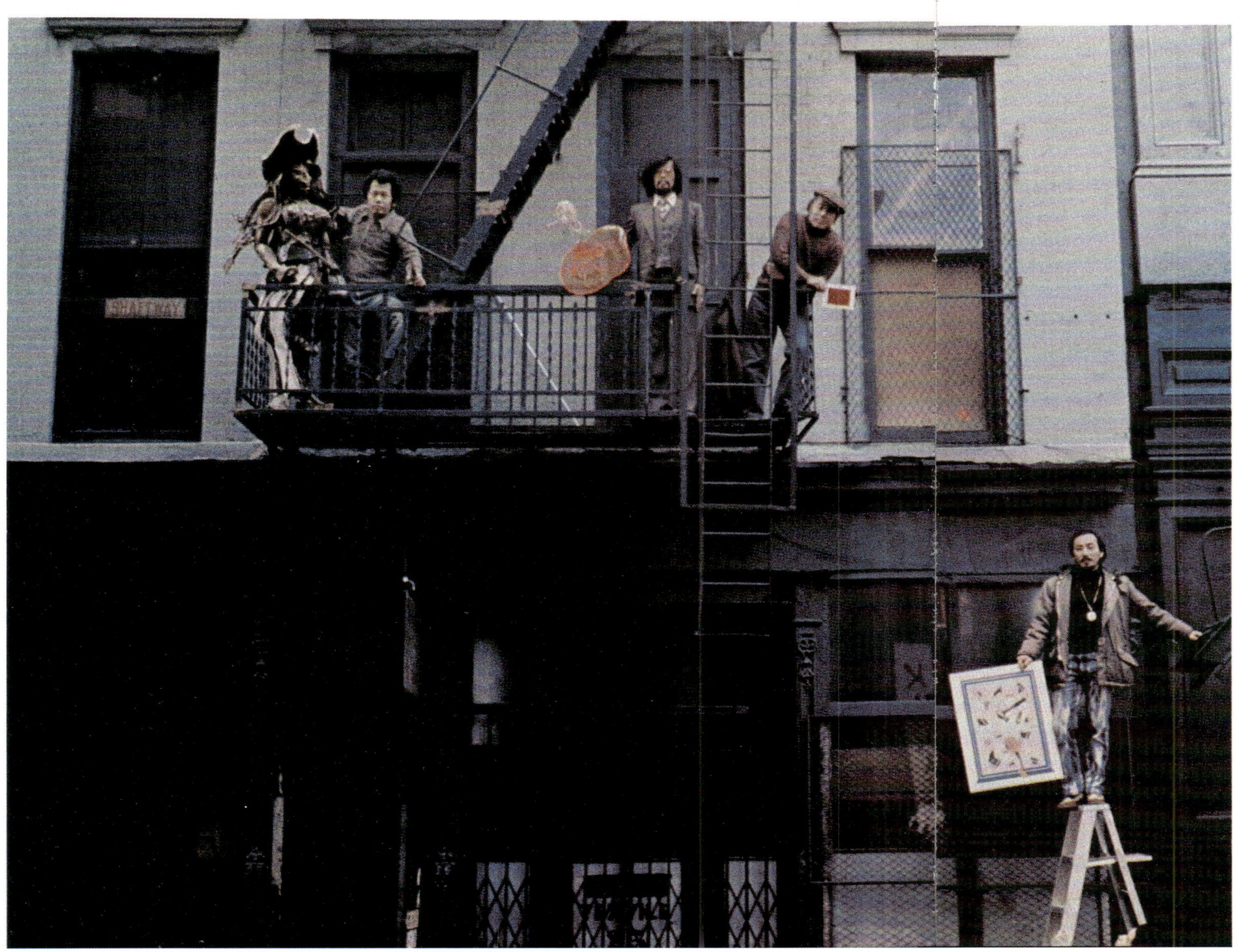

FIGURE 4.15

First pages of "Japanese Artists in SoHo,"
Trends, no. 9 (1973?). From left: Ushio
Shinohara, Minoru Yoshida, Risaburō
Kimura, and Kunio Iizuka

Notes

I am grateful for the generosity of Beate Sirota Gordon, Alexandra Munroe, Naoto Nakagawa, and Okamoto Shinjirō, who took time to talk to me and write to me in the course of preparing this essay. I am also thankful for the research assistance of Nakajima Yasuko, Nakajima Masatoshi, and Kondō Tatsuo in Tokyo, Yūko Teshima and Eleni Cocordas in New York, and Miho Fang, Haruko Hoyle, Mari Eijima, and Reiko Sassa at Japan Society.

All translations from Japanese are by the author.

1   While the painting was taken down, I had a chance to examine her inscription on the back, which reads: KUSAMA / 1961 / NET. S.P.

2   This account is based on my phone conversations with Alexandra Munroe (March 14, 2007), Mari Eijima (on the Society's staff since 1960; March 19, 2007), and Eleni Cocordas, formerly Exhibitions Manager and Interim Director of the Gallery (2001–06; March 30, 2007). The Gallery's Kusama file indicates that the existence of this painting was noted when Japan Society's art collections were appraised in 1995 under Gunhild Avitabile, the third Gallery Director (1990–98).

3   Edwin O. Reischauer, *Japan Society, 1907–1982: 75 Years of Partnership Across the Pacific* (New York: Japan Society, 1982), 21; Frederick William Gookin, *Japanese Colour-Prints and Their Designers* (New York: Japan Society, 1913). Gookin's book, as noted on its title page, contains Gookin's lecture on the subject at Japan Society on April 11, 1911, and reproductions of some works in the exhibition. Interestingly, this *ukiyo-e* project as well as the Japanese garden with a teahouse that the Society built atop Hotel Astor, which also proved to be extremely popular, were deficit-ridden endeavors, although then Society president Lindsay Russell optimistically observed that the money spent was "a good investment" to generate publicity, further the educational effort, and insure institutional prestige. See Reischauer, 21–22.

4   Rand Castile, "Remembering Japan Society," *Impressions: The Journal of the Japanese Art Society of America*, no. 28 (2006–07): 76–98.

5   For "international contemporaneity," see Reiko Tomii, "Historicizing 'Contemporary Art': Some Discursive Practices in *Gendai Bijutsu* in Japan," *Positions* 12, no. 3 (2004), especially 615–19.

6   Robert Rauschenberg visited Tokyo in 1964, in conjunction with the world tour of Merce Cunningham Dance Company, when he created *Gold Standard* before a live audience in the program entitled "Twenty Questions to Bob Rauschenberg" at the Sōgetsu Art Center, a hotbed of avant-garde activities. Jasper Johns had two solo exhibitions at Minami Gallery, one of a few dealers specializing in contemporary art in Tokyo, in 1965 and 1967. *Two Decades of American Painting* was held at the National Museums of Modern Art in Tokyo and Kyoto in 1966–67, then traveled to New Delhi, Melbourne, and Sydney. This exhibition included work by Pollock, Rauschenberg, and Johns, as well as Warhol and Lichtenstein.

7   For Rauschenberg's activities in 1964, including his visit to Tokyo, see Hiroko Ikegami, "Dislocations: Robert Rauschenberg and the Americanization of Modern Art, Circa 1964," Ph.D. diss. (Yale University, 2007).

8   Two more grantees are added in the following issue dated October 10, 1956, making the total 29 for this fiscal year; Japan Society's fiscal year spans July to June of the following year.

9   "Japan Society Fellows, 1956–57," *Japan Society Forum* (June 22, 1956): n.p.

10   Reischauer, 39–42.

11   Ibid., 61.

12   "The Coming Year," *Japan Society Forum* (July 1, 1954): n.p.

13   "Annual Report of the Executive Director, July 1, 1954–June 30, 1955," *Japan Society Report 1955*, n.p. See also Reischauer, 62.

14   The phaseout is announced in *Japan Society 1960 Report* (p. 6). *Japan Society 1961 Report* gives the aggregated total at 198, while announcing two fellows for 1960–61 (p. 5); *Japan Society 1962 Report* announces five fellows for 1961–62 (p. 6), thus making the total 203. The average amount of $1,000 is first given in *Japan Society 1959 Report* (p. 7), while *Forum* (February 12, 1954) states "The size of each grant will be determined in the light of individual need, but in no case will exceed $1,500" (cover), while the reduced maximum amount, $1,200, is first mentioned in *Japan Society Forum* (June 15, 1958) and thereafter repeated.

15   Nagasaka Kenjirō, a Fulbrighter who arrived at Columbia University in New York in 1962, recently recalls that he was awfully poor, despite the monthly stipend of $120 (or $1,440 for one year), which was the highest amount the Fulbright Foundation would then give to an individual student; after paying half for room and board, he couldn't even buy books, spending most of his time at the library. See "Nagasaka kaichō gofusai intabyū" [An interview with Mr. Nagasaka, the new association president, and his wife], *Tokyo Fulbright Association Newsletter* (December 2006): 2.

16   Reischauer, 61.

17   *Japan Society Forum* (July 1, 1954): n.p.

18   *Annual Report 1955*, n.p.

19   Reischauer, 62.

20   The account of Matsuzawa's life and following quotations derive from his autobiographical accounts in *Kikan* [Organ], no. 13, special issue of Matsuzawa Yutaka (1982): 36–73, and his interview with author, July 23, 2000.

21   I thank Prof. Linda Henderson of the University of Texas at Austin for identifying some of these names.

22   For Matsuzawa's conceptualism, see Reiko Tomii, "Concerning the Institution of Art: Conceptualism in Japan," in *Global Conceptualism*, exh. cat. (New York: Queens Museum of Art, 1999), 19–20.

23   For excerpt translation, see *Global Conceptualism*, 19.

24   Unless otherwise noted, my description of Gordon's activities in this section is based on Beate Sirota Gordon, interview with author, March 6 and April 16, 2007.

25   Gordon's biographical account is mostly based on Beate Sirota Gordon, *The Only Woman in the Room: A Memoir* (Tokyo/New York/London: Kodansha International, 1997), and her notes to author, postmarked May 16, 2007.

26   Reischauer, 64.

27   Gordon, 147; Reischauer, 68; Erika Duncan, "A Link to Pre-War Japan Builds Bridges in the Arts," *New York Times*, Long Island Weekly Desk, August 4, 1996; Gordon, interview with author, March 6, 2007.

28   Gordon, 147–48.

29   For the Association's board members, see *The 1st Japan Art Festival*, exh. cat. (Tokyo: Japan Art Festival Association, 1966). I thank Beate Gordon

for sharing with me her Japan Art Festival folder.

30 Asō Yoshikata, "Dai 1-kai Japan āto festibaru o owatte" [After the 1st Japan Art Festival], *Kokusai Geijutsu Mihon'ichi Kyōkai kaihō/Japan Art Festival*, no. 3 (July 1, 1966): 4.

31 According to Gordon, Mari Eijima has located no paperwork in the Society's archives to indicate Japan Society's institutional involvement with the Festival. However, the day-to-day operational details are chronicled by Mizumoto Kiyoshi, a former staff member of the Association in 1966–69, in his recent blog, "Kokusai geijutsu mihon'ichi (Japan āto fesutibaru) shimatsuki" [Report of *Japan Art Festival*], http://gastrocamera.cocolog-nifty.com/blog/2007/01/index.html (accessed May 10, 2007). Mizumoto acknowledges the extensive assistance by John D. Rockefeller 3rd (blog entry, January 21, 2007), Japan Society's influential leader. His diary entry dated January 21, 1966 (blog entry, January 23, 2007) reports Gordon sent a telegraph to the Ministry of Foreign Affairs, requesting the payment of her salary. This indicates the Association's semi-governmental status and the fact that the Association paid her salary.

32 See *Japan āto fesutibaru 10-shūnen kinen ten* [10th anniversary exhibition of Japan Art Festival], exh. cat. (Tokyo: Japan Art Festival Association, 1977).

33 *Contemporary Japanese Art: Fifth Japan Art Festival Exhibition*, exh. cat. (New York: The Solomon R. Guggenheim Museum, 1970), n.p.

34 During the Society's centennial celebration, a series of special archival displays is installed outside the Society's auditorium, organized by Cynthia Sternau, Publications Manager, together with Mari Eijima and Maria Oda, Archives; Christine Knorr, Design; and Jeff Nemeth, Production. The 1916 annual report and other early documents, including Frederick Gookin's 1913 book on woodblock prints, are exhibited in the first of the five-part archival exhibition (February 1–May 31, 2007).

35 *Japan Society 1965 Report*, 8.

36 Haryū Ichirō, "Okamoto Shinjirō no geijutsu to taishū bunka" [Okamoto Shinjirō's art and popular culture], in *Okamoto Shinjirō no sekai: Tokyo shōnen/The Exposition of Shinjiro Okamoto* [Tokyo boy], exh. cat. (Niigata: Niigata City Art Museum, 1988), 4. This catalogue is a good source for the artist's life and work.

37 See *Yangu sebun-ten/Young Seven*, exh. cat. (Tokyo: Minami Gallery, 1964).

38 *Nagaoka Gendai Bijutsukan-shō kaikoten 1964–1968* [A retrospective of the Museum of Contemporary Art, Nagaoka, Prize Exhibition, 1964–1968], exh. cat. (Niigata: The Niigata Prefectural Museum of Modern Art et al., 2002), 15–17.

39 The account of Okamoto's New York experience is based on Okamoto Shinjirō, "Chubby's Blues: *Komochi no Kuinī* ni tsuite (Shitsumon ni kotaete)" [On *Queenie the Mother* (In response to the questions)], handwritten letter to author, April 21, 2007. All quotations are from this letter, unless otherwise noted.

40 Miki Tamon, "Kūru na yūmoa no miryoku" [Appeal of cool humor], *Betty Boop's Country*, exh. cat. (Tokyo: Fuji Television Gallery, 1974), n.p.

41 Okamoto Shinjirō, response to "'Gendai bijutsu no shin-sedai' ten shuppin sakka eno ankēto" [Questionnaire to artists in *New Generation of Contemporary Art*], *Gendai no me* [Contemporary eye], no. 135 (February 1966): 6.

42 For example, in 1953, Japan Society arranged the first American exhibition of the oil painter Arai Tatsuo at the Riverside Museum, according to *Report to the Board of Directors* (1953). The exhibition received a review: Howard Devree, "In Modern Veins," *New York Times*, February 23, 1953.

Japan Society 1957 Report (p. 9) mentions that it co-organized the gallery exhibitions of Inokuma Gen'ichirō, Shinoda Tōkō, and Hasegawa Saburō (probably with Willard Gallery, Nippon Club, and Bertha Shaefer). See S.P., "Art: Religious Motifs," *New York Times*, January 4, 1957; D[ore] A[shton], "Genichiro Inokuma Has First Show Here," *New York Times*, April 6, 1957; Ashton, "Art: Pre-Columbian Work," *New York Times*, April 25, 1957; Ashton, "Art: Oriental Painters," *New York Times*, October 23, 1957.

Under "Young Japanese Exhibit," *Japan Society Report: 1968–69* (p. 12) describes the exhibitions of a dozen artists—including Shirai Akiko, a printmaker and Japan Society Fellow—that Japan Society organized in collaboration with the New York Board of Trade at the board's Fifth Avenue offices in the fall–winter season.

43 Castile, 88.

44 Munroe, conversation with author, January 16 and May 23, 2007.

45 The account of Nakagawa's life is based on Nakagawa Naoto, interview with author, May 2, 2007, as well as author's running conversation with him in the winter of 2006–07. All quotes by Nakagawa are from these interviews. For Nakagawa's work in the 1960s and 1970s, see *Triple X: Extended, Exploded, Extracted—Naoto Nakagawa, 1965–1975*, exh. cat. (New York: White Box, 2007).

46 For Nakagawa's knowledge of Gutai, see Reiko Tomii, "Biography, Exhibition History, Bibliography," in *Triple X*, 57.

47 John Perreault, "Word Works." *Village Voice*, June 13, 1968, 15.

48 Aikō Kenji. "Teimei no naka no seishin-na jojō: Nyūyōku no wakai Nihonjin gaka: Nakagawa Naoto, Wakita Aijirō" [Fresh lyricism in stagnation: Young Japanese painters in New York, Naoto Nakagawa and Wakita Aijirō]. *Bijutsu techō*, no. 295 (March 1968): 162–65.

49 Perreault, "The Terror of a Wooden Match," *Village Voice*, January 20, 1972.

50 Kondō was so busy shooting other artists that he forgot to include himself in the mix. Kondō Tatsuo, interview with author, March 26, 2007.

51 Kōichi Saekawa, "Sōho no Nihonjin ātisuto" [Japanese artists in SoHo], *Trends* 9 [possibly 1973]: 25. This number is probably not so far off the mark: "Young Japanese Artists Exhibit" in *Japan Society Report: 1968–69* (p. 12) gives an estimated number of some 600. A notable study on this subject is Mary Hale Bereday, "Japanese Artists in New York City," dissertation (Teachers College, Columbia University, 1972).

52 "About Us," http://www.jaa-ny.org/aboutus.htm (accessed May 14, 2007).

53 Kondō's extensive reviews and texts published in *Geijutsu Shinchō* are anthologized in his memoir, *Nyūyōku gendai bijutsu/New York Art 1960–1988* (Tokyo: Shinchōsha, 1988), illustrated by numerous photographs he took. Gen Hikage's anthology *360-do no Nyūyōku: Āto mūbumento 1994–2000* [New York 360-degree: Art movements 1994–2000] (Tokyo: Gallery Station, 2000) is also useful.

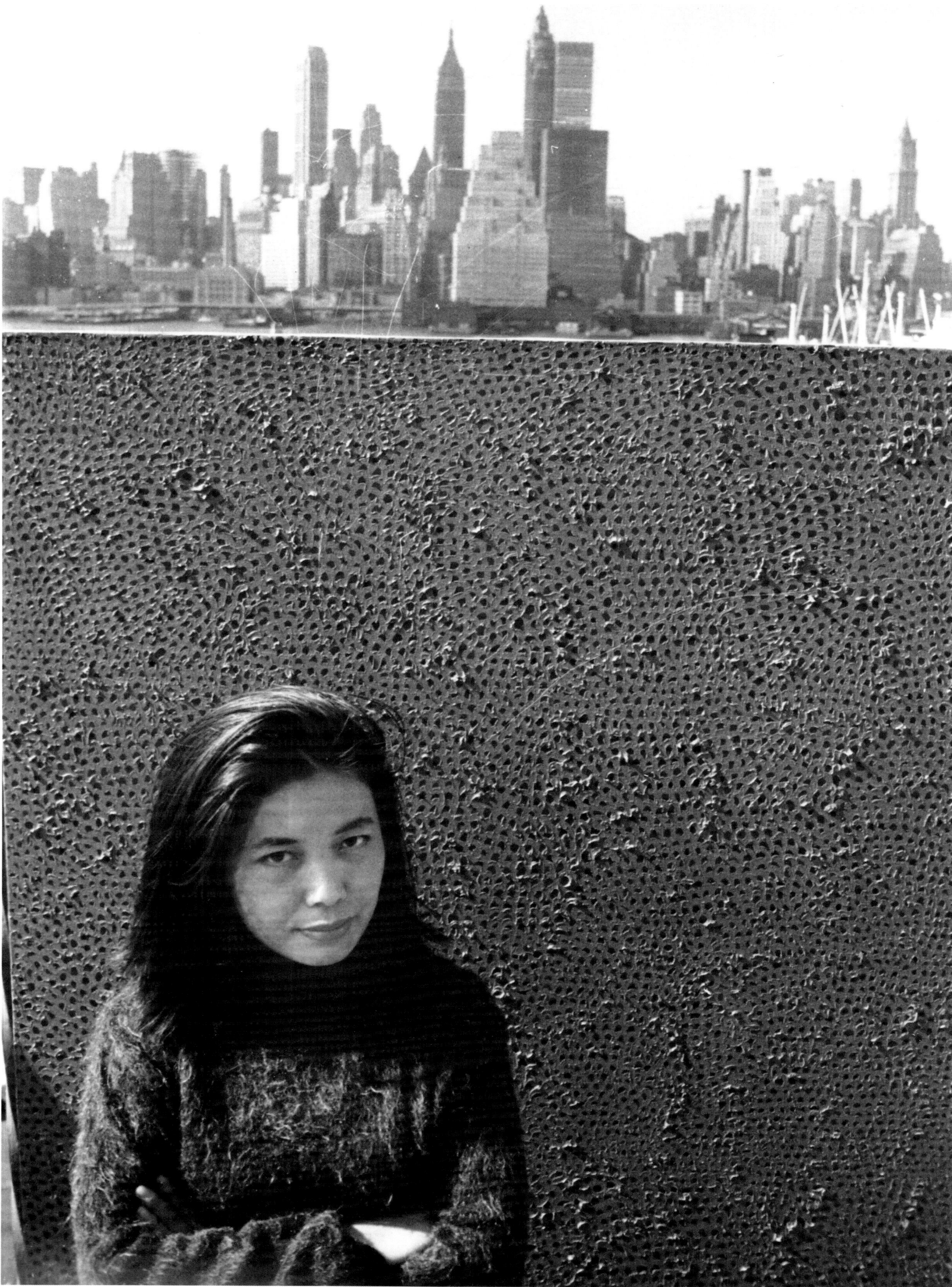

KUSAMA YAYOI'S EARLY YEARS IN NEW YORK
A Critical Biography

MIDORI YAMAMURA

"Eye of the Art World Shifts from Paris to New York." When the August 11, 1958 issue of the general-interest magazine *Weekly Shinchō* reported the latest trend among Japanese artists, the article included—together with the names of respected masters Okada Kenzō and Inokuma Gen'ichirō—that of Kusama Yayoi, who had just moved to the world's new art capital in June of that year.[1] By June of 1962, Kusama was exhibiting with such young luminaries as Robert Morris, Claes Oldenburg, James Rosenquist, and Andy Warhol, all on their way to stardom as Pop and Minimal artists, at Green Gallery, a prominent vanguard venue in New York (Fig. 5.2).

Kusama's quick emergence in New York, however, was not easy. It was preceded by long years during which a young woman born and raised in the regional city of Matsumoto found her calling in art and pressed her way toward recognition first in Japan, then in Seattle, and eventually in New York. This period of her life, including her early years in New York, has been known primarily through her autobiographical accounts. Still, some details have long remained obscure. For example, how did she survive in New York? What was the history of her now well-known psychiatric problems? When and how did she begin her signature "soft sculpture" series, which she first exhibited at Green Gallery in 1962?

This essay offers a brief account of Kusama's life in Japan and Seattle, followed by a close re-examination of her early years in New York, from 1958 to 1963, drawing on materials uncovered by new research. They include Kusama's calendar-diaries (1960–63); three notebooks that reveal her activities and ideas; and a scrapbook that was, judging by the handwriting, compiled by her mother. Through a focused and critical look at her biography, this essay explores the life of an important Japanese artist who made New York her home in the crucial decade of the 1960s.

1942–1955: A "Tireless Path of Art"

Kusama Yayoi was born in mountainous Matsumoto in central Japan in 1929 to an affluent family that owned a plant nursery. Surrounded by the Japanese Alps, Matsumoto was a secluded place whose residents back then dreamed of going beyond the mountains to see the Pacific Ocean. Kusama's impressionable teen years occurred during World War II, when the military government controlled every corner of civic life. She detested the "conservative" and "backward education" tainted by nationalism provided by her high school and preferred to stay home and draw.[2] In 1942, following Japan's attack on Pearl Harbor, Hibino Kakei (Teruo), a practitioner of *Nihonga* (Japanese-style painting), came to her school as a new art teacher, replacing the predecessor specializing in *yōga* (Western-style painting). Kusama, then 13, frequented

his studio to watch him paint; by 1943, she started taking private lessons from him.[3] In July 1944, together with her classmates, Kusama was mobilized to sew parachutes at a military factory. As the U.S. air raids intensified in November 1944, Kusama glimpsed "American B29s flying in broad daylight." This was her first contact with the U.S. The parachute factory's poor working conditions made her pneumonic, forcing her to stay home, and she spent hours upon hours "drawing flowers and fruits." A sketchbook full of peony drawings from 1945 demonstrates her skills in *Nihonga* (Fig. 5.3). In the "dark, dead-end" days of the war, she began to consider the life of a professional artist and going overseas, so that she could "communicate with a wider audience, especially people abroad, through my art."[4] In a sense, the war "put me on a tireless path of art."

In 1945, the war ended with Japan's defeat in August—the outcome that Kusama had been "certain" of and "prayed for every day." In November 1945, she promptly began her career as a professional artist by participating in regional "open call" competitive exhibitions. In 1948, she moved to Kyoto to formally study *Nihonga* for one year

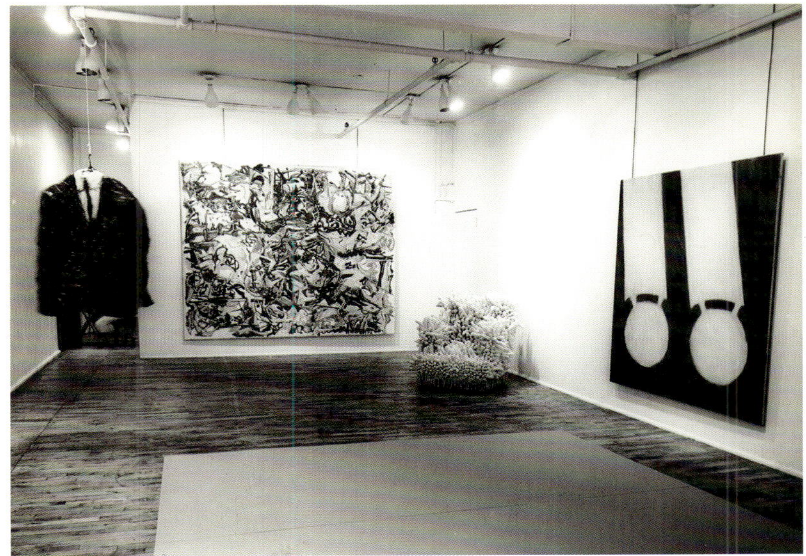

FIGURE 5.2

Installation view of a group exhibition at Green Gallery, June 1962. Visible are Claes Oldenburg's suits (extreme left); Robert Morris's floor piece (foreground); and Kusama's *Accumulation #1* (far end, right corner)
PHOTO: RUDOLPH BURCKHARDT; COURTESY OF KUSAMA YAYOI STUDIO, TOKYO

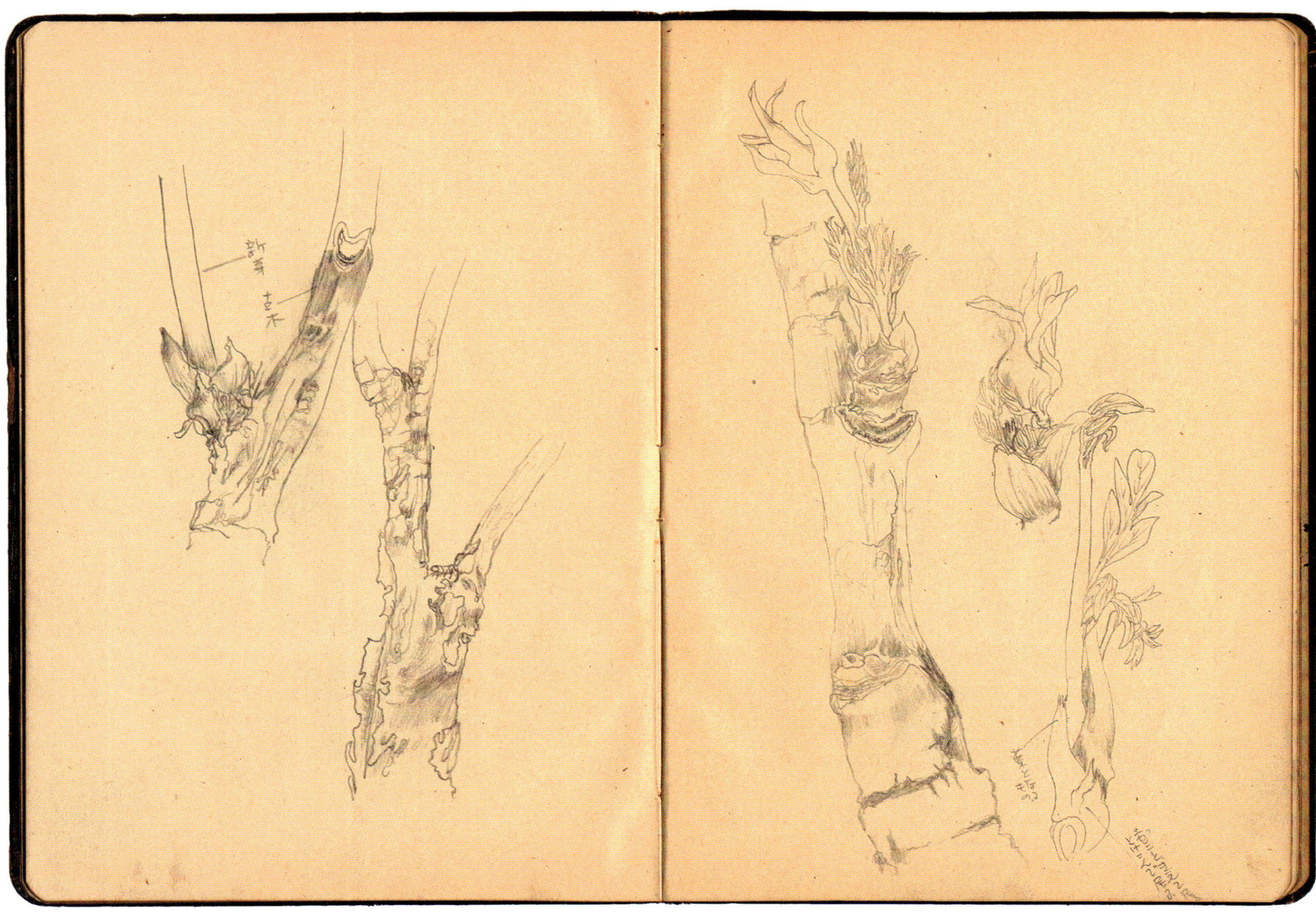

at the Kyoto Municipal School of Arts and Crafts. After completing her coursework, she tried a few directions to further her career, but eventually gave up on *Nihonga*, partly stymied by its strict patriarchal system and partly in search of an environment in which she could pursue her free and original expression. In 1952, to create a tradition-free environment for herself, she organized two solo exhibitions in Matsumoto in March and October, showing some 200 and 280 new works respectively (Figs. 5.4–5). Her energetic production and exhibition activities continued in Tokyo through 1955, when she redirected her energy to securing a visa to go abroad; upon her arrival in New York three years later, she resumed her artistic activities in full force.

Her independent streak, as well as her faith in the power of art, is also evident in her essay "Ivan the Fool," published in 1955:

> The Devil is at once an enemy of art and an ally of art. He resides only in freedom. No sooner had something been established, he would leave it…. Such devilish power is the power that provokes the earnest desire for spiritual freedom in eternity. A rising of that which is inexplicable allows people to see the world of yonder, wherein our spirit will be inspired to free itself…. Flowers thus bloom.[5]

Kusama's words point to her aspiration to defend the essential human instinct against the orderly rational world—an idea which resonated with the increasing skepticism that characterized the thought of postwar intellectuals in the aftermath of Hiroshima and the Holocaust.[6] Yet, as the writer Fukushima Tatsuo observed in the same year, she straddled the "rationalist ground" and "resistance to anti-humanism," while producing "metaphysical mysterious work"—an enduring quality that threads throughout her art.[7]

The second solo exhibition caught the attention of Nishimaru Shihō, a professor of psychology at the local Shinshū University, who studied the brains of preeminent people, especially those of artists. At an exhibition he happened upon, Nishimaru believed he recognized traits of schizophrenia in the artist's face. He interviewed her on the spot and determined she suffered from hallucinatory cenesthopathy. (That is, though there was physically nothing wrong with her, she nonetheless experienced strange bodily sensations.) Since Kusama appeared to him quite capable of controlling herself in both manic and depressive conditions, he merely noted her bipolar tendencies.[8] On December 13, 1952, Nishimaru presented a paper on Kusama and her art at the annual conference of the Kantō Psychiatric and Neurotic Association, held at the University of Tokyo. Notably the title was "Genius Woman Artist with Schizophrenic Tendency," *not* diagnosing her with "schizophrenia."[9] An encounter with Nishimaru marked the beginning of Kusama's interest in psychiatry.

1955–1958: Toward Seattle

Immediately after the war, Paris was still the Japanese government's officially sponsored destination for artists. However, Japan's cultural orientation as a whole gradually shifted away from Paris to the U.S. through the concerted effort of the U.S. Information Service, the continuing U.S.-Japan cultural exchanges, and the policy that made English mandatory in school curricula during the Occupation (1945–52). A decisive event that prompted Kusama to shift her eye to the U.S. was her participation in the 18th International Watercolor Exhibition at the Brooklyn Museum in 1955. This little-known biennale was one of the first to introduce progressive Japanese contemporary artists to New York.[10] Sales of two works from this exhibition appeared promising to Kusama, who was determined to make her living as a professional artist.[11] By November 1956, after a failed effort to go to Paris with government sponsorship, she contacted American artists Georgia O'Keeffe and Kenneth Callahan to explore the possibility of mounting her exhibitions in the U.S.[12] Kusama first wrote to O'Keeffe on November 15, saying that she had seen *Black Iris (II)* in the collection of John C. Denman, an art collector, chief pilot of Northwest Airlines, and Tokyo resident. (This was the beginning of a continuing correspondence with O'Keeffe.) She could have seen this work in a publication or at an exhibition at the Bridgestone Gallery in Tokyo in 1954.[13] She would have known of Callahan from the effort of the U.S. government to popularize in Japan such American artists as Callahan, Morris Graves, and Mark Tobey of the Pacific Northwest school whose work reflected their interests in Asian culture and philosophy.[14]

Callahan was instrumental in bringing Kusama to the U.S. He brought Kusama's works to his dealer Zoe Dusanne, an African-American woman who promoted Pacific Northwest artists including Graves, Tobey, Kenjirō Nomura, and George Tsutakawa. Seattle's first dealer specializing in modern art, Dusanne was known for her "astute and critical eye." She immediately offered Kusama an exhibition.[15] But Kusama did not quickly accept the offer. She had to first make sure Dusanne was the right dealer for her. She sent detailed queries to Neil Meitzler, Callahan's student, asking about Dusanne's roster of artists, her willingness to support emerging artists, the gallery's location, attendance, and modernist credentials.[16] It is this professionalism and aggressive attitude that later enabled her to achieve quick success in New York City.

Getting a proper visa was difficult, since there existed no official route for professional artists to immigrate to the U.S. at that time. Determined to avoid a student visa, Kusama spent almost two years to find a sponsor in the U.S. to petition her visa.[17] On November 18, 1957, with full financial support from her parents,[18] Kusama left Japan for Seattle. (In 1956, in anticipation of what she thought to be her daughter's imminent departure, Kusama's mother began compiling a scrapbook of clippings about her; it contains more than a dozen newspaper clippings reporting on her departure in 1957.)

Kusama's exhibition at Zoe Dusanne included 26 water-based works out of 100 she had brought with her. It previewed to the press and collectors on December 8 and 9 and opened to the public on the 10th. The show was a critical success, but in the first three months of her stay in Seattle, Kusama spent $1,167.77 on her exhibition and other expenses, excluding room and board.[19] Concerned about her finances, Kusama first tried to move to Los Angeles, where a cousin had once lived.[20] Her petition for a six-month visa was denied, because Los Angeles was not a center of the art industry; only when she changed her destination to New York did she succeed in securing her visa.[21]

1958: Arriving in New York

I am writing this letter [to Georgia O'Keeffe] on the eleventh day of my stay in New York City.... I do not know

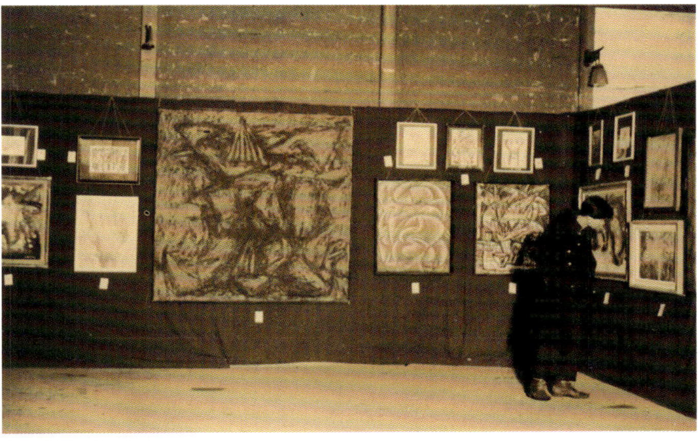

Installation view of Kusama's first solo exhibition at a civic center in Matsumoto, March 1952
PHOTO COURTESY OF KUSAMA YAYOI STUDIO, TOKYO

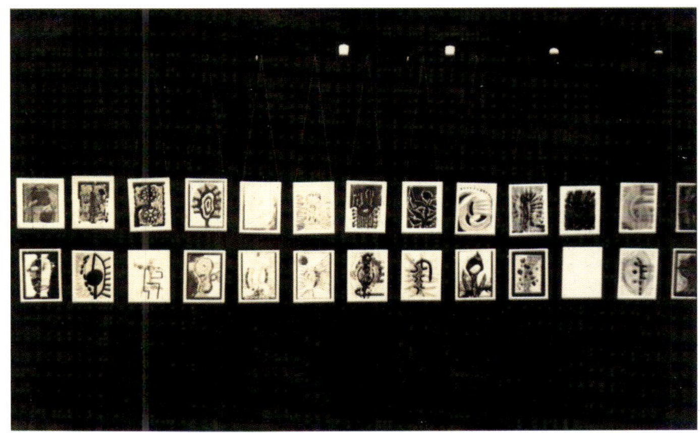

Installation view of Kusama's second solo exhibition at a civic center in Matsumoto, October 1952
PHOTO COURTESY OF KUSAMA YAYOI STUDIO, TOKYO

any of the dealers and have no friends in New York, so I intend to compile a list of dealers and galleries from the phonebook and visit each one with an armload of paintings. I am hoping that I will be able to establish some sort of connection in this way and sell some paintings. I am truly amazed at the large number of galleries listed in the phone book. There must be well over 100 galleries in the area.

—July 8, 1958[22]

I made many friends after I came to New York. Painters, sculptors, photographers, actresses, playwrights, poets, and magazine editors—all sorts of people visit my studio. All these people live near my studio. I also became acquainted with such leaders of New York-ism as [Willem] De Kooning, Franz Kline, and Philip Guston. I met many times with the poet Frank O'Hara, the painter Sam Francis, and the editor of *It Is*, Philip Pavia, etc.

—March 26, [1959][23]

I am planning to create a revolutionary work that will stun the international art world. This will show the New York art world a decisive direction for the future.

—June 1959[24]

On June 28, 1958, Kusama arrived in New York City without knowing anyone, speaking little English, and with scant funding but with an immense conviction in her art. She first mingled with the local Japanese and Japanese-American communities in order to gather information about the New York art world. Soon, she decided to launch her career from the downtown art scene. By the end of 1958, Kusama moved from her Upper West Side apartment to a spacious Greenwich Village loft at 70 East 12th Street; her co-tenants included Michael Goldberg, a second-generation Abstract Expressionist painter.[25] Among the artists she recorded meeting, the name of Philip Pavia is significant. In 1949, he initiated a loosely knit artists' organization, The Club, and hosted a Friday evening lecture series at The Club's loft on Eighth Street. Kusama likely attended at least one of these meetings.

Going to The Club was the way for young artists to make the right connections in the 1950s. The majority of artists gathered at The Club showed their works at the artists-run cooperative galleries on and around Tenth Street, established in reaction to commercialized uptown galleries. These cooperatives operated in a truly democratic spirit: after being admitted and paying a small monthly fee, the members could freely exhibit their works. Many women and minority artists, such as Marisol and Louise Bourgeois, showed in these galleries early in their careers.[26] Because generating revenue was not the main concern, the cooperatives were also seedbeds for such experiments as Happenings and figurative and geometric-abstract tendencies that would become

dominant modalities of Pop and Minimalist arts in the 1960s. In the late 1950s and early 1960s, Donald Judd, Allan Kaprow, Claes Oldenburg, and Tom Wesselmann all showed their works in the cooperatives. When seven galleries on Tenth Street held their openings on the same night, almost the entire New York art world gathered, giving emerging artists the best possible exposure. Promising artists were spotted by commercial dealers, who moved them to uptown galleries. Kusama joined the cooperative Brata Gallery through the African-American member Ed Clark. Her calendars of 1960 and 1961 indicate her dealings with Brata, including paying monthly dues and framing expenses. It is at Brata that she mounted her first New York solo exhibition.

1959–1961: *Infinity Net*

I rented a large studio and faced a black canvas so huge that I could not reach [its top] without using a stepladder. I began painting an expanse of particle-like white nets, almost devoid of tonality, as minute as I could possibly hope.... In the bustle of a competitive and hectic New York, at the bottom of light and shadow of a contemporary civilization that moves forward with creaking noises, in the midst of this metropolis which symbolizes American pragmatism, I keep painting uninteresting paintings. This is a form of my resistance....

This infinitely repeatable rhythm and monochrome surface constitute a new painting, through an unusual "light"... And these paintings absolutely defy a single fixed focus or center. This is my original idea, which time and again surfaced in my work for the past ten years. In mountainous Shinshū, I drew assemblies of black dots in *sumi* ink, cell-like structures in pen, magnified interior views of the plant stem, countless chains of unknowable indivisible things.... I have long wanted to release this "unknowable something" from me, release it from the muddy lake of emotion into the spiritual yonder of eternity. Now, I am just releasing it into a vacuum chaos.

—May 1961[27]

In October 1959, Kusama presented five large canvases, which initiated what is now called the *Infinity Net* series, at Brata. They won immediate attention: *New York Times* critic Dore Ashton wrote in her review that they were "dry, obsessional repetitions" and "infinitely extending compositions"[28]—an observation which established the basic view on the series that has continued to date. However, the series had its origin in smaller watercolor paintings, as seen in a 1958 photograph of Kusama working in her studio (Fig. 5.6). Specifically, Kusama once explained to Beatrice Perry, her dealer in Washington, D.C., that her small watercolors titled *Pacific Ocean* were her first *Infinity Net* paintings.[29] She also told a Japanese newspaper reporter that the series was inspired by the

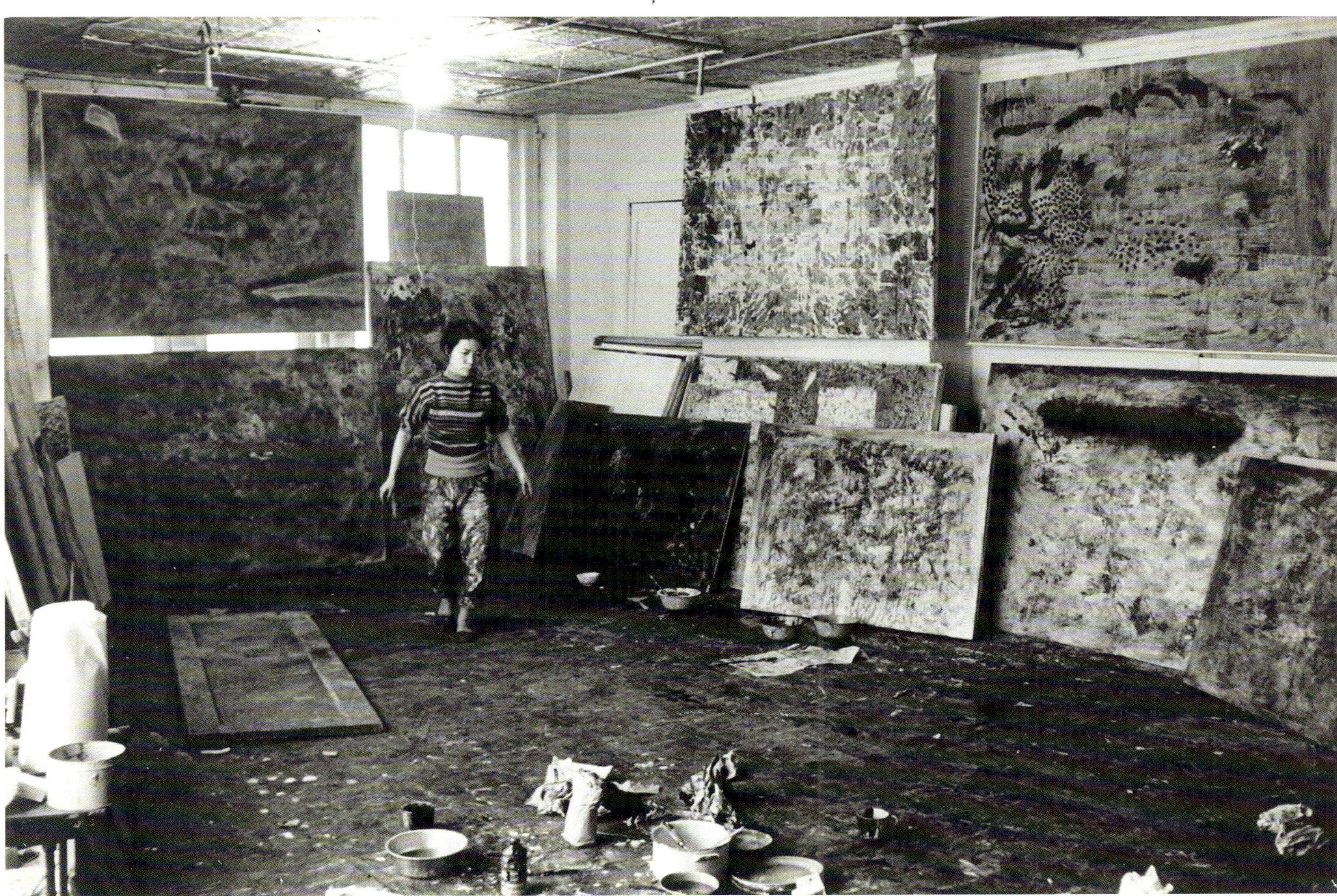

expanse of a "shallow space" made up of tiny waves spreading over the Pacific Ocean, which she had seen during her trans-Pacific flight to Seattle.[30] The artist also spoke of her *Infinity Net* in relation to light, with white being a color that absorbs maximum light.

The *Infinity Net* series also represents Kusama's response to the Abstract Expressionism she encountered in New York City. A 1960 photograph in her archives that shows her in her studio provides a clue to her relationship with the New York School (Fig. 5.7). Here, Kusama is preparing what appears to be a 33-foot canvas that would cover the longest wall of Stephen Radich Gallery at her second New York solo exhibition in May 1961. She clearly referenced Hans Namuth's famous photographs of Pollock at work in his studio, published in *Life* magazine in 1949. Kusama is working on a large, unstretched canvas, making it an "arena," just as the critic Harold Rosenberg famously alluded in 1952 to Pollock's poured painting.[31] However, unlike Pollock, whose "action" painting asserted the uniqueness of his work with his distinctively cluttered colored lines, Kusama stands coolly in front of the camera, opening up her arms to point to the tedious process of applying foundation to her spectacular canvas—twice the size of the largest works by Pollock—as though to imply that anyone can paint like her. Hence not individuality but banality becomes a thrust of her art-making.

This photograph also suggests mechanical and industrial qualities. The way Kusama hung one end of the canvas over a stretcher that leans against the studio window makes it look like an enormous dark conveyor belt. With the canvas blocking the natural light from the window, the scene is lit with artificial lighting. "I feel as if I were driving on the highways or carried on a conveyor belt without ending until my death": she would soon articulate a feeling characteristic of modern industrialized life, as she progressed to the next stage of her art comprising soft sculptures and macaroni-strewn environments.[32] In 1960, however, she was still working in an abstract language, as if to "release my spirit into a vacuum chaos."

Around 1959, the names of Mark Rothko, John Cage, and Jasper Johns appear in Kusama's notebook (No. 1), pointing to her interest in, indeed, her close study of, their works. Her embrace of the tedious process of an *Infinity Net* painting makes a marked contrast with Pollock's heroic action painting, resonating more with Johns's restrained canvases. Like John Cage's silent music, *4' 33"*, wherein noises from the audience made his music, Kusama too created an almost white canvas, giving her audience a larger responsibility in configuring its meaning. Kusama's effort to make her *Infinity Net* paintings as large as gallery walls to create an engulfing environment parallels the practice of Rothko and Barnett Newman hanging their large color-field paintings intentionally lower in order to invite the audience into their painterly environment (Fig. 5.8). (Kusama admired Newman's work.) However, her preoccupation with an enveloping space was already evident in her October 1952 exhibition in Matsumoto, where she lined an entire wall with a black cloth on which hung two rows of similarly framed drawings of equal size, giving a unified look to the wall (Fig. 5.5). The New York art world thus helped Kusama to expand her innate strengths and concerns in her art. Step by step, she became a genuine member of its vanguard scene.

Kusama's interest in photography as a tool of publicity also dates back to her Matsumoto years, but she evolved into a capable publicist for herself in New York.[33] This photograph is very likely among a set of photographs she sent to *Life* reporter Kathleen Shortall in 1961 (Fig. 5.4); Kusama in a sense was competing with Pollock as depicted in the Namuth photographs published in 1949. In her notebook (No. 2), she kept a log of publicity photographs sent to the media, including Shortall. In her early New York years, she had her photograph taken primarily for publicity. Between 1958 and 1962, she published essays on New York in newspapers and magazines in Japan, often accompanied with her portraits. These images were usually provided to explain who she was and where she was based. In one calculated endeavor, she brought her gigantic *Infinity Net* painting to the Brooklyn Heights Promenade to pose herself and her work against the skyline of Manhattan (Fig. 5.1). Professional photographers Kusama hired to shoot her included Rudolph Burckhardt, Hal Reiff, and Peter Moore.

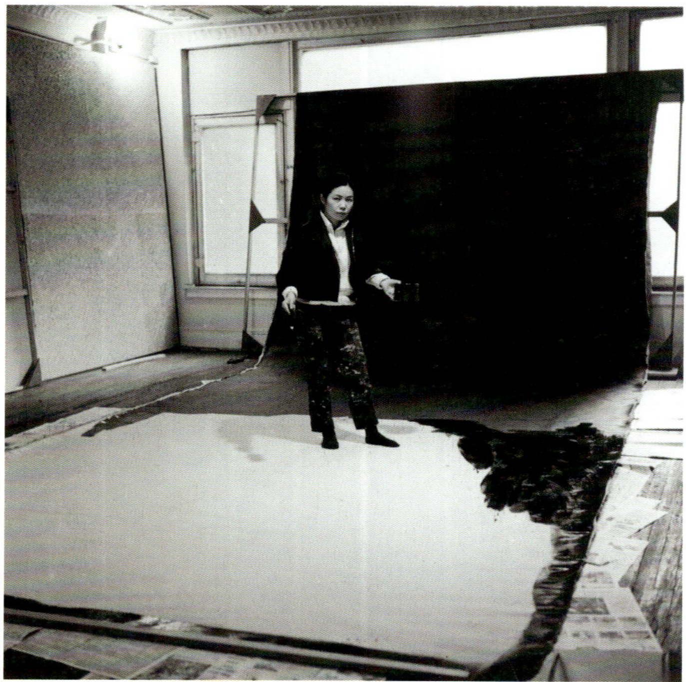

Kusama working on her 33-foot *Infinity Net* at her New York studio, 1960

1960–1963: Art of the Poor

Here, in the most expensive city in the world, where people feed on money, I was so poor back then that I didn't even have 15 cents for bus fare. I was absorbed in creating net paintings, famished, eating nothing for two days in a row.

—May 1961[34]

February 1960
5th: Admitted to League
8th: League
9th: Go to Immigration; Brata takes money
18th/24th/29th: Go to League
26th: Buy paint; buy lacquer

July 1960
6th: Pay $12.35 to Katagiri; pay $20.12 for telephone; buy fur
12th: Go to Martha at 10; go to Staempfli; 2 paintings returned from Stephen
17th: Perry comes back; ask her money
22nd: Sick
25th: Roose[velt] Hospital

January 1961
2nd/9th/16th: J.S. 5–7
23rd: J.S. 5–7; go to photo store
25th: Go to photo store
26th: Judd finishes writing and comes
30th: J.S. 5–7; telephone Stephen; send text

March 1962
1st: Telephone fabric shop
5th/10th: Get egg cartons
9th: Borrow a sewing machine
13th: Go to Immigration
23rd: Mother telephones; get egg cartons

December 1963
10th: Telephone Taketomo; Perry's house at 1
14th: Truck; go at 11
17th: Solo exhibition opening 5–7
21st: Art International comes
23rd: Geldzahler at 10; Rudy's photo at 10:30
28th: Give $10 to Rudy; give $50 to Gertrude; $50 from Hanford

—Excerpted from Kusama's calendar-diaries

Kusama's Brata Gallery exhibition in 1959 was reviewed in the *New York Times*, *Arts Magazine*, and *Art News*. By 1960, she was represented in New York by the uptown gallerist Stephen Radich, with whom she had her second solo exhibition in New York in May 1961 (Fig. 5.8). She was represented outside New York by the Washington, D.C.–based Beatrice Perry of Gres Gallery. The reproduction of *Work No. 2* in *Arts* attracted the attention of the young German curator Udo Kultermann, who invited Kusama to participate in his exhibition *Monochrome Malerei* in March–May 1960. The show featured an international monochromatic tendency in painting that was gaining global prominence. Kusama's participation in *Monochrome Malerei* resulted in invitations to a long

list of exhibitions at European venues, including Galleria Del Naviglio in Milan and the Stedelijk Museum in Amsterdam, both of which played a crucial role in the development of postwar art in Europe.

Critical success did not readily translate into financial success, however. The record of expenses Kusama kept in her calendars reveals the hard reality of her life. A majority of the money she made from selling her work went to art supplies and related expenses. Very rarely did she go to Chinese restaurants with her friends to taste Asian food; she bought only minimal household goods, such as a blanket, a gas stove, and a clock. After 15 years of being a professional artist, she still struggled to make a living from her work. (Her parents monthly sent her money, "secretly hiding Japanese yen in airmail envelopes," against the stringent foreign currency control by the Japanese government.[35]) To make matters worse, with her visa expired in 1959, Kusama had to switch to a student visa, and she enrolled in Julian Levy's life-drawing class at the Art Students League in February 1960. However, "my attendance was low," because she was preoccupied with the preparation for her next solo exhibition, and "the school office called me and told me not to miss classes."[36] An ambitious plan to show several mural-size *Infinity Nets* added to her financial burden, forcing her to procure a huge quantity of paint. On July 22, 1960, out of deep depression, Kusama jumped from her second-floor window. The day is marked on her calendar as "sick" (*byōki*) in red

(Fig. 5.9). When she regained consciousness, she realized she hit her ribs on a bicycle parked beneath her window. She recalls, "It hurt *so* much."[37]

To buy costly art supplies for her Radich Gallery exhibition to be held in May 1961, Kusama might have taken some measures to supplement her income. Immediately before the exhibition, between January and March 1961, her calendar has the notation of "J.S. 5–7" on every Monday. Although further archival research is necessary, she could have found some way to supplement her income at Japan Society. Later in 1962, Beatrice Perry wrote that in order for Kusama to "continue her work, buy materials, and live, she must have some outside help,"[38] and asked for financial support from the Graham Foundation for Advanced Study in Fine Arts.

In May 1961, Kusama's Radich show opened and closed as planned. On September 1, 1961, she moved to a new loft at 53 East 19th Street, as marked in her calendar. Notably, Kusama's inventory notebook lists two new works of "stickers" in the fall of 1961, indicating the shift of her focus away from expensive oil paint to new media. They were followed by a series of experiments with readily available and free-of-cost materials, such as airmail stickers and egg cartons. This shift may have possibly been inspired by a historically important, yet largely forgotten, exhibition, *New Forms–New Media* at Martha Jackson Gallery in June 1960.

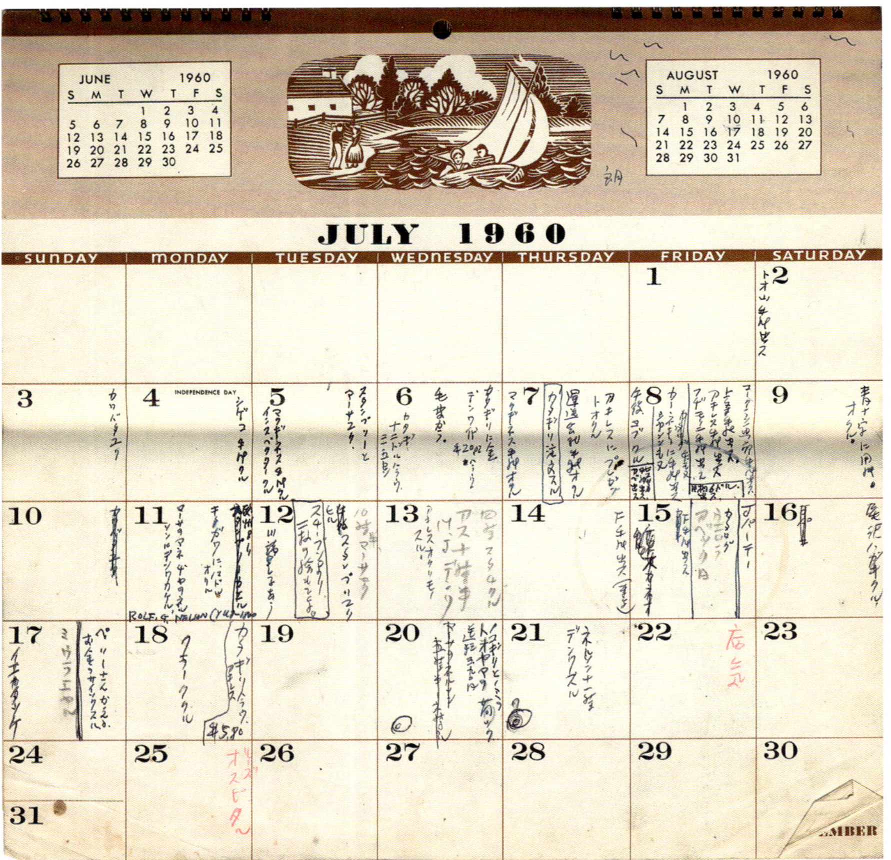

Figure 5.9

Kusama's calendar-diary, July 1960

was also financially exhausted, as she needed to reimburse the gallery for its purchase of the advertisement pages in various art magazines, amounting to $1,700.[42] Being serious about her career, Kusama did not give a second thought to these expenses. The cost-free "junk culture," advocated by Alloway—her close associate in the early 1960s—took concrete form after the Radich exhibition.

In the fall-winter season, Kusama underwent an exhausting exhibition schedule, which included her solo exhibitions at both the Chicago and Washington, D.C. branches of Gres Gallery, as well as such major group exhibitions as the Whitney Annual and the Carnegie International. In March 1962, she extended her use of cheap and readily available materials from collages to three-dimensional objects. As indicated by her calendar entries, she started working on her first soft sculpture (armchair), *Accumulation No. 1*, and a relief made of discarded egg cartons at the same time. The psychosexual nature of her soft sculpture, with its phallic fabric-made protuberances that densely cover various household objects, has been a topic of discussion. Donald Judd wrote in his review that the new works—having obvious association with human organs—project Kusama's "psychological preoccupations."[43] Oldenburg, another practitioner of soft sculpture, observed that Kusama's obsessively repeated components made her anxiety palpable to her audience.[44] In interviews Kusama herself has often discussed her fear of the male sexual organ.[45] This association of visual form and psychological anxiety was informed by Kusama's abiding interest in psychiatry that dates back to her meeting with Nishimaru Shihō in Japan. Kusama indeed considers psychiatry as one of the most important intellectual discoveries of the modern era.[46]

Furthermore, this hitherto unknown fact—the concurrent launch of two seemingly different series, soft sculpture and egg-carton reliefs—has another psychosexual significance: while the fabric-made protuberances of her soft sculpture stand for male sexuality, the egg stands for female sexuality and the carton's concave form also alludes to the concept of female passivity. In other words, the two series constitute a conceptual binary of male/female, which parallels her portrayal of pistils and stamens, or female/male plant motifs, in her earlier watercolors. A photograph from 1963–64, which graced the cover of the Dutch publication *De nieuwe stijl/The New Style* (1965), captures these two works in the same frame (Fig. 5.10), confirming that they formed a conceptual binary pair.

The exhibition was a genealogical survey of works by 75 artists, from Kurt Schwitters to Jasper Johns and Robert Rauschenberg, who paid attention to commonplace objects and "junk culture," as described in the introductory essay by the celebrated Pop art pundit, Lawrence Alloway.[39] It took place four months prior to the declaration of Nouveau Réalisme in Paris and almost one and a half years before Sidney Janis Gallery's now famous exhibition, *The New Realists*. The show was international in its scope: participants included Yves Klein, Gutai's Motonaga Sadamasa and Yoshihara Jirō, Antonio Tàpies, Teshigahara Sofū, and Walasse Ting. It attracted massive public attention, including television coverage by CBS,[40] and a sequel, *New Media–New Forms, Version 2*, opened on September 27, 1960. The exhibition loudly claimed realism as the new form of artistic expression after Abstract Expressionism.

The time lag of more than a year between *New Forms–New Media* and Kusama's first sticker-collages may be explained by her preoccupation with the Radich show, as she received the contract from the dealer in September 1960. Due to her thorough and deliberate personality, Kusama would conceive each solo exhibition as a "project," attaching it to a distinct concept. This is especially true when she began creating environments under such titles as *One Thousand Boat Show* and *Driving Image Show*.[41] She could begin planning for a new body of work only after she mounted her most ambitious monochrome exhibition. By the summer of 1961, Kusama

The inventory kept in her notebook (No. 2) indicates the consignment of two soft sculptures (armchair and couch) and four sticker collages to Richard Bellamy, probably around early June 1962.[47] These sculptures are documented in two photographs found in her archives, taken at a group exhibition at Bellamy's Green Gallery (Fig. 5.2). An astute connoisseur of 1960s art, Bellamy very likely visited Kusama's studio in early May and asked her to participate in a June group show. Kusama must have felt one sculpture was not powerful enough to convey her new idea; she quickly began another sculpture on May 16, as indicated in her calendar. Since the show was slated to open in early June, she had precious little time to rush through the production. She mobilized her friends to help complete *Accumulation No. 2*, a large couch covered with stuffed phallic protuberances. Kusama's upstairs neighbor between 1961 and 1964, Judd remembers that assisting her meant "days [of] unending stuffing."[48]

In the Green Gallery group exhibition, Kusama showed her armchair and couch together with works by Robert Morris, Claes Oldenburg, James Rosenquist, Richard Smith, Robert Whitman, Andy Warhol, and Philip Wofford. The date of this show has long been mistakenly assigned to September 1962, an error made by Kusama herself and followed by others. But it was reviewed by Brian O'Doherty in the *New York Times* on June 17, 1962, and the paid exhibition advertisement, which includes the names of the participating artists, appears on the same page with his review.[49]

The participation of Kusama and Oldenburg in the same exhibition at this particular juncture begs attention, as Oldenburg, too, soon developed his own version of soft sculpture. Kusama recalls that Oldenburg presented a "stiff suit made out of papier-mâché,"[50] an observation affirmed by the installation photograph, while Oldenburg states, "I remember the sofa that probably was the first time I saw her work."[51] This recollection must have been made in reference to the 1962 Green Gallery exhibition.

According to Kusama, Bellamy originally offered her a solo exhibition at Green Gallery in September 1962. However, she had to turn the offer down, because she did not have enough works to show due to financial strain. In retrospect, this may have been the source of the mistaken date.[52] Oldenburg began using his sewn soft props in *Store Days* performances around May 1962. It was Oldenburg who instead showed in the September slot. During the summer of 1962, his former wife, Patty Mucha, sewed his version of soft sculptures, developed from his soft props. She recalls, "I was very proud of the work I did for Claes. Their existence had a lot to do with my ability to sew … and his need to make big sculpture."[53] On September 18, 1962, Oldenburg premiered his soft sculptures at Green Gallery with accompanying Happenings. As noted in her calendar, Kusama attended the opening with Judd; a photograph of a visibly anxious Kusama exists in Oldenburg's archives.[54] In the wake

of New Realism and Pop Art, the show received rave reviews. Such art magazines as *Arts*, *Studio International*, *Kunstwerk*, *Art News*, and *Art International* carried large reproductions of his soft sculptures, which immediately brought Oldenburg to international attention. More specifically, the November 1962 issue of *Arts Magazine* carried Sidney Tillim's lengthy three-page review of Oldenburg's exhibition,[55] which Kusama would have known through Judd, who worked as a critic for the magazine.

Following this chain of events, Kusama entered psychotherapy for the first time, although the artist herself has never responded to my query on this. On November 17, 1962, Kusama made the first call to Yasuhiko Taketomo, a psychiatrist in New York, with whom she had become acquainted probably at a party at his home in December 1961, according to her calendar. On November 24, she was rushed to the hospital by ambulance. She noted in her calendar that she felt dizziness without detectable causes. The doctors dismissed it as her being a hypochondriac. On December 6, Kusama again called up Taketomo and, despite the financial strain, began to have regular psychotherapy sessions from December 9, 1962.

On May 6, 1963, her long-awaited permanent-residency visa was granted. By then, she had truly become a New Yorker, suffering from the psychological frictions of heightened competition in the art world and seeing her psychiatrist biweekly. The names of people she met recorded in her calendar in 1963 included André Emmerich, Henry Geldzahler, Eva Hesse, Ivan Karp, and Georgia O'Keeffe, along with her new dealers Gertrude Stein and Richard Castellani. In December 1963, Kusama finally held a solo exhibition of her soft sculpture, *Accumulation: One Thousand Boat Show*, at Gertrude Stein Gallery. The curator, Alice Denney, remembers performing a Happening during the exhibition, along with four other young women all wearing red leotards.[56] With her Green Card in her hand, Kusama was now free to travel to Europe, where she gathered considerable attention as an American artist in the mid-1960s.

Since 1977, Kusama has voluntarily lived in a Jungian art therapy institution in Tokyo. This fact, amplified by her eccentric behavior witnessed by the denizens of the New York art world, has led to the frequent interpretation of her art in the context of her presumed mental illness. However, while she lived in New York City, she was never known as a mentally ill artist. Moreover, as this critical biography demonstrates, Kusama and her art were clearly an integral part of the New York art world. If she entered psychotherapy, her decision was indeed informed by a rational, self-preserving impetus often absent in the depressed: as an artist, she needed to save herself from a distressed life. Living and working in New York City, she learned from yet competed with concurrent tendencies, and developed them into her original and imaginative art, drawing from the dual aspects of her identity—being Japanese and being a woman.

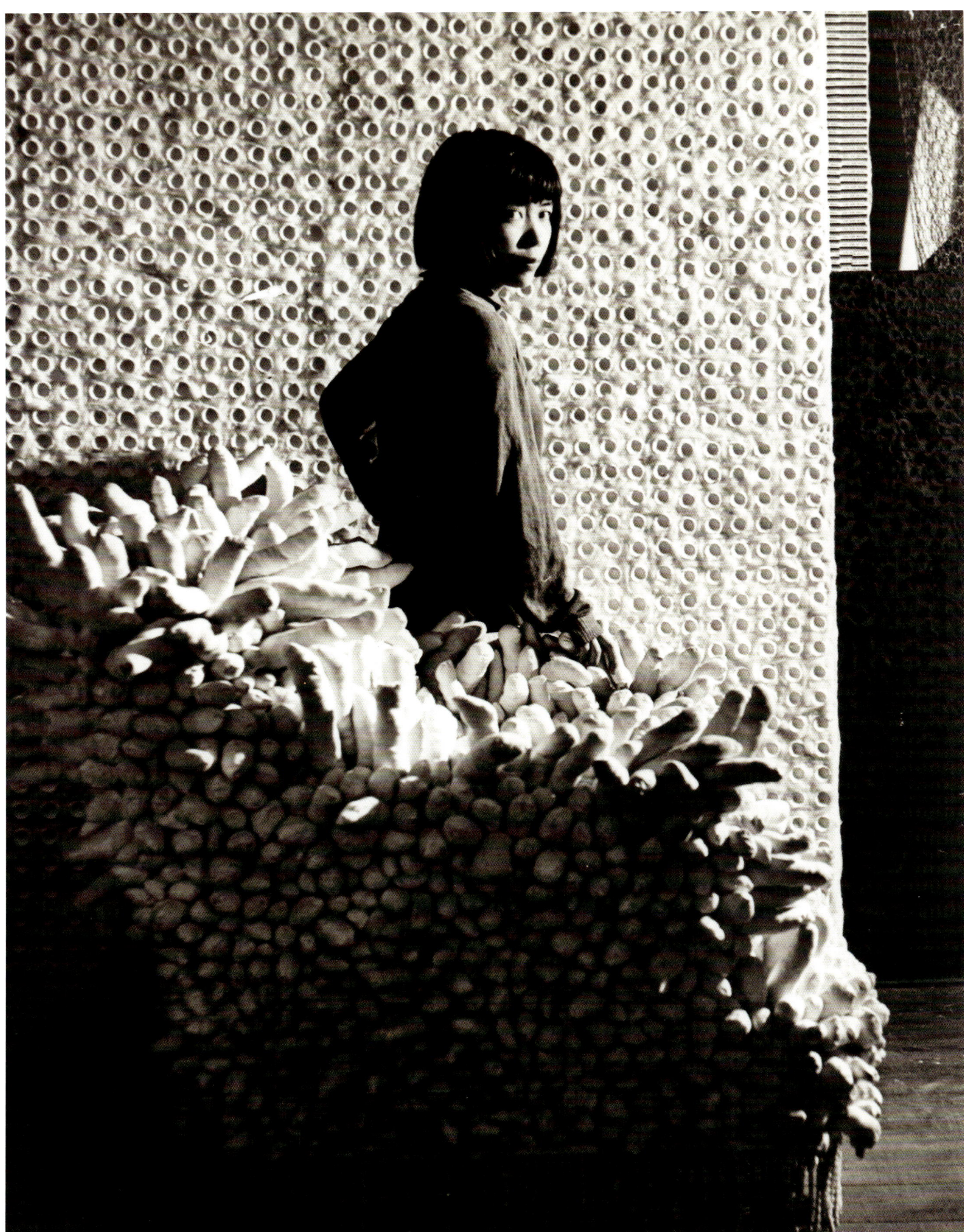

FIGURE 5.10

Kusama with *Accumulation #1* (1962)
and an egg-carton relief (1962) at her
New York studio, ca. 1963–64

Notes

I would like to extend my utmost gratitude to the artist Kusama Yayoi for granting me interviews and to the staff of Kusama Yayoi Studio, Fujibayashi Takako and Kawasaki Yōko, for making valuable materials accessible and patiently responding to my lengthy questions and requests. I am also indebted to and honored to work with Dr. Reiko Tomii, who conducted extensive research for Kusama's first retrospective in this country in 1989; I have inherited the project she initiated to compile the profile of this extremely complex and difficult artist. I thank Geoffrey Batchen, Ed Clark, Jerome Feldman, the Francia-Reyes Family, Justin Jesty, Henk Peeters, Cynthia Navaretta, Franklin Odo, Shibutami Akira, Judith Stein, Matthew Waldman, Carol Willis, the Terra Foundation for Arts, the Ford Foundation, the staff and fellows at the Smithsonian American Art Museum and the Archives of American Art, the staff of the Stedelijk Museum library, and the staff of the Museum of Modern Art, New York, Education Department for their support. Terai Akie—my mother, a native of Matsumoto, and an alumna of the same high school as Kusama—has been an invaluable source in my research. Last but not least, I am deeply thankful to my graduate advisor Anna C. Chave and my husband Luis H. Francia for their continuing support.

Unless otherwise noted, all translations are by the author and Reiko Tomii.

Major archival sources referenced in this essay are as follows.
A) Personal archives housed at Kusama Yayoi Studio in Tokyo include Kusama's calendars (1960–63); notebooks (No. 1, ca. 1959–60, with black-and-white marble cover; No. 2, 1961–64, with green-and-white marble cover; No. 3, 1965, spiral bound); and Kusama Shigeru's scrapbook (ca. 1956–68). Other papers and documents are noted as "Kusama Personal Papers."

B) Among Kusama's personal archives, those organized by Reiko Tomii at the Center for International Contemporary Arts (CICA), New York, in 1988–89 and returned to the artist are indicated by the ID code beginning with CICA/YK/.

C) CICA Oral History Archive, consisting of audio tape recordings and housed at the Fine Arts Library, The University of Texas at Austin, are indicated by ID code beginning with CICA/ATT/001.

1   "Gadan no me wa Pari kara Nyūyōku e: Shintenchi ni dekakeru Nihon gaka-tachi" [Eye of the art world shifts from Paris to New York: Japanese painters go to a new world], *Shūkan Shinchō* [Weekly new trends] (August 11, 1958): 15.

2   Unless otherwise noted, all quotes by Kusama in the pre–New York sections are taken from her letter to author, March 1, 2007.

3   Hibino Kakei (Teruo), letter to Harada Heisaku, April 24, 1989 (CICA/YK/HH.01); Kitazawa Kiyoji, "Kusama Yayoi-san" [Ms. Kusama Yayoi], *Dōsōkai kaihō* [Alumni association newsletter] (March 15, 1956): n.p.

4   Kusama, "Tobei o mae ni shite: Watashi no yume wa kakushite jitsugen suru" [On the eve of departure for the U.S.: My dream is thus about to come true], [unidentified magazine, probably 1957], in Kusama Personal Papers.

5   Kusama Yayoi. "Iwan no baka" [Ivan the Fool], *Geijutsu Shinchō* (May 1955): 164–65.

6   See for example, Herbert Marcuse, *One-Dimensional Man: Studies in the Ideology of Advanced Industrial Society* (Boston: Beacon Press, 1964); and Hannah Arendt, *Eichmann and the Holocaust* (London: Penguin Books, 1977).

7   Fukushima Tatsuo, "Shinpifū-na sakuhin, chūmoku sareru Kusama Yayoi no koten," [Mysterious work, remarkable exhibition of Kusama Yayoi], [unidentified newspaper], April 6, 1955 in Kusama Personal Papers.

8   Nishimaru Shihō, *Hōkōki: Kyōki o ninatte* [Records of wandering: Taking on insanity] (Tokyo: Hihyōsha, 1991), 171–74.

9   I thank Shibutami Akira, the curator of the Matsumoto City Museum of Art, who shared with me the conference proceedings and Kusama's exhibition catalogues from 1952, which he had uncovered in 2004 among Kusama Personal Papers.

10 Yoshida Hodaka, "Nihon no gendai sakuhin ni tsuyoi kanshin: Burukkurin kokusai suisaiga ten o miru" [Strong interest in contemporary Japanese art: International watercolor exhibition in Brooklyn], *Shinano Mainichi shinbun* [Shinano Mainichi newspaper], May 17, 1955.

11 "Kōhyō yonda ichi josei no e" [Painting by a Japanese female artist recognized at the international watercolor exhibition in Brooklyn], *Chūnichi shinbun* [Chūnichi newspaper], September 24, 1955.

12 Kusama, letter to Neil Meitzler, December 17, 1955 (Neil Meitzler papers, accession no. 2761, Special Collection Division, University of Washington Library, Seattle); Kusama, letter to Georgia O'Keeffe, November 15, 1955 (CICA/YK/GO.01).

13 Kusama recently recalls that she did not have a chance to see O'Keeffe's work in person in Japan in response to the author's query (Kawasaki Yōko, Kusama Yayoi Studio, e-mail to author, March 20, 2007). A publication of work she could have seen is Abe Nobuya, "Shichinin no Amerika gaka no sakuhin" [Works by seven American artists], *Atorie* [Atelier] (February 1951): 34–35. For the exhibition history of *Black Iris (II)*, see Barbara Buhler Lynes, *Georgia O'Keeffe Catalogue Raisonné*, vol. 2 (New Haven: Yale University Press, 1999), 1154.

14 For example, see John C. Denman, "Amerika no sakka-tachi" [American artists], *Atorie* (May 1951): 38–40.

15 Zoe Dusanne, letter to Kusama. January 14, 1956 (Zoe Dusanne papers, accession no. 2430-4, Box 6, Folder 4, Special Collections Division, University of Washington Libraries, Seattle); *Tribute to Zoe Dusanne*, exh. cat. (Seattle: Modern Art Pavilion of the Seattle Art Museum, Seattle Center, 1977).

16 Kusama, letter to Neil Meitzler, January 25, 1956.

17 Kusama, letter to O'Keeffe, April 25, 1958 (CICA/YK/GO.18); Kusama, letter to author, March 1, 2007.

18 Kusama, letter to Neil Meitzler, November 17, 1956.

19 "Expense Account for Yayoi Kusama, Nov. 15 1957 to Feb. 15, 1958," probably created by Kusama's hostess in Seattle, Mrs. Shinano Ōta, in Kusama Personal Papers.

20 Kusama, letter to O'Keeffe, January 26, 1958 (CICA/YK/GO.15).

21 Kusama, letter to O'Keeffe, July 8, 1958 (CICA/YK/GO.19).

22 Ibid.

23 Kusama, "Amerika…" [partial clipping from unidentified magazine, text signed as "In New York, March 26," probably 1959] in Kusama Personal Papers.

24 Kusama, "Pīpuru" [People], *Geijutsu Shinchō* (June 1959): 31.

25 Kusama, interview by author, July 28, 2006.

26 Joellen Bard, Ruth Fortel, and Helen Thomas's Exhibition Records of *Tenth Street Days: The Co-Ops of the '50s*, Series 1: Records of *Tenth Street Day: The Co-Ops of the '50s, 1953–1977* (Box 1 and OV), The Archives of

American Art, Washington, D.C.

27 Kusama "Onna hitori kokusai gadan o yuku" [A lone woman goes in the international art world], *Geijutsu Shinchō* (May 1961): 127, 128–29.

28 Dore Ashton, "Art: Tenth Street Views," *New York Times*, October 23, 1959.

29 Hart Perry (son of Beatrice), interview by author, May 1, 2007.

30 Ōgane, "Nyūyōku de hyōka sareta Kusama Yayoi no monokurōmu kaiga" [Kusama's monochrome painting critically acclaimed in New York], *Yomiuri shinbun* [Yomiuri newspaper], January 10, 1961, in Kusama Shigeru's Scrapbook.

31 Harold Rosenberg, "The American Action Painters," *Art News* (December 1952): 22.

32 Kusama, "Miss Yayoi Kusama: Interview Prepared for WABC Radio by Gordon Brown, Executive Editor of *Art Voice*," in *De niuewe stijl/The New Style* 1 (1965): 162–64.

33 Midori Yamamura, "Body and Counterculture: Yayoi Kusama's Photographic Experiments, 1958–1969," unpublished paper presented at ラジカル！ (*Rajikaru!*) *Experimentations in Japanese Art 1950–1975: Graduate Workshop*, Hammer Museum, Los Angeles, April 29, 2007.

34 Kusama, "Onna hitori," 127.

35 Kusama, letter to author, June 4, 2007.

36 Kusama, letter to author, February 20, 2007.

37 Kusama, interview by author, July 28, 2006.

38 Beatrice Perry, letter to Graham Foundation for Advanced Study in Fine Arts, New York, May 31, 1962 (CICA/YK/6180.2).

39 Lawrence Alloway, "Junk Culture as a Tradition," in *New Forms–New Media I*, exh. cat. (New York: Martha Jackson Gallery, 1960), n.p.

40 Martha Jackson, "New Media–New Forms," in *New Forms–New Media I*, n.p.

41 Kusama, letter to Henk Peeters, March 3, 1965 (CICA YK/920.79). When she planned her European exhibitions, she discussed them in terms of these rubrics.

42 Stephen Radich Gallery Records, 1956–76, file 5, box 5, The Archives of American Art, Washington, D.C.

43 Donald Judd, "Yayoi Kusama," *Arts Magazine* (September 1964): 69.

44 Claes Oldenburg, interview by Alexandra Munroe and Reiko Tomii (Oldenburg's studio, New York), February 21, 1989 (CICA/ATT/001.47).

45 Kusama, interview by Munroe (Kusama's apartment, Tokyo), December 15, 1988 (CICA/ATT/001.03).

46 Kusama, interview by Munroe (Cozy Corner coffeeshop and Kusama's apartment), December 18, 1988 (CICA/ATT/001.10).

47 Kusama's notebook (No. 2) does not include a precise date for this transaction, but Green Gallery's entry immediately precedes and follows that of late May and early July. The documentary photographs indicate that Bellamy did not show four collages, all dated 1962, in the main gallery.

48 Judd, interview by Munroe and Tomii.

49 Brian O'Doherty, "Seasons End: Abstractions and Distractions," *New York Times*, June 17, 1962, 103. The exhibition date is also mistakenly given as "April" in Barbara Rose, *Claes Oldenburg* (New York: The Museum of Modern Art, 1970), 201.

50 Kusama, interview by author, June 14, 2004.

51 Oldenburg, interview by Munroe and Tomii.

52 Kusama, interview by author, June 14, 2004.

53 Patty Mucha, e-mail to author, September 20, 2006.

54 A photo of Kusama and Judd at the opening is reproduced in *Claes Oldenburg: An Anthology* (New York: Guggenheim Museum, 1995), 167. Oldenburg also discusses how he found this photo in his archive (Oldenburg, interview by Munroe and Tomii).

55 Sidney Tillim, "Month in Review," *Arts Magazine* (November 1962): 36–38.

56 Alice Denney, interview by author, December 20, 2006.

Addendum

Right before press time, a hitherto unknown egg-carton relief was brought to my attention. Bearing the date of 1960, this untitled work was shown at *Art/38/Basel* by the New York–based Robert Miller Gallery in June 2007. Significantly, the artist recycled one of her earlier canvases painted with scale-like net patterns, which are visible on the back of the work. Measuring 49 ½ x 58 inches, it is much smaller than two extant egg-carton reliefs, both dated 1962 and measuring 70 x 78 inches. These two aspects indicate that this relief was probably the first piece in her egg-carton series, although further research is necessary to fully understand the circumstances of its production. At this point, we can only speculate, but Kusama might have shown this work to Martha Jackson on June 30, 1960, six days after the closing of *New Forms–New Media I*, when the artist visited the gallerist, as noted in the former's calendar-diary. I thank Yūko Teshima for informing me of its display at the Basel art fair and Dr. Reiko Tomii for sharing her first-hand inspection of this work with me.

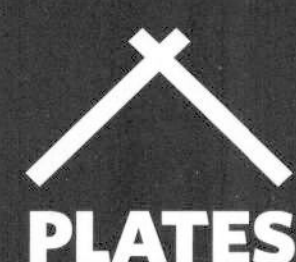

PLATES

⌂ 01 ON MEGUMI AKIYOSHI

ON Pollinating Contemporary Art
ERIC C. SHINER

Certain artists, diverse in their processes and methods of presentation, draw near to the role of honeybee, one of nature's most enduring sources of creation. Busy as it is constructing intricate hives for shelter, protection of the Queen, and communion with its colony mates, flitting about from flower to flower for nourishment and the promotion of pollination, and producing the sweet nectar honey that draws human and animal alike close enough to warrant a mighty sting, the bee is in essence nature's artist. It builds; it protects; it produces; it sustains; it stings; it is respected and feared in equal measure. These activities are all tied to the corpus of the bee: its legs gather pollen; its wings propel it to and fro; its stinger stabs deep in times of crisis. In this vein, the semantic and physical associations of "bee" are the same as those of "artist."

ON megumi Akiyoshi is a prime example of this anthophilic-human connection, as her production, processes, and persona mimic the actions of the honeybee in more ways than one. Perhaps best known for her massive wall murals and full-room installations bursting with brightly hued flowers in neon pinks, yellows, and greens, Akiyoshi creates florid environments within which the viewer is able to commune with nature, albeit a larger-than-life and synthetic version that overwhelms the eye with celebratory color and intrinsic joie-de-vivre (Pl. 1.3). The artist offsets these playful murals with gaudy gold Baroque picture frames that act as a buffer between the exploding pinks of the mural and the bare white wall exposed within the frame. By forcing the subject matter of the work onto the wall, and stripping the space of the missing canvas bare, Akiyoshi supplants the viewer's gaze from the picture hung on the wall to the wall itself, while at the same time providing a bare space upon which the viewer's imagination may project its own meaning and outcome. Like the bee, Akiyoshi pollinates the imagination amidst a sea of flowers pregnant with beauty, potential, and life itself.

Another central tenet of the artist's oeuvre is mobility, as found in her continuing project *ON gallery* (Fig. 1.1, Pl. 1.2). In this performance-based work, the artist dons a variety of costumes—some floral, others white—laden with small works of art hung directly on her body. She thus becomes a roving art gallery, a spectacle that moves through the streets of a given locale delivering art to those in her wake, and indeed to those who might not otherwise visit a museum. From a linguistic standpoint, the artist's childhood nickname, ON-chan, takes on greater significance: the work is hung ON her body; it is the site of the performance first and foremost. Thus, the performance is played out *ON* megumi Akiyoshi. The artist again replicates the bee, delivering not pollen but art to the masses in an act of pollination that feeds the intellect of the viewer while perhaps giving a little sting to the seriousness of the art world thanks to her light-hearted and somewhat sarcastic critique of the art gallery system.

Akiyoshi addresses the issues of the gaze and spectatorship in her work by placing herself at the center of attention in *ON gallery* and by positioning the blank wall in a central location in her floral installations. Her work *Dress the Dress—Think of Marie Antoinette Era* of 2005 also manipulates the viewer's gaze by throwing it right back (Pl. 1.1). An opulently appointed French queen in petticoats and powdered wig hangs on the wall of the gallery, formed in paper clay and just over 14 inches in height. Her face is a mirror that reflects the viewer's gaze; the viewer becomes the famous monarch, regardless of race, gender, or persuasion. Again, cross-pollination is at work here; the worker bee–cum-artist plants an idea in the mind as she stings with the realization that identities are in flux: you too can become the queen of France whether you want to or not.

For *Making a Home*, Akiyoshi creates a new installation covered with lush and vivid flowers. The space will become a garden of meditation, a space within which guests can revel in the artist's sweet gift—a little taste of honey to nourish the soul.

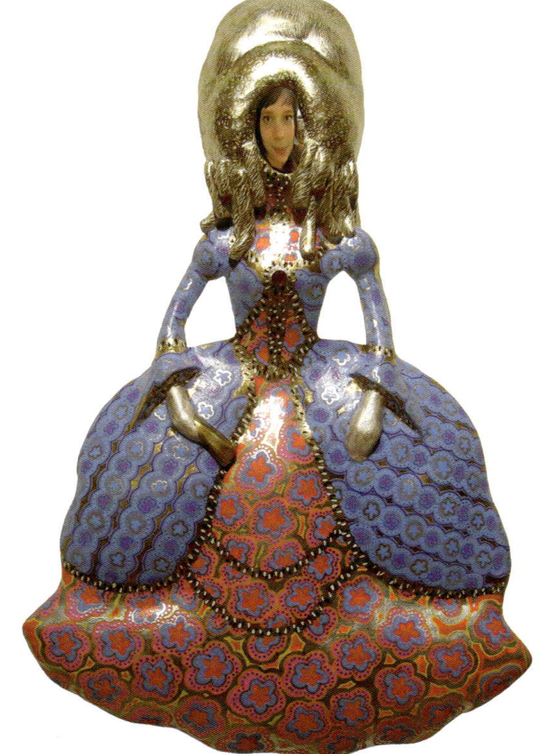

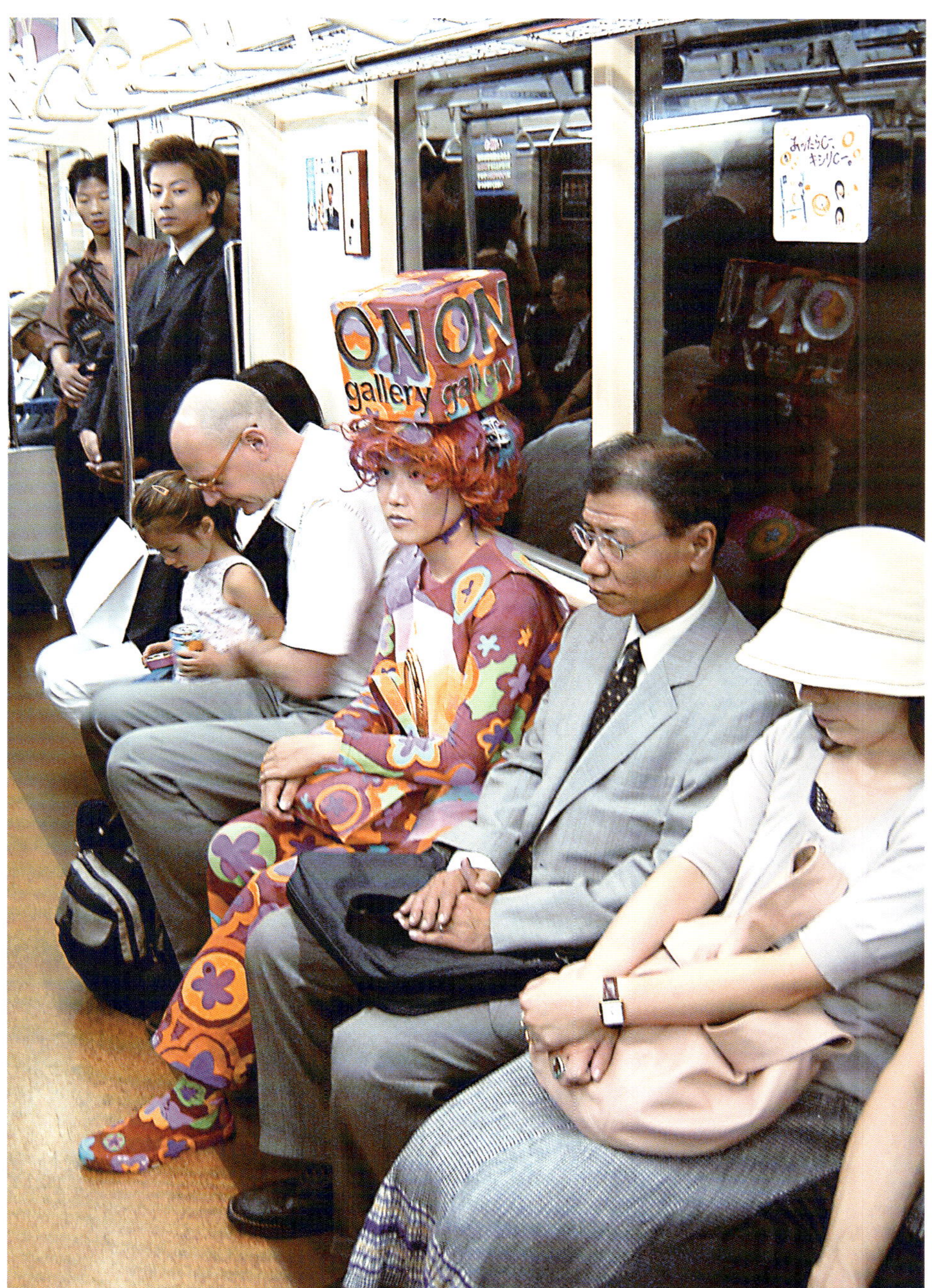

When and how did you first realize that you wanted to be an artist?
ON: When I did the elimination process I felt "Nothing left but to pursue art," and the motivation behind this was the vision "I want to die happy."

Why did you decide to leave Japan?
ON: I simply wanted to get out of Japan at least once in my lifetime.

Why did you choose New York as your ultimate destination?
ON: New York had the strongest gravitation.

Has the experience of living in New York changed your style or process significantly?
ON: I felt much freer and that led me to expand into uncharted mediums. However, I don't think my style itself has changed remarkably. I am influenced by a mixture of both worlds.

What experience has given you the most satisfaction as an artist in New York?
ON: In New York, when I was performing and wandering around the Dumbo Art Festival in 2006, some people were saying, "Oh, you became a museum, last year you were just a gallery!"

In this age of globalism, do you consider yourself to be a Japanese artist, an American artist, an international artist, or a hybrid of all three?
ON: As I start to experience wherever I am inside or even outside of Japan, I hear the slight intro fade-in of the melody ♪ It's a Small World ♪ and think of the lyrics. I consider myself a New York–based/ Japanese/international artist.

PLATE 1.2

ON megumi Akiyoshi
ON gallery in Tokyo Subway (Ginza Line)
2004
Moving gallery performance by artist exhibiting
FLOWER gallery
Courtesy of the artist

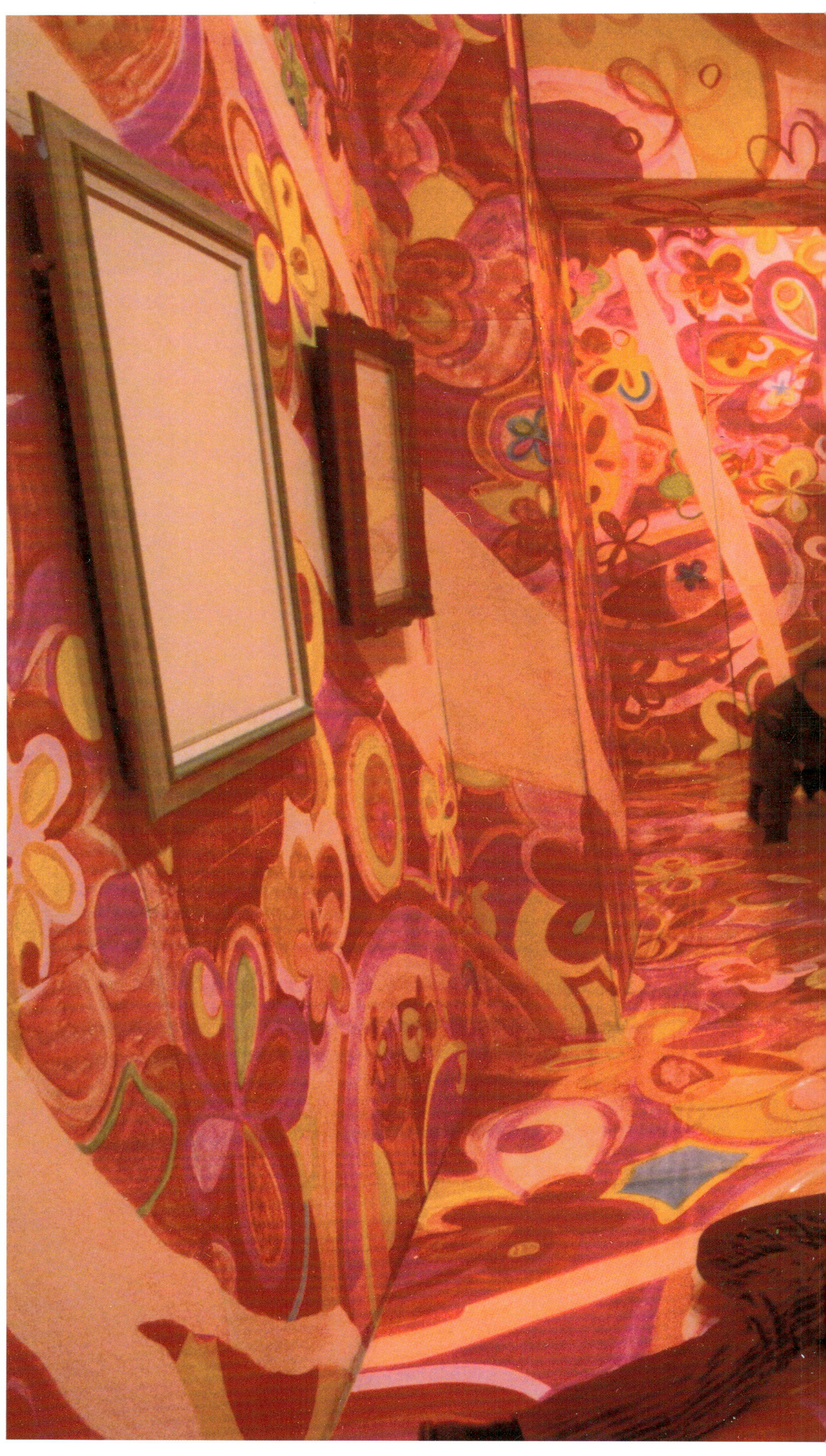

Plate 1.3

ON megumi Akiyoshi
FLOWER gallery
1999
Frames, acrylic paint, plywood, cardboard,
transparent plastic sheet
10' 10'' x 12' 9 ½'' x 26' 3'' (3.3 x 3.9 x 8 m)
Collection of the artist
PHOTO: ON MEGUMI AKIYOSHI

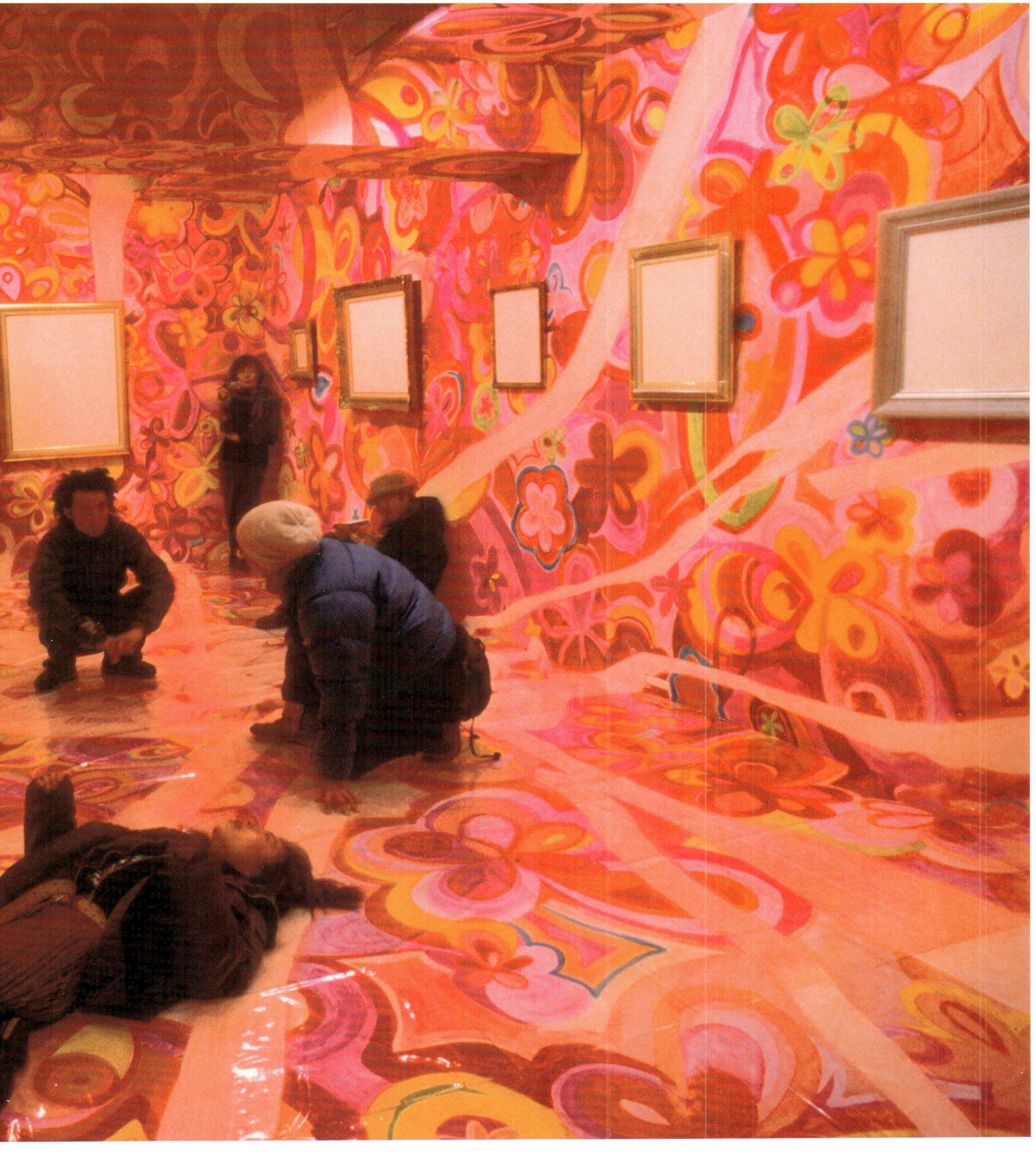

02 NORIKO AMBE

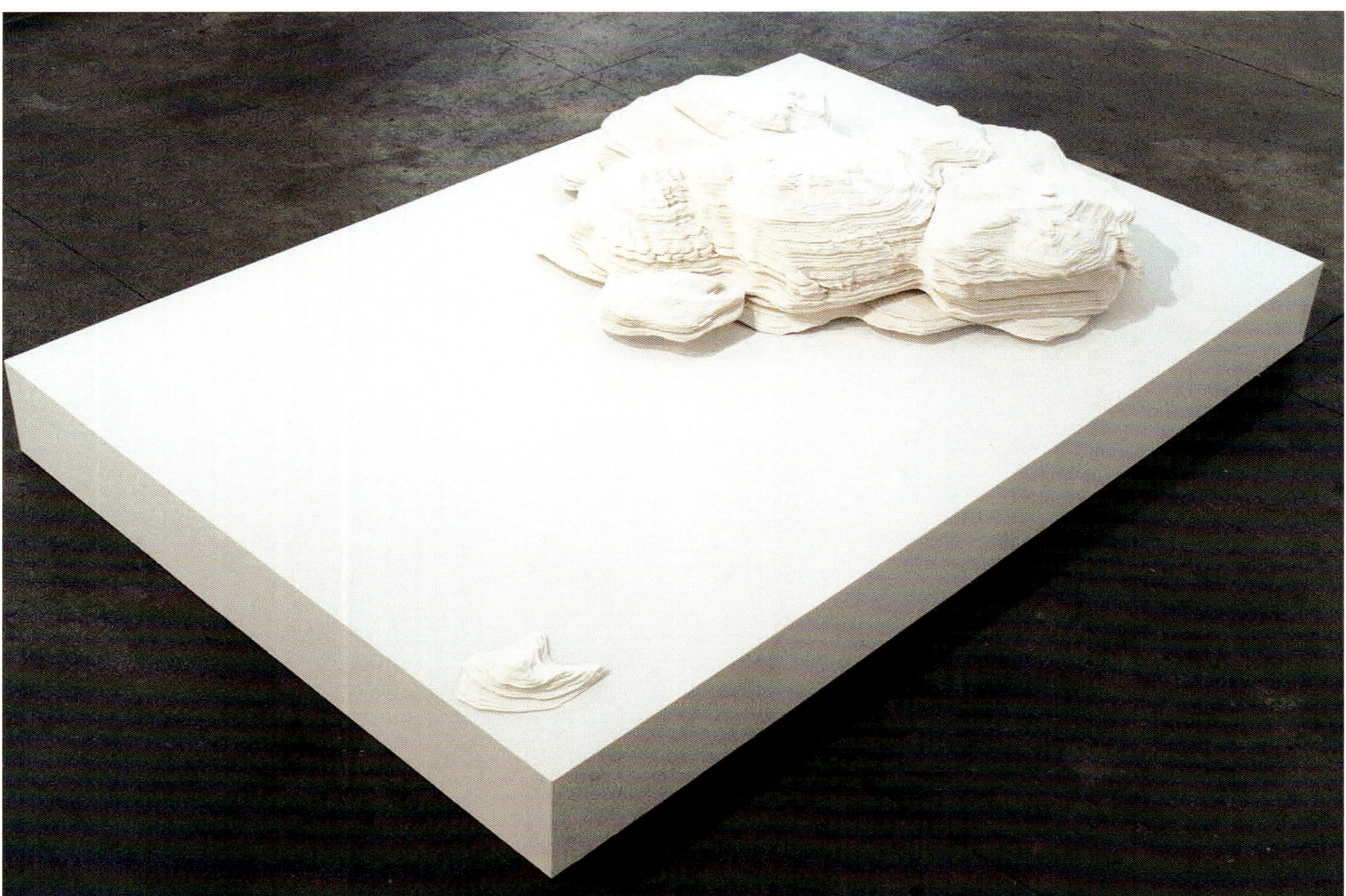

Noriko's Line, or the Language of Infinity
LUIS CAMNITZER

I first met Noriko Ambe in the summer of 1997, in a small village in Tuscany. At the time she was undergoing a long crisis in her art. "I'd been in chaos for three years," she recalls. "I'd been losing my way. What had my art been for?!? What is my original?!? I doubted myself. Then I started systematic work, etching to be simple." She spoke no English then. Within a month her life had changed.

At a dinner party one night where everyone was speaking English, Noriko heard someone refer to a grocery store in the village as a 7-Eleven. Her eyes lit up; she erupted from her linguistic confinement and, to everyone's surprise, practically screamed: "*Seven-Eleven, convenience store!*" A few weeks later she was able to communicate with the rest of the group. A similarly intense change occurred in her art. Her chaos-stance disappeared over one night—nobody knows if it was sleepless—and the next morning her work was to be meditative. The question was: What is art for me?

Changes were not made on a whim; she was slowly preparing to embark on what she later called "a ten-year journey." It certainly involved a change in body language (hesitation became slow hand movements), but it was much more than that. While the early work was sustained by disconcertion and who-knows-what mixture of emotions, she now stopped. She radically changed her pace to observe how her body felt while working. More importantly, she also started to inhale and process reality as one of the many symbols of infinity. In a more trivial way, one could simply say that Noriko had discovered the line.

For Noriko this was not a trivial matter. In her own terms, the line was her pulse, her heartbeat, her breathing, and even more, her control of all the above. The line was not a thing, but a verb. Even in terms of that new-found reality, the line continued being a verb, but here meaning a different action. For this, the line served to build a spiderweb, a knitted platform of reference from which she could not only observe the world, but also extend her reach to touch her surroundings and absorb them. In fact it became an antenna, her synonym for exploration. It became what in 1999 Noriko decided was her visual voyage.

It is this shift of the line from formal element to action that allowed her to engulf things rather than describe them. When the line met the slices of a tree trunk, she performed an act of recognition. It was realizing an awareness of relatedness that went far beyond formal similitude. Both she and the tree performed the same operation over time: they grew lines. When they met, it was not the discovery of resemblance that took place, but an intersection of times of growing. Together they create a graph rather than a replication.

When her line met topography, yes, Noriko delimited territory, but not to describe existing canyons and mountains or to give an impression of them (Pls. 2.1–2). Instead, her line became a frontier. It burrows into materials and separates them from space. When applied to books, it burrows into knowledge and separates it from space and from other knowledge (Pl. 2.3). Deceptively, the results of the process seem to be landscapes, but are not. Landscapes— their descriptions—are finite, a verb; her line, is not. When Noriko's line stops, it is not because a description is finished. It is because the material is exhausted and shows its end by presenting its own limits. It is then, when she just goes to another material, that all temporary supports for her verb are designed to reach infinity.

Meanwhile, eight of the ten years of her planned voyage have passed. The self-imposed deadline now elicits both curiosity and fear. The curiosity is about the questions: in what language(s) will Noriko eventually erupt, and what consequences will it have on her art? The fear is that her exploration of infinity will stop cold, as it did when she started a decade ago, which led to this trip. It is only her fear of repetition that causes these shifts. But for the viewer there is still a seemingly inexhaustible task to be performed, one that we would hope continues, for our sake.

NA: When I was a child, I liked picture books and art class at school. When I was 16, I decided to go to *yobikō* (art cram school). And when I was 32, I found my way, and started the *Linear-Actions Project*.

NA: Seven years ago, after I participated in a residency program in Italy during the summer, I came to New York. Then I met the gallery director whom I work with now.

NA: Joy, excitement, expectation, and anxiety.

NA: As a foreign artist, I face many difficulties such as language, moral and cultural gaps, etc. The first highlight was when a gallery director in Brooklyn picked me up for a solo show in 2003. Since then, things began to move.

NA: My close artist-friends and I have been helping each other in many ways, though we are very independent from each other. I feel as if they are a second family to me nowadays.

NA: Bringing New York speed into my work is challenging physically and practically. I have also been working with industrial materials (such as cabinets). In this way I feel that the New York sensibility has been an influence on my work.

NA: Never. Of course I miss Japan, my family, friends, food, hot springs, etc.

NA: I am aware of my Japanese identity here in the U.S. on a daily basis. That is my destiny. It never changes. Being in the U.S. has helped me to have a broader perspective in respect to Japanese culture and tradition. I want to be a Japanese artist who is international.

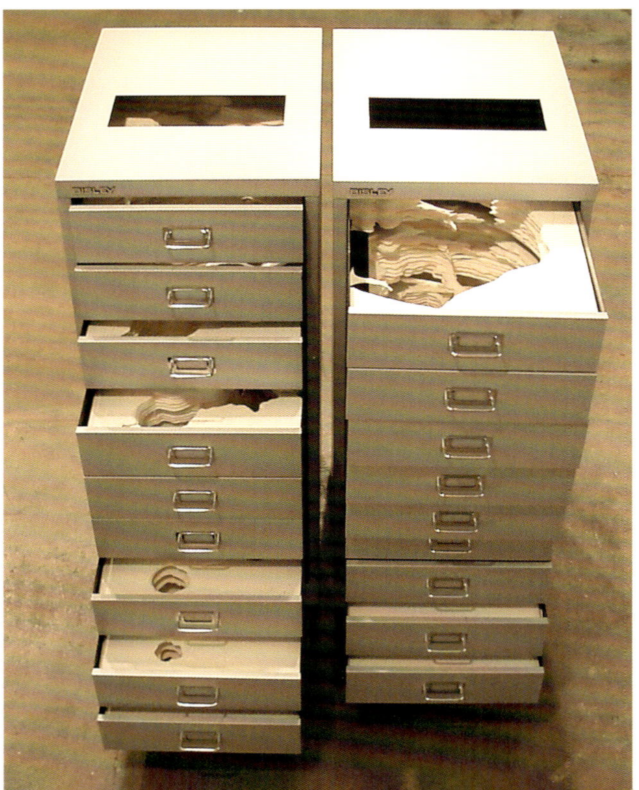

PLATE 2.2

Noriko Ambe
Flat File Globe 3A, B
2006
Cut Yupo synthetic paper, metal cabinets
Each 37 x 13 ¾ x 18" (94 x 34.9 x 45.7 cm)
Courtesy of the artist and Josée Bienvenu Gallery, New York
PHOTO: NORIKO AMBE

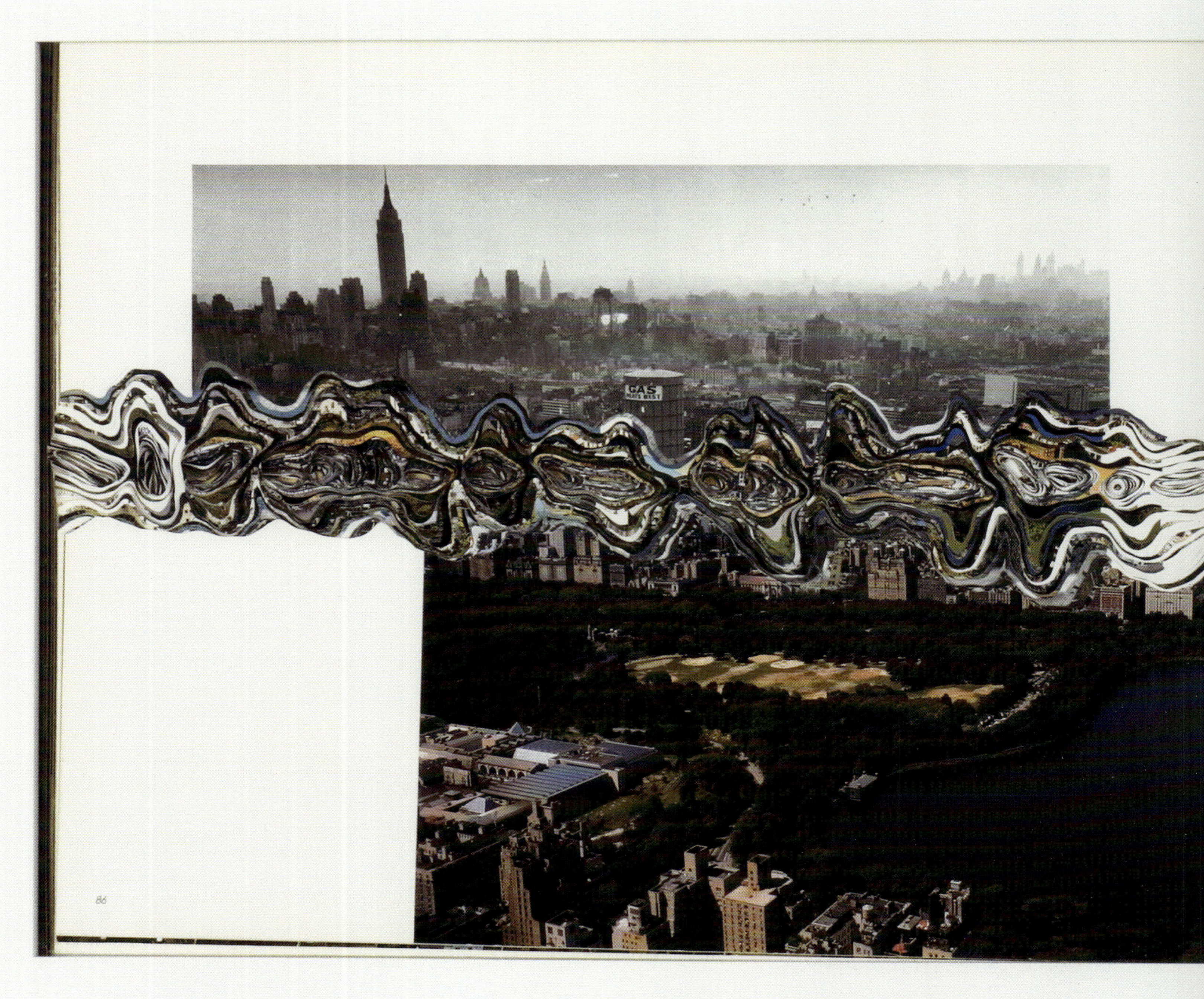

PLATE 2.3

Noriko Ambe
Flat Globe: Above NY
2006
Altered book, cut pages, framed
12 ¹⁄₁₆ x 29 ³⁄₁₆ x 1 ½" (30.6 x 74.1 x 3.8 cm)
Whitney Museum of American Art, New York. Purchase, with
funds from Francis Greenburger, T.2006.100

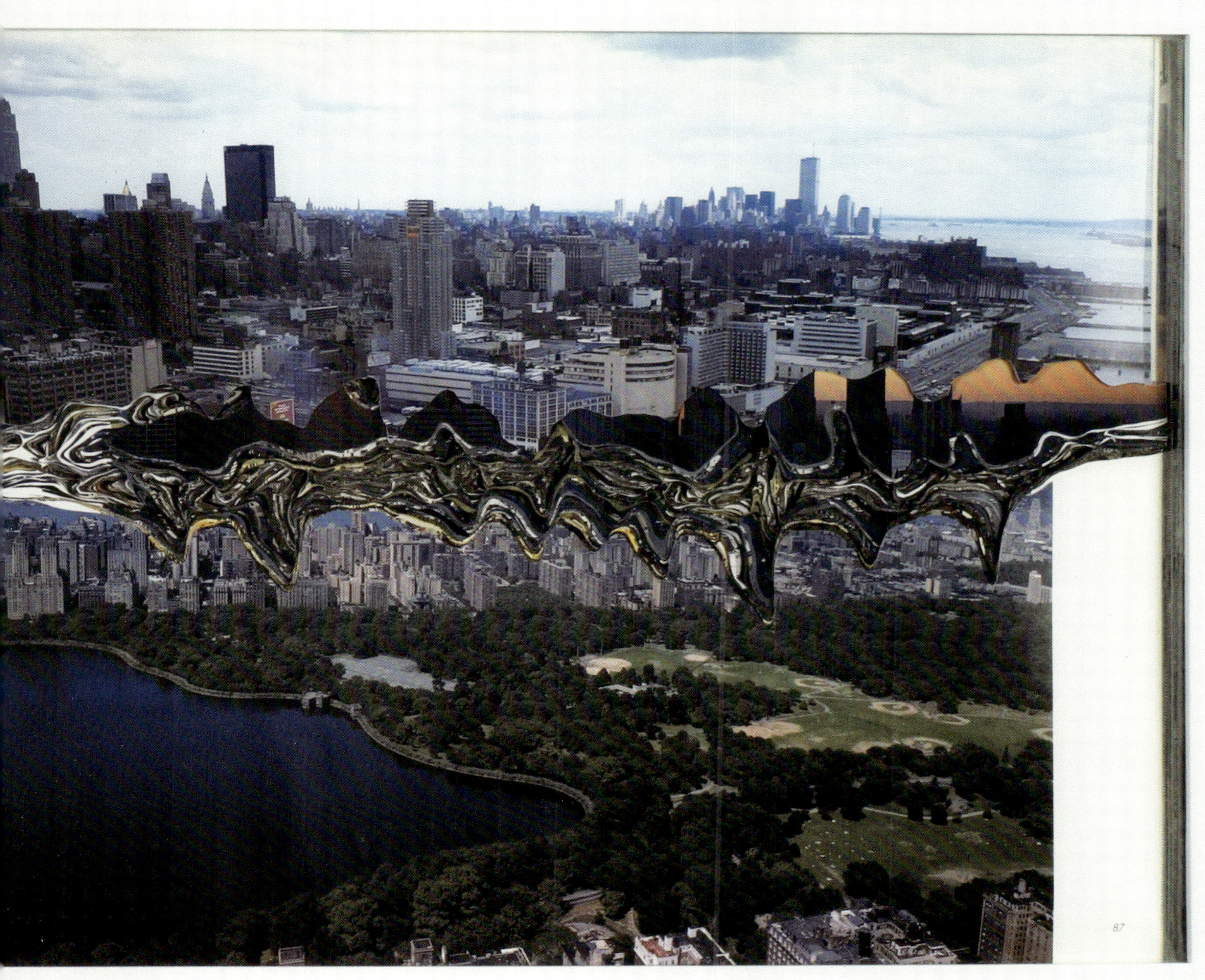

87

⌂ 03 EI ARAKAWA

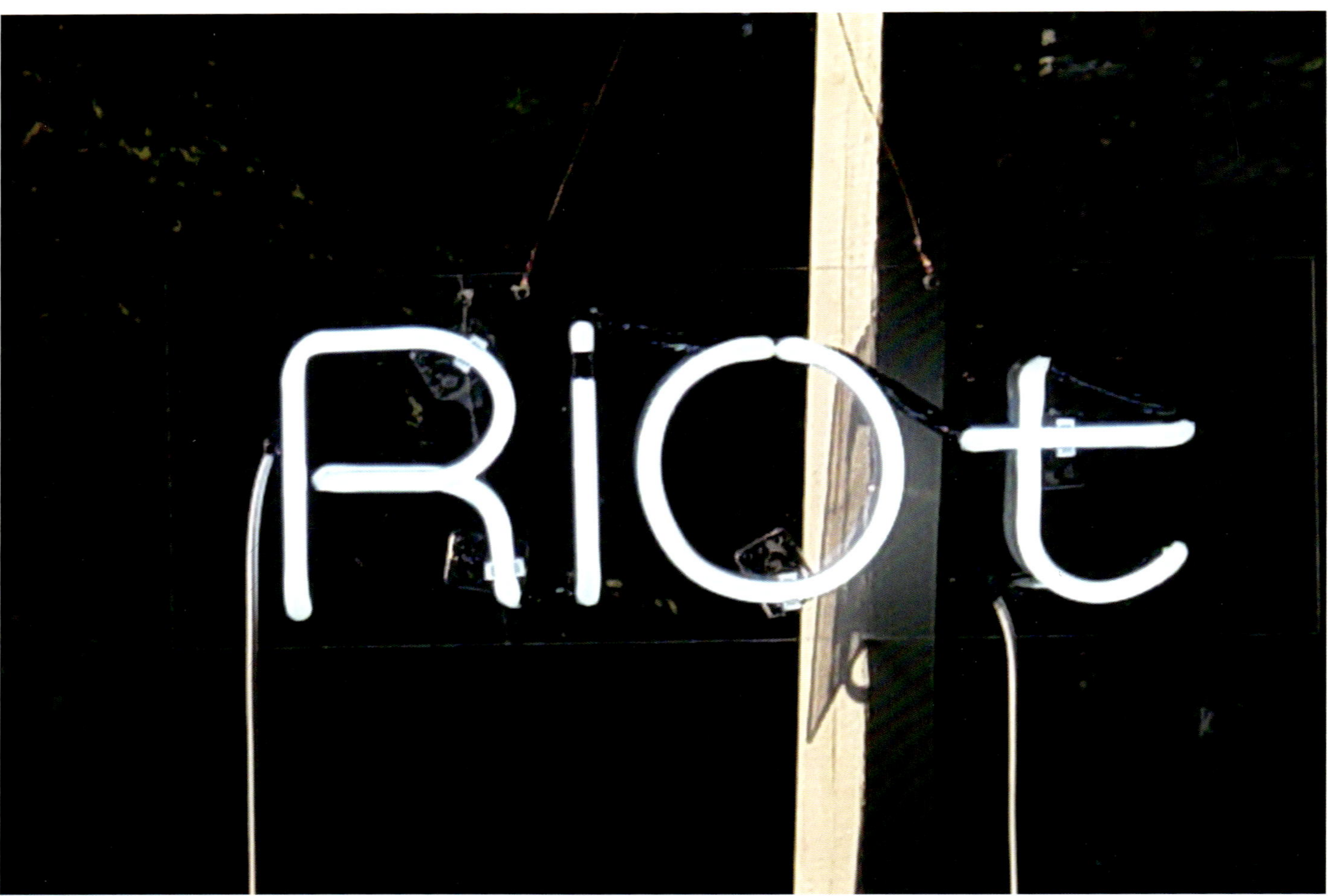

Dictionary of Ei Arakawa
Excerpts from a Preliminary Edition
REIKO TOMII

Arakawa: This lexiconic study concerns Ei (b. 1977), a performance artist who came to New York in 1998, not Shūsaku (b. 1936), a conceptualist who came to New York in 1961. Just like the younger filmmaker Kurosawa Kiyoshi who has to contend with the qualifier, "not Akira, no relation," Ei stands in the shadow of his well-known predecessor.

Collectivity: Arakawa's *modus operandi* is characterized by collectivism. For his breakthrough performance, *Mid-Yuming as Reconstruction Mood* (2004), he gathered together six non-artist women to perform with him. Since then, gathering a team of collaborators became an integral part of his work. While he mobilized eight fellow international art students from the National Academy School of Fine Arts (NASFA) and the Art Students League in *On Kawara's Esperanto* (2004), he invited eighteen fellow international students from the Peridance Center to dance in *Metropolis* (2005). (He was a student at NASFA and Peridance at those times.) Although his conception and deployment of collectivism is highly fluid and temporal, he has recently formed two groups, "Grand Openings" (with Reena Spaulings affiliates) and "Togawa Fan Club," whose memberships are relatively stable.

Construction: See *Mood*.

Grand Openings: See *Collectivity*.

History: Historically conscious, Arakawa makes frequent historical references in his work. Artists to whom he has paid homage or otherwise alluded include: Kusama Yayoi; Gutai's Murakami Saburō; Tezuka Osamu (*Astro Boy*); Donald Judd; and Dan Graham. *RIOT THE BAR 2005* was inspired by the Stonewall Riot of 1969 (Pl. 3.1). *See also* Kawara, On.

PLATE 3.1

Ei Arakawa
RIOT (neon sign) from *RIOT THE BAR 2005*
2005
Performance at Bard College, Annandale-on-Hudson, N.Y.
Neon sign: 5 x 16" (12.7 x 40.6 cm),
edition of 3 + 1 A.P.

Kawara, On: A prominent conceptualist known for his *Date Painting* series, On Kawara presents Arakawa with the riddle of internationalism and identity, compelling the younger artist to create a series of works. Arakawa first made a fake *Date Painting* while flying back from Tokyo to New York. Having incorrectly translated "Duty Free" into Esperanto in this airborne project, he devised a performance, *On Kawara's Esperanto*, in which international art students mass-produced *Date Paintings* on wood with the correct word, *Senimposta*, written on them. These fake On Kawaras were immediately "deconstructed" and turned into constructivist sculptures. The two projects, together with his research paper on Kawara's signing practice in the *Bathroom* series (1952), were then turned into a video, *Make Your Name Foreign* (2005), which premiered at PoNJA-GenKon's* first art-history conference, held at Yale University (Pl. 3.3).

Mood: Arakawa on "mood" in *Mid-Yuming as Reconstruction Mood*: "If 'reconstruction' is our group's desire, the performance is a temporal condition of our desire that creates 'mood.' This 'mood' signifies music that is mid-Yuming. It's about a 'construction' of mood. Mood is the installation. Mood seems more spatial than objects in my performance." Arakawa on "mood" in *On Kawara's Esperanto*: "If the 'constructivist' objects at Greene Naftali are art works of Ei Arakawa, then what are the other parts of the performance that happen all at the same time? Maybe these objects look like art works, but, in fact, they are a part of the production of mood as art."

Music: Arakawa's use of blasting music, selections of which are often informed by historical references, is instrumental in creating a "mood" in his performance. *See also* Mood.

Multiplicity: Performative *scenes* Arakawa choreographs are deliberately chaotic. In his work, the artist himself is hardly the center of attention. Neither are the performers' bodily acts the sole element of his work, be it a grand jeté in *Metropolis* (2005) or crawling in *Two Grahams* (2007) (Pl. 3.4). His works are varyingly comprised of multiple elements—including "construction" of some sort (which is often followed by destruction), blasting music, artist's books (produced in advance or during the performance), and video projections—which, together with task-oriented or mundane movements, generate a multifaceted "spectacle" that refuses to offer a single meaning but encourages his audience to be multitasking in their observation.

Name: Name is closely tied to identity in Arakawa's mind. To create a fluctuating identity, Arakawa authored *Make Your Name Foreign* as Huang-chuan Yi, using the Chinese reading of his Japanese name. *See also* Kawara, On.

Reena Spaulings: A fictional gallerist, created by John Kelsey and Emily Sundblad, with a cast of collaborators that includes Arakawa. The namesake gallery was opened in 2004 in New York's Chinatown, where Arakawa presented *Mid-Yuming as Reconstruction Mood*, *Toward A Standard Risk Architecture* (2006), and *Two Grahams*.

Temporality: A perennial multi-tasker, Arakawa introduces multiple layers of temporality in his performative work: the physical time of performance; the temporal existence of the team assembled; and historical time(s). *See also* History.

Togawa Fan Club: *See* Collectivity.

Yuming: A female singer-songwriter active and popular in Japan since the 1970s.

*PoNJA-GenKon (Post-1945 Japanese Art Discussion Group/Gendai Bijutsu Kondankai) is a scholarly listserv group.

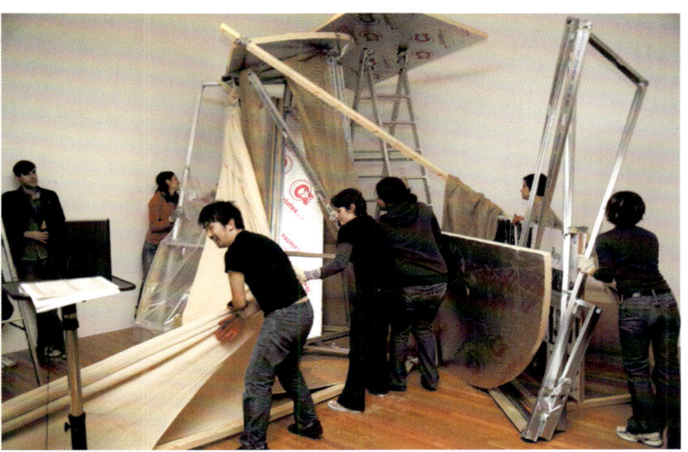

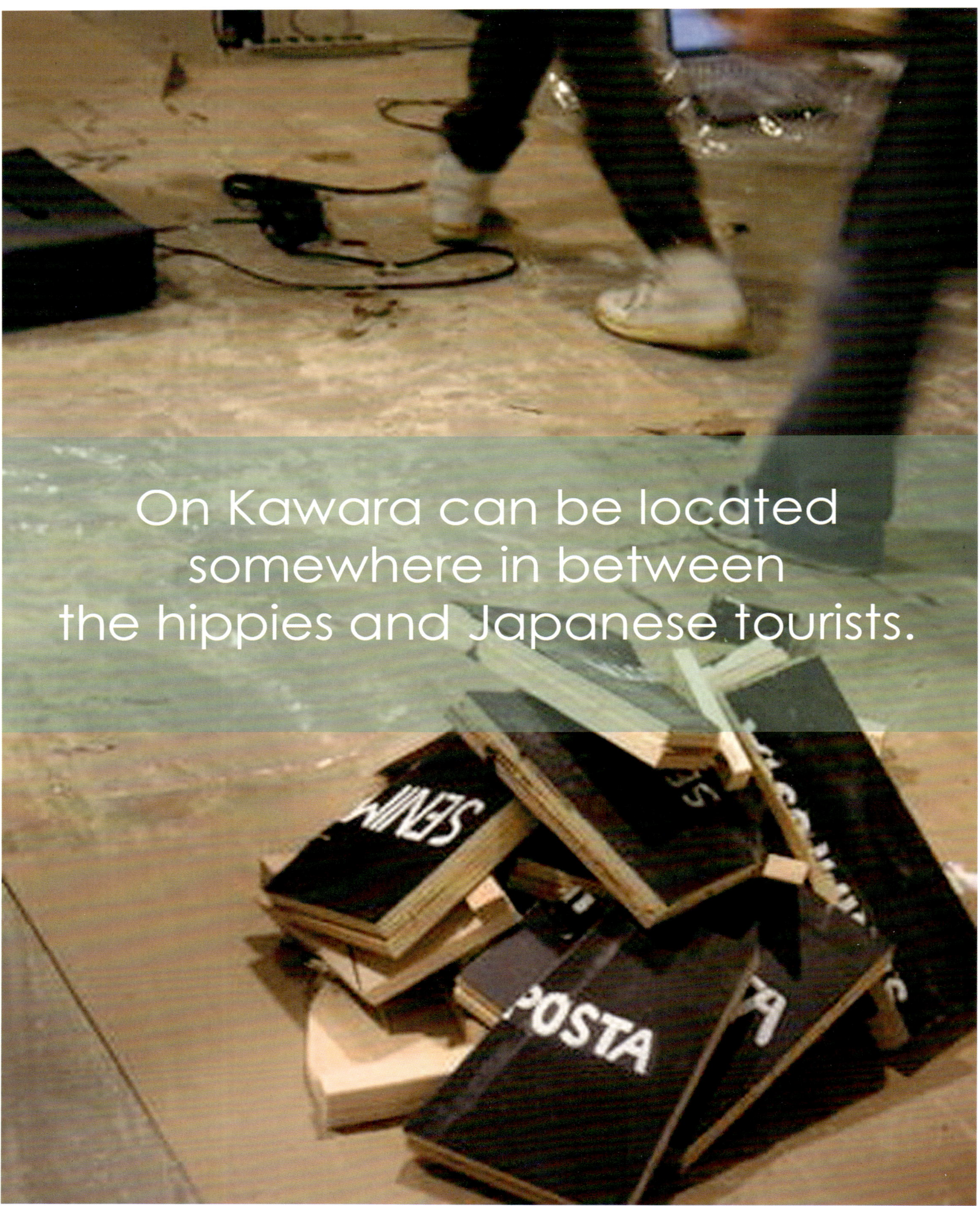

Plate 3.3

Ei Arakawa
Still from *Make Your Name Foreign*
2005
Video
13 minutes 39 seconds
Collection of the artist

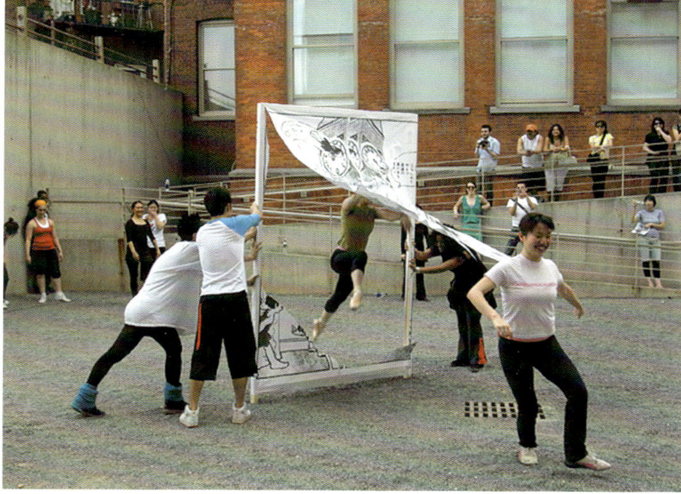

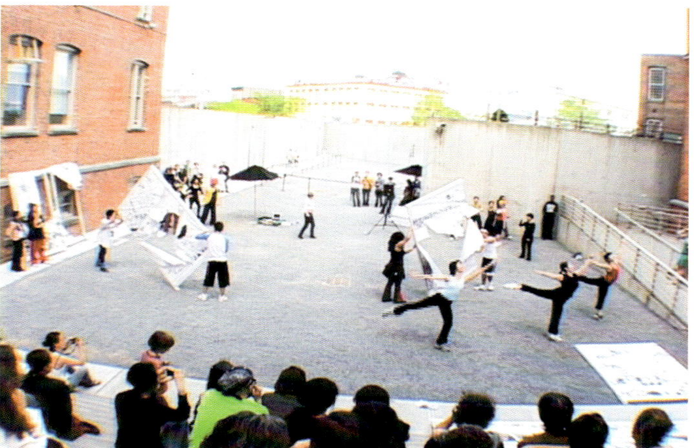

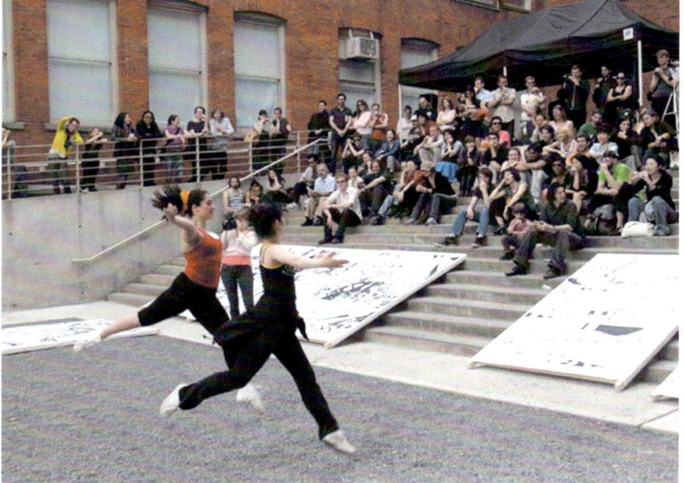

PLATE 3.4

Ei Arakawa
Scenes from *Metropolis*
2005
Performance at P.S.1 Contemporary Art Center, Queens

What was your first impression of New York City?
EA: The people don't care what other people do.

Did you have any interactions with other artists or supporters that were especially beneficial to you and your work?
EA: I found Seth Price amazing even before he started to make sculpture. He and I met at Dia where I was volunteering. Jutta Koether was the really early person who encouraged me to do a performance. I am particularly interested in the people from Cologne in the 1980s. Jan Avgikos welcomed me to be a participant of her seminar on *Documenta 11* at the School of Visual Arts (SVA). This seminar led me to Reiko Tomii, the art historian, with whom I did a one-on-one study. John Kelsey often reminds me of what I find very interesting. He is a co-owner of Reena Spaulings, through which I met many interesting artists in Europe. Sam Lewitt, a friend I met at John Miller's class at SVA has an impressive library of obscure knowledge. He recommended me for the Whitney Independent Study Program. Mari Mukai, a frequent supporter of my performance, is not an artist but is very unconventional. She was the first Japanese person I met in New York in 1998.

What experience has given you the most satisfaction as an artist in New York?
EA: To learn that what the publicity says is not always right. It is easier for me to keep a critical autonomy from them here.

In this age of globalism, do you consider yourself to be a Japanese artist, an American artist, an international artist, or a hybrid of all three?
EA: I feel this question is dated. I am a Japanese artist, but legally and intellectually, I am not stable as Japanese, American, international, nor a hybrid of whatever.

04 SATORU EGUCHI

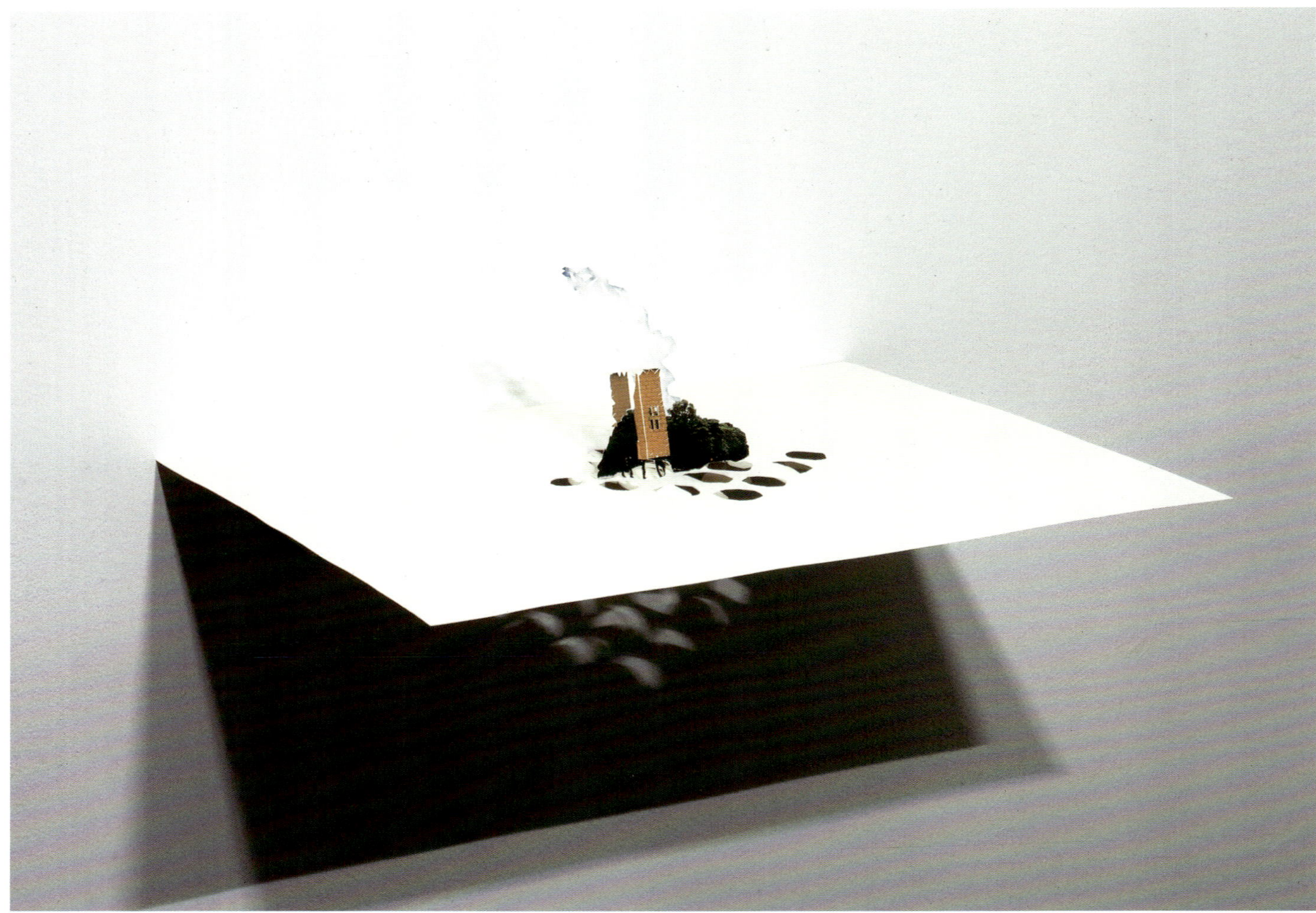

Drawing a Home
HIROKO IKEGAMI

For *Making a Home* Satoru Eguchi has chosen a most appropriate subject. His contribution is a room-sized installation in which he re-creates his "home" space as an artist: his studio. *STUDIO* invites viewers to enter and encounter a variety of objects that surround the artist in his everyday environment—a work desk, a plant, bottles of paint, and stationery (Pl. 4.2). Using common materials such as cardboard and wood, Eguchi re-creates these items casually but painstakingly, in a way reminiscent of an artist drawing a landscape to grasp its fleeting impression. In other words, *STUDIO* is a three-dimensional, tactile drawing that captures traces of the artist's transient, yet successive, perceptions.

Although Eguchi's career as an artist is relatively short—he arrived in New York in 1998 to enroll in the BFA program of the School of Visual Arts, where he completed his MFA degree in 2004—he has already been lauded for his photo-collages. One such work,

among the earliest Eguchi exhibited, is *Untitled* (2003), an ethereal construction made of a piece of paper and a snapshot, in which he creates a kind of imaginary landscape by combining negative and positive forms of cutout materials (Pl. 4.1).

Like his materials, Eguchi's cutout technique may seem rather basic and unpretentious; but with this method he produces works of striking beauty and delicacy. In *Swimming Pool* (2005), he removed numerous leaf-shaped forms from a snapshot, which he pinned down to a support as if the piece were a specimen of a rare insect (Pl. 4.3). As the picture casts an intricate shadow on the support, the work assumes a sculptural quality as well as displaying a complex interplay between the figure (a snapshot, whose original image has become barely identifiable) and the ground (the support, which now holds the abstract pattern of the shadow).

Plate 4.1

Satoru Eguchi
Untitled
2003
Paper, cut-out photo, glue, variable shadow
cast on the wall
14 x 16 ½ x 4 ½" (35.6 x 41.9 x 11.4 cm)
Collection of the artist
PHOTO: GŌ SUGIMOTO

Plate 4.2

Satoru Eguchi
Model for *STUDIO*
2007
Paper, wood, glue, paint, etc.
15 x 24 x 12" (38.1 x 61 x 30.5 cm)
Collection of the artist
PHOTO: GŌ SUGIMOTO

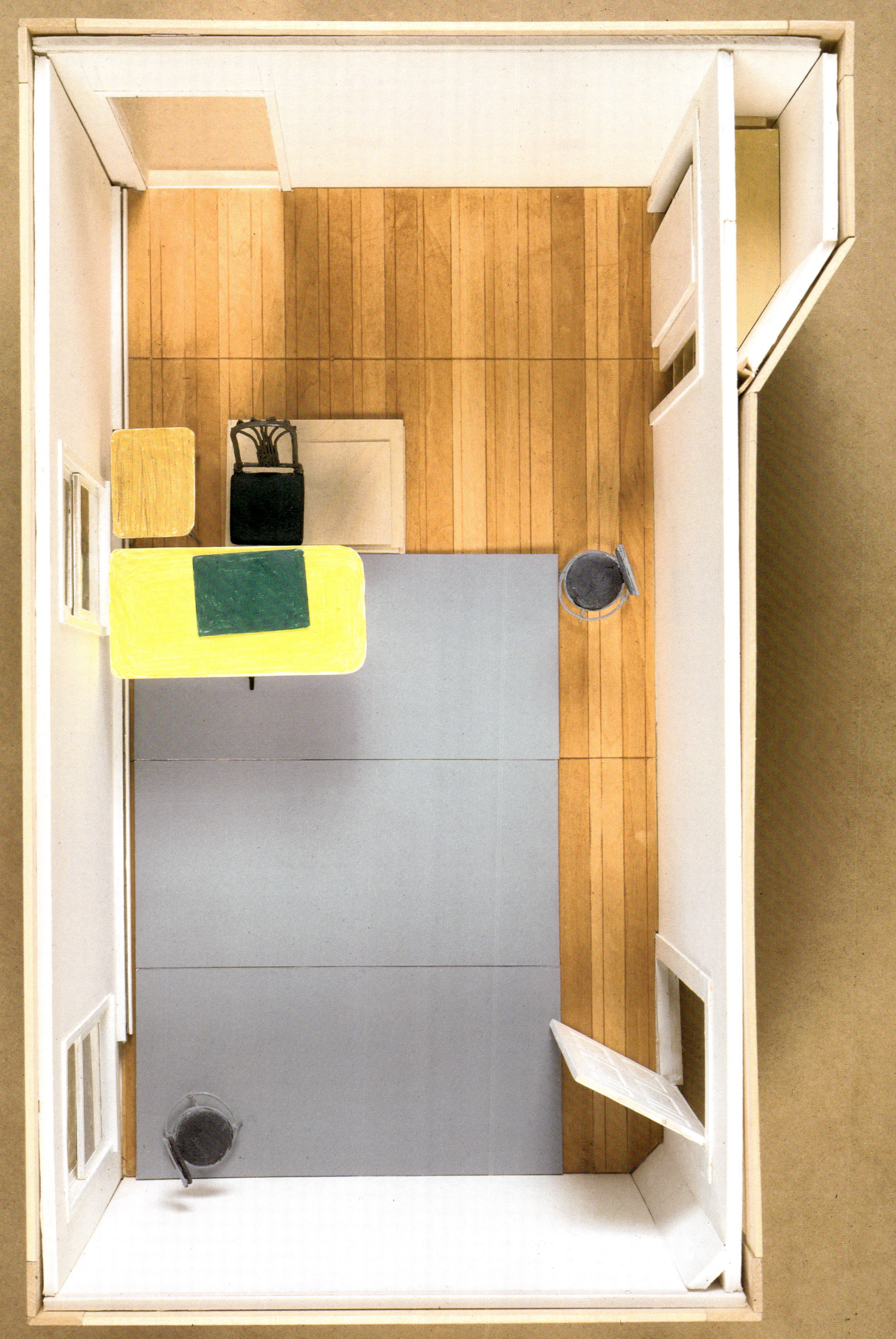

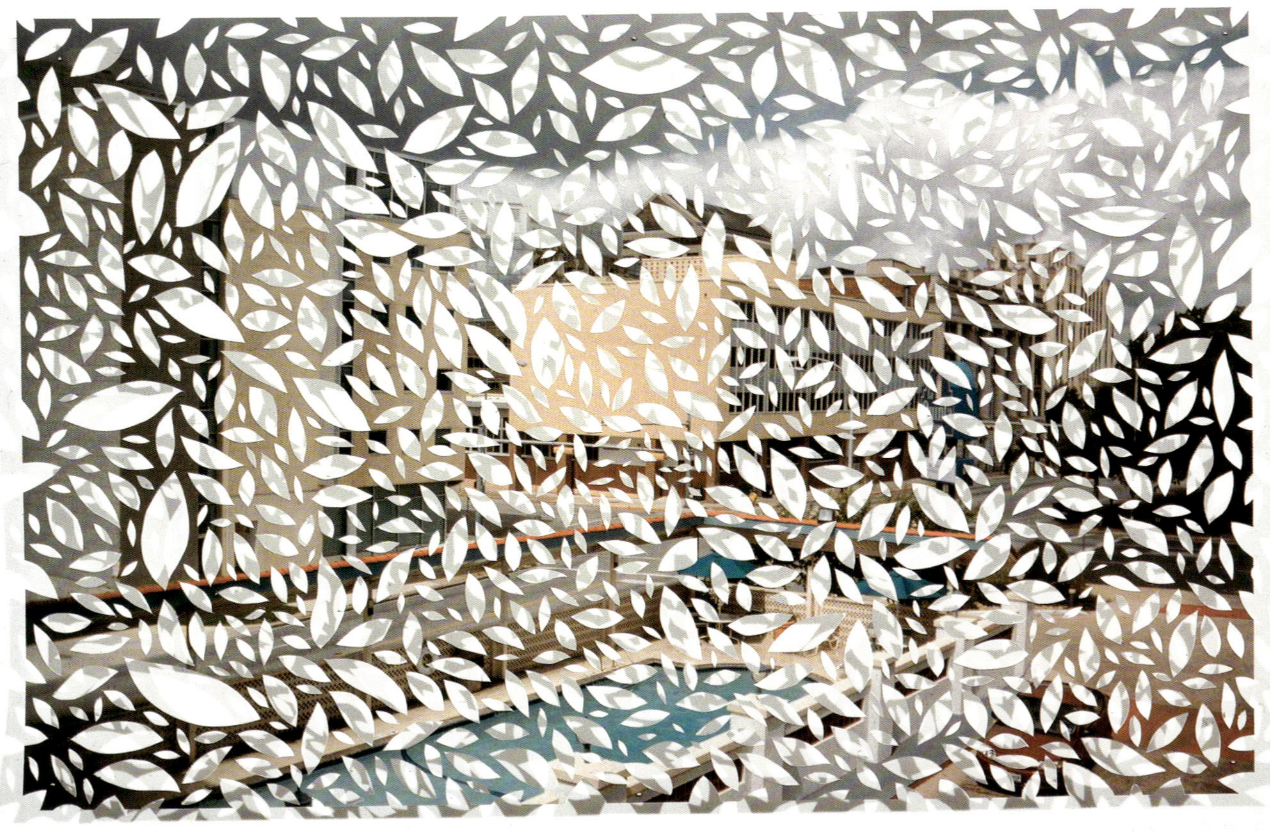

Eguchi has also produced sculptures by reversing this process. For instance, he used torn-off pieces of his own old clothes to create *Shoebox* (2004) (Pl. 4.4). In a reverse of the way in which he reduced an existent, yet anonymous, landscape to abstraction in cutout snapshots, he created a recognizable object from personal fragments of his own life. A pair of shoes eight feet in length, housed in a huge box made of cardboard, *Shoebox* is not a traditional sculpture in that the piece is not about the mass or volume of a real pair of shoes. It is more about how Eguchi sees things as an artist in real life. He first observes an object of interest with his eyes, and then traces its visual impression with the materials of his choice. The process is essentially the same as that of drawing.

Thus, Eguchi's concept of drawing is a working principle that lies at the heart of his production, whether it results in the delicate beauty of altered pictures or in the nonchalant humor of collaged sculptures. In fact, his cutout technique should be seen as a way of drawing, as a method with which Eguchi transforms his perception into a visual form. As the most basic, daily practice for an artist, drawing is a way for him to confirm the ground on which he stands. By utilizing readymade, mundane materials, Eguchi tries to link his art-making process to other daily activities in his life. To put it differently, drawing is not only a way of visual thinking, but also a way of being for the artist.

In this sense, *STUDIO* occupies a special position among Eguchi's output, since he re-creates the studio in his own living space. Through this piece he contemplates what it means to create a work of art, and how it can be—or *cannot* be—differentiated from other everyday acts that he conducts in his apartment. This tactile drawing may well be the artist's attempt to catch a transient moment of his life in New York. He knows that a "home" is perhaps only a temporary condition; as a matter of fact, his apartment building has been sold. *STUDIO* is therefore Eguchi's self-reflective work about being an artist in New York, his tentative "home" at the moment. Whether or not he will find—or even create—another one in the future, this piece surely marks a turning point in his artistic career.

When and how did you first realize that you wanted to be an artist?

SE: When I was around 12 or 13, I spent all summer making a small-scale model of a Japanese castle with balsa wood. It was something that relates to my studio practice today. But I didn't think about wanting to be an artist until I was around 20. I started to go to the library on Sundays to look up works by contemporary artists in monographs, copying different painting techniques.

Did you face many obstacles in establishing your career in New York?

SE: I feel that I am just working on it right now. Where I grew up, I don't remember having choices. It is possible to have choices or to make choices in New York. Perhaps I cannot completely get used to that idea of having choices. I am talking about in general but also about my own work. I used to work at galleries installing exhibitions. It was an interesting experience to witness the working environment of the art world. I met some nice artist-friends there whom I still hang out with.

Has the experience of living in New York changed your style or process significantly?

SE: My work really begins after I moved to New York, perhaps even recently. Living in New York makes me look at each day differently. I feel everyday life is a part of the bigger process that goes beyond my existence. In my current project I am re-creating a working environment and the process of living, in the scale of my private space.

In this age of globalism, do you consider yourself to be a Japanese artist, an American artist, an international artist, or a hybrid of all three?

SE: New York is still my present, but tentative, "home." For these reasons it doesn't make sense to give myself a singular category. Having said that, I am a Japanese artist based in New York at this moment.

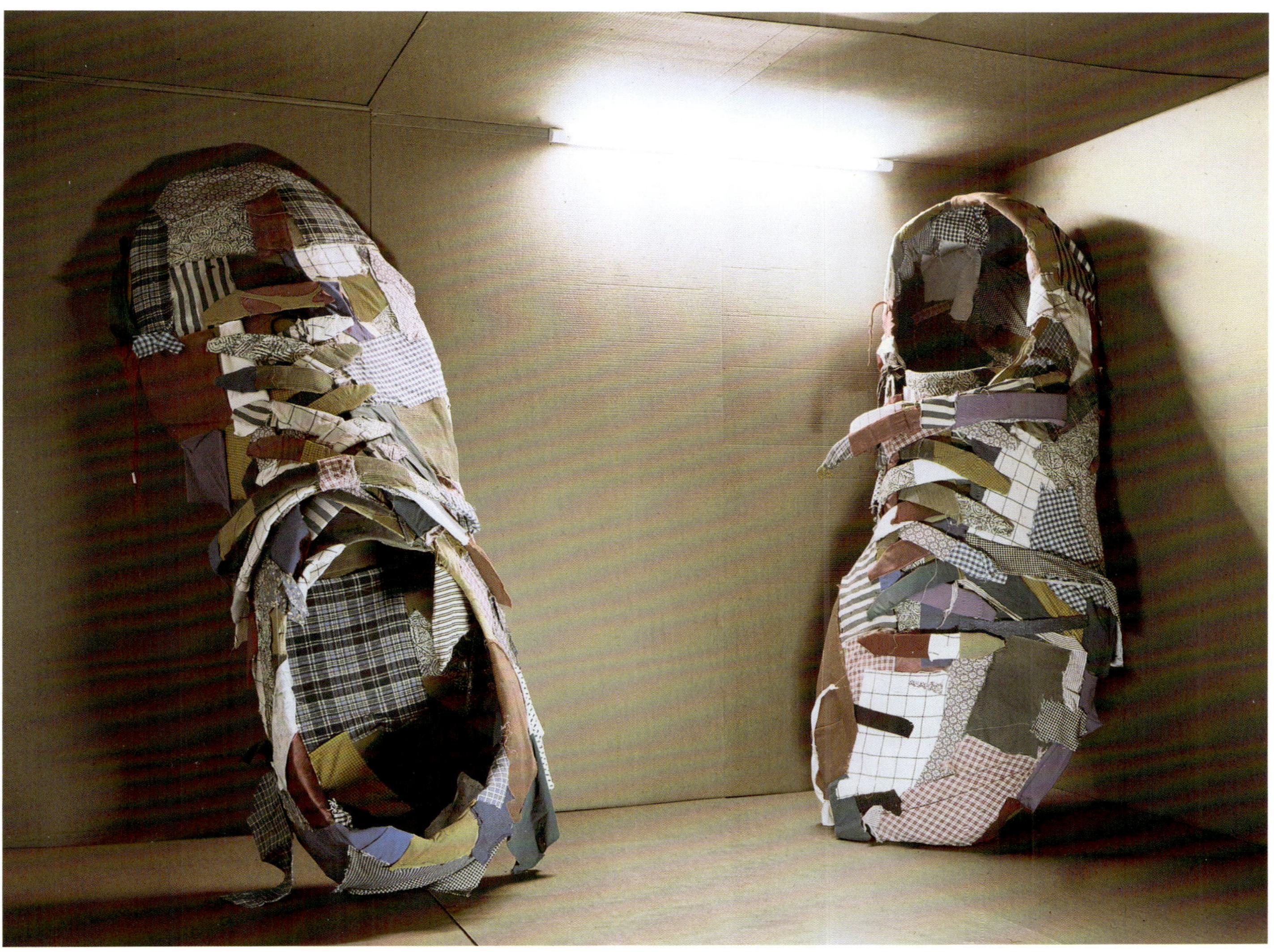

PLATE 4.4

Satoru Eguchi
Shoebox
2004
Fabric torn from artist's used clothing, cardboard room, fluorescent light
8 x 12 x 8' (243.8 x 365.8 x 243.8 cm)
Collection of the artist

AYAKOH FURUKAWA

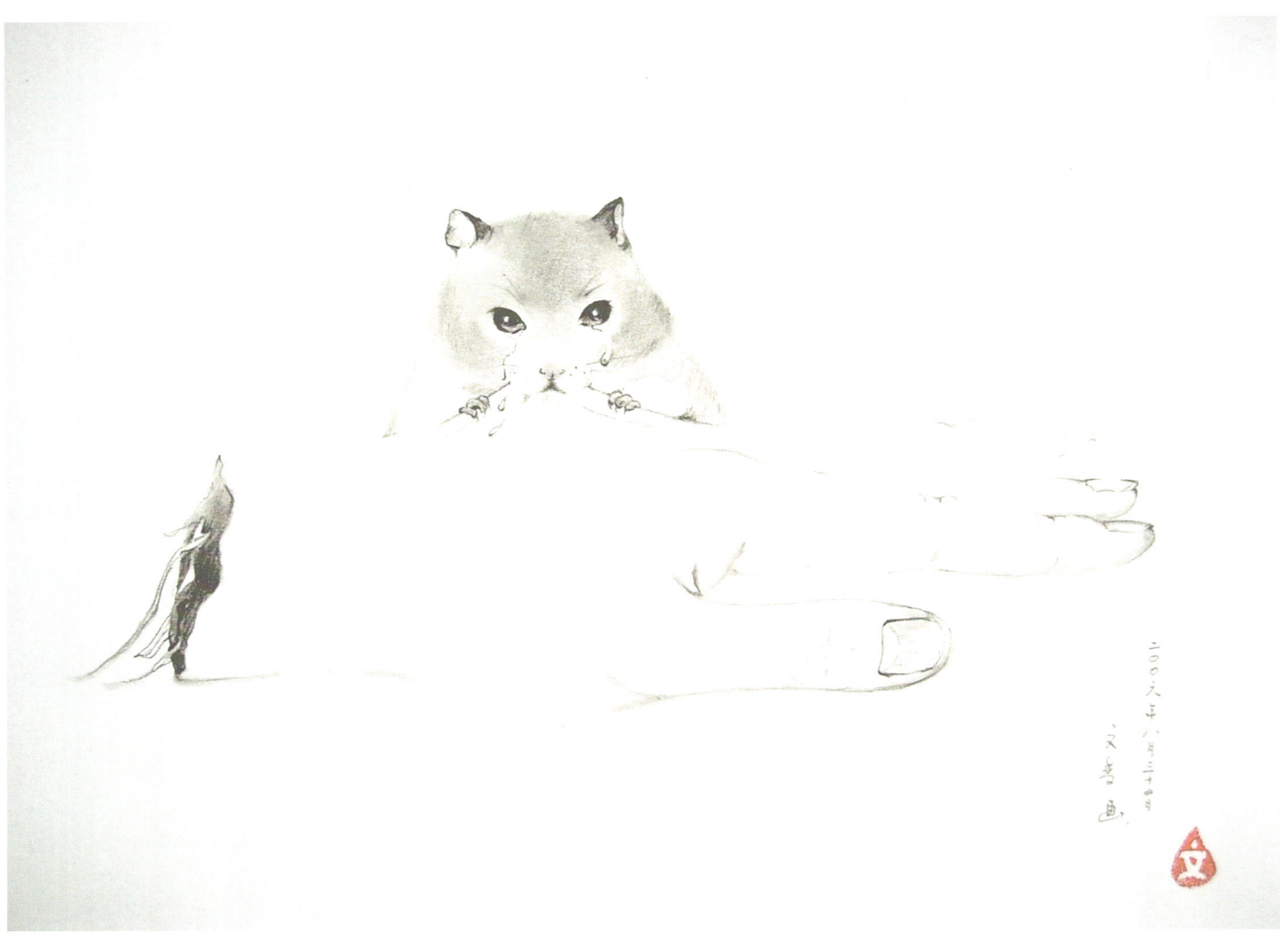

Plate 5.1

Ayakoh Furukawa
August 31, 2006 from *100 Ways
to Torture the Innocent*
2006
9 x 12" (22.9 x 30.5 cm)
Pencil on paper
Collection of the artist
PHOTO COURTESY OF THE ARTIST

Loss in Lead
ERIC C. SHINER

In *Making a Home*, artist Ayakoh Furukawa presents selections from her most ambitious work to date, *100 Ways to Torture the Innocent (Part of My/Your Mind)*. A cathartic narrative presented in 100 scenes, the work is Furukawa's ode to her beloved pet hamster Wachacha, who unexpectedly died while the artist was visiting her family in Japan. In many ways, Wachacha was more than a pet to the artist: she was the security blanket with which Furukawa took shelter; the main source of comfort for an artist quite unsure of her place in the world.

For years, Furukawa dreamt of coming to New York to be an artist. She worked in an office in Japan to save funds for the trip and, once here, would make periodic trips back to Japan to work for several months in order to sustain her study and life in her new home. After completing her BFA at Hunter College, Furukawa enrolled in the MFA program at that institution and graduated this year. She continued drawing and painting at a feverish pace to establish her art career and exhibited her work each year in the Japanese Artists Association of New York (Jaany) show. When Wachacha died, however, it was as though Furukawa hit a brick wall at full speed. Her interior world became heavy with guilt and grief; she knew something had to be done to recover.

After struggling for so long to achieve widespread recognition for her work, and at the point, reached by many artists, where she began to question the success of her output, a sign of hope fell into Furukawa's lap when she was awarded a juror's prize during a student exhibition held at New York's Ise Cultural Foundation Gallery in the summer of 2006. The work on display, *The Ghost of 108 Ill Desires*, is a massive pencil drawing from the artist's *Coded Portraits* series (Pl. 5.2). It

Plate 5.2

Ayakoh Furukawa
The Ghost of 108 Ill Desires
2006
Pencil on paper
36 x 52" (91.4 x 132.1 cm)
Collection of the artist
PHOTO COURTESY OF THE ARTIST

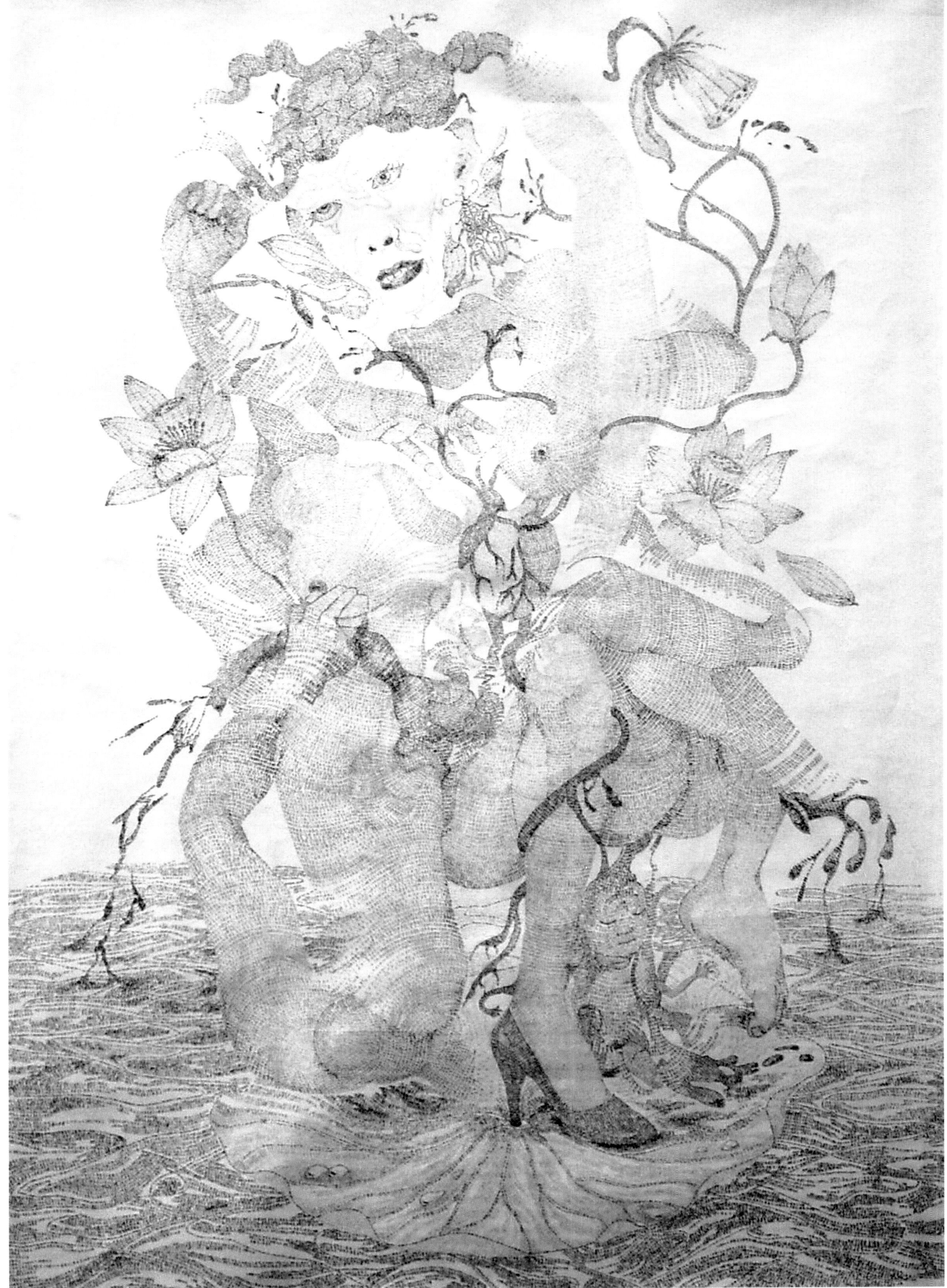

depicts a woman growing out of a lotus blossom, her body shredded apart in an organic explosion of violence and angst. Upon close inspection, the viewer realizes that the figure is not made up of simple lines in pencil. Instead, it is composed of numbers and letters spelling out the words 108 Ill Desires hundreds of times over. The work is about the construction of femininity, the absurdity of sexism, and the beauty industry's attempts to make women more beautiful. It takes the idealized imagery of "woman" and boils it down to its roots. Here, beauty is farmed and the feminine grown. Furukawa deconstructs the notions of the ideal woman, and in so doing, repossesses the vocabulary of sexism, emasculating it in a powerful burst of language-based line and unbridled obsession.

With this timely nod to her artwork, Furukawa realized that in order to go on, she needed to cleanse her spirit and overcome the death of her dear pet, Wachacha. Instead of holding Wachacha on high through formal portraiture or abstract ode, Furukawa decided to make 100 variations of her fluffy darling being tortured and in some cases conducting torture herself. For Furukawa, the only way to take the pain away was to inflict it once again.

And like renowned *ukiyo-e* master Kuniyoshi and his portfolio of prints depicting ghoulish apparitions, Furukawa set about drawing a series, scene after scene of Wachacha engaged in macabre acts that repel and attract the viewer in equal measure. In one image, Wachacha becomes victim, trapped in a small log, blood dripping from her nose (Pl. 5.3). In another, she takes on the role of torturer as she nibbles on the stub of a human finger (Pl. 5.4). Other images depict large hamster faces with cartoonish eyes, tears falling down in a cascade of sadness and loss, or a hamster chewing on a dismembered human hand (Pl. 5.1). Using a pencil to draw, Furukawa borrows the centuries-old aesthetic technique of ink painting to realize these works, yet conflates the serenity of the genre with her frightening scenes depicting anguish in its rawest form. For her, the only way to feel at home in New York was to examine the darkest recesses of her soul, to release Wachacha on a violent journey that both heroicizes and empowers her in one fell swoop. To that end, Furukawa has finally come to terms with her unexpected loss, and in so doing has created a powerful body of work that will celebrate the closeness she savored with Wachacha for eternity.

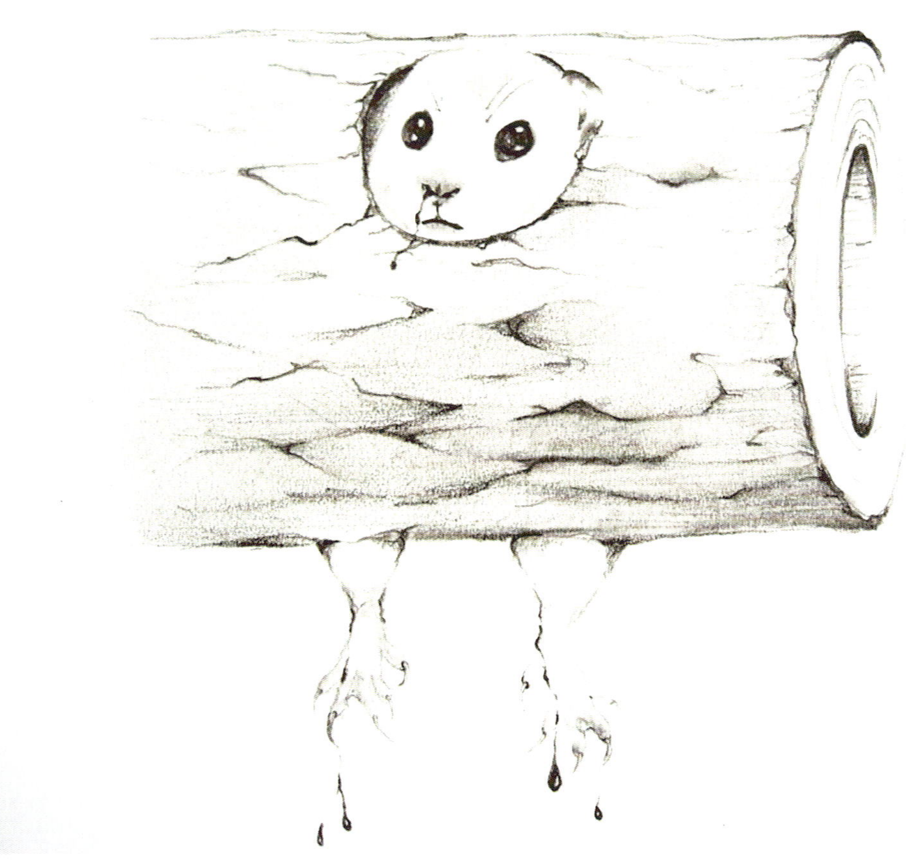

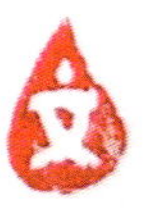

PLATE 5.3

Ayakoh Furukawa
April, 2006 from *100 Ways to Torture the Innocent*
2006
Pencil on paper
9 x 12" (22.9 x 30.5 cm)
Collection of the artist

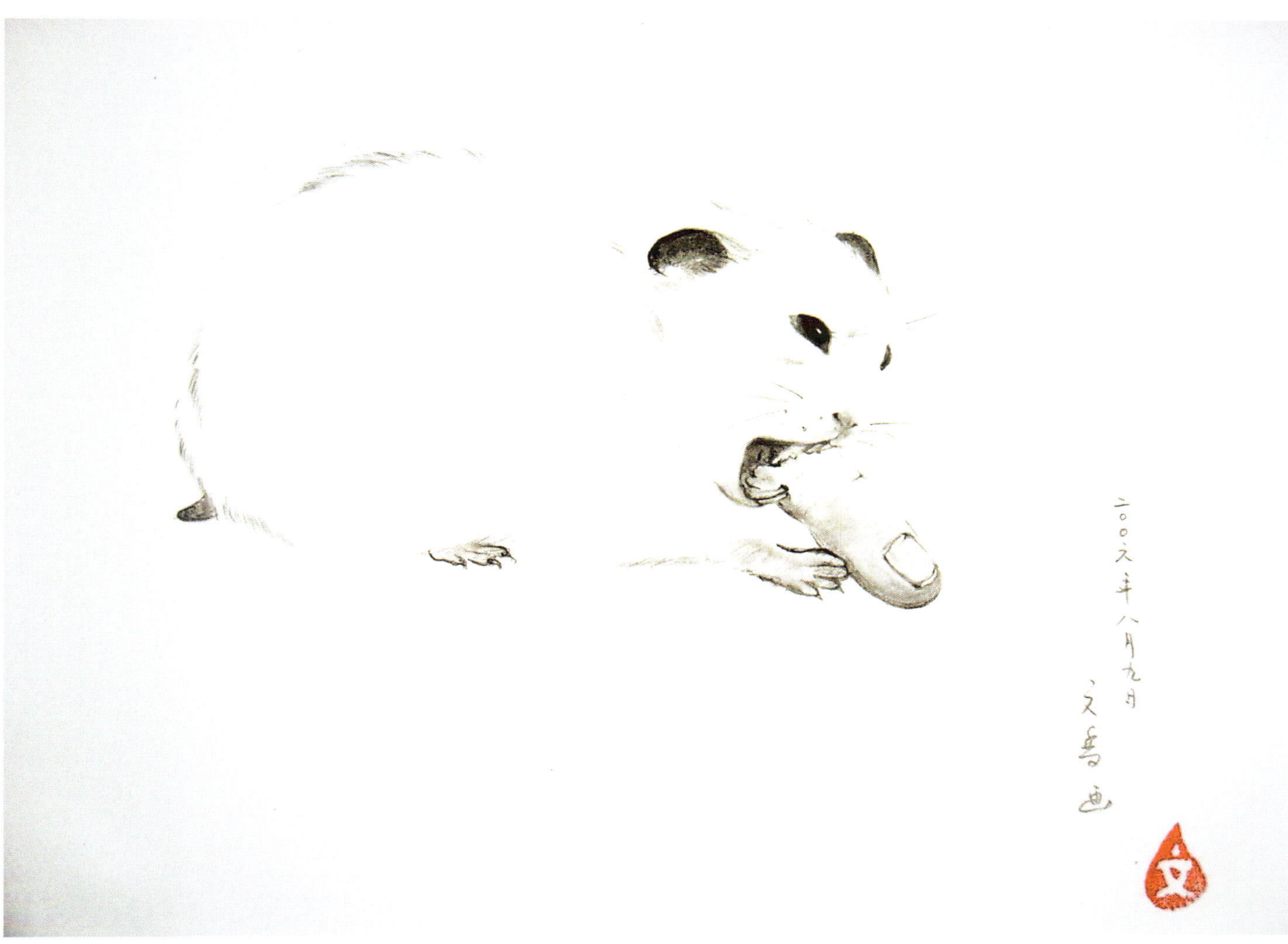

When and how did you first realize that you wanted to be an artist?
AF: I just wanted to be a good painter for a long time. Only recently I started wanting to be an artist, a good one.

Why did you choose New York as your ultimate destination?
AF: I am not sure if New York is my ultimate destination or not.

What was your first impression of New York City?
AF: I felt so much energy in the air.

Did you have any interactions with other artists or supporters that were especially beneficial to you and your work?
AF: I've had occasions to talk to artists who have engaged in art for a long time, like half a century. Their words about living life as an artist are always profound and real to me.

Has the experience of living in New York changed your style or process significantly?
AF: After I experienced many different styles/expressions in New York, I have realized there is always something special in any style. That something special is an essential part of my expression. Japanese aesthetics is a strong influence in my works.

Do you ever regret leaving Japan?
AF: No regret. But I sometimes miss my family, especially my mother in Japan.

In this age of globalism, do you consider yourself to be a Japanese artist, an American artist, an international artist, or a hybrid of all three?
AF: I usually do not think about my ethnic background or what category I belong to. I am in my world. However, some people want me to be a little Asian/Japanese artist.

PLATE 5.4

Ayakoh Furukawa
August 9, 2006 from *100 Ways to Torture the Innocent*
2006
Pencil on paper
9 x 12" (22.9 x 30.5 cm)
Collection of the artist

06 **TŌRU HAYASHI**

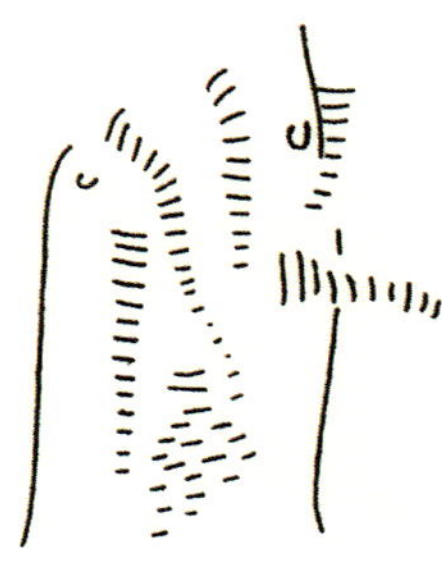

Conceptual Landscapes of Tōru Hayashi
REIKO TOMII

Tōru Hayashi is a conceptualist who creates endearing images. Up close, for instance, each drawing of his signature work *Equivocal Landscape* reveals no more than a handful of lines registered in a white void (Pls. 6.1, 6.4). Precious yet intently drawn, his "trees" evoke a warm, tender feeling, intriguing us to examine what is going on.

Born in Kōbe, Japan in 1963, Hayashi came to art at the age of 20, when he happened upon drawings by the renowned fashion illustrator Nagasawa Setsu in magazines. This encounter led him to enroll in a night program at Nagasawa's school in Tokyo in 1987 and, subsequently, end his employment at a notable research institute as a systems analyst. In 1990, having learned the basics of picture-making, Hayashi left Japan for New York. The usual struggle of a would-be artist from a foreign country ensued. In his search for a voice truly unique, he long experimented with diverse media, with mixed results.

In retrospect, his 1997 performance, *T*A*K*A* Out of Business*, indicated two aspects that saliently characterize his art today: conceptualism and ingenuity to uncover intimate details of our mundane life (Pl. 6.3). That summer, he gained the use of a Japanese restaurant in Greenwich Village where he then worked, while it was closed for a holiday. Every day for a week he sat in the dining room and painstakingly whited out the characters T, A, K, A, as they appeared in this order (which constituted the eatery's name) in the pages of the Business section of that day's *New York Times*. The result was a pointillist abstraction that literally documents the days when the restaurant, as well as the artist, was "out of business."

A breakthrough came with *Equivocal Landscape*, a drawing project he began in January 1998. At the time, as he recalls, he "just felt like drawing a tree." He set up the task of drawing trees every day

PLATE 6.1

Tōru Hayashi
Equivocal Landscape/Inwood II
2005
Etching, edition of 40
Image: 5 x 7 ⅜" (12.7 x 18.7 cm)
Courtesy of the artist

in a sketchbook of some 140 sheets. Now at the 27th volume (as of April 2007), he has filled his sketchbooks, leaf after leaf, with animated scenes portraying the daily doings of one or two or sometimes more trees: thinking, loitering, embracing, chatting, reaching out, playing. What has sustained him in this "endless" undertaking was a discovery, perhaps at the second sketchbook, that he was indeed creating a sort of self-portrait, because the Chinese ideograph of his name Hayashi (meaning "forest") comprises two trees side by side.

In 2000, Hayashi devised a new scheme, founding a conceptual company called *Travel Agency Garden*. In the company's précis, the artist-cum-C.E.O. declared the offer of "another form of travel." The idea was saliently borne out in its initial production, *View to View: A Manhattan Tour*. A group of a dozen or so canvases (re)present famous sites of New York City, from the Statue of Liberty to Grand Central Station to Times Square, for the exclusive enjoyment of its inhabitants. Highly abstract, the sites are undecipherable without the accompanying title plates, at once confounding and amusing New Yorkers who know these places so intimately.

Since then, he added a number of sites to the *Travel Agency Garden* series, including Brooklyn, Kyoto, Disneyland, and World Wide Museum (a tour of famous museums in the world, including the New York Guggenheim and the Louvre) (Pl. 6.2). They reveal his fluid pictorial interpretations of these cities, presenting his "memory image" of these metropolises. In 2003, the series evolved into *Metropolis Mandala Series*, each of which presents a visual compendium of his impressions of a given city. He explores the city (where he stays for an extended period of time) through daily observation to seek out subtle changes, and he organizes them into a format that he calls *mandala*, borrowing from Buddhist cosmology. He explains: "The term *mandala* in Sanskrit can be translated as 'integration of truth.' I reinterpreted it to demonstrate the 'integration of time,' which I express through countless dots and markings.... The resulting image looked as though it were a three-dimensional space on paper—an idea rooted in the original *mandala* paintings." He also compares his constellation of dots and other markings on paper to the infinite stars in the sky: both evoke a "feeling of endless space." After working on *Metropolis Mandala* of New York, Paris, Tokyo, and Prince Edward Island, he has just completed *Delhi Mandala* in India, the land where mandala cosmology originated (Pl. 6.5).

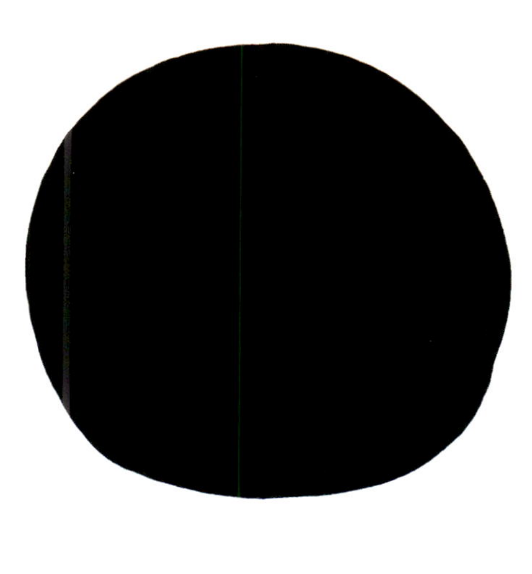

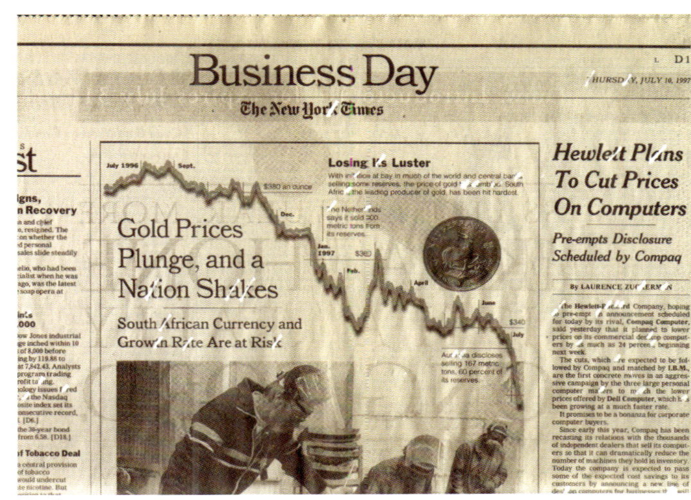

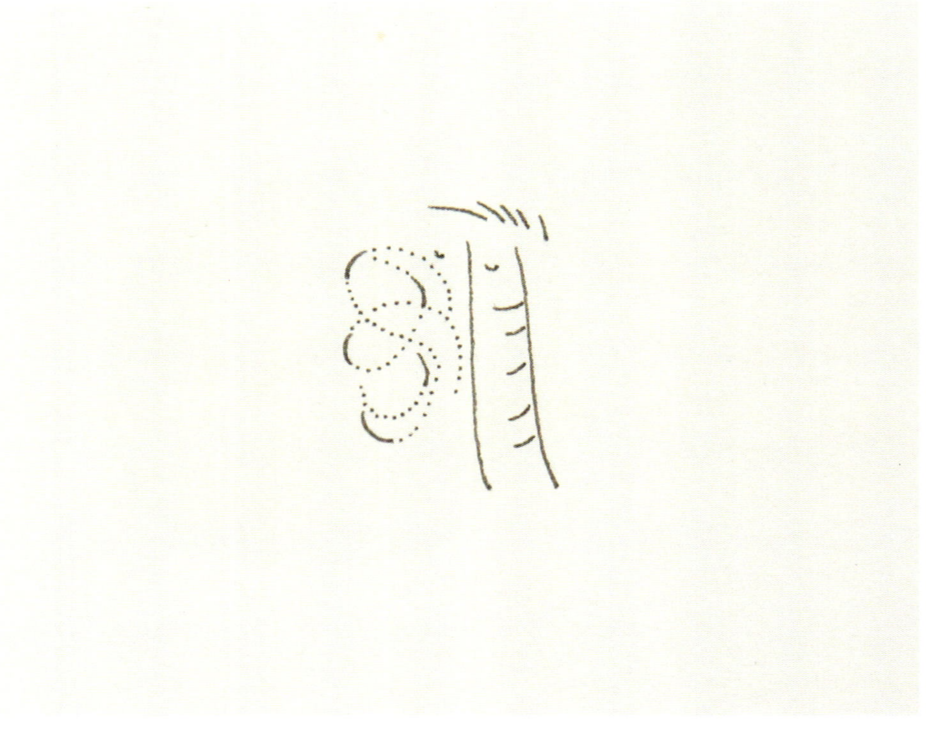

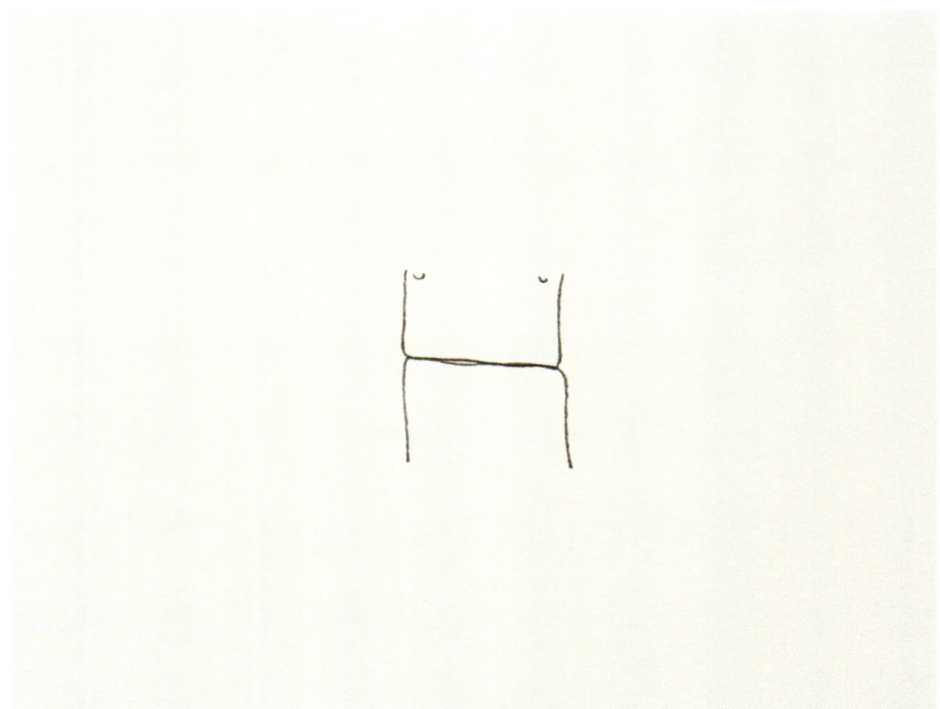

When and how did you first realize that you wanted to be an artist?

TH: I read the book *Boy Art* [*Shōnen āto* by Nakamura Nobuo, 1986] in 1989 while studying at Setsu Mode Seminar in Tokyo, and I realized that art, especially contemporary art, could make "a new language." But I was not sure of what being an artist should be at that time. The school, Setsu Mode Seminar, gave me a chance to change my life to do something else rather than being a businessman.

Why did you choose New York as your ultimate destination?

TH: New York called me to come over somehow. I came to New York directly from Tokyo in 1990. It took 26 hours due to engine trouble.

What was your first impression of New York City?

TH: I felt the city was sexy.

Did you face many obstacles in establishing your career in New York?

TH: I haven't established my art career yet. It has been hard to live and to work in New York over keeping a job to make ends meet. The Artist in the Marketplace program at the Bronx Museum opened the door to the New York art world. It was in 1994.

In this age of globalism, do you consider yourself to be a Japanese artist, an American artist, an international artist, or a hybrid of all three?

TH: Being in New York easily allows me to sense that many different people exist on the globe. New York often makes me feel that the world is not that big, but getting smaller and smaller year after year. I consider myself as Tōru Hayashi.

PLATE 6.4

Tōru Hayashi
Equivocal Landscape Vol. 25
top: sheet 56; bottom: sheet 24
October 21, 2006–January 9, 2007
Sketchbook; ink on paper
5 ½ x 8 x ¾" (14 x 20.3 x 1.9 cm)
Collection of the artist

PLATE 6.5

Tōru Hayashi
Delhi Mandala III (Red)
2007
Watercolor, color pencil, and ink on paper board
11 ⅝ x 8 ¼" (29.7 x 21 cm)
Private collection

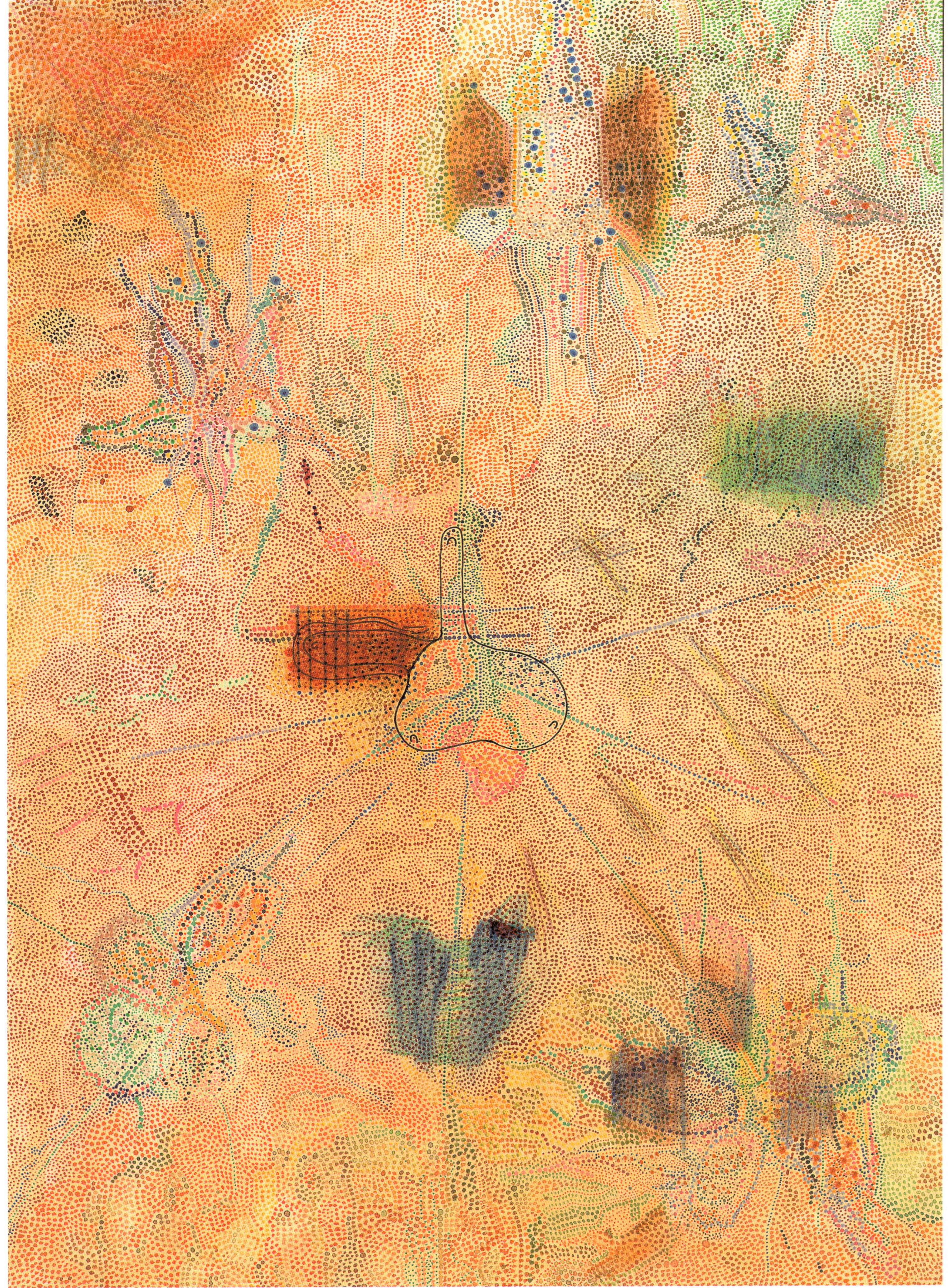

07 NORITOSHI HIRAKAWA

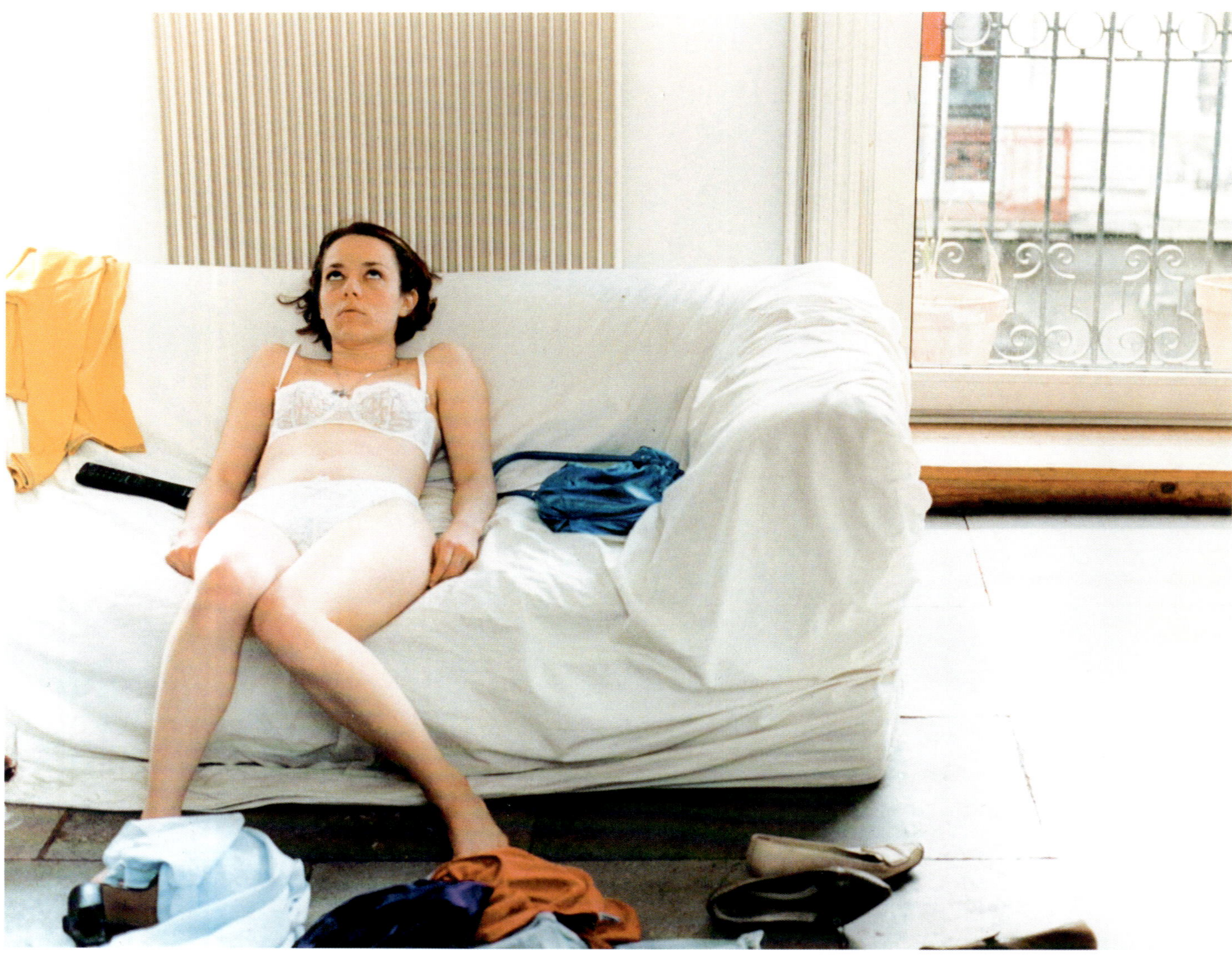

The Exploits of an Art Trickster Par Excellence
ERIC C. SHINER

The politics of sex permeate all of Noritoshi Hirakawa's videos, photographs, and performances. He has been called a pervert, a voyeur, a sexually frustrated artist. Yet, once these labels are stripped away, it becomes evident that Hirakawa is none of these things. In fact, he is a barometer of our times, an artist who has his finger on the pulse of the sexual currents of our era, a topic that he exposes without apology. He is a trickster who utilizes the graphic and the raw to stir emotions—indeed, to encourage dialogue on one of the most taboo subjects in the world. His work is not easy to stomach, yet it hits a nerve in its probing study of the intersection of sex, society, and art. It is a necessary examination of the inner workings of the psychosexual that uncovers social injustices not only in the realm of the flesh, but also race, economics, and identity. Hirakawa might well be the pink elephant in the room, yet his work is important in that it unearths the Freudian kinks that define our contemporary society.

Using shock tactics to engage the viewer is Hirakawa's speciality. He has made luscious pink C-prints of a magnified anus, hired a model to defecate in a booth at an international art fair, and even produced a film about a father's incestual relationship with his daughter. Although brutally direct in subject matter, Hirakawa's finished products are always eloquent portrayals of the lascivious; as works of art, they are polished, even refined. In different ways,

PLATE 7.1

Noritoshi Hirakawa
Les temps de rien à Montpellier—Un Jour II
2001
C-print
16 x 20" (40.6 x 50.8 cm)
Collection of the artist

PLATE 7.2

Noritoshi Hirakawa
Virtue in Vice — Rachel / 24 /
St. Andrew's Roman Catholic Church,
September 4, 1997
1997
Duraflex print
60 x 40" (152.4 x 101.6 cm)
Collection of the artist

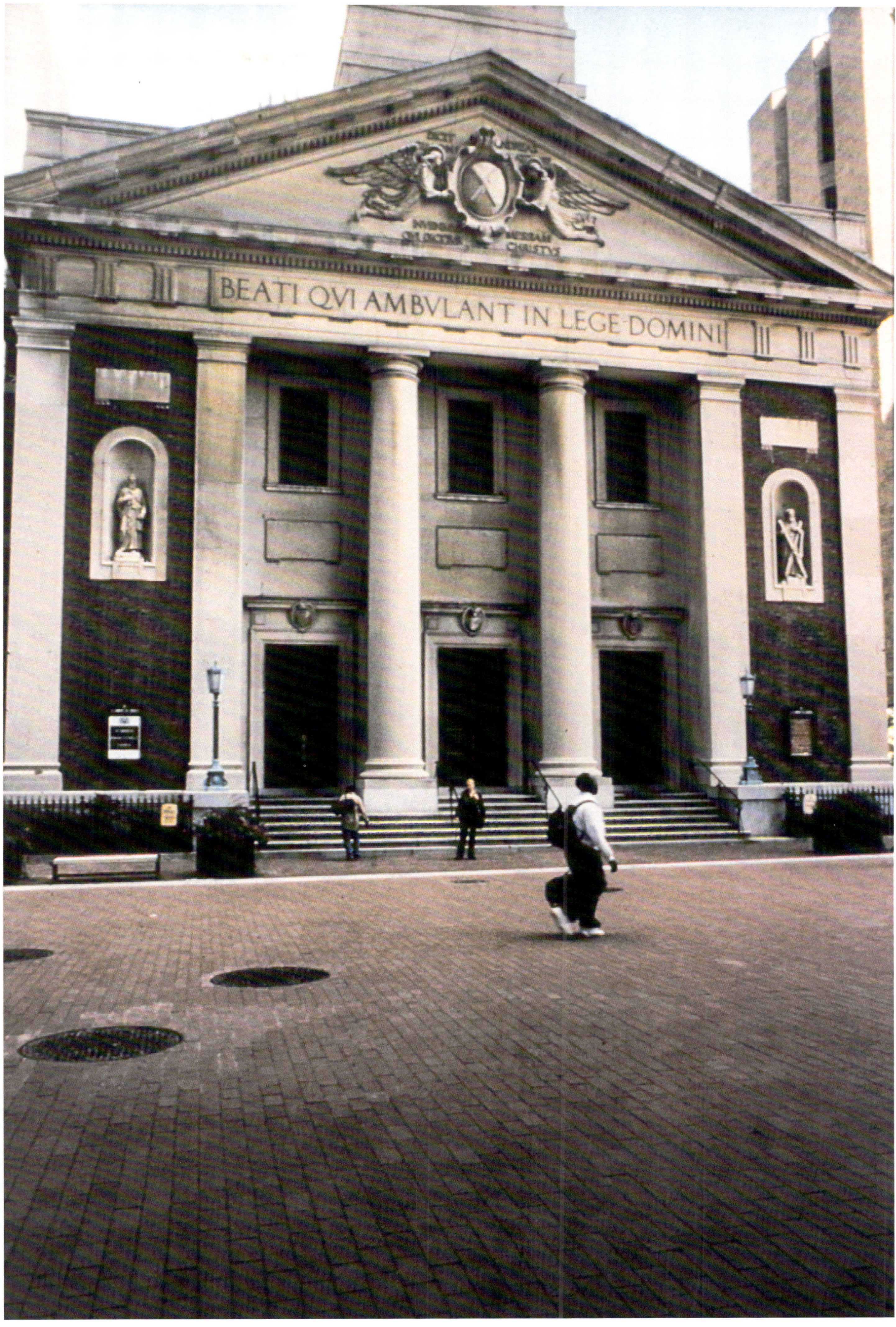
BEATI QVI AMBVLANT IN LEGE DOMINI

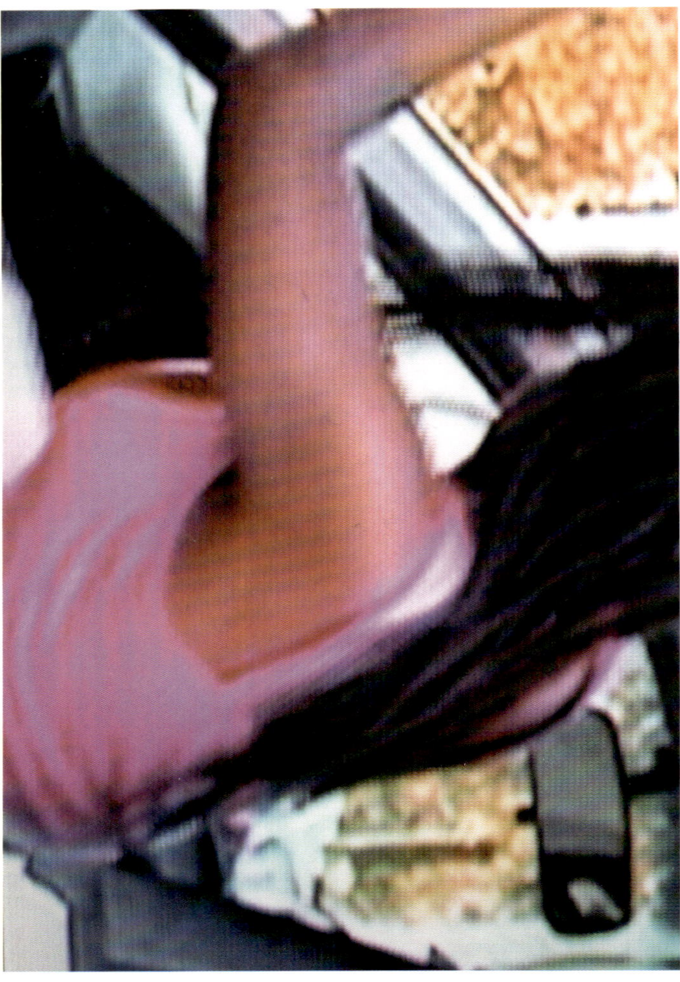

the artist sugar coats, almost camouflages, the true nature of his work. For example, his *Virtue in Vice* series of photographs at first glance appears to be completely mundane (Pl. 7.2). A grouping of seven large-scale photographs executed in 1997, the work depicts seven young women, each standing in front of a different church located in New York City. Without knowing the artist's trick, these images would be nothing more than tourist snapshots. It is only after one reads the wall label that the truth comes out. Every model was being sexually gratified by a battery-powered vibrator when the shutter was tripped. Hirakawa takes an image of pious dedication and flips it on its head to reveal the human propensity for vice over virtue.

In his film *Les temps de rien à Montpellier* of 2001, Hirakawa worked with professional dancers to orchestrate a finely tuned ballet based on courtship rituals (Pl. 7.1). Enacted not on a stage, but in a church, on the TGV high-speed train, and in a museum gallery, the dancers flirt with and cajole one another in places not normally designated "sexual zones." Likewise, in the 1999 film *La Va et Vient* that appears in *Making a Home*, Hirakawa traveled to the Caribbean island of Martinique to film Afro-Caribbean contemporary dancers—two women and one man—engaged in a sexually charged dance at a gasoline stand (Pl. 7.3). Two brief shots at the beginning and end of the film depict white party goers in formal attire. In truth, it is a shot of an annual reunion of the descendants of the European settlers of the island—in other words, a whites-only tradition that reifies the hidden racism that plagues Martinique to this day. The "go and come back" of the title references not only the tide of the sea so integral to the island, but also the sexual friction of the dance itself. By celebrating the strong Afro-Caribbean tradition of dance and the music of birds native to the island in the main portion of the film, Hirakawa makes a judgment call, valuing the African and local culture of the island over that of the persnickety Europeans who act as straight-edged bookends at either end of the film. In many ways, it is the artist's direct reference to the state of race relations in the United States.

Through exposing that which is often left unspoken, Hirakawa has opened a can of worms time and again over the course of his career. Acting as a sort of virus to the immune system of the art world, he is engaged in a nonstop attack on the status quo. With any viral attack, if the organism is able to weather the initial plague, its immunity to the virus grows over time. Thanks to Hirakawa's trickster strategies, however, he remains an ever-mutating virus that successfully stays one step ahead of its host's immune system, a constant threat to be reckoned with, like it or not.

PLATE 7.3

Noritoshi Hirakawa
Still from *Le Va et Vient*
1999
Video
10 minutes
Collection of the artist

NH: I did not decide it. I haven't even decided it now. Sometimes you do not make any conscious decision, you are just out of place automatically.

NH: I was not motivated to move to New York and live here such a long time. Originally, my New York lawyer applied for my Green Card without informing me (this could be my fate). So, I think New York has never been my ultimate destination. I have never thought of it. Here is only a relay station but at the same time, sometimes I feel I was sent on a mission to New York as…because the existence of New York is built upon a wrong assumption.

NH: Smell of pee.

NH: An artist simply functions like a gold mining digger for the art world in New York. And I am still living in a cave and digging gold (or, something like gold) every day.

NH: Artist hates artist in New York, the same as lovers hate each other. Especially in New York, often money only initiates the motivation for supporters (investors) to step into art interactions with artists.

NH: I am against the way New Yorkers recognize art. People here love an artist who repeats, creating the same thing over, over, over again until people don't need to think anymore about what the name of the artist was when they see the work. Japanese aesthetics is a familiar exoticism, one such factor to create easy recognition. So, New Yorkers could not manage to change my style of creation yet.

NH: Globalism is completely an illusion. There is only human interaction between people.

08 YOSHIAKI KAIHATSU

Art Invented from Everyday Life
MIDORI YOSHIMOTO

In Japanese the word *kaihatsu* means development or invention. Yoshiaki Kaihatsu has invented art out of everyday life through novel concepts, forms, and means. Since the early 1990s he has been keeping a diary of shopping receipts and photographic self-portraits in order to record his daily consumption patterns and aging process. He then displays these documents in his exhibitions. In 1995–96, Kaihatsu also exploited a popular television show to present his *365 Project*, for which he sent a life-sized wooden box in his own form to 365 people across Japan. He visited a different person every day for a year, revealing how each participant modified the box with his/her ideas and incorporated it into his/her life. Foreshadowing American reality TV shows, Kaihatsu's TV-based communication art circumvented the established commercial gallery system to offer alternative modes of artistic presentation. In 2000, Kaihatsu also started *The Day of 39@rt*, or "Thank You Art," marking March 9 as an annual holiday to appreciate contemporary art. Participating museums and galleries were asked to provide visitors with "small gifts," be they discount admissions, small works of art, or refreshments. (3/9, *"san kyū"* in Japanese, rhymes with "thank you.")

To make art out of himself, or as a proof of his devotion to his art-filled life, Kaihatsu started wearing all gray clothing in 1992. The gray color represents the ambiguity and neutrality between black and white and the typical business suits worn by the Japanese office workers dubbed salarymen. The artist also identifies gray as the color of social conformity. Graduating with an MFA from Tama Art University in 1993, Kaihatsu witnessed the burst of the bubble economy and downfall of Japanese work ethics. One of his early performances, *Baby Salaryman* (1992), satirized the infantalization of Japanese businessmen with the artist standing in a busy intersection in Tokyo, wearing a baby costume and carrying an attaché case filled with baby toys.

Kaihatsu's art has often been fashioned from worthless non-art materials such as dust and plastic foam packaging. His floor installations using dust started in 1994, when he collected several days' worth of accumulated dust from a three-story junior high school building in Tokyo and laid it out neatly on three quarters of the floor in a classroom, preserving the "holy" platform for a teacher. As its title *Existence and Nonexistence* suggests, the gray dust functioned as a physical metaphor for the frail existence between two opposites. In 1997, the dust work developed into *The Stardust Memory* series in which the artist would form a gray star out of the dust gathered from a selected location, such as his studio, a private residence, or a nuclear power plant in Japan. In 2002, while Kaihatsu was in New York, he collected dust remaining in the area around Ground Zero to create a circular pond of dust in the Ise Cultural Foundation Gallery in SoHo (Pl. 8.1). While the pond was based on the Japanese gardening concept of *karesansui* ("dry landscape") often found in a Zen temple, this pond included two small pointed projections in the center, representing two teardrops—and, unwittingly—the destroyed twin towers.

Kaihatsu is perhaps best known for his polystyrene foam sculptures and environments which he started in 1990. An imperishable industrial material (called *happō suchirōru* in Japanese), the disposable plastic is for Kaihatsu a metaphor for a hollow society. Beginning with an installation in Hong Kong in 2000, he has built numerous architectural structures out of polystyrene packaging found on the streets near his exhibition venues. Instead of gluing the foam pieces together, he uses toothpicks or skewers to connect them, combining various shapes and molds which were used to package electric appliances and other products. He often emphasizes the three-dimensional quality of the packing pieces by lighting his works from the inside with fluorescent lights. Recycling the city's waste and presenting it in the context of art, Kaihatsu infuses a new aesthetic life into the discarded objects of a city's consumer society.

For this exhibition, Kaihatsu presents *Happō-En Teahouse*, a structure made of foam packaging, which was originally conceived in Japan in 2001 (Pls. 8.2–3). Since then, he has re-created the work in international venues including Bregenz, Austria and Berlin and Wiesbaden, Germany. In each location, the artist offered his version of the tea ceremony to volunteer participants, using a polystyrene bowl and plastic utensils. Although the materials used are contemporary, the Zen spirit of avoiding unnecessary waste is at the heart of this recycled art. Kaihatsu, in the end, serves up that which is usually thrown away.

Plate 8.1

Yoshiaki Kaihatsu
Tear's Pond (installation view with Clouded Sky, 1997 on the wall at Ise Cultural Foundation Gallery, New York)
2002
Dust from Ground Zero
Diameter: approx 10' (3 m)
Collection of the artist

When and how did you first realize that you wanted to be an artist?
YK: I thought that I became an artist at 13 years old. I would have been a cook if it was not possible to become an artist. I liked thing-making.

Why did you choose New York as your ultimate destination?
YK: Because of the desire that the United States is a heartland of art.

Did you have any interactions with other artists or supporters that were especially beneficial to you and your work?
YK: I met Midori Yamamura and an exhibition was planned for me.

Has the experience of living in New York changed your style or process significantly?
YK: I think my work changed greatly after I came to the U.S. I began to create works that were more consciously Japanese.

In this age of globalism, do you consider yourself to be a Japanese artist, an American artist, an international artist, or a hybrid of all three?
YK: I will think about the place and the society that stays. However, I might be a Japanese artist through all eternity.

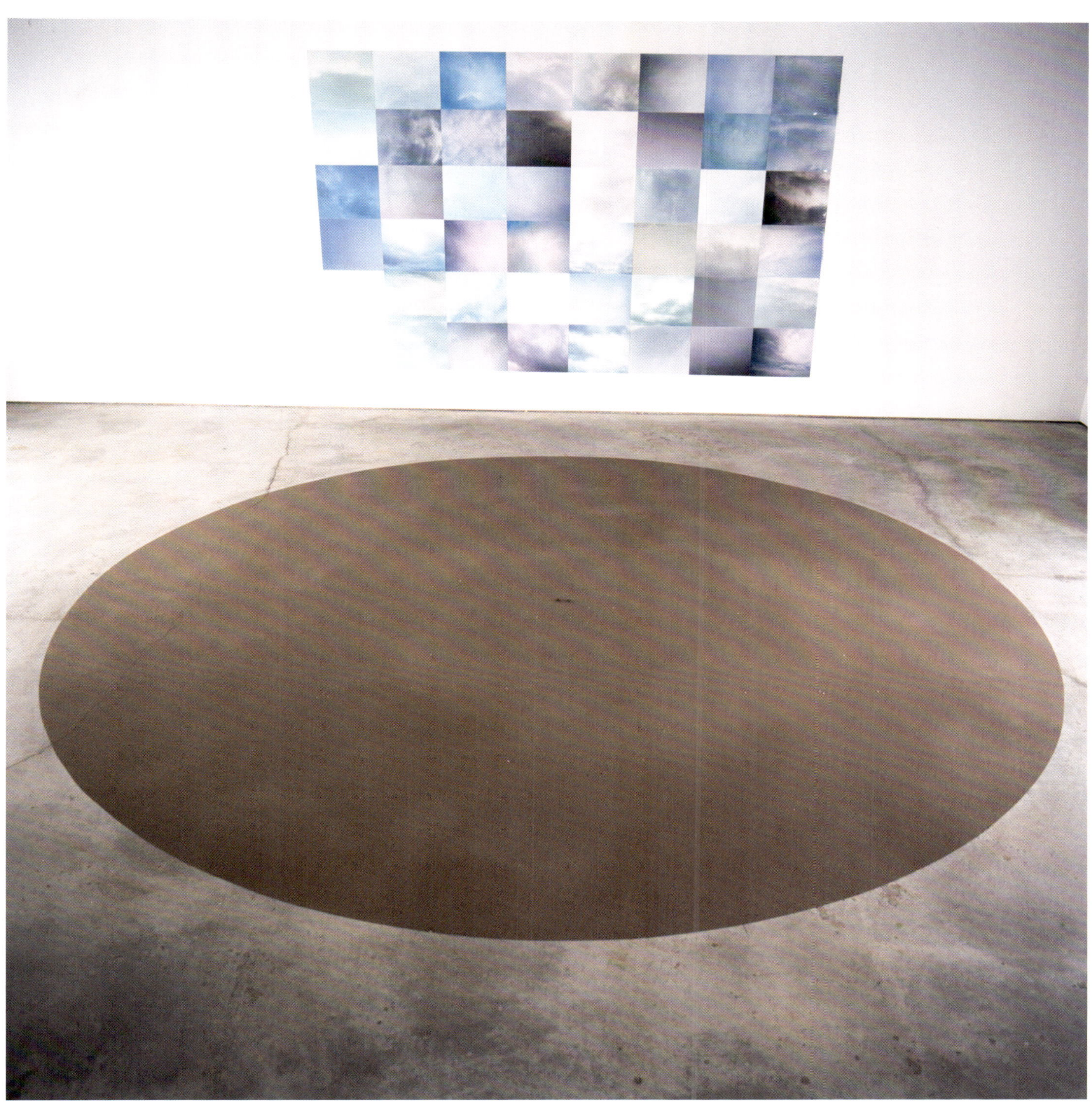

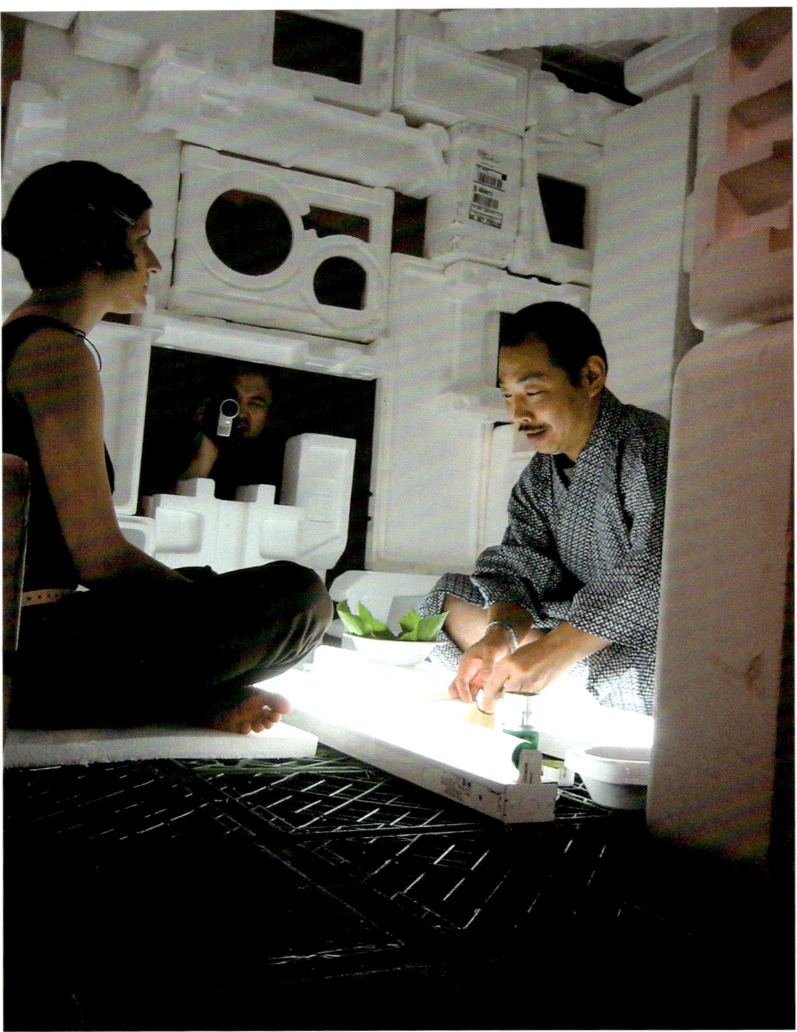

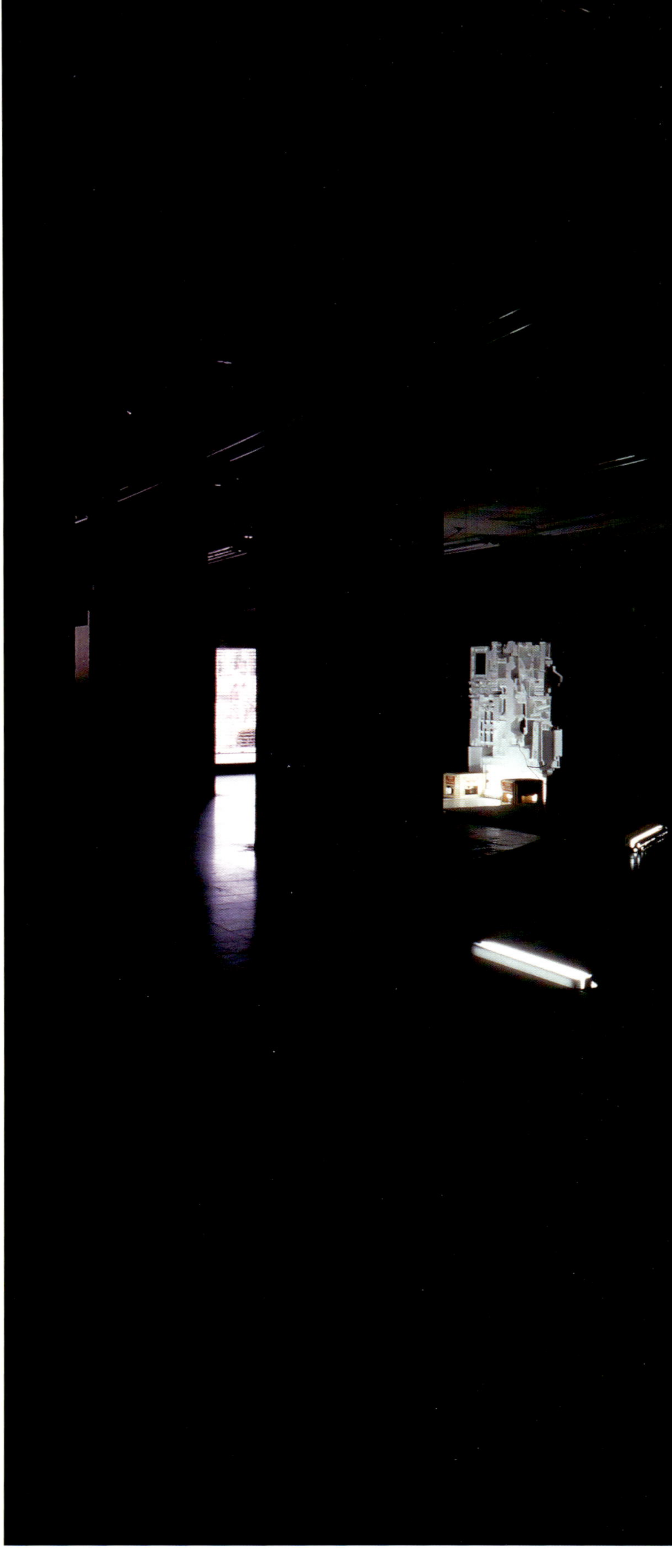

PLATE 8.2

Yoshiaki Kaihatsu
Scene of tea ceremony performance in *Happō-En Teahouse* at Ise Cultural Foundation Gallery, New York
2002
Courtesy of the artist
PHOTO: YOSHIAKI KAIHATSU

PLATE 8.3

Yoshiaki Kaihatsu
Happō-Tei Teahouse (installation view at Art Tower Mito)
2004
Polystyrene foam, fluorescent lights, plywood board, plastic cases
75.5 x 8.9 x 7.9' (23 x 2.7 x 2.4 m)
Collection of the artist
PHOTO: TANIOKA YASUNORI

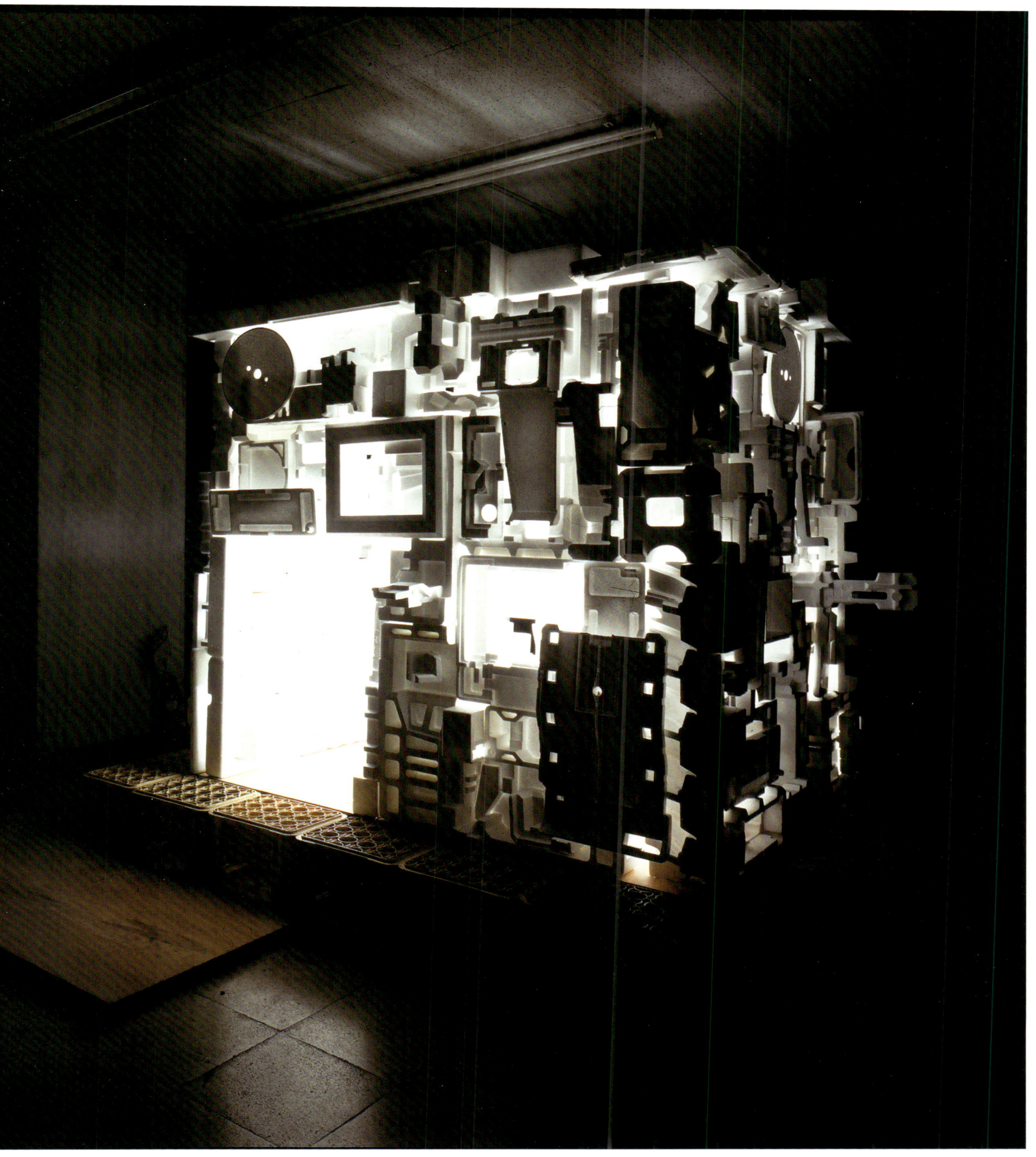

⌂ 09 TAKAHIRO KANEYAMA

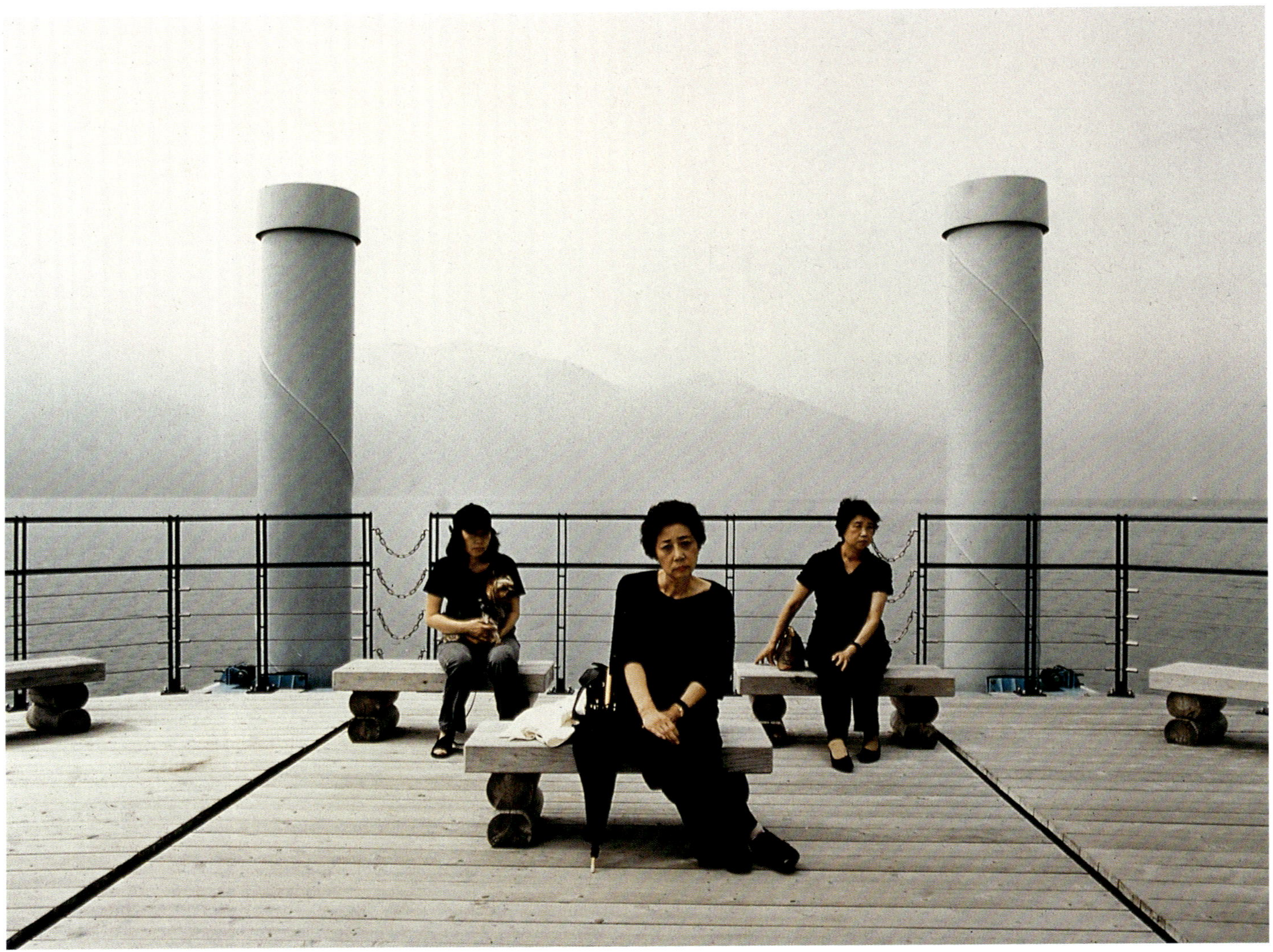

The Kaneyama Sisters
ERIC C. SHINER

Photographer Takahiro Kaneyama came to his chosen medium not through formal training, but through necessity. When his grandmother died in 2000, the artist had an epiphany of sorts, realizing that life is ephemeral and that without recording it on film he would lose the memories of his close-knit family, so dear to his heart. He decided to begin taking portraits of his mother Sayoko, her older sister Miyako, and their younger sister Noriko. These were the women who raised Kaneyama, and, to this day, remain inseparable. Add to this the facts that the artist's aunts never married and that his mother has suffered from schizophrenia since his teenage years, and the artist's intimate family portraits begin to morph into a documentary narrative of a family's complex secrets, hopes, and despairs.

Since starting this project, Kaneyama has snapped portraits of his mother and her sisters each time he returned home to Japan. Images of the sisters on the beach, in public parks, at home, and in a temple record the passing of time as they grow older year by year. Noriko's pet dog makes regular appearances in the photographs, as does the hospital that Kaneyama's mother regularly enters when her schizophrenia worsens and she is in need of care. Juxtaposed with these intimate portraits of his family, the resultant *While Leaves Are Falling* series features still-life photos of nature and architecture, mundane street scenes, and close-ups of interior spaces. These images are slightly off: a bush has no leaves; trees are wrapped in black netting (Pl. 9.3); a building juts into the sky at a strange angle as if it may topple over at any time. They fit well

PLATE 9.1

Takahiro Kaneyama
Nikko 1 from *While Leaves Are Falling* series
2000
Chromogenic print
20 x 24" (50.8 x 61 cm)
Collection of the artist

with the family portraits: both types of image become historical documents that trace the *condition* of things. In this way, Kaneyama records the ups and downs, the health and the sickness, the very essence of his family *and* the physical spaces that they inhabit and traverse. *While Leaves Are Falling* then becomes a work about the ephemeral nature of not only life, but of *things*. It is a contemporary tale inspired by the aesthetics of *wabi sabi*, the literature of Tanizaki Jun'ichirō, and the drama of the American soap opera all rolled into one. A selection of family portraits from the series will be featured in *Making a Home*, instilling a sense of connection to Japan and to Kaneyama's family members remaining there.

In addition to this expansive portfolio of photographs, Kaneyama has been working on a series called *1971*, the year of his birth. In order to draw connections with—and indeed to distinguish himself from—others born in the same year, Kaneyama has sought out people born in 1971 and asked them to pose for portraits. In addition to the visual component of the work, Kaneyama has conducted interviews with his subjects, asking each to talk about the ways s/he copes with change in his/her life. The models include Amy Thoelen, who was born in South Korea on "approximately January 22, 1971" and adopted by an American family at the age of two; the actor David Kaplan who often plays in gangster films; and John Pamer, a skateboarding drummer with a day job (Pl. 9.2). For all of Kaneyama's subjects, a certain sense of confidence coupled with uncertainty resides in their eyes. As the children of baby boomers, these Generation X'ers have often excelled in their lives, but still feel that something remains unfulfilled. For Kaneyama, the series is a way to help him make sense of his own life in New York City where he studies for his upcoming CPA exam by day, and takes pictures whenever he has the time. The portraits in *1971* are perhaps best read as documents of a generation, as the alternate paths that Kaneyama might have taken had he been dealt a different fate.

In his never-ending pursuit to freeze the present on film, Kaneyama protects his past while ensuring his future. He has created a series of works that allows him to reference his family's sorrow and love and his generation's ambivalence and fear. He is a documentarian with a perfect eye and a deep soul. His pictures reveal both of these qualities in equal measure as they spell out a story of one man's journey into the apparently familiar—yet completely unknown—realm of the self.

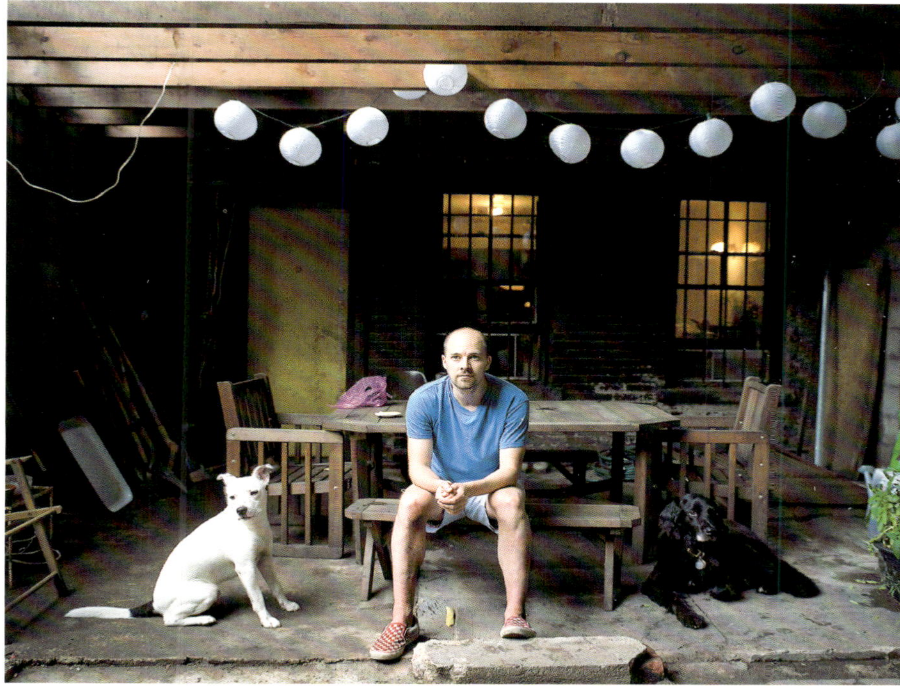

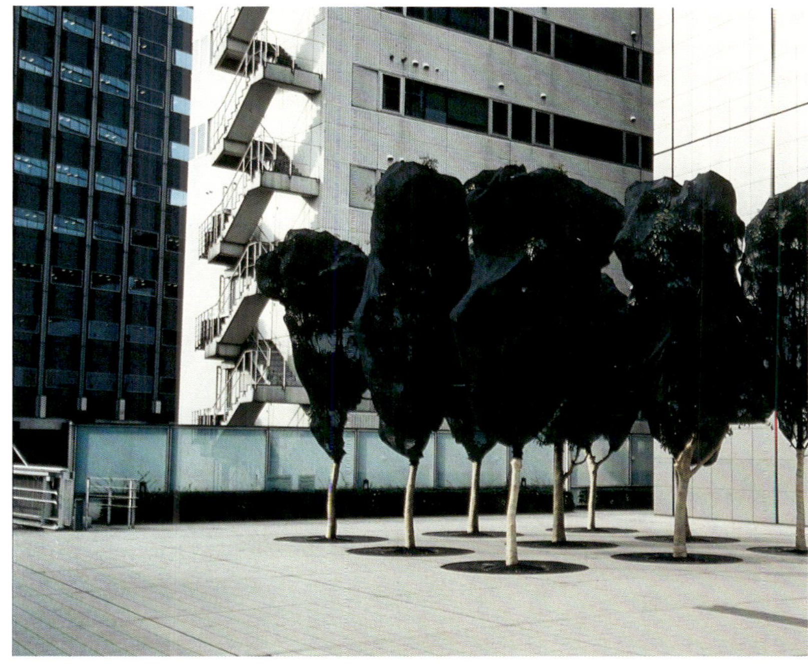

PLATE 9.2

Takahiro Kaneyama
John Pamer from *1971* series
2003
Chromogenic print
20 x 24" (50.8 x 61 cm)
Collection of the artist
PHOTO COURTESY OF THE ARTIST

PLATE 9.3

Takahiro Kaneyama
Untitled from *While Leaves Are Falling* series
2003
Chromogenic print
20 x 24" (50.8 x 61 cm)
Collection of the artist
PHOTO COURTESY OF THE ARTIST

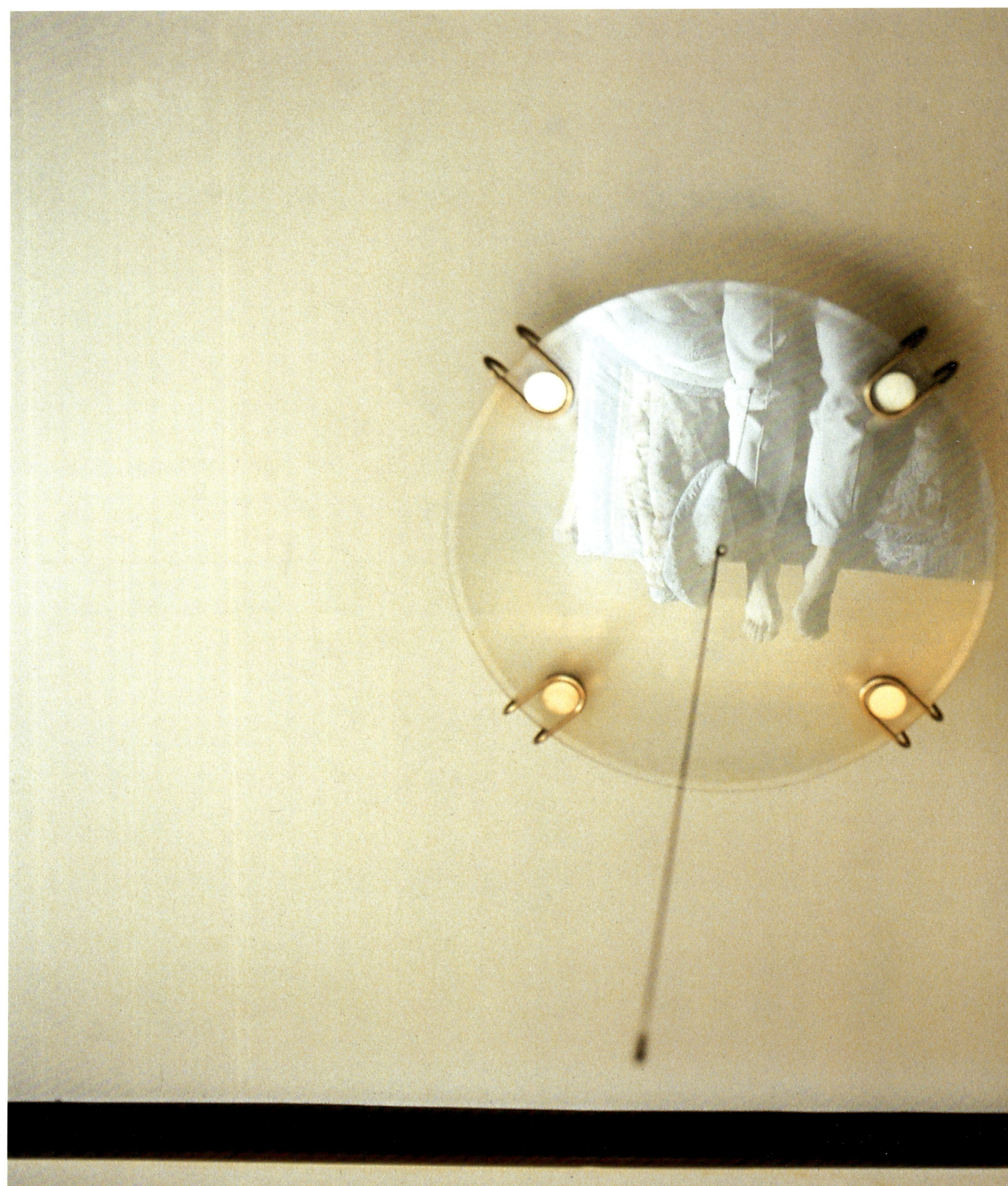

Why did you decide to leave Japan?

TK: When I first came to the U.S. 13 years ago, I was a film major. I got into photography by accident…. However, my ultimate goal remains the same; I haven't given up on making films.

Why did you choose New York as your ultimate destination?

TK: The first obvious area of influence/inspiration comes from movies, especially the ones made in New York: Scorsese's *Taxi Driver*, Ridley Scott's *Someone to Watch Over Me*, *Tootsie*, and others. I… just loved the New York I saw in these movies.

What was your first impression of New York City?

TK: The real New York I saw with my own eyes seemed unreal to me. It may not make any sense, but the New York I saw on television and in movies before I actually came to New York…proved to be the real New York in my perception…. In a way two different New Yorks exist within me.

Do you ever regret leaving Japan?

TK: Yes, I admit that I do have some what-ifs floating around in my head (what if I had stayed in Japan, what if I were a salaryman down there…), but it doesn't happen as often as it used to.

In this age of globalism, do you consider yourself to be a Japanese artist, an American artist, an international artist, or a hybrid of all three?

TK: Every work I create and how I see/visualize things have a lot to do with my past experiences (memories of childhood and adolescence), ethnic/cultural background, etc. I noticed there are viewers who almost force themselves to find some sort of Japaneseness in my work: Zen spirits, Murakami world (Haruki Murakami, the writer), and whatnot. If that makes me unique and different from other non-Japanese artists, I'll take full advantage of it. I consider myself a genuine Japanese artist.

PLATE 9.4

Takahiro Kaneyama
Mother's Feet from *While Leaves Are Falling*
series
2003
Chromogenic print
20 x 24" (50.8 x 61 cm)
Collection of the artist

10 EMIKO KASAHARA

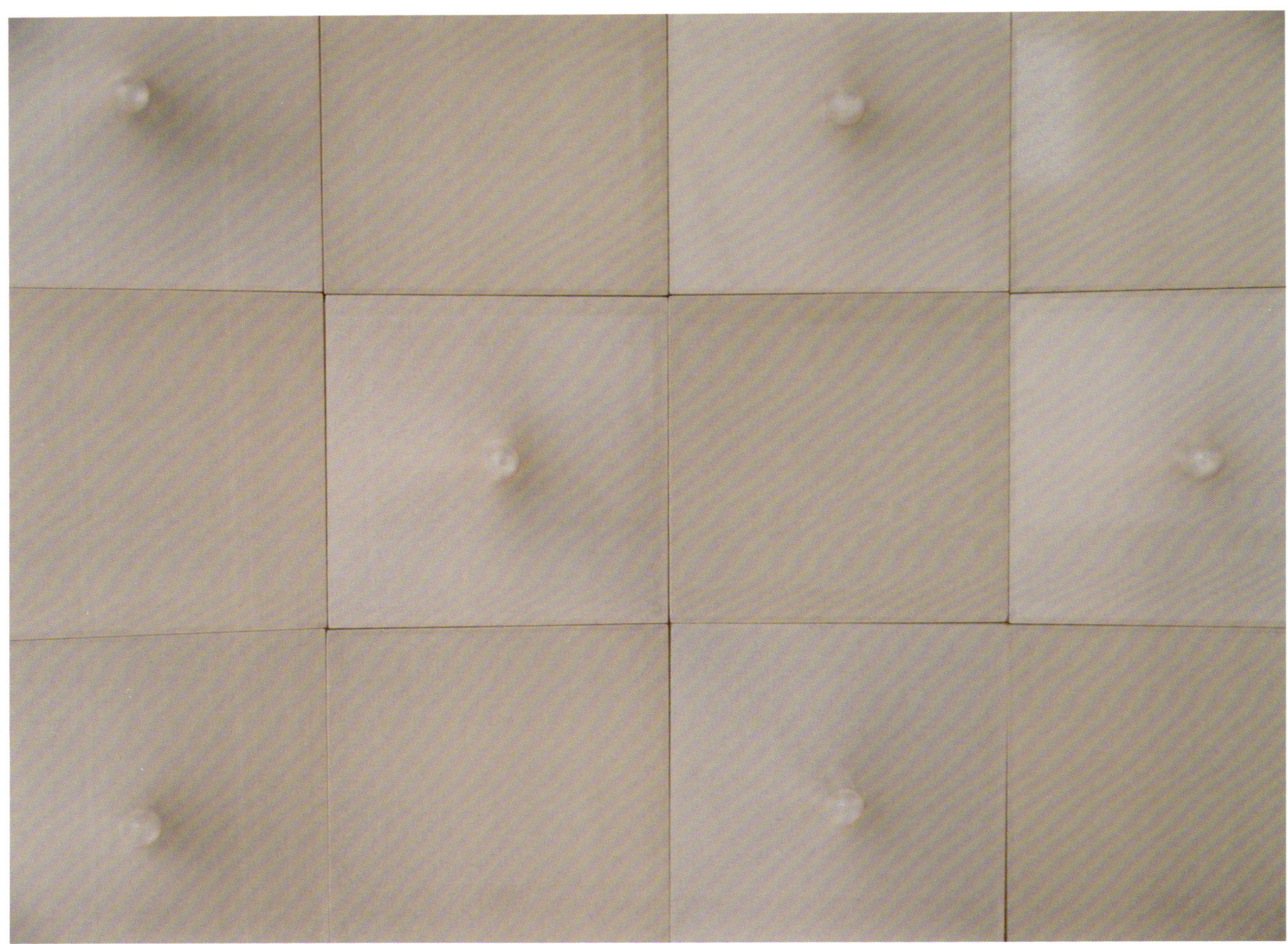

The Body Delivered
ERIC C. SHINER

Conceptual artist Emiko Kasahara is engaged in a career-long examination of the female body and signifiers of femininity and sexuality, both internal and in interaction with the world outside. She uses the staid materials of marble or wood in certain sculptures, the revolutionary materials of wig hair, nail polish, make-up, and false eyelashes in others, to both elicit and confront stereotypic femininity. They are celebratory and damning in equal measure.

Kasahara's early works from 1993 to 1995 are beautifully crafted but disturbing marble sculptures that conflate female sexual anatomy and institutional toilet fixtures of sinks, urinals, and a bedpan. They are made more unsettling by being filled with a bleach and water solution that disseminates an antiseptic odor that fills the room. *Untitled—Double Urinal* (1993) takes the form of a pair of pinkish breast-shaped urinals each set with a nipple

beneath. The nurturing or sexual breasts of flesh, now refigured and carved in stone, present a challenging vision of utilitarian public fixtures for male use. The breasts/urinals are also offered for contemplation as receptacles of fluids, male and female, bodily and chemical, nurturing, excreted, and sterilizing.

In the same period, Kasahara created a seminal work: *Untitled –Three Types–* of 1993 (Pls. 10.4–5). Three beds with crisp linen sheets sit in a row, each inset with a small valve. The shining steel lid and casing of each valve hides a sexualized orifice made from pink rubber. The valve is set at a different place on each bed—corresponding, the artist says, to the mouth, vagina, and anus of a woman, the three openings of a woman's body associated with sex and the entrance/exit of the inner/outer body. The three types from the title refer to her three stages of life—birth, procreation, and

PLATE 10.1

Emiko Kasahara
Study for *SHEER* (detail)
2007
Nylon stocking, acrylic plastic
Each unit: 7 ½ x 7 ½ x 3 ⅝" (19 x 19 x 9.2 cm)
Collection of the artist
PHOTO: EMIKO KASAHARA

death—or to three sexualities. Kasahara again conflates the organic and sexual with the clinical, institutional, and machine-made.

In her exploration of the construction of beauty and the production of femininity, Kasahara embarked on a project based on paint, though not of the sort used on canvas. Her *MANUS-CURE* portfolio from 1998 comprises 1,050 small rectangles bathed in color and spread out over 30 sheets (Pl. 10.3). The shiny surfaces of rainbow explosion recall Damien Hirst's colorful dots, yet here each hue has an individual label, alphabetized from "accent rose" to "zip zap pink." These are not art shop enamels for certain, but commercially available nail polishes, both highend and lowbrow. For Kasahara, these whimsical colors are healing devices on the one hand, and enablers of feminine beauty ideals on the other. The manicure makes one feel pretty, while at the same time objectifying the customer to ogling eyes. Here, as elsewhere, the duality of beauty infuses and defines Kasahara's work.

In the *Structure* series from 1998 to 2001, Kasahara uses false eyelashes to create extensive grid patterns encountered in her daily life: the patterns found in the chicken wire set in the windows of her Williamsburg studio, a sidewalk grate, and bathroom tiles. From afar, the works look like geometric studies in formalism; encountered at close range, they become a microcosm of cilia-infused beauty. *La Charme* from 2001 explodes this microcosm to

a grand scale: mammoth disks of shimmering wig hair populate the gallery in blondes, brunettes, reds, and blacks (Pl. 10.2). Live models with their own hair dyed to match perform atop these synthetic discs, playing out the production of beauty before the viewer's eye. Spaced out like the formations in a Japanese rock garden, the artist references her upbringing in Japan while placing the female body and its accoutrements at the center of the gaze.

For *Making a Home*, Kasahara has created a new piece, *SHEER* (Pl. 10.1). Composed of plastic boxes and skin-toned panty hose, the work invites viewers to enter a room covered with hundreds of blocks—many sprouting nipples from which soft whispers emit, enticing the viewer to draw near and listen. These voices, in languages from around the globe, relate personal tales of loss. Many are unattainable due to inherent language barriers; some strike straight to the heart. "When you lean in to listen to the nipple, it will remind you of when you were a baby breast-feeding," Kasahara has said. "The sense of sucking on your mother's nipple will conjure the emotional memory of this loss." In the safe confines of the installation, we realize that these intimately relayed words and the stories behind them rely on us for the inscription of meaning. This is the space in which tears can be shed, where we all can be one in the pulsating realm of loss.

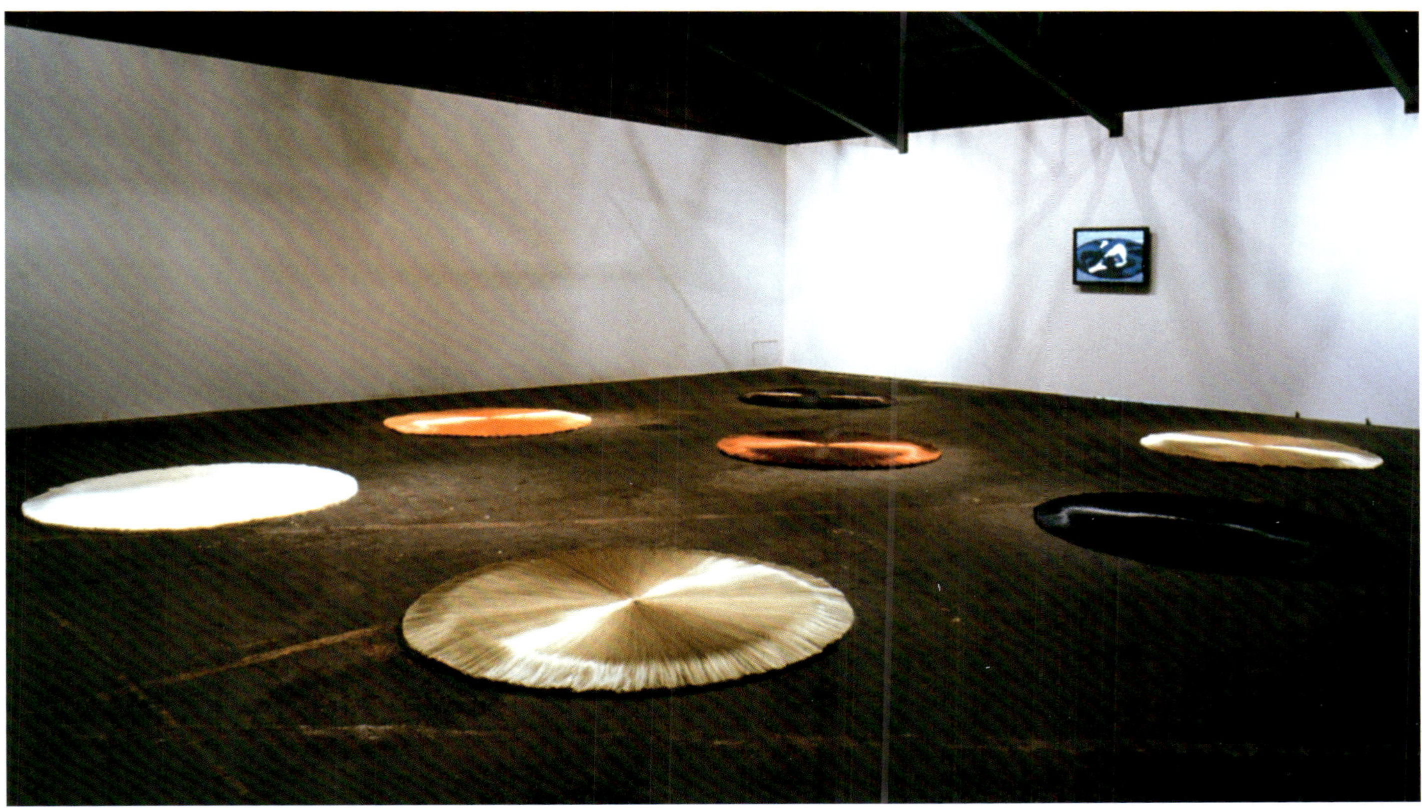

Emiko Kasahara
La Charme #1
2001
Installation and performance at *Yokohama Triennale 2001*;
synthetic hair, wood, cloth, DVD and monitor
7 pieces: each diameter: 60" (150 cm)
Collection of the artist
PHOTO: SAKATA MINEO

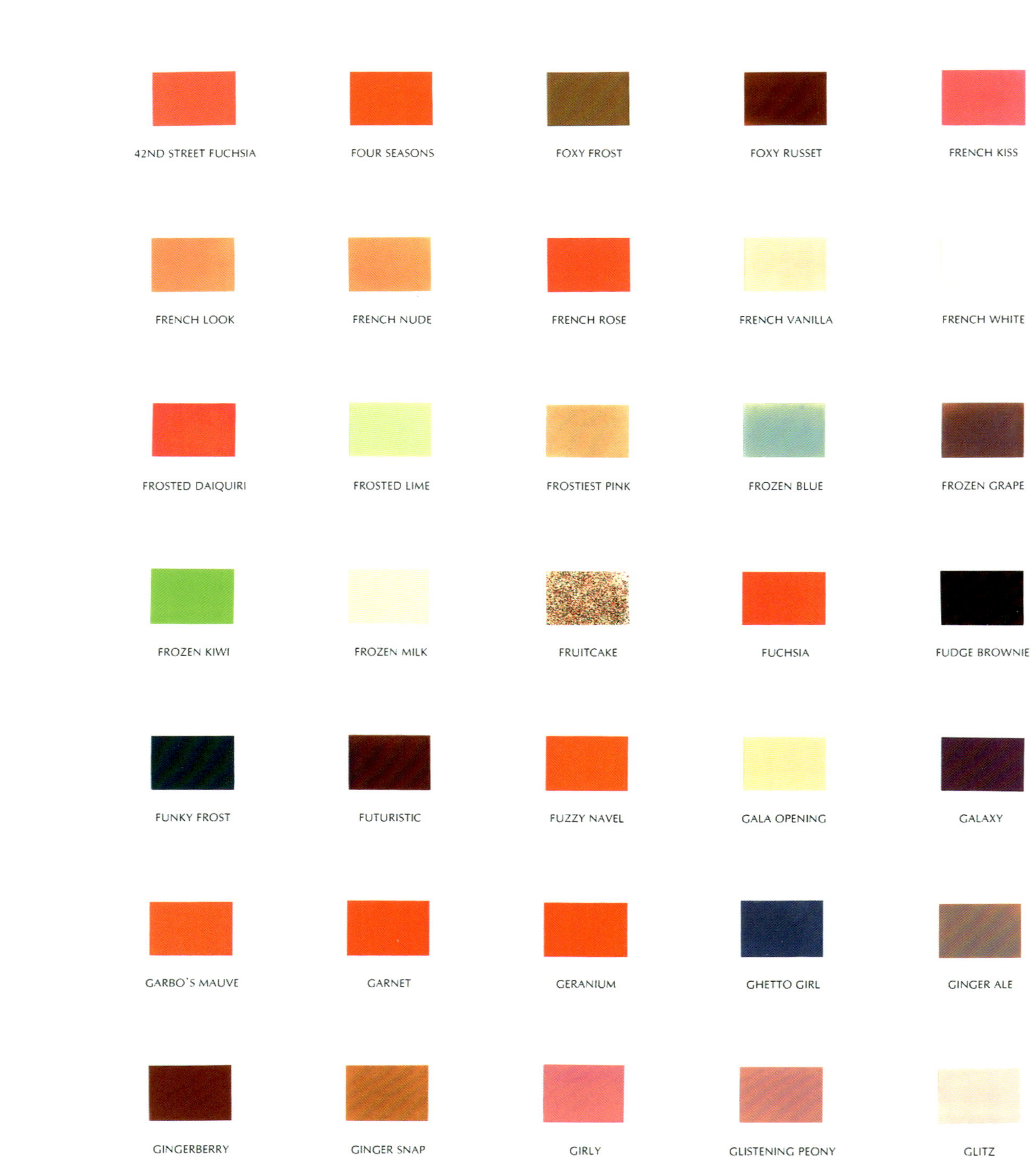

PLATE 10.3

Emiko Kasahara
MANUS-CURE (detail)
1998
Boxed portfolio of 32 sheets; 1,050 nail colors, polyester
film, stainless steel case, museum board, cotton ribbon
Each sheet: 18 ½ x 14 ½'' (47 x 37 cm)
The National Museum of Modern Art, Kyoto, Japan

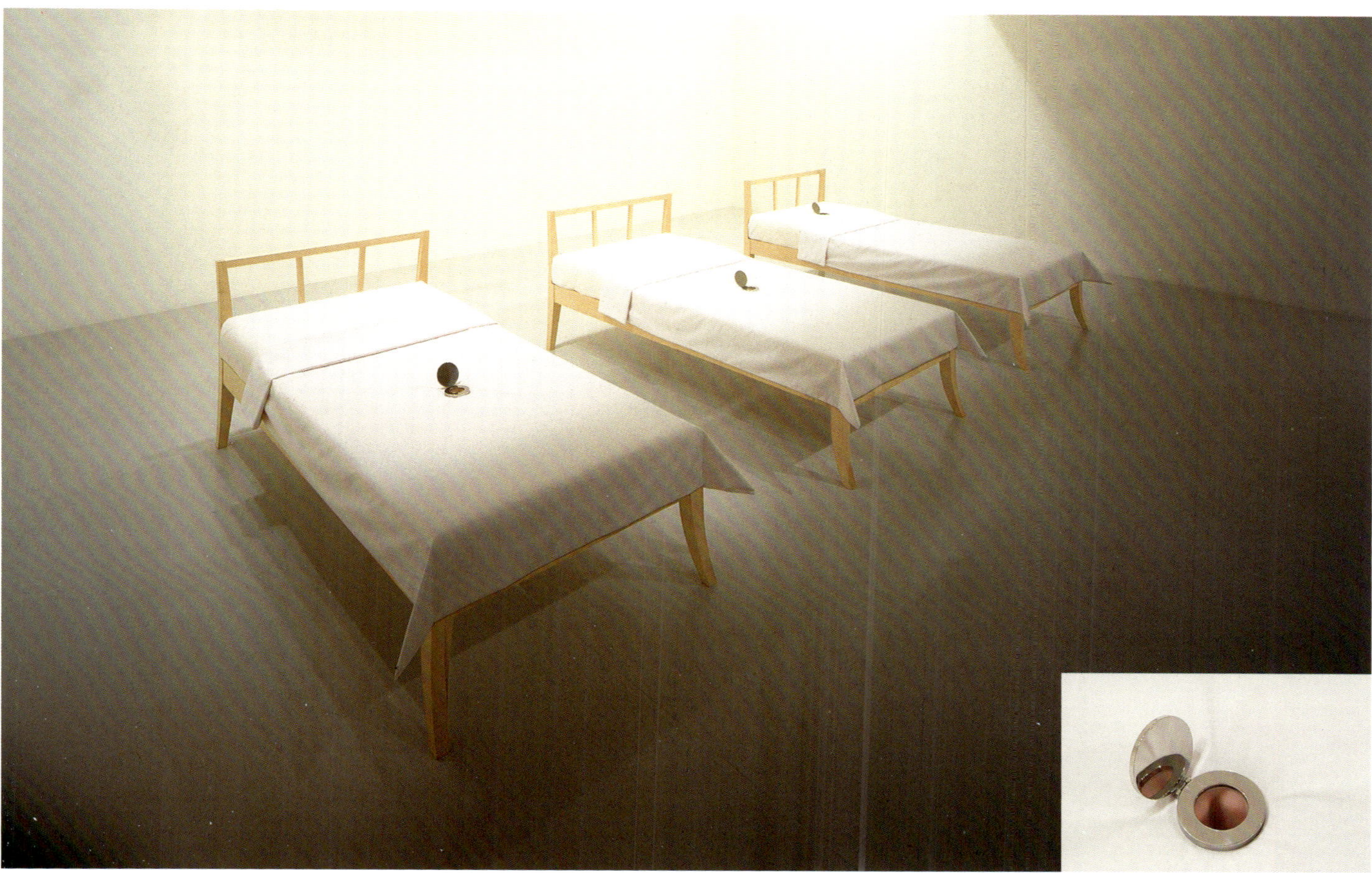

Why did you decide to leave Japan?

EK: I received a full-year grant from the Agency for Cultural Affairs of Japan, and it required me to be out of Japan for one year. I had already started my art career in Japan and had difficulty supporting myself as an artist. I needed to take any grant or artist-in-residence I could to continue my creation of art.

Why did you choose New York as your ultimate destination?

EK: I was in an artist-in-residence program in France for a few months before I came to New York. It was rather difficult since I didn't speak French. Considering my language ability (Japanese and English only), one of my limited choices outside of Japan was the U.S.

What was your first impression of New York City?

EK: People here need to know a reason first before doing something. In Japan, people do things first, then discover the meaning along the way. This difference in working was hard for me to understand in the beginning.

Has the experience of living in New York changed your style or process significantly?

EK: I became more conscious of Japaneseness and that initiated the conceptual aspects of my work. I don't think my style has changed much, though.

Do you ever regret leaving Japan?

EK: New York is a great place for me as long as I can go back to Tokyo. I try to be in Tokyo as much as I try to be in New York. I would regret it if I had to leave one or the other.

In this age of globalism, do you consider yourself to be a Japanese artist, an American artist, an international artist, or a hybrid of all three?

EK: I see myself now as a part of the diversity of the world and that cultivates the essential part of my political stance and my belief in the equality of people. I will always see myself as a Japanese artist, but certainly an international Japanese one.

PLATE 10.4

Emiko Kasahara
Untitled –Three Types–
1993
Wood, stainless steel, silicon rubber, cloth
Each 28 x 30 ½ x 65" (71.1 x 77.5 x 165.1 cm)
Stiftung für Gegenwartskunst, Balzers, Lichtenstein

PLATE 10.5 (inset)

Emiko Kasahara
Detail of Pl. 10.4

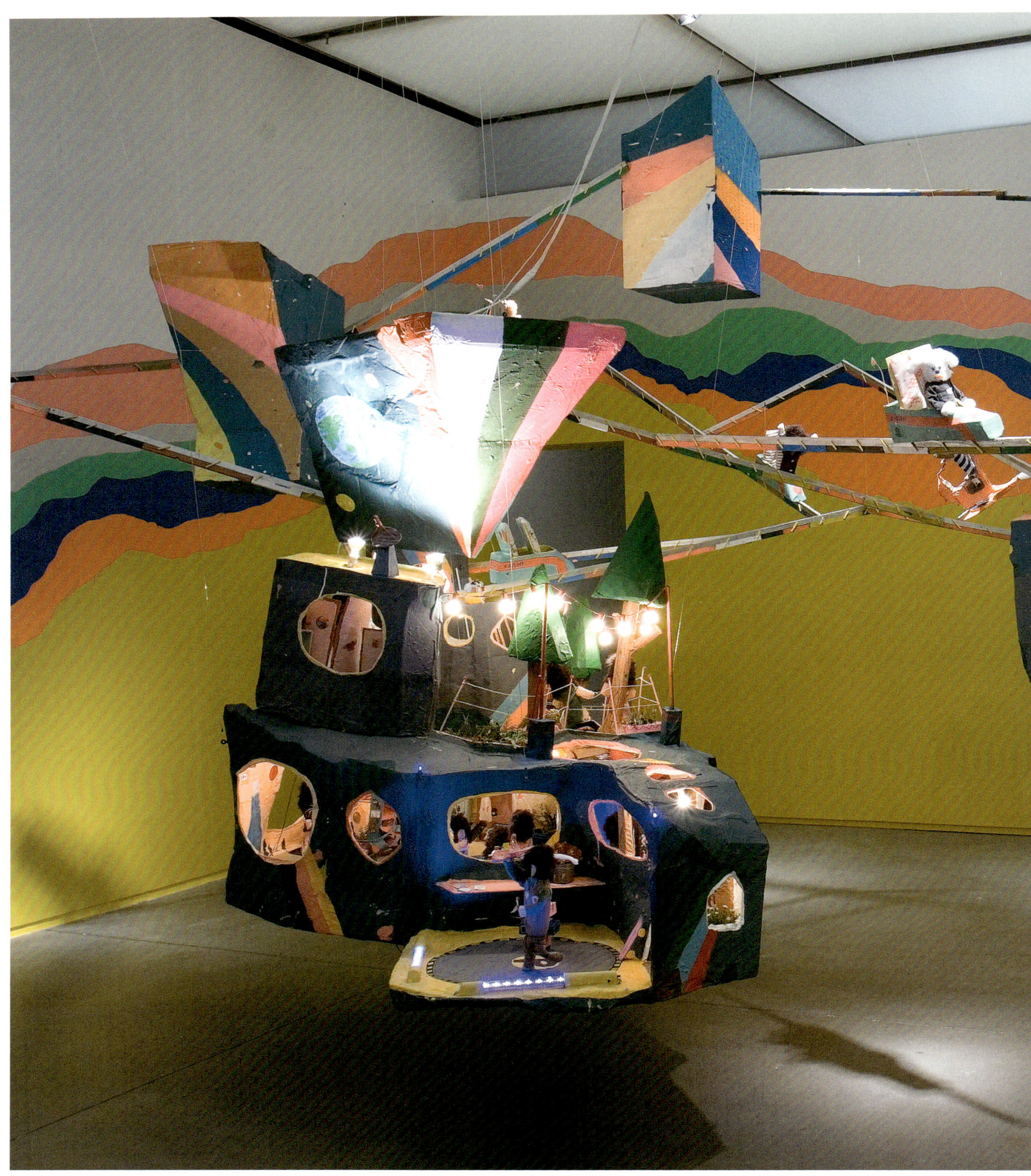

PLATE 11.1

Misaki Kawai
Space House (installation view at Institute of
Contemporary Art, Boston)
2006–07
Acrylic, fabric, cardboard, wood, wire, plastic,
lighting, video monitors
Dimensions variable
Collection of the artist
PHOTO: JOHN KENNARD

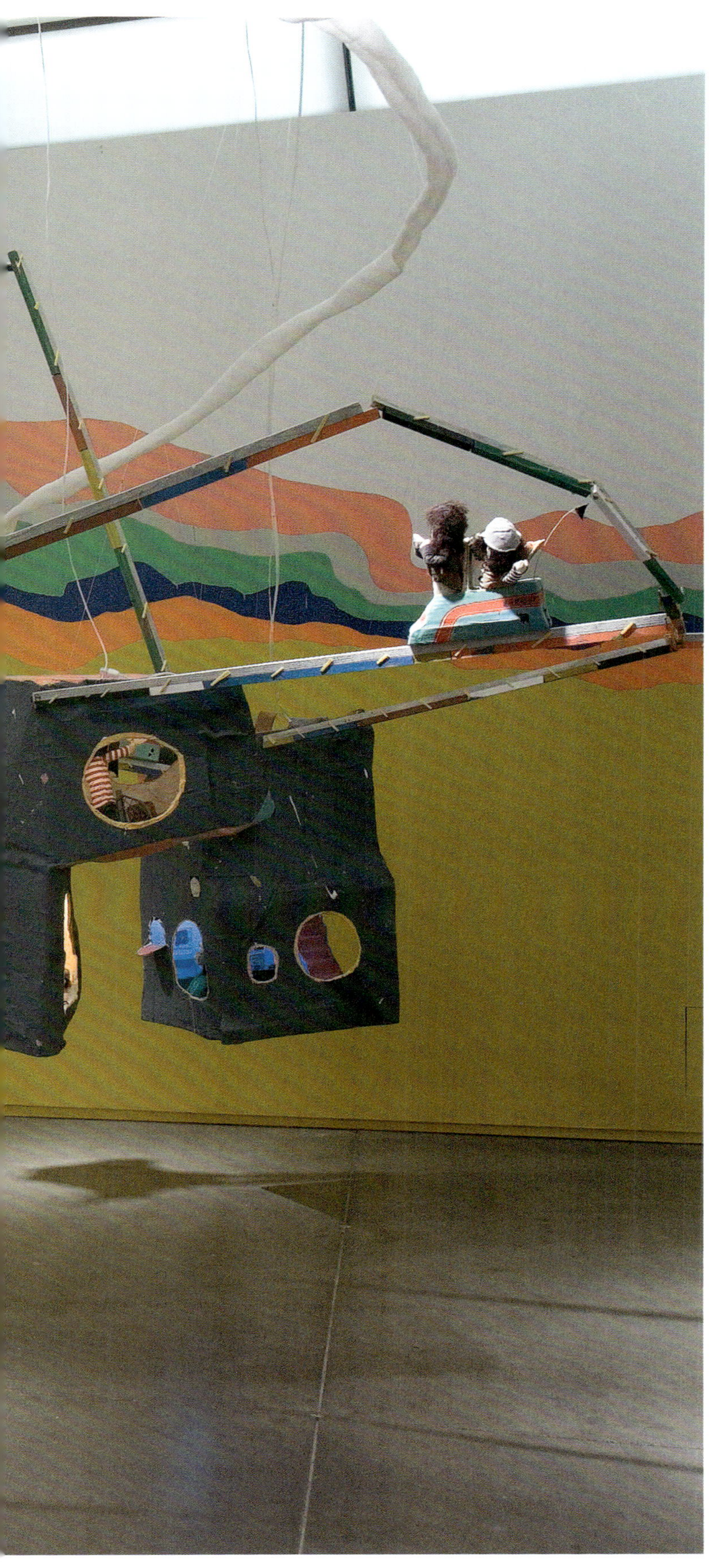

In the Maelstrom of Kawai(i)
ERIC C. SHINER

Misaki Kawai creates outlandishly cute dream worlds from the detritus of life. One need only glimpse the artist at work in her studio to begin to understand her process: with piles of paper and pots of glue all around, she clips and pastes to the board or object in front of her with an incredibly focused, yet seemingly reckless, abandon. She seems to have an intimate and direct relationship with the work before her; she becomes a young and female Jackson Pollock engaged in a ballet infused with the fuzzy animals, buxom blondes, and fast cars that often take form on or in her creations. She uses colorful drips of paint here and there, no doubt an indexical mark of her interaction, or perhaps a visual nod to the fact that her works literally overflow with cute. As if an ironic foreshadowing of her output, the artist's family name Kawai needs only an extra "i" attached to phonetically (not textually) change it into the Japanese word for "cute," thus producing a pun that inextricably links the artist Kawai to the *kawaii* worlds she produces.

Kawai arrived in New York not knowing a soul. She started to hang out with the Williamsburg art crowd and sold her work on the streets to make ends meet. It happened that the group of young artists she befriended was the vanguard of New York's young art scene—including Taylor McKimens and James Benjamin Franklin— who spoke in a visual vocabulary similar to Kawai's. The group met often, exchanged ideas, and even made collaborative works, all in the service of youth culture set against a backdrop of pastel dreams and whimsical characters. They focused on sex and drugs and rock and roll, but in a subtle way. Kawai made sculptures filled with dolls sporting her friends' faces; McKimens created a comic book and series of work called *The Drips* starring a toxic sludge character; Franklin made small resin-dipped canvases featuring oversized heads. Theirs was the new voice of the streets; today it is the new voice of Chelsea.

Kawai made her entrée into the commercial art world when London-based gallerist Kenny Schachter saw her work and put her in a group show in 2002. She had her first solo show at the gallery in the summer of 2003 and another small solo show at P.S.1 in New York later that year. In 2004, New York gallerist extraordinaire Jeffrey Deitch included Kawai in a group show, thus cementing her place in the New York art zeitgeist. Today, Kawai, McKimens, and Franklin are together again, showing at the same Chelsea gallery, Clementine.

Kawai's work started off big. She often created large-scale sculptures made out of cardboard, paint, dolls, and video elements. *Himalaya Space Station* is a massive snow peak that houses a control center manned by stuffed animals, blinking lights, and dolls, one of which—the pilot—is a self-portrait of the artist (Pl. 11.3). Spaceships zoom around the sky above the mountain, with trails of white smoke cotton spreading out behind them. The work requires close examination through the portholes cut out at various points around it, and surely the viewer will discover something new on each visit. This thriving dream zone portrays Kawai's own rambling imagination, a mindscape that becomes a maelstrom of cute set on swirling overdrive. Her 2006 installation *Space House*, a portion of which is shown here in *Making a Home*, features a multi-room living space with additional pods connected by a monorail (Pl. 11.1).

Recently, Kawai has created two-dimensional works on board depicting characters similar to those found in her sculptures. However, these works signal a decidedly new direction in subject matter, as Kawai's stuffed animals and dolls have been replaced by characters that are unabashedly risqué. *G-String Riders* features two plus-sized women with large posteriors zooming down the street on bicycles, wearing only G-strings and bikini tops (Pl. 11.2). *Workout Wind* shows a gym bunny passing gas on a muscle stud behind her. Needless to say, Kawai isn't embarrassed by the playful nature of her work, itself an extension of a most upbeat and outgoing soul rooted in the international culture of cute.

Why did you decide to leave Japan?
MK: After graduating from art school, I wanted to keep making art. I visited a friend in Los Angeles, then traveled to San Francisco, where an old man I met said to me, "If you want to be an artist, you should go to New York." While in New York, I realized that in order to make a living as an artist you have to be in New York.

What was your first impression of New York City?
MK: I was unhappy. I had no friends and the people were cold. I really wanted people to see my artwork. At first, I took some artwork and showed it to some galleries, but nobody would even look at it. So I decided to show my artwork on the street. This was how I started to meet other artists and people who were interested in my art.

Did you have any interactions with other artists or supporters that were especially beneficial to you and your work?
MK: When I first came to New York, I got a lot of support from artists like Taylor McKimens, Kiki Smith, and Donald Baechler which really helped me a lot. And of course Kenny Schachter was a big help. He put me in some of my first shows in New York, which introduced my work to the New York art community.

Do you ever regret leaving Japan?
MK: Culture differences really are difficult. What would be best would be a place where the best parts of Japan are mixed with the best parts of America.

In this age of globalism, do you consider yourself to be a Japanese artist, an American artist, an international artist, or a hybrid of all three?
MK: Since I am Japanese, of course I'm a Japanese artist. Since I live and work in New York, I am also a New York artist. But since I've had shows in Europe, the United States, Canada, and Japan, I'm an international artist, too, right?

Translated by Ryan Holmberg

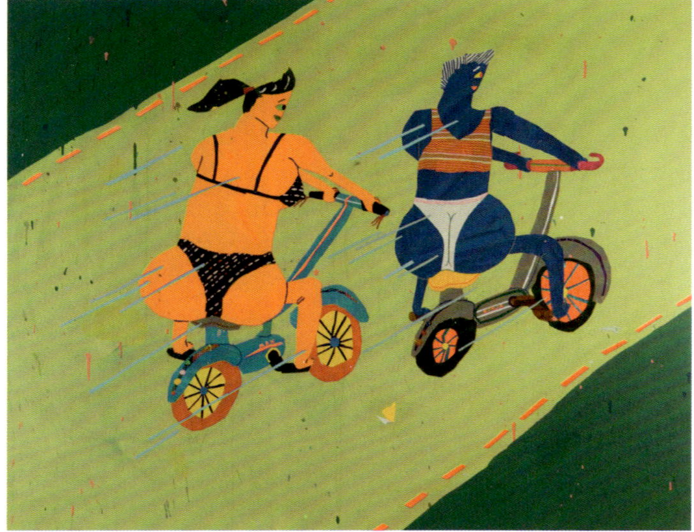

PLATE 11.2

Misaki Kawai
G-String Riders
2007
Acrylic, paper, and fabric on canvas
48 x 60" (121.9 x 152.4 cm)
Collection of Nancy Derene Seltzer, New York

PLATE 11.3

Misaki Kawai
Himalaya Space Station
2004
Cardboard, wood, acrylic, fabric, paper, wire, lighting, video monitors
8' 6" x 7' x 6' 3" (2.6 x 2.1 x 1.9 m)
Collection of Ray Otis, Golden Beach, Fla.

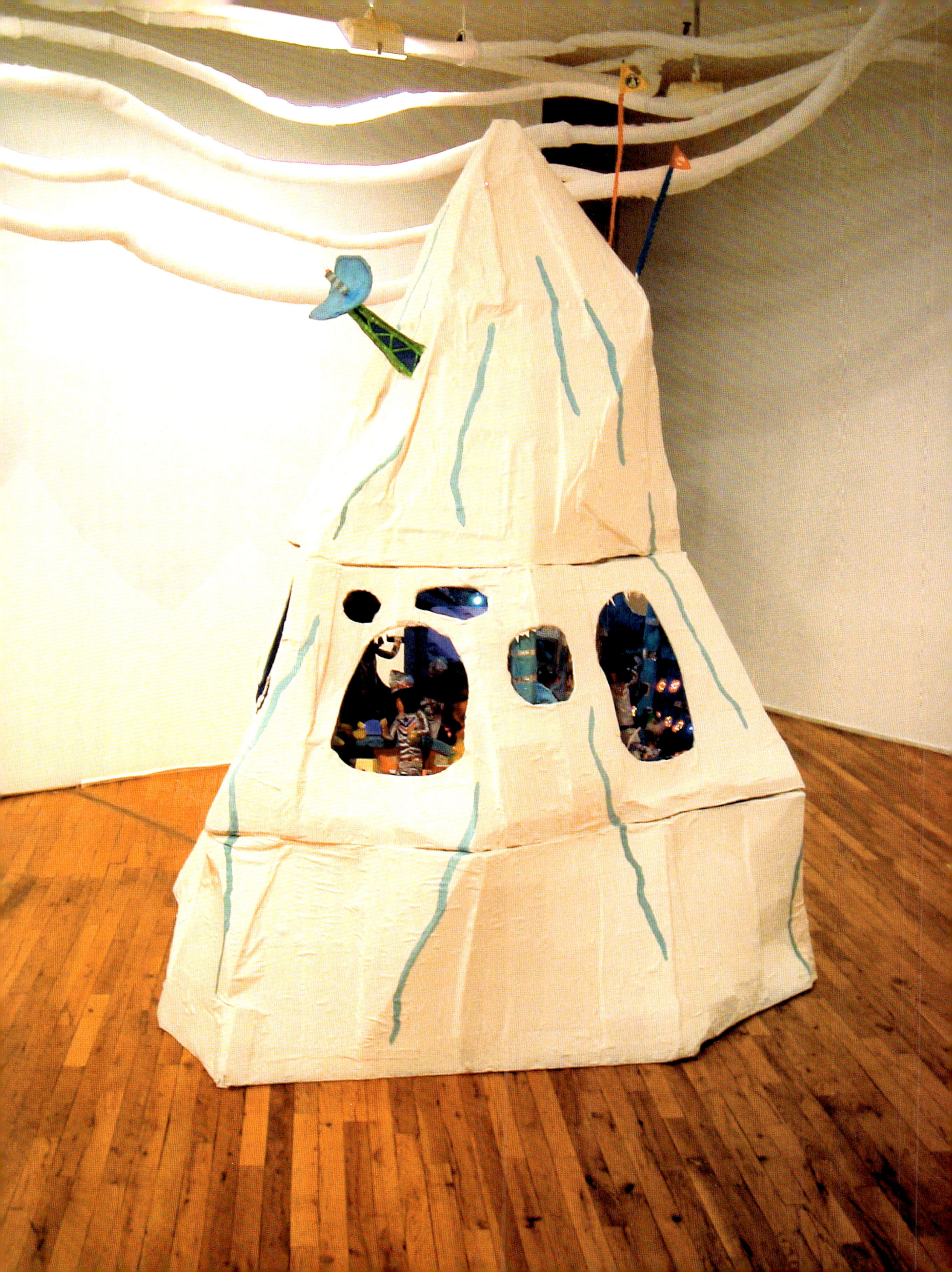

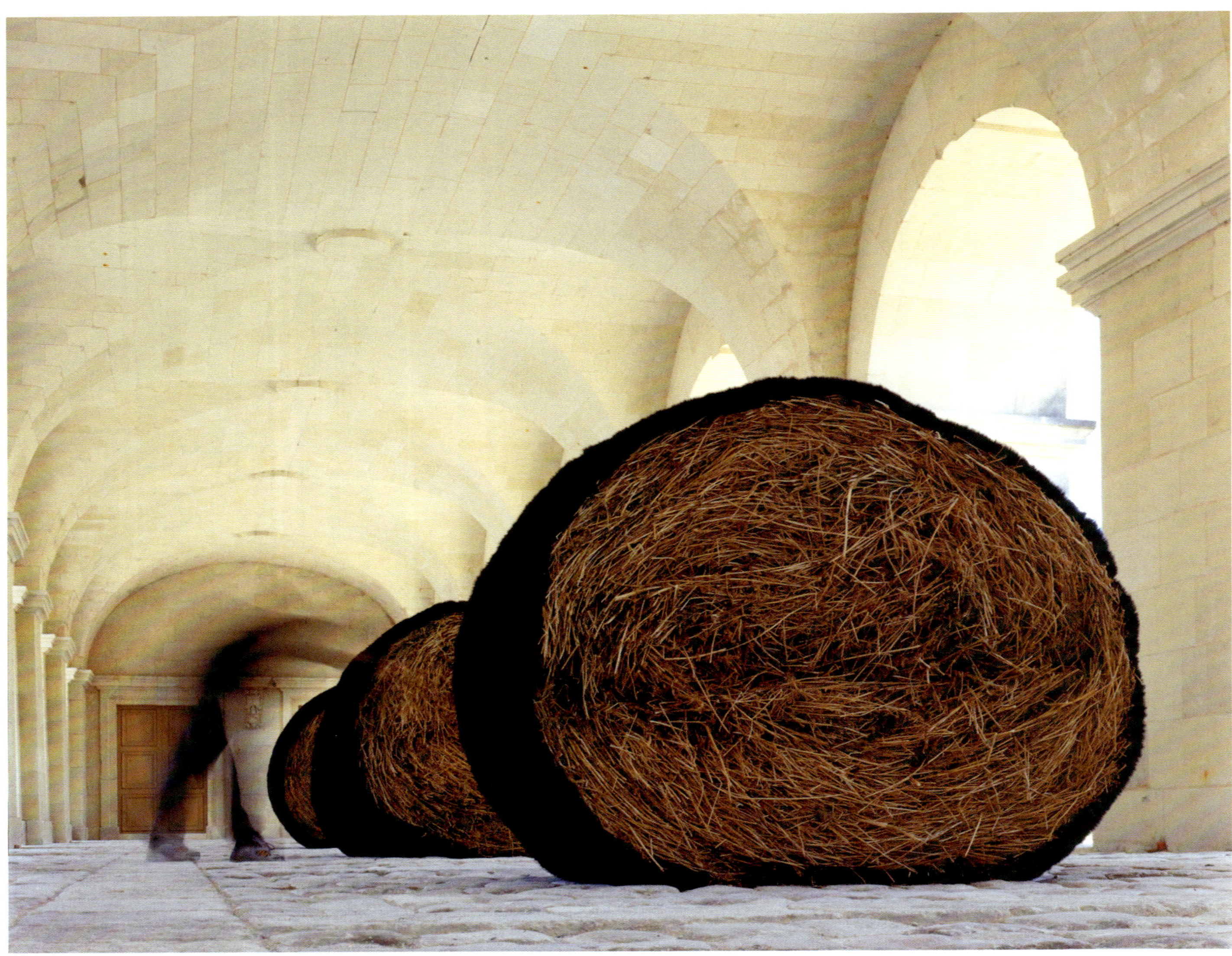

Food Is a Many-Splendored Thing
SHINYA WATANABE WITH REIKO TOMII

"American people eat in an American way, Japanese people eat in a Japanese way." This seemingly simple observation informs the complex art of Miwa Koizumi, who uses food to "cut through cultural differences and underline them with an immediacy unmatched by any other medium." Simply put, she examines the conditions of globalism through a mundane yet intimate eye.

Koizumi's transnational attitude was nurtured by the many trips she made, especially in her student years, through several former Communist countries, Western Europe, the U.S., and South and Southeast Asia, during which she developed a layered view on the differences of human existence. This is already evident in *Tranches Empailles*, a site-specific installation she created in 1998

near Poitiers in west central France, while she was a student at the École Nationale Supérieure des Beaux-Arts in Paris (Pl. 12.1). It consisted of three hay bales of a man's height, wrapped in synthetic fur. The hay bales, kept in a farmer's barn over the winter, exuded strong animal smells, an integral element of the work that forced the viewer to take note of what may have disappeared from our modern life. The title was a word play in French, adding a linguistic dimension to the already layered composition of the work: slices (*tranches*) of hay (*pailles*) dressed like stuffed animals (*empailles*).

Koizumi lived in Paris from 1996 until she and her husband moved to New York in 2001. In Paris, she was troubled that craftsmanship was regarded as an attribute of artisans, not contemporary artists.

However, outside Paris she noticed that some artists displayed a great degree of craftsmanship *and* received critical recognition. (Tara Donovan, Brian Jungen, and Ernesto Neto, for example, whom she encountered in New York.) At issue for them is not necessarily craftsmanship per se but the conceptual essence that the artist expresses through it. The borderless nature of New York further liberated her, for the city has "no containers," unlike Paris, where she had to have a relationship with "French culture."

One of her New York works is the *PET's* series (2005–), in which she reveals an exquisite inventiveness in handling one element of the ubiquitous trash of our time, PET (polyethylene terephthalate) bottles (Pl. 12.2). She scavenges and recycles variously colored water bottles—San Pellegrino green, Volvic blue, and assorted brands that are clear. She transforms them into primitive life forms of sea anemones and jellyfish by cutting them, molding them by heat, and puncturing them with a soldering iron. Her recycling links geologic time when oceanic life was turned into fossil fuel with our time when fossil fuel is consumed to sustain almost every aspect of our consumerist life style, including bottled water. She thus figuratively completes a cycle of reincarnation for fossilized sea creatures by returning them to approximations of their original forms.

If Koizumi's *PET's* series alludes to our food culture through the material object, her food-based performances, begun in 1999, provide her with an arena to directly explore cultural differences in a global age. Among them, *SuperSpa*, presented in *Making a Home*, is a most ambitious project (Pls. 12.3–4). What is "super" about this spa, another obsession of metropolitan life today, is her subliminal mixing of spas and professional wrestling (which is more show business than sport) and her purposeful application of organic foods for the good of our health. Seated on the wood benches set up in the ring, two unknowing "clients" are first prepped by "uniformed attendant-trainers." They are then given three courses of "treatments," each of which consists of edible ingredients. The first, "Forest Bomb Hand Scrub," is made of celery, parsley, lemon, and brown rice bran that help "exfoliate the hands"; the second, "Royal Rumble Energy Buster," is a foot bath of fresh picked mint and green tea infused with ginseng and honey that "provides the ultimate foot glow." The ingredients and indication of each treatment are slowly announced in a recorded voice coming from a speaker, which also subliminally prepares the clients to become a "blood pumping champion." By the time the third treatment, "Rest in Peace Facial Mask," made of yogurt and cucumber, is done, the clients' hands, feet, and heads are covered by gloves, boots, and masks, ostensibly to enhance the effect of the initial three treatments but, in fact, to dress them for a championship match. In the gentle world of Miwa Koizumi, however, everybody is a winner: a *SuperSpa* performance always ends with the raising of both clients' hands to declare success.

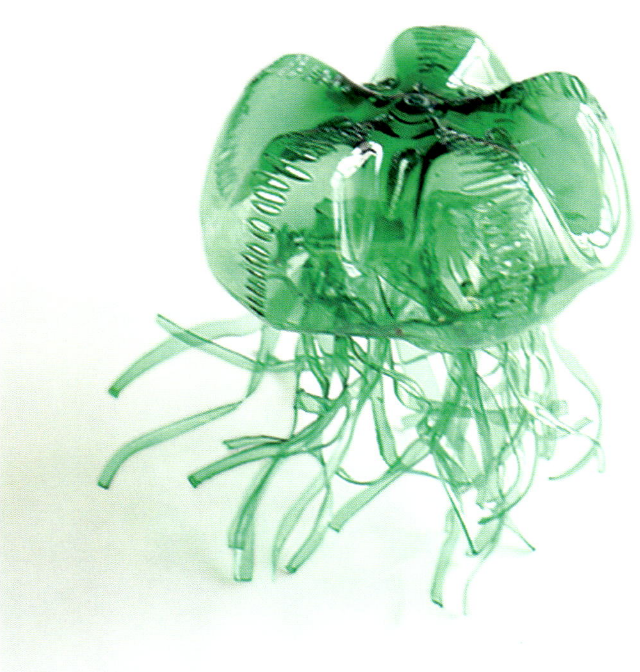

Miwa Koizumi
PET's
2005
PET (polyethylene terephthalate) San Pellegrino bottle
24 x 14 x 28" (61 x 35.6 x 71.1 cm)
Collection of the artist
PHOTO: MIWA KOIZUMI

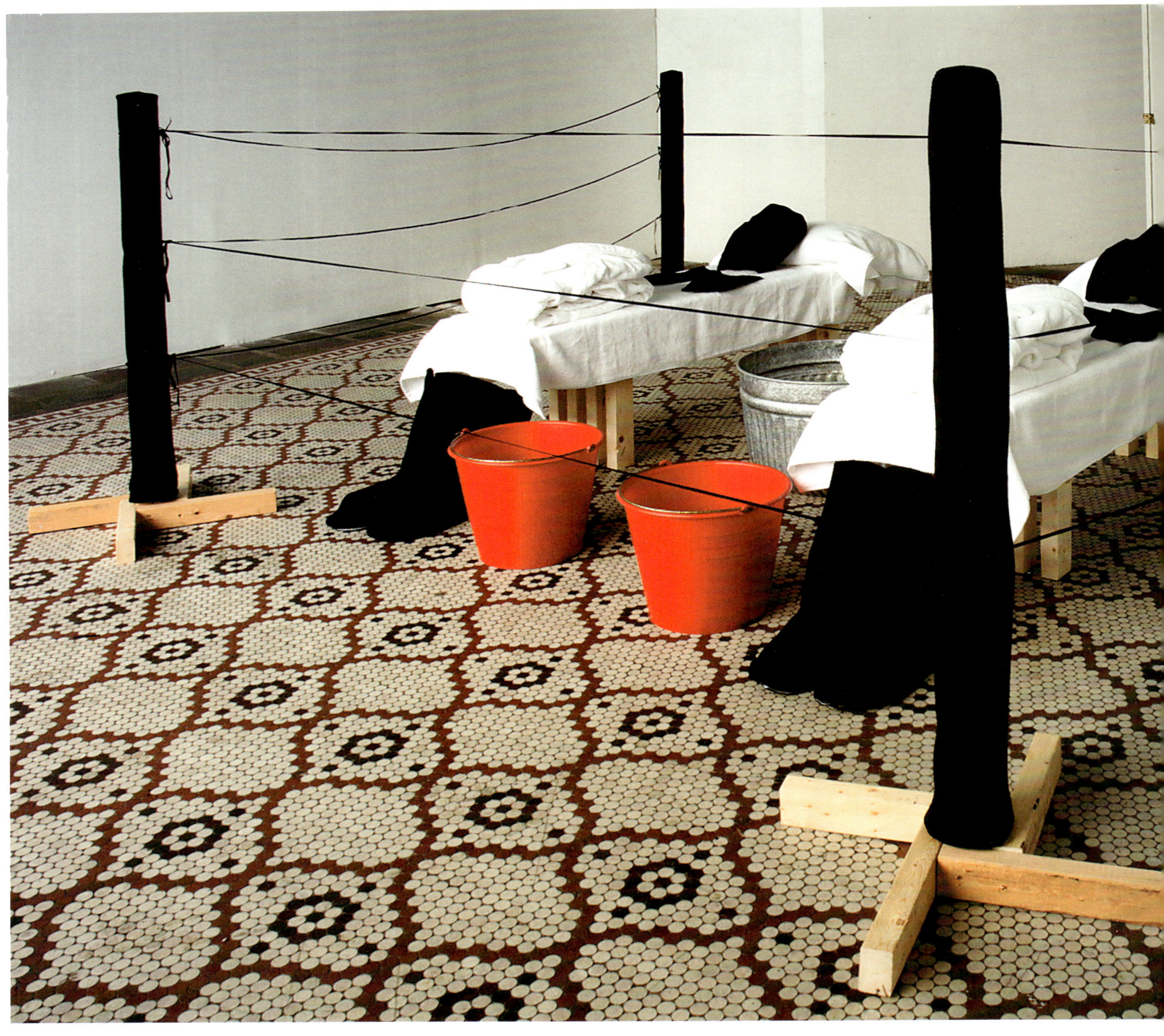

PLATE 12.3

Miwa Koizumi
SuperSpa
2006
Performance/installation; masks, gloves, boots, bathrobes, white towels,
ring, benches, buckets, recorded voice, ambient music, foodstuffs
Ring: approx. 10 x 10' (3 x 3 m)
Collection of the artist

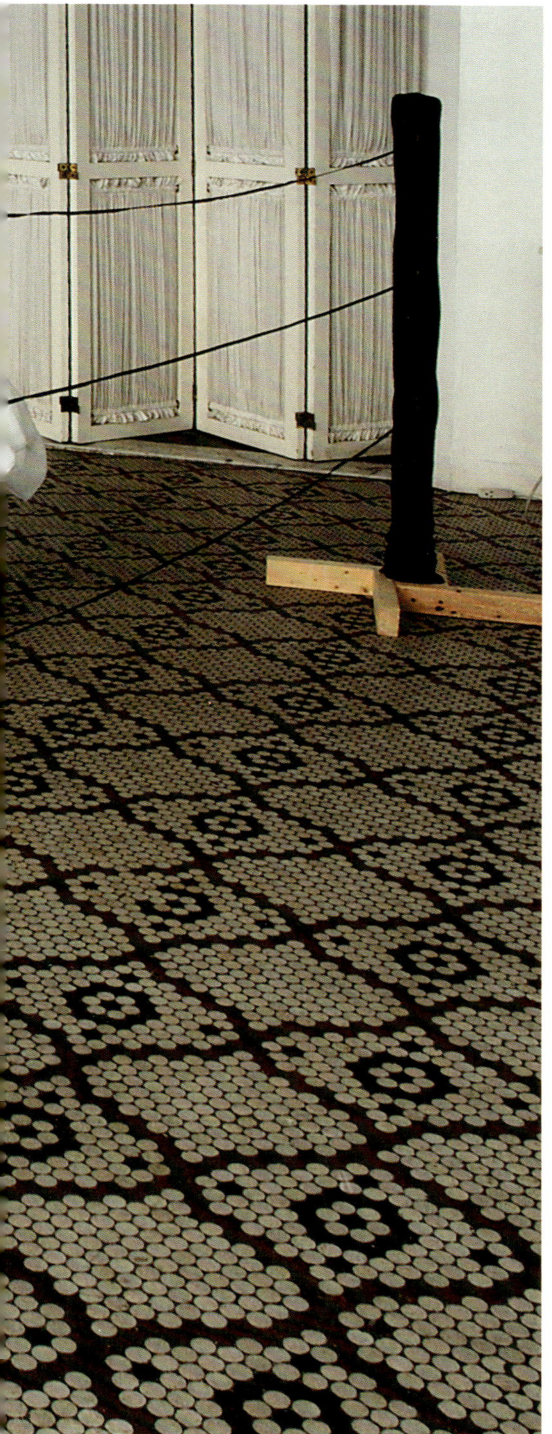

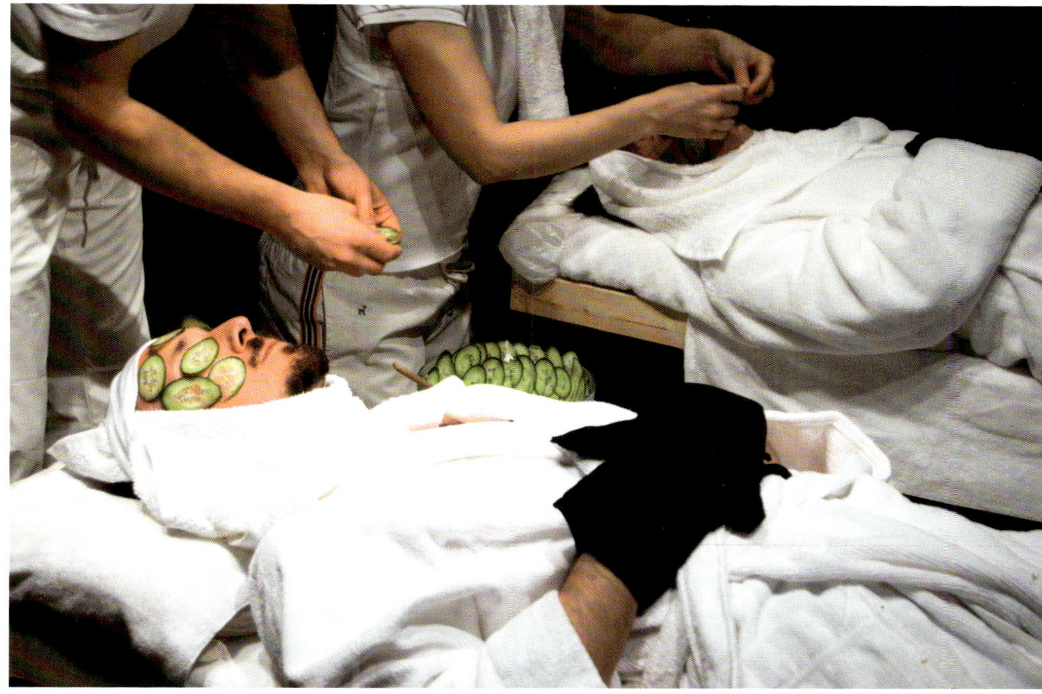

When and how did you first realize that you wanted to be an artist?

MK: When I was young I dreamed of being many things: pianist, composer, dancer, poet, designer, photographer, journalist, ethnologist, biologist, chef. So I wound up pursuing the only career that lets me do all these things.

Why did you decide to leave Japan?

MK: When I finished my BA in Japan, the Japanese economy was really strong, Japan was investing in culture.... I felt like I could do anything. I had no fear. I decided to go to France to learn contemporary art. I felt that Paris, geographically at least, was more in the center of the world than Japan and France of course has a rich culture of food. The French seemed to nurture and respect individuality. And France has borders with many other European countries. Coming from an island, I was fascinated by the idea of many countries and cultures sharing the same land.

Why did you choose New York as your ultimate destination?

MK: I am so happy to observe how all the world's cultures clash in New York City. It is not a homogeneous culture like Japan. Everyone is free to do and think and eat what they want.

What was your first impression of New York City?

MK: For one week, I ate tortilla chips from a huge, huge bag and got meals from the all-you-can-eat counters in delis where I did not have to read a menu or ask for anything.

Do you ever regret leaving Japan?

MK: No. If I didn't leave I couldn't find out myself.

In this age of globalism, do you consider yourself to be a Japanese artist, an American artist, an international artist, or a hybrid of all three?

MK: I don't know. I am Miwa. I like to make interesting things, and create events which hopefully people will remember. The rest is for someone else to figure out.

PLATE 12.4

Miwa Koizumi
Third Treatment: Rest in Peace Cucumber and Yogurt Facial from *SuperSpa*
2006
Performance/installation
Collection of the artist
PHOTO: MARCO SCOFFIER

13 YUMI KŌRI

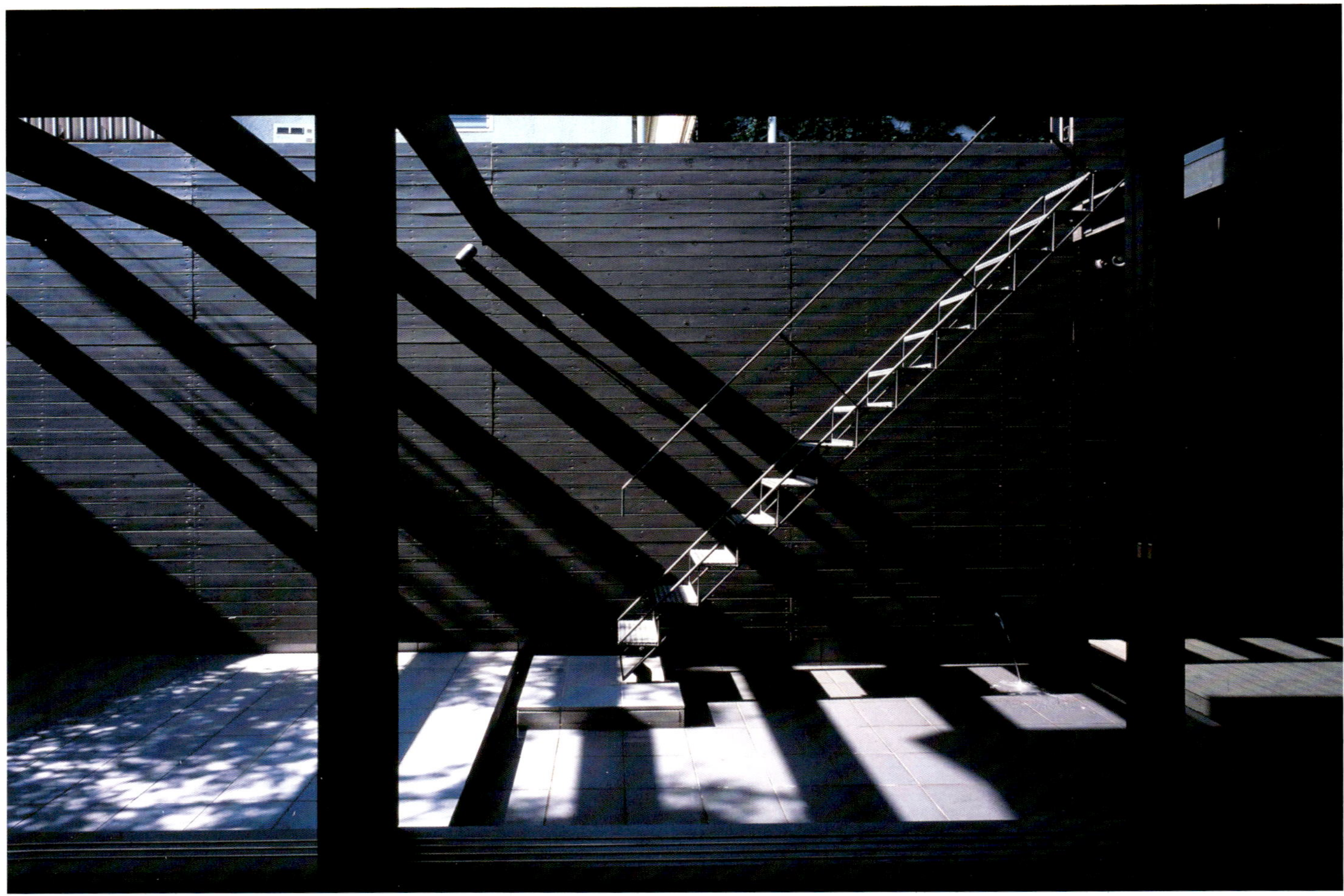

Yumi Kōri Builds with Light
YASUFUMI NAKAMORI

Using the ephemeral and transcendental qualities of light, architect-artist Yumi Kōri affects the way we see and feel the world. Her art installations and architecture challenge our conventional sense of space and the relationship of our physical "self" to the space around us.

Having studied architecture both in Japan and the U.S., Kōri established the architects' office Studio MYU in Tokyo with her partner Endō Toshiya in 1991. She has since designed many residences and buildings in Japan. *House of Shadows* (2002) that she designed in Musashino, on the outskirts of Tokyo, was highly commended and received the prestigious London-based AR Award for Emerging Architecture in 2002 (Pl. 13.1). She wrote on this house: "I aspired to 'vanish' architecture by using 'shadows' and 'corridors.' Shadows eclipse the materiality of architecture…. Shadows erode architecture." A multitude of shifting shadows in and around the house resonate with Tanizaki Jun'ichirō's influential essay "In Praise of Shadows" (In'ei raisan), which embraces the richness of shadows and the infinite nature of darkness.

For Kōri, light and shadow imply the passage of time, induce human activities, and deconstruct and construct space, as demonstrated in her installation project at Maison Hermès Forum in the commercial district of Ginza in Tokyo in 2002 (Pl. 13.3). The work was titled *Panta Rhei*, or "all things are in constant flux," an axiom of the ancient Greek philosopher Heraclitus. It simply consisted of eleven tons of gravel named *Shirakawa jari* (the type used at the Zen temple Ryōanji in Kyoto) raked in concentric circles around structural steel columns of the building. The whole scene, reminiscent of the *karesansui*-style sand garden, can be viewed from a wooden deck also created by the artist. The gravel becomes the medium of light and shadow, reflecting the sunlight that enters through the gallery's glass block walls and enabling the viewer to see the changing color of light, as the day goes by. At night, the

---

PLATE 13.1

Yumi Kōri
House of Shadows (view of courtyard from living room)
2002
Private two-story passive-solar house in Musashino, Tokyo

PLATE 13.2

Yumi Kōri (with sound by Bernhard Gal)
Defragmentation/red (installation view at Prenzlaure Berg, Berlin)
2000
Site-specific installation at an underground water reservoir; light bulbs, film, acrylic cylinders, water
Reservoir: diameter 131' 2 ¾" (40 m)

artificial light of nearby neon signs adds color to the otherwise monochromatic space, which is illuminated by white fluorescent tubes installed beneath the viewing deck.

Kōri deems light a medium for transcending the measurable world to a sensual, visceral, and subliminal experience. In *Defragmentation/red* (2000), an installation in Prenzlauer Berg, Berlin, Kōri guided the visitor through the dark, concentric, labyrinthine corridors in a 19th-century underground water reservoir by strategically installing vertical red light bars (Pl. 13.2). Sounds composed by sound artist Bernhard Gal and human echoes permeated the space. The light bars were spaced to lure visitors on to explore the tunnel-like passage. The experience was at once disorienting and mesmerizing, as though time had stopped. This installation, which won another AR Award for Emerging Architecture in 2001, and *House of Shadows* marked points of departure for Kōri's more recent light-based installations. Since these projects, she has worked as an artist as much as an architect. Her dual career development, as a female architect in Japan's male-dominated architecture world, and simultaneously as an artist, is unique, perhaps made possible by her conscious selection of the U.S. and Europe as her main artistic venues.

The importance of sound in Kōri's art derives from the artist's comparison of physical "space" to the "pause" between sounds, both of which are expressed by the Japanese word *ma*. She argues that both architecture and music create space and environment and they have to be experienced over time. For her, in music, the space between sounds is as important as the sound itself, as in architecture, the space between walls is as important as the built work itself. In her installation art, she desires to bring these two types of *ma* into a dialogue and create a hybrid space.

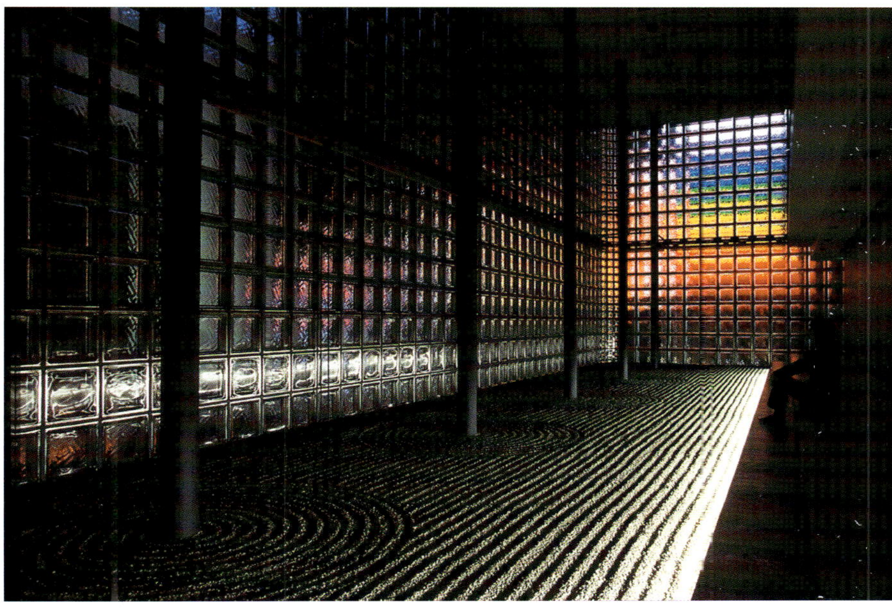

The installation *Shinkai* (meaning "deep sea") created for *Making a Home* is an example of such hybridity (Pl. 13.4). Kōri created the first version of this work for her 2006 solo exhibition at the Ise Cultural Foundation Gallery in New York. Here, the gallery's white cube is transformed into a space filled with tiny red lights which seemingly float in space. A mixture of ambient sounds of the site and water sounds, produced in collaboration with Gal, creates a deep ocean effect. The lights seem like myriad squiggling neon tadpoles suspended in water. In reality, she uses only seven or eight lights, which reflect on the surface of thousands of clear balloons that fill the gallery. Kōri thus invites the audience to physically engage with the otherworldly transformed space and with their own changing reactions within it.

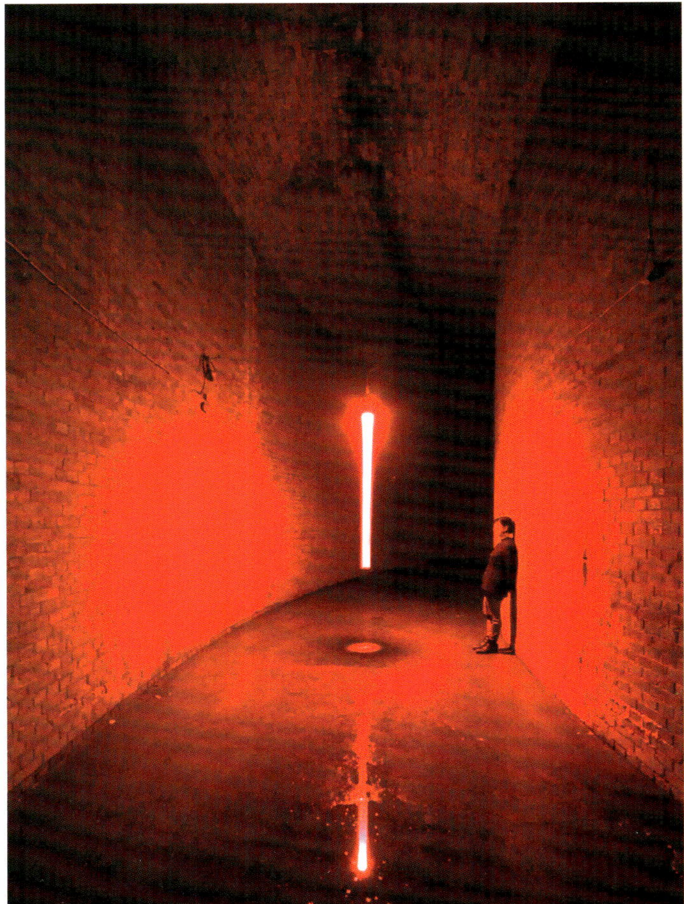

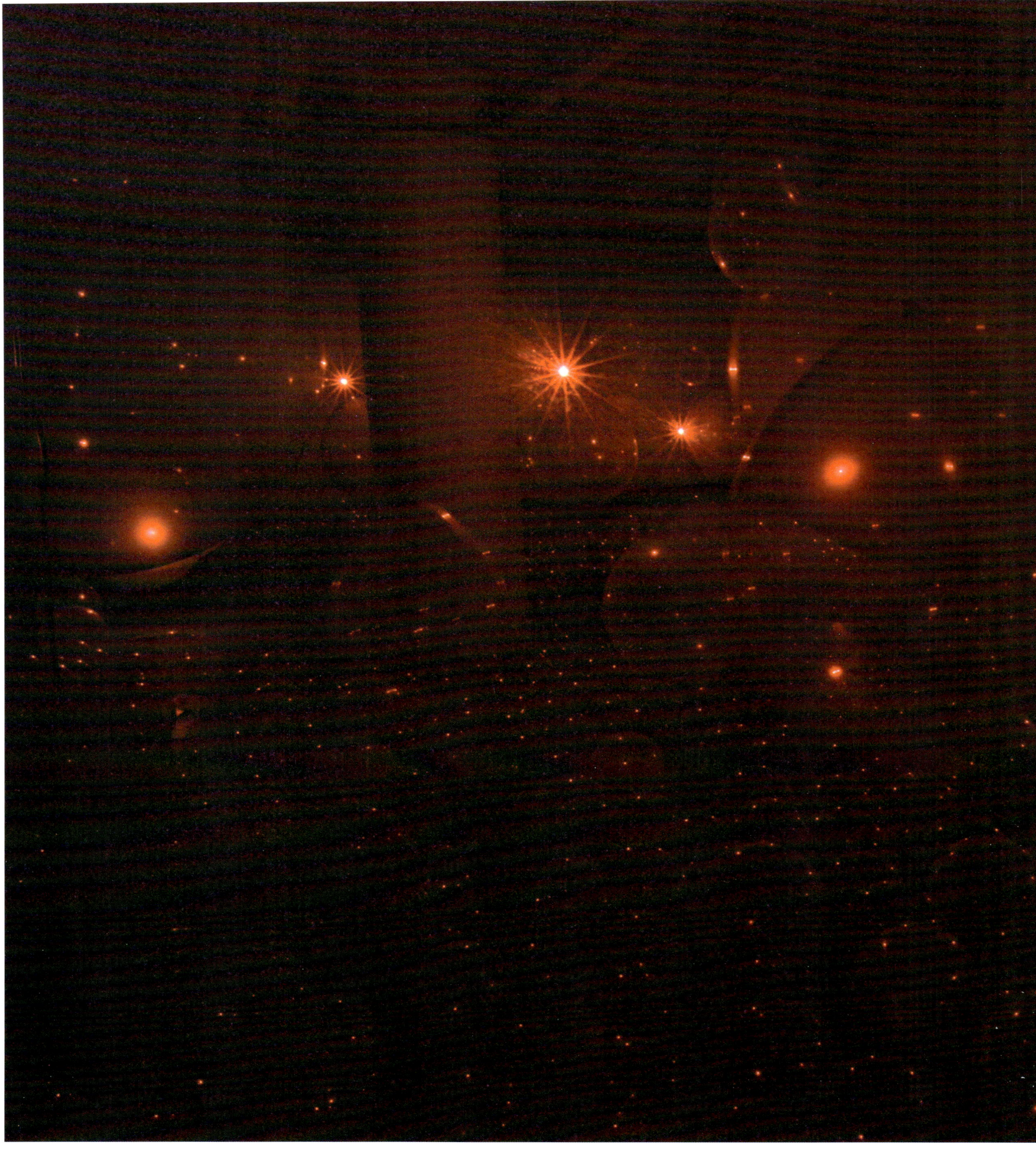

PLATE 13.4

Yumi Kôri (with sound by Bernhard Gal)
Shinkai (installation view at Ise Cultural Foundation Gallery, New York)
2006
Balloons, light bulbs, plywood platform, speakers, DVD player
Dimensions variable
Courtesy of the artist

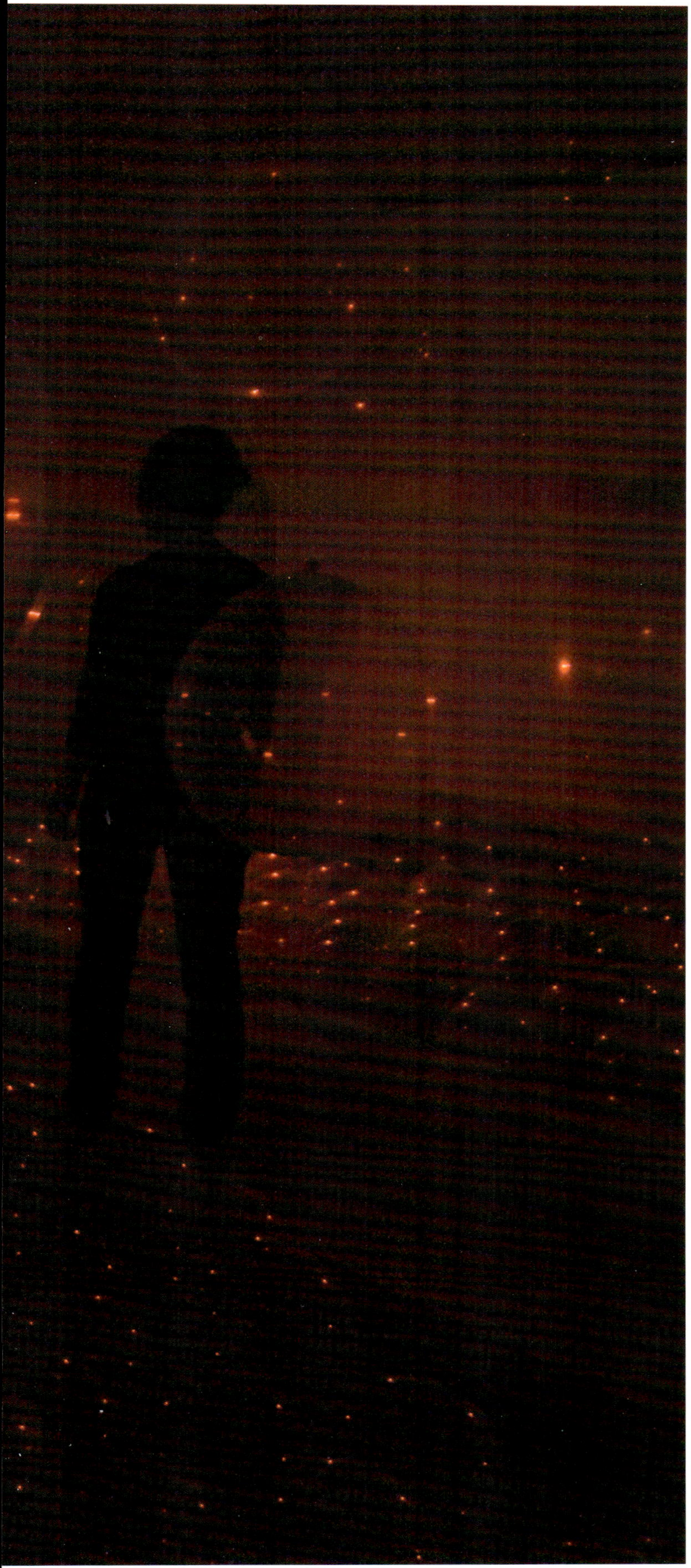

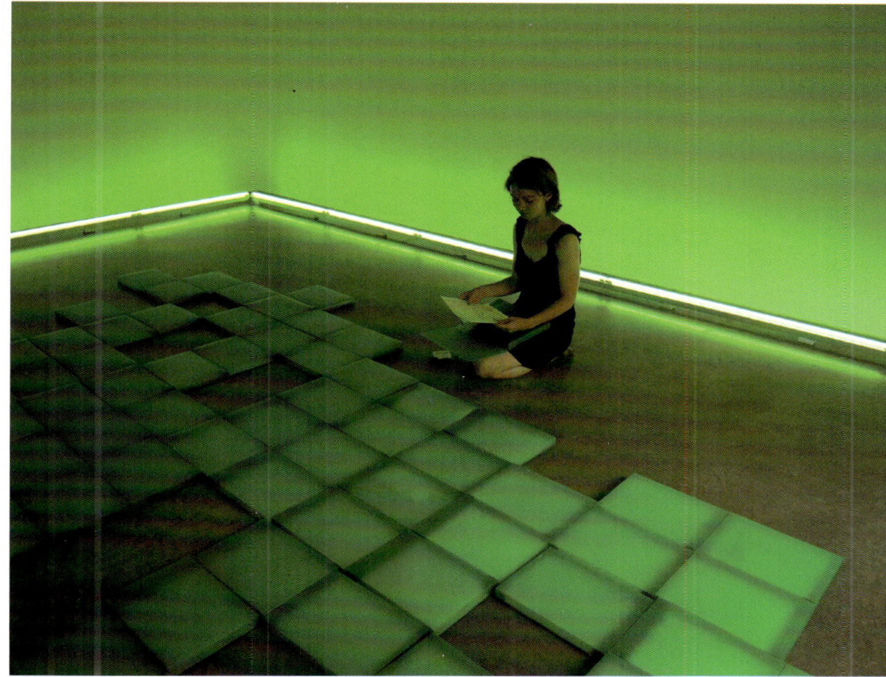

What was your first impression of New York City?

YK: In 1989, after traveling to Europe for three months, I flew from Rome to New York. It was my first visit but I felt I was returning to my hometown. I was very comfortable, and I felt that I would live in New York some day.

Did you have any interactions with other artists or supporters that were especially beneficial to you and your work?

YK: I have found my friendship with artist Phill Niblock the most important. Phill, who runs the organization called Experimental Intermedia, began his career as a photographer, and now is engaged in sound art and video installation. His work influenced the way I think of the interactive quality of sound and space. In his loft, where he hosts great artists from all over the world, I have met numerous really wonderful artists.

Do you ever regret leaving Japan?

YK: These days, I believe the word "living" has adopted an entirely new meaning. With a fast Internet connection, I can "live" in multiple places. While I "live" in New York, I "live" in Japan and other countries. Moreover, since I always work site-specifically, I work with the local people and the local place. I feel that I live in the site where I work. For example, last year I "lived" in Switzerland by participating in an artist-in-residence program. I also "lived" in Brazil for the preparation of my art installation. I am constantly traveling: I "live" in the cities I stay in.

Translated by Yasufumi Nakamori

PLATE 13.5

Yumi Kōri
Green Box/VT (installation view at *Human = Nature*, Victoria Anstead Firehouse Gallery, Burlington, Vt.)
2002/2006
Polypropylene, paper, seamless line lamps, automatic dimmer, objects provided by participants (in boxes)
Each box: 9 x 12 ½ x 1 ¼" (22.9 x 31.8 x 3.2 cm)
Courtesy of the artist
PHOTO: YUMI KŌRI

14 NOBUHO NAGASAWA

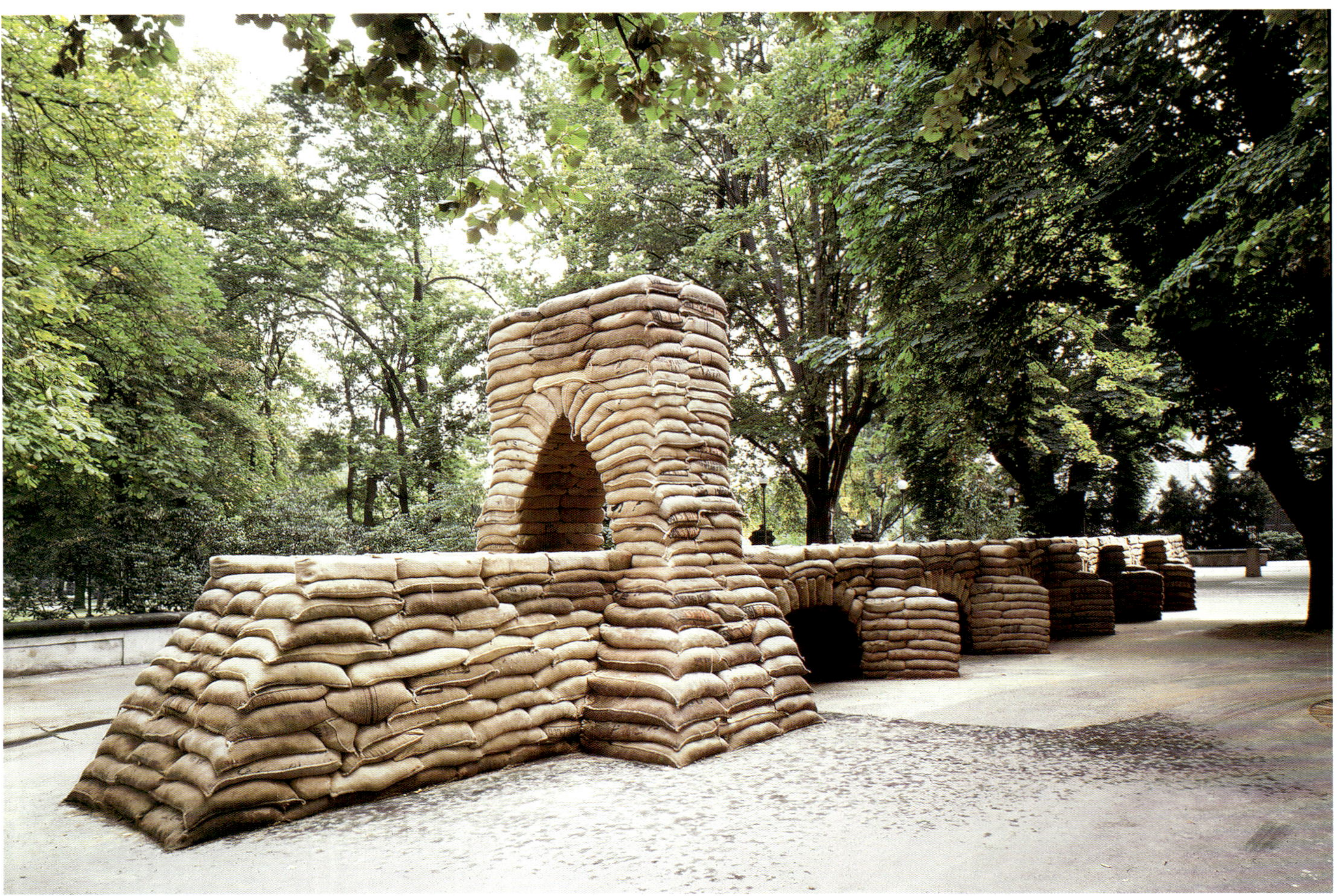

Planting Minefields of Engagement as Far as the Mind Can See
ERIC C. SHINER

An artist who travels the world often and vigorously, a wanderer who soaks in the essence of cultures and peoples, mindsets and values: such is Nobuho Nagasawa, whose exhibitions span Europe, the Middle East, Asia, and the United States. Her work is informed not only by local conditions where she creates, but also by the hybrid cultural identity that she has developed on her endless journeys. She is an installation artist, a social scientist, and an ardent observer of politics, religion, and the human condition; a nomad who plants peaceful minefields of social engagement across the battlefield of contemporary culture.

Nagasawa left Japan when she was 18 to attend the Art Academy in the Netherlands and earned her MFA at Hochschule der Künste in Berlin. There, she started to engage with the local history and political climate of Cold War Berlin, still divided by the Wall. Her first major earthwork, *Noyaki* (literally, "field burning"), took place in the countryside of Japan in 1984, after

she took the Trans-Siberian Railroad across the continent from Berlin to Beijing, and returned to Japan and back by herself. Inspired by the sight of the Great Wall of China vanishing into the desert, she built a sculpture of a wall that would gradually return to dust, unlike the Berlin Wall. After the construction, she lit the sculpture on fire for a week. It whistled in the wind and allegorized the futility of using earth to divide humanity and nature in one graceful, yet fiery, action (Pl. 14.2).

In 1985, Nagasawa created *Navel of the Earth* in West Berlin by excavating earth in a bomb site, the ruin of a Jewish synagogue. She built a fire each day to purify the earth and the atrocities that had befallen the city in prior decades. The following spring, new life arose from the site of destruction and disuse. It was an action of resistance, an ode to the conflict of the past. It was also a statement of power, Nagasawa becoming handler of the flame; the archaeologist-cum-artist who, with her own hands, dug deep

PLATE 14.1

Nobuho Nagasawa
Where are you going? Where are you from?
1992
Site-specific work at The Royal Garden of
the Prague Castle, Prague, Czech Republic;
sandbags, barbed wire
15 x 82 x 15' (4.5 x 25 x 4.5 m)

into Berlin to excavate the past and then set it on fire to let loose a phoenix born from the flames. These seminal works mark the beginning of a journey in which the artist took the elements of earth, air, water, and fire, and inscribed them with meaning close to her soul and the cultures within which they unfolded.

In 1986, Nagasawa was invited to the California Institute of the Arts as a visiting scholar where she studied visual arts, music, and critical theory. By this time, she was undertaking monumental projects; she erected not only massive structures in Prague, Budapest, and Aachen but also built connections with the local community and the history of philosophy, science, aesthetics, and art history that she had researched. In 1993, when Czechoslovakia peacefully split into the Czech and Slovak republics, she constructed a sandbag bridge at the Royal Garden of the Prague Castle with youths from the two nations to "bridge" the communications between them (Pl. 14.1).

Nagasawa traveled to a small coastal town in Denmark in 1995 to realize *Bunker Motel: Emergency Womb*, a project commemorating the 50th anniversary of the end of WWII (Pl. 14.4). Working closely with local children, she installed 500 plaster eggs the size of a human brain in several bunkers built by the Nazis and long abandoned. After the war, the bunkers were often used by local lovers for privacy, and Nagasawa addressed both histories in identifying the spaces as realms of renewal. The eggs and beds furnished with sandbag pillows and blankets, along with the motel signs she mounted on top of several bunkers, turned a military fortification into a life-bringing refuge.

Nagasawa again used the egg motif in the large-scale installation *her render: she gives back naturally what is true in her nature* (Pl. 14.3). First realized at the Sharjah Biennale in United Arab Emirates in 2003, at the start of war in Iraq, the work comprises hundreds of *male* and *female* eggs cast in salt—a life-essential mineral—and a film of running water projected on a bed of rock salt. In Sharjah, the *female eggs* wrapped in women's undergarments (nylon stockings) carried Arabic script describing secrets that Nagasawa's young women collaborators would never dare discuss. The work reveals secrets of the soul using the rejuvenating materials of the earth. Nagasawa again populates a field with mines that, once viewed, explode the intellect and infect the imagination.

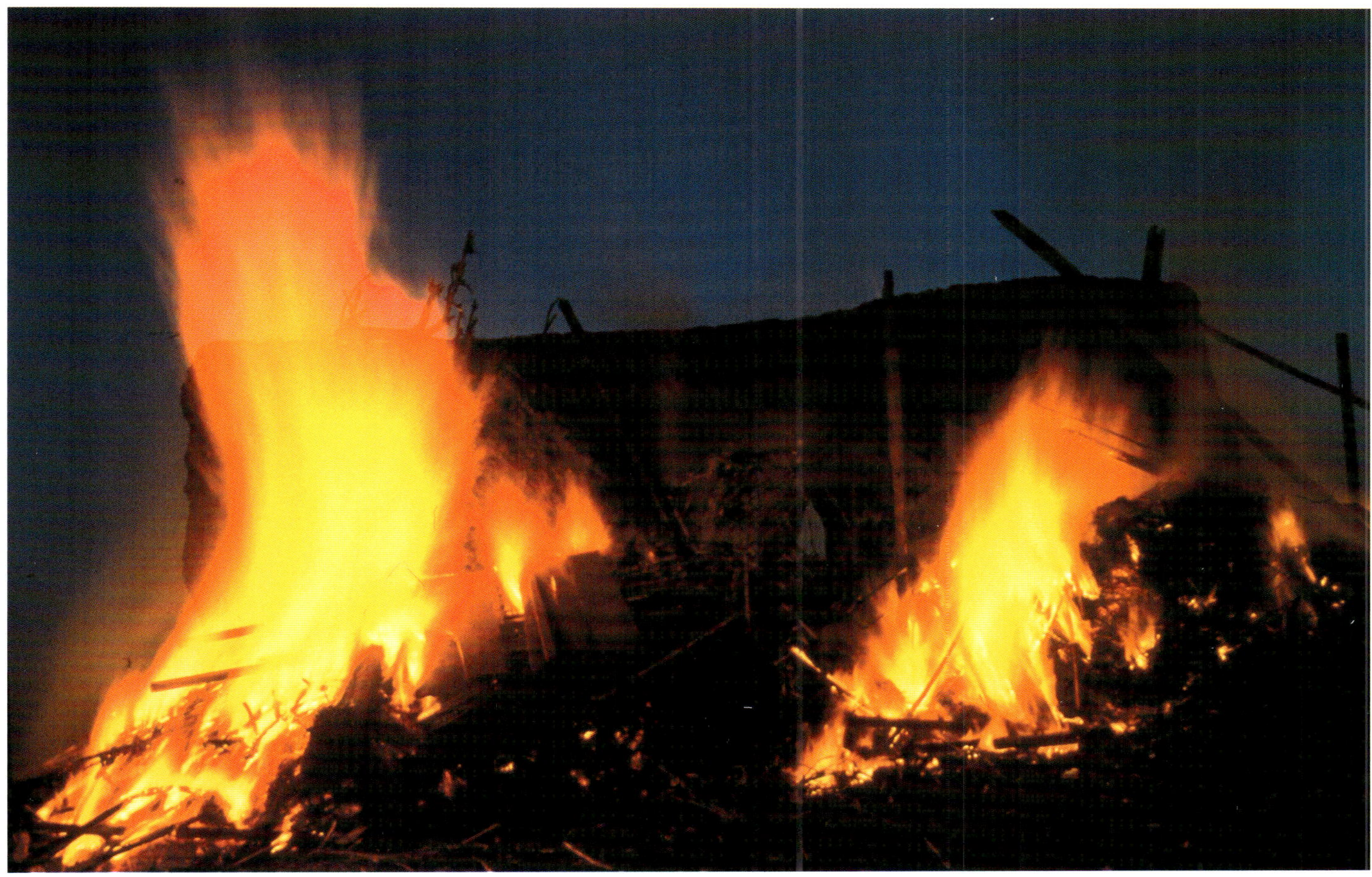

PLATE 14.2

Nobuho Nagasawa
Noyaki
1984
Site-specific work at Tokoname, Japan;
earth, sea water, fire
7 x 17 x 5' (2 x 5.3 x 1.6 m)

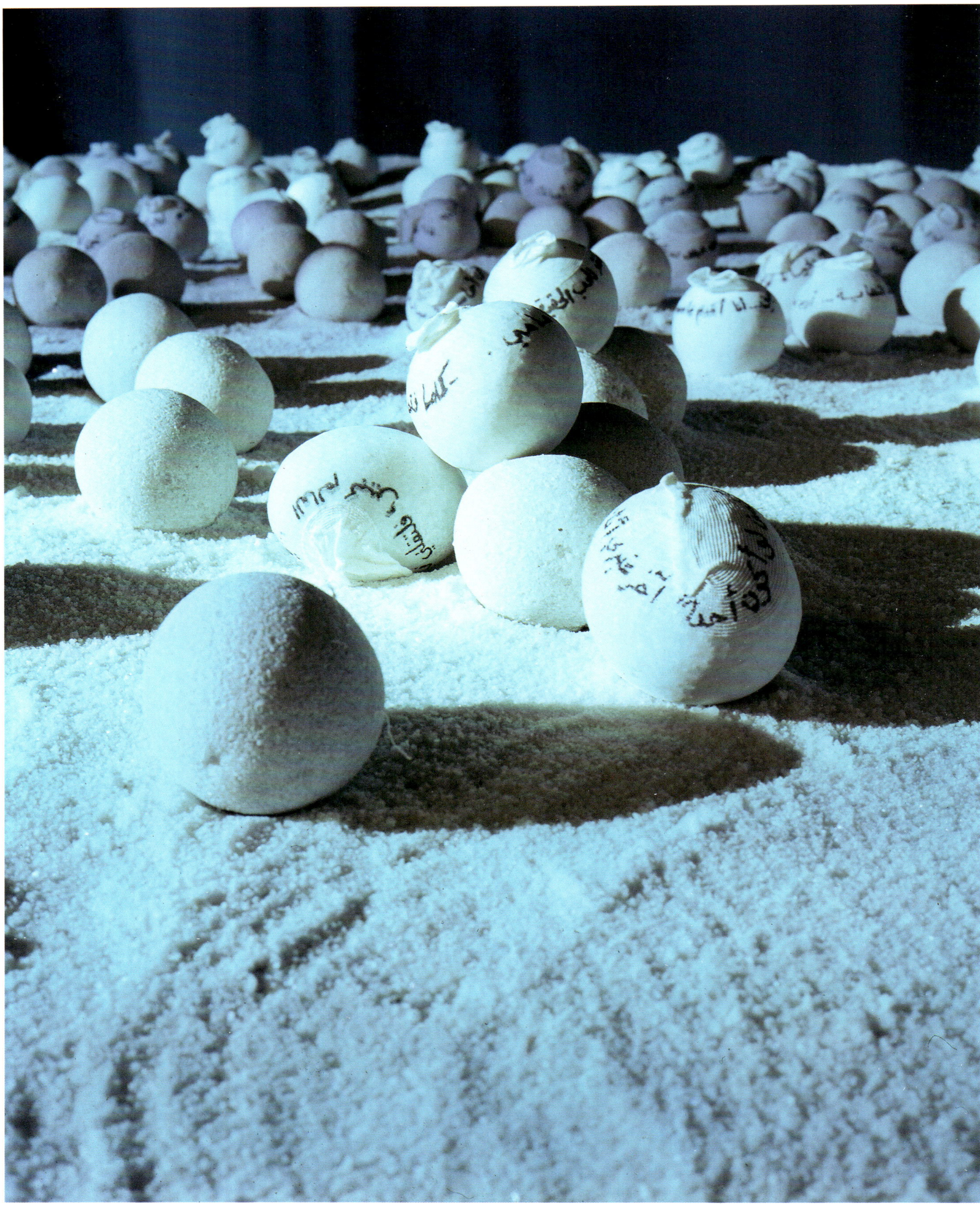

Plate 14.3

Nobuho Nagasawa
her render: she gives back naturally what is true in her nature
(installation view at Sharjah Museum, Sharjah, United Arab Emirates)
2003
Rock salt, nylon stockings, script, film projection
Measurements variable
Collection of the artist
PHOTO: SHIN'ICHI YOKOYAMA

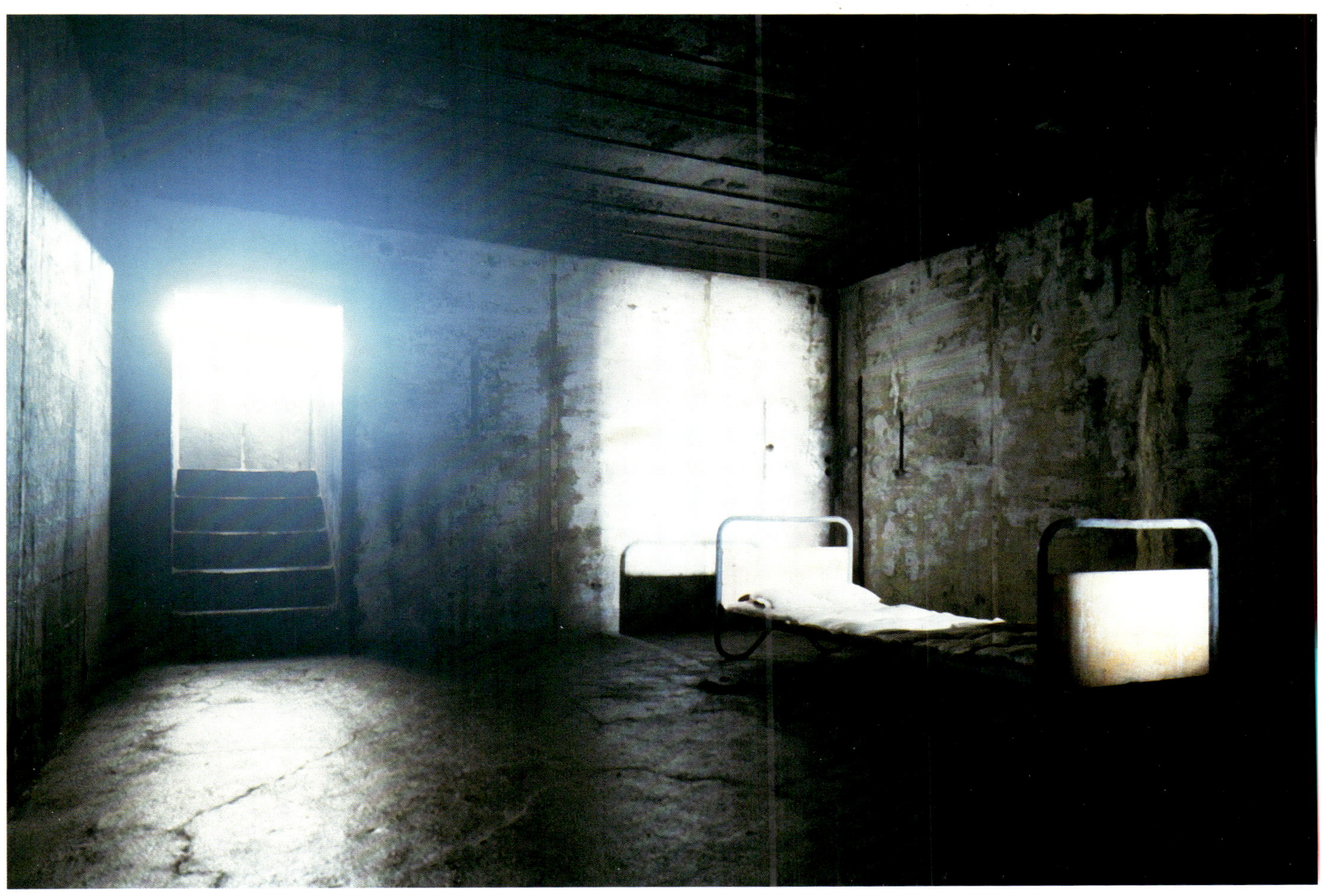

When and how did you first realize that you wanted to be an artist?

NN: When I was 15, I assisted an excavation at an ancient village site and found a prehistoric pottery fragment. This piece had a distinctive rope pattern known as Jōmon, and a finger impression of the person who coiled the raw earth, which left an impression on my palm. Holding this small fragment, I felt as if I was communicating with my ancestor. This was the moment I knew that I wanted to create a "piece of life" with my hands. I still have this ancient piece of clay in my toolbox, and hold it in my hand once in a while.

What was your first impression of New York City?

NN: 9/11 happened within my first weeks of arriving in New York, and my studio was near Ground Zero. In many ways, the new chapter of the 21st century seemed to have started on 9/11.

In this age of globalism, do you consider yourself to be a Japanese artist, an American artist, an international artist, or a hybrid of all three?

NN: I think of myself as a citizen of a planet, who is comfortable to be nomadic. My "home" can be anywhere. All the places I lived in in the past have proven to be important in my life.

I see my artist's identity as inevitably "hybrid"—part sculptor, journalist, poet, architect, and urban designer. Materials and methodology follow upon the necessary diversity of evolving concepts as a project reveals its conditions. I see this process as an *excavation* of meanings that lie hidden within the materials themselves. By revealing personal memories, collective histories, unacknowledged myths, and contradictory issues, I try to open up key social and personal reserves that can galvanize public interaction. My goal is to create artwork that provokes and revives a site and wakes people up to the poetry of place.

PLATE 14.4

Nobuho Nagasawa
Bunker Motel: Emergency Womb
1995
Site-specific installation in Thyborøn, Denmark; steel, sand, sugar, military bags, army cots, plaster, light, candles
Dimensions variable

15 HIROYUKI NAKAMURA

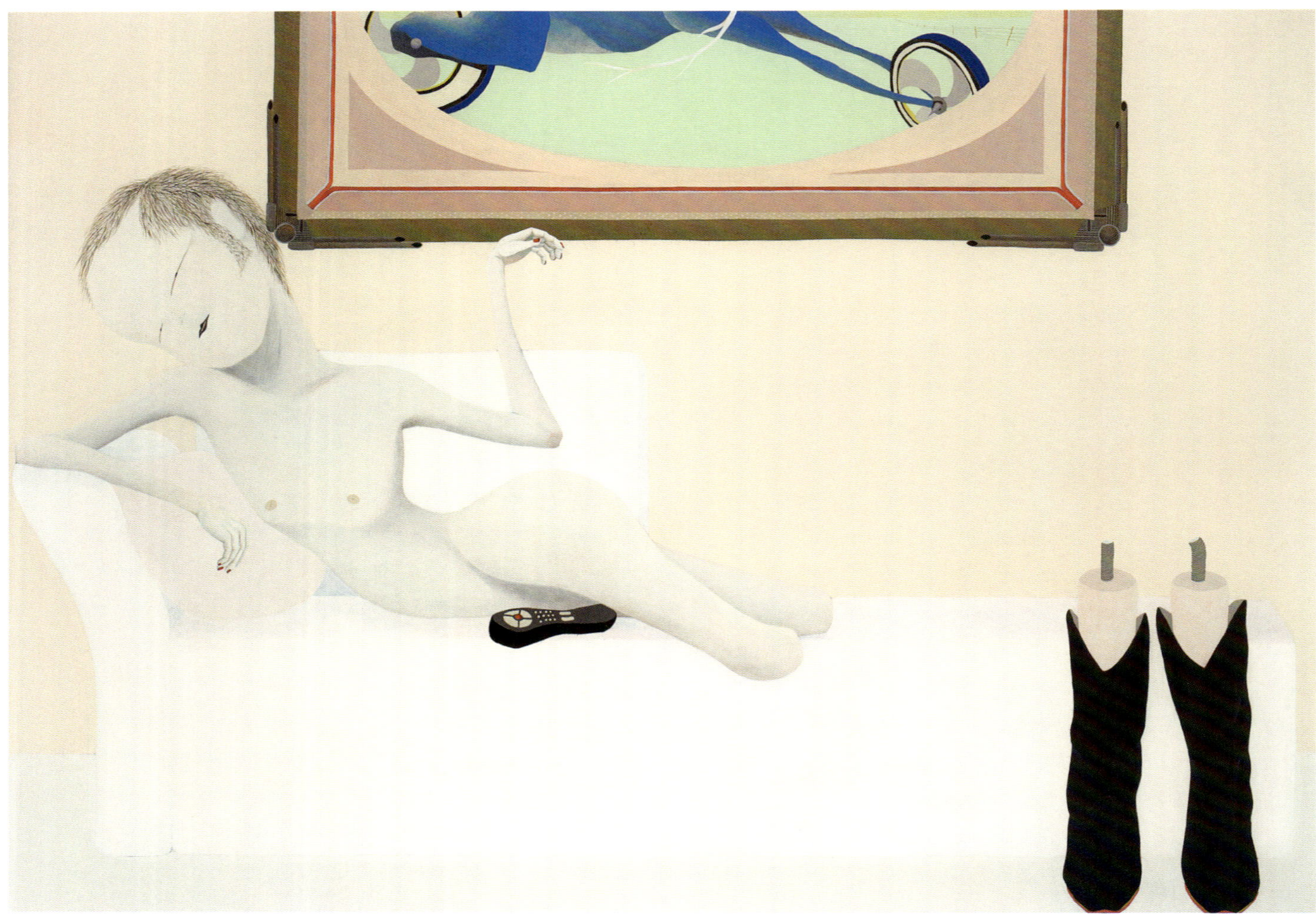

Lonesome Cowboy
ERIC C. SHINER

The Wild West as psychic paradigm played out by haunted and androgynous figures consumed with playing cowboy and their morning ablutions—such sexually charged introspection and experimentation has become the chief project of painter Hiroyuki Nakamura. Trained as a photographer at New York's School of Visual Arts, Nakamura has been influenced by the tropes of photography (framing, snapshot imagery, and tourism photo-as-memento) and has carried those elements across to his visual lexicon in paint. His fixation with the inherent machismo of the American West drives his production, yet he sublimates the masculine bravado of the Marlboro Man by painting pictures of young Asian cowboys much more concerned with shaving their legs, holstering their sex organs, or binding their corsets than with the outward display of manliness so often depicted through the brooding cowboy atop his mighty steed.

From a heterosexual male painter, Nakamura's images are complex and mysterious. An air of homoeroticism fills his work, yet this initial response might be drawn not only from the perceptions the viewer brings to the canvas, but also via the artist's personal examination of his relationship with America and its ideals of manliness and sexuality. Perhaps better positioned as deeply self-reflexive explorations tinged in equal measure with prideful boasting and lack of self-confidence, Nakamura's paintings expose the absurdity of gender roles while at the same time referencing his own maturation process on American soil.

Coming to the United States with his parents at the age of 11, Nakamura attended a Japanese expat junior high school in Chicago, and then an American public high school for one year before he decided not to return to Japan with his family, but to attend a military academy. At the age of 16, Nakamura found himself in the

PLATE 15.1

Hiroyuki Nakamura
everybody loves remotes and detachable penises, and so does a cowboy—LANDMINE JUNKIE is gonna hit another head
2007
Acrylic on canvas
36 x 50" (91.4 x 127 cm)
Collection of Ann Schaffer, South Orange, N.J.;
courtesy Mehr Gallery, New York

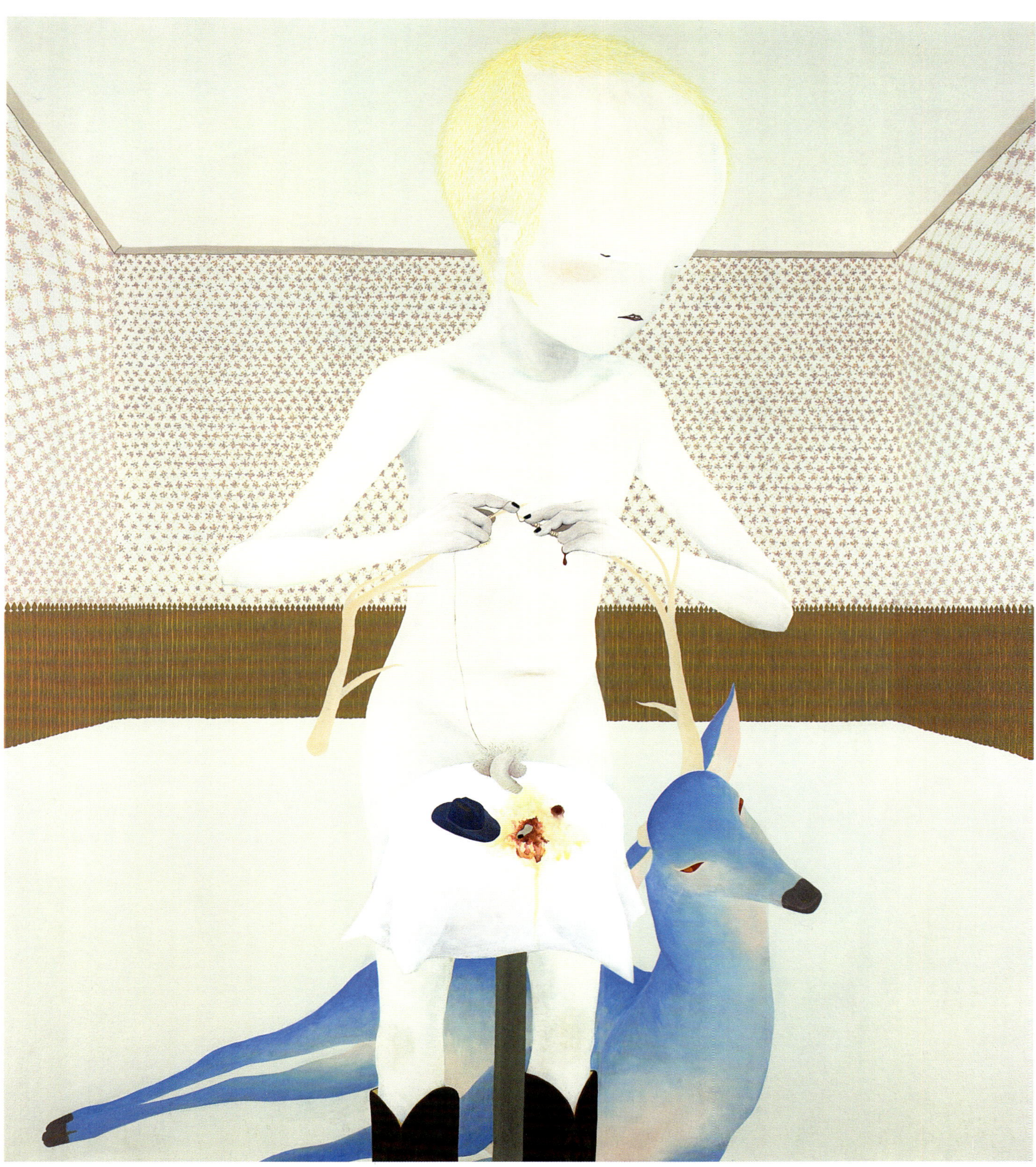

PLATE 15.2

Hiroyuki Nakamura
sweet cowboy knitter
2007
Acrylic on canvas
42 x 37'' (106.7 x 94 cm)
Collection of the artist;
courtesy Mehr Gallery, New York
PHOTO: HIROYUKI NAKAMURA

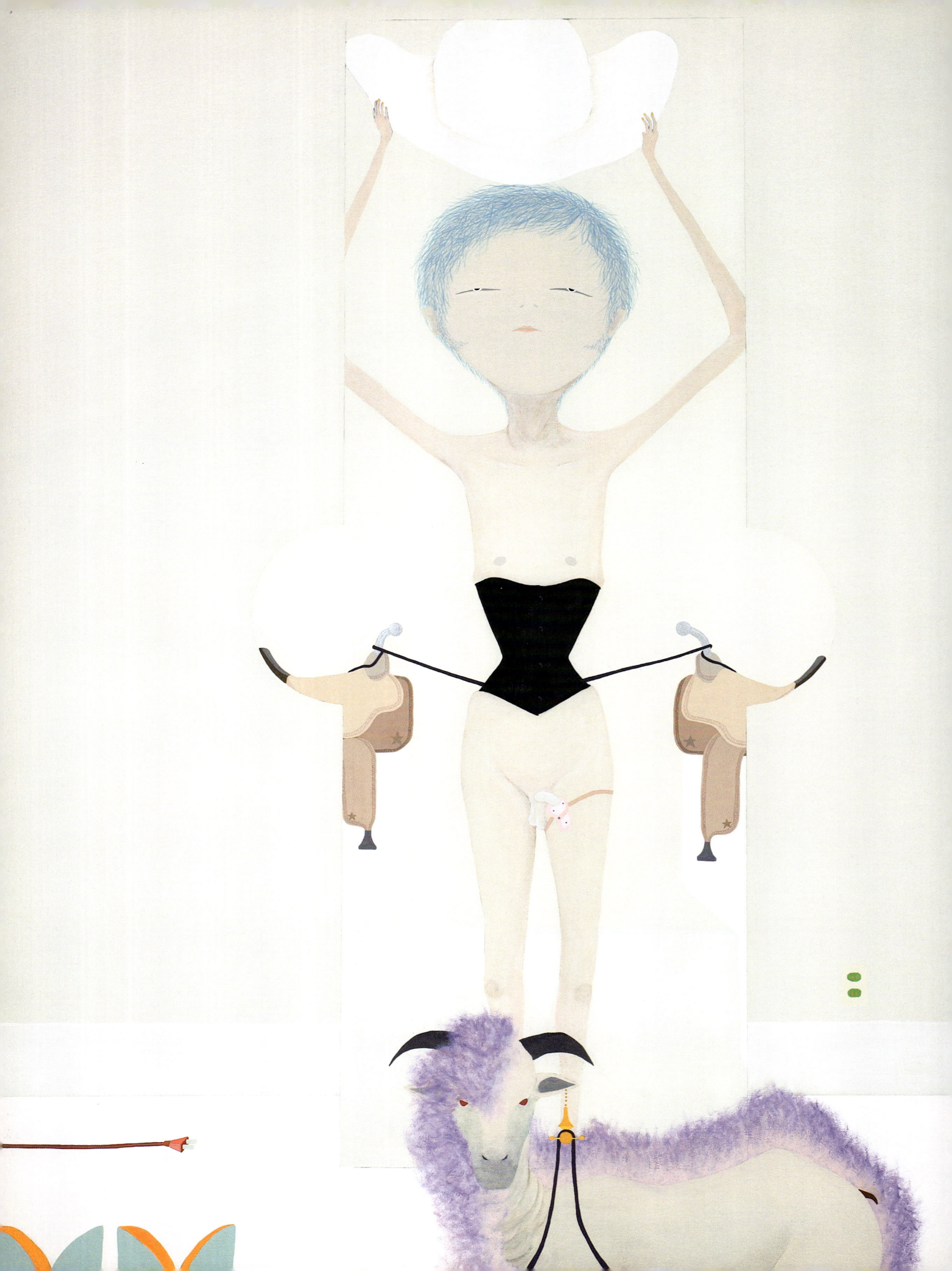

epicenter of teenage testosterone, and the rituals of the academy—
uniform, weaponry, pomp and circumstance—that he encountered
there provide the basic building blocks from which he constructs
his visual narrative. His ambiguous cowboys are no doubt self-
portraits of a young man thrown into a hyper-masculine world and
the experiences he had there. As they prepare for the world beyond
the safe interiors in which they preen and play, Nakamura's figures
try on the socially constructed trappings of Western valor and take
them off again to expose their inner nature. They prove that gender
coding rests on external elements, worn and removed at will.

The underlying ambiguity of gender and sexuality in Nakamura's
work is further displayed in images of male legs shaved in the outline
of cowboy boots, which, once put on, would hide the hairless skin
beneath. Other works see naked cowboys gathered in a group
querying a pile of empty boots on the floor before them. Are they
simply utilitarian protection for the foot or meaning-laden social
constructs best avoided? In another painting, a single waif stands
naked save for his boots and requisite cowboy hat; these are the
main ciphers of masculinity it seems—to wear them is to be a man.

Nakamura further complicates the sexual conundrum in his
paintings through the frequent application of breasts and penises
in places they don't belong. One cowboy nurses himself from his
own ample bosom, while another cowboy rides a mystical beast
with breasts for the saddle horn and a penis for a tail. Once again,
Nakamura's cowboys conflate perceptions of sexual normativity
in favor of alternate realities and unbridled fantasy. They are on
a mission of self-examination through experimentation. Their
cowboy hats, holsters, and boots are costumes through which
they perform masculinity; their shaved legs and interest in beauty
products point to so-called feminine pursuits. Nakamura blends
these socially constructed markers of sexuality into his paintings to
challenge stereotypes of all variety and in so doing comes to terms
with his own skin, covered as it once was with the coded costume
of a military academy uniform.

The processes of cleansing, primping, and dressing depicted
in Nakamura's paintings represent the artist's own identity-
construction in the environs of the American military academy,
and perhaps beyond. His works become deeply personal studies
infused with play, pensiveness, angst, and discomfort. They capture
the essence of not fitting in—the universal feeling of not belonging
familiar to us all.

HN: It is a bit silly, but most likely the closest thing was when I
realized that I wanted to be Keith Richards playing his telecaster
with open-G tuning while other kids in school were going crazy for
Kurt Cobain. I always wanted to be an individual who thinks like
Bob Dylan, behaves like Keith Richards, is as curious and foreign as
Bjork, is in the body of Ziggy Stardust, and sings with the voice of
Billie Holiday over Tori Amos's sensitively hysteric melody. I actually
never wanted to be an artist and I still don't, but the funny ironic
fact is that I am.

HN: I moved into a tiny New York dormitory room that was
converted from an old hotel in Brooklyn Heights. The thing I
remember is the sight of the Brooklyn Bridge and the World Trade
Center in the misty rain from the Brooklyn Promenade... I couldn't
even see the top half of the WTC because it was in the clouds... and
that says it all about my impression of New York City.

HN: I am a Japanese artist made in the U.S.A. I am always Japanese
as a person and Japan is always in me, however I am American as
an artist. Therefore, I consider myself to be an American artist. I
was totally educated and manufactured as an artist here, not in
Japan, like Toyota is assembling their hybrid cars somewhere in the
Midwest by people of all those different cultural backgrounds.

PLATE 15.3

Hiroyuki Nakamura
100% Pure American Saturated Fat
2006
Acrylic on canvas
43 x 37" (109.2 x 94 cm)
Collection of Jeremy Kost, New York;
courtesy Mehr Gallery, New York
PHOTO: HIROYUKI NAKAMURA

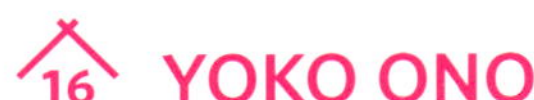 **YOKO ONO**

Woman of the World
KEVIN CONCANNON

Emerging within a New York art world intrigued with Asian philosophy and aesthetics, Yoko Ono established herself as a major player in the nascent Fluxus movement. Inspired to create what would become the first concert and performance series of its kind in Lower Manhattan, Ono rented a loft in 1960 for this purpose. Immediately joined in this venture by La Monte Young, she co-produced the influential Chambers Street series. Operating within a matrix of experimental artists and composers, Ono presented both concerts and visual art exhibitions from the very start of her career. Moving sometimes indistinguishably between art and music, Ono's unique sound and vision has fascinated audiences throughout the world. Her peripatetic family background—a childhood spent traveling back and forth between the United States and Japan—has positioned her notably between Eastern and Western cultures.

Ono had her first solo gallery exhibition at George Maciunas's AG Gallery in New York in July 1961. Some of the works featured written instructions alongside their realizations. *Painting To Be Stepped On* (1961), for example, was a piece of canvas on the floor that viewers could walk over. It referred to Japanese *fumie*, religious pictures on which suspected Christians were required to step, symbolically renouncing their (Western) religious beliefs. Ono redeployed this usage from Japanese history as a challenge to the conservative tradition of easel painting.

In 1962, she returned to Japan, performing and exhibiting at Sōgetsu Art Center in Tokyo. Her exhibition there featured *Instructions for Paintings*, texts hung on the wall and presented not as calligraphy, but as conceptual works to be completed in the minds of viewers. In 1964, she published the first edition of her classic book of instructions, *Grapefruit*. Returning to New York that September, she told friends she was "going home."

It was at her first London exhibition, in 1966, that she met John Lennon, with whom she would regularly collaborate (and ultimately marry). Their *Bed Ins* and *War Is Over!* campaigns of 1969, innovative works spreading their message of peace, brought performance and conceptual art to their widest audiences ever.

Over several years during this period, Ono made a series of works in the mediums of mail art and magazine advertisements, in addition to performing and exhibiting. *Hole To See The Sky*, for example, created as a concept in 1964, was initially realized as a postcard in 1971 and packaged as an insert in her *Fly* LP of that year (Pl. 16.2). (The work will be realized again for *Making a Home*.) The sky pieces, which date to the earliest years of her career, remind us that regardless of national borders, the sky is something we all share—something that connects us.

After a major retrospective at the Everson Museum in Syracuse in 1971, Ono presented a relatively low profile as a visual artist and made a series of inventive pop records. Following Lennon's death in 1980, much of her energy was devoted to managing his legacy. In the late 1980s she re-emerged as a visual artist.

Ono has stated: "All my works are a form of wishing. Keep wishing while you participate." Since 1996, *Wish Trees* have often been featured in Ono's exhibitions (Pl. 16.3). "As a child in Japan, I used to go to a temple and write out a wish on a piece of thin paper and tie it around the branch of a tree. Trees in temple courtyards were always filled with people's wish knots, which looked like white flowers blossoming from afar." In April 2007, her city-wide project called *Imagine Peace*, which included a billboard, was launched in Washington, D.C. *Wish Trees*, part of this campaign, then became part of the Washington D.C. Cherry Blossom Festival, challenging a new generation to use the power of positive wishing to realize the "unfinished work" for which we are all responsible. A new *Wish Tree* is featured in the current exhibition as well.

Ono, however, is not blind to the realities of our present situation. *Freight Train* (1999–2000) consists of an actual German boxcar, approximately 18 feet high and 38 feet long (Pl. 16.1). Through a large hole in its roof and bullet holes that riddle its walls, an intense light from within shines toward the heavens, like so many dematerialized spirits. A haunting soundtrack, concluding with the sound of chirping birds, gives voice to the spirits within. Based on a news story of Mexican immigrants left to die in a boxcar in the desert after being smuggled across the border into Texas, the work suggests another 20th-century tragedy: the Holocaust, specifically the trains that brought victims to the death camps. Ono describes it as "a work of atonement for the injustice and pain we've experienced in this century, expressing resistance, healing, and hope for the future."

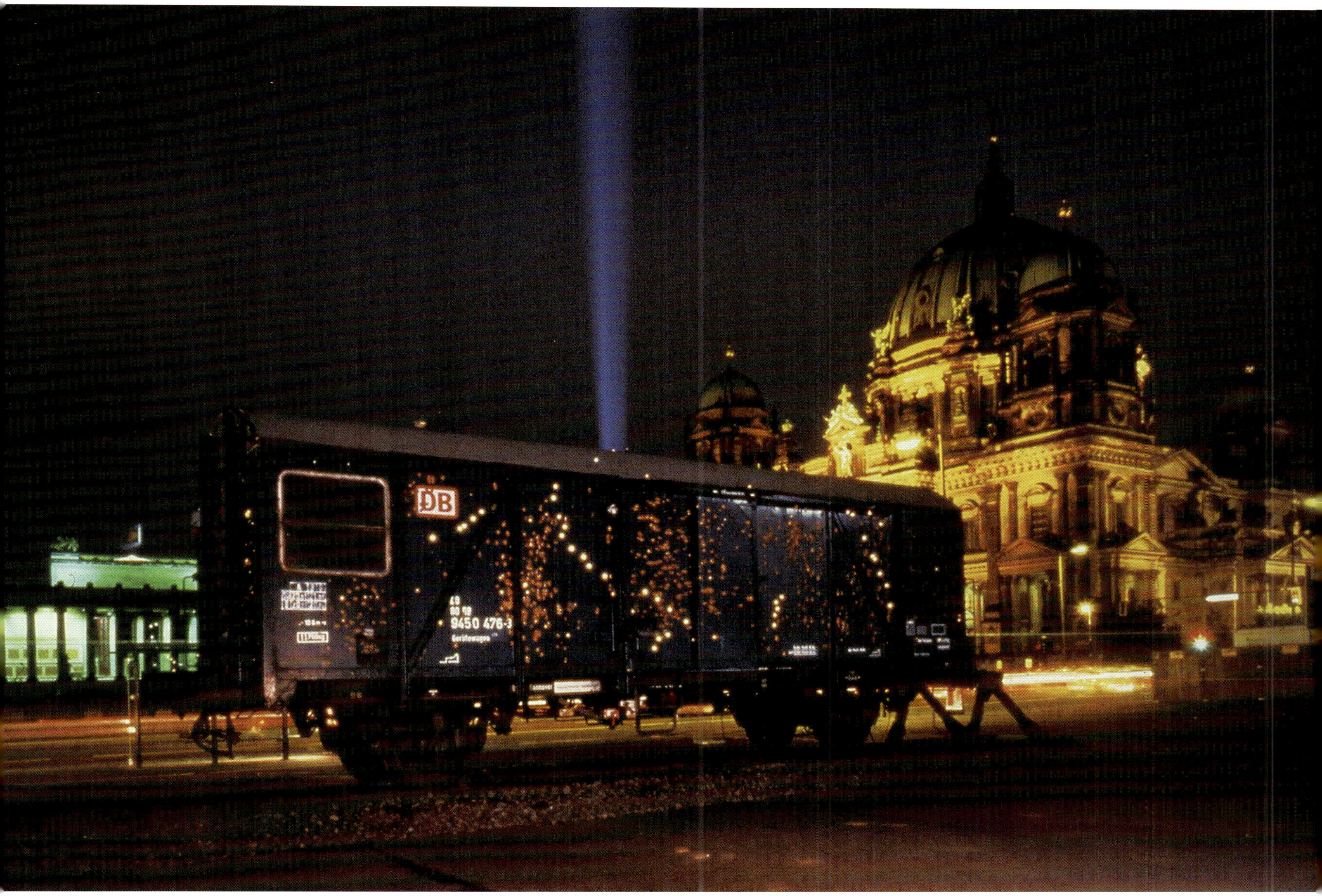

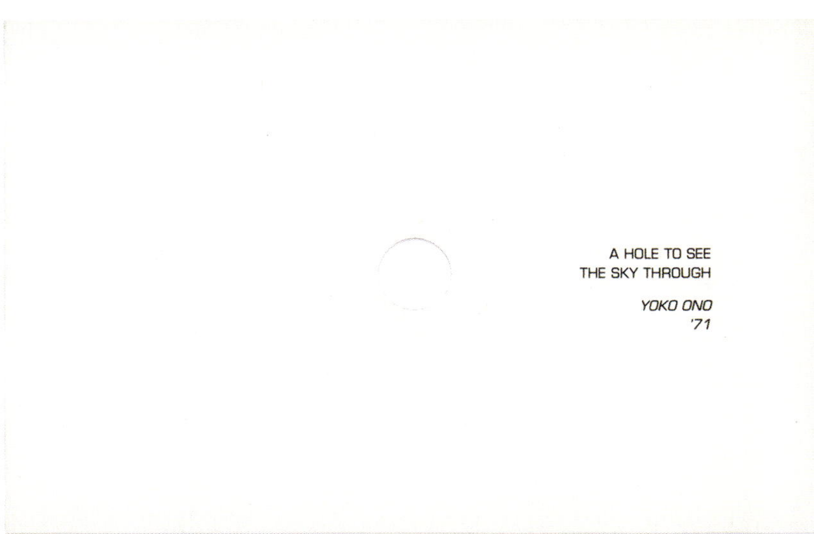

PLATE 16.1

Yoko Ono
Freight Train (installation view in Berlin, Germany)
1999–2000
Freight car with bullet holes, searchlight, engraved
text in German, Japanese, English, and Spanish
Soundtrack: atmospheric music with percussion and
vocals by Yoko Ono; 16 minutes looped
Train: approx. 14 x 38 x 10' (4.15 x 11.6 x 3.15 m)
PHOTO COURTESY OF LENONO PHOTO ARCHIVE

PLATE 16.2

Yoko Ono
A Hole To See The Sky Through
1964/1971
Offset printing on card stock (postcard), die-cut hole
3 11⁄16 x 5 ¾" (9.4 x 14.6 cm)
Courtesy of the artist

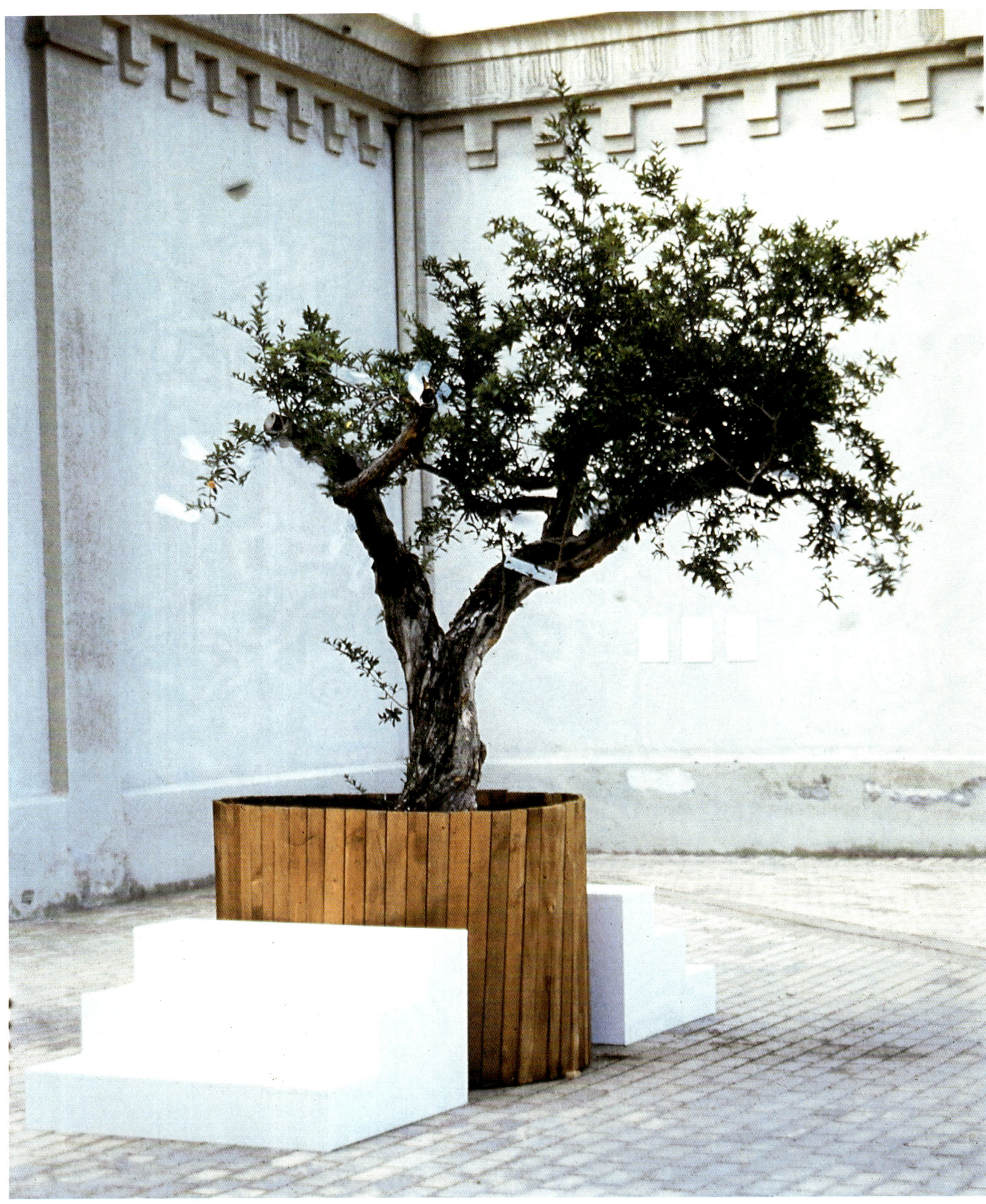

Plate 16.3

Yoko Ono
Wish Tree (installation view at *EnTrance*, 1997)
1996
Living tree, wishes written by viewers on paper tags
with string in pen, printed instructions
Lonja del Pescado, Alicante, Spain
Courtesy of Lenono Photo Archive
PHOTO: MIGUEL ANGEL VALERO

What does New York mean to you?
It's where I gave my blood, sweat and tears. It's my home. Y

17 HIROKI ŌTSUKA

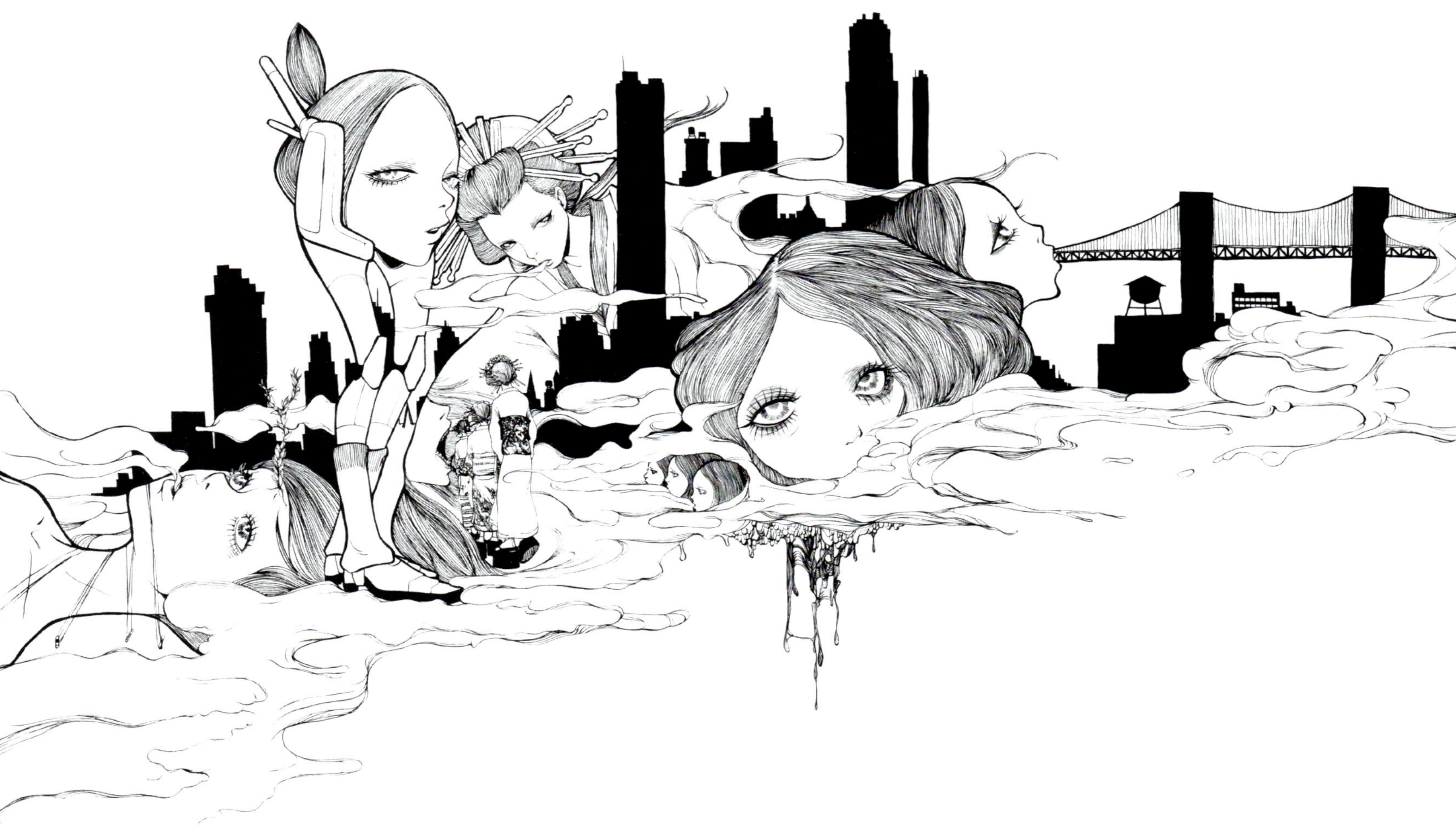

Plate 17.1

H* in the inking
RYAN HOLMBERG

Hiroki Ōtsuka began as a manga author in 1998. Over the course of nine years, he has (sometimes under the pen name Pirontan) created ten volumes of manga, nine in Japanese, one in English (Pl. 17.5). Most of these are pornographic in content, with a majority burlesque in the handling of courting and copulation. Since 2005, however, he has focused on original works of *sumi* ink and acrylic on panel, wall, or paper, all figurative and derived, in style, from manga (Pl. 17.4). These works are largely monochrome with occasional highlights of lurid color. Ōtsuka creates inkings, a graphic practice between drawing and painting. Inking is a noun as it is a verb in its progressive aspect. In concept as in practice, inking is a double portmanteau: it is short for both ink drawing and ink painting. As in drawing, Ōtsuka renders shape and mass through line. As in painting, he obscures underdrawing and deictic marks through the smooth application of an opaque and liquid substance. As such, inking fixates on finish. But as a practice of liquid line, it lends itself

to the figuration of process: inking as progressive liquescence. An artist rooted in porn, Ōtsuka eroticizes this process. He draws out the rising coming in the inking.

Ōtsuka's inkings are at some odds with the conventional erotics of pornographic manga. The genre is typically wet. Its pages are soaked in buckshot globs of semen and puddles of vaginal excretions. The male is a cannon and the female a loaded sponge. Upon this wetness, coupling occurs as an act of violent collision, creating a soggy din of sucking, smacking, pumping, and plunging. In 2005, Ōtsuka captured this soundscape with *Sex Sounds*. Sets of onomatopoeia—from the squishing "zuputs zuputs" to the pounding "DOPYUTS DOPYUTS"—were inked, in Japanese, in one case on a gallery wall, in another on a hanging scroll, each forming a symphony of aggressive wet sex (Pl. 17.3). A related verbal work, *Dialogue* (2005) features a violent/passionate exchange during sex that centers on "No, no" (Pl. 17.2). These works are a parody,

PLATE 17.1

Hiroki Ōtsuka
Evening Calm Union
2007
Sumi ink on paper
15 x 21 ¼" (38 x 54 cm)
Collection of the artist
PHOTO: HIROKI ŌTSUKA

for when Ōtsuka figures sexual intercourse, he tends to avoid brute combustion. For him, erotic coupling, when it is true, entails a silent and sensual coalescing.

The legacy of Art Nouveau is strong in Ōtsuka's inkings, even if the inspiration is indirect. Its spirit lives in his patterning of ornament and limbering of the human figure, and in his devotion to the sensuality of organic form. Ōtsuka eroticizes liquid lines, thematizing the fluid materiality of inking as a process of erotic dissolution. He fills his pictures with ganglia, most often in the form of *rocaille* rivulets of hair, nesting faces in tresses that curl and break in undulations of sexual stimulation, the erotic subject reduced to a nervous system and its facial registration. These faces swoon, however, only rarely. His inkings are only infrequently tableaus of orgasm. They are instead rapt with horror or tranquilized with a quiet deeper than sleep. His inkings, in other words, are filled with death masks, some with lifeless eyes wide open. And likewise, the tapering forms that figure the loss of self in coming draw out at times instead a violent undoing. Organic becoming hardens into elastic synthetics, materials for the masochist to stretch and to bind.

Time is coagulated in all of these liquidities. In this, Ōtsuka's plasmatic forms contain a remnant of the practice in which his inking originated. For time is the root of narrative, and narrative

the basis of manga. In his inkings, fluidity and elasticity maintain a latent narrativity, but a narrativity without sequence, a state without a before or after, without a beginning or an end, but still a state in process. His inkings figure not the pregnant moment that tells of its dramatic preparation and coming conclusion. He fixates on the climax itself, and labors to keep it going, in full intensity. His inkings are no longer, as were once his manga, pornographic. The moments of penetration and orgasmic release, basic to the pornographic narrative, are rejected, in his inkings, in the name of an ideal: continuous coming, autonomous from the act of intercourse.

* A capital H from the Roman alphabet is a common way to represent the Japanese word *etchi* (perversion, perverted, pervert), foremost for the phonetic similarity between the two. According to the *Kōjien* (the standard dictionary of the Japanese language), H is also short for *hentai* (pervert). It is only appropriate, then, that H is the first letter in the given name of Hiroki Ōtsuka.

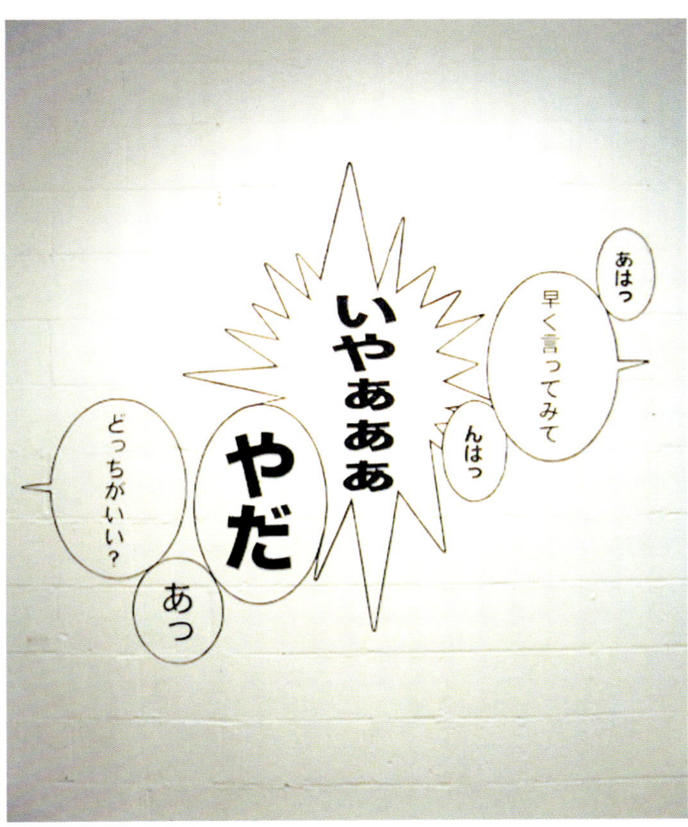

Plate 17.2

Hiroki Ōtsuka
Dialogue
2005
Sumi ink on wall
Dimensions variable
Collection of the artist

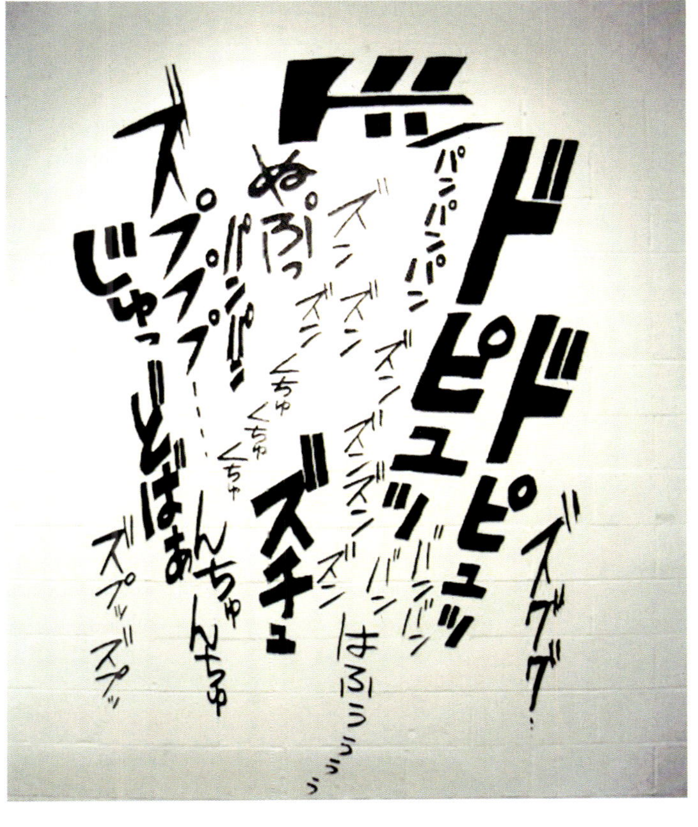

Plate 17.3

Hiroki Ōtsuka
Sex Sounds
2005
Sumi ink on wall
Dimensions variable
Collection of the artist

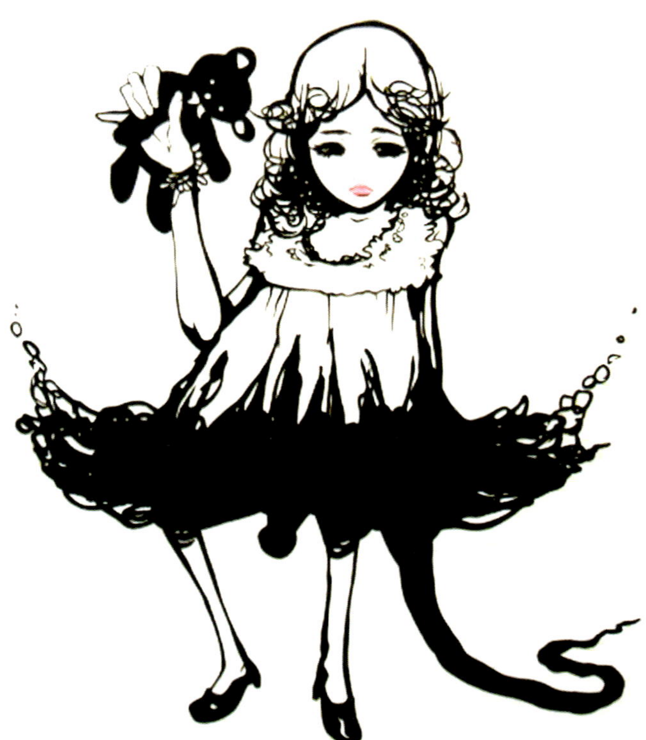

When and how did you first realize that you wanted to be an artist?
HO: I wanted to be a manga author since I was three. My dreams came true at 19. At some point, I began drawing manga on canvas. I don't think I had any intention of becoming an artist. I suppose a current just carried me to where I am now.

Why did you decide to leave Japan?
HO: At around 28, I realized that working in manga meant not drawing what I wanted to draw, but rather what current fashion trends, editors, and the mass media demanded. I decided to leave Japan before my sense of self and my own original "voice," sunk deep inside me, were lost. I thought I would be able to hear my own true "voice" in a country where I did not understand the language.

What was your first impression of New York City?
HO: The highlight of the New York art world was that, no matter where I was or where I looked, I was surrounded by art that is free in expression and speaks to me. I was struck by how natural it all was.

Has the experience of living in New York changed your style or process significantly?
HO: I have begun drawing more and more images that are extremely dark in their handling of emotion and sex. I think getting in touch with the inner side of my spiritual world has brought out these expressions.

In this age of globalism, do you consider yourself to be a Japanese artist, an American artist, an international artist, or a hybrid of all three?
HO: I don't know why, but I feel that I am a Japanese artist. I was born Japanese in a body named by my parents "Ōtsuka Hiroki," I was raised within the inheritance of Japanese culture, I have been influenced by manga and anime. Whatever the means, I make work with the hope that the viewer will enjoy it, even if just a little.

Translated by Ryan Holmberg

PLATE 17.4

Hiroki Ōtsuka
Little Monster
2005
Sumi ink and acrylic on board
30 x 40" (76.2 x 101.6 cm)
Private collection, New York
PHOTO: HIROKI ŌTSUKA

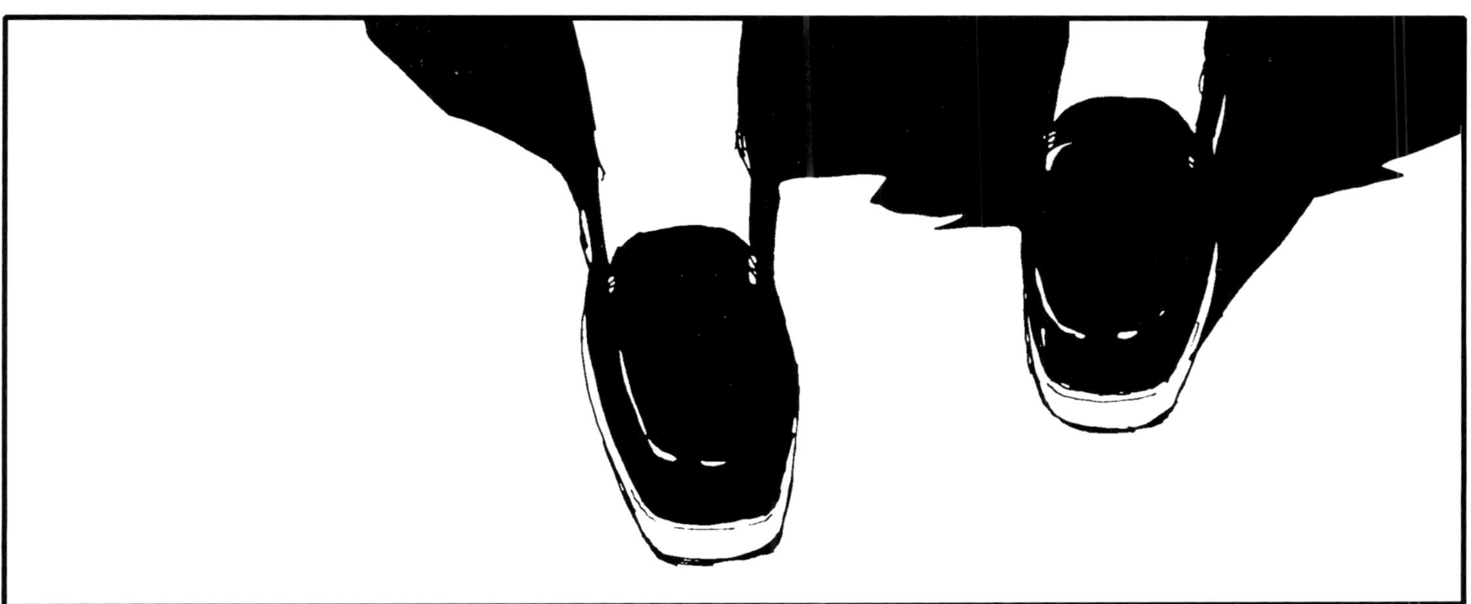

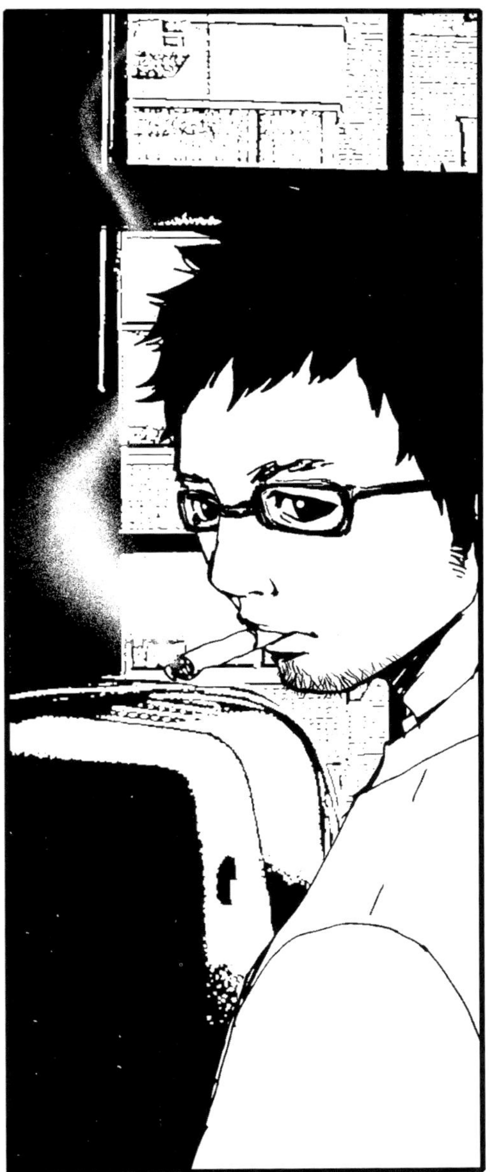

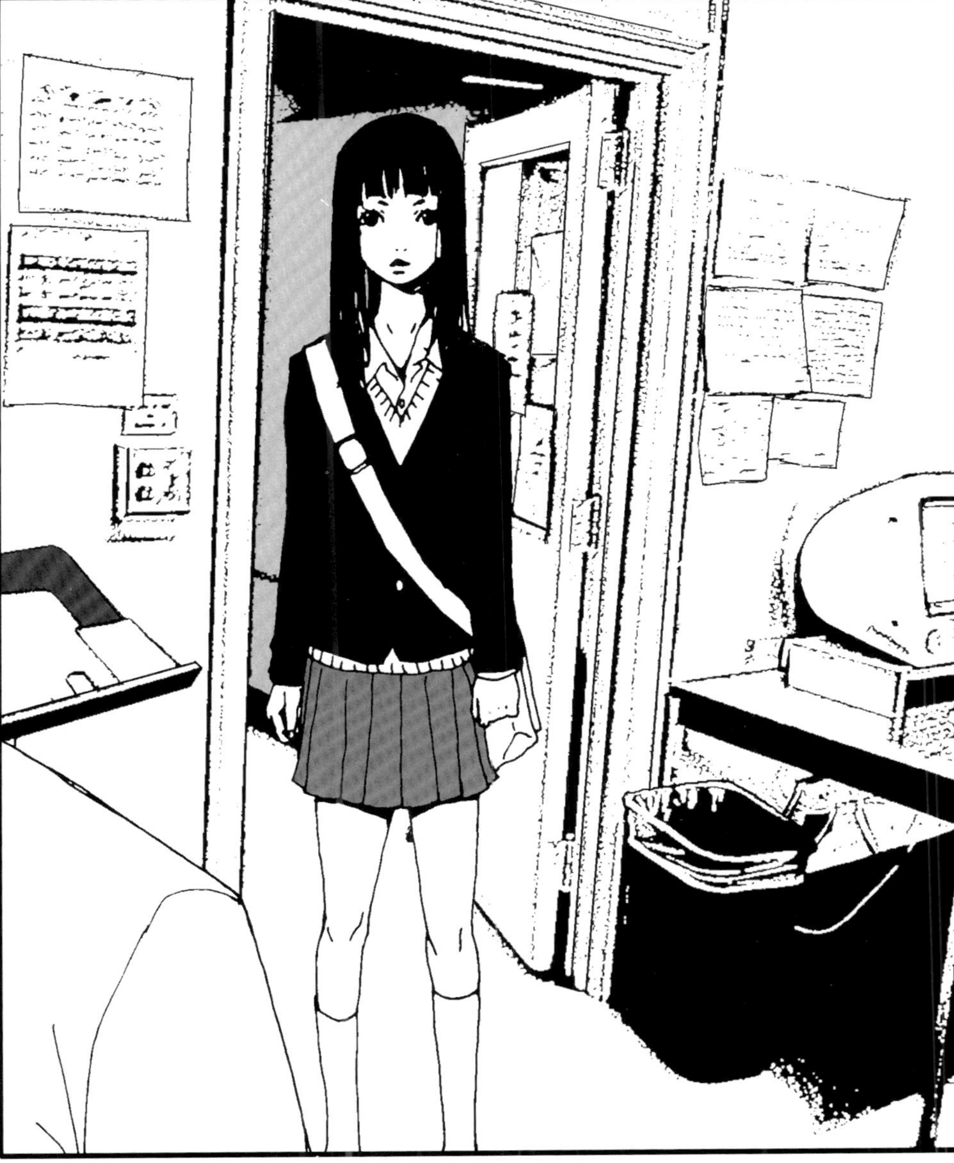

PLATE 17.5

Hiroki Ōtsuka
BLACK and WHITE
2004
Sumi ink on paper
11 ⅝ x 8 ¼" (29.7 x 21 cm)
Collection of the artist

18 KATSUHIRO SAIKI

A Photographic Experiment to Capture the World
YUKIE KAMIYA

Although photography is the principal mode of expression for Katsuhiro Saiki, he does not use this medium to simply record scenery and copy reality. Instead, he employs a camera as an artistic device, as a distinctive means to depict and examine an alternate reality.

Saiki's first tool of expression was a paintbrush. His switch to the camera was influenced by the American photographer Lewis Baltz, an icon of the New Topographics movement of the 1970s, whose work Saiki viewed at an exhibition in Tokyo. Baltz and the New Topographics artists depicted the landscape without emotional description, sometimes working against the sublime beauty of unfettered nature, taking pictures of man-made landscapes like suburbia at the peak of the industrialization of the American economy. Saiki had his eyes opened, becoming aware that photography could maintain an objective distance from the subject matter, making it possible for him to insert his conceptualism into the philosophical space between. With his discovery of the strong conceptual currents in photography of the 1970s, Saiki moved to New York in 2002 to participate in the International Studio Program at P.S.1 Contemporary Art Center and has lived and worked in New York ever since.

Although it is straight photography, Saiki's work captures minimal, almost abstract elements and his practice consistently blurs the boundaries of photography. In his earliest series, *Frames* (1998–2001), one finds cubical forms floating against a white background. At first glance, they look like monochrome paintings of geometric shapes. Upon closer inspection, we can see that the artist is playing with optical perception. The works are pure photography without computer manipulation. Saiki composes three-dimensional cubical models from stainless steel wire within an exquisitely white-lit

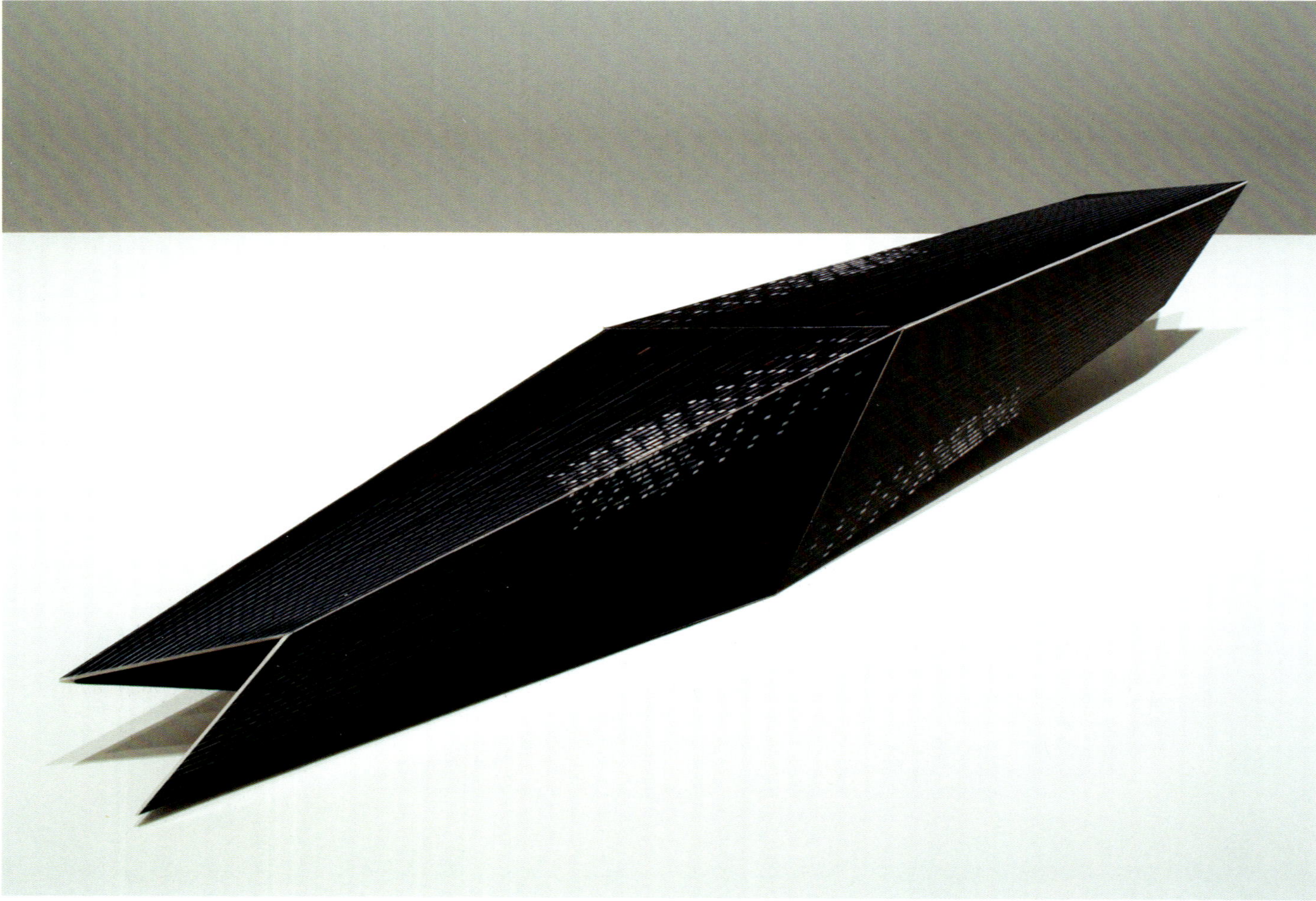

Katsuhiro Saiki
Study for Metropolis #2
2006
C-print, paper board, watercolor
4 ¾ x 23 ⅝ x 4 ⅜" (12.1 x 60 x 11.1 cm)
Collection of Fujiwara Fumiko and
Tatsuo, Tokyo
PHOTO: KATSUHIRO SAIKI

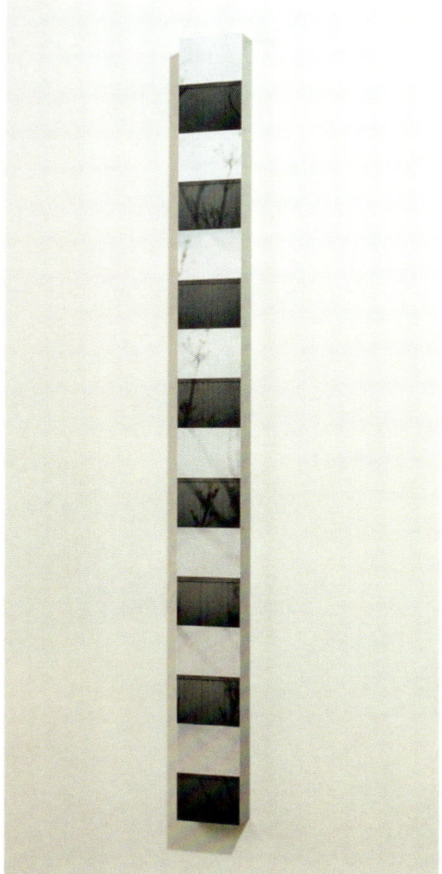

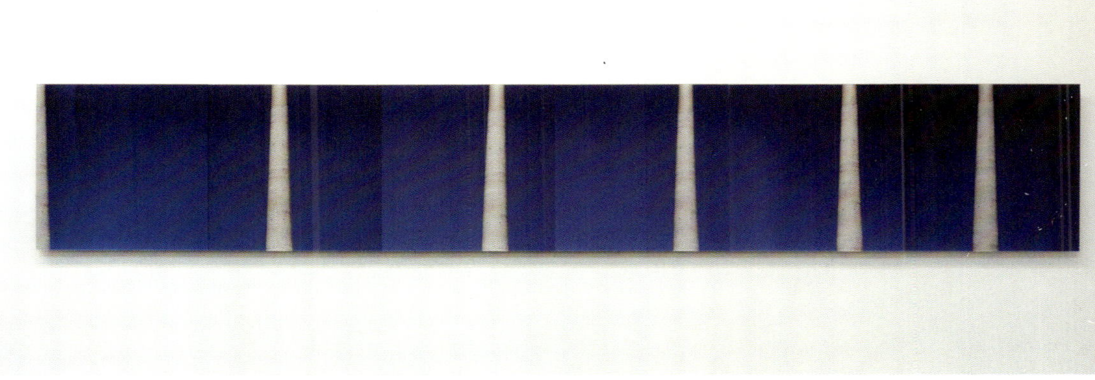

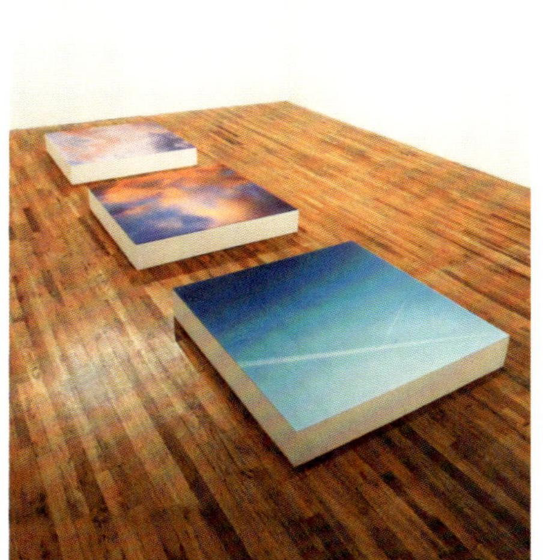

When and how did you first realize that you wanted to be an artist?

KS: When I was a high-school student. Being an artist is a way to live a life, as much as being a baker is a way to live a life.

Why did you choose New York as your ultimate destination?

KS: I was interested in American art theory. I was inspired by the theories of Michael Fried and Rosalind Krauss. Both Minimalism and photography deal in relations with actuality. I have been living and working in New York since I moved to the United States; however, I have never thought of this city as my final destination or a goal.

What was your first impression of New York City?

KS: New York is dirtier than Tokyo. But now, I feel Tokyo is too clean.

Has the experience of living in New York changed your style or process significantly?

KS: My work has not changed so much even after moving to New York. I have been inspired by various genres in various countries, e.g. film, music, literature, dance, and art. I am interested in how the works treat the actuality and the world.

In this age of globalism, do you consider yourself to be a Japanese artist, an American artist, an international artist, or a hybrid of all three?

KS: New York is the city for immigrants from all over the globe. Inevitably, I began to think about nations and races. I have Japanese nationality and am recognized as a Japanese artist at exhibitions. However, I have never considered my work to represent Japan in any respects. Categorization is a determination from outside. Nationality is also determined from outside.

A nation exists independently aside from the people who live there…. You just happened to be born in a certain country. To consider a hypothesis of being born in the United States or in an African country such as Somalia could help you to reconsider your own nationality.

Translated by Yukie Kamiya

PLATE 18.2

Katsuhiro Saiki
Arrangements #18
2000
C-prints, aluminum
37 ¾ x 3 ⅛ x 1 ⅝" (95.9 x 7.9 x 4.1 cm)
DZ Bank, Frankfurt, Germany

PLATE 18.3

Katsuhiro Saiki
Place (installation view at Artists Space, New York, 2003)
2002
C-prints face-mounted to acrylic, plywood, paint
Each 7 ⅛ x 47 ¼ x 47 ¼" (18 x 120 x 120 cm)
The Japan Foundation, Tokyo

PLATE 18.4

Katsuhiro Saiki
Split #3
2002
C-prints face-mounted to acrylic (6 panels)
17 ¾ x 106 ¼" (45 x 269.9 cm)
Collection of the artist

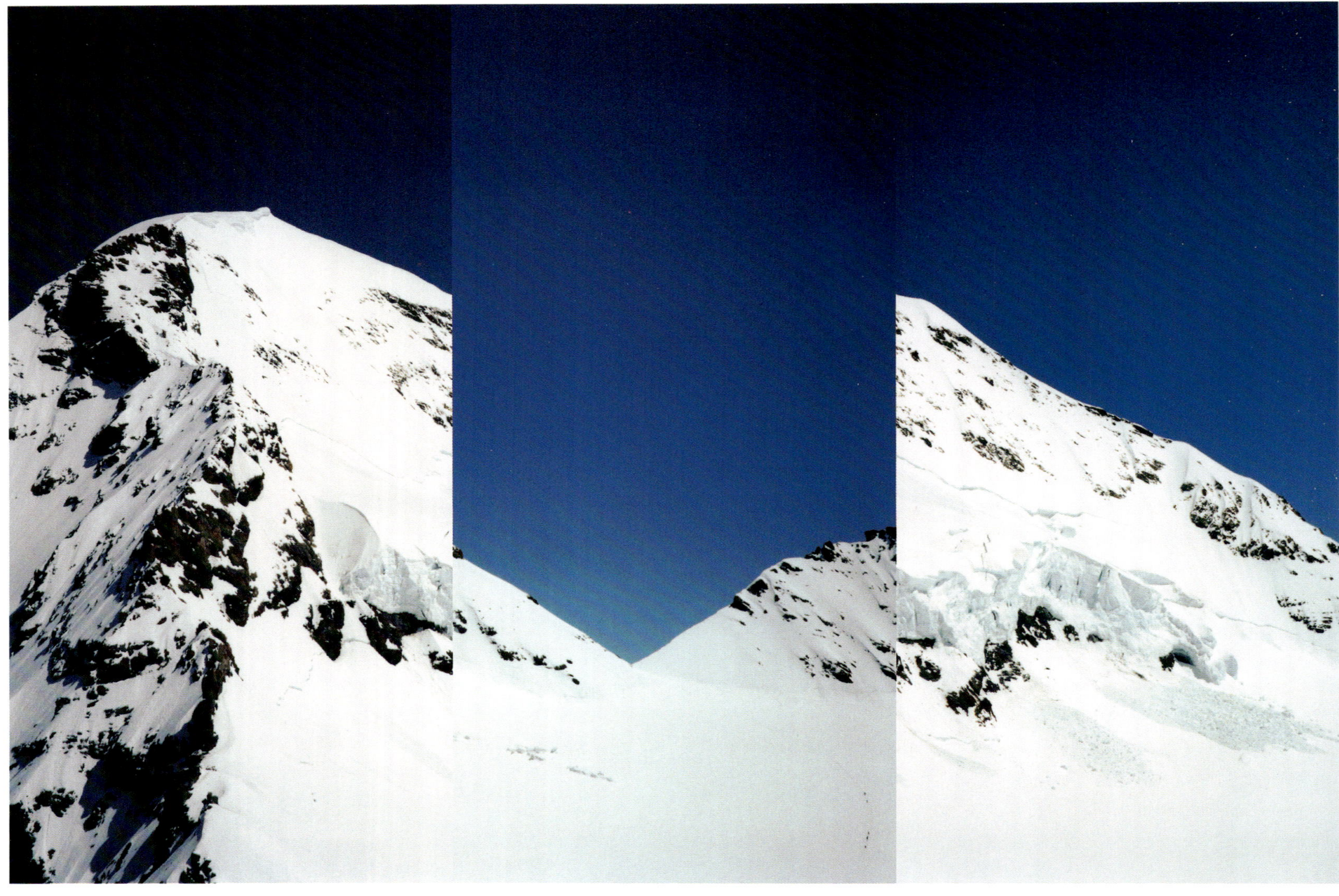

environment, in which the shadows of the frames are eliminated. His perspective perplexes our visual senses and makes viewers reconsider real physical presence versus virtual perception.

Next, Saiki turned his exploration of geometric forms into actual landscapes. He is fascinated by the counter-aesthetic in a monotonous cityscape, and photographs such things as the surface of a wall, a section of concrete tower, and the exterior of a building whose composition is split in two (Pl. 18.4). The artist puts the consecutive images side by side and the sequence of a fragmental landscape in an oblong picture carries a complex visual impact. In *Arrangement* (1999–2005) Saiki sets these photographs in a vertical line on the surface of an aluminum square pillar (Pl. 18.2). Here, the sequence of photographic images evokes a feeling of movement like a montage. He continues this practice both in Tokyo and in New York in a continuing artistic exploration that incorporates photography into the three-dimensional experience of sculpture.

In *Place* (2002–04), Saiki further explores formalist imagery in a series of C-prints face-mounted to acrylic panels, which are placed atop wood boxes, and displayed on the floor (Pl. 18.3). Each photograph depicts a skyscape; a tiny airplane flies like a bird in the scene, emphasizing the sense of scale of the wide swath of sky depicted. Viewers can look down on heavenly images at their feet while the surfaces of the acrylic panels reflect images of the room. The piece is not just photography, but a spatial installation designed in response to features of the exhibition space, thus creating a chance for the audience to physically engage with the work. The instantaneous potential for photography to capture a moment in time is transformed into a sustained object.

Saiki photographs a postcard-like image of a beautiful snow-covered mountain in *Divide* (2003) and reassembles the order of the mountain range to create an alternate photographic reality (Pls. 18.5–6). His new series of works, *Study for Metropolis* (2006–) also

PLATE 18.5

Katsuhiro Saiki
Divide #1
2003
C-prints face-mounted to acrylic (3 panels)
48 x 71 ⅝" (121.9 x 181.9 cm)
Collection of the artist

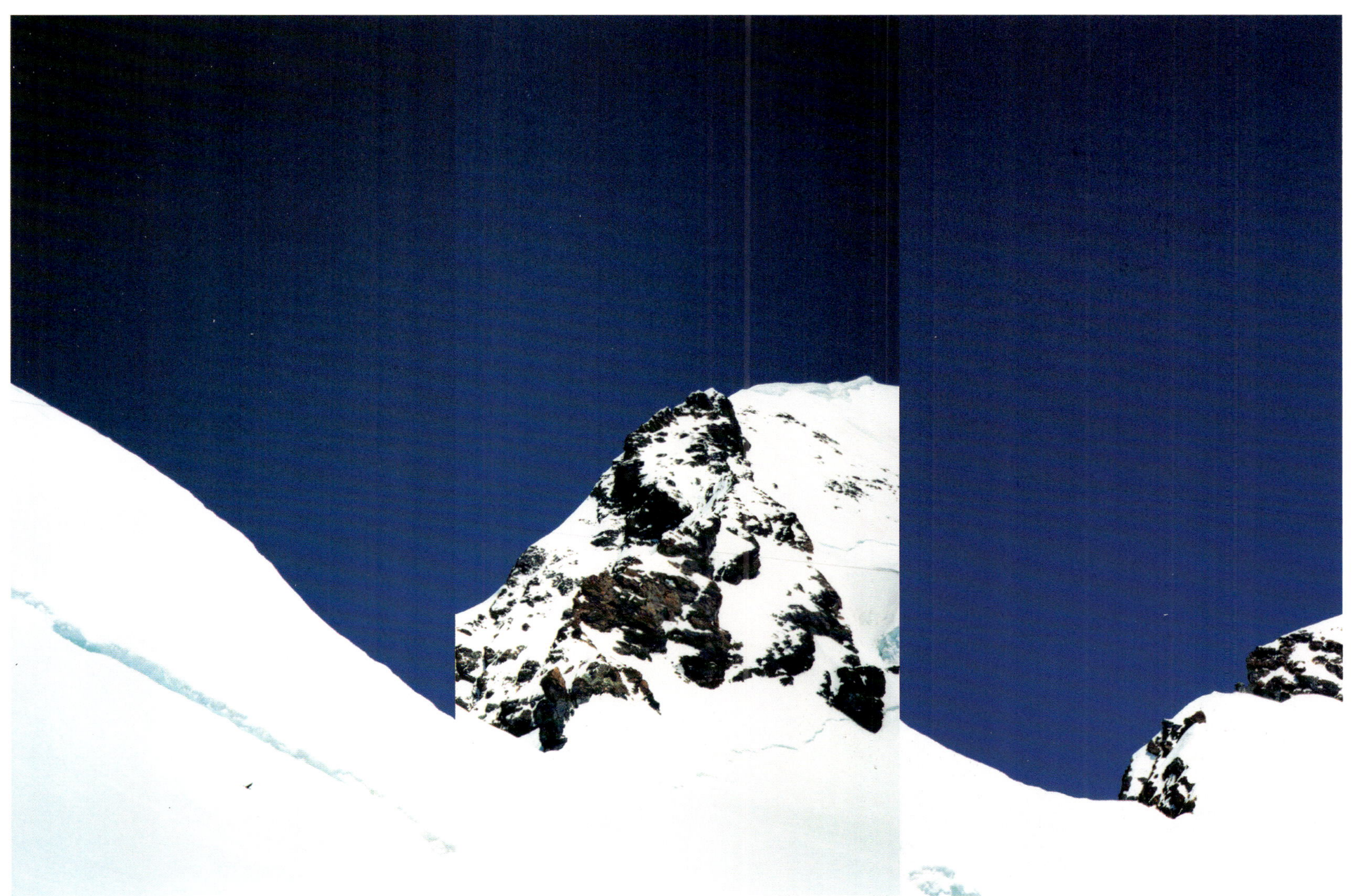

examines the deconstruction of iconographic images (Pl. 18.1). Saiki is documenting modernist buildings that make up the Manhattan skyline and are symbolic images of the artist's current home. He creates a polyhedron from each photographed building's image, manipulating the architectural volume and the coercive dominance of the building into a portable, handcrafted object. A new version of the work is on display in *Making a Home*.

The landscape that we perceive firsthand and its photographed representation are never the same. Saiki's photographic practice attempts to present an alternative perspective from which to see the world. He immerses himself in the urban environment, surrounded by the human landscape, in order to explore the far reaching potential of photography.

PLATE 18.6

Katsuhiro Saiki
Divide #II
2003
C-prints face-mounted to acrylic (3 panels)
48 x 71 ⅝" (121.9 x 181.9 cm)
Collection of the artist

19 · KYŌKO SERA

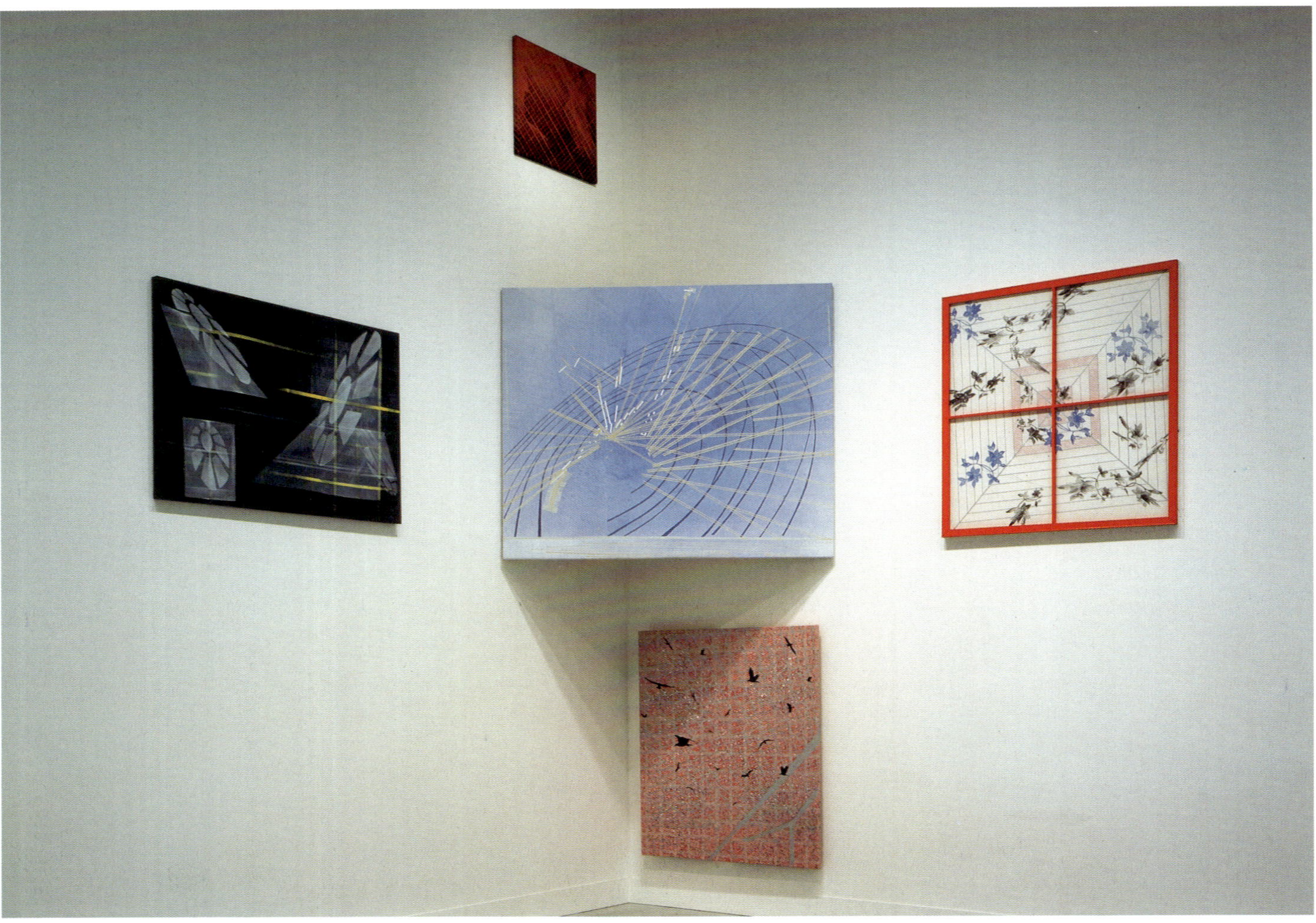

Time and Space Stretched and Structured
ERIC C. SHINER

Artist Kyōko Sera paints, yet she is not a painter per se. She also creates installations and constructions, still she is not necessarily a sculptor. She blurs the line between the two mediums, using paintings as objects to populate her installations. Her canvases thus become physical forms positioned in space, usually in contorted and unthinkable ways. Sera is apt to hang a large canvas at the juncture of two walls, at ceiling height. The next canvas, perhaps unstretched, might be stapled to the wall below and to the right. Power cords or other found objects may connect gallery wall and floor, somehow making the paintings above seem to float in space. For the traditionalist, Sera's works might lean to the absurd; for Sera, they reflect a life-long search for order, a way to make order of chaos, to quite literally stop it in its tracks.

Beyond the materiality of Sera's canvases, the subject matter of the works provides a complex spatial depth rooted in mathematical equations, black holes, physics, and frames. The artist gives birth to the impossible, turning the rules of science and math on their ears in her studies of galaxies, both potentially real and fully imagined. In *Seeking an Unfragmented Life: Cross Model 0-1* from 2005, Sera hung five canvases of various dimensions in the corner of Tokyo's Shiseidō Gallery as part of the annual Tsubaki-kai group exhibition (Pl. 19.1). The central panel, a blue-hazed painting with a looming Ferris wheel whirling across the picture plane, is positioned between the two walls of the gallery, forming a new angled surface in the installation and, as a result, a new way of looking at the world. It is flanked above, below, and to the sides by four additional canvases. The flanking canvas to the left plays with light (Pl. 19.2); Gothic rose windows are seemingly projected onto the canvas, marked with yellow dashes evoking speed and luminosity. The picture above features a scene of two young boys holding rifles painted in a rich red on black fabric, an effect that draws the eye to the top of the high gallery wall. The image was found in a newspaper article about the war in Iraq and appropriated by the artist as a political reminder of the times. To the right, a painting morphs into a red window frame, within which flowers float through space against a squared-off spider web of a grid. And to the bottom, pink fabric with a white grid is overlaid with another image of the Iraq war, here in the form of birds caught in the barbed-wire fence of a military prison. The overall effect of this powerful cross-shaped work is based in academics, theology, politics, and theory, yet displayed with strong attention to color, placement, and order. Sera creates her own universe, providing a window onto her deeply philosophical explorations of the limits of time, space, and contemporary society.

In the *Goddess Spear's Sutra* series from 2000, Sera again conflates concepts of space, puncturing it with an imaginary spear and ripping it to shreds. These large works on paper are grayish washes of ink that give rise to a multi-layered world swarming with playing-card queens (P s. 19.3–4). Spades lurk within the murky confines of the image in some; they stand out in the foreground in others. Peering queens blend in and out of clarity, staring the viewer square in the face here, becoming barely visible there. For Sera, these works are not a literal examination of playing cards, but instead stand as a metaphor for the violence of war and the power of goddesses watching from the heavens above. They are spiritual works for the artist, images that reveal the myriad definitions and roles of governments and religions the world over.

It seems that Kyōko Sera is on a journey of sorts, perhaps a pilgrimage to a higher visual plane. Her painterly contortions and spatial undermining are not just technical studies of the limitations of materials; they become theoretical examinations of society, religion and the bodies that populate space in real time. Sera searches for new possibilities in the display of art, art that folds in upon itself and opens a door to an alternate universe of ordered chaos ruled over by goddesses and a most intelligent creator who hopes to heal and warp space every chance she gets.

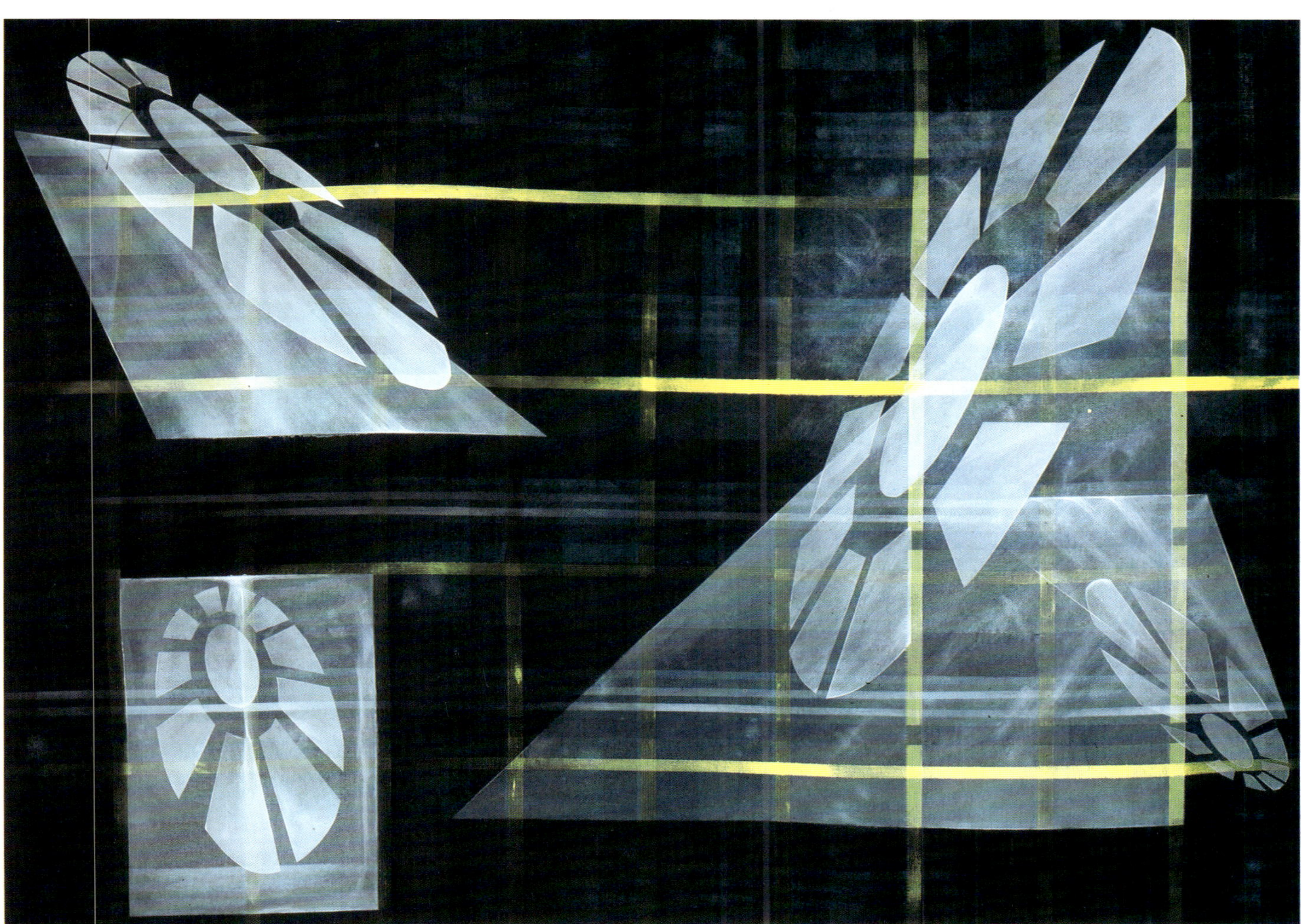

PLATE 19.2

Kyōko Sera
Left canvas from *Seeking an
Unfragmented Life: Cross Model 0-1*
2005
Acrylic on cloth
39 x 54" (99.1 x 137.2 cm)
Shiseidō Art House, Kakegawa
PHOTO: YAMAMOTO TADASU

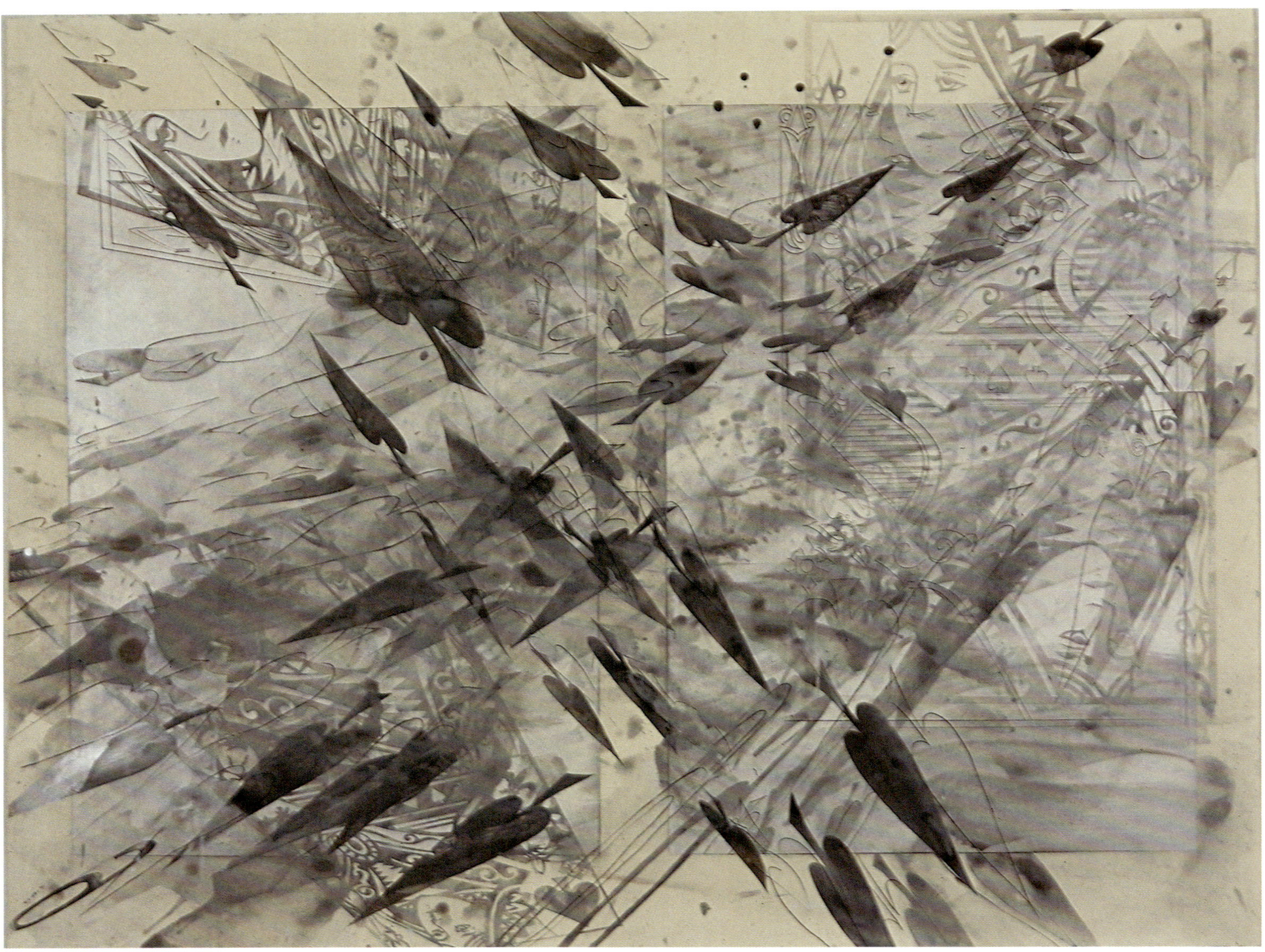

When and how did you first realize that you wanted to be an artist?
KS: At around age 11, I thought I wanted to become a poet or a musician. Connection and expansion.

Why did you decide to leave Japan?
KS: I chose to be in an environment in which I could be immersed in my work.

Why did you choose New York as your ultimate destination?
KS: By living here, I feel that I can truly experience life.

What was your first impression of New York City?
KS: Lots of freedom, brightness, dryness, and directness.

Did you face many obstacles in establishing your career in New York?
KS: I am still working on it. I need to obtain visas and learn the language. I enjoy the frequent opportunities to meet with artists as well as to see their work.

Did you have any interactions with other artists or supporters that were especially beneficial to you and your work?
KS: Through relationships with a violin maker and a healer, I have discovered and learned much.

What experience has given you the most satisfaction as an artist in New York?
KS: When I have an idea, I am now able to manipulate its image with greater ease. I am now able to accept it when that idea takes on a life of its own in a way that I find interesting.

Do you ever regret leaving Japan?
KS: Not at the moment.

In this age of globalism, do you consider yourself to be a Japanese artist, an American artist, an international artist, or a hybrid of all three?
KS: Not in particular. Here, I can find it meaningful to make a work. To me, New York is that kind of place.

Translated by Ryan Holmberg

Plate 19.3

Kyōko Sera
War No. 7 (Goddess Spear's Sutra)
2004
Acrylic, carbon, pigment on paper
38 ½ x 50" (97.8 x 127 cm)
Collection of the artist
PHOTO: NOGUCHI MASAHIRO

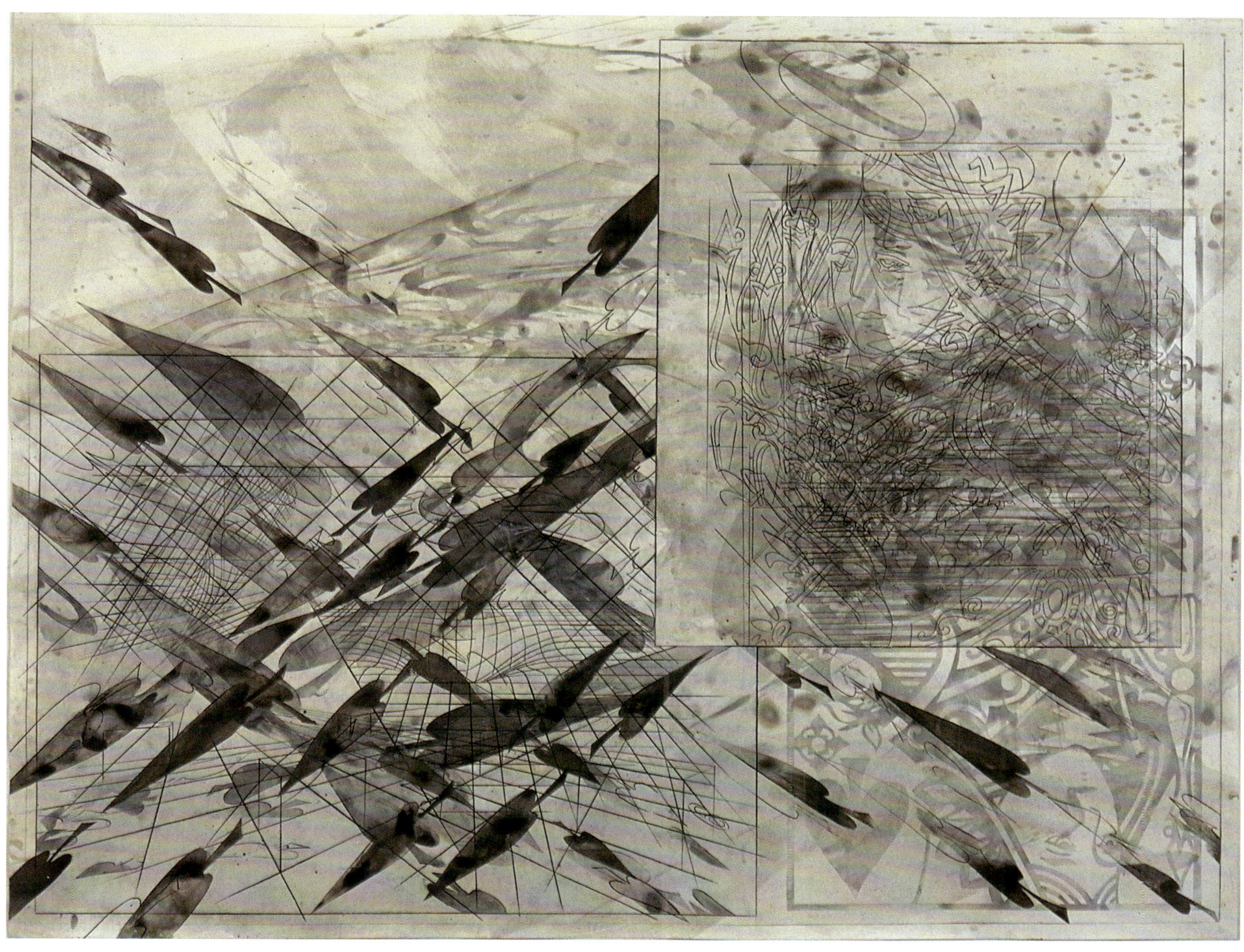

PLATE 19.4

Kyōko Sera
*Who Made This World? (Goddess
Spear's Sutra)*
2004
Acrylic, carbon, pigment on paper
37 x 48 ½" (94 x 123.2 cm)
Collection of the artist

20 NORIKO SHINOHARA

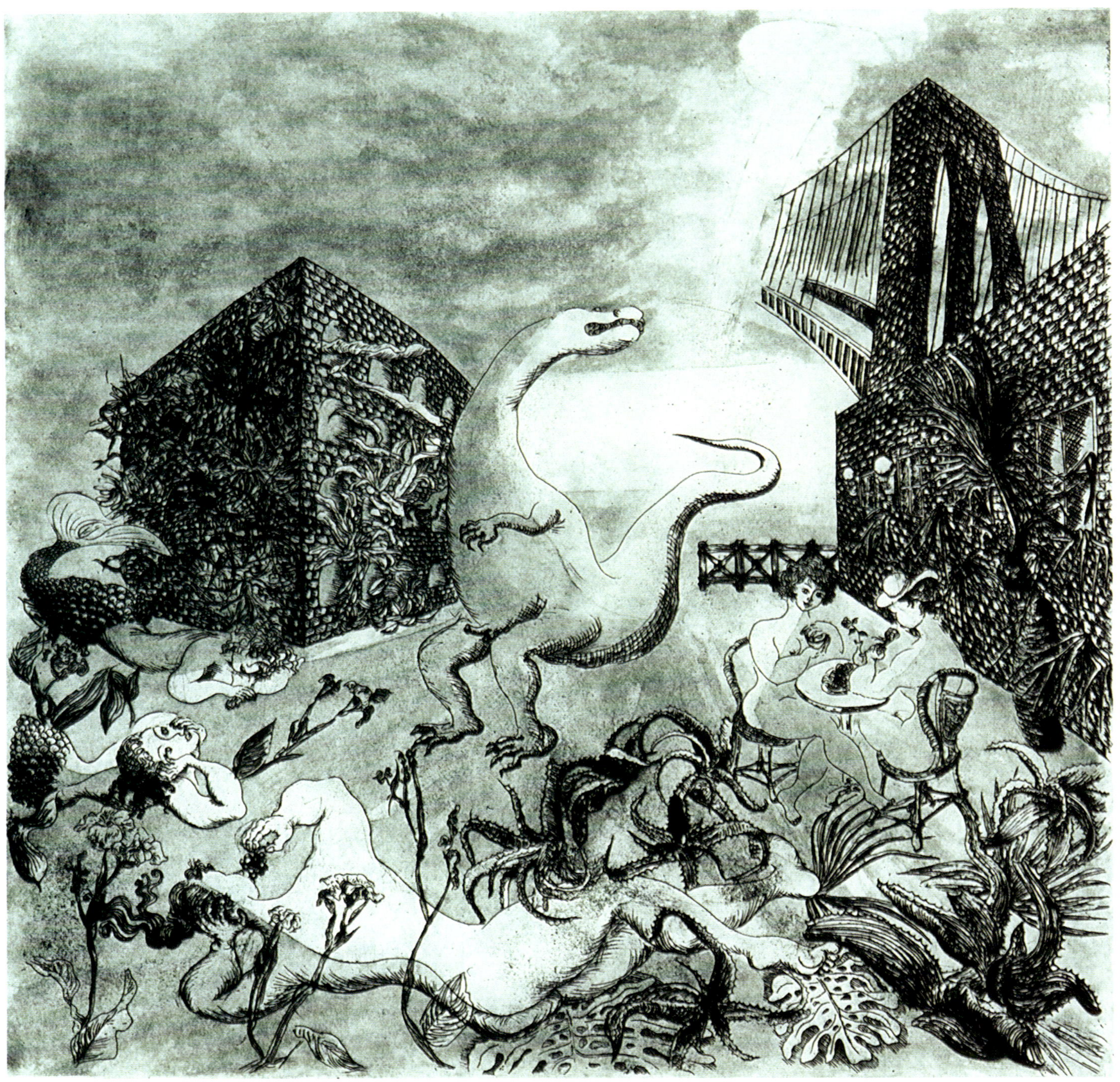

PLATE 20.1

Noriko Shinohara
If Everybody Has Gone—After Sept. 11th
2003
Etching and aquatint
12 x 12" (30.5 x 30.5 cm)
Collection of the artist

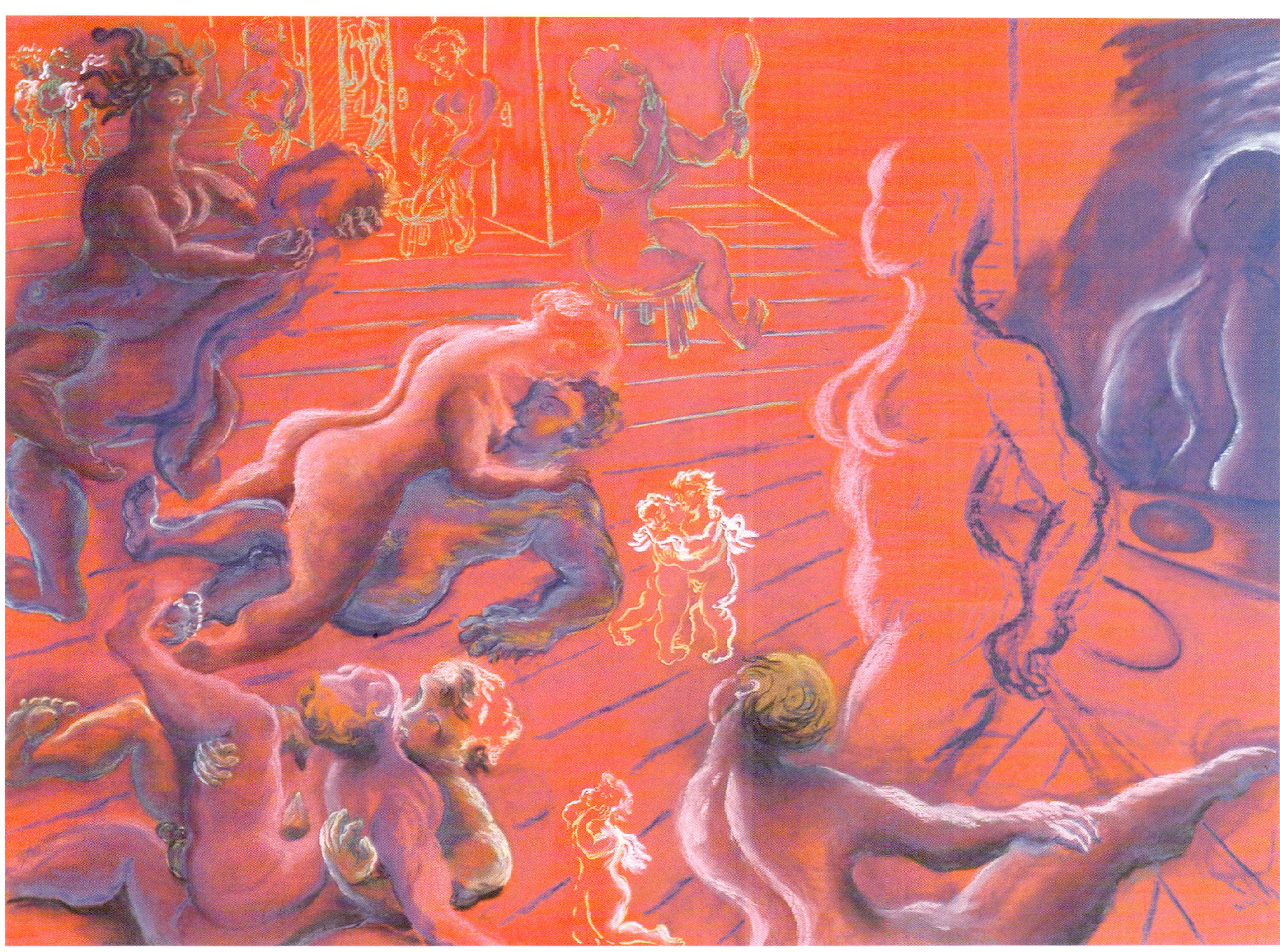

Cutie Strikes Back

ERIC C. SHINER

Noriko Shinohara came to New York in 1972 at the age of 19 to take on the art world. After six short months of joyous learning at the Art Students League, Noriko had an encounter that would in many ways change her life forever: she met and fell in love with her future husband, renowned painter Ushio Shinohara (who was 21 years her senior). In fact, her newfound love was her undoing in terms of her meditative student years. On a three-day-long sojourn with Ushio, Noriko missed class, and the powers-that-be revoked her student visa. What was young Noriko to do? Her solution was to move in with Ushio (although she started paying the rent immediately), have a son (Alex, who would grow up to be an artist), and become lifelong business partner, babysitter, and muse of her wild and crazy partner. To understand this nonstop drama, we only have to turn to a novella she published in 1994, *Sigh of New York* (Tameiki no Nyūyōku), whose semi-autobiographical narrative centers on vivid accounts of her husband's escapades and how she put up with it all.

Luckily, throughout the crama, this gifted artist never stopped making art. Over the decades, she eventually learned to create her own sanctuary—her "queendom"—to which the uninvited intruder, her husband included, is banned from physical entry. In her own realm of art, she chose to channel the unpleasant aspects of her life into a body of paintings, drawings, and prints steeped in a colorful and orgiastic explosion of woman power, sensuality, and fantasy that acts as a counterbalance to the reality of Ushio. "To change things with special magic"—that was Alchemy, the talent that motivated her to become an artist, at the age of 17. Noriko shares many interests in art history with Ushio, ranging from Hokusai's *ukiyo-e* to Renaissance painting, but their interpretations are completely different: If Ushio specializes in bravado, Noriko works meticulously and intimately in diverse pictorial media. Her 1999 pastel, *Locker Room Series IV: Homage to Hokusai Shunga*, is a good example, peopled with copulating couples reminiscent of protagonists from her favorite Greek myths (Pl. 20.2). Her fantastic imagination recently found an effective outlet in the medium of the artist's book: she has created a series of exquisitely collaged accordion books, in which she narrates stories for children of all ages. She is also an accomplished printmaker (her queendom is equipped with her own printing press), as demonstrated by *If Everybody Has Gone—After Sept. 11th*, dated 2003 (Pl. 20.1). This work, depicting a dinosaur that stamps over mythological figures felled under a truncated Brooklyn Bridge, marked an important turning point for her: it was her first pictorial production in which the reality of the external world threatened her fantasy.

Around this time, Noriko decided to take up the nickname Cutie, after a young man on the street greeted her, "Hi, Cutie." The liberating power of this nickname has become tangible this past year in a series of works titled *Cutie's 3 Wine-Bottle Box*, which began with souvenir boxed wine she brought back from one of her trips to Europe with her husband. As an extension of her book-making projects, she turned these wine boxes, seven of which are included in *Making a Home*, into the beautiful European-inspired townhouses she saw in her beloved Buenos Aires. Yet, the backsides of these painted wonders display a shocking surprise: the trials and tribulations of Cutie as she puts up with a character who bears incredible resemblance to one Ushio Shinohara. Drawn in black against white ground, the mixture of fantasy and reality is uncanny. On the box titled *Alchemy*, Noriko depicts Ushio dreaming of becoming "a Cinderella boy" and following a rich lady to her limousine with puppy dog eyes. In a subsequent episode, Cutie wields an axe and a knife, "becom[ing] mad and jealous." So what does Cutie do to save the day? "Cutie decided to study Alchemy!" And in so doing, her hair turns platinum and, in a way, she takes on the superpowers necessary to rein in her wayward hubby. On another box, *Sweet and Tender Love*, Cutie's "gay friend recommended me [to] dress as dominatrix and punish him with dildo!" (Pl. 20.3). A strong feminist statement, the story of her alter-ego Cutie getting even with Ushio fascinates the author herself so much that she is planning to turn this series into a book-length manga.

When and how did you first realize that you wanted to be an artist?
NS: When I was 17 years old, I felt that I had a talent for Alchemy—to change things with special magic—and that my Alchemy would be Art.

Why did you decide to leave Japan?
NS: In Japan then the entry exam for art colleges called for endless drawings of Greek sculpture. I loved those Greek statues but I yearned to drench their pure white forms with emerald green or hot pink paint—alchemy with which the art colleges in Japan wanted nothing to do.

Why did you choose New York as your ultimate destination?
NS: Something new, like Pop Art, was happening in New York. Even Abstract Expressionism of the 1940s and 1950s looked very new in the early 1970s to me, pretty much isolated in a rural part of Japan.

What was your first impression of New York City?
NS: Looking out from the window of a cheap hotel in Times Square, I wondered to myself, "Where am I? Where is Hollywood? Where is Elvis Presley?"

Has the experience of living in New York changed your style or process significantly?
NS: On first arrival here, I started to paint like an expressionist, with free mind, colors, and brush strokes. After my husband had skimmed off my paint, canvas, and ideas, nothing remained in me. It took more than a quarter century to find and establish a new identity, which drew richly from my early encounter with those Greek stories and forms.

Do you ever regret leaving Japan?
NS: Raised by a middle-class family, as a girl I had quite a good life, even with luxury. After I started living with my husband, I learned what poverty was and regretted leaving Japan.

In this age of globalism, do you consider yourself to be a Japanese artist, an American artist, an international artist, or a hybrid of all three?
NS: My friend Mr. Makoto Saeki wrote in a Japanese magazine that I'm an alien from outer space. I think it is true.

PLATE 20.3

Noriko Shinohara
Cutie's 3 Wine-Bottle Box No. 2
Sweet and Tender Love
2006
Oil on collaged cardboard
4 x 10 ½ x 13 ½" (10.2 x 26.7 x 34.3 cm)
Collection of the artist

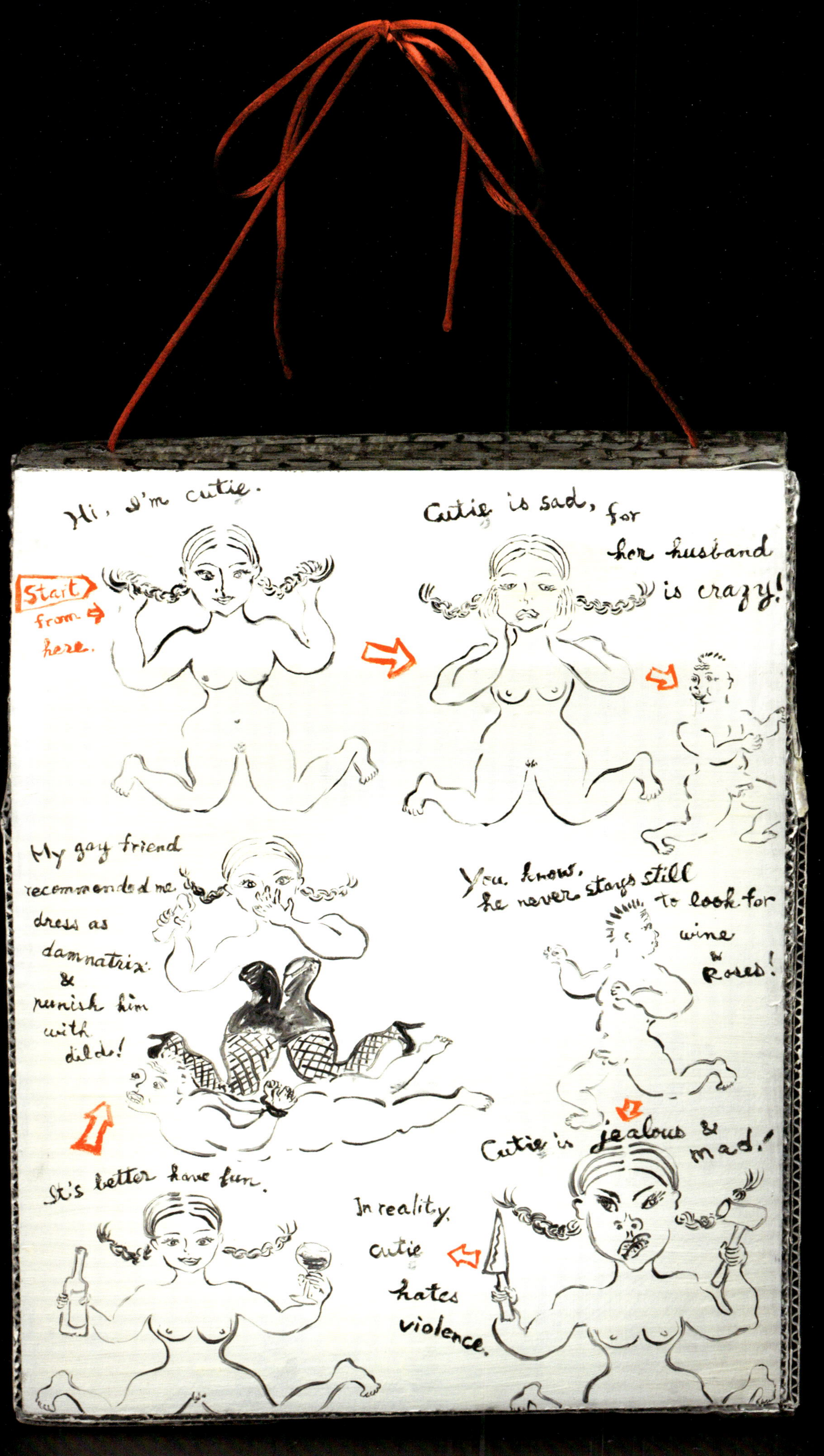

Hi, I'm cutie.
Start from here.
Cutie is sad, for her husband is crazy!
My gay friend recommended me dress as damnatrix & punish him with dildo!
You know, he never stays still to look for wine & Roses!
It's better have fun.
Cutie is jealous & mad!
In reality, cutie hates violence.

21 USHIO SHINOHARA

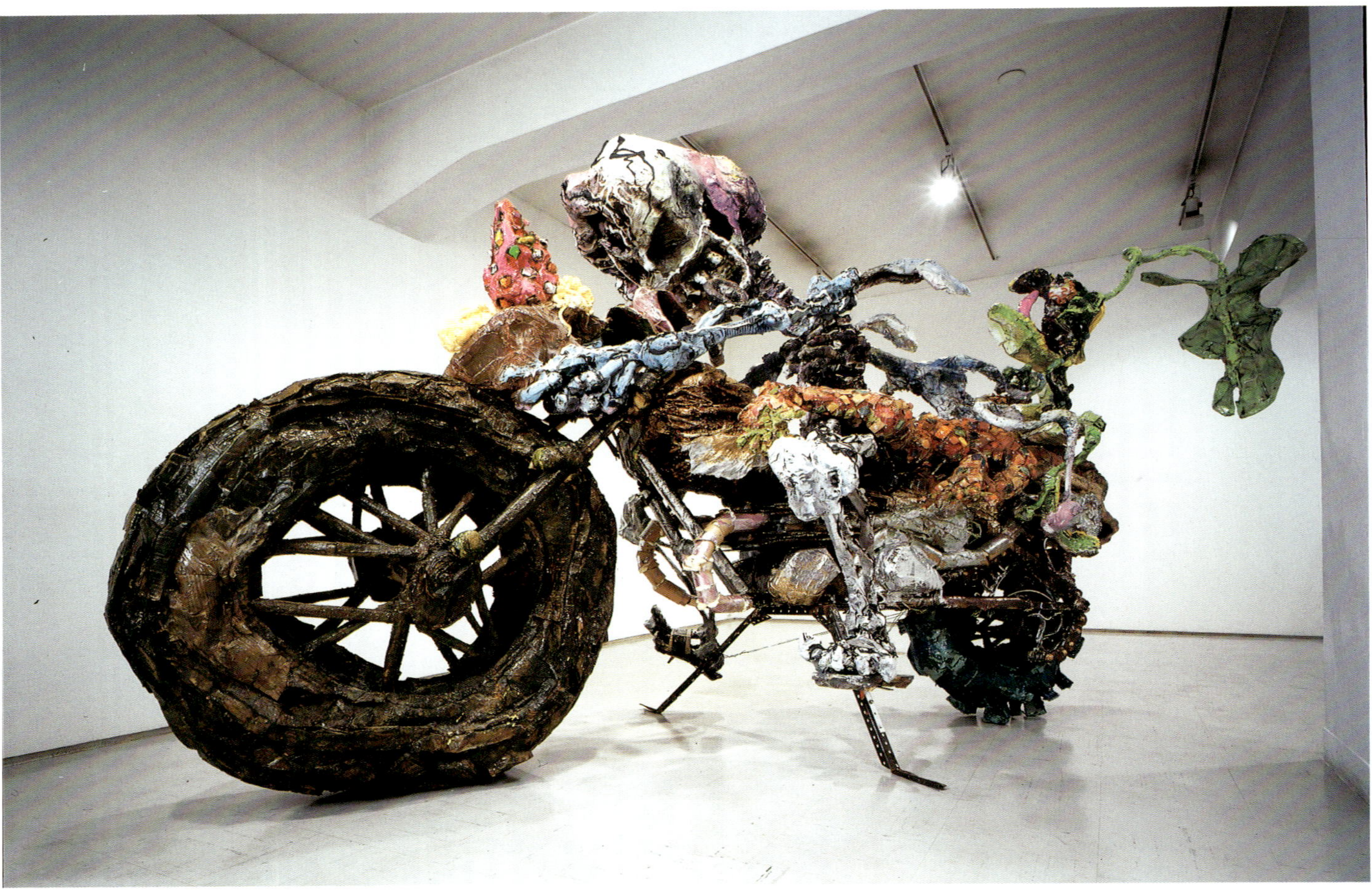

Canal Street Cornucopia
ALEXANDRA MUNROE

Ushio Shinohara paints cinematic reality. He lifts tableaux from what he sees—gritty East Village street scenes, garish Coney Island beach bars, packed Manhattan subways bright with Bubblicious ads—and then compresses multiple views into a single canvas or junk-art sculpture. Speed, picture, and action appear all at once, like a movie whose scenes are transposed into a single frame. Yet within this visual chaos, Shinohara's multiple narratives emerge as legible, even plausible, scenes of life. His subject is our reality, saturated and intensified, ripe for devouring.

Affectionately known to the Japanese art community by the nickname "Gyū-chan,"* Shinohara was born in Tokyo in 1932. His artist parents instilled in him a love for Cézanne, van Gogh, and Gauguin. Like others of his generation who were raised during Japan's wartime years, Shinohara developed a deep fascination for the culture that so spectacularly defeated his world. He experienced what his contemporary, the photographer Tōmatsu

Shōmei, called the Americanization of Occupied and postwar Japan—jazz culture, Hollywood bravado, hellacious comic book dramas, and a rough disregard of social convention. In 1952, Shinohara entered the prestigious Tokyo National University of Fine Arts and Music, where he majored in oil painting. Disappointed by the school's conventional curriculum, he left before graduation. It was the artist and critic Okamoto Tarō's radical call to overthrow beauty for the power of "repulsive" art championed in his influential 1954 book, *Today's Art* (Konnichi no geijutsu), that served as Shinohara's creative catalyst. From that moment on, he was committed to the revolutionary "path of the avant-garde."

Shinohara emerged as a central figure in the legendary Yomiuri Independant Exhibition, participating every year but one from 1955 until 1963. This unjuried, anti-salon forum for young artists became *the* staging ground for Japan's postwar avant-garde and was the stimulus for Shinohara's early unbridled antics—including

Ushio Shinohara
Skeleton Rider Licking Strawberry Ice Cream Accompanied by Woman, Rabbit, and Frog (Just After Terrorist Attack on New York)
2004
Cardboard, plastic, varieties of paint, iron, aluminum
81 ½ x 145 ⅝ x 54 ¾" (207 x 370 x 139 cm)
Courtesy of the artist and Gallery Yamaguchi, Tokyo
PHOTOGRAPH: SUEMASA MAREO

his sculpture of found objects that gained critical recognition as "junk art." In 1960, he was a founding member—along with Yomiuri Independant artists Akasegawa Genpei, Shūsaku Arakawa, and Yoshimura Masanobu—of the group Neo Dada (initially Neo Dadaism Organizers), whose exhibitionist Happenings thrust improvised performance and junk-art assemblage towards the center of Japanese avant-garde expression. His fame as the quintessential art rebel was secured in 1961, when he performed a *Boxing Painting* that was reported in the illustrated weekly *Mainichi Graph*, with text by the novelist Ōe Kenzaburō. Dipping his cloth-bound fists in *sumi* ink, he punched his way rapidly across an expanse of paper, creating a mural of black drips and splashes that gave literal meaning to the popular term "action painting." In 1964, Shinohara again made history when he exhibited a copy of Robert Rauschenberg's 1958 combine, *Coca-Cola Plan*, and called it "imitation art."

The JDR 3rd Fund, under the direction of Porter McCray, was instrumental in advancing contemporary Japanese art by supporting young artists in their dream to travel to New York for extended periods of work and study. Some, like Shinohara who came in 1969, never returned home. He loved the city's luscious filth, its anything-goes spirit, its ethnically mixed multitudes. He loved being an eternal tourist, snapping away at whatever enthralled him, expressing the speed and sensuality of American culture in whatever medium he could afford, including cardboard found on the street. He constantly reinvented the art he loved: American comics, Neo-Dada, and the spirit of Vincent van Gogh.

Shinohara has a special history with the Japan Society Gallery. His one-person show in 1982, *Tokyo Bazooka*, shocked the Society's traditional supporters but attracted serious critical review, emboldening Gallery Director Rand Castile to commit his program further still to showcasing contemporary Japanese art. *Tokyo Bazooka* was also my first project as a young museum professional on Castile's team. I had recently returned to New York after several years of study in Japan, prepared to pursue a curatorial career in Japanese art, a field that I still imagined "ended" in the mid-19th century. What I saw in Shinohara's Howard Street studio radically and instantly changed the course of my research and curatorial focus, and led directly to my 1994 exhibition and book *Japanese Art After 1945: Scream Against the Sky*. Shinohara, it turns out, not only stimulated Tokyo's postwar avant-garde in historic ways; he has also been an inspiration and a mentor to me and over time to many young scholars who now recognize the giant of his genius, and the genius of his cultural significance.

Gyū is the alternate pronunciation of *ushi* for the character meaning "bull"; *chan* is a suffix for proper names that designates an endearing or informal relation, usually reserved for children.

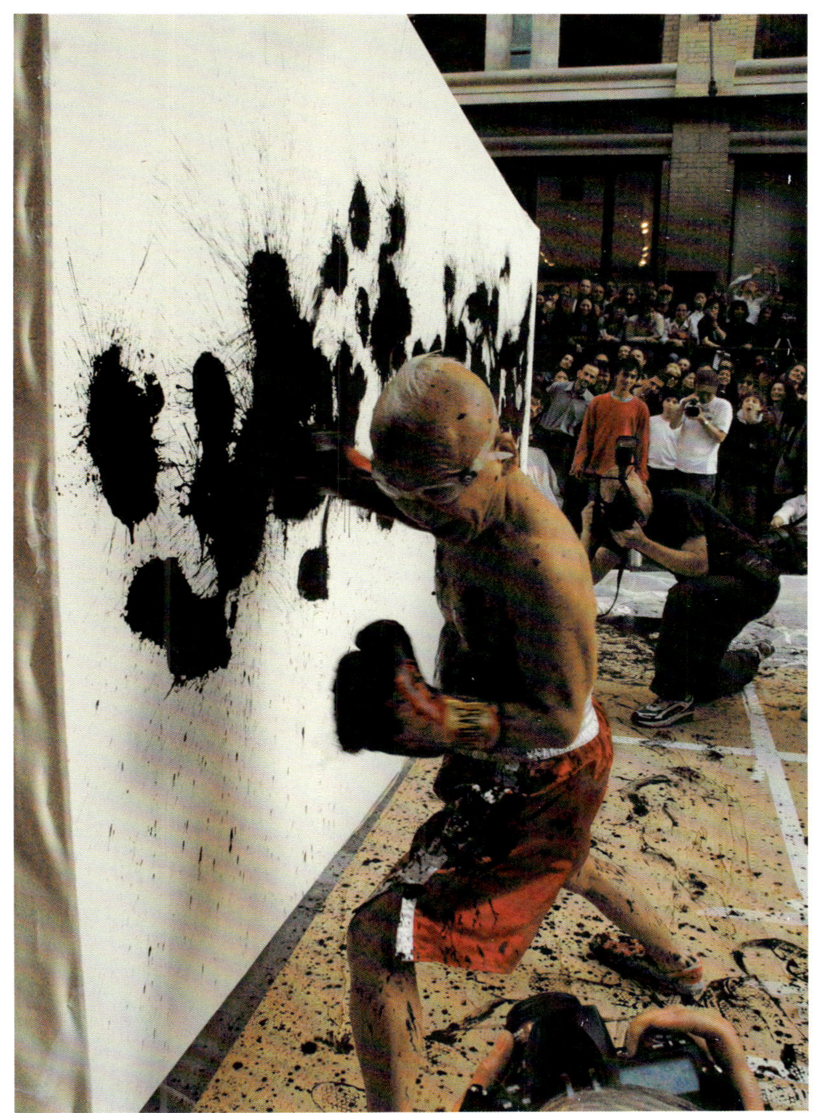

 PLATE 21.2

Ushio Shinohara
Scene from *Boxing Painting*
2006
Performance on Jay Street, New York
for *Action Painting Street Battle! Ushio Shinohara vs. Ryōga Katsuma*
Courtesy of Ethan Cohen Fine Arts, New York
PHOTO: ARVIN FANG/ECFA

When and how did you first realize that you wanted to be an artist?
US: My father was a poet and my mother was a *Nihonga* [Japanese-style painting] artist. This environment motivated me to pursue an artistic career.

Why did you decide to leave Japan?
US: From 1955 to 1965, in my youth, avant-garde art in Japan was strongly influenced by the international art world. I wanted to see what was going on in Europe and America.

What was your first impression of New York City?
US: The first, most exciting thing I did was to sit down in a shabby downtown bar and sip a drink, like protagonists in my favorite American detective stories.

Has the experience of living in New York changed your style or process significantly?
US: I set up my studio to work in New York's downtown. I got energy from the immigrants' city, New York. My English was poor and I knew very few people in the art world, but with these hardships, my work became more intense in expressing my ideas.

Even now, my ideas and energy are as strong as the 1960s, when I was engaged in avant-garde activities in Japan.

In this age of globalism, do you consider yourself to be a Japanese artist, an American artist, an international artist, or a hybrid of all three?
US: I become happy, sad, and emotional when I read or watch what happened in the world in the papers and on TV. I think of how my artistic expression can help this chaotic world. I consider myself to be a Japanese, especially in the multiethnic city, New York.

Translated by Sachiko Hisajima

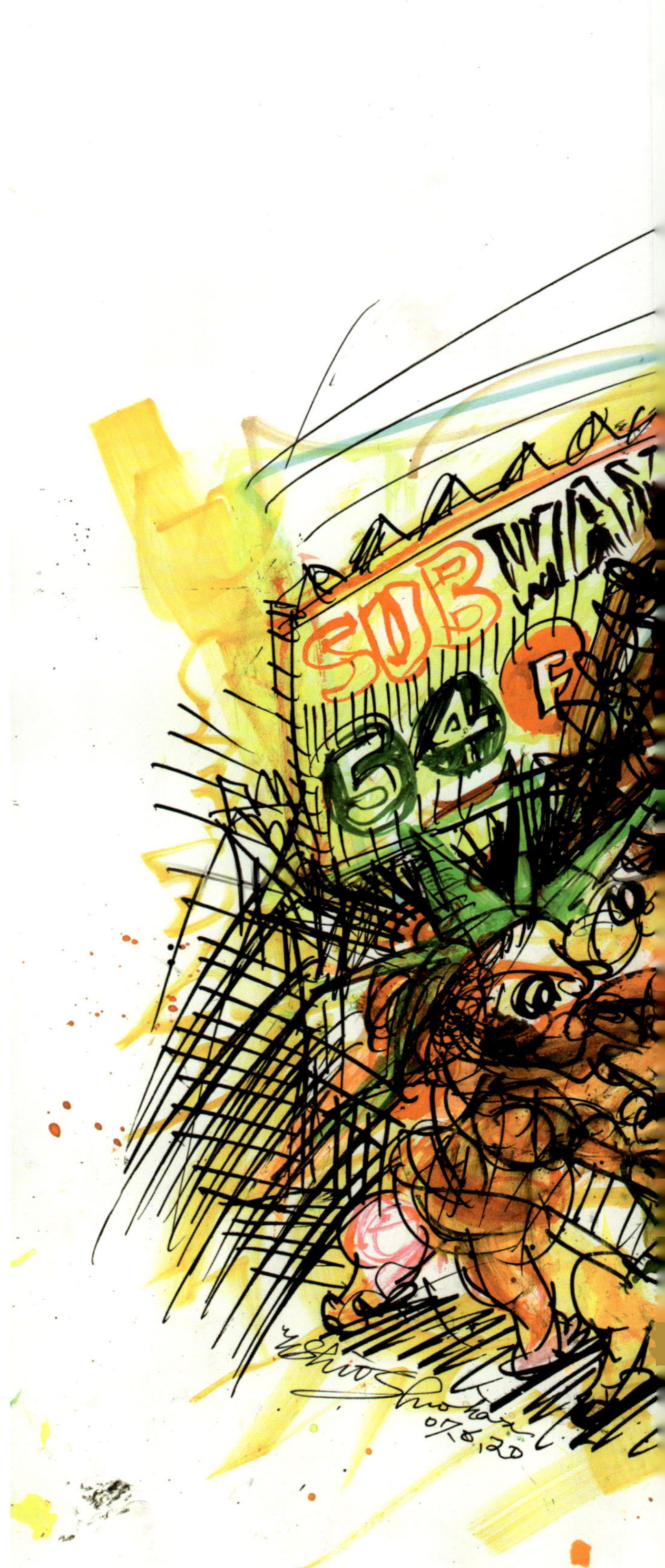

PLATE 21.3

Ushio Shinohara
New York Subway Entrance
2007
Color ink and acrylic on paper
19 x 24" (48.3 x 61 cm)
Collection of the artist

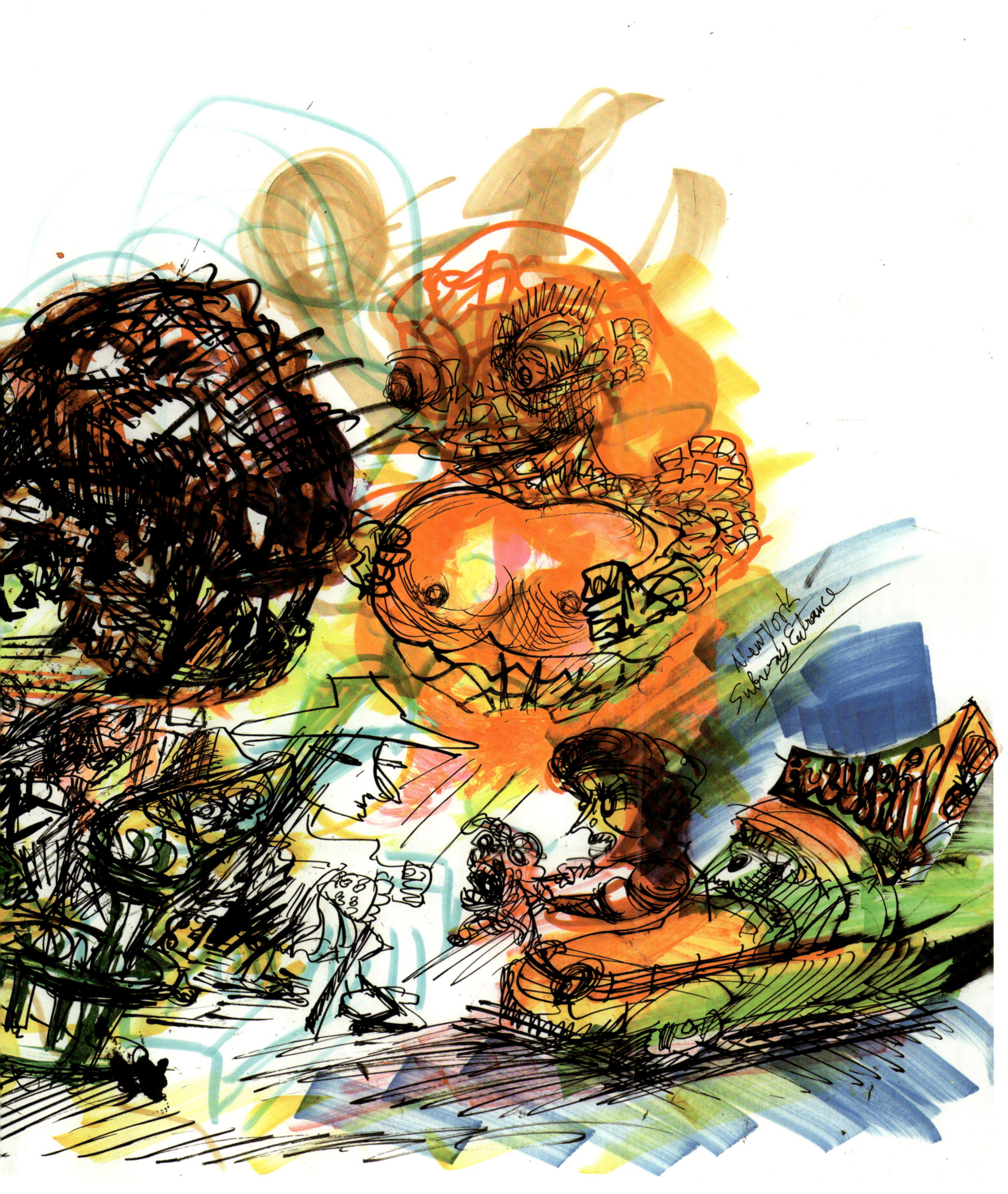
New York
Subway Entrance

⌂ 22 GŌ SUGIMOTO

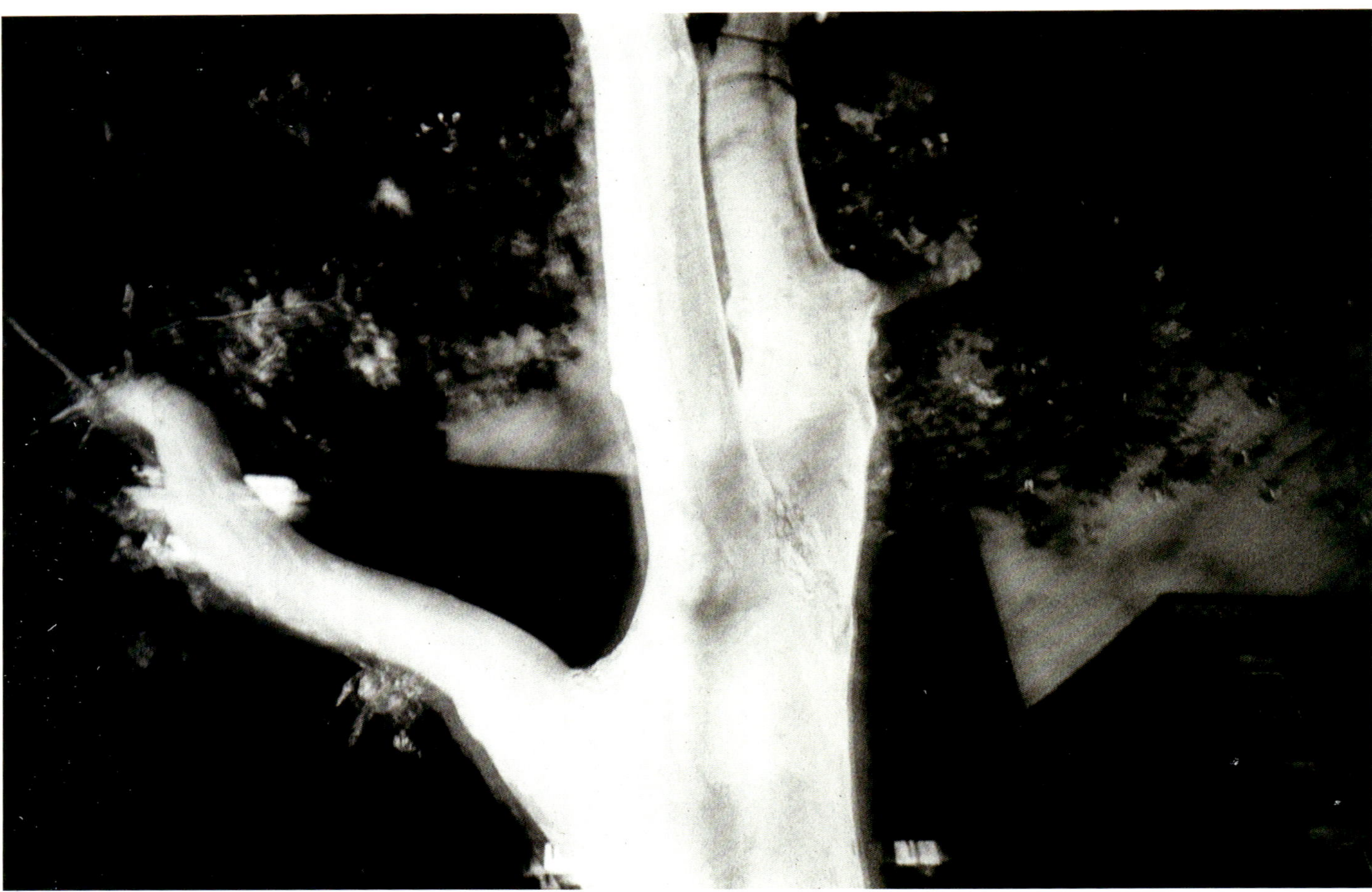

The Exquisitely Extreme Photography of Gō Sugimoto
REIKO TOMII

Gō Sugimoto has the exquisite eye of a painter. To realize his vision in photography, he challenges the camera to an extreme task that it is not routinely asked to perform—shooting at night with scarcely any light or shooting white on white. By doing so, he literally "photographs," that is, by light (*photo*) he draws (*graph*).

Sugimoto is the purist of all purists. He feels little affinity with color photography. His medium of choice is black-and-white, in which, he observes, "Night creates rich black, forcing long exposures." Above all, he loves the winter night: "The black is intense, revealing the bottom of the night." He finds that clouds especially photograph beautifully in the crisp winter air (Pl. 22.2). His first mature series, *Walk in the Night*, resulted from four years of shooting the cityscapes of New York at night, from 2002 to 2005 (Pls. 22.1–3). His shooting period started in November, when trees shed their foliage. The first three months of the year were his favorite; the warmer months were reserved for the darkroom. In the

first year of the project, he was still a student at the International Center of Photography (ICP) and he shot every night, roaming the desolate streets of downtown Manhattan (in the East Village and West Village) and the Brooklyn neighborhoods of Sunset Park and Williamsburg. If he went to Times Square, he stayed on the side streets. He disliked the clutter of people even at night, perhaps because they brought with them the "reality situation" of daytime. Besides, night is more "obvious" to him: "If photography is a means to capture reality, I can still make a completely different world at night, by working in the gradations of black."

The night photography of Sugimoto makes a ready comparison with that of Provoke, a group of radical photographers working in Tokyo almost four decades ago. The works of all are grainy, often blurred, and out of focus. However, whereas the Provoke photographers—especially Moriyama Daidō and Nakahira Takuma—endeavored to document urban life as it was lived and

PLATE 22.1

Gō Sugimoto
Untitled from *Walk in the Night*
2004
Gelatin silver print
20 x 24" (50.8 x 61 cm)
Courtesy of the artist and M.Y. Art
Prospects, New York
PHOTO: GŌ SUGIMOTO

seen by denizens of the underground world, Sugimoto creates a study in abstraction, intent on seeing a netherworld of the city invisible to the ordinary eye.

Scenes captured in his *Walk in the Night* are phantasmic. A tree is not like any tree we know, seemingly glowing from within (Pl. 22.1). It is accorded an iconic presence against the nocturnal air. A church stands as an ethereal void of itself (Pl. 22.3). The camera did its job, and so did the artist. With the tree, he found one angle wherein the fluorescent light of a streetlamp hit its trident trunk like a spotlight. With the church, the camera faithfully captured the detail of sculptural ornaments on the illuminated facade; the artist then keyed up the contrast in the printing process to kill the detail, depriving the edifice of its corporeality.

It may come as a surprise, but Sugimoto produced *Walk in the Night* with a point-and-shoot, which was his first ever camera. He purchased it when he enrolled at ICP in 2002 at the age of 22, after a few years in New York. Long fascinated by photography, he had never had a chance to study it. His interest in making things first took the form of small collages and assemblages, which were obsessive and even stifling. Photography might have taught him to maintain a

distance from his own vision, intervened by the mechanics of the film camera and the chemical processes of the darkroom.

In the next project, *Paper_work* (2004–05), Sugimoto took the completely opposite direction in every way (Pls. 22.4–5). This time, he shot in pure white with a bare hint of shade. He retreated from the street into a makeshift studio in the corner of his room; he used a medium-format camera he borrowed from ICP over the weekend; he set up a meticulous composition of a sheet of white paper; he fussed over the lighting—all these in order to create a light-filled vision which is, again, phantasmic, in a sense that it is barely perceptible.

Sugimoto works slowly and deliberately in series. He still has a few more ideas in his arsenal to realize, which he developed during his year at ICP by dutifully following the inspiring advice of his instructor, "You must find what you want to do, find your own expression, and you graduate with these ideas." We just have to wait to see what's next with Gō Sugimoto.

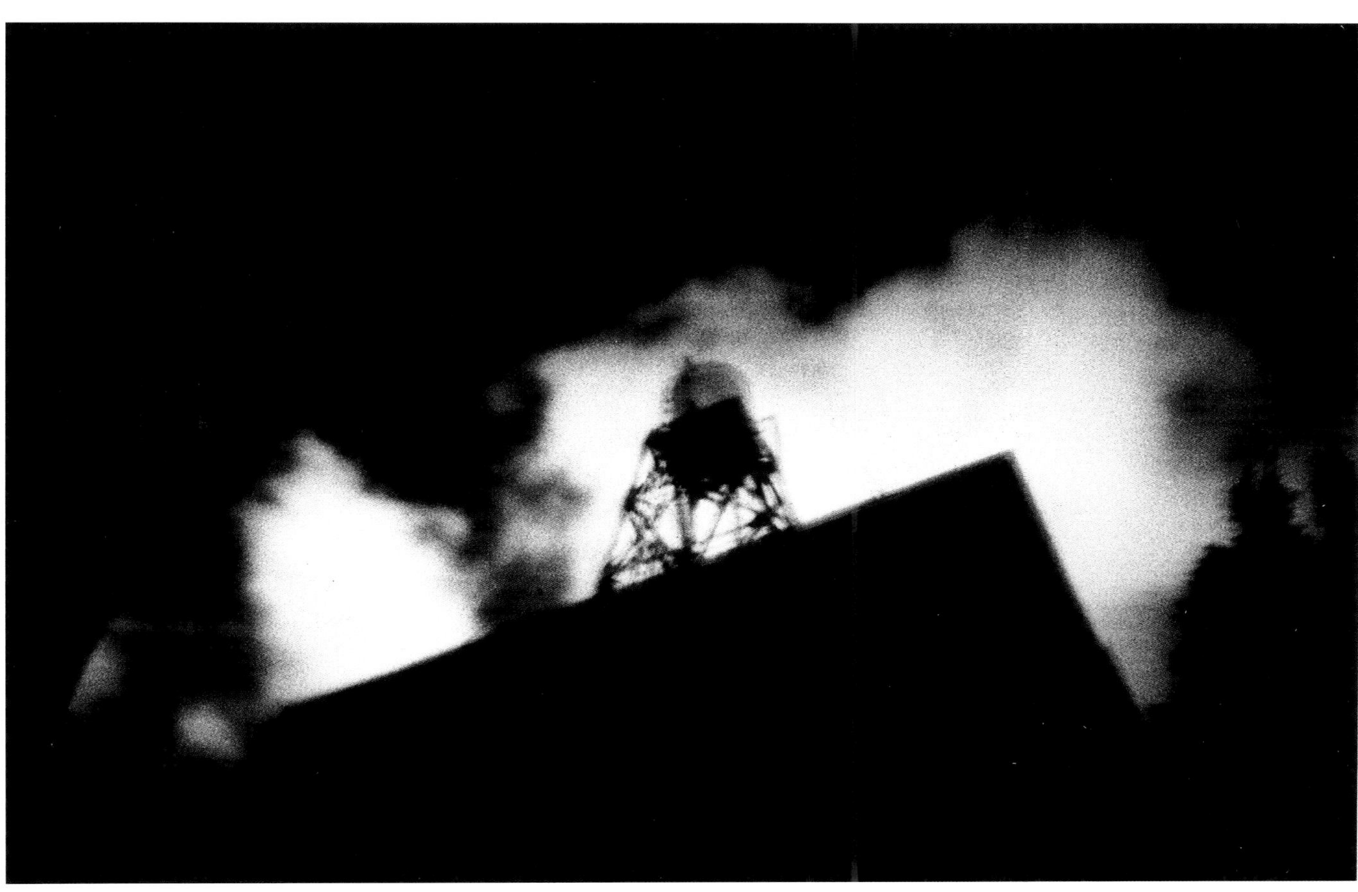

Gō Sugimoto
Untitled from *Walk in the Night*
2004
Gelatin silver print
20 x 24" (50.8 x 61 cm)
Courtesy of the artist and M.Y. Art Prospects, New York
PHOTO: GŌ SUGIMOTO

Why did you decide to leave Japan?

GS: I planned to make a trip to New York since I had always wanted to go. I even remember that I got really excited about going to New York when I was very little and watching a kids' television program in the morning before going to school. It's called *Ponkikki*. They always had some report from New York, so I often dreamed about it quietly. New York is a good place to be beaten up for a while when I am young, to experience lots of important things in my life. I basically thought I could grow more here than living in Tokyo.

Why did you choose New York as your ultimate destination?

GS: I came here directly and I never lived elsewhere before. I am not sure New York will be my ultimate destination, but I am hoping it will be.

Has the experience of living in New York changed your style or process significantly?

GS: I started making my work since I moved here. I am influenced by Japanese aesthetics and global culture.

Do you ever regret leaving Japan?

GS: No. However, when I am hungry and eating pasta all the time, I miss Japanese food.

In this age of globalism, do you consider yourself to be a Japanese artist, an American artist, an international artist, or a hybrid of all three?

GS: I would like to consider myself as a hybrid artist. However, I might be called a Japanese artist because of my work. It also depends on what I make in my future.

PLATE 22.3

Gō Sugimoto
Untitled from *Walk in the Night*
2003
Gelatin silver print
20 x 24" (50.8 x 61 cm)
Courtesy of the artist and M.Y. Art Prospects, New York
PHOTO: GŌ SUGIMOTO

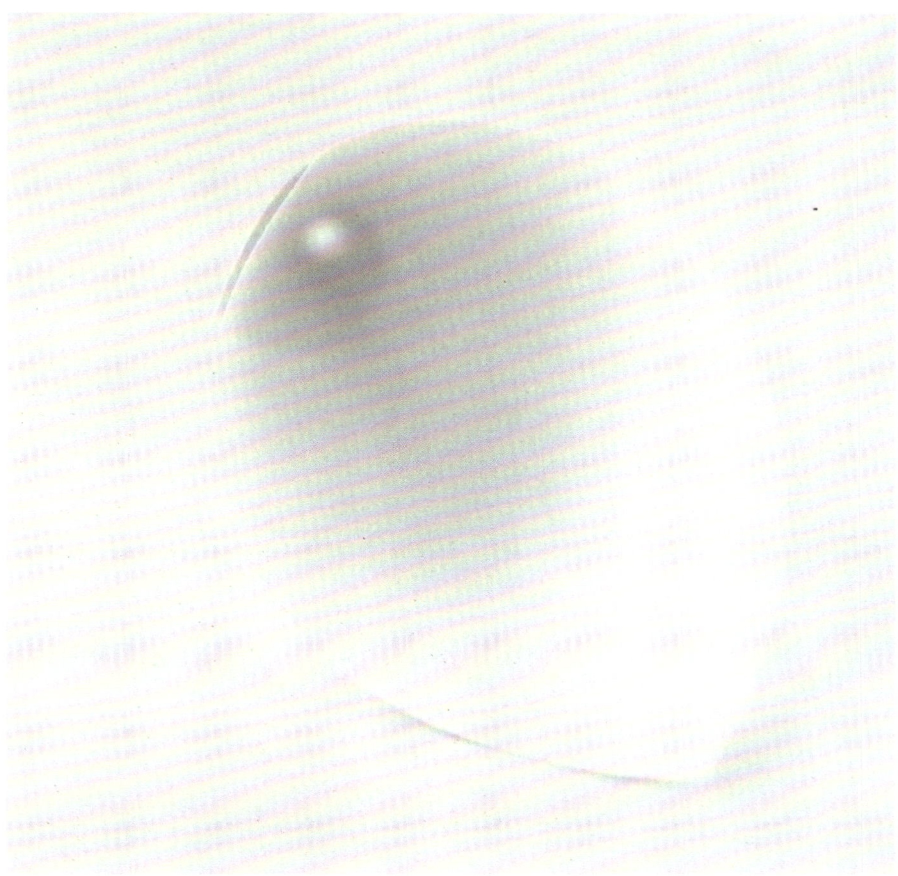

PLATE 22.4

Gō Sugimoto
Untitled from *Paper_work*
2006
Gelatin silver print
20 x 20" (50.8 x 50.8 cm)
Courtesy of the artist and M.Y. Art
Prospects, New York

PLATE 22.5

Gō Sugimoto
Untitled from *Paper_work*
2006
Gelatin silver print
20 x 20" (50.8 x 50.8 cm)
Courtesy of the artist and M.Y. Art
Prospects, New York

23 KUNIE SUGIURA

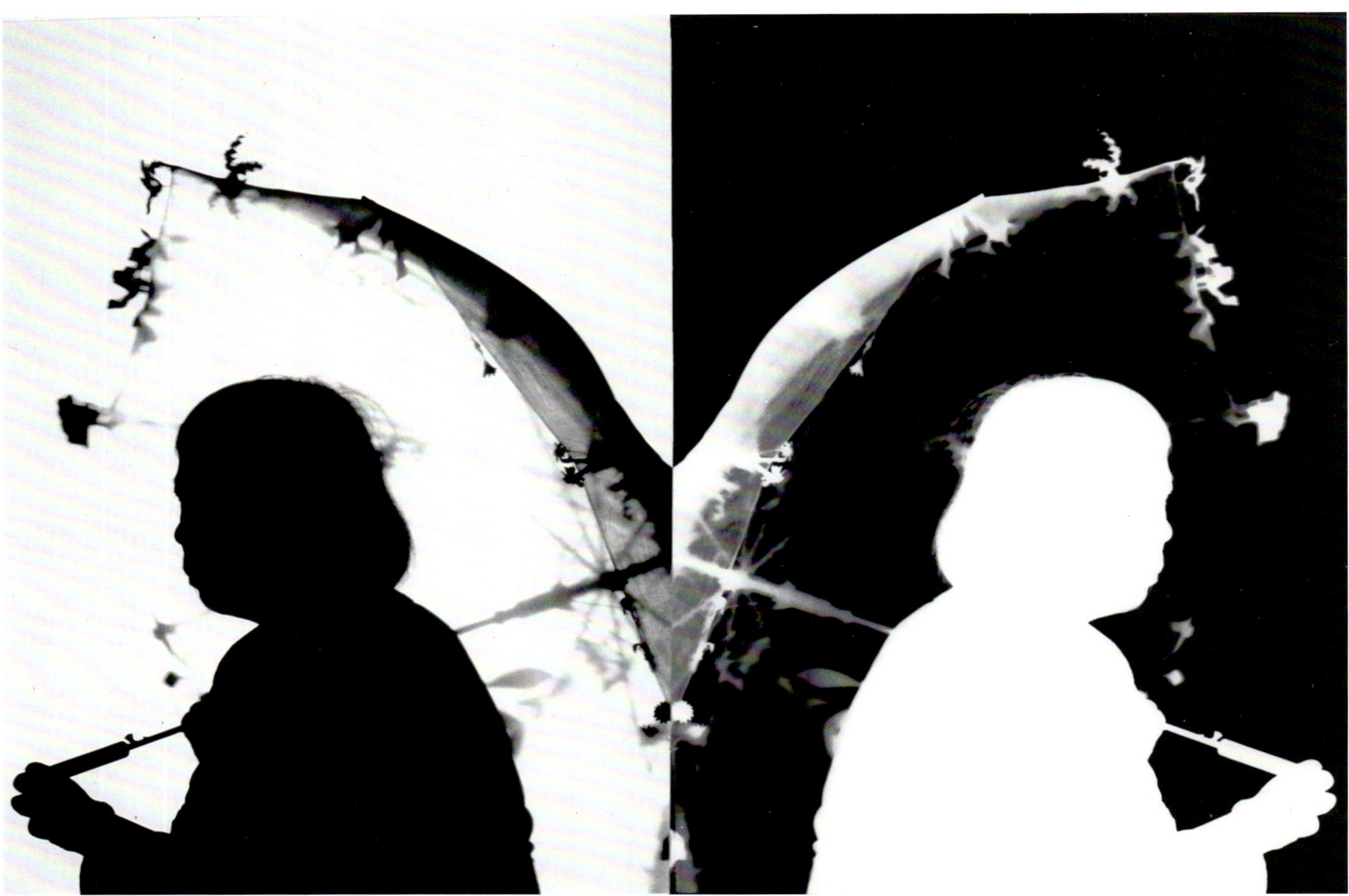

Holding Paper to the Sun
ERIC C. SHINER

Artist Kunie Sugiura has been on a decades-long quest for shadows and ghosts. Simply, she has revolutionized the contemporary usage of a venerable photographic technique, the photogram. Her works are studies of bodies, flowers, and forms, mostly in monochrome, created from light shone on objects and people set against photographic paper. Once exposed, they become the archival remains of that which covered the surface for a brief moment in time. Perhaps best known for her flower pictures, in their X-rayed rawness, Sugiura uses her chosen medium not only to capture the idea of a flower, but also to bore into that concept, exposing not just the stalks and stamens of physical flowers, but the metaphysical essence of blooms laid bare before her. In a rare experiment from 2005–06, Sugiura infused one series of her flower photograms with color, allowing an even deeper understanding of beauty in Technicolor radiance; the works burst with an emotional energy that tricks the viewer into thinking that the stems are very much alive, though they are but ghosts of long-dead buds that only the artist had the luxury of savoring (Pl. 23.2).

Her monochrome photograms of flowers range in density from lightly strewn assemblages of stems in swoops and swirls, as in *Trocoids Positive* (2003), to densely populated pictures that use natural forms to create clearly unnatural constructs, as in *Stacked Tulips A8* (1999). In either case, Sugiura takes simple flowers and contorts them into formal arrangements that are both beautiful and academic at the same time. Her grids and ellipses become landscapes and still lifes infused with energy, yet completely devoid of the essence of flowers as found in nature. These works become receptacles for flowers that never die, flowers that become spectral forms contorted into space for eternity.

In this vein, Sugiura has made a career of capturing ghosts in her alchemical project of holding paper, conceptually, to the sun. The act of exposing chemically treated paper to the bright burst of a manmade flashbulb is like the process of capturing an image on film within the confines of a camera. With the photogram, the set itself becomes a camera of sorts, the subject an internal

PLATE 23.1

Kunie Sugiura
Yayoi Kusama C and Cp
2003
Unique gelatin silver prints (2 panels), framed
39 x 59" (99.1 x 149.9 cm)
Collection of Lewis and Diana Meyers, New York;
courtesy Leslie Tonkonow Artworks + Projects, New York
PHOTO: JEFF STURGES, NEW YORK

element of this scenario; it becomes etched on the paper once the light source is triggered. The entire process holds other historical references. It is akin to the capturing of shadows in the blinding rays of light let loose from a nuclear bomb: here, the city becomes a camera populated with subjects frozen in time by a murderous flash. Hiroshima was one such mangled camera, and the horrific shadows left in Little Boy's wake no doubt stand in direct juxtaposition to Sugiura's images of beauty captured in a most familiar way. Although Sugiura was born in Nagoya and raised in postwar Tokyo, far from the wreckage of Hiroshima and Nagasaki, she no doubt was aware of the effects light can have, for better or for worse.

For *Making a Home*, Sugiura displays three works from her *The Artist Papers* series, in which she asked luminary artists to pose for her. In addition to such American masters as Jasper Johns and Robert Wilson, she photographed many Japanese art stars, including Takashi Murakami and Kusama Yayoi. The Murakami piece shows the artist in profile placing his bright anime-inspired paper eyes on a gallery wall (Pl. 23.3); Kusama's work positions the artist in profile with a large umbrella adorned with flowers behind her (Pl. 23.1). In addition to these two works, an image of Ushio Shinohara, a fellow featured artist in *Making a Home* is displayed in a Mylar room (Pl. 23.4). The shadows of these Japanese contemporary artists, all current or former residents of New York, are reflected on the shiny mirrored surfaces of the gallery floor; the viewer sees her or himself and shadows of the artists simultaneously, evoking an otherworld populated by apparitions of a most productive variety. All of these artists are currently alive and well, yet their spirits float for an eternity in Sugiura's honorific homage made real by a flash of light as ephemeral as life itself.

KS: I was eight years old. In art class we were taken to the park and were supposed to paint pink cherry blossoms but I painted a big green pine tree. The teacher praised my painting and I realized I could be rebellious and accepted in art.

KS: I was studying physics then and wanted to get out of that situation. I went to the School of the Art Institute of Chicago to study industrial design and changed to photography and film later.

KS: It was during the Vietnam War and in the middle of the Hippie movement. People, the street, and art in New York are so fascinating and exciting to me. People looked expressive, liberated, and hopeful. A lot of art slides I saw in art history classes were on the wall in the museum. Many galleries every month had terrific new shows— qualities, diversities, and media activities.

KS: Richard Bellamy and David Hickey. They put me in touch with other artists and found outlets for my works.

KS: No. But I wish I could live in Japan simultaneously while I lived here, like if I could have a clone, for I think Japan is a very interesting place.

KS: People see me as Japanese or woman or a Japanese woman artist constantly, so that I have to recognize what I am made of. I think I am all of the above and I probably act like what others expect from me even as I try to ignore that. But art can be a thoughtful, meaningful personal discovery, and free to share with all people who come into contact with it.

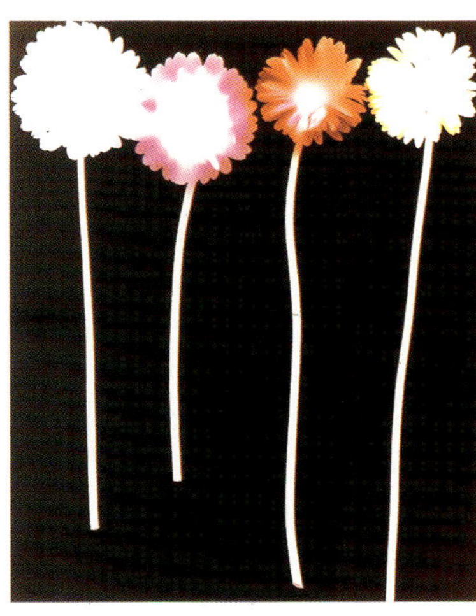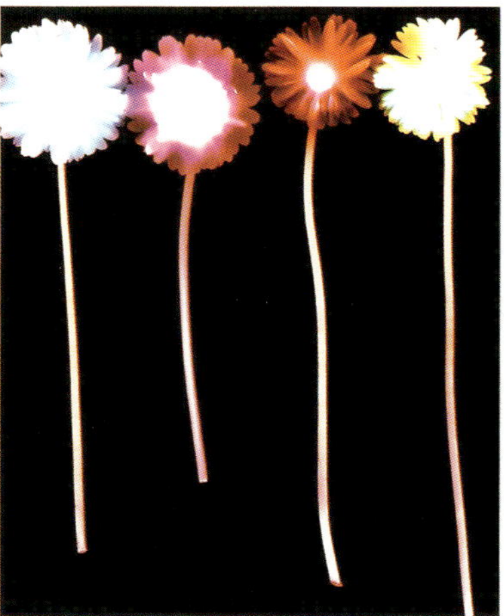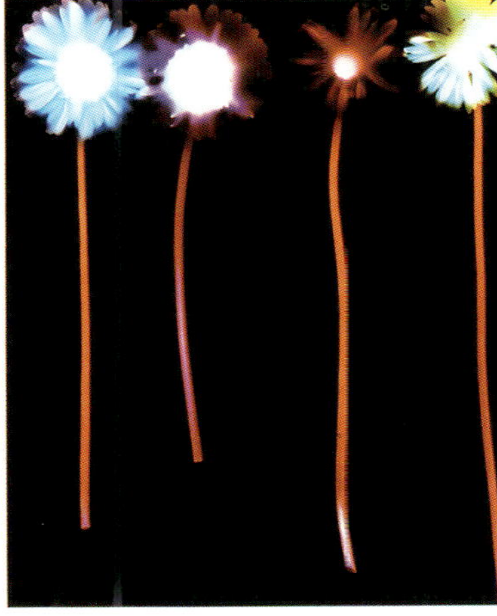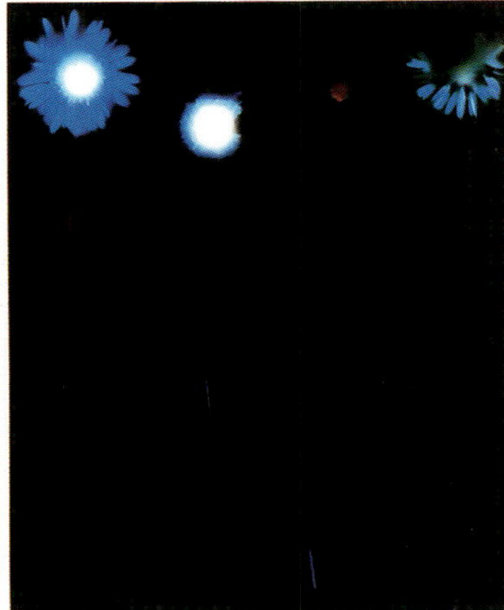

PLATE 23.2

Kunie Sugiura
Gerbera 4 Times
4 C-prints
2006
Each 20 x 16" (50.8 x 40.6 cm)
Collection of Nakahara Hiroshi, Tokyo
PHOTO: GO SUGIMOTO AND LEANDO VILLARO

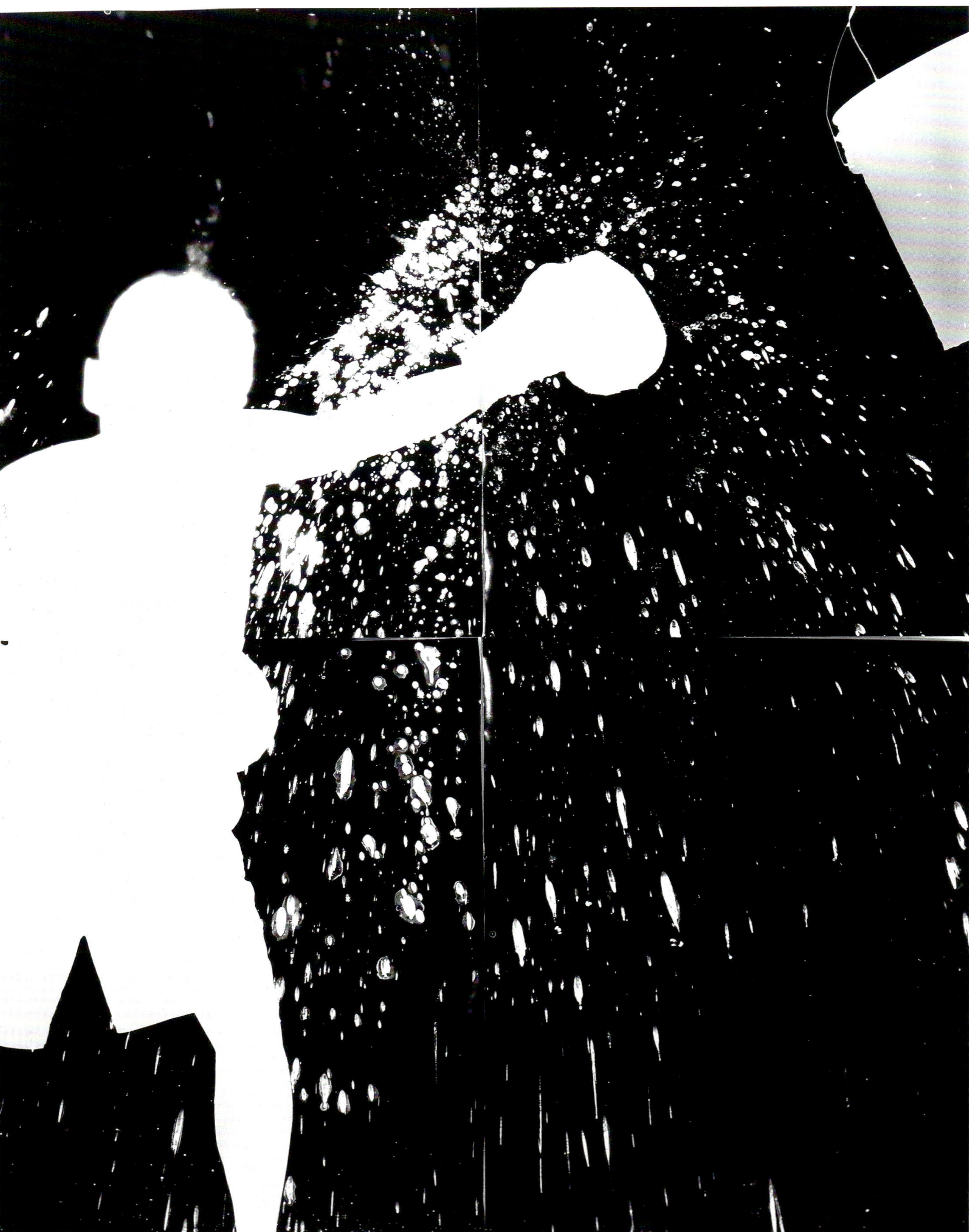

PLATE 23.3

Kunie Sugiura
The Boxing Papers (Shinohara B)
1999
Unique gelatin silver prints (4 panels), framed
80 x 60" (203.2 x 152.4 cm)
Collection of Robinson and Nancy Grover, West
Hartford, Conn.; courtesy Leslie Tonkonow
Artworks + Projects, New York

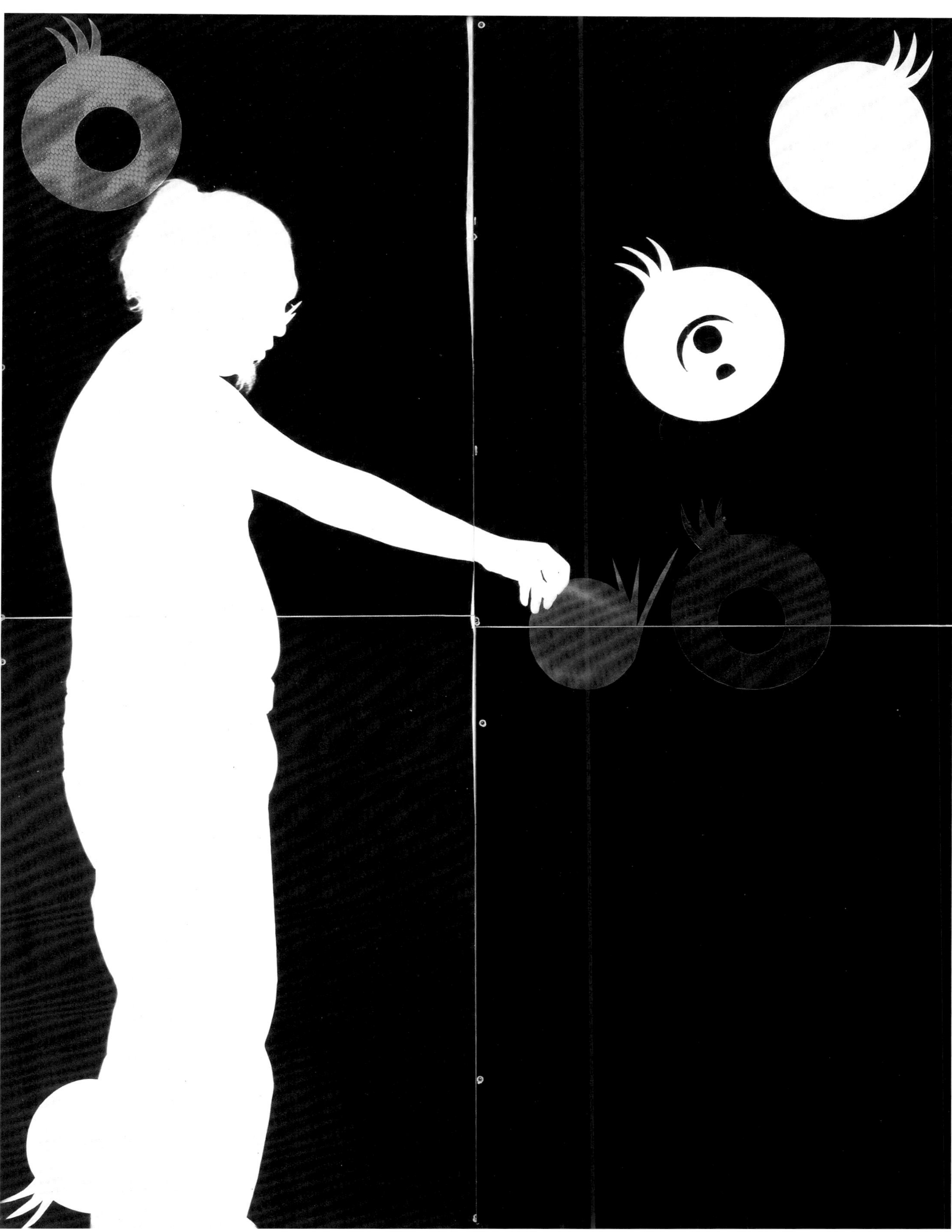

PLATE 23.4

Kunie Sugiura
Takashi Murakami A
2002
Unique gelatin silver prints (4 panels), framed
78 ¼ x 57 ½" (198.8 x 146.1 cm)
Collection of Dr. & Mrs. Thomas Loeb, Old Westbury, N.Y.;
courtesy Leslie Tonkonow Artworks + Projects, New York
PHOTO: JEFF STURGES, NEW YORK

⌂ 24 HIROSHI SUNAIRI

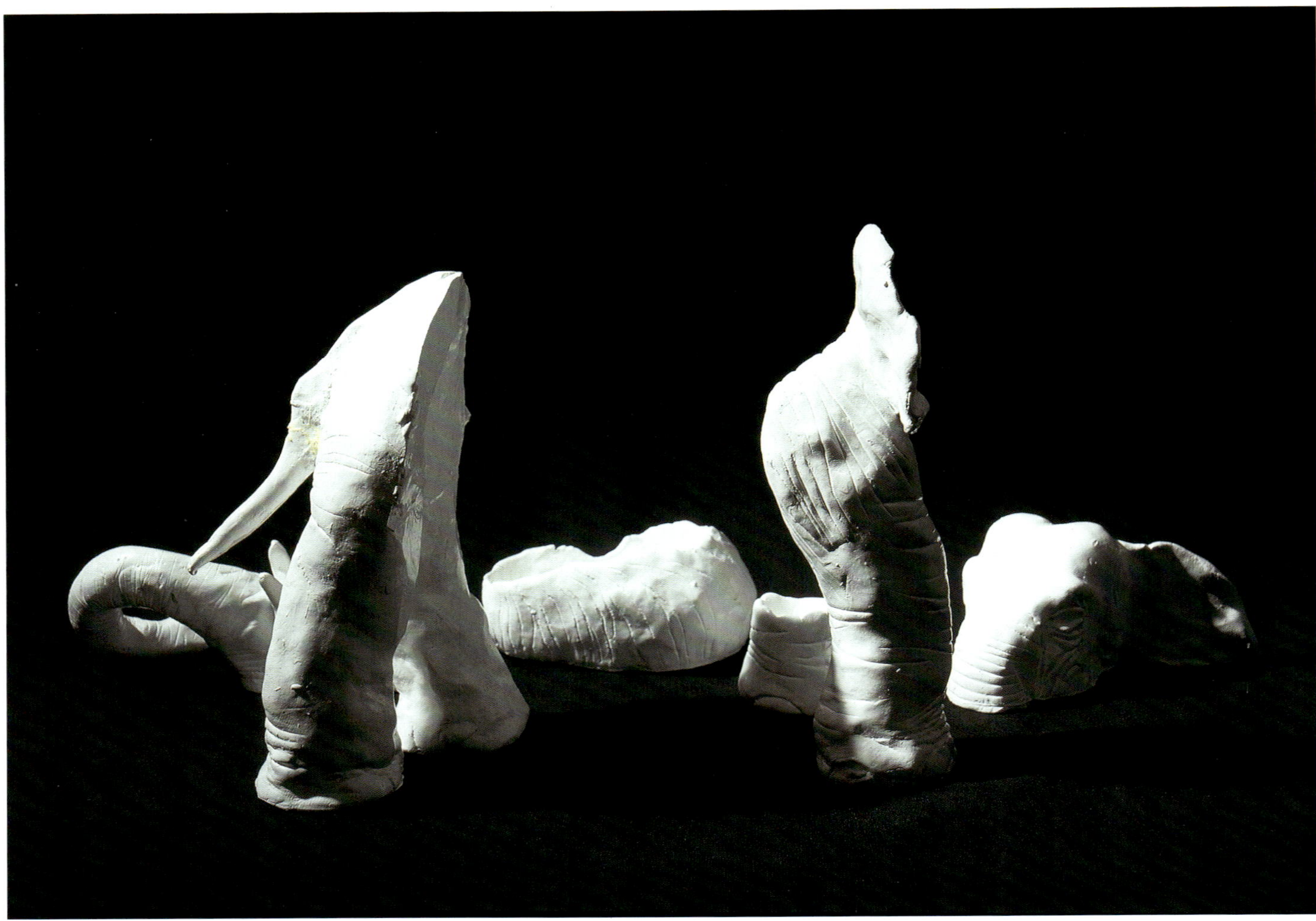

Memento Mori for New York
BARBARA LONDON

On September 11, 2001 at 9:15 AM, Hiroshi Sunairi sat in an A train stalled at the Church Street Station, anxiously wondering why the doors remained shut. Suddenly a woman appeared on the platform, screaming and gesticulating wildly. He assumed, "Oh, another crazy New Yorker." Sunairi could only think about how late he would now be for his immigration appointment with the INS. When the subway doors finally opened, he sprinted up the stairs toward his destination. Of course he never made it to the meeting, becoming entangled in the melee on the street (Pl. 24.2). Ignoring policemen's attempts to stop him, he reached the destruction site and captured the flying debris and billowing devastation with the fresh film that happened to be in his camera.

Sunairi's first-hand experience with the World Trade Center disaster resonated with childhood memories. For several decades, his prosperous-again hometown of Hiroshima has had a bifurcated public face, most visibly with the new shiny buildings standing next to shards of old ones. Although he is two generations removed

from the fateful event, as a Hiroshima dweller the history of horror and destruction was imprinted on him. Since childhood he saw the influx of international crowds making annual pilgrimages to demonstrate for peace, as they gathered at the iconic site memorializing August 6, 1945.

At 18, Sunairi left Japan to pursue art in the United States. After his BA he moved to New York and became a denizen of the downtown club scene. Freer than he ever could have been in hierarchical Japan, he moved from painting to photography and then to performance (that interdisciplinary forum of new ideas). He approached identity politics through trans-gendering, drawing on the sensibility of Noh and Kabuki, where men dress and masquerade as female characters while still retaining the dignity of their masculinity. He focused on "enlightening" the role of Asian men and wanted to project empowerment of the Asian male in his art. His campy, geisha-like demeanor attracted a following, but he felt that his political intentions were misunderstood and decided

PLATE 24.1

Hiroshi Sunairi
White Elephant (miniature model)
2007
Clay
Height: 1 ½–6" (3.8–15.2 cm)
Collection of the artist
PHOTO: TAKAHIRO KANEYAMA

to go beyond the narcissistic tendency in art to something more universal but personally felt.

In 2005 Sunairi returned to his hometown, invited to do a workshop with students and to create a new installation for the Hiroshima City Museum of Contemporary Art. While beginning this work he discovered that his mother was irradiated by the atomic bomb when in her mother's womb. (This type of irradiation is called *tainai hibaku* in Japanese.) He was closer to the event than he realized. Sunairi focused on elephants, inspired by the saying that "elephants never forget" and the storybook legend that the animals have the ability to find their way back to their birthplace. Sunairi went off to do preliminary research in India, where elephants are considered offshoots of a god, not friendly Dumbos or zoo or circus animals as viewed in Japan and the West. To a small child, the actual colossi are closer to monsters, sometimes frightening because of their imposing scale.

Sunairi's installation in Hiroshima, *A Night of Elephants*, became a community art project (Pl. 24.3). Based on the drawings he did in India, he designed a mesh cage in the shape of a life-size, recumbent elephant. He spent the next several months working with locals, collecting *hibaku*, or irradiated, objects: a leather

backpack once owned by an elementary schoolgirl who perished in the bombing, wooden walls from a demolished gymnasium, a skirt stained by ointment that soothed a young woman's wounds, and tattered, abandoned socks. Sunairi also worked with local gardeners, who provided prunings from trees that miraculously survived the bombing. He then filled the elephant cage with the cut branches and displayed the other objects along the back wall of the gallery, each with its own memories and history. The scruffiness gives the work a humble charm.

Sunairi's latest work, *White Elephant* (2007), is made of porcelain (Pl. 24.1). The life-size adolescent elephant's body has been broken down into many parts. Viewers are free to walk around the apparition and confront the wizened units: the large head, stumpy feet, and amphora legs. The behemoth feels domesticated and controllable. Arranged across the floor, the elephant resembles a still life, and elicits ruminations on life and death and regeneration.

Hiroshi Sunairi's thoughts take him back to the morning of 9/11, when his clothing turned gray with dust and he gasped for breath as debris floated from the sky. The impermanence of life remains on Sunairi's mind in this memento mori, a memorial to Manhattan by an artist who draws inspiration from being rooted to New York.

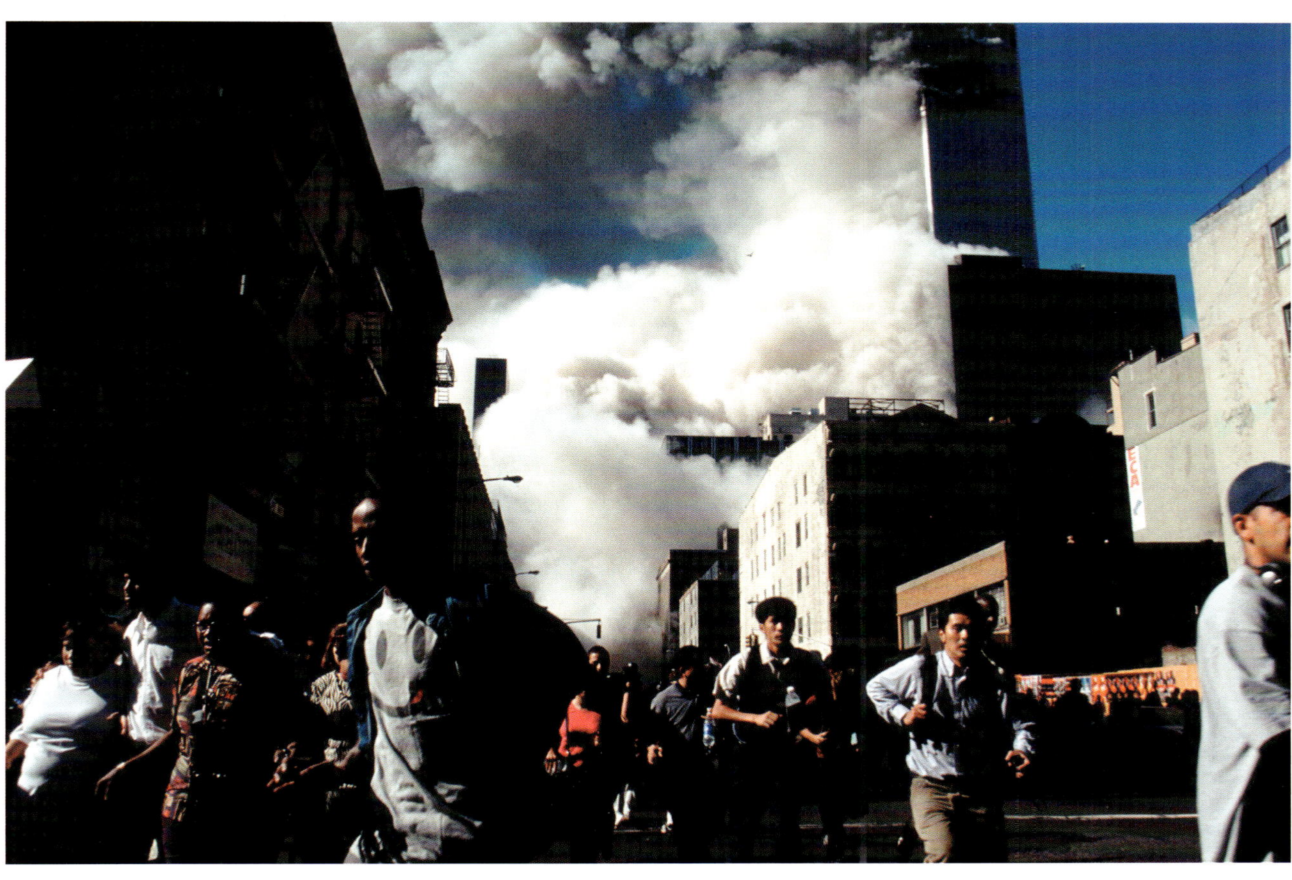

When and how did you first realize that you wanted to be an artist?
HS: I grew up with a sign company my parents owned. So, the scene of production was naturally my playground. I used to draw the Disney animation *101 Dalmatians* to get attention from people in my preschool. Then I had a vague idea about being an artist. But, then, one day I discovered the biography of Andy Warhol. When I read the book, I became fascinated with Warhol and Pop Art. It hit me strongly that art could be as fluid as music.

Why did you choose New York as your ultimate destination?
HS: I lived in Utah, Washington State, then upstate New York, enjoying the different cultures, landscapes, and people over some time. But I knew that ultimately I wanted to come to New York. I wanted to get in the middle of the hybrid culture that New York was famous for.

What experience has given you the most satisfaction as an artist in New York?
HS: When Roberta Smith wrote an article on me in the *New York Times*, which really dealt with the progress of my artmaking in such a caring way. It really moved me and I realized that someone out there was watching me.

In this age of globalism, do you consider yourself to be a Japanese artist, an American artist, an international artist, or a hybrid of all three?
HS: I am a Japanese artist living in New York, an artist who was educated in American art, an artist who exhibited in the West all at the same time. I experience globalism, migration, and the international art world in fragments just as I am partly all of a Japanese artist, an American artist, and an international artist. I experience rather unique encounters because of the particularity of my work, so it has been such a liberating experience to be where I am.

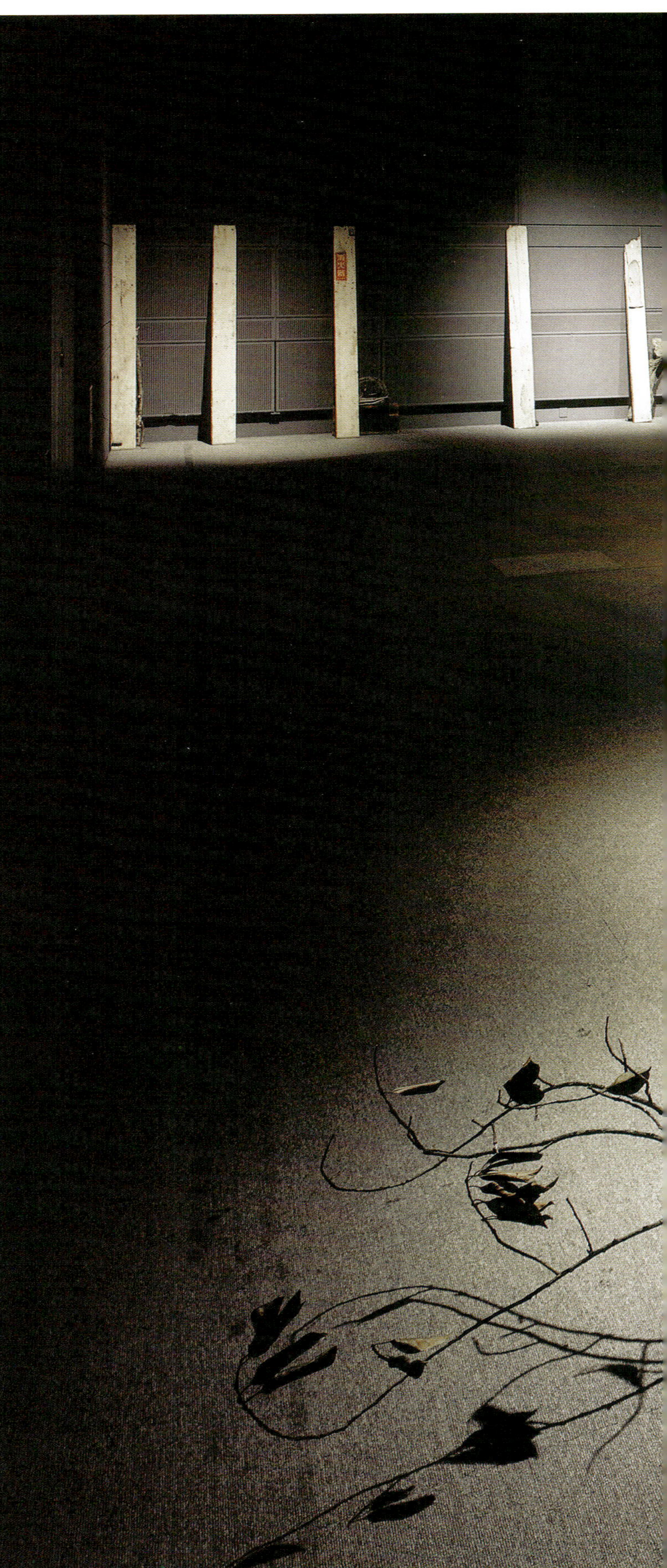

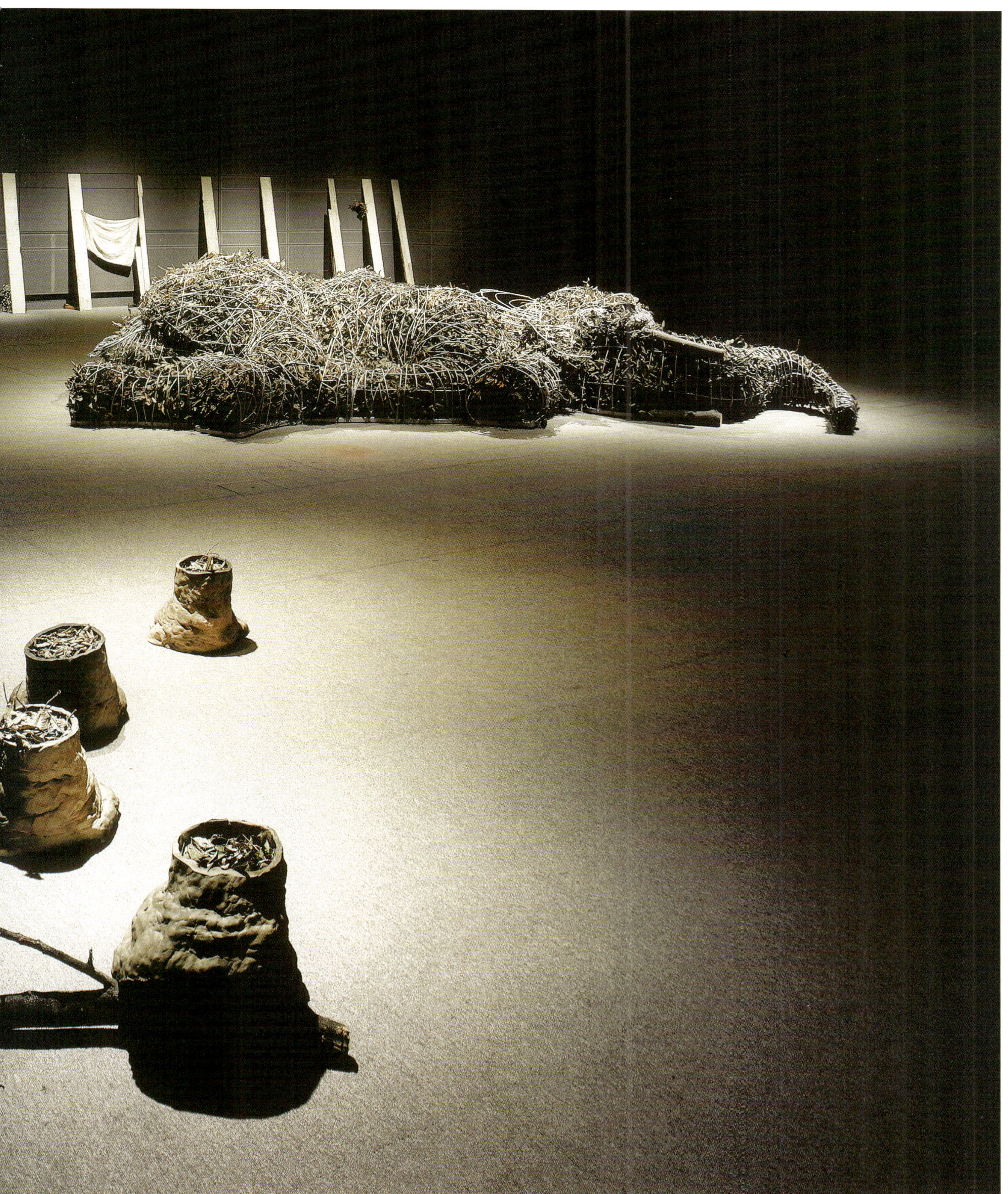

PLATE 24.3

Hiroshi Sunairi
A Night of Elephants
2005
Elephant: steel, metal board, Japanese Hackberry trees, *kuroganemochi* trees, and *nuku* trees; elephant foot: ceramic; *hibaku* objects: leather backpack, wooden walls, a woman's skirt, and a little boy's sock
Elephant: 39 ⅜ x 118 ⅛ x 196 ⅞'' (1 x 3 x 5m); elephant foot: each 15 x 15 x 15'' (38.1 x 38.1 x 38.1 cm)
Collection of the artist
PHOTO: ŌSHIMA STUDIO, HIROSHIMA

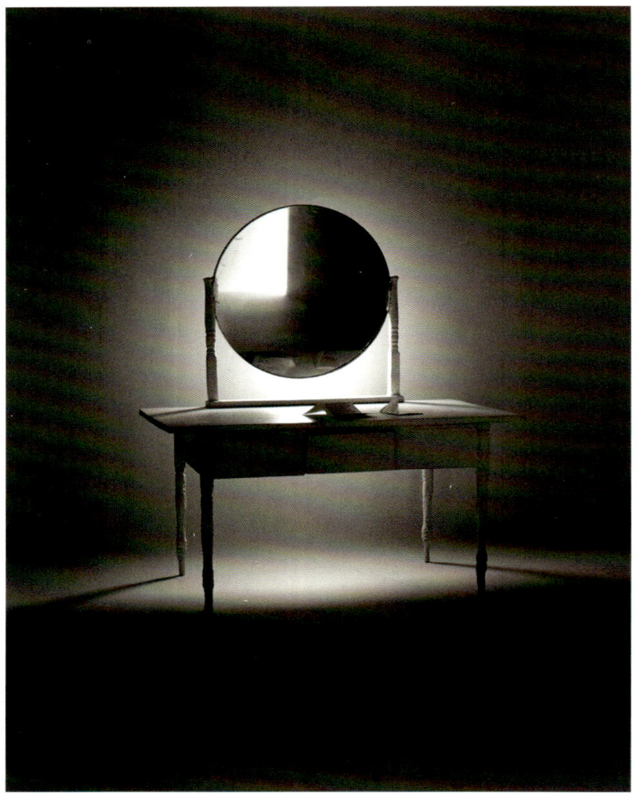
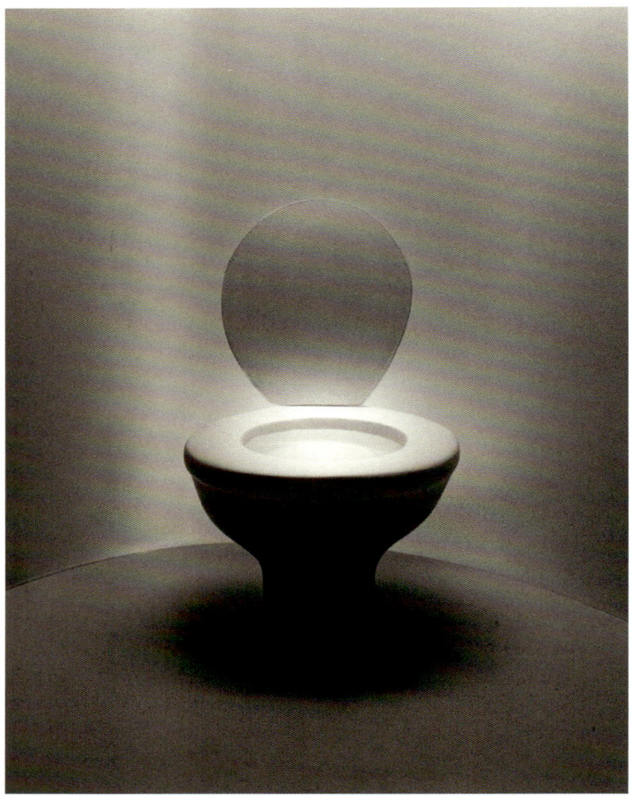

25 MAYUMI TERADA

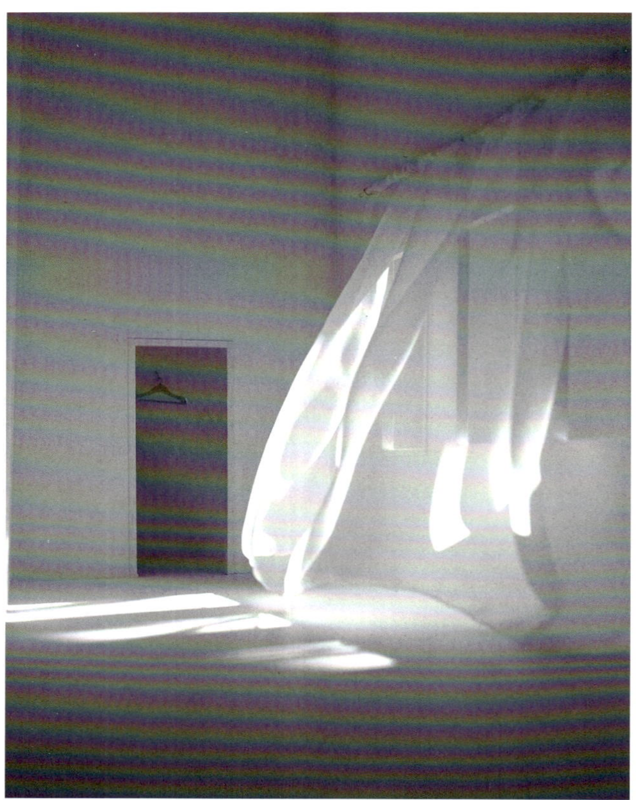

PLATE 25.1

Mayumi Terada
Dresser
2003
Gelatin silver print
22 ½ x 17'' (57.1 x 43.2 cm)
Courtesy Robert Miller Gallery,
New York

PLATE 25.2

Mayumi Terada
Toilet
2003
Gelatin silver print
22 ½ x 17'' (57.1 x 43.2 cm)
Courtesy Robert Miller Gallery,
New York

PLATE 25.3

Mayumi Terada
Curtain
2001
Gelatin silver print
55 x 41 ½'' (139.7 x 105.4 cm)
Courtesy Robert Miller Gallery,
New York

PLATE 25.4

Mayumi Terada
Shower
2001
Gelatin silver print
22 ½ x 17'' (57.1 x 43.2 cm)
Courtesy Robert Miller Gallery,
New York

Intimate Absence
JONATHAN GOODMAN

Mayumi Terada moved to New York from Japan in 2001. Beginning her artistic career as a sculptor, she began photographing her three-dimensional models of interior space in Japan, shortly before coming to New York. When the all-white, simply furnished mock-ups are finished, she goes on to photograph the miniature tableaux under natural light. The result is a haunting sequence of images, based upon a transparent facture and miniature size that produces anomalies in the picture, underscoring its exquisite artificiality. Terada remains a sculptor, working out, in a method similar to that of James Casebere, three-dimensional sets that are evocatively imaged in the photograph that is shown as the finished work. But whereas Casebere has been concerned with the social constraints of public spaces, Terada attracts her audience through imagery that can best be called poetic and melancholic; she seems to be most interested in the lyric approximation of loss. Her doors and windows let in light which is surrounded by shadow, and which offsets the deep darkness of the interior space.

When Terada first began making models of architectural interiors, the three-dimensional works were the final objects of contemplation. She photographed the models as a record of her work, only to find that the photographic images were so evocative that they were art in their own right. As an artist interested in how models might, and might not, fool her audience, she gives clues that undermine the seeming reality brought forth in her work. In an early piece titled *Curtain* (2001), light moves through the drapes to illuminate the floor of a room with one doorway and no furniture (Pl. 25.3). The only other element in the scene is a wooden clothes hanger hanging inside the suggested closet behind the doorway; its detailed manufacture and appropriate scale suggests a believable verisimilitude, yet there is something about the way the curtains catch the wind and light that argues against the certainty that the image is real. In fact, the curtains look false, like replicas of the real thing. This disconnect between the seeming truthfulness of the overall picture and the particulars that regularly undermine it says a considerable amount about the relations between artifice and authenticity; in fact, the account as it is and as we believe it to be is marvelously compounded in a photograph that encompasses certainty and pretense at the same moment in time.

The images of Terada evoke a delicate realism that, surprisingly, is most believable when most dreamlike. In the more recent works, the windows open out onto beautiful vistas of trees and dappled sunlight. In fact, Terada has in these pictures photographed tiny photographs of the natural world, adjusting them so they look convincing to the viewer. In one image, *Glass Door with Path* (2006), an open door looks out onto a shadowed path with foliage on either side (Pl. 25.7); and in another, titled *View of Bridge & Bed* (2006), one sees a bedroom with a horizontal window looking out onto a pedestrian bridge, over which tree branches hang (Pl. 25.6). The intimacy of the bed and gauze curtains, visible by indirect light, contrasts with the direct light of the view outside, which seems as public as the interior is private. In *Rocking Chair and Window* (2005), a particularly resonant image, the seat of a modern rocking chair catches the light reflected from a seascape that shines through a window before the chair (Pl. 25.5). In each of these images one senses an ongoing theme of isolation, in which the absence of people actually fills the picture with an atmosphere of longing.

The poetry and realism of Terada's images are perfectly balanced, effortlessly erecting a diminutive monument of isolated intimacy. How is it that these works are melancholic in ambience? Terada has built, in her ongoing sequence of imagistic loneliness, a world in which people do not appear—yet somehow contribute—to the artist's poetics of loss. Her audience is a part of this imagined, and imaginative, isolation; we project our emotions onto what is basically impartial and uninhabited, so that the sublime is completed in the life of feeling the images produce. Terada's indirect aesthetic, available both as constructed model and theme, visualizes a world in which nature offers solace in unspoken ways. Surprisingly, its beauty gives consolation even as she takes the comfort away.

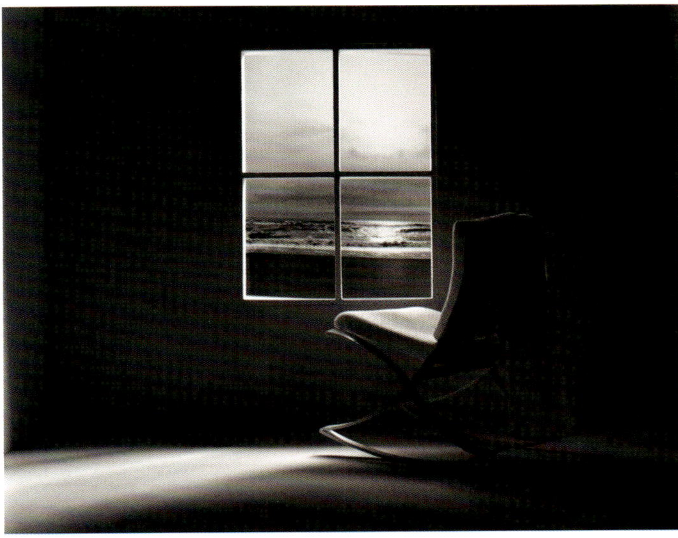

Mayumi Terada
Rocking Chair and Window
2005
Gelatin silver print
17 x 22 ½" (43.2 x 57.1 cm)
Courtesy Robert Miller Gallery, New York
PHOTO COURTESY OF THE ARTIST

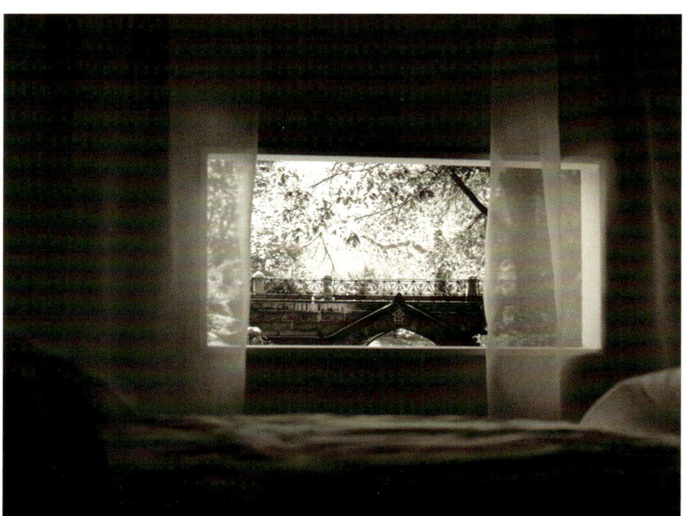

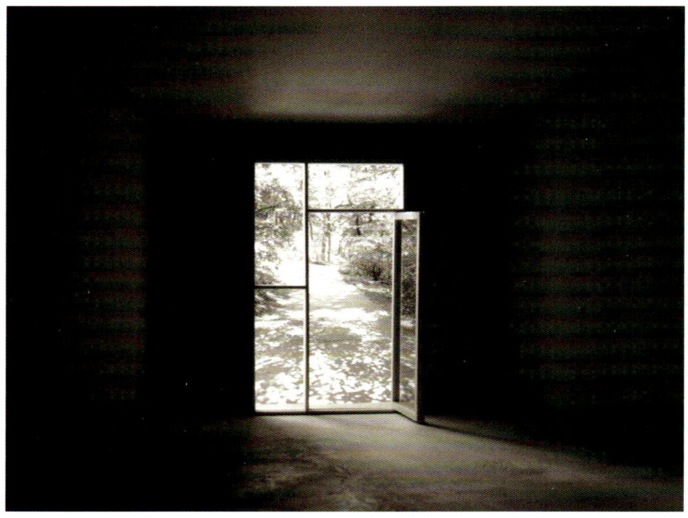

When and how did you first realize that you wanted to be an artist?

MT: I made an outscale and transparent jacket titled *Jumper Johns* in 1985. This was the beginning of my making art but I don't remember why I made it.

Why did you choose New York as your ultimate destination?

MT: I came to New York directly because I felt like it. I can see myself here more than anyplace else but I can't explain why.

What was your first impression of New York City?

MT: I first came to New York when I was three years old with my family and we stayed four years in the early 1960s. My first memory is the airplane. I remember my father taking me inside of the Statue of Liberty when my mother was in the hospital giving birth to my brother. I remember the view of the towering skyscrapers. About 40 years later I visited my old house. The building and backyard still remained and I had a sentimental moment. I have beautiful memories of New York.

Did you have any interactions with other artists or supporters that were especially beneficial to you and your work?

MT: Making a work is a process of confronting myself. It's a lonely act, so I have no interaction with anybody. Still, I am sometimes inspired by films and paintings by other artists. I love visiting the Metropolitan Museum to see paintings there. Every time I see Pollock's life-size abstraction, I am overwhelmed. I wish I could have met him!

In this age of globalism, do you consider yourself to be a Japanese artist, an American artist, an international artist, or a hybrid of all three?

MT: I think that the issue is personal and universal. If people from anywhere appreciate my work, it is fine.

PLATE 25.6

Mayumi Terada
View of Bridge and Bed
2006
Gelatin silver print
17 x 22 ½" (43.2 x 57.1 cm)
Courtesy Robert Miller Gallery, New York

PLATE 25.7

Mayumi Terada
Glass Door with Path
2006
Gelatin silver print
17 x 22 ½" (43.2 x 57.1 cm)
Courtesy Robert Miller Gallery, New York

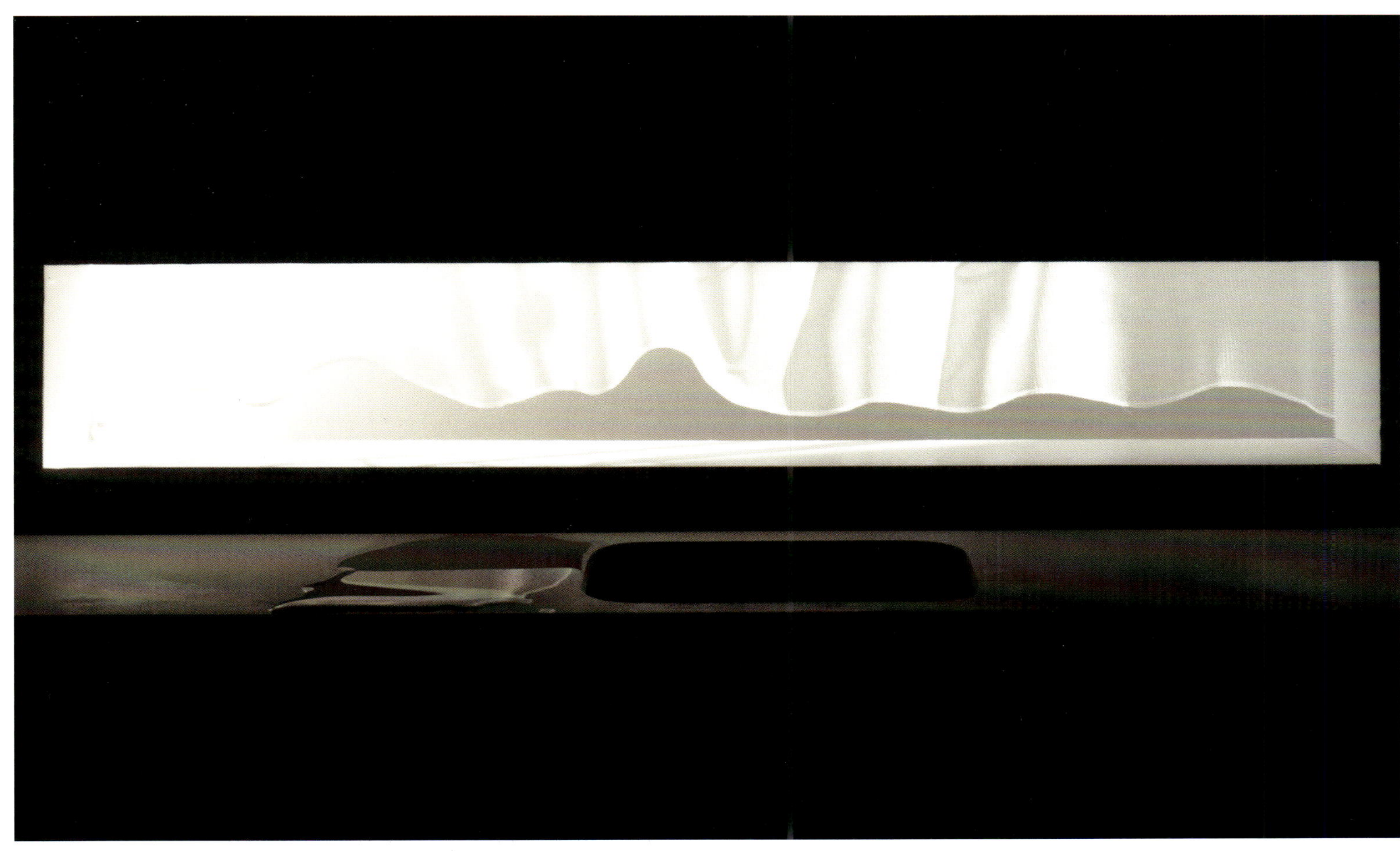

PLATE 25.8

Mayumi Terada
Kitchen Sink (horizontal)
2004
Gelatin silver print
17 x 22 ½" (43.2 x 57.1 cm)
Courtesy Robert Miller Gallery, New York

26 YŪKEN TERUYA

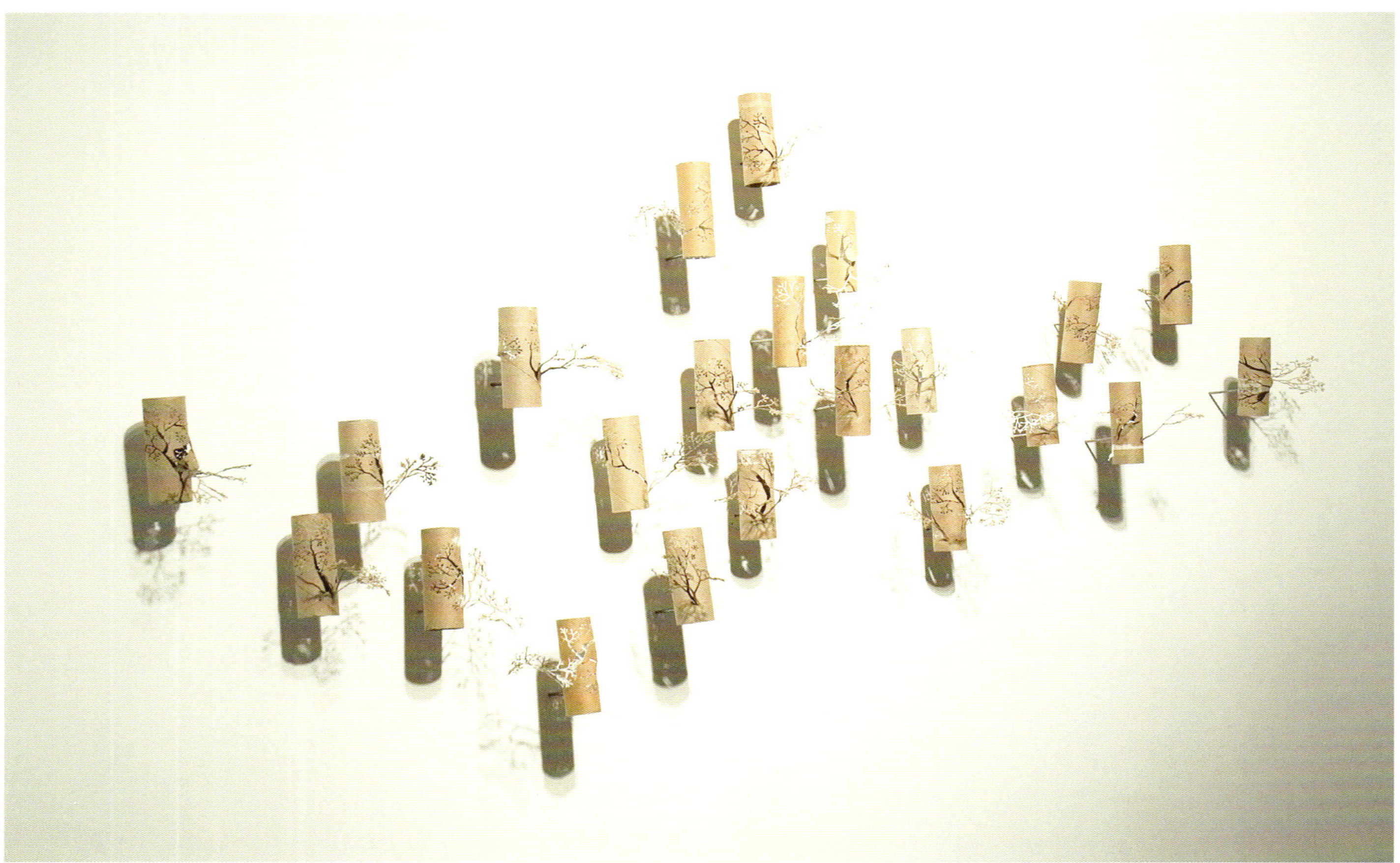

What Comes Around Goes Around
MIWAKO TEZUKA

A compulsive hoarder makes a great artist. Yūken Teruya finds and saves materials that are common everyday items, particularly those that are easily overlooked in the nitty-gritty of our fast-paced world. So far, objects that have become Teruya's source of inspiration—recycled and morphed into his artwork—range from things as prosaic as cardboard toilet paper tubes to often incomprehensible and negligible road signs. Common among his work is a sense of humor, which acts as a trigger to invoke hidden meanings in familiar materials and phenomena.

Teruya's artistic career is defined by movement: first from Okinawa to Tokyo, then to New York, his residence since 1998. Born in 1973, just one year after Okinawa's so-called "return" to Japan from the jurisdiction of the United States, he moved to Tokyo to attend Tama Art University and received his BFA in 1996. This first move made him aware that he was already an outsider, coming from the remote southern island. The realization prepared him for his next move to New York, where he seems at home today.

In 2002, he translated the geopolitical dynamics of Okinawa into a kimono design of *bingata*, a uniquely Okinawan stencil-dye technique. *You-I, You-I*, created in collaboration with an Okinawan artist trained in *bingata*-dye technique, represents Teruya's idea of his home (Pl. 26.3). Merged into traditional motifs of water, clouds, birds, and flowers are fighter planes and parachuting soldiers. For centuries, Okinawa's strategic location has brought to its people not only conflict and contestation, but also the confluence of varying cultures, Japanese, Chinese, and American. The largest U.S. military base in East Asia still operates there today, and its presence has become a fact of life in the region. However, Teruya's *bingata* kimono is not so much a simplistic criticism of this condition as an appreciation of the Okinawan strength, the people's ability to live with ideological complexity and sustain life's fragile balance, suggested by the title of this work: *You-I* is "you and I" in English and sounds like *yui*, "making," in archaic Japanese.

Teruya has since found in New York City a cacophonic mixture of things and people, turning his studio into a recycling bin. In fact, a series of works utilizing a pile of salvaged paper bags became his signature (Pl. 26.2). Among them, *Notice-Forest* was shown at the exhibition *Greater New York* at P.S.1 Contemporary Arts Center, New York, in 2005. It consists of seven small, extremely economical (in fact, free) paper shopping bags and take-out food bags. Sitting quietly on shelves with their openings to the front, they appear unassuming and negligible from afar. However, these bags are small dioramas housing trees, basking in light from above. The outline of these small trees is cut out from the top portion of the bags, then folded inward so that the roots affix to the inside bottom. Paper is returned to its original tree, and the space far from nature is transformed into an arborous environment. As each tree is uniquely based on an actual tree, the forest they create together represents the idea of individualism in a mass-consumer society.

In *Making a Home*, Teruya's alchemical magic turns the bamboo grove in Japan Society's lobby pond into a dense "rain forest." This is a continuation of another series, called *Rain Forest*, that utilizes toilet paper tubes from which cutout paper tree branches are sprouting (Pl. 26.1). The Japan Society installation echoes the natural growth of bamboo stalks as the tubes are hung vertically like raindrops falling from the sky. Strikingly, the paper branches are much more resilient than one might imagine. Made from recycled paper, the tubes' curved structure naturally gives each branch tautness and a slightly coiled swerve. The incongruous combination of the bamboo and the tubes comes harmoniously together as we learn that such formal resilience of bamboo is traditionally respected as a symbol of moral virtue. This installation may also bring to attention the fact that bamboo is one of the most environmentally friendly lumber substitutes.

Many facts of life lie buried under the world of complexity and entanglement. Teruya sifts through everyday life to carefully recover the seeds of meaning and potential that neglected materials inherently possess In essence, his approach begins in a Platonic vein: a seed of a tree already contains the *idea* of a fully grown tree. But Teruya goes further to create his own theory; he believes in the resilience of everyday ephemera and their potential to make a full circle, being reborn before our eyes.

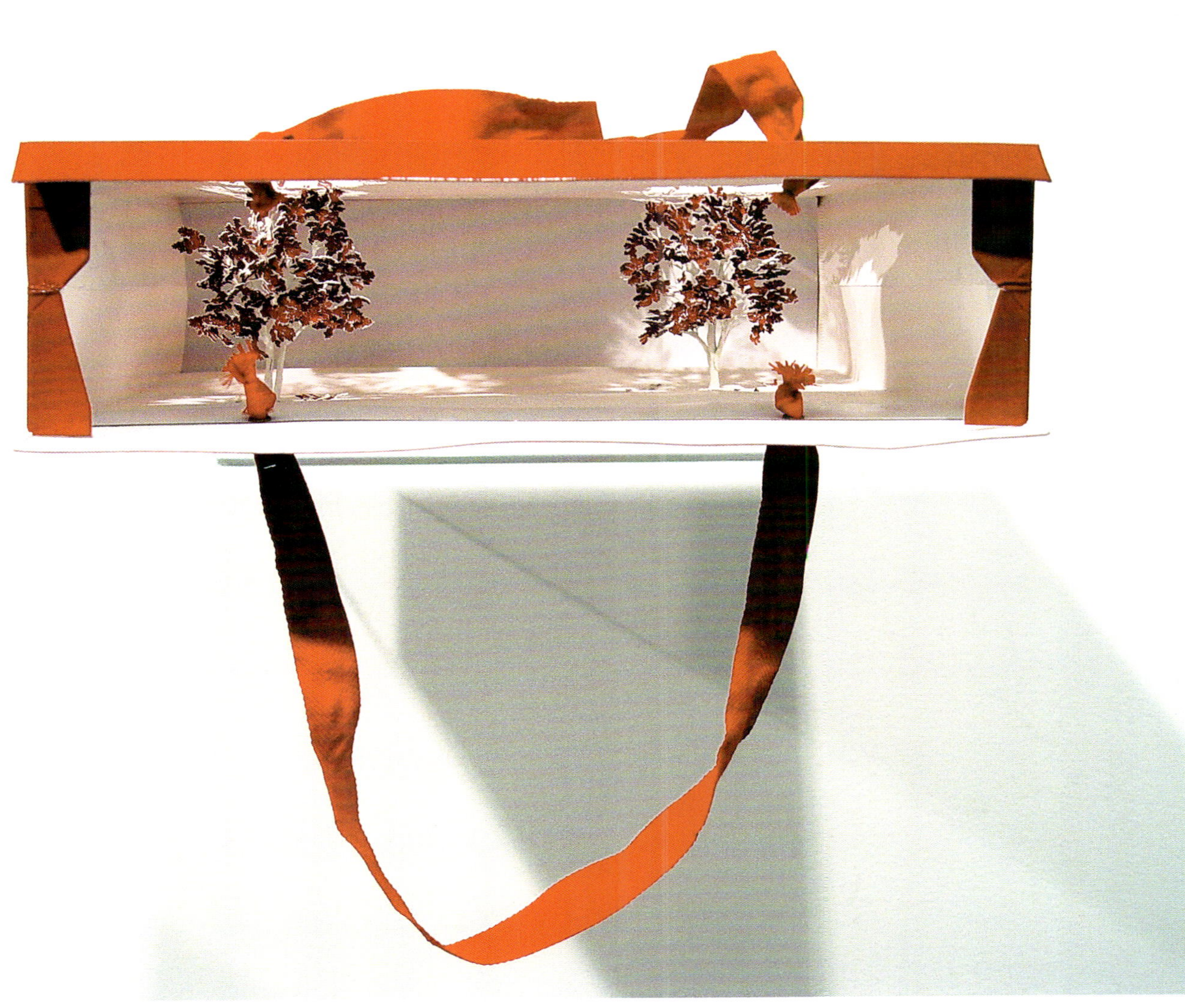

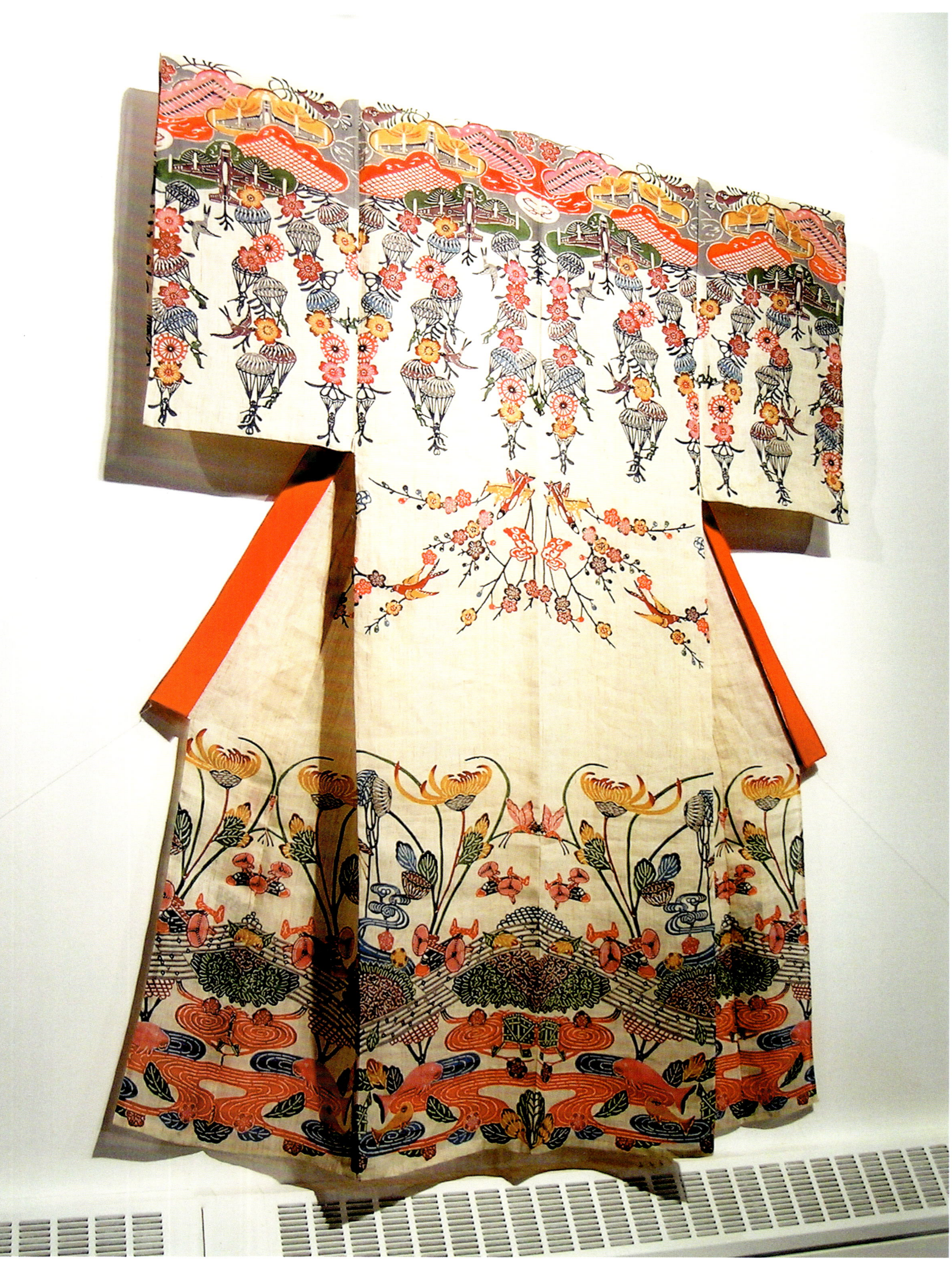

Why did you decide to leave Japan?
YT: When I was in Japan, when I introduced myself, I was recognized as either someone who was a student or someone who had a job; and I was introduced as an Okinawan before I was introduced by my name. In New York, I can be just Yūken as an individual. When I first came to New York I found many shortcuts that I could use to keep myself, and at the same time, I realized that I am a part of the diversity of Asian culture, and an Asian as a part of the world.

It's clearer for me to see myself in the world if I am in New York.

Did you have any interactions with other artists or supporters that were especially beneficial to you and your work?
YT: I have started interviewing individual collectors and making video documentations. I had provided these collection of interviews to art colleges in Japan so that they can introduce collectors' ideas and encourage more art students in Japan.

What experience has given you the most satisfaction as an artist in New York?
YT: When my works go to a good collection, I feel it's a greatly satisfying action for my career. At the same time, I feel a great confusion about the responsibility of my works and feel sad that my works with all my effort and time wouldn't be in my studio any more.

In this age of globalism, do you consider yourself to be a Japanese artist, an American artist, an international artist, or a hybrid of all three?
YT: By taking advantage of being an Asian contemporary artist, I was invited to show at the Asia Society. And I got a chance to introduce Okinawan culture through my new works for the Asia Society show. But eventually I hope this show will have a more international intersection when Okinawan art works are introduced in New York through the context of Asian contemporary arts.

PLATE 26.3

Yūken Teruya
You I, You I
2004
Bingata dyed linen
Length: approx. 69" (175 cm)
Courtesy of the artist and Josée
Bienvenu Gallery, New York

27 YASUNAO TONE

Technology/Noise
CALEB KELLY

Yasunao Tone has been involved in the discovery of chance, through indeterminate techniques in composition, performance, and recording, for close to 50 years. Though his utilization of indeterminacy dates back to the early 1960s, he is also at the forefront of the use of glitches, cracks, and unstable systems for sound production. His later compositions are harsh in their intensity and volume but compelling in their radical and unexpected outcomes. At the center of the Tokyo Fluxus movement in the 1960s,Tone was closely linked with Fluxus artists Ichiyanagi Toshi, Takehisa Kosugi, Nam June Paik, Yoko Ono, and others, as well as composers such as John Cage and David Tudor. The links between Fluxus in Japan and in New York are numerous and most Japanese artists involved spent time in the city during the 1960s or later, like Tone, permanently relocated here.

Born in 1935, Yasunao Tone attended the national Chiba University in Japan, but did not study music. His first public works were musical in nature and pointed to the future direction of his practice. In August 1960 Tone founded the improvisational music unit Group Ongaku, with Takehisa Kosugi, Mizuno Shūkō, and Shiomi Mieko, one of the first of such groups to be formed around a fully improvisational structure. Tone's early work in the 1960s was heavily involved in indeterminate composition, the outcomes of which resemble the "event" scores being written in the U.S. only slightly earlier. Works such as *Anagram for Strings* (1962) and *Geodesy for Piano* (1962) point to an interest in the boundaries of systems and their various outcomes, and how these can be used to create compositions.

A parallel theme in Tone's work involves the use of recently developed technologies. When technologies are newly released there is a period where the specific future of their function is unknown. During this phase they may be creatively employed by artists, often in unexpected ways. Tone's use of very new technologies is exemplary. His *Theater Piece for Computer*, first performed at the *Biocode Process* festival in Tokyo in December 1966, is an example of an early use of the computer in the arts. The work was a Happening that used computer-generated random instructions, combined with binary-like "on" and "off" alternatives, that directed the performers to choose different actions.

The most productive and cited approach to new technology taken by Tone developed in 1984 when he came across a method of preparing a commercially recorded music CD that he thought could be used to cause discrepancies in its playback. The technology had only recently been made available on the market and most people would not have actually handled it then. Tone took a new CD and placed Scotch tape on the playing surface of the disc causing the CD to skip and jump erratically when played. At the time there was much talk about the high-tech nature of the CD and the lack of noise and errors on playback. Tone's approach was anything but high tech in his use of the tape and in his later performance of the "wounded CDs" in which he banged the player with his hand to force it to jump from one glitch to the next.

Tone's interest in digital technologies continued in the work *Musica Iconologos* (1993), a piece created from 187 scanned images of Chinese characters and photographs representing the script. The scans were run through an "optical music recognition" program and the sound files produced were processed digitally to form a sonification of the characters themselves. Tone's *Musica Simulacra* (1996) was produced in a similar manner and then additionally wounded to form the Golden Nica–winning work, *Man'yo Wounded 2001*, at the 2001 Prix Ars Electronica (Pls. 27.2–3). More recently, for the installation *Parasite/Noise* at the 2001 Yokohama Triennale, Tone used the gallery's in-house museum headsets to display the work. Visitors expecting the device to deliver a commentary as they viewed the exhibition instead heard a computerized voice reading Walter Benjamin, juxtaposed with noise, subverting their preconception of the role of the apparatus in the gallery.

Silent Staircase, Tone's proposed creation for *Making a Home*, makes use of newly developed ultra-directional speakers and their employment in the museum as information guides to specific displays. The speakers emit sound in a cone shape, in effect allowing sound to be directional rather than radiating around the room. Tone will use these speakers to cancel out the sound of a waterfall in the lobby and, in a similar manner to his work *Parasite/ Noise*, cancel out institutionalized sound produced by the museum with noise.

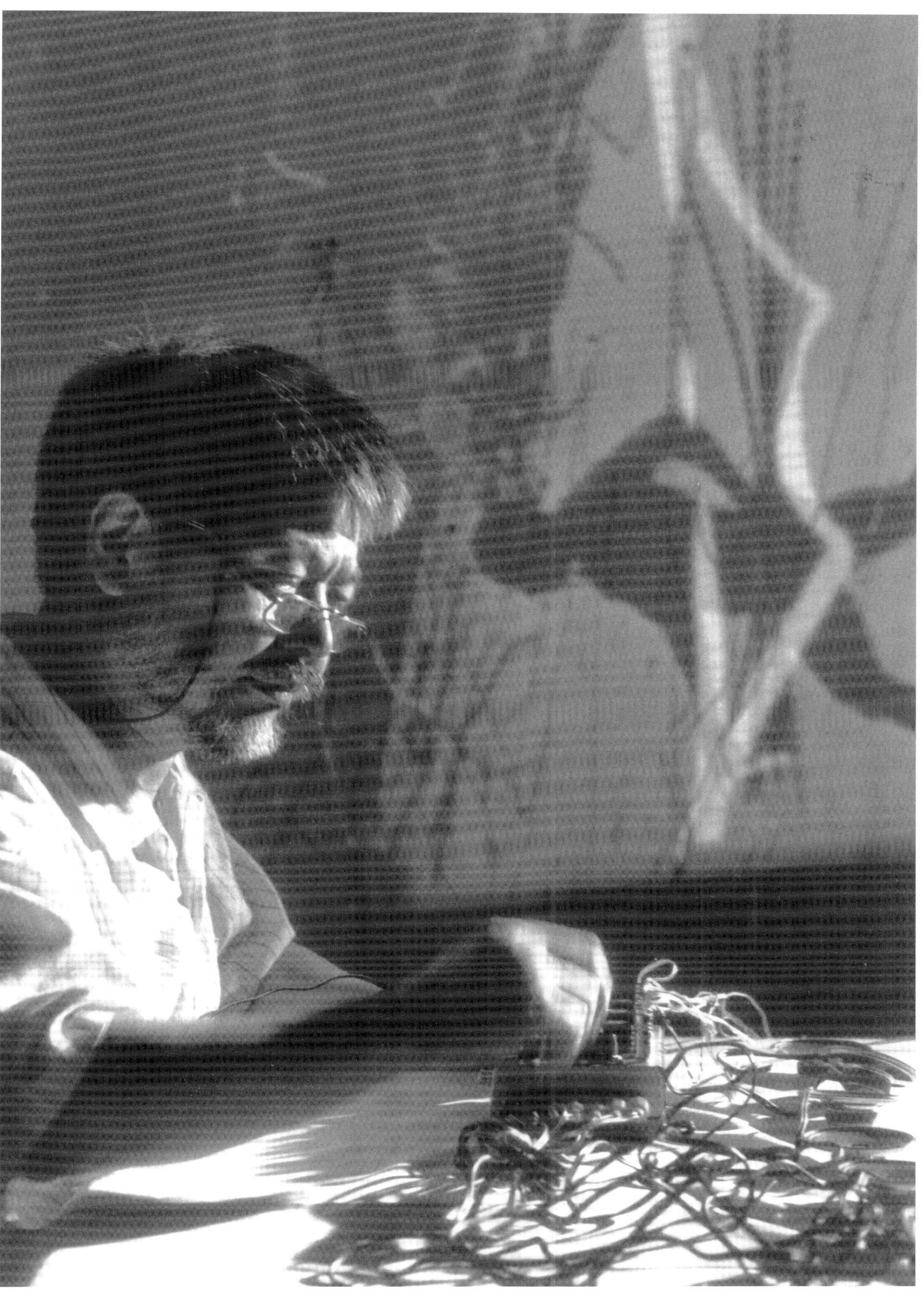

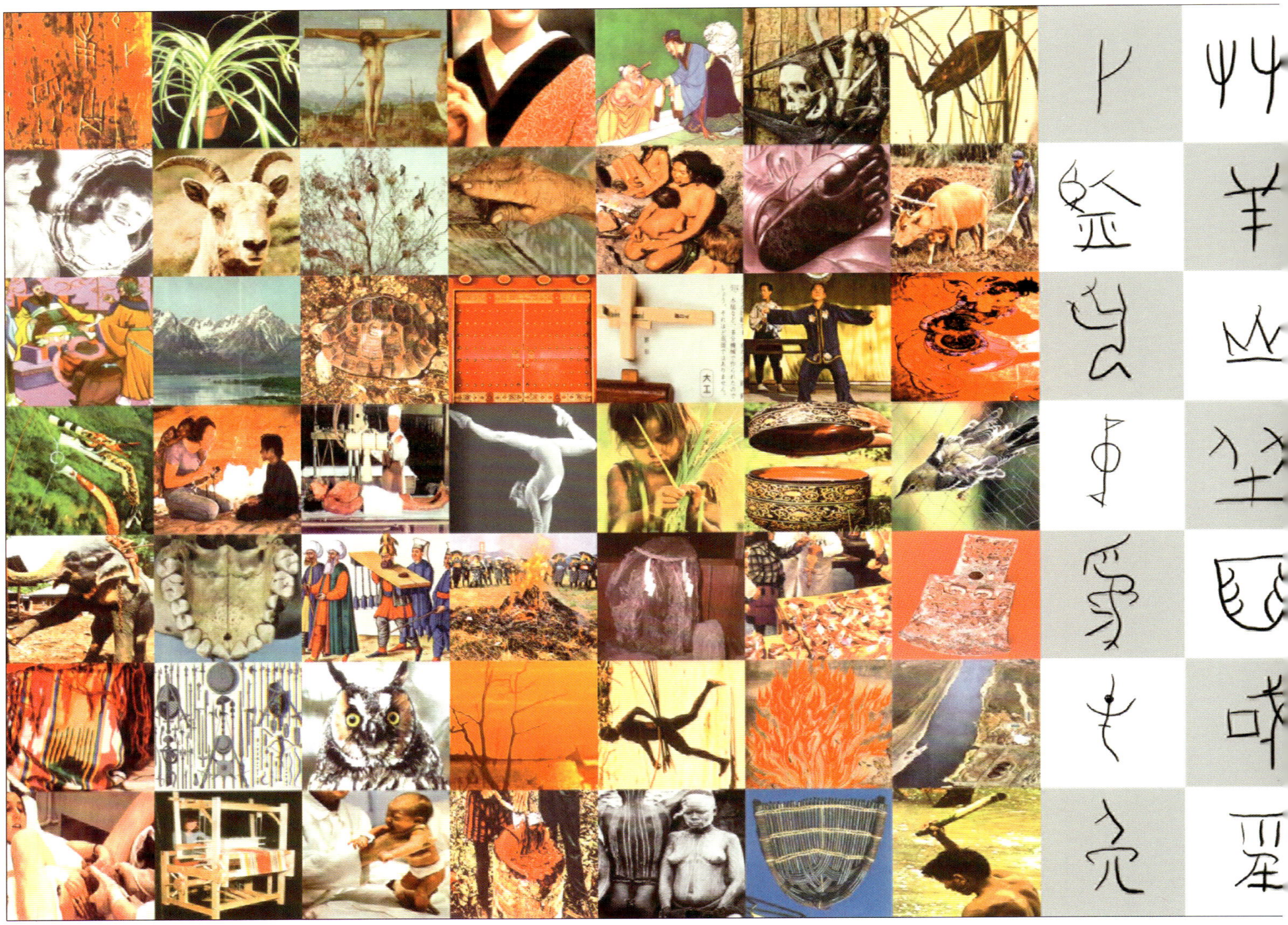

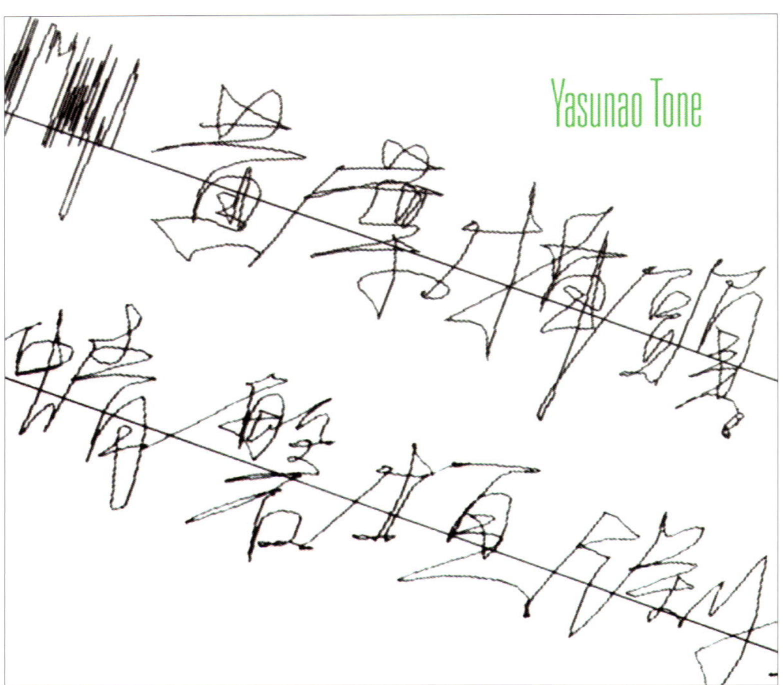

PLATE 27.2

Yasunao Tone
Yasunao Tone (Asphodel 2011)
2003
CD inner sleeve

PLATE 27.3

Yasunao Tone
Yasunao Tone (Asphodel 2011)
2003
CD cover
This CD features *Wounded Man'yo 2/2000,*
Wounded Man'yo, No. 36-7, and *Wounded*
Soutai Man'yo

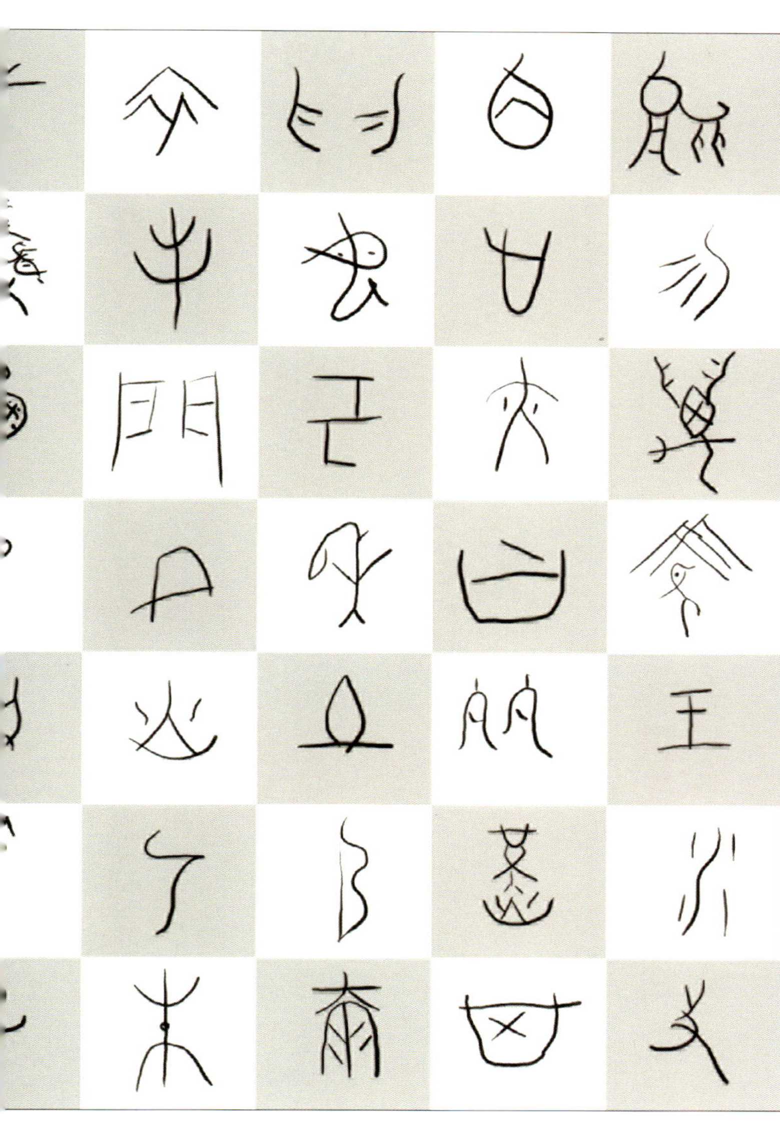

When and how did you first realize that you wanted to be an artist?
YT: I don't remember when (sometime in high school), but probably I wanted to become a poet and art critic when I read a short story where the protagonist had contempt for vulgar novelists and wrote poems and art criticism. I didn't like poetic art criticism so I tried to become as logical as possible, but as a result I seemed to deviate to music.

What was your first impression of New York City?
YT: I came here from San Francisco by bus. It was exciting to watch between coasts but it looked so boring. New York was dirty but so exciting in the 1970s.

Did you face many obstacles in establishing your career in New York?
YT: The difficulty is that I was recognized as a Fluxus artist (actually there is no such thing because it does not belong to art) and it was not easy to get rid of that.

Has the experience of living in New York changed your style or process significantly?
YT: Living in New York and being based in New York has made my hatred towards East Asian traditions disappear. That made it easier for me to practice some traditional things like calligraphy, reading Tang dynasty poems, *Man'yōshū*, and Zen books, and then made those things my material sources.

In this age of globalism, do you consider yourself to be a Japanese artist, an American artist, an international artist, or a hybrid of all three?
YT: I would be thinking global wherever I am, and migration itself is not an issue unless you are in a situation like political exile. I am drifting all the time conceptually and physically.

28 MOMOYO TORIMITSU

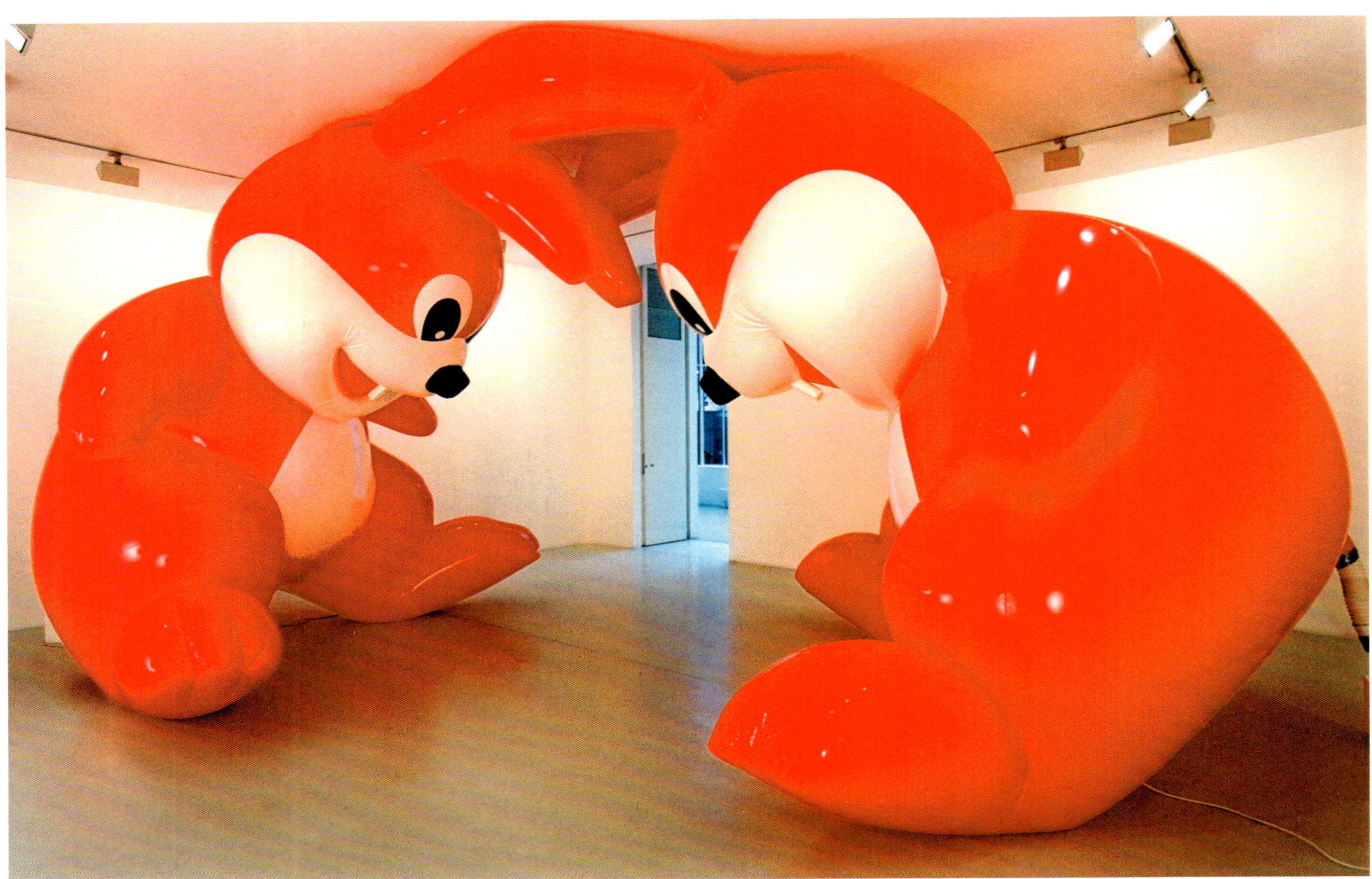

Torimitsu Confronts Global Corporate Culture
MIDORI YOSHIMOTO

Primarily a sculptor and installation artist, Momoyo Torimitsu has consistently addressed timely social issues in superbly executed three-dimensional forms and in video. Coming of age during the decline of the Japanese bubble economy, Torimitsu shares a keen critical sensibility of Japanese society with artists of her generation, including Yoshiaki Kaihatsu. Among her earliest works was *Pleasure of Destruction Merry-Go-Round* (1995) which positioned resin-cast sculptures of two high-school girls in sailor uniforms on their hands and knees alternating with two white goats on a red turntable. Actually functional as a merry-go-round, the sculptures were offered for visitors to ride. The red turntable symbolized Japan as the rising sun while the goats and girls represented scapegoats or the damned of society. The work uncannily suggested the degeneration the bubble economy triggered in Japanese society, which shed its traditional boundaries and momentarily sought the sheer pleasure of consumerism and the flesh.

Of the many topical issues that captured Torimitsu's interest, those associated with corporate culture became her main focus. Soon after graduating from Tama Art University in 1994, she premiered *Miyata Jirō*, a lifelike robot of a stereotypical "salaryman" (a Japanese loanword from English for a white-collar worker) that crawled through the streets of Tokyo's business districts. Torimitsu dressed as a nurse and followed the robot to change its battery and steer it away from obstacles. The absurdity of a young nurse tending to a groveling middle-aged salaryman was not only farcical, but also satirical of the corporate soldiers who sacrificed their private lives for their employers' and country's interests. The frequently reported news of salarymen deaths from overwork (*karōshi*) made this work poignantly relevant in the late 1990s.

Inspired by the overwhelming response to *Miyata Jirō* in Japan, Torimitsu took the opportunity to come to New York in 1996 to explore the reaction to the robot in varied social settings. With a scholarship from the Asian Cultural Council, Torimitsu participated in the P.S.1 International Studio Program and staged the crawl of *Miyata Jirō* on Wall Street and near Rockefeller Center (Fig. 3.1). These performances drew large crowds and major press coverage, allowing Torimitsu to go on a world tour with the robot, showing the piece in Amsterdam, Graz, London, Paris, Rio de Janeiro, and Sydney.

This international experience led to her next work, *Inside Track* (2004), shown at Deitch Projects in New York. The work consisted of three new male robots of different ethnicities crawling about an office floor: *Lee* (Asian), *Gunter* (Anglo-Saxon European), and *Mark* (Caucasian-American). In a video included in the exhibition, the three businessmen raced through a corridor of an office building, evoking the fierce competition of the American business world. At the nearby Swiss Institute, Torimitsu simultaneously presented *Horizons*, an Astroturf diorama, decorated with plastic foam buildings and mountains and swarming with 100 G.I. Joe doll–derived robots in business suits (Pl. 28.3). The allusion to the American war in Iraq was apparent when corporate soldiers crossed over oceans and national borders to take control of cities and oil fields. Although many robots broke down and their suits wore out by the end of the exhibition, a few dozen remaining robots kept fighting the never-ending corporate battle.

While life in New York expanded Torimitsu's interest to global issues, living away from Japan also permitted her to view her country from a critical distance. In her installation *Danchizuma-Endless Sunrise* (1998), she highlighted the monotonous, conformist lives of four middle-aged Japanese housewives residing in a suburban apartment complex through idealized photographic portraits and a diorama of their town encased in a yellow plastic bubble. Similarly, the two gigantic, identical, inflatable plastic rabbits in her *Somehow I Don't Feel Comfortable* (2000) physically expressed the cramped and repressed feeling of Japanese society as well as her subversion of the country's *kawaii* (cute) popular culture (Pl. 28.1).

In 2001, Torimitsu created a series of site-specific works in collaboration with small family-run factories in Sumida Ward, Tokyo. After discussions with the factory workers, she incorporated in her work many of their final products and the waste derived from their production, such as plastic suction cups, toys, metal scraps, and machine sounds (Pl. 28.2). This collaborative experience suggested her potential for public art. For *Making a Home*, Torimitsu presents an interactive installation of sleek office furniture to heighten the corporate aesthetic of efficiency and monumentality.

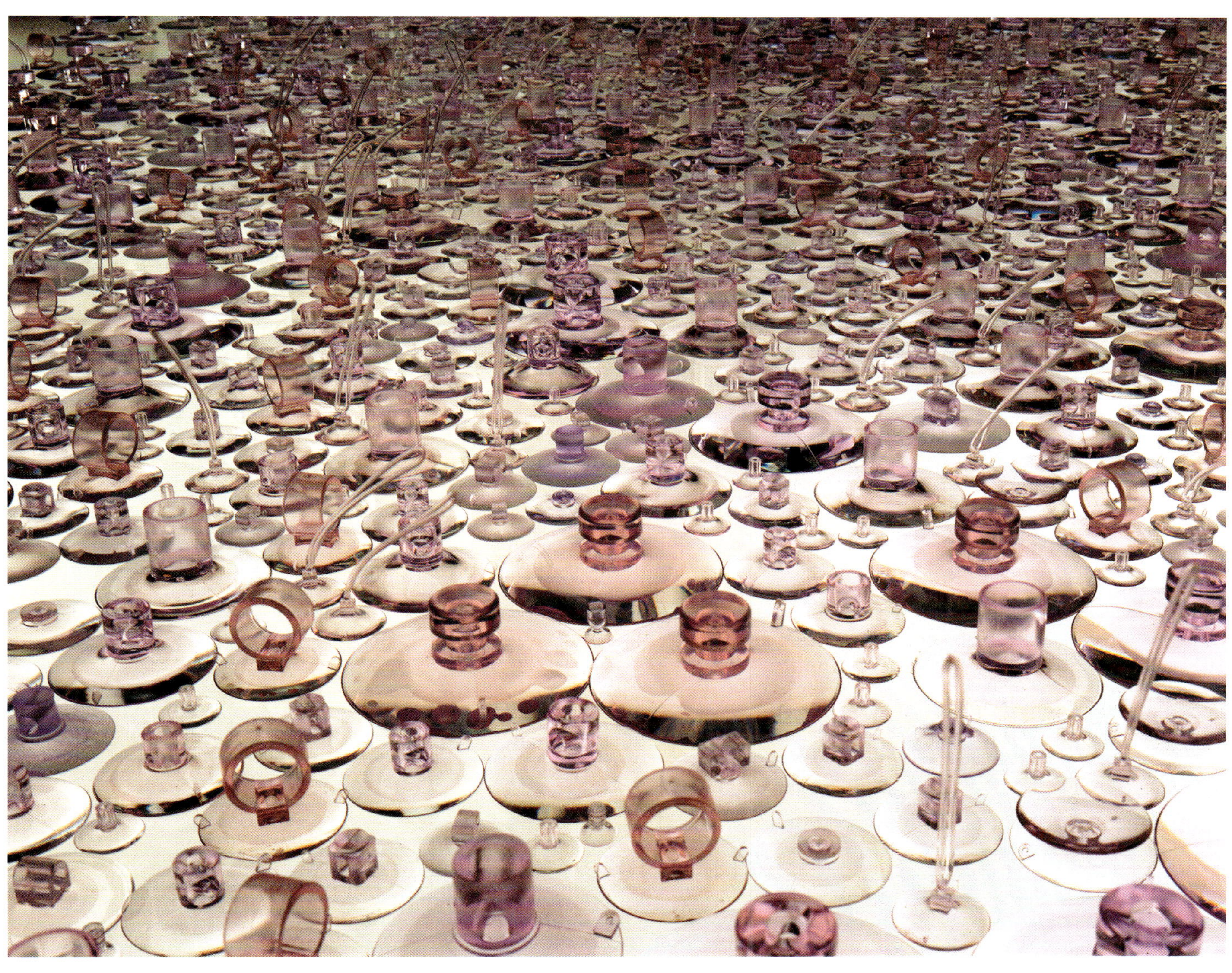

When and how did you first realize that you wanted to be an artist?

MT: I originally wanted to study graphic design, for which I failed the entrance exam three times in Japan. Then I was working at a topless club as a hostess/spotlighting person for the show. I had been hanging out with those dancers—actually, they were emerging Butoh dancers. It inspired me to be an artist rather than a commercial creator.

Why did you decide to leave Japan?

MT: I didn't have an idea to leave Japan, I applied for a grant to do my crawling businessman performance in New York. Concerning the concept of my performance, I thought I should do it somewhere overseas, on a business street. It was my luck, I got a grant for P.S.1 one-year residency program— it wasn't my original plan. One year after, my old boyfriend convinced me to stay, otherwise I wouldn't have done so.

Why did you choose New York as your ultimate destination?

MT: When I got media attention in Japan over 10 years ago, people recognized me as spectacle, entertainment, not as art. But in New York I realized that people listened to me seriously, to what I want to say.

Did you face many obstacles in establishing your career in New York?

MT: When I lost two of my closest people within one year, I completely lost creative energy. I seriously thought to quit being an artist.

Has the experience of living in New York changed your style or process significantly?

MT: Before I moved to New York, I was very conscious that I was making art as a Japanese artist. My thinking on Japan's rapid economic growth [in the 1960s and 1970s] went into the Miyata piece. I am still Japanese, but after 10 years away, my knowledge of Japan is outdated. If I tried to base a work on the current trends in Japan, it would lack reality.

In this age of globalism, do you consider yourself to be a Japanese artist, an American artist, an international artist, or a hybrid of all three?

MT: I'm a Japanese artist, working internationally.

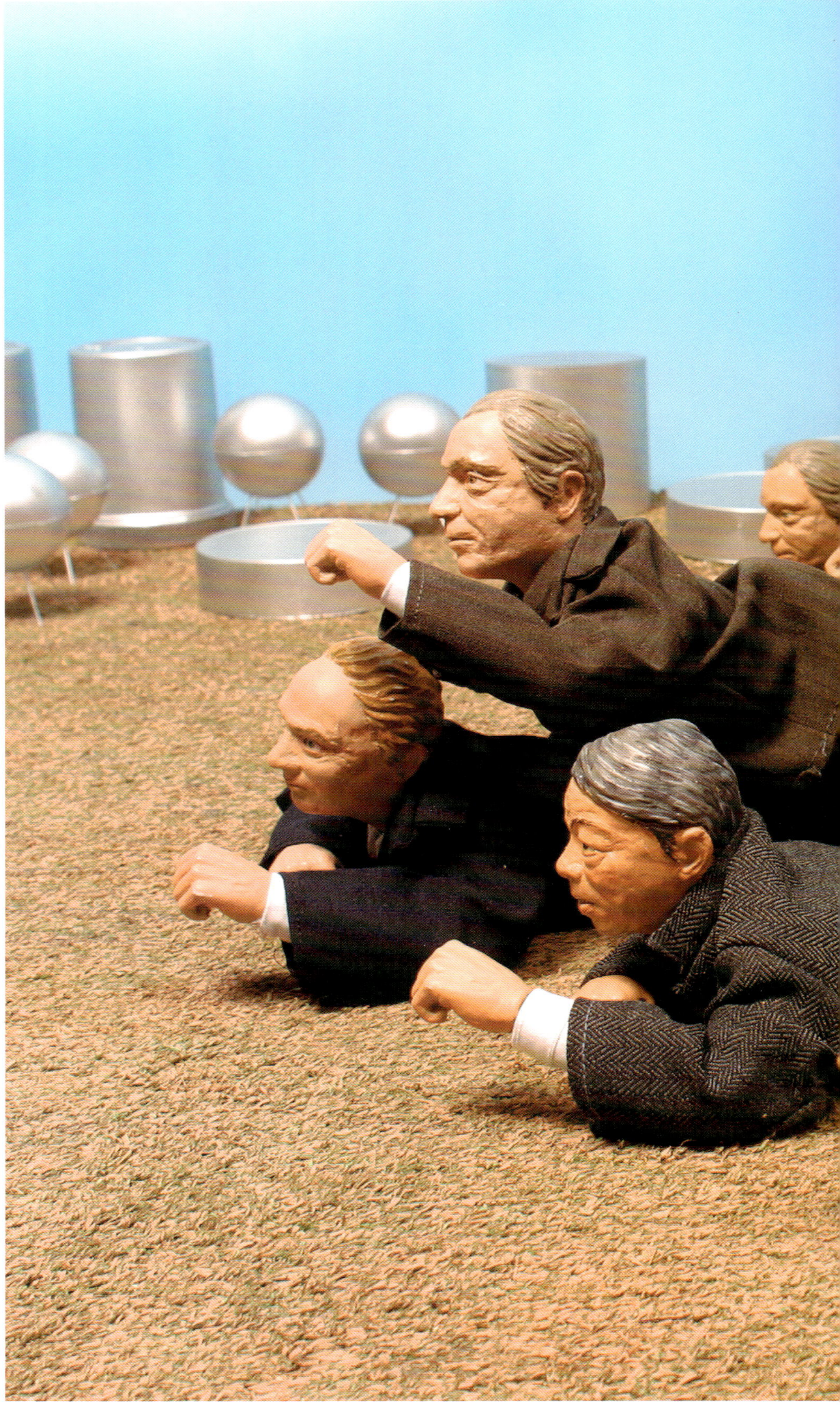

PLATE 28.3

Momoyo Torimitsu
Horizons
2004
Video still
Collection of the artist

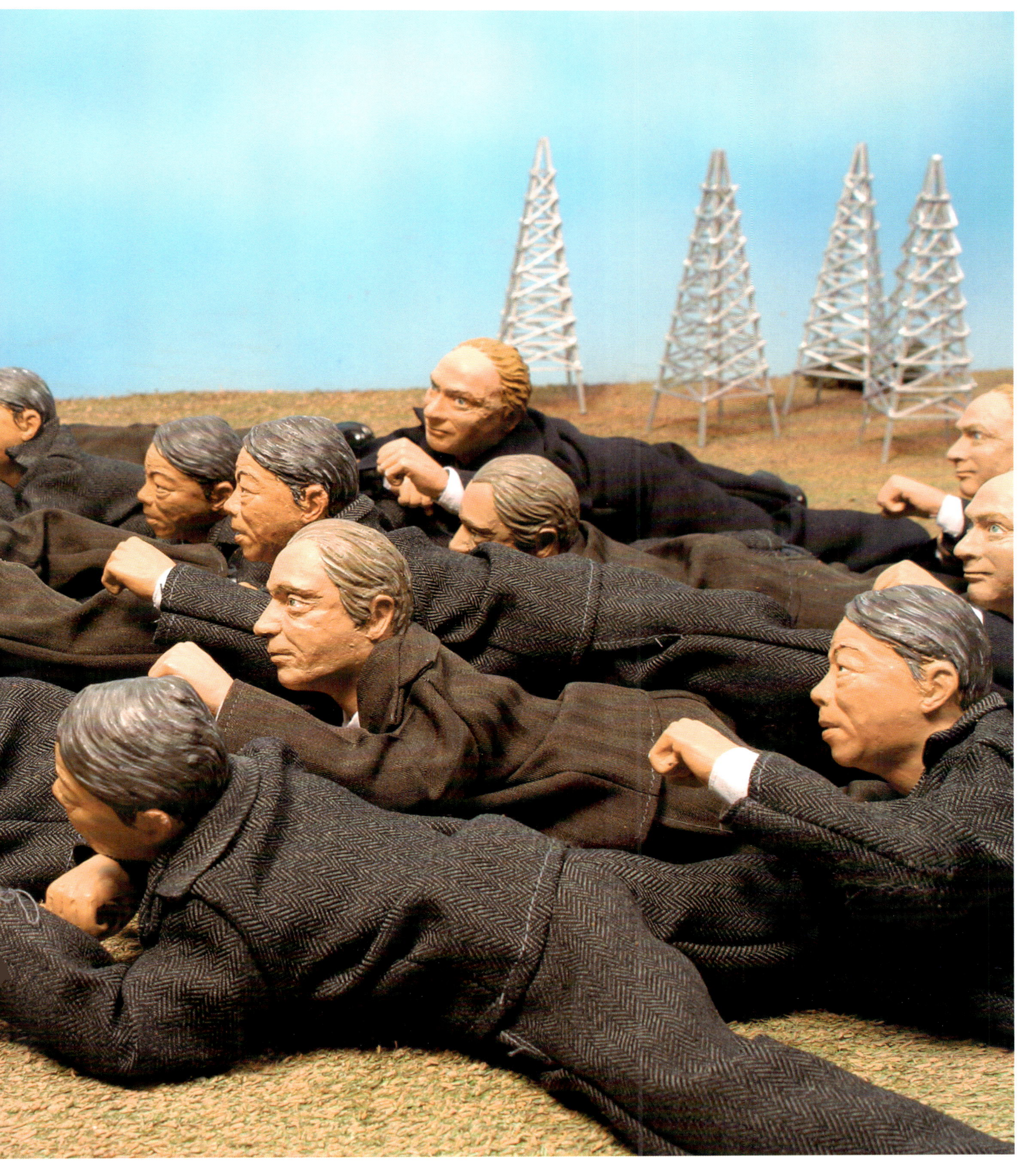

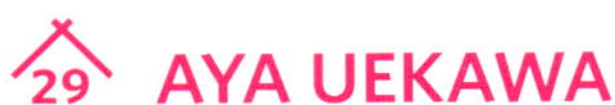

AYA UEKAWA

Ambiguous Images of a New Floating World
ERIC C. SHINER

Painter Aya Uekawa depicts ambiguous women in peculiar positions, not in terms of physical arrangement on the canvas, but of racial makeup and corporal presence in space. In other words, the figures that Uekawa gives birth to are at once Asian and African-American, perhaps Latin, or a mix of all three. They inhabit fantastical interiors with flocked wallpaper, or are set in strange exterior scenes with flowers and joy in some, dead trees and fear in others. Uekawa creates images of a contemporary floating world, a snapshot of our present society and its proclivity toward the internationalization of bodies through cultural hybridity and the common language of anonymous space that could be found nearly anywhere. At the same time, she reveals her inner emotions in the works, perhaps best described as psychic mindscapes of that which the artist might become, or that which she has already been.

Although the heritage of Uekawa's subjects and the sites within which they are positioned remain vague, her women are anything but. They develop individual identities in their rich complexity laid bare through the artist's strict attention to detail in clothing, hairstyle, and accessories; the ambiguous bodies become secret microcosms in which braids of hair house miniature worlds populated by tiny sheep, or in which lace frocks become hiding places for entire cities crafted with a meticulous hand. Uekawa makes bodies that are repositories of culture upon which not only her personal history finds a home, but indeed through which the age of globalism finds painterly representation. She borrows from the ideas of *ukiyo-e* as she references her lived reality and its fantasy potential, while at the same time drafting social documents in the form of human melting pots of race, class, and national identity. The women found in Uekawa's striking paintings are no doubt self-portraits of a complex soul engaged in a search for her own cultural roots, played out across two countries with vivid accompaniment from the myriad cultures that confront and sustain the artist's life in New York on a daily basis.

In *Japanese Team Player Candidate* of 2005, a gorgeously elongated woman sits in a red dress, her hands stuffed into two plastic bags—one black, the other white—on her lap (Pl. 29.1). She is surrounded by the whimsical grayish silver curlicues of a tree-like form which explodes into a cloud of lace. Flowers populate the lawn upon which she sits; her well-kept braids replicate the natural beauty encircling her. The figure's face, however, is not so easily read. She could be pensive or panicking, enrapt or enraged. Uekawa offers up a snapshot of a woman engaged in a dream, or perhaps trapped in a nightmare. The richness of the scene might complement her joie-de-vivre, or stand in direct juxtaposition to her sadness. The plastic bags represent the artificiality of the picture and act as a visual pun highlighting the racial binary of black versus white, as though the figure might pull a lucky number from one or the other to decide her fate. Is she a Japanese team player, or a member of a rival team? Her candidacy might well be linked to her position in the world; her identity hinging on her inclusion or exclusion from Team Japan. In this way, Uekawa surfaces in the work, perhaps questioning her position as a Japanese-born artist now part of a new multicultural playing field.

Chrysanthemum Syndrome and *A Euro Lover* (both 2006) in kind address the issues of race and identity in contemporary society (Pls. 29.2–3). The former work features a pretty woman in a flowery dress standing on a balcony adorned with potted plants; the latter depicts a woman in a houndstooth suit striking a demure pose in an urban scene harboring several leafless trees and an apartment building with terraces in the background. The flowers in the first work seem to grow out of the pots and into the figure's dress; her face is again open to multiple interpretations. In the second work, the ominous black trees lurk behind the figure as though the branches might indeed be spikes and horns growing from her back. In both, organic vegetation blends with the human body to conceptually root the figure to the composition. The women's ambiguity in terms of race and emotion, however, allows Uekawa unlimited possibilities for her own outcome, and indeed that of all womankind.

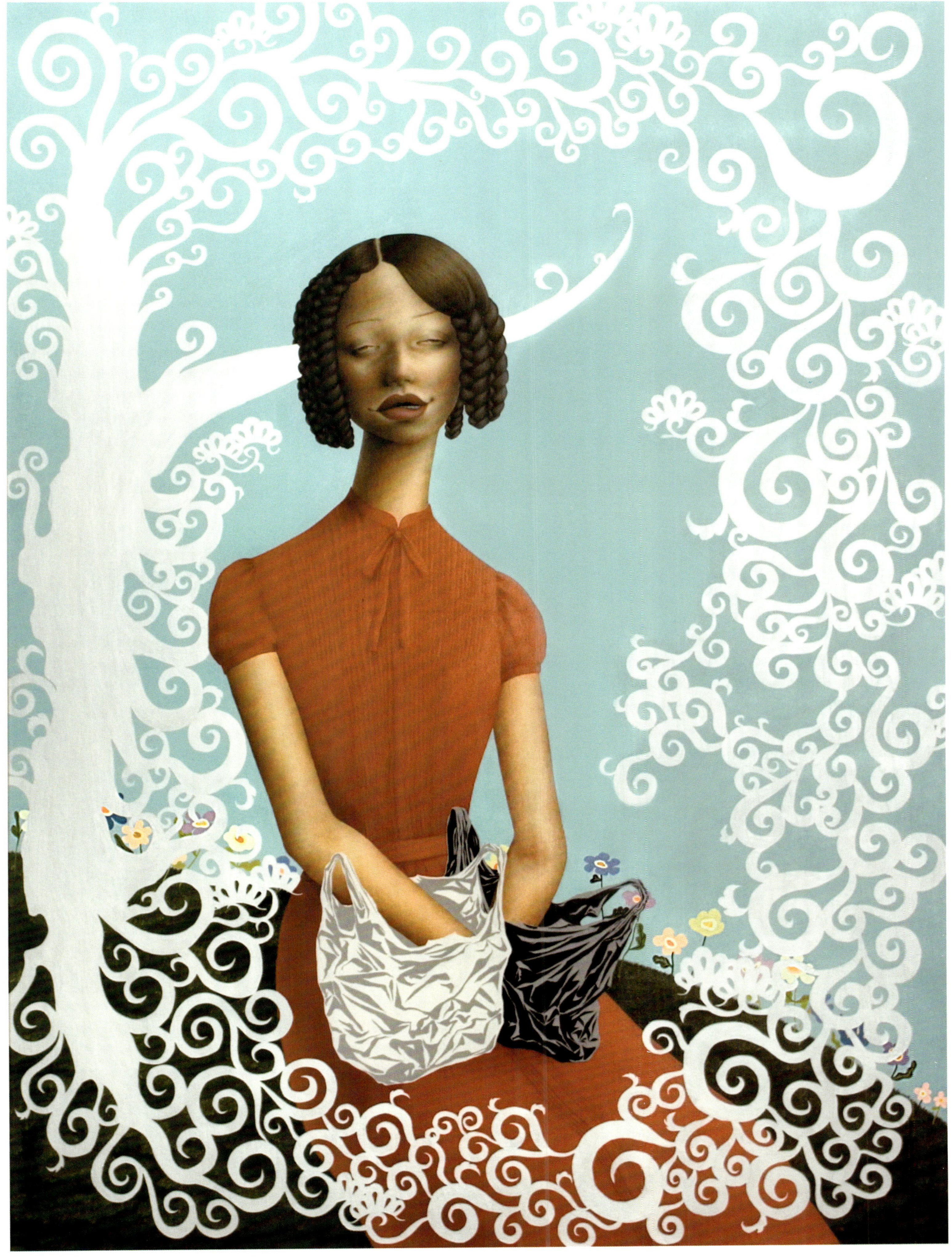

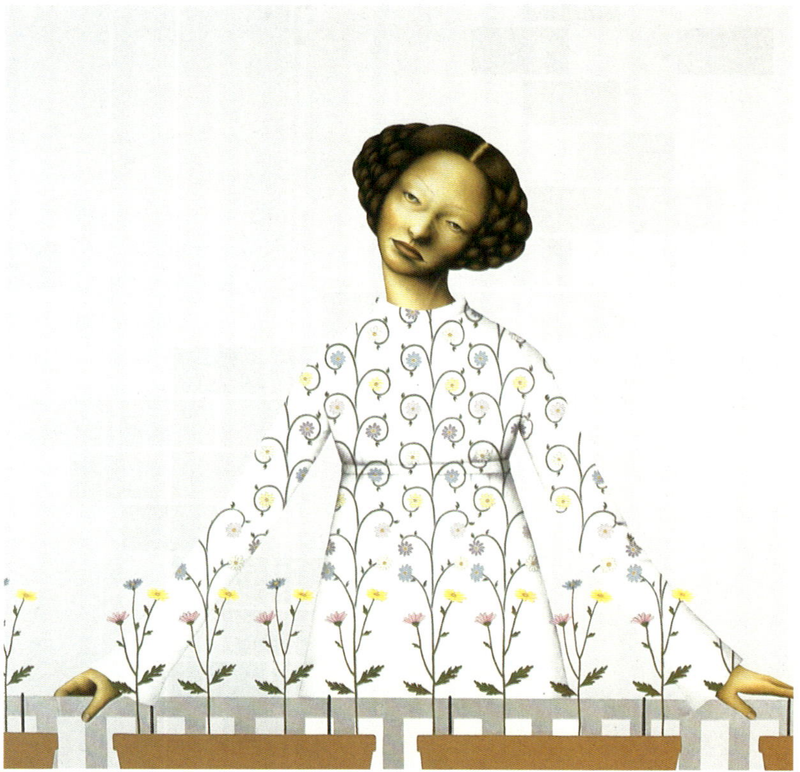

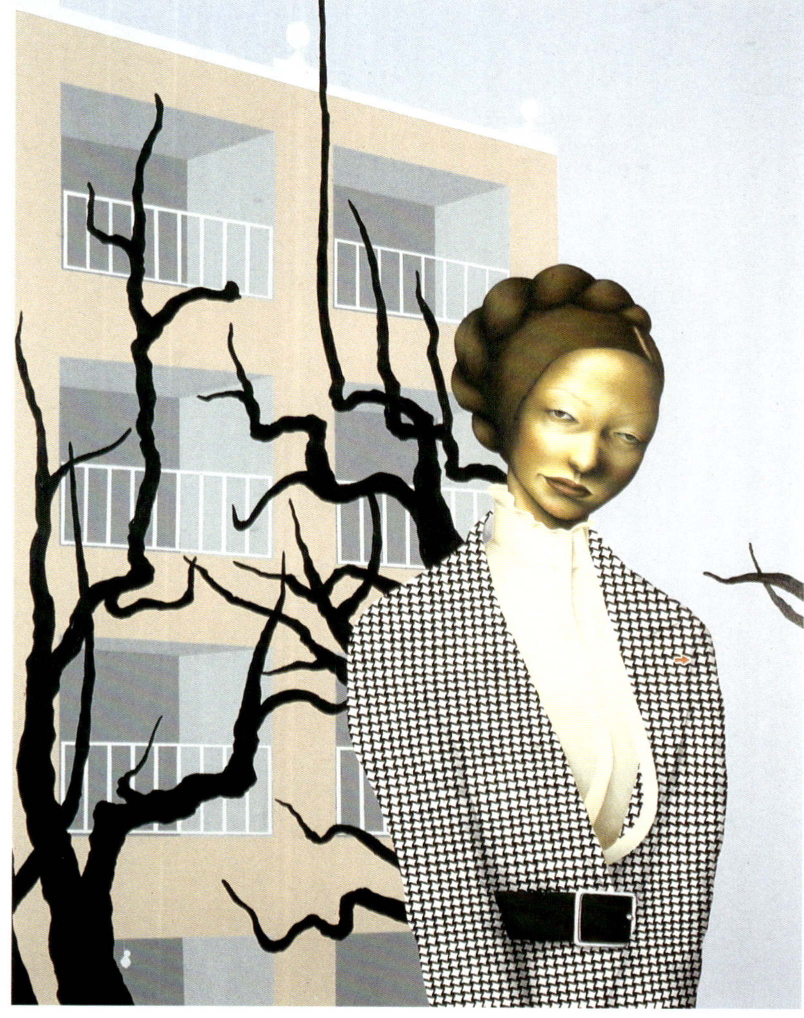

When and how did you first realize that you wanted to be an artist?

AU: The motivation to pursue my dream was that I wanted to express myself directly, and also I feared that I would have to have a job only to make a living for the rest of my life. If I had to struggle for something, I wanted to choose something I really like.

Why did you decide to leave Japan?

AU: Japanese art schools cost as much as studying abroad. I thought it would be good for me to study art and English together. Also, I thought it would be beneficial for me to live in New York, since it seemed to be a capital in the art world.

What was your first impression of New York City?

AU: Unexpectedly disorganized! Also, people are friendly on the streets, but cold at offices. However, I could feel this city gives us the feeling of freedom and self-independence. This is a place where artists don't feel boundaries.

Has the experience of living in New York changed your style or process significantly?

AU: My influence is both Japanese aesthetics and global trends, as well as Western aesthetics. Leonardo da Vinci and Picasso are more famous than Hasegawa Tōhaku in Japan. I believe I learned both Japanese and Western aesthetics naturally since I was a child.

In this age of globalism, do you consider yourself to be a Japanese artist, an American artist, an international artist, or a hybrid of all three?

AU: As a minority in America, I became very conscious of my identity as Japanese. However, I am realizing it basically originated from America's virtue of fostering minorities' identity. Showing Japanese visual tradition is respected, but we don't wear kimonos. Our daily life is very similar to Americans except in social customs and little differences, which sometimes look strange to non-Japanese.

I am a global artist, but at the same time, I am a hybrid of a Japanese and Western artist.

PLATE 29.2

Aya Uekawa
Chrysanthemum Syndrome
2006
Acrylic on panel
44 x 44" (111.8 x 111.8 cm)
Collection of Craig Robins; courtesy Kravets/Wehby Gallery, New York

PLATE 29.3

Aya Uekawa
A Euro Lover
2006
Acrylic on panel
40 x 30" (101.6 x 76.2 cm)
Private collection, New York; courtesy Kravets/Wehby Gallery, New York

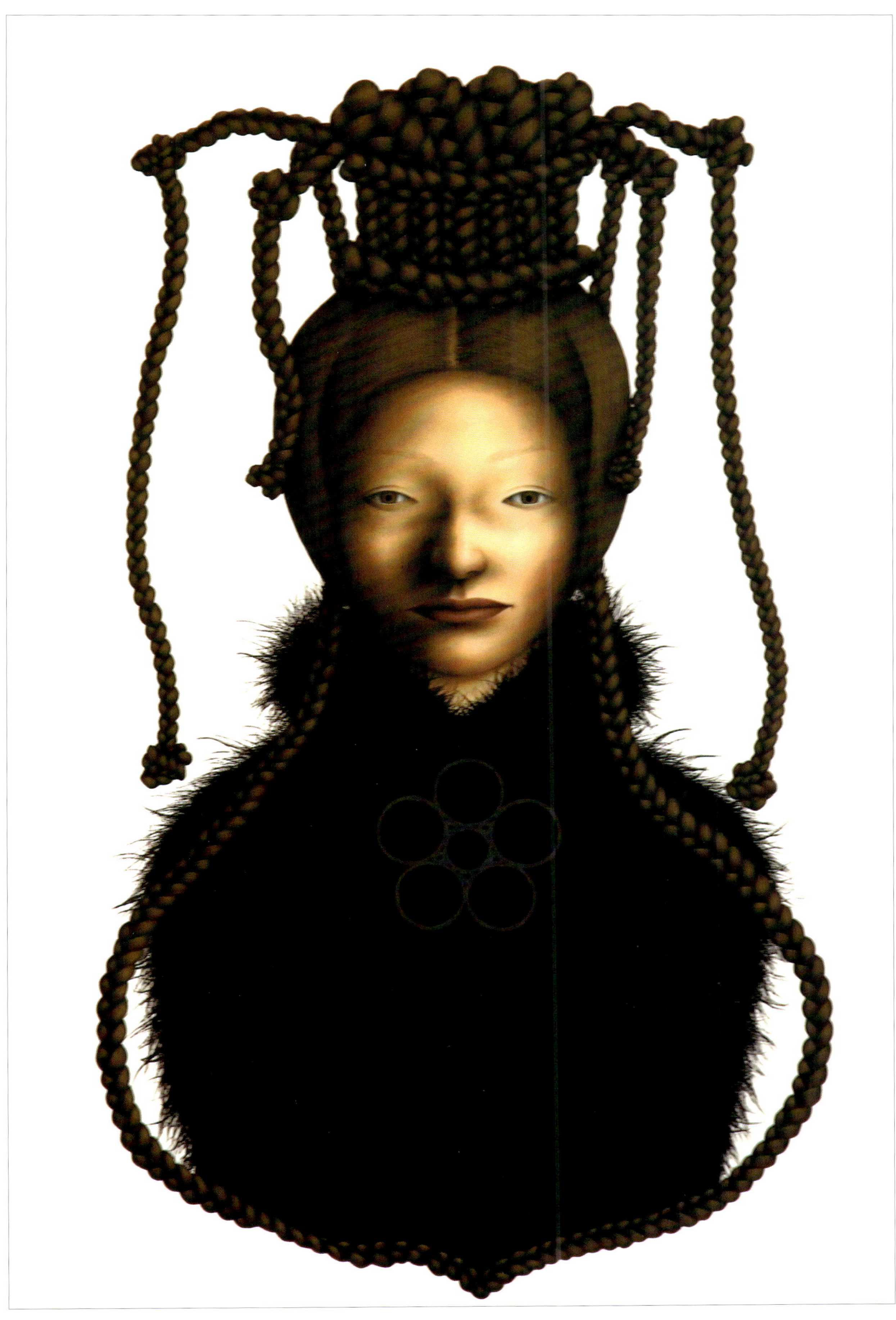

PLATE 29.4

Aya Uekawa
A Safety Crown
2007
Acrylic on panel in artist's frame
36 x 26" (91.4 x 66 cm)
Collection of Dorothy and Martin Bandier;
courtesy Kravets/Wehby Gallery, New York
PHOTO: DOUGLAS EMMETT

⌂ 30 UNITED BAMBOO

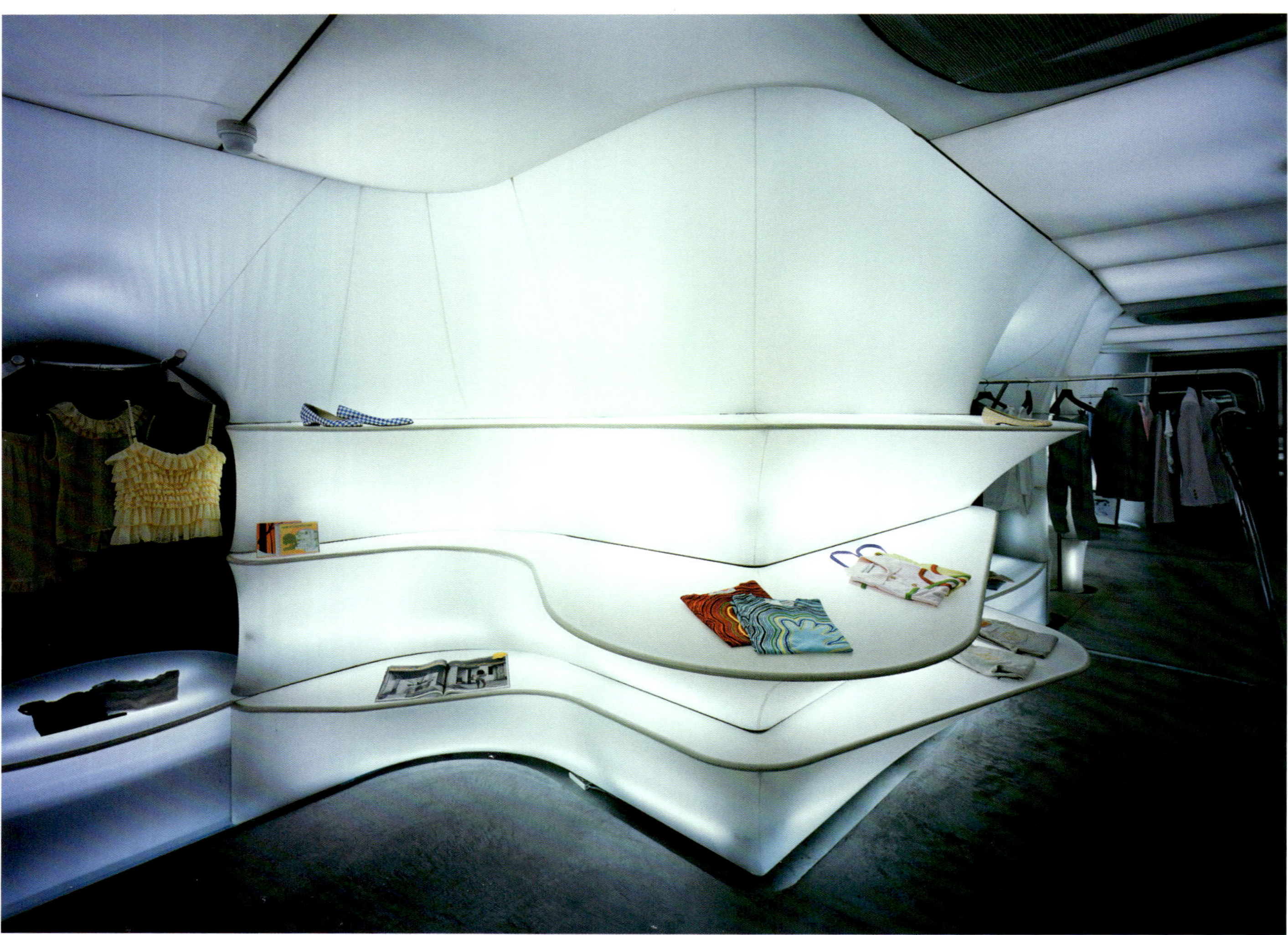

Fashioning Asia in[to] America

ERIC C. SHINER

Designers Miho Aoki and Thuy Pham are bent on changing the face of fashion, using the vocabulary of American style to redefine the shape and feel of clothing and the bodies that it adorns. Operating within and beyond the tradition of vanguard Japanese fashion designers in New York, they have crossed not only cultures but genres, interacting with downtown artists and musicians to create clothing as art and fashion as concept within an art-leaning ambience. Aoki, originally from Japan, and Pham, from Vietnam, infuse their clothing with aesthetic traditions from around the world, including Caribbean-inspired prints and origami-like folds influenced by Japanese design. For United Bamboo, internationalism is worn on the sleeve and style is sewn into every detail.

Aoki and Pham first met in New York when they worked at the trendy downtown fashion house Bernadette Corp. in the mid-

1990s. They teamed up as United Bamboo in 1998 with the dream that the label would not focus solely on functional fashion, but would grow to encompass an entire lifestyle reflective of contemporary American culture. They held their first New York fashion show in 2004. When they opened their first free-standing boutique in 2003 in Tokyo's hip Daikan'yama district, they initiated a collaboration with high-profile artist and architect Vito Acconci, asking him to create an "environment" instead of a "store." The end result is a proud two-story structure in which video, lighting, and sculpture are integrated with the retail nature of the boutique, giving shoppers the satisfaction of buying a unique piece of clothing and giving them an art experience at the same time (Pls. 30.1–2). The design received a gold prize at 2005 Art Basel Miami Beach. Their men's store in Tokyo's Omotesandō district opened in

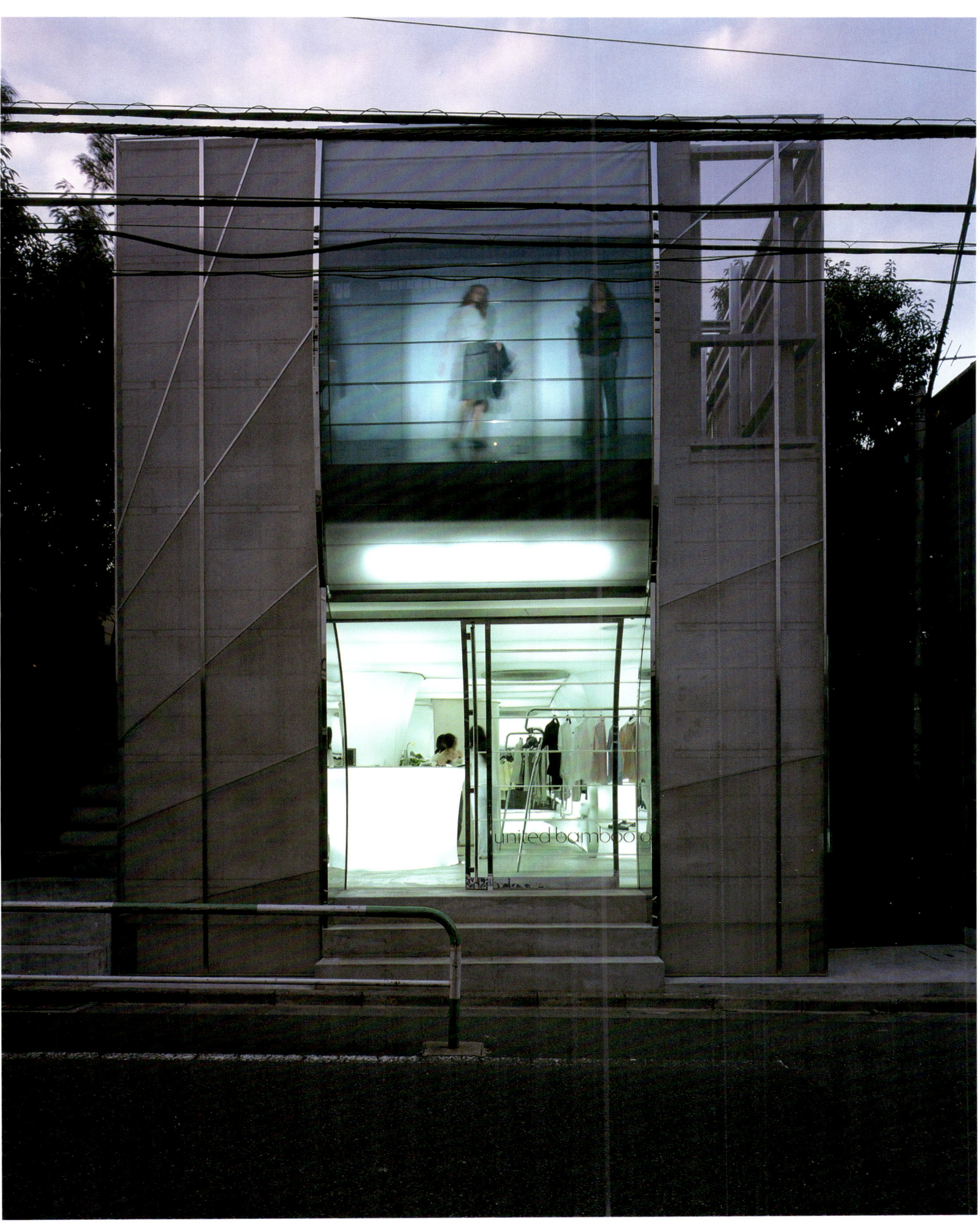
united bamboo

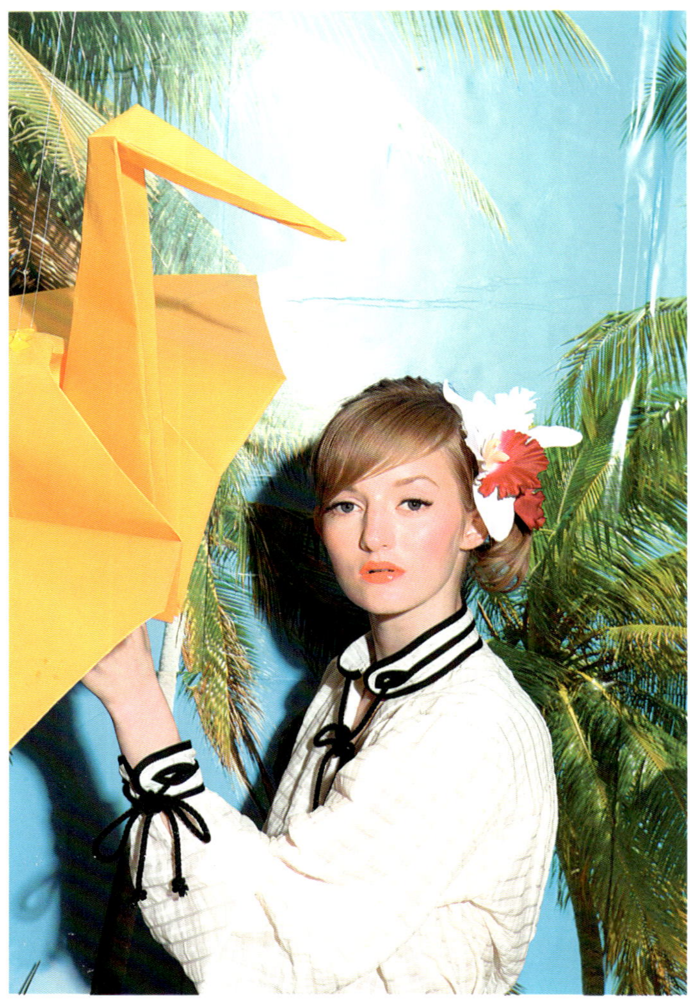

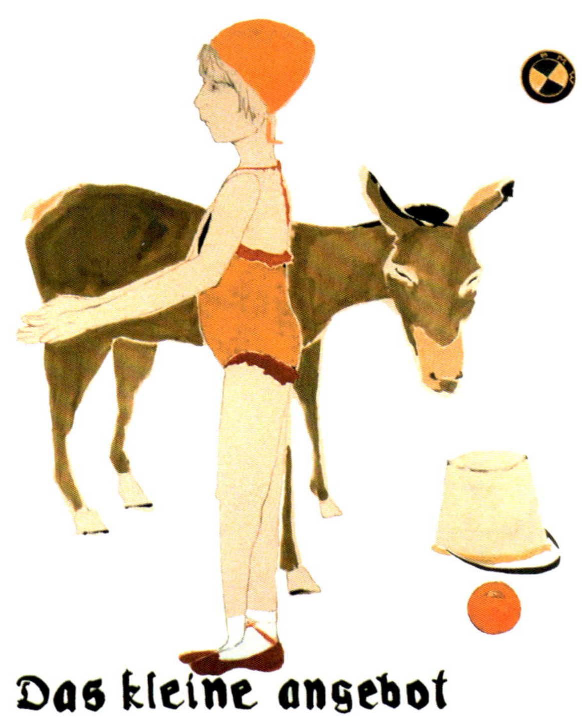

2006 and similarly blends art and fashion into a seamless and chic whole.

In addition to two annual collections, the designers have promoted the work of emerging artists with periodic projects curated by art world friends and musicians, in which works are printed on T-shirts that take to the streets in a life well beyond gallery walls. In 2003 Hiroshi Sunairi, a fellow artist in *Making a Home*, curated the T-shirt project *University of Girls: T-shirts by Female Artists of NY*. The collection, the first curated by an artist from Japan, included designs by Amy Gartrell, who has created concert posters and cover art for rock bands, and Shannon Lucy, who reproduced one of her large-scale paintings (Pl. 30.4). Sunairi later offered artworks for sale in the 2006 United Bamboo event in Tokyo, "Yankee Doodle Flea Market." The designers are also interested in avant-garde music, and in 2003 launched their first compilation of the sounds of downtown New York under the label United Acoustic Recording. They pay special attention to the relationship between form and music, often commissioning young composers and musicians to create the soundtracks for their fashion shows. Beyond their art and music projects, Aoki and Pham have become

an integral part of the art scene through their many customers who inhabit that world. *Making a Home* artist Yoko Ono is a fan, as is actress Chloë Sevigny.

For *Making a Home*, United Bamboo presents several designs from its Spring/Summer 2008 collection. The pieces are shown on mannequins strutting down a conceptual runway in the form of the small stream that meanders through the bamboo garden on the second floor of Japan Society, thus literally tying United Bamboo to a grove of the same name. In addition to the actual clothing on display, the entire runway show is broadcast on a flat-screen monitor installed within the garden, giving viewers the chance to experience a New York fashion event in a most unlikely setting. Aoki and Pham, and their propensity for invention, have contributed to the ongoing modern tradition of fashion-as-art that plays out on stylish bodies in New York, Tokyo, and cities around the globe. They have challenged the fashion world to expand its horizons while demanding attention from the art world. United Bamboo is a thread that weaves the beautiful together across disciplines and cultures.

PLATE 30.3

United Bamboo
New York Collection
Spring/Summer 2007
(advertisement)
PHOTO: MARCELO KRASILCIC

PLATE 30.4

Shannon Lucy
Little Offering (Das Kleine Angebot)
2003
T-shirt design
Courtesy of United Bamboo

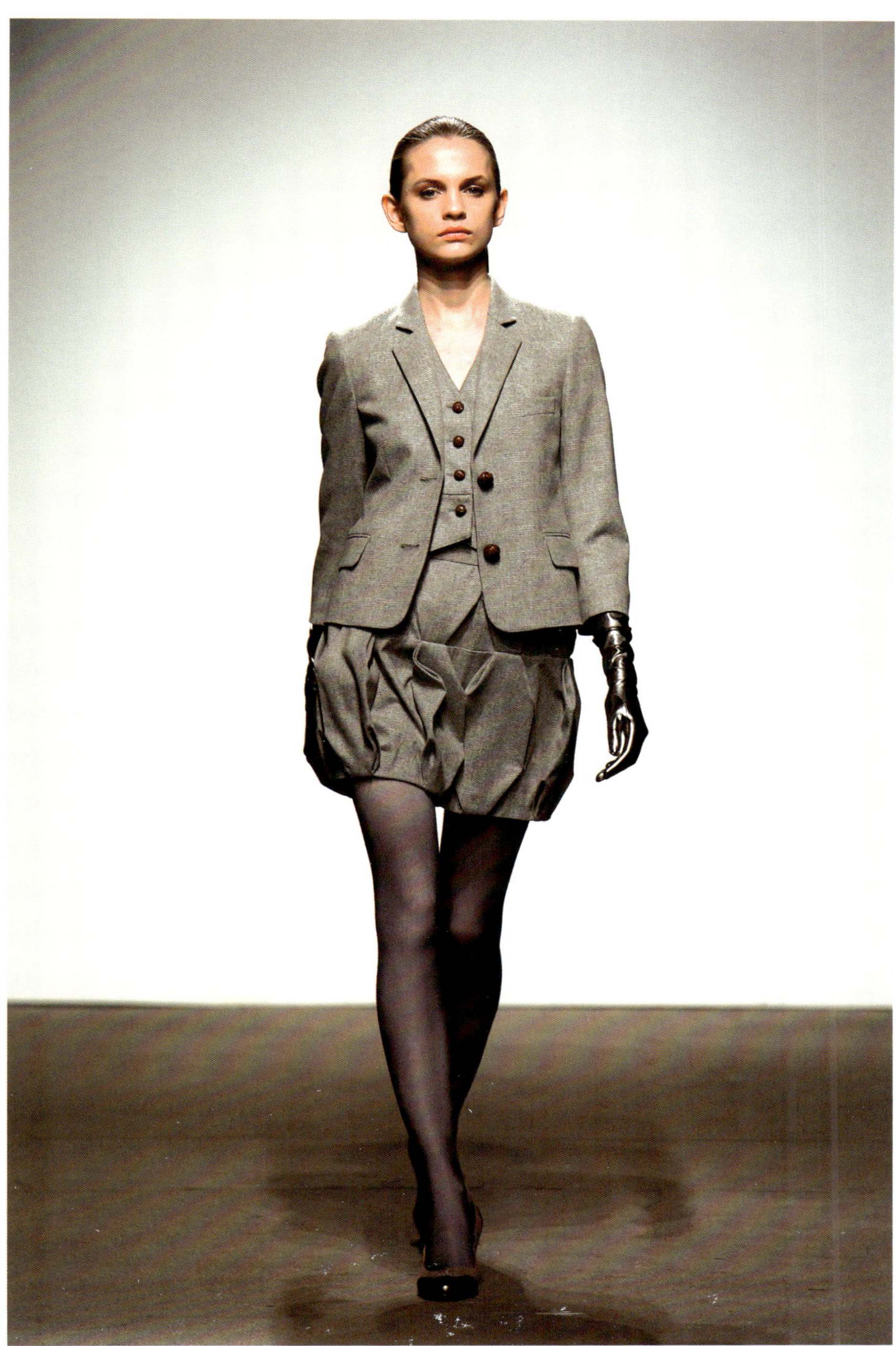

Why did you decide to leave Japan?

MA I left Japan because I was in love with the United States. At the time, I was completely immersed in the *Shibu-kaji* and *Ame-kaji* fashion [in the style of "Shibuya casual" and "American casual"]. Eventually, I persuaded my parents to send me abroad to an American boarding school. I had no thoughts of becoming a fashion designer when I left Japan. But once I entered Stoneleigh-Burnham, art class became my favorite and I knew I wanted to pursue a career in a creative field.

Why did you choose New York as your ultimate destination?

MA: When I attended the boarding school in Massachusetts, every two weeks or so my friends and I would take the Peter Pan bus to hang out in New York. I was mesmerized by the stimulation of the big city. It was at this point that my eyes truly opened to fashion. When I graduated high school, I had no doubt that I would move to New York.

Did you have any interactions with other artists or supporters that were especially beneficial to you and your work?

MA: We asked the famed artist/architect Vito Acconci to design the first United Bamboo store, in Tokyo. The architectural underpinnings of United Bamboo designs and the cultural affinity toward art made Acconci Studios a natural match. The resulting store is an amazing environment that showcases the clothes and contextualizes the collection as both conceptual and fun and hip.

In this age of globalism, do you consider yourself to be a Japanese artist, an American artist, an international artist, or a hybrid of all three?

MA: My work has taken me to different countries, where I have the opportunity to experience different things and be absorbed in new environments. As such, I want to be a hybrid person. I have been fairly conscious of the connections between the work I produce in the context of fashion and the trends of contemporary globalism.

Translated by Ryan Holmberg

Miho Aoki with Thuy Pham form the design team United Bamboo.

PLATE 30.5

United Bamboo
Runway view of New York
Collection
Fall/Winter 2007

31 JUNKO YODA

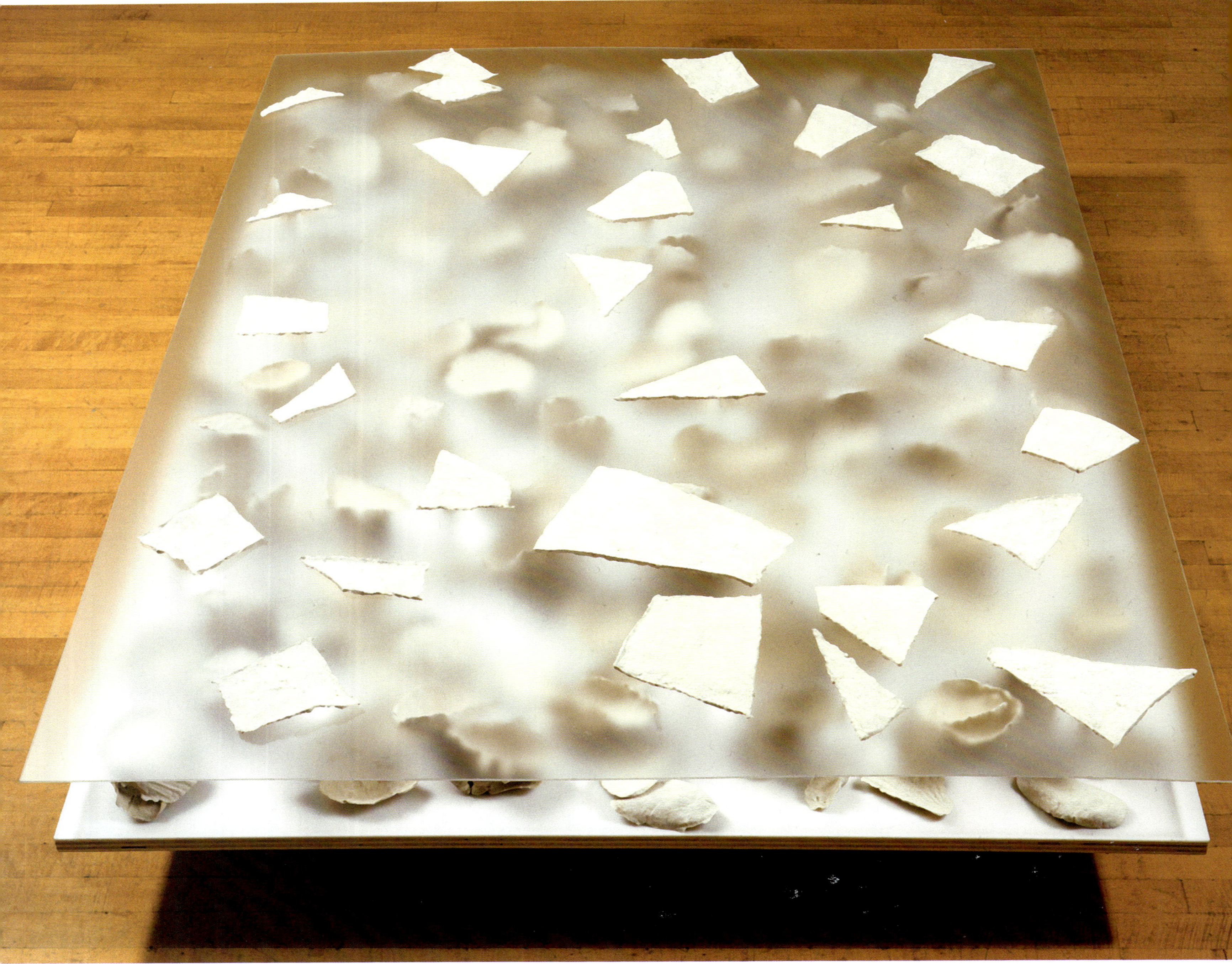

Dripped Topographies

JONATHAN GOODMAN

An artist of unusual craft, Junko Yoda creates paintings dense with texture, in which one can see her determination to render a surface that reads like Abstract Expressionism; at the same time, the composition suggests such actual objects as a terrain map or the twisting course of a river in an aerial view. The texture of her paintings is remarkably packed, the result of an intricate process:

a ground layer is made by paint dripped on paper stretched over wood; after this first layer, Yoda colors sheets of Japanese rice paper by more paint dripping, applying each separate hue after the previous color has dried. She then cuts up the paper into small, butterfly-shaped pieces, which are pasted onto the ground layer and add a texture of considerable force. The surface is all the

PLATE 31.1

Junko Yoda
Ice Floe
2004
Papier-mâché, acrylic sheet, plywood
76 x 50 x 4" (193 x 127 x 10.2 cm)
Collection of the artist; courtesy
Zabriskie Gallery, New York
PHOTO: JEFFREY STURGES

more remarkably evocative when one realizes that it has not been touched by a painterly hand.

A recent work entitled *The Hudson* (2006) resulted from a flight that brought Yoda over Ithaca and the Finger Lakes region of New York (Pl. 31.2). Inspired by seeing the lakes one by one as she passed over them, the artist decided to include in *The Hudson* a rendering of slender bodies of water, which take a moment to recognize amid the dense reddish-green color of the painting. On the right-hand side of the painting, the viewer sees a thin black line that feels very much like the representation of a river on a map; its vertical alignment corresponds to the geographical north-south position of the Hudson River. These slightly obscured references to natural features add complexity to the painting, which is a tour de force declamation of dripped color in the tradition of Pollock. However, rather than dripping paint onto a single surface, Yoda creates a double layer of ground and surface, which complicates and enlivens the picture plane with numerous brilliant colors. The tension between abstract markings and references to natural bodies of water results in a work of considerable refinement, in which the artist attracts her spectators by creating a design of nearly limitless complexity that, even so, refers to genuine topography.

To see *The Hudson* and Yoda's recent drawings and sculptures is to recognize her long residence in New York City, to become aware of affinities between her work and the process-oriented art of the New York School (Pl. 31.1). Yet it may also be said that the artist's procedures are rooted in craft, the exquisite nature of which inevitably reminds her viewers of a Japanese aesthetic. Yoda's alliance with a beauty of unusual subtlety is all the more fleeting because of its intensity. Her work offers a reading of nature that emphasizes an allover patterning that may well involve a reaction to traditions in New York, where paint as the record of its own activity has been championed for decades. Indeed, it is hard to dismiss the ambient influence of her adopted city, which has been a host to artists from all over the world. Her viewers remember that the technique of dripping paint is an American innovation, freeing the artist from the physical record of the paintbrush's touch. By participating in both Western and Asian aesthetics, Yoda reminds us that the principles of painting need not remain exclusively within the confines of a single culture. The cut pieces of Japanese paper construct, ever so slightly, a surface in which the layers are not utterly flat, with the result that the painting's exterior reflects light more intricately than a work with an entirely smooth surface. This is an acknowledgment of the efficacy of artisanal effort, as well as a recognition that painterly effects cannot be ascribed to a single tradition. In this way, Yoda speaks eloquently to the duality of her experience.

When and how did you first realize that you wanted to be an artist?
JY: When I was in junior high school. I was living in the countryside of Japan and I had no chance to see actual masterpieces of art works. One day, my teacher lent me a book of van Gogh paintings. I could hardly remove my eyes from the book. At that time, it was the first time that I realized that there was an occupation called "An Artist." I was delighted.

Why did you decide to leave Japan?
JY: In 1966, there was a great exhibition at the National Museum of Modern Art, Tokyo. It was called *Two Decades of American Painting*. It was an important exhibition that introduced American paintings to Japanese people for the first time. The show included works by Pollock, De Kooning, Morris Louis, Newman, Johns, Rauschenberg, Warhol, and many other artists. I saw the paintings of all the artists for the first time. It was shocking enough for me to decide to go to New York.

Did you have any interactions with other artists or supporters that were especially beneficial to you and your work?
JY: As an artist, I liked to have dialogues with paintings by Jackson Pollock while sitting on the benches at MoMA and the Metropolitan Museum. I learned so much from his paintings.

Do you ever regret leaving Japan?
JY: As an artist, I have never regretted leaving Japan. However, I miss my family very much.

In this age of globalism, do you consider yourself to be a Japanese artist, an American artist, an international artist, or a hybrid of all three?
JY: I do not see a relationship between globalism or migration and my work. On the contrary, I am afraid that the mystery of the world might die from growing globalism. I think great art won't be born without mystery.

PLATE 31.2

Junko Yoda
The Hudson
2006
Acrylic, Japanese paper, and charcoal on wood panel (diptych)
96 x 144" (243.8 x 365.8 cm)
Collection of the artist; courtesy Zabriskie Gallery, New York

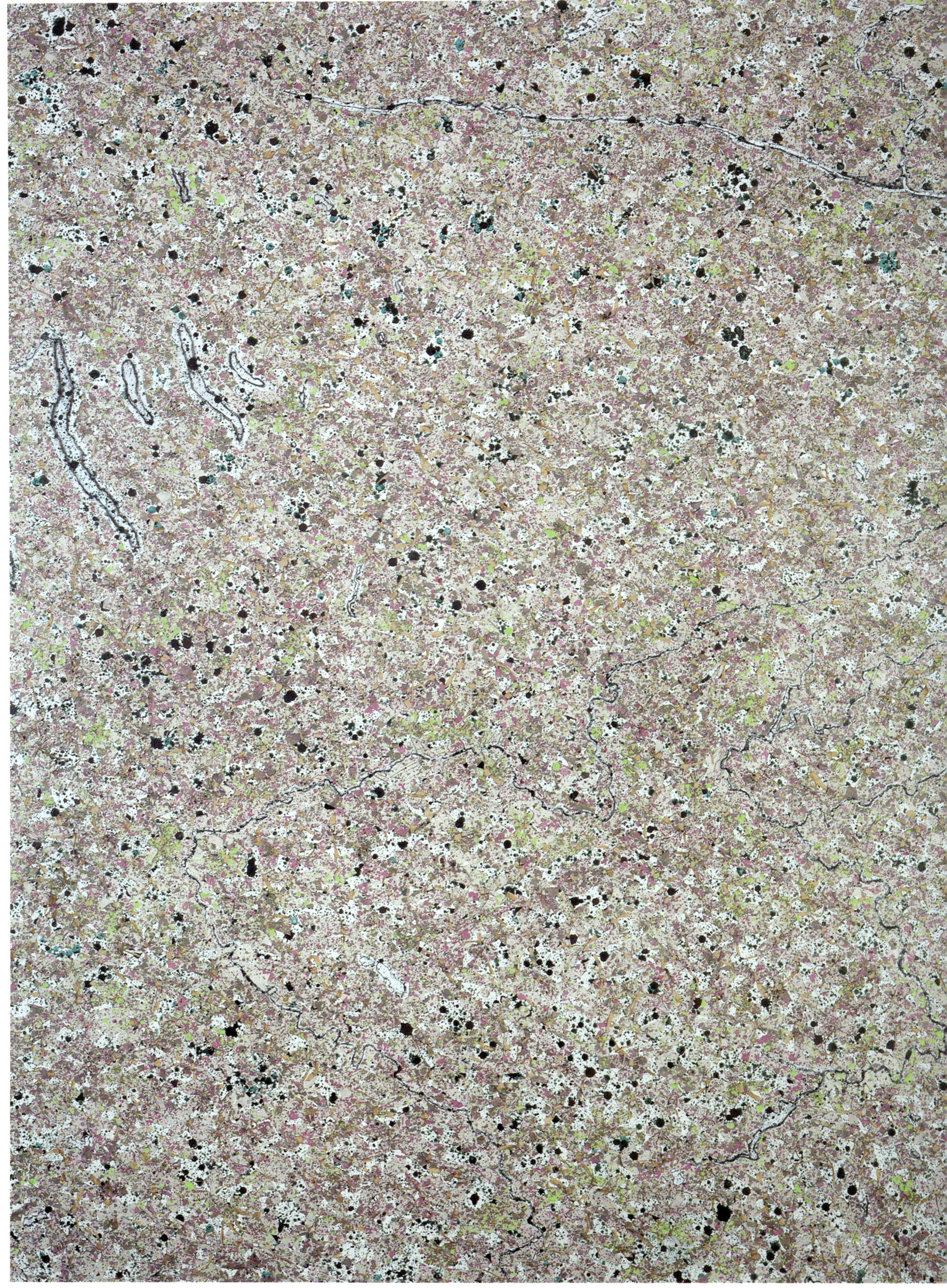

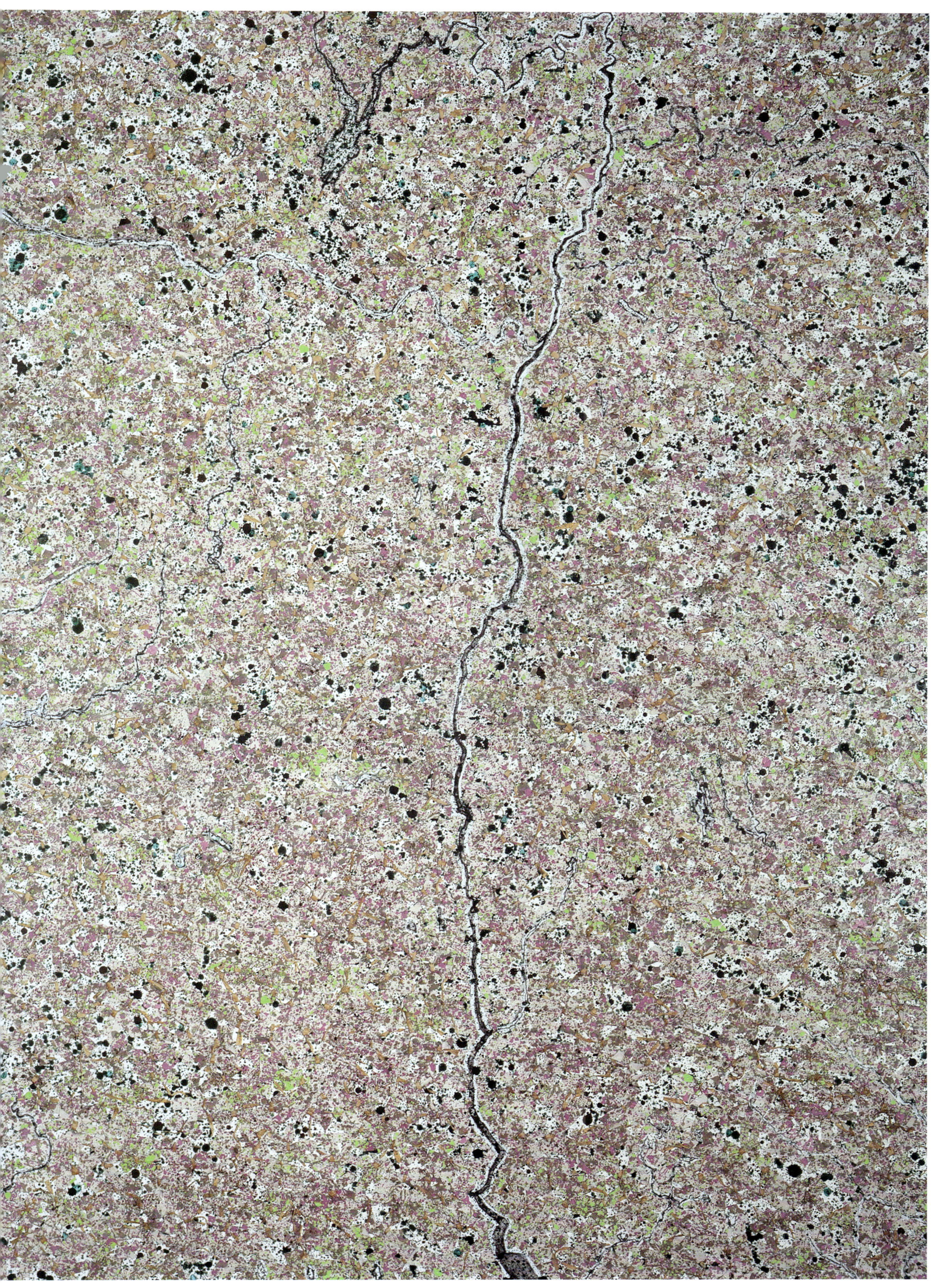

32 TOSHIHISA YODA

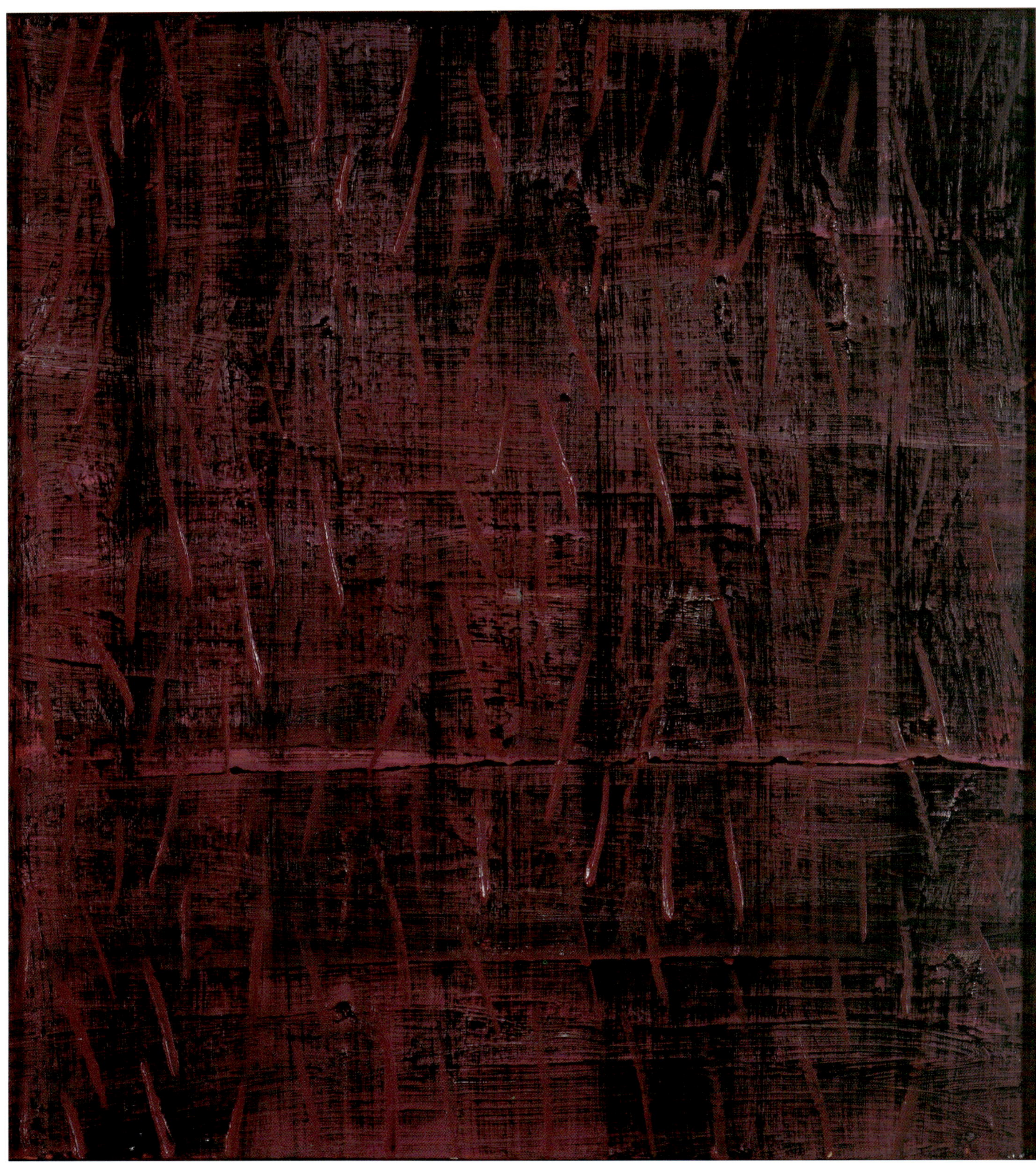

PLATE 32.1

Toshihisa Yoda
Untitled
1981
Oil on canvas
18 x 14" (45.7 x 35.6 cm)
Collection of the artist
PHOTO: JACQUES DEMELO

Tremors of the Air
REIKO TOMII

Like any enduring work of art, a canvas by Toshihisa Yoda at once demands and rewards an attentive mind and a persistent eye. His art may generally be called formalist: Yoda's dedication to the medium of painting has never wavered since he arrived in New York in 1967. As he lived through the lean years of painting, he steadfastly and determinedly explored the potential of abstraction in the best possible sense of late-modernist tradition. But he is no mere formalist, having managed to break open formal strictures to express what he calls "tremors of the air" (*kūki no furue*) in pictorial space.

Yoda's early inspirations included Jasper Johns, whose 1965 exhibition at the influential Minami Gallery in Tokyo fatefully changed his destination from Paris to New York, as well as Jackson Pollock and Paul Klee, whose retrospectives he saw at the Museum of Modern Art, New York and the Guggenheim Museum, respectively, upon his arrival. He was nonetheless touched by fashions of the time, first simulating the style of Op Art, then that of Hard Edge abstraction. It was not until the late 1970s that he found his own voice, creating in his canvases a subtle but clarified order that is punctuated by fragmentary marks. A small untitled work of 1981 kept in his studio exemplifies a breakthrough he achieved around that time (Pl. 32.1). (All his paintings are *Untitled*.) Like his recent canvas in this exhibition, its "structure," as Yoda calls it, consists of a series of layers: he first applied paint or molding paste to create horizontal bands which are minimalist yet show a rough materiality along their edges; he then applied the ground color of purple, followed by a dry, see-through layer of black, and literally put on "final touches" with short, organic, vertical lines in opaque purple. The resulting picture reveals an unexpectedly light pictorial space, "full of air" (*kūki ga ōi*), in his own words.

The critic Fujieda Teruo took note of this body of work. An acquaintance of the artist from the late 1960s onward and a frequent visitor to New York, Fujieda included Yoda in an exhibition of three emerging painters, subtitled "The Problems of Painting," which he guest-curated for the Seibu Museum of Art in Tokyo in 1980. In the world of contemporary art in Japan, there was a renewed interest in painting, especially in formalist-minimalist veins, since the late 1970s. Yoda's lone effort in New York unexpectedly coincided with a Japanese critical concern.

In the next two decades, his organic strokes more and more densely covered his canvases: some were filled with quivering vertical strokes, some with a mixture of verticals and horizontals, and yet others with short crosshatches. His unassuming marks were reminiscent of long stems, blades of grass, or foliage; the artist himself acknowledged his indebtedness to nature. These works represented his effort to generate a "tension on the surface as a whole" and "assured colors" through minimalist palettes dominated by black and dark red. Opaque and dense as these canvases may appear, his goal remained the same—to evoke "tremors of the air."

Around 2000, Yoda took up "tiny triangles," jettisoning his densely drawn organic strokes (Pl. 32.2). Triangles were not a new motif, as he used them both in his painting and sculptural experiments during his Hard Edge period. This time, after he started using the triangular unit, he learned the shape also had a vegetative association: the stem of *kayatsurigusa* (*Cyperus microiria*), a kind of sedge, is trigonous. (Native to East Asia, the weed is in the same genus as papyrus.) With the new series, Yoda in a sense returned to his own principles, or "structure," from about 1980: he introduced a simple stem-like armature of composition—no longer minimalist but more morphological—and radically reduced the number of visible strokes, which together engender a liberated sense of open space. Much more complex in the process of layering than his circa-1980 series, the new paintings complicate and deepen our experience of "seeing." A large two-panel canvas, shown in this exhibition, reveals a rich set of his strategies (Pl. 32.3). In particular, the translucent veil-like layers made up of almost imperceptible vertical white strokes create different levels of blurriness, even transforming some triangles into ghostly apparitions. Ultimately, to paraphrase the recent words of the critic Fujieda, seeing and making are two acts that are inseparable in Yoda's painting.

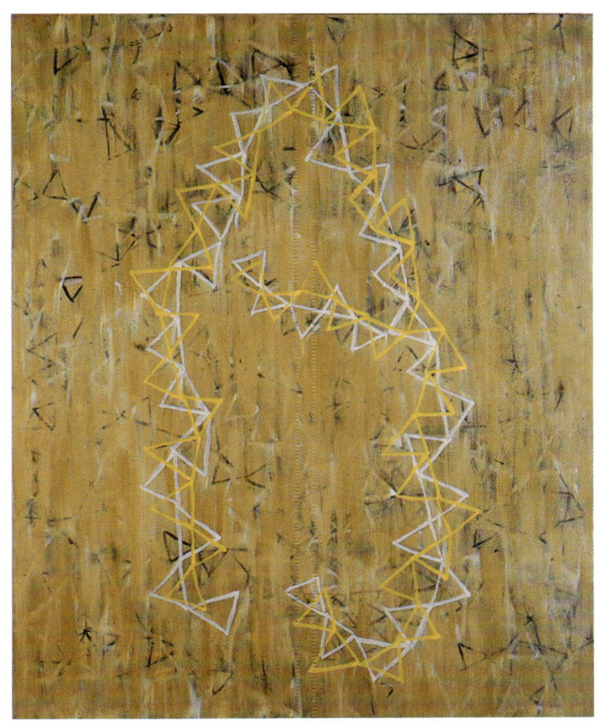

PLATE 32.2

Toshihisa Yoda
Untitled S-15
2002
Oil on canvas
50 x 40" (127 x 101.5 cm)
Collection of the artist

Why did you choose New York as your ultimate destination?

TY: At first, I was thinking about going to France. However when I saw Jasper Johns's exhibition at Minami Gallery in Tokyo, I changed the direction to New York. In August 1966, I left the port of Yokohama bound for Los Angeles. In L.A., I worked for eight months and made $5,000. Then I got a Greyhound bus ticket to New York. It read "$99 for 99 Days."

What was your first impression of New York City?

TY: I saw a performance by Yayoi Kusama at Washington Square Park. I asked several questions to Ms. Kusama. She replied, "Don't you know about Body Painting?" with an angry face.

Did you face many obstacles in establishing your career in New York?

TY: I think it took me about 14 or 15 years. I had a hard time finding the right studio. I had to move six times. At the beginning, I was in group shows at the Berkshire Museum in Massachusetts, the Aldrich Museum in Connecticut, and others.

Did you have any interactions with other artists or supporters that were especially beneficial to you and your work?

TY: When I was working for the gallery at the New School for Social Research (the gallery became the first space of the New Museum of Contemporary Art), director Mr. Paul Mocsany helped me so much to make a living and he gave me very important art books. An artist named Mr. Philip Pearlstein talked to me about his college friend Andy Warhol and many other artists.

In this age of globalism, do you consider yourself to be a Japanese artist, an American artist, an international artist, or a hybrid of all three?

TY: I don't think much about globalism or migration because I experienced the art of the late 1960s, 1970s, and 1980s and built my art with it as the base. I consider myself an international artist.

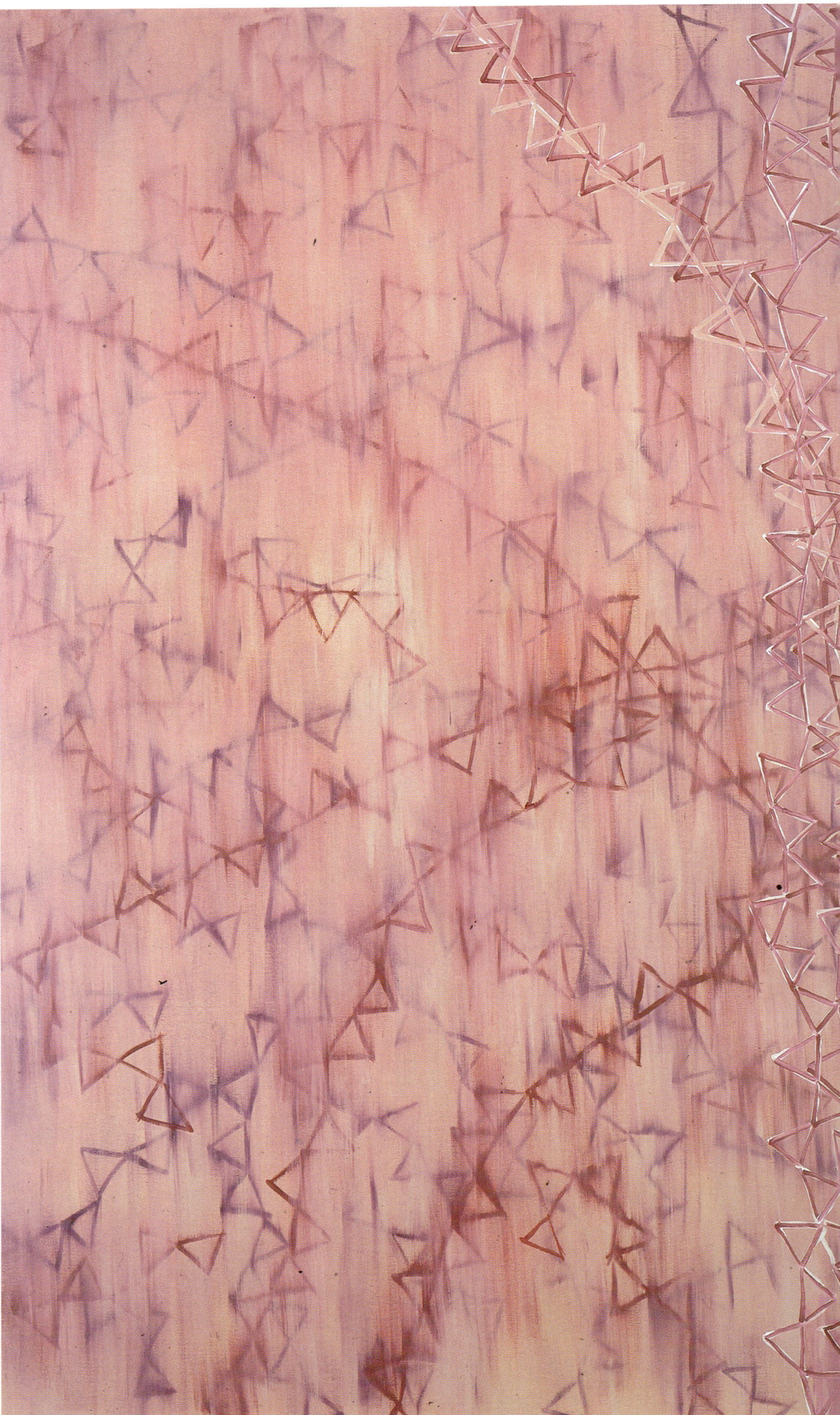

PLATE 32.3

Toshihisa Yoda
Untitled #12-03
2003
Oil on canvas (diptych)
90 x 144"(228.6 x 365.8 cm)
Collection of the artist
PHOTO: JACQUES DEMELO

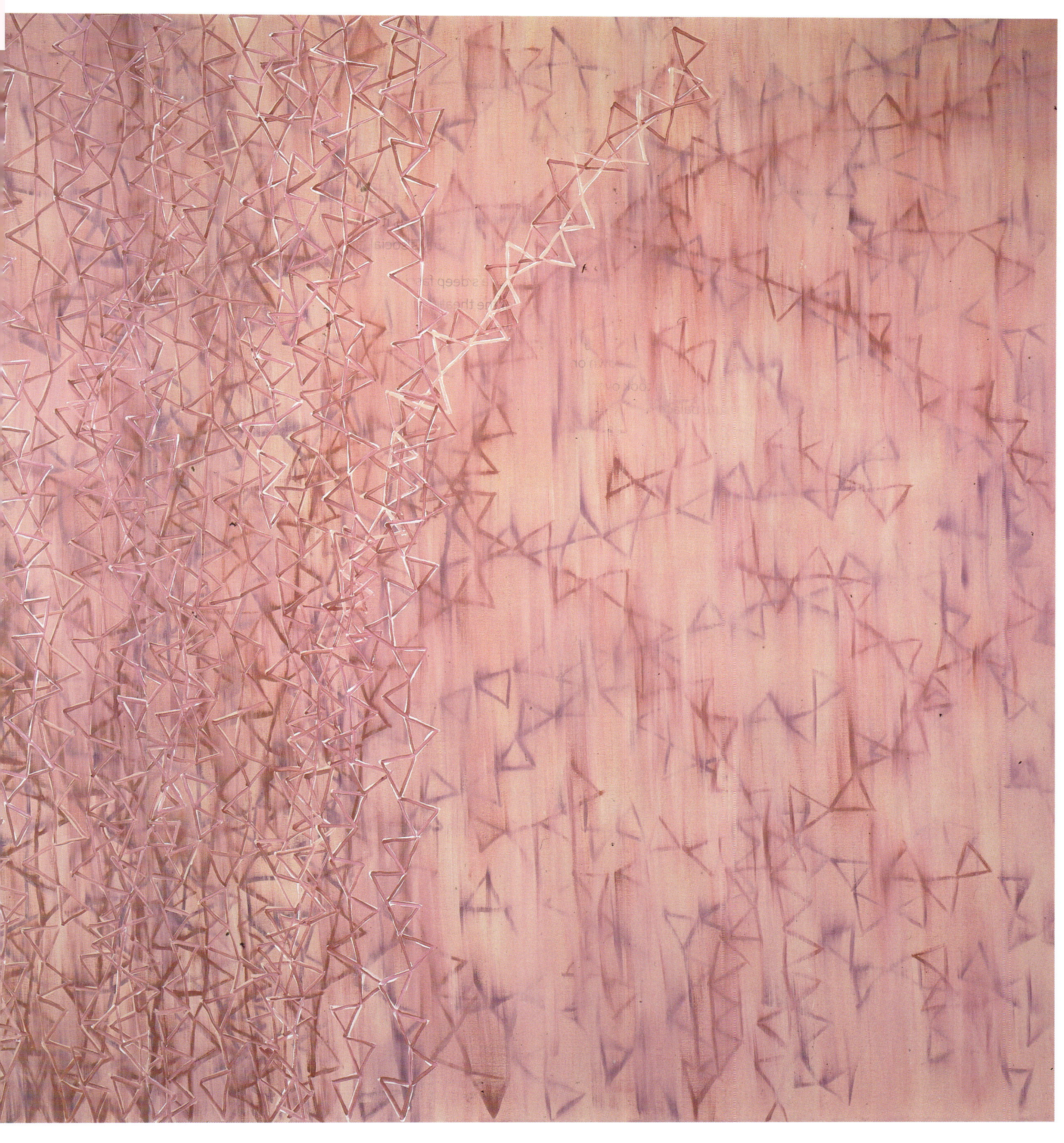

⌂ 33 YŌICHIRŌ YODA

Projecting the Past into the Future
ERIC C. SHINER

Painter Yōichirō Yoda is equal parts historian, social scientist, and artist. Since the early 1990s, he has been engaged in a series of works documenting the so-called Great White Way, New York City's Broadway theater district. For more than 20 years, that portion of Midtown Manhattan has been undergoing a slow-but-sure metamorphosis from seedy red-light district to gentrified tourist trap. As a sort of urban renewal renaissance in the 1990s, New York City toughened laws against the many porn theaters that set up shop in the neighborhood in the 1970s and 1980s, shutting them down or forcing them out of business. Eager developers often took over the old theaters, turning them back into pleasure palaces for a newly vibrant Broadway or, in many cases, destroying them completely to erect office buildings, wax museums, and multiplex movie theaters where the grand stages of New York once stood. With camera in hand, Yoda was there to record it all. His work captures the ghosts of Broadway in architectural and painterly forms.

Yoda's paintings are eerie glimpses of the darkened halls of now-defunct theaters such as the Selwyn, the Empire, and the Harem. One painting, *Times Square Theatre Seats*, shows row upon row of red velvet seats in a state of impending decay (Pl. 33.2). It is clear that these dingy seats have not hosted a genteel audience in years, although the possibility of XXX film–viewing is a high probability from the recent past. Yoda would often explore and record these theaters, sometimes befriending guards and construction workers who would allow him to sneak inside days before the theater was set for demolition. Video camera at the ready, Yoda filmed the interiors, stages, and film screening rooms of these theatrical behemoths. His resultant video work, *Last Days of 42nd Street*, is a

compendium of these images shot from 1994 to 2003 (Pl. 33.1). Decidedly noncommercial and grainy, the video is as much brilliant cultural critique as it is useful document of an important part of New York City's social history.

Yoda's deep fascination for Times Square may be rooted in his love of the theatrical. As an artist, he has always been intrigued with the world of fantasy, Hollywood, and the starlets that inhabit that world. In his own life, his tastes run to the extremes of performance: his musical attention leans to heavy metal; his favorite movie is the 1939 film *The Roaring Twenties*, starring James Cagney. Yoda supports his art career by working as a security guard at the Metropolitan Museum of Art. He is there surrounded by art, as well as the swarming crowds that populate the museum day in and day out. That his paintings are often devoid of people hints that the artist is just as compelled by the realms of art when they are empty as he is with those same spaces teeming with people eager to look at the most beautiful things the world has to offer.

Yoda is truly surrounded by art around the clock. He lives and works in the same SoHo loft as his parents, Junko and Toshihisa, painters also featured in *Making a Home*. For the Yoda clan, art making is a family affair. Their massive loft is stocked floor to ceiling with canvases from years of shared production. Each of them works in a separate vein, but the smell of paint runs heavy in the air and acts as a common link to the family's production. Only three months old when he moved here, Yōichirō grew up in the thriving art world of New York, surrounded by his parents' paints and artist friends, thus gradually soaking in the stuff that mandated his own future path.

In the end, though, young Yoda has established a voice fully independent from the vocabulary of his parents, steeped as it is in the idioms of the New York School. Yōichirō has established a career as a painter engaged in reportage and social critique. His paintings *Movie Projector (Selwyn Theatre) #1* and *#2* are fully representative of the artist and his oeuvre (Pls. 33.6–7). They show the lone source of magic and light in an otherwise dark environment, just as Yoda brings life to the now destroyed theaters of New York's own realm of musical magic.

  PLATE 33.1

Yōichirō Yoda
Still from *Last Days of 42nd Street*
(Empire Theatre moving)
1994–2003
Video
60 minutes
Collection of the artist
PHOTO: JACQUES DEMELO

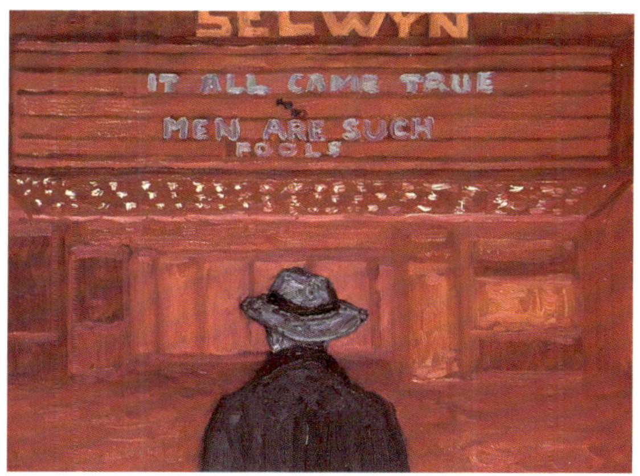

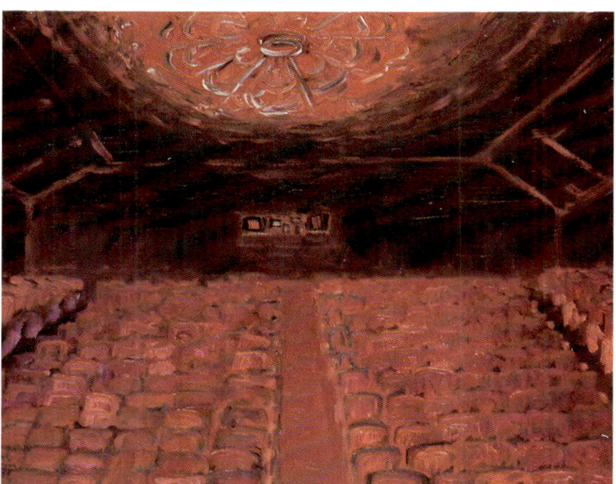

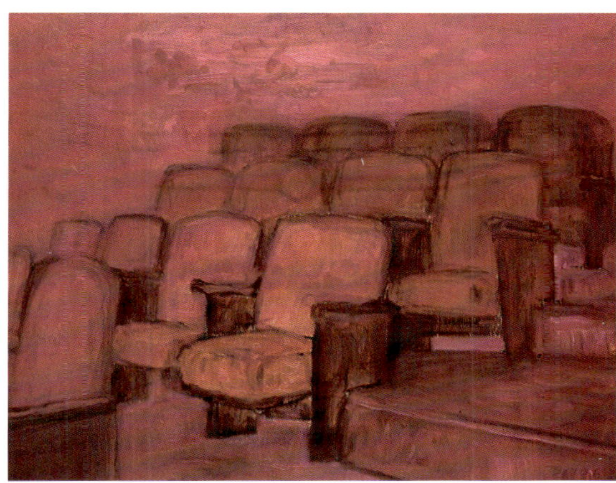

Why did you decide to leave Japan?

YY: I came to New York City with my parents three months after I was born.

What was your first impression of New York City?

YY: The earliest thing I remember growing up in Midtown Manhattan is my childhood home at 885 Third Avenue. Back in the mid 1970s to early 1980s, it was still a family-based neighborhood. I feel very lucky to have had the chance to go to such great New York institutions as Zum Zum, Chock Full of Nuts, Automat-style cafeterias, Woolworth's, and many single screen movie theatres. Sadly, it was in 1982 that we (42 families) were evicted from our homes on Third Avenue to make way for several office buildings, thanks to greedy developers. Little did I know that this was my introduction to a theme I would explore years later in my paintings.

In this age of globalism, do you consider yourself to be a Japanese artist, an American artist, an international artist, or a hybrid of all three?

YY: As a New York–based Japanese artist, I feel that I have always been and still am influenced by what is going on in New York City, especially the loss of countless historical theaters, buildings, and hotels, rather than the influence of globalism. I feel that there is no time to lose and therefore I have to document as much as possible in my paintings and videos before more is lost. I consider myself an American artist, but I hope that my work will appeal to a wider audience around the world.

PLATE 33.2

Yōichirō Yoda
Times Square Theatre Seats
2004
Oil on canvas
20 x 16" (50.8 x 40.6 cm)
Collection of the artist

PLATE 33.3

Yōichirō Yoda
Selwyn
2003
Oil on canvas
16 x 20" (40.6 x 50.8 cm)
Collection of the artist

PLATE 33.4

Yōichirō Yoda
RKO Theatre
2004
Oil on canvas
16 x 20" (40.6 x 50.8 cm)
Collection of the artist

PLATE 33.5

Yōichirō Yoda
Harem Theatre Seats
2004
Oil on canvas
16 x 20" (40.6 x 50.8 cm)
Collection of the artist

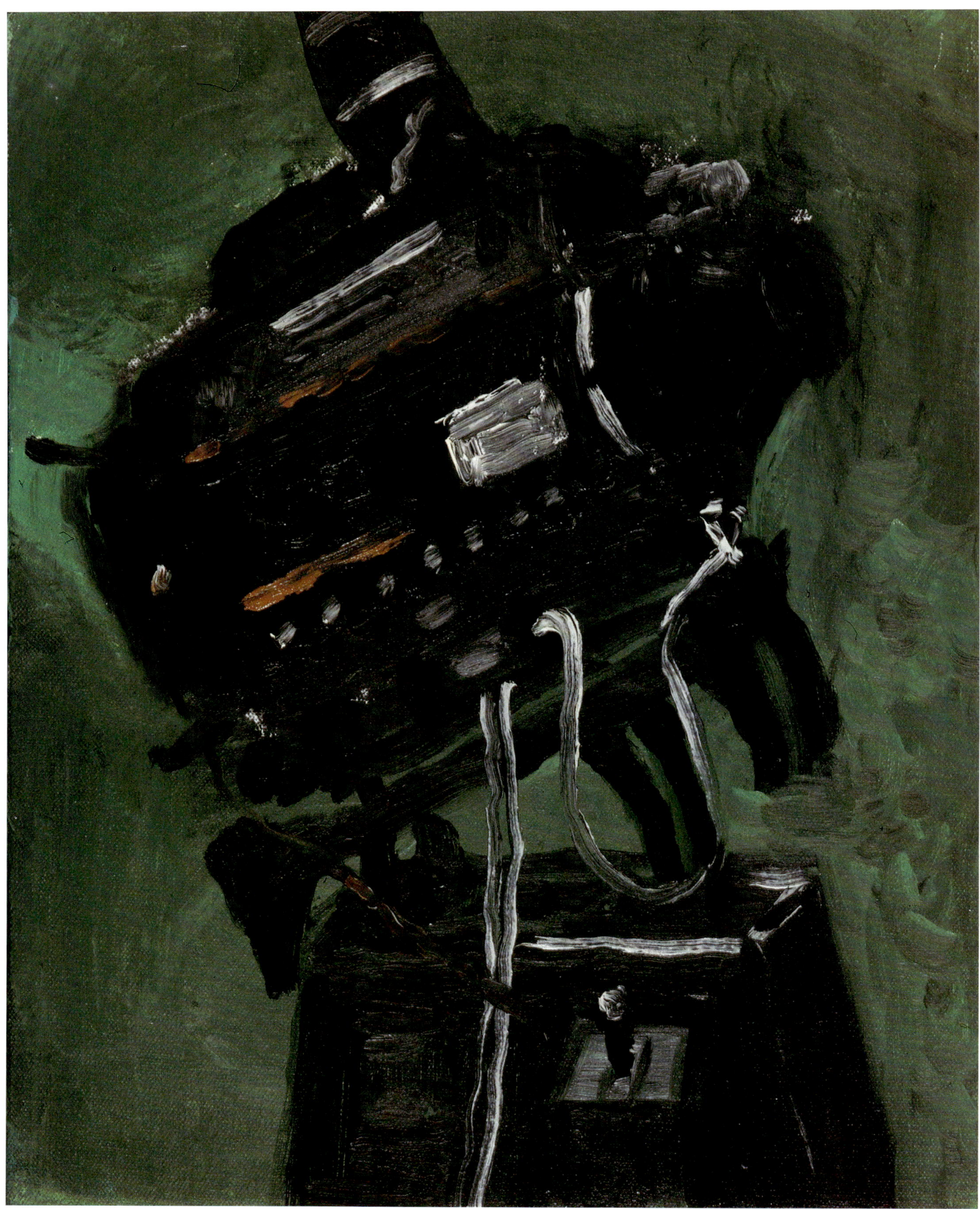

PLATE 33.6

Yōichirō Yoda
Movie Projector (Selwyn Theatre) #1
2001
Oil on canvas
14 x 11" (35.6 x 27.9 cm)
Collection of the artist

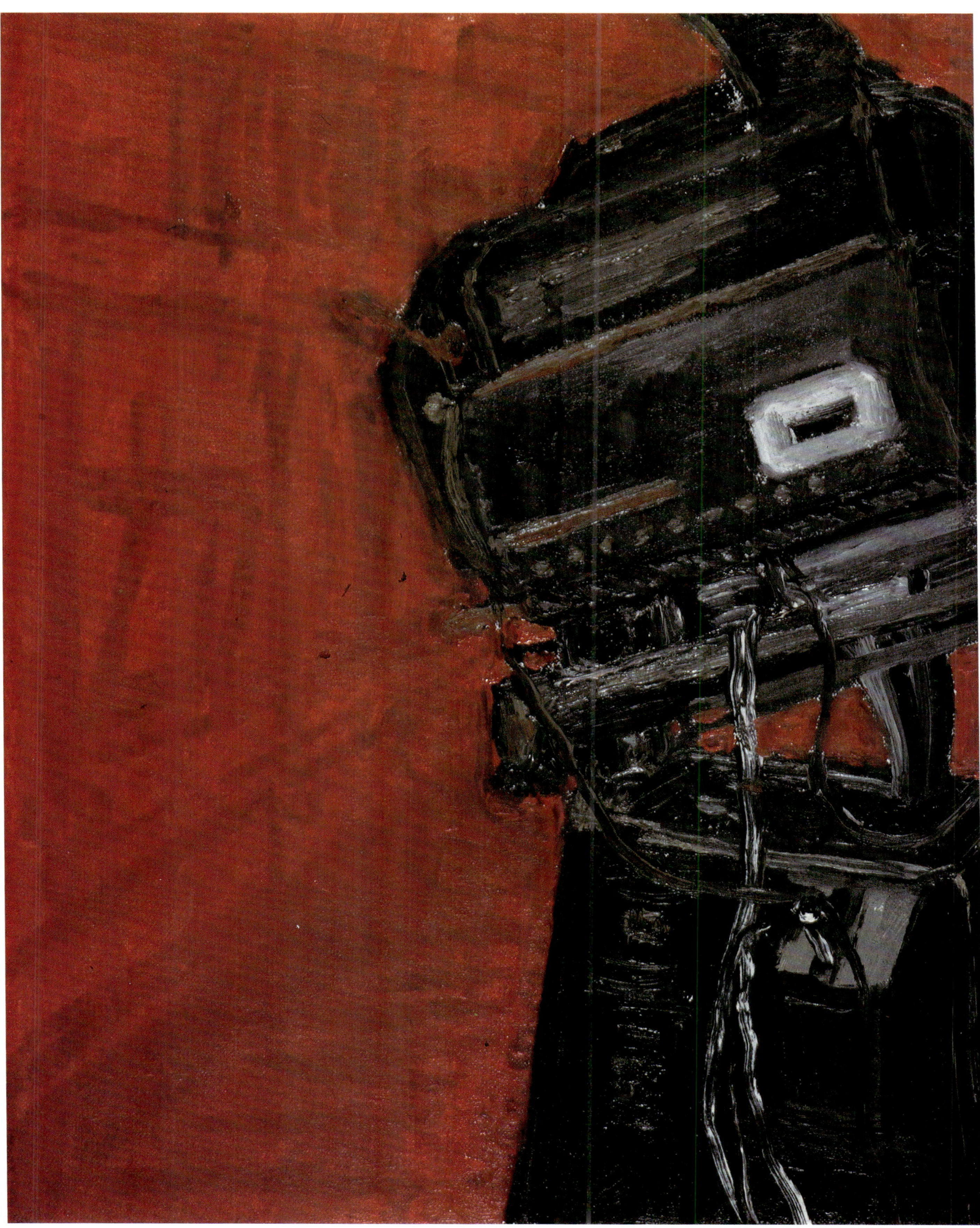

PLATE 33.7

Yōichirō Yoda
Movie Projector (Selwyn Theatre) #2
2001
Oil on canvas
14 x 11" (35.6 x 27.9 cm)
Collection of the artist
PHOTO: JACQUES DEMELO

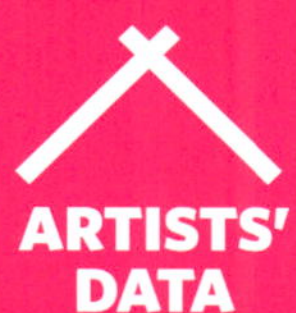
ARTISTS'
DATA

ARTISTS' DATA

Compiled by Sachiko Hisajima

This data section offers selected information on the biography, exhibition history, and publications of artists in *Making a Home*.

1   When an artist-in-residence culminates in a solo or group exhibition, the residency is noted following that exhibition.

2   In selecting publications, emphasis was given to those published in New York and the U.S.

3   Exhibition catalogues are indicated by asterisks (*) in the exhibition listings.

4   As a rule, titles of Japanese publications are given in English translation only, and noted by [Japanese text].

5   Some artists chose not to provide certain data and portrait photographs.

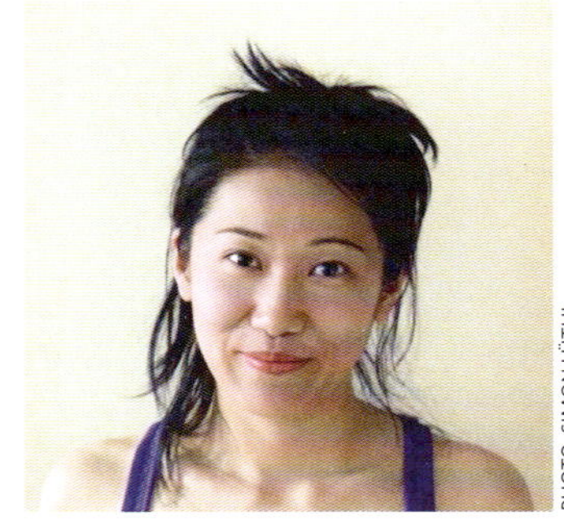

PHOTO: SIMON LÜTHI

⌂ 01
ON MEGUMI AKIYOSHI
秋好恩

Born in Utsunomiya, Tochigi Prefecture, Japan, 1972; lives and works in Brooklyn

1997
BFA in oil painting, Tokyo National University of Fine Arts and Music

2002
MFA in fine art, School of Visual Arts, New York

2005
Awards, Manhattan Community Arts Fund, Lower Manhattan Cultural Council and New York City Department of Cultural Affairs

Solo Exhibitions
2004
Two-person show with Shih Chieh Huang, Vox Populi, Philadelphia

2005
xanadu*, New York

2006
ON museum @ Times Square, New York

Group Exhibitions
2000
Rounding & Rounding, Sakima Art Museum, Ginowan, Okinawa Prefecture, Japan

2002
Autoritratto, Sesto Senso, Bologna

Installations, West Side Gallery, New York

2003
Echigo-Tsumari Art Triennial 2003, Niigata Prefecture, Japan (as part of Tsumari Gei)

The Mythical Nation, Artspace, New Haven, Conn.

2004
Fiction Love, Museum of Contemporary Art, Taipei

Vector: Este-Oeste, Centro de Arte Caja de Burgos, Spain

Voice of Site: Tokyo-Chicago-New York, Chinretsukan Exhibition Hall, Tokyo National University of Fine Arts and Music

2005
Gravity News, NewYorkRioTokyo, Berlin

Hors Cadrage, Ise Cultural Foundation Gallery, New York

Red Beans and Rice, Atlanta Contemporary Art Center

2006
Beyond Measure, Taipei Cultural Center, New York

Dumbo Art Under the Bridge Festival, Brooklyn

Fiction @ Love, Singapore Art Museum and Museum of Contemporary Art, Shanghai

2007
Catapult, Maryland Hall, Annapolis

Jamaica Flux 2007, Jamaica Center for the Arts and Learning, Queens (award)

Sakura Matsuri, Brooklyn Botanic Garden

Sustainable Art Project, org. by Environmental Process Art and Tokyo National University of Fine Arts and Music, JR Ueno Station, Tokyo

The Reality Show, 2 x 13 Gallery, New York

Publications
Benjamin Genocchio, "Art Review," *New York Times*, July 27, 2003

Stefano Pasquini, "NRG: It's Good to Be Back," *NY Arts Magazine* (November 2003): 59

Seth Clark Silberman, "Review from Red Beans and Rice Show," *ArtAsiaPacific* (Spring 2006): 90–91

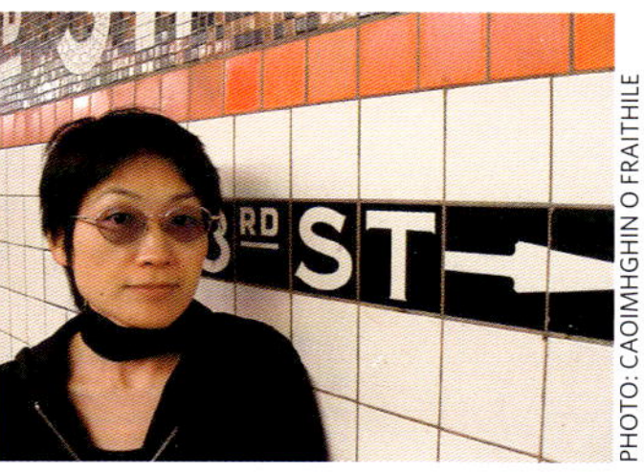

PHOTO: CAOIMHGHIN O FRAITHILE

⌂ 02
NORIKO AMBE
安部典子

Born in Fukaya, Saitama Prefecture, Japan, 1967; lives and works in Queens

1990
BFA in oil painting, Musashino Art University, Tokyo

1994
8th Holbein Scholarship, Japan

1997
Summer printmaking program, Studio Camnitzer, Valdottavo, Italy (also '98, '99)

1999–2000
Pola Art Foundation grant, Tokyo (lives in New York and Italy)

2003
Freeman Fellowship (artist-in-residence, Vermont Studio Center)

2004–05
Japanese Government's Overseas Study Program fellowship (lives in New York)

Studio residency program, Lower Manhattan Cultural Council

2005
Artist-in-residence, Art Omi International Arts Center, N.Y.

2007
The Pollock-Krasner Foundation grant

Solo Exhibitions
1993
Gallery Natsuka, Tokyo (also '02, '03*)

2003
Pierogi, Brooklyn

Vermont Studio Center, Johnson, Vt. (after artist-in-residence)

2004
Snug Harbor Cultural Center, Staten Island (after artist-in-residence)

2006
Josée Bienvenu Gallery, New York

2007
d.e.n. contemporary art, Culver City, Calif.

Group Exhibitions
1997
Mostra di Incisione, Barga, Italy (also '97, '98)

2002
Dumbo Art Festival, Brooklyn

Looking East, Looking West, Brattleboro Museum, Vt.

The Philip Morris Art Award, Tokyo International Forum

2003
Cristinerose/Josée Bienvenu Gallery, New York (also '04)

Japan: Rising—Contemporary Art from Japan, Palm Beach Institute of Contemporary Art, Lake Worth, Fla.

Line Dancing, Islip Art Museum, N.Y.

Take Out, Zabriskie Gallery, New York

2004
Microwave, Sicardi Gallery, Houston

Talespinning: Selection Fall 2004, Drawing Center, New York

Troy Stories, Hosfelt Gallery, San Francisco

2005
Bonds, Ise Cultural Foundation Gallery, New York

Ground Work, d.e.n. contemporary art, Culver City, Calif.

Pulp, Tyler Gallery, Tyler School of Art, Philadelphia

2006
Art on Paper Biannual 2006, Weatherspoon Art Museum, Greensboro, N.C.

Force of Nature, Halsey Gallery, College of Charleston, S.C. (after artist-in-residence)

Trans-Boundary Experiences, Spool Mfg, Johnson City, N.Y.

Publications
Grace Glueck, "Working Words into Images," *New York Times*, September 24, 2004

Merrily Kerr, "New Paper Sculpture," *Art on Paper* (March–April 2005): 62

Jonathan Goodman, "Flat Globe," *Sculpture* (November 2006): 73–74

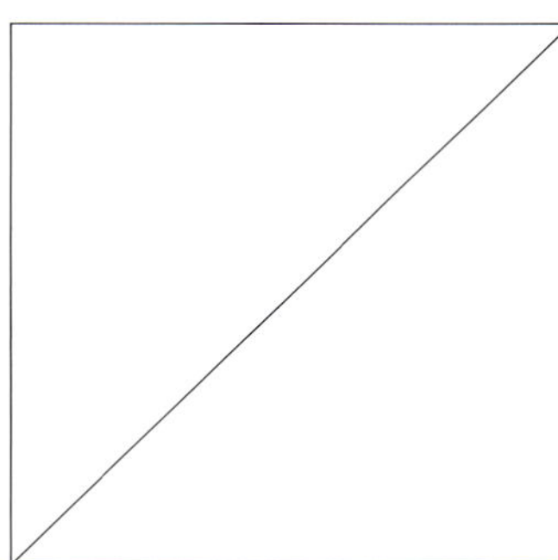

EI ARAKAWA
荒川医

Born in Iwaki, Fukushima Prefecture, Japan, 1977; lives and works in Brooklyn

2004
BFA, School of Visual Arts, New York

2005–06
Independent Study Program, Whitney Museum of American Art, New York

2006
MFA in film/video, Bard College, Annandale-on-Hudson, N.Y.

Group Exhibitions
2004
Don't Think About Me, I'm Alright, Greene Naftali Gallery, New York (with performance)

Succeeding Where the Hippies Failed, LeRoy Neiman Gallery, Columbia University, New York (with performance)

2006
Bunch Alliance and Dissolve, Contemporary Arts Center, Cincinnati

Continuous Project 8, CNEAI, Paris/Chatou

Keep Passing the Open Windows or Happiness, Galerie Gisela Capitain, Cologne (with performance)

2007
For the People of Paris, Sutton Lane. Paris (with performance)

Syntropia, Neue Gesellschaft für bildende Kunst, Berlin (with performance)

Various Small Fires, Royal College of Art Galleries, London (with performance)

Performances
2004
Reena Spaulings Fine Art, New York (also '06, '07)

2005
Bard College, Annandale-on-Hudson, N.Y. (also '06)

Empty Space with Exciting Events, Artists Space, New York

ETC, Andrew Kreps Gallery, New York

Greater New York 2005, P.S.1, Queens

Performa 05, New York

2006
Echigo-Tsumari Art Triennial 2006, Niigata Prefecture, Japan

Movement Research at the Judson Church "About Town," New York

2007
One Season in Hell, Gavin Brown's Enterprise, New York

Screenings
2005
Japanese Art Since 1945: The First PoNJA-GenKon Symposium, Yale University, New Haven

2006
Tbilisi 3: Let's Stay Alive Till Monday, Children National Gallery, Tbilisi, Georgia

2007
Our Land Is Our Land, Henry Art Gallery, Seattle

Publications
Cay Sophie Rabinowitz, "Ei Arakawa's Six Degrees of Subtlety," *Art Papers* (September/October 2005): 25–27

John Kelsey, "Best of 2005," *Artforum* (December 2005): 252–53

Holland Cotter, "Whitney Independent Study Program," *New York Times*, May 12, 2006

Nick Stillman, "An Art Brand," *Flash Art* (May/June 2006): 96

Emily Speers Mears, "On the Verge of the Audience," *Texte zur Kunst* (September 2006): 199

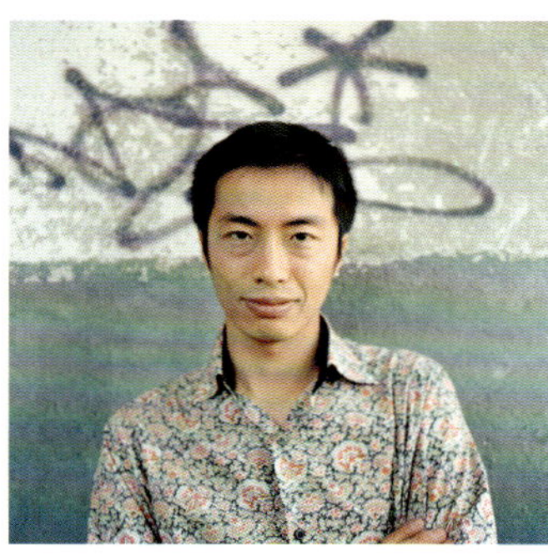

SATORU EGUCHI
江口悟

Born in Shibata, Niigata Prefecture, Japan, 1973; lives and works in Brooklyn

2002
BFA in painting, School of Visual Arts, New York

2004
MFA in mixed media, School of Visual Arts, New York

2006
Artist-in-residence, Yaddo, N.Y.

Solo Exhibitions
2005
Voyeur Project View, Lisbon

Yoshiko Matsumoto Gallery, Amsterdam

Group Exhibitions
2003
Night of 1000 Drawings, Artists Space, New York

Re-Interpreting Landscape, Office Ops, Brooklyn

2004
Articles and Waves, Geoffrey Young Gallery, Great Barrington, Mass.

New American Talent 19, Arthouse, Austin, Texas

Northwest Annual, Center on Contemporary Art, Seattle

Sleight of Hand, Lemon Sky: Projects + Editions, Miami

The Luggage Project, Denver International Airport

The Neon Forest Is My Home, Sixtyseven, Brooklyn

2005
Let the Players Play, Geoffrey Young Gallery, Great Barrington, Mass.

Sleep Spaces, Dumbo Arts Center, Brooklyn

2006
Emotional Landscape, Rotunda Gallery, Brooklyn

What a Beautiful Day, Ise Cultural Foundation Gallery, New York

MetLife, Morgan Lehman Gallery, New York

Nina Lora Bachhuber, Satoru Eguchi & Takako Hamano: Drawings, Toshiko Matsumoto Gallery, Amsterdam

Publications
Oneil Edwards and Satoru Eguchi, "Off-Ramp," *Zingmagazine* (Winter/Spring 2003): 235–51

Holland Cotter, "Sampling Brooklyn, Keeper of Eclectic Flames," *New York Times*, January 23, 2004

Nana Kano, "Nine," *NY Arts Magazine* (March/April 2004): 49

Serge Onnen, ed., *Drawings on Geology* (New York: J&L, 2005)

Kai van Hasselt, "Een Collage van Dimensies en Perspectieven," *Tubelight* (February 2005): 12–13

Emily Wei and Kunst Nu, "Portfolio," *S.M.A.K.* (April 2005): 30–37

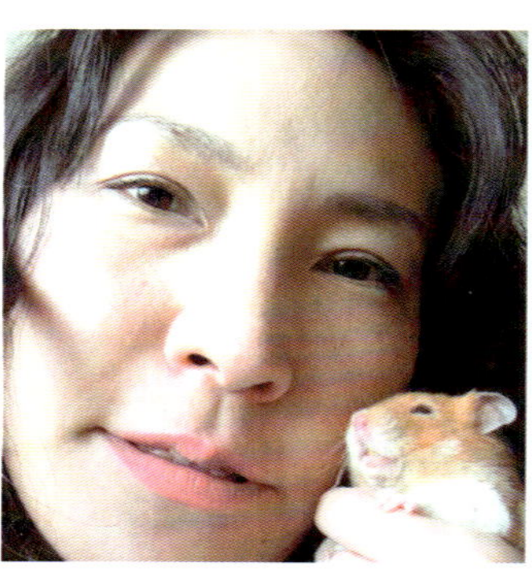

AYAKOH FURUKAWA
古川文香

Born in Sakai, Osaka Prefecture, Japan, 1962; lives and works in Queens

1993
AA in painting, Los Angeles Valley College

1997
Osaka Twenty-First Century Association award

2000–02
Art Students League of New York (merit scholarship)

2004
BFA in painting, Hunter College, New York

2007
MFA in painting, Hunter College, New York

Appointed president, Japanese Artists Association of New York, Inc. (Jaany)

Solo Exhibitions
1994
Gallery Ichi, Osaka

1997
Gallery Yamato, Osaka

1998
Two-person show with Higuchi Taeko, Gallery Yamato, Osaka

Group Exhibitions
1999
Annual Exhibition of Japanese Artists Association of New York, Broome Street Gallery, New York, (also '00, New Century Gallery, New York; annually '02–'06, Tenri Cultural Institute of New York)

Apocalypse 1999, Williamsburg Art & Historical Center, Brooklyn

2001
Collage & Assemblage, Concourse Gallery, Art Students League of New York

2001 International Group Show, Cealum Gallery, New York

2002
Tribute Exhibition to 9/11, Gallery 128, New York

2004
Dialog I, II: RENKA, Consulate General of Japan, New York

2005
East Wind in the Stroll Garden, Hammond Museum, North Salem, N.Y.

Summer Festival Art Students' Show 2005, Ise Cultural Foundation Gallery, New York (receives commendation; also '06, receives Janet Koplos Juror Award)

2006
Contemporary & Traditional: Two Aspects of Jaany, NYCoo Gallery, New York

Reverie: Visions of Mystery, 58 Gallery, Jersey City

2006 CUNY Arts Gala: Fiction, Film, Poetry, Video, Martin E. Segal Theatre Center, The Graduate Center, New York (receives award)

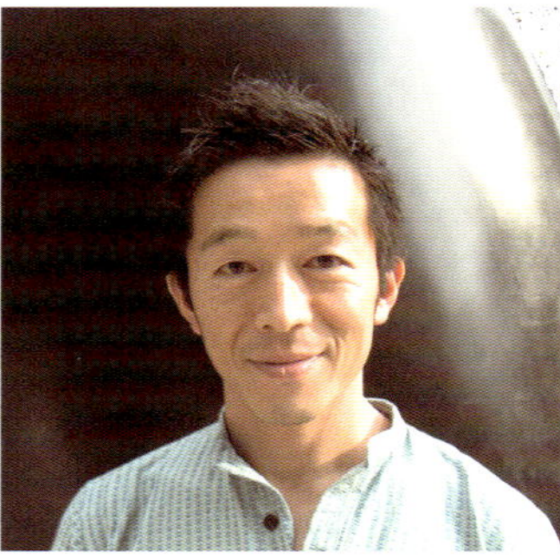

TŌRU HAYASHI
林亨

Born in Kōbe, Japan, 1963; lives and works in Manhattan

1988
BS in mathematics, Hokkaidō University, Sapporo, Japan

1990
Setsu Mode Seminar, Tokyo

1994
Artists in the Marketplace, Bronx Museum of the Arts

1999
Change, Inc. grant, New York and The Wheeler Foundation grant, Brooklyn

2004
Tenot Foundation grant, France

2007
Artist-in-residence, Sanskriti Kendra Culture Center, New Delhi

Solo Exhibitions
1997
Taka, New York

2001
Ise Cultural Foundation Gallery, New York

Group Exhibitions
1994
Artists in the Marketplace Exhibition, Bronx Museum of the Arts

**Shouts and Whispers*, Venue Gallery, Philadelphia

1995
Makers of Identity, Gallery Korea, New York

1996
Momenta Art, Brooklyn

SoHo Arts Festival 1996, New York

1997
Downtown Arts Festival, New York (also '98, '00)

1999
Outer Boroughs, White Columns, New York

2000
**20 Years of the Artist in the Marketplace Program: Good Business Is the Best Art*, Bronx Museum of the Arts

2001
Pioneering Spirit: Colbert Art Walk 2001, Hermes, New York

2002
Asian Contemporary Art Week, New York

2003
**Japan: Rising—Contemporary Art from Japan*, Palm Beach Institute of Contemporary Art, Lake Worth, Fla.

2004
Wedding, Space Force, Tokyo

2005
Influence, CAMAC, Marnay-sur-Seine, France (after artist-in-residence)

2006
Perceiving Beauty: Art, Science, and Human Nature, Confederation Centre Art Gallery, Prince Edward Island, Canada (after fellowship/artist-inresidence)

Publications
Holland Cotter, "A Showcase for Artists Learning Their Business," *New York Times*, August 19, 1994

Tōru Hayashi, "Equivocal Landscape" (artist's portfolio), *Open City*, no. 12 (2001): 43–48

Roberta Smith, "Art in Review," *New York Times*, July 6, 2001

Jay Wesley, "Travel Agency Garden," *Dutch* 37 (2002): 17

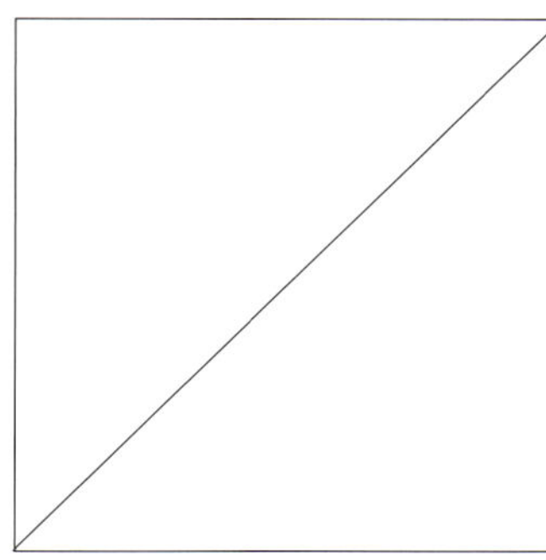

07
NORITOSHI HIRAKAWA
平川典俊

Born in Ukiha, Fukuoka Prefecture, Japan, 1960; lives and works in Manhattan

Solo Exhibitions (from 1994)
1994
*American Fine Arts, New York

Art & Public, Geneva, Switzerland (also '00, '02)

Wako Works of Art, Tokyo (also '98*, '02, '05)

1995
Galerie d'Eendt, Amsterdam

Galerie Emmanuel Perrotin, Paris (also '97)

1996
*Hiroshima City Museum of Contemporary Art

Zeno X Gallery, Antwerp (also '04)

1997
Centre d'Art Neuchâtel, Switzerland

*Deitch Projects, New York (also '98)

Gabriele Rivet, Cologne

1998
Galleria Massimo De Carlo, Milano

*Taka Ishii Gallery, Santa Monica

1999
*Kunsthalle St. Gallen, Switzerland

2001
*Magazin 4, Bregenz, Germany

2002
*Maison Hermès Forum, Tokyo

Noirmont Prospect, Paris

2003
*BMW Group Pavilion, Munich

2004
Frieze Art Fair (Wrong Gallery), London

The Eric Arthur Gallery, University of Toronto

2005
In Situ, Paris

Salon 94, New York

2006
Baukunst Galerie, Cologne

Galerie Ferdinand van Dieten, Amsterdam

Gallery HAM, Nagoya

Group Exhibitions (from 1994)
1994
*A Vision of Japan for 21st Century, Sezon Museum of Modern Art, Tokyo

1995
*Campo, Corderie dell'Arsenale, Venice

*Feminin, Masculin, Centre Georges Pompidou, Paris

*4th Istanbul Biennial

*Ripple Across the Water, Watari-um, Tokyo

*Shift, De Appel, Amsterdam

1996
Shopping, Yohji Yamamoto, New York

*Traffic, CAPC, Bordeaux, France

1997
*Absolute Landscape, Yokohama Museum of Art

Heaven: Public View, Private View, P.S.1, Queens

Truce, SITE Santa Fe

1998
Live and Let Die, Apex Art, New York

1999
*Missing Link, Kunstmuseum Bern

2001
*Casino 2001, S.M.A.K., Ghent, Belgium

*The Beauty of Intimacy, Gemeentemuseum, The Hague

2003
*False Innocence, Fundació Joan Miró, Barcelona

*The History of Japanese Photography, Museum of Fine Arts, Houston

2004
*Mixed Farming, Nederlands Fotomuseum, Rotterdam

2005
*Le Mois de la Photo à Montréal

*Lichtkunst aus Kunstlicht, Museum für Neue Kunst, Karlsruhe, Germany

*Tirana Biennale 3, National Gallery of Arts, Albania

2006
*Into Me/Out of Me, P.S.1, Queens

The Garden Party, Deitch Projects, New York

2007
*Mulher, Mulheres, SESC, São Paulo

*Lost Format, Be-Part, Waregem, Belgium

Publications
Noritoshi Hirakawa, *No More Pains of Isaac Newton* [Japanese text] (Tokyo: Yōbisha, 1990)

Noritoshi Hirakawa, *I Am Here, But I Am Not Here* [Japanese text] (Tokyo: Seikyūsha, 1991)

Noritoshi Hirakawa, *To Be Dharma* (Middelburg: de Vleeshal, 1991)

Noritoshi Hirakawa 1988–94 (Tokyo: Wako Works of Art and Nagoya: Gallery HAM, 1995)

Noritoshi Hirakawa, *Matters* (New York: Deitch Projects and Antwerp: Zeno X Gallery, 1998)

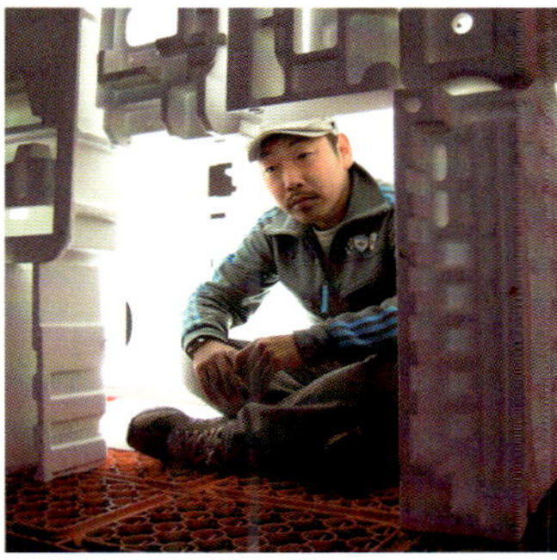

08
YOSHIAKI KAIHATSU
開発好明

Born in Kōfu, Yamanashi Prefecture, Japan, 1966; lives and works in Manhattan

1991
BA in oil painting, Tama Art University, Tokyo

1993
MA in oil painting, Tama Art University, Tokyo

1998–99
Asian Cultural Council fellowship, New York

2000
Artist-in-residence, Banff Art Centre, Alberta, Canada

2001–02
Artist-in-residence, International Studio & Curatorial Program, New York (also '05)

Pola Art Foundation grant, Tokyo

2004–05
Japanese Government's Overseas Study Program fellowship (lives in New York)

Solo Exhibitions
1990
Gallery Natsuka, Tokyo (also '91, '92, '93, '94, '96, '97, '04)

1995–96
365 Project, Japan

1999
Westbeth, New York

2000
FADs Art Space, inaugural exhibition, Tokyo

Other Gallery, Banff, Canada

Para Site Art Space, Hong Kong

2001
Contemporary Art Factory, Tokyo

*IBM Kawasaki City Gallery

2002
Ise Cultural Foundation Gallery, New York

Magazin 4, Bregenz, Austria

2003
Murata & Friends, Berlin (also '05)

2004
Neru, Sendai, Japan

Yamanashi Prefectural Museum of Art, Kōfu, Japan

2005
*Museum für Ostasiatische Kunst, Cologne, Germany

Staatliche Museen zu Berlin

2006
Kuenstlerhaus Bethanien, Berlin (after artist-in-residence)

*NKV, Wiesbaden, Germany

Group Exhibitions
1990
New Works, Setagaya Art Museum, Tokyo (also '91, '93, '94, '98, '99)

1992
COM ART Festival, Suon, Korea

1999
Tea, Asia Society, New York

2000
*Echigo-Tsumari Art Triennial 2000, Niigata Prefecture, Japan (also '06)

2001
Neo-Tokyo, Museum of Contemporary Art, Sydney

Tokyo Rabbit Paradise Project, Selfridges, London; and C/O Careof, Milan ('04)

2002
Dia del Mar/By the Sea, P.S.1, Queens

The Day of Thank You Art Memorial, FADs Art Space, Tokyo

2003
*Imagine, Parthenon Tama, Tokyo

MAD'03, Madrid

Revolving Door: ISCP Asia, Chambers Fine Art, New York

2004
Isst du gerade meinen Tofu?, Backfabrik, Berlin

Melbourneconnectionasia 2004, Australia

Pro Tsubo, Neue Galerie Landshut, Germany

Soweit Japan, Kunstallianz 1 Berlin

The Venice Biennale 9th International Architecture Exhibition

Triangle Artists' Workshop 2004, open studio, Brooklyn (artist-in-residence)

2005
Impression: Sunrise, Murata & Friends, Berlin

Light Art from Artificial Light, ZKM Museum for Contemporary Art, Karlsruhe, Germany

Views from Abroad, Stadtgalerie Kiel, Germany

When No Leaf Moves …, Palais für aktuelle Kunst, Glückstadt, Germany

2006
Berlin-Tokyo/Tokyo-Berlin, Neue National Galerie, Berlin

Sculpture @ City Nord Hamburg 2006, City Nord Park, Hamburg

Publications
Kevin Kwong, "It Has Become Chic," *South China Morning Post*, July 24, 2000

Kunie Sugiura, "Yoshiaki Kaihatsu Exhibition" [Japanese text], *Bijutsu techō* (July 2002): 184

Kaihatsu Yoshiaki, "My Favorite Animators" [Japanese text], *Art It* (July 2004): 61

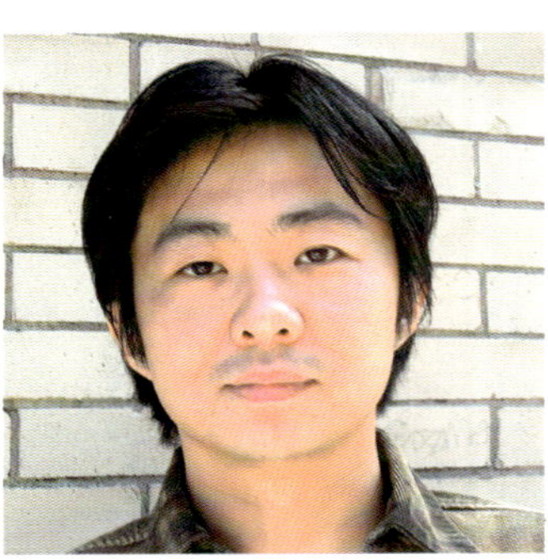

TAKAHIRO KANEYAMA
金山貴宏

Born in Tokyo, Japan, 1971; lives and works in Manhattan

1998
BA in photography, The City College of New York

2000
The New Face Prize, Fujifilm/Fuji Photo Salon, Japan

2001
Hitotsubo-ten Award, Guardian Garden, Tokyo

MFA in photography and related media, School of Visual Arts, New York

New Cosmos of Photography Award, Canon, Japan

2002–03
Certificate program in photojournalism and documentary, International Center of Photography, New York

2003
Fellowship, Guardian Garden/ Recruit, Tokyo

Solo Exhibitions
2000
Fuji Photo Salon, Tokyo

Group Exhibitions
2000
Lightness of Being: Tokyo & New York, Fuji Photo Salon, Osaka

2001
Canon New Cosmos of Photography, Morta Politica Gallery, Tokyo

Children of Japan, Galerie Grand Paris, Paris

Hitotsubo-ten, 3.3 m x 3.3 m Exhibition, Guardian Garden, Tokyo

2003
Mindfactory, Jody Monroe Gallery, Milwaukee

Young Portfolio Acquisitions 2002, Kiyosato Museum of Photographic Arts, Japan

2005
Art Fair Tokyo, Tokyo International Forum

Because I Dream, I'm Not, Capsule Gallery, New York

Central East Tokyo 2005: ROJI CULtural/logical/radical TOKYO

Kunst 05 Zürich, 11th International Contemporary Art Fair

2006
Milwaukee International Art Fair

Publications
Going 1992–2002 Guardian Garden, Hitotsubo-ten, 20th Anniversary (Tokyo: Guardian Garden/Recruit, 2003), 134, 158–60

"Snapshot," *New York Times Magazine* (Sophisticated Traveler, part 2), March 2, 2003, 24

Krissa Corbett Cavouras, "1971," *American Photo on Campus* (November 2003): 22–23

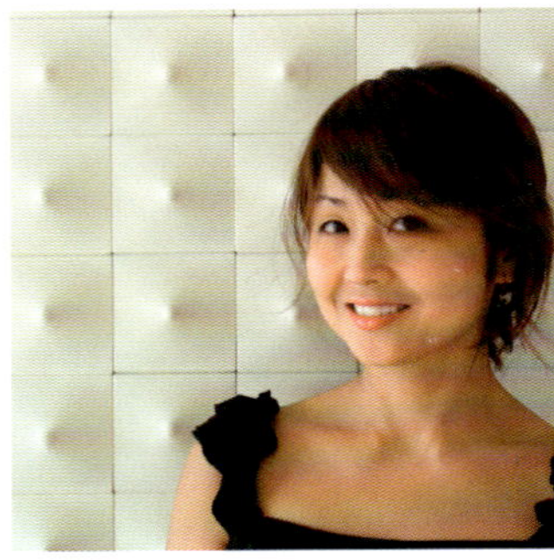

EMIKO KASAHARA
笠原恵実子

Born in Komae, Tokyo Prefecture, Japan, 1963; lives and works in Brooklyn

1988
MFA in sculpture, Tama Art University, Tokyo

1990
Asian Cultural Council fellowship, New York

1991
Artist-in-residence, Fondation Cartier pour l'Art Contemporain, Paris

1994
Japanese Government's Overseas Study Program fellowship (lives in New York)

1997
Pola Art Foundation grant, Japan

2003
New York Foundation for the Arts fellowship

Solo Exhibitions
1990
Gallery Kobayashi, Tokyo (also '92, '93)

1997
Deitch Projects, New York

2001
White Box, New York

2003
Scope, Dylan Hotel, New York

2005
Volkskunde Landesmuseum Joanneum, Graz, Austria

2007
Haydee Rovirosa Gallery, New York

Group Exhibitions
1989
Floating Scale, Spiral/Wacoal Art Center, Tokyo

1990
Japanese Kunst der Achtziger Jahre, Frankfurter Kunstverein, Frankfurt

1991
A Hybrid Garden, Bigi Art Space, Kyoto

Cabinet of Signs, Tate Liverpool; Malmo Kunstverein, Sweden ('02); and White Chapel Gallery, London ('02)

Zones of Love, Touko Museum of Contemporary Art and Museum of Contemporary Art Sydney

1994
Space, Time, Memory: Photography and Beyond in Japan, Hara Museum of Contemporary Art, Tokyo; Rufino Tamayo Museum, Mexico; Vancouver Art Gallery; Los Angeles County Museum of Art; Corcoran Gallery of Art, Washington D.C.; and Denver Art Museum

1995
Art in Japan Today 1985–1995, Museum of Contemporary Art, Tokyo

The Age of Anxiety, The Power Plant, Toronto

1996
Asia-Pacific Triennial of Contemporary Art, Queensland Art Gallery, Brisbane

Nowhere: Incandescent, Louisiana, Copenhagen

1997
Floating Image of Women in Art History, Tochigi Prefectural Museum of Fine Arts, Utsunomiya, Japan

Japanese Art Exhibition, National Museum of Contemporary Art, Korea, Seoul

1998
Tastes and Pursuits: Japanese Art in the 1990s, National Gallery of Modern Art, New Delhi and Metropolitan Museum of Manila

1999
Visions of the Body: Fashion or Invisible Corset, National Museum of Modern Art, Kyoto and Museum of Contemporary Art, Tokyo

2000
3rd Kwangju Biennale

2001
Made in Asia, Duke University Museum of Art, Durham, N.C.

Yokohama Triennale

2004
Auckland Triennale

*Sydney Biennale

2005
*Chikaku, Kunsthause Graz, Austria; Marco, Vigo, Spain; and Tarō Okamoto Museum of Art, Kawasaki ('06)

Publications
Dana Friis-Hansen, "Review," *Flash Art* (November/December 1993): 123

Carol Latfy, "Emiko Kasahara," *ARTnews* (November 1994): 129

Kim Levin, "Review," *Village Voice*, January 28, 1997

Jonathan Napack, "Review," *ArtAsiaPacific* (Spring 1997): 91

Janet Koplos, "Emiko Kasahara at White Box," *Art in America* (March 2002): 131

Stephanie Cheung, "Seeing Self," *Asian Art News* (September/October 2005): 81

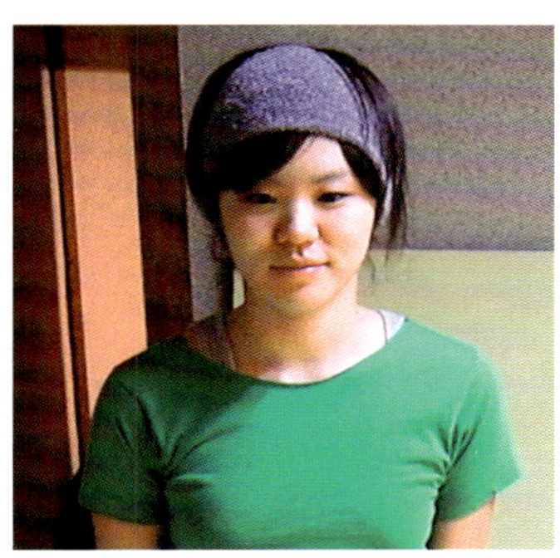
PHOTO: TAYLOR MCKIMENS

11 MISAKI KAWAI
河井美咲

Born in Ōkawa-gun, Kagawa Prefecture, Japan, 1978; lives and works in Brooklyn

1999
AA in visual design, Kyoto College of Art, Kyoto

Solo Exhibitions
2002
Kenny Schachter Contemporary, New York (also '03)

Two-person show with Mica G. Scalin, Transformer, Washington D.C.

New Image Art, West Hollywood (also '03, two-person show with Taylor McKimens)

2003
Inman Gallery, Houston

P.S.1, Queens

2004
Jack Hanley Gallery, San Francisco

2005
Kantor/Feuer Window, New York

2006
Two-person show with Taylor McKimens, Watari-um, Tokyo

2007
Clementine, New York

Perugi Artecontemporanea, Padova, Italy

Institute of Contemporary Art, Boston

Group Exhibitions
2002
Tensionism, Perry Street Rove, New York

2004
Five Artist Shows, Kenny Schachter Rove, London

Majority Whip, White Box, New York

Trunk of Humours, Deitch Projects, New York

2005
Desired Constellations, Daniel Reich Gallery, New York

Tiger Drip, Galleri Loyal, Stockholm

Greater New York 2005, P.S.1, Queens

Hanging by a Thread, Moore Space, Miami

Live Through This, Deitch Projects, Miami Design District

2006
A Thousand Things, MU Museum, Eindhoven, The Netherlands

Don't Abandon the Ship, Allston Skirt Gallery, Boston

It's a Beautiful Day, Ise Cultural Foundation Gallery, New York

Unwrapping the Wing, The Invisible Museum, Denver

2007
Five Painters, Galleri Loyal, Stockholm

Publications
Roberta Smith, "Art Review," *New York Times*, January 17, 2003

Jerry Saltz, "Rays of Light," *Village Voice*, January 22, 2003

Kristin Poor, "The Wow-wee World of Misaki Kawai," *ArtAsiaPacific* (Summer 2005): 96

Air Show (Los Angeles: Broken Wrist Project, 2005)

Wendy Goodman, "Home Is Where the Art Is," *Modern Painters* (March 2006): 100–103

Cate McQuaid, "In Her Whimsical Installation, She Plays with Dolls," *Boston Globe*, March 27, 2007

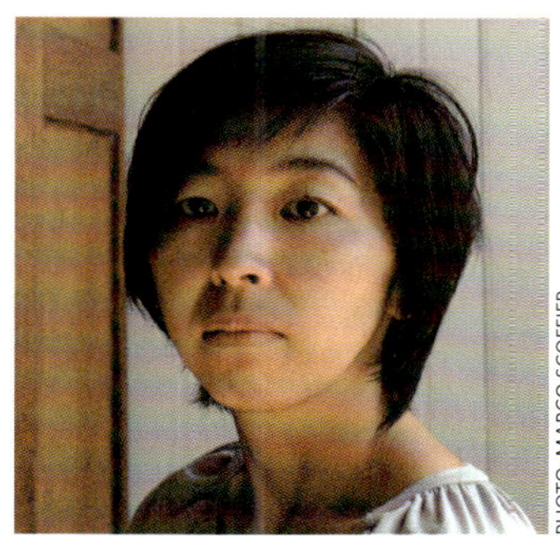
PHOTO: MARCO SCOFFIER

12 MIWA KOIZUMI
小泉美和

Born in Nagoya, Japan, 1969; lives and works in Brooklyn

1995
MFA in editorial design and photography, Tama Art University, Tokyo

T-Brain Club Techno Art Museum award, Tokyo

2000
Diploma with distinction, École Nationale Supérieure des Beaux-Arts, Paris

2002
Artist-in-residence, Greenwich House Pottery, New York

2005
Lecturer, Simons Center for the Arts, Charleston, S.C.

Honorable mention, *Transmediale*, Berlin

Solo Exhibitions
2002
Jane Hartsook Gallery, New York

2004
Tattfoo Temple of Art and Design, Staten Island

2006
Two-person show with Marc-Antoine Dupont, KBP, Brooklyn

2007
*Two-person show with Andrea Dezsö, Hungarian Cultural Center, New York

Group Exhibitions
1992
Promising Photographers 4, Parco Gallery, Tokyo and Osaka

1998
Toxic, Château d'Oiron, Val de Loire, France

1998
Gesture of Photography, Soko Gallery, Tokyo

1999
Galerie St Eustache, Paris (also '00)

2000
Project, Caisse des Dépôts et Consignations, Paris

2001
About Vase (open studio), Corcoran College of Art and Design, Washington, D.C.

2003
New No York, Subtonic, New York

Open-G, Goliath Visual Space, Brooklyn

Flux Factory, Queens (also '04, '05, '06)

2004
Surface to Air, Ise Cultural Foundation Gallery, New York

2005
Sawaguzo, Redux Contemporary Art Center, Charleston, S.C.

2006
The Cook, the Thief, His Wife, Her Lover, and Their Dinner Guests, New General Catalog 224, Brooklyn

Dumbo Art Festival, Brooklyn

2007
L.I.C., NYC, Socrates Sculpture Park, Queens

Unlikely Materials, Alpan Gallery, Huntington, N.Y.

Volume, 3rd Ward, Brooklyn

Publications
Joshua M. Bernstein, "Candy Land: A Golden Ticket into Flux's Chocolate Factory," *New York Press* (December 2003)

Tiffany Jow, "PET Project," *Surface* (March 2007): 108

Josh Ozersky, "6C. Liquid Nitrogen + 3 Tbsp. Meat Glue + 1 Sonic Wave Blaster," *American Way* (April 2007)

Benjamin Genocchio, "Art Review," *New York Times*, April 8, 2007

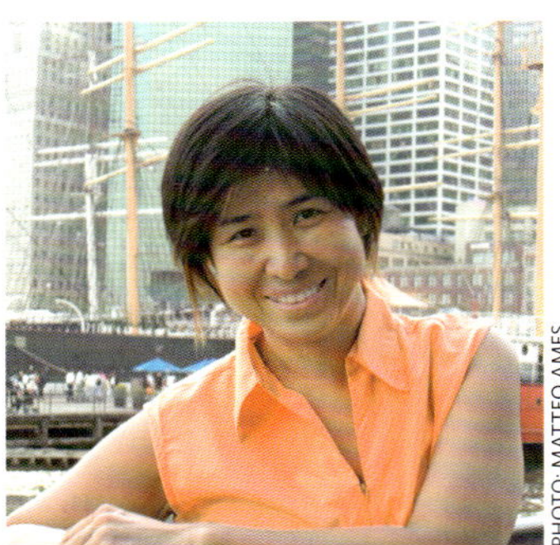
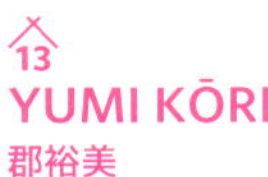
PHOTO: MATTEO AMES

13 YUMI KŌRI
郡裕美

Born in Nagoya, Japan, 1960; lives and works in Manhattan and Tokyo

1983
BA in architecture, Kyoto Prefectural University

1990
First-class architect license, Japan

1991
Founds Studio MYU Architects Co. Ltd., Tokyo

1995
MS in architecture, Columbia University, New York

1996–2006
Adjunct assistant professor, Barnard/Columbia College, New York

1997
Design consultant, Nationality Rooms Program, University of Pittsburgh

Lecturer, Parsons The New School for Design, New York

Residential Architecture Award, Tokyo Society of Architects & Building Engineers

1998
Tokyo Architecture Award, Tokyo Association of Architectural Firms

2000
Architectural Cultural Award, Chiba Prefecture, Japan (also '06)

2001
AR Award, Architectural Review, London (also '02)

2003
Lecturer, Yale School of Architecture, New Haven

2005–present
Lecturer, Nagoya Institute of Technology

Solo Exhibitions
** with sound by Bernhard Gal

1999
Studio Five Beekman, New York**

2000
6th Kryptonale, Berlin**

2002
Die Franziskaner-Klosterruine, Berlin**

Old Public Library, Musashino, Tokyo

2003
*Maison Hermès Forum, Tokyo

2004
International Studio & Curatorial Program, open studio, New York

The Phatory LLC, New York

2005
Center on Contemporary Art, Seattle**

Minoriten Church Kapitelsaal,

Krems-Stein, Austria**

Swing Space, Lower Manhattan Cultural Council, New York**

2006
Ise Cultural Foundation Gallery, New York**

Warteck, Basel, Switzerland**

2007
Bell Gallery, Brown University, Providence, R.I.

Two-person show with Shinji Turner-Yamamoto, Shigeko Bork Mu Project, Washington, D.C.

Group Exhibitions
2004
Paper Works, Ozone Plaza, Tokyo

2006
Human = Nature, Firehouse Gallery, Burlington, Vt.

Light of Light, SESC Pinheiros, São Paulo**

2007
Kōbe Biennale

Architecture Projects
1997
Loop A, apartment complex, Tokyo

1999
Kugayama Post Office, Tokyo

2000
Volks F, prototype house design with passive solar system, Tokyo

2002
House of Shadows, residence, Musashino, Tokyo

2003
Atelier K, artist studios and apartment complex, Tokyo

2004
White House/Black House, Mitaka, Tokyo

2005
Kichijōji Honchō, senior citizens center, Musashino, Tokyo

2006
Cafe Shieto, historical renovation, Sawara, Chiba Prefecture

Publications
Asami Nagai, "Ex-library Gets Reprieve for Exhibition," *Washington Post*, November 16, 2002

"House of Shadows," *Architectural Review* (December 2002): 62–63

"Contemplating Ginza's Neon Beach," *Herald Tribune*, March 6, 2003

Asami Nagai, "Luxury and Nothingness at Maison Hermes," *Washington Post*, March 20, 2003

Gayle Clemans, "Infinitation,"

Seattle Times, July 1, 2005

Jonathan Goodman, "Yumi Kori," *Sculpture* (June 2006): 54–59

Michael O'Sullivan, "'Japan': Reaching for the Unreachable," *Washington Post*, May 25, 2007

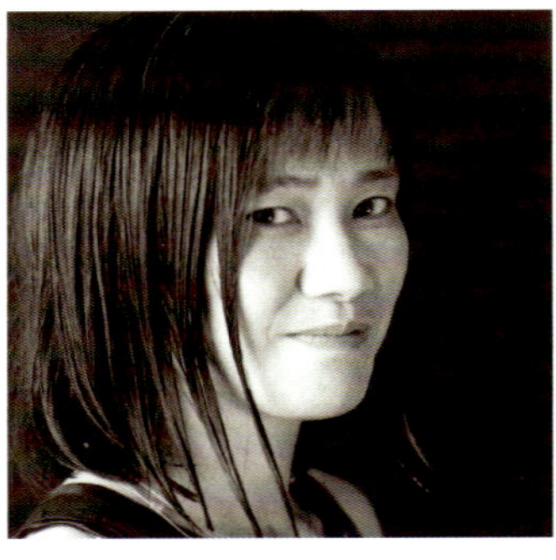

14
NOBUHO NAGASAWA
長澤伸穂

Born in Tokyo, Japan, 1959; lives and works in Manhattan

1978–82
Fine Arts Academy, Maastricht, The Netherlands

1982–85
MFA, Hochschule der Künste Berlin

1986
DAAD grant

1986–87
Visiting scholar, California Institute of the Arts

1992–96
Assistant professor, Scripps College, Claremont, Calif.

1996–01
Associate professor, University of California, Santa Cruz

1997
Design Excellence Award for Architecture and Public Art, Department of Cultural Affairs, Los Angeles

2001
Marie Walsh Sharpe Art Foundation grant, New York

2001–present
Associate professor, Stony Brook University, N.Y.

2004
Established Artist Grant, Urban Glass, Brooklyn

2007
2006 Art Commission Awards for Excellence in Design, Art Commission of New York

Solo Exhibitions
1992
Daniel Saxon Gallery, Los Angeles

1999
Aquarena Springs, San Marcos, Texas

2000
Post Gallery, Los Angeles

Museum of Art and History, Santa Cruz, Calif.

Group Exhibitions
1991
Beyond the Manifesto, Mito Annual, Art Tower Mito, Japan

1992
Invisible Nature, Royal Garden of the Prague Castle, Prague; Ludwig Museum, Budapest; and Ludwig Forum für Internationale Kunst, Aachen, Germany

1994
Connections 2, Getty Center for the History of Art and the Humanities, Santa Monica

1995
Peace Sculpture 95, Jutland, Denmark

1996
Between Earth and the Heavens— Aspects of Contemporary Japanese Art II, Nagoya City Art Museum and Rufino Tamayo Museum, Mexico

Origin of Myth and Fire, Saitama Museum of Modern Art, Japan

2002
Artist to Artist, Ace Gallery, New York

Imagining the Books, Royal Library of Alexandria, Egypt

10th Asian Art Biennale Bangladesh, Dhaka

2003
Echigo-Tsumari Art Triennial 2003, Niigata Prefecture, Japan

6th Sharjah International Art Biennial, Sharjah Museum, United Arab Emirates

2005
Atomica, Esso Gallery and Lombard-Freid Fine Arts, New York

2006
First Sinop Biennial, Turkey

2007
Exquisite Corpse in the Garden, Beacon, N.Y.

Zone Chelsea, New York

Public Art Commissions
1996
Vermont Square Library, Los Angeles

2000
National Government Buildings, Saitama, Japan

2004
City Hall and Public Plaza Art in Public Places, Austin, Texas

2005
City Hall and Civic Plaza, Seattle

2007
Third Street Light Rail Project, San Francisco

in progress
Columbia Street Percent for Art Project, Brooklyn

Metro East Project, San Francisco

Soto Station, Los Angeles

UCLA Hospital, Los Angeles

Publications
Grady T. Turner, "Report from the U.A.E.," *Art in America* (November 2003): 88

Holland Cotter, "Art Review," *New York Times*, July 8, 2005

Laura Dillon, "Water Weaving Light Cycle," *Sculpture* (November 2006): 19

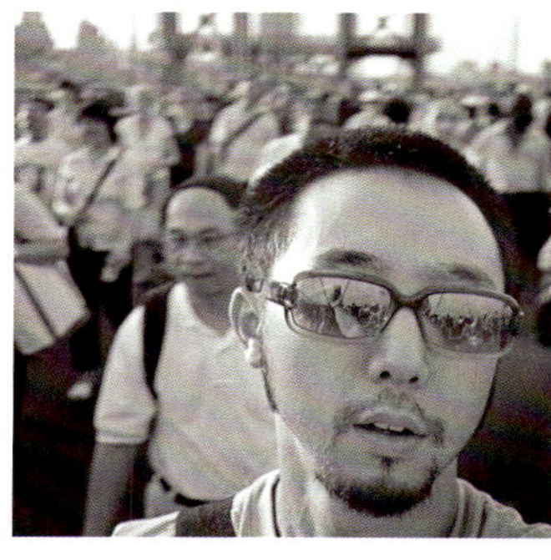

HIROYUKI NAKAMURA
中村裕之

Born in Tokyo, Japan, 1977; lives and works in Brooklyn

2000
BS in photography, Drexel University, Philadelphia

2001
Summer studio residency, School of Visual Arts, New York

2002
MFA in photography and related media, School of Visual Arts, New York

2006
Artist-in-residence, Gilfélagið (Gil Society), Akureyri, Iceland

2007
Artist-in-residence, Newark

Museum, Newark, N.J.

Artist in the Marketplace (AIM), Bronx Museum of the Arts

Artist-in-residence, Millay Colony for the Arts, Austerlitz, N.Y.

Solo Exhibitions
2006
Gilfélagið, Akureyri, Iceland

Group Exhibitions
2000
Drexel students thesis exhibition, Auxiliary Art Space, Philadelphia

2002
Plain, Visual Art Gallery, New York

2004
Sympathetic Nerve, Capsule Gallery, New York

2005
A Knock at the Door…, org. by Lower Manhattan Cultural Council, Cooper Union, New York

Brooklyn Artists, Alpan Gallery, Huntington, N.Y.

Point of View, Alpan Gallery, Huntington, N.Y.

Summer Residency Group Exhibition, Cooper Union, New York

Sweet Tragedy, Planaria Gallery, New York

2006
Arcaute Arte Contemporaneo, Monterrey, Mexico

Little Monsters, AG Gallery, Brooklyn

Please Open the Door, NURTUREart Gallery, Brooklyn

2007
AIM27 Here and Elsewhere, Bronx Museum of the Arts

Publications
New American Paintings (February 2007): 102–5

"Museum Selects New Artists for 2007 Residency Program," *Access* (Winter 2007): 12

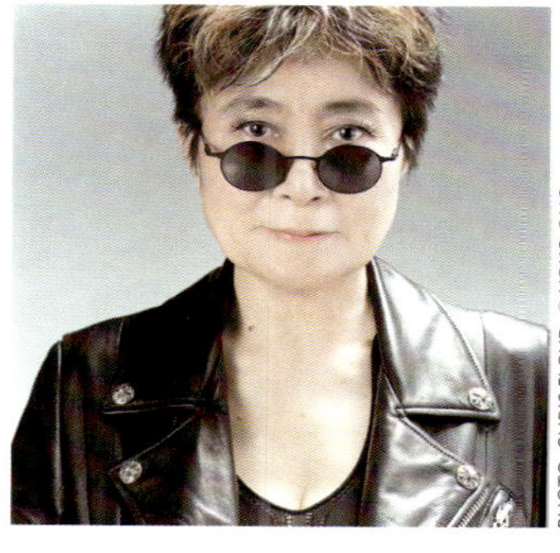

YOKO ONO
オノ・ヨーコ

Born in Tokyo, Japan, 1933; lives in Manhattan

Yoko Ono is an artist who works in numerous media. Since the early 1960s, she has had solo exhibitions in museums and galleries throughout the world, done performances, performed her music, and worked in such diverse media as film, satellite radio, newspaper advertising space, billboards, and interactive public installations.

Data before 2000 may be found in the catalogue YES YOKO ONO *(New York: Japan Society, 2000).*

Solo Exhibitions
2000
*Japan Society, New York (traveled to 12 venues)

*Museo Vostell Malpartida, Malpartida de Cáceres, Spain

*Palacio de Sástago, Zaragoza, Spain

Schloßplatz Berlin Mitte, Berlin

2001–02
Gallery 360°, Tokyo (also '04, '05, '06)

*Galerie Vostell, Berlin

2002
*Palau de la Virreina, Barcelona

SECCA, Winston-Salem, N.C.

Shoshana Wayne Gallery, Santa Monica

2003
Deitch Projects, New York (also '05)

Kampa Museum, Prague

*Musée d'Art moderne de la Ville de Paris

P.S.1, Queens

2003–05
Detroit Institute of Arts

2004
Institute of Contemporary Art, London

*Kulturhuset, Stockholm

Portsmouth Cathedral, Portsmouth, U.K.

Printed Matter, New York

The Women's Museum, Århus, Denmark

2005
*Astrup Fearnley Museet for Moderne Kunst, Oslo, Norway

*Migros Museum für Gegenwartskunst, Zürich

Museum Moderner Kunst, Passau, Germany

Tokachi Millennium Forest, Hokkaidō, Japan

2006
*Centre A, Vancouver

Galerie Davide Di Maggio-Mudimadue, Berlin

St. Paul's Cathedral, London

2007
Kasa Galeri, Sabanci University, Istanbul

*Kunsthalle Bremen, Germany

Multiple outdoor installations org. by Street Scenes, Washington, D.C.

*TSUM Department Store, Moscow

in progress
Imagine Peace Tower, Reykjavik, Iceland

Group Exhibitions
2000
Sydney Biennale

2001
Yokohama Triennale

2002
Open 2002, Venice

2003
Venice Biennale

2004
Open 2004, Venice

Concerts and Performances
2002
The Kitchen, New York

Théâtre Le Ranelagh, Paris

2004
Tate Britain, London

2005
Tonic, New York

2007
92nd Street Y, New York

THEARC, Washington, D.C.

Recordings
Blueprint for a Sunrise (Hollywood: Capitol, 2001)

Yoko Ono: Night of the Half-Moon (New York: Tonic Limited Edition, 2005)

Open Your Box (Remixes) (New York: Astralwerks, 2007)

Yes, I'm a Witch (New York: Astralwerks, 2007)

Publications by the Artist
Grapefruit: A Book of Instructions and Drawings by Yoko Ono (New York: Simon & Schuster, 2000)

Yoko Ono Yes Box (Lund: Bakhåll, 2004)

Imagine Yoko (Lund: Bakhåll, 2005)

Give Peace a Chance, with John Lennon (Lund: Bakhåll, 2007)

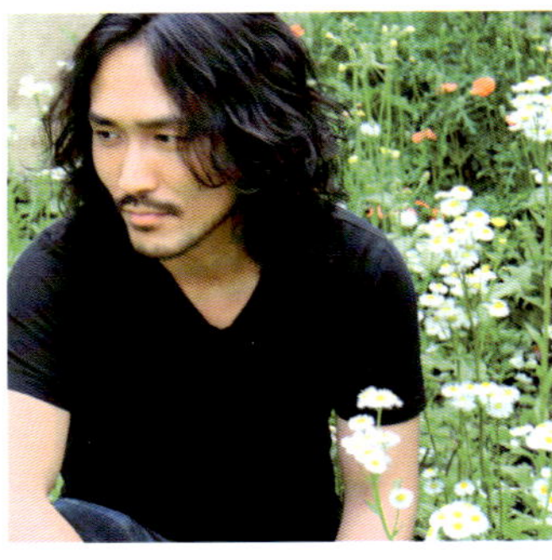

17
HIROKI ŌTSUKA
大塚弘樹

Born in Nagahama, Shiga Prefecture, Japan, 1972; lives and works in Brooklyn

1994
Certificate in graphic design, layout design, drawing, and painting, Tokyo Designer Gakuin, Nagoya

2003–04
Internship, Kaikai Kiki, Brooklyn

Solo Exhibitions
2005
Studio Connect, Brooklyn

Stay Gold Gallery, Brooklyn

Group Exhibitions
2003
Nth Art Exhibit 001, OLS&CO Gallery, London

2004
Parakeet Salon #2, Parakeet Project Space, Brooklyn

2005
Ab Ovo, Yerba Buena Center for the Arts, San Francisco and Arena 1, Santa Monica ('06)

Viva! Stay Gold, Stay Gold Gallery, Brooklyn

8, Stay Gold Gallery, Brooklyn

Moleskine Group Exhibition, Kinokuniya Bookstore, Tokyo and Keibunsha, Kyoto ('06)

2006
The Armory Show (Fredericks Freiser Gallery), New York

Volta Art Fair (Fredericks Freiser Gallery), Basel

Pleasure Little Treasure, Stay Gold Gallery, Brooklyn

Fruitcake & Casserole, Stay Gold Gallery, Brooklyn

The Outsider, Stay Gold Gallery, Brooklyn

Publications
Bryony Roberts, "Art in the City," *L Magazine* (August 31, 2005): 47

"Galleris-Brooklyn," *New Yorker* (September 5, 2005): 34

Chuck Austen and Hiroki Ōtsuka, *Boys of Summer*, vol. 1 (Hamburg and Los Angeles: Tokyopop, 2006)

Eric Shiner, "Hiroki Otsuka: from Ero-Manga to Ero-Pop," *ArtAsiaPacific* (Spring 2006): 42

Ken Takeuchi "Hiroki Otsuka, on the Tipping Point" *Persu Asian* (Winter 2006): 30

Jason Sheftel, "Leave It to Balazs," *Daily News*, March 2, 2007

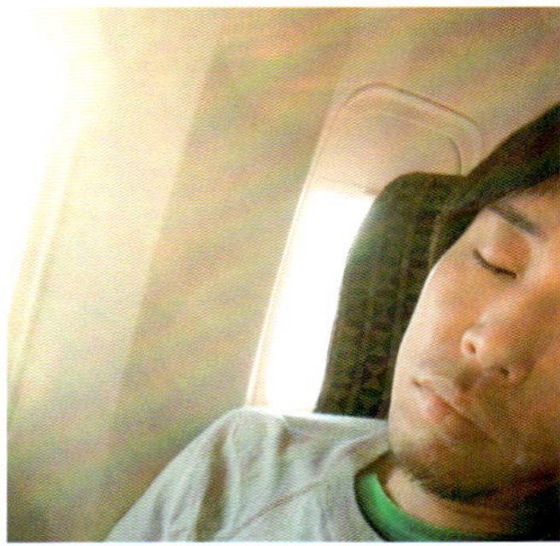

18
KATSUHIRO SAIKI
齋木克裕

Born in Tokyo, Japan, 1969; lives and works in Queens

1992–93
Sōkei Academy of Fine Art and Design, Tokyo

1994–96
Tokyo College of Photography, Yokohama

2002–03
International Studio Program, P.S.1, Queens (with Asian Cultural Council grant)

2004–06
Japanese Government's Overseas Study Program fellowship (lives in New York)

Solo Exhibitions
1999
Light Works, Yokohama

2000
Murata & Friends, Berlin (also '02, '04)

2001
Gallery Maki, Tokyo

2002
SCAI The Bathhouse, Tokyo (also '06)

2003
Artists Space, New York

2006
*Two-person show with Christoph Weber (*Sumazo 2006*), KunstMarke, Vienna

Group Exhibitions
1999
Up Above the World, Gallery Nikkō, Tokyo

2000
The J-Way, Lydmar Hotel, Stockholm

2001
Outer/Inter: Aspects of Contemporary Photography 2001, Kawasaki City Museum

SCAI The Bathhouse, Tokyo (also '02, '04)

Surface: Contemporary Photography, Video, and Painting from Japan, Nederlands Foto Instituut, Rotterdam

2002
Anstiftung zu einer neuen Wahrnehmung, Neues Museum Weserburg, Bremen, Germany

Good Luck!!: An Aspect of Contemporary Art, Parthenon Tama, Tokyo

VOCA '02, Ueno Royal Museum, Tokyo

2003
Breaking Away, P.S.1, Queens

Da Sein, Ernst Barlach Museum, Ratzeburg, Germany

Raum, Zeit, Oldenburger Kunstverein, Oldenburg, Germany

2004
Das Versprechen der Fotografie, Moscow House of Photography

Passage to the Future: Art from a New Generation in Japan, Istituto Giapponese di Cultura, Rome

So Weit Japan: Junge Kunst aus Japan, Kunstallianz 1 Berlin

2005
FotoFest 2005; Photography in Houston Galleries, McClain Gallery, Houston

2006
Minimal Illusions: Arbeiten mit der Sammlung Rik Reinking, Villa Merkel/Bahnwäterhaus, Esslingen am Neckar, Germany

2007
Active Constellation, The Brno House of Arts, Brno, Czech Republic

Publications
Nagoya Satoru, "Katsuhiro Saiki, SCAI the Bathhouse," *Flash Art* (May/June 2002): 220

Kusumi Kiyoshi, "A Drill in Vision and Perception," *Art Star: Pictures—Katsuhiro Saiki*, CD-ROM (Tokyo: Toppan 2005)

Monty DiPietro, "Seeking the Abstraction in Suspension," *Japan Times*, November 23, 2006

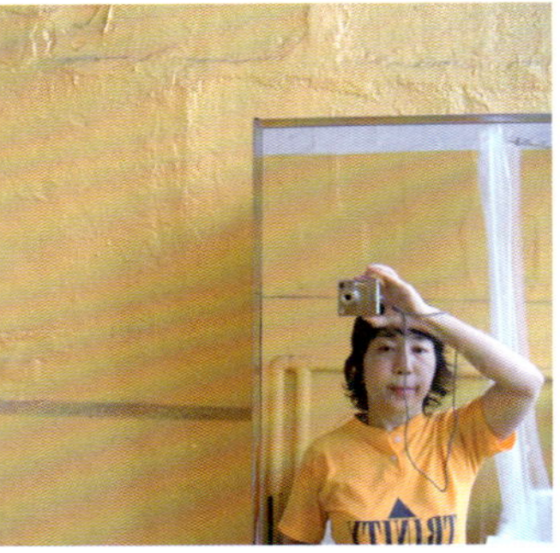

19
KYŌKO SERA
世良京子

Born in Kurate-gun, Fukuoka Prefecture, Japan, 1957; lives and works in Brooklyn

1981
BFA in sculpture, Tokyo Zōkei University

1994
Vision of Contemporary Art (VOCA) prize, Tokyo

2000–01
Japanese Government's Overseas Study Program fellowship (lives in New York)

Solo Exhibitions
1988
Gallery Sano, Ayauta-gun, Kagawa Prefecture, Japan (also '93)

1991
Fukuoka Art Museum Civic Gallery, Fukuoka

Ten Gallery, Fukuoka

1992
*Gallery Sano Warehouse, Sakaide, Kagawa Prefecture

1993
*Gallery Yamaguchi, Tokyo (also '94)

2001
*Snug Harbor Cultural Center, New York

Group Exhibitions
1992
*6th Pusan Biennale, Korea

1994
*Prospects of Contemporary Art: Fukuoka '94, Fukuoka Prefectural Museum of Art

*VOCA '94, Ueno Royal Museum, Tokyo

1995
*Allegory of Seeing 1995: Painting and Sculpture in Contemporary Japan, Sezon Museum of Art, Tokyo

*Nagoya Contemporary Art Fair

1996
*The Structure of Painting, Bumpōdō Gallery, Tokyo

1999
*5th Kitakyūshū Biennale: The Aesthetics of Repetition and Continuity, Kitakyūshū Municipal Museum of Art

*An Overview of Contemporary Japanese Painting, Tokyo Station Gallery, Tokyo

2001
*Tsubaki-kai, Shiseidō Gallery, Tokyo (also annually '02–'05)

2003
*Traffic: Art Exchange Between Kitakyūsyū and Fukuoka, Fukuoka Art Museum and Kitakyūshū Municipal Museum of Art

The Fifth Tsubaki-kai Group Exhibition, Shiseidō Art House, Shizuoka

2004
VOCA 1994–2003, Ōhara Museum of Art, Kurashiki

2006
The Present State of Contemporary Art: Selected Works from the VOCA Concours, Utsunomiya Museum of Art

Publications
Yofu Katsuhiko, "Artist Now: Kyōko Sera" [Japanese text], Yomiuri Newspaper, October 15, 1994

Takashina Shūji, "Seeking an Unfragmented Life: Cross Model" [Japanese text], Hon (August 2006): cover, 68

Tatehata Akira, Incomplete Past: Painting and Modernism [Japanese text] (Tokyo: Goryū Shoin, 2000), 167–68

Michael J. Fressola, "Solo Exhibition Reveals Depth of Ambition," Staten Island Advance, August 24, 2001

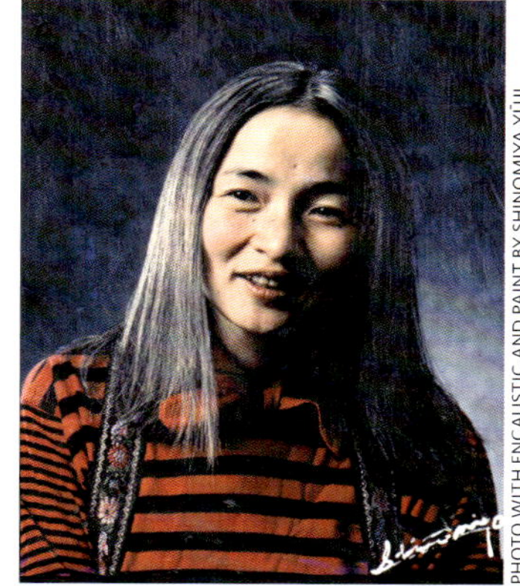

20 NORIKO SHINOHARA
篠原乃り子

Born in Takaoka, Toyama Prefecture, Japan, 1953; lives and works in Brooklyn

1972–73
Art Students League of New York

1973–77
Pratt Graphics Center, New York

1995
Takes printmaking courses, Kyoto City Art University and Tokyo National University of Fine Arts and Music

Solo Exhibitions
1986
The Cat Club, New York

1991
Two-person show with Ushio Shinohara, Jain Marunouchi Gallery, New York

1994
Bokushin Gallery, Tokyo

1999
Galleria Grafica, Tokyo

2005
Gallery Niigata Eya, Japan

2006
Gallery Now, Toyama, Japan

Almondine, New York

Group Exhibitions
1995
Art of Godzilla, The World Children's Art Museum, Okazaki, Aichi Prefecture, Japan

1999
Firehouse: AAAC 25th Anniversary, Asian American Art Centre, New York

2003
Art for Peace from N.Y., Print Show 2003, Nasu-Kōgen Museum, Tochigi Prefecture, Japan

New Prints 2003/Summer, International Print Center New York

In the Shadow of 9/11: A Chinatown Memorial Exhibition, Silk Road Place, New York

2005
New Prints 2005/Autumn, International Print Center, New York and A+D Gallery, Columbia College Chicago ('06)

Publications
Shinohara Noriko, Tameiki no Nyūyōku [Sigh of New York: A novella] (Tokyo: Sanshindō, 1994)

Abe Satoshi, "Carrel Interview: Noriko Shinohara" [Japanese text], Carrel (April 20, 2005): 4–7

Shikimura Yoshiko, "Love and Hate: An Expression of Human Saga" [Japanese text], Niigata nippō, May 3, 2005

21 USHIO SHINOHARA
篠原有司男

Born in Tokyo, Japan, 1932; lives and works in Brooklyn

1960
Co-founder, Neo Dada (initially Neo Dadaism Organizers), Tokyo

1969
Grant, JDR 3rd Fund (moves to New York)

2007
Mainichi Art Award, Japan

Solo Exhibitions (from 1982)
1982
*Japan House Gallery, New York

1983
Gallery Yamaguchi (also '84, '87, '88, '90, '91, '95, '01*, '05)

1992
Hara Museum Arc, Shibukawa, Japan

*Hiroshima City Museum of Contemporary Art

Tokushima Modern Art Museum, Japan

Tsukashin Hall, Amagasaki, Japan

2001
*Fuchū Art Museum, Tokyo (also Boxing Painting performance)

2005
*Museum of Modern Art, Kamakura & Hayama, Japan (also Boxing Painting performance)

2006
Kirin Plaza Osaka (also Boxing Painting performance)

Kirishima Open-Air Museum, Kagoshima Prefecture, Japan (also Boxing Painting performance)

Group Exhibitions (from 1994)
1994
*Japanese Art After 1945: Scream Against the Sky, Yokohama Museum of Art; Guggenheim SoHo; and San Francisco Museum of Modern Art

1997
*Japanese Summer, 1960–64, Art Tower Mito

1998
*Neo-Dada Japan, 1958–1998, Art Plaza Ōita, Japan (also Boxing Painting performance)

*Out of Action: Between Performance and the Object, 1949–79, Museum of Contemporary Art/Geffen Contemporary, Los Angeles (traveled to Vienna, Barcelona, and Tokyo; also Boxing Painting performances at Vienna and Tokyo)

2000
Et l'art se met monde, Institut d'art contemporain, Villeurbanne, France (also Boxing Painting performance)

*Homage to Tarō Okamoto from Seven Artists, Tarō Okamoto Museum of Art, Kawasaki

2004
*Resounding Spirit: Japanese Contemporary Art of the 1960's, Gibson Gallery, SUNY Potsdam, N.Y. (also Boxing Painting performance)

2007
*Art, Anti-Art, Non-Art: Experimentations in the Public Sphere in Postwar Japan, 1950–1970, Getty Research Institute, Los Angeles (also Boxing Painting performance)

Performances (Boxing Painting)
1991
National Museum of Art, Osaka

2003
Ise Cultural Foundation Gallery, New York

2005
Expo 2005 Aichi Japan

2006
Ethan Cohen Fine Arts, New York

Publications
Shinohara Ushio, *Avant-Garde Road* [Japanese text] (Tokyo: Bijutsu Shuppan-sha, 1968; reprint, 2006)

Grace Glueck, "Art," *New York Times*, October 1, 1982

Julia Cassim, "Ushio Shinohara at Tsukashin Hall," *Art in America* (February 1993): 121

Edward M. Gomez, "Art/ Architecture," *New York Times*, August 20, 2000

Janet Koplos, "Clamor and Quiet," *Art in America* (March 2006): 58–61

Ushio Shinohara, *Revenge of the Poison Frog: Ushio Shinohara Drawings* [Japanese text] (Tokyo: Bijutsu Shuppan-sha, 2006)

Be Swift, Beautiful, and Rhythmical: Conversations with Ushio Shinohara [Japanese text] (Tokyo: Bijutsu Shuppan-sha, 2006)

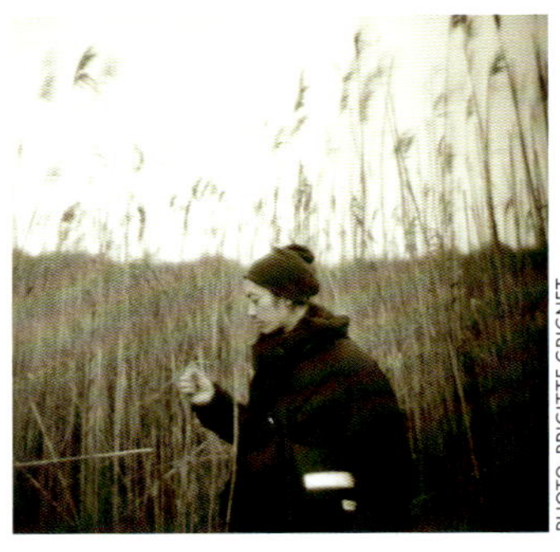

22 GŌ SUGIMOTO
杉本剛

Born in Iwakuni, Yamaguchi Prefecture, Japan, 1979; lives and works in Brooklyn

2002–03
Certificate program in general studies and photography, International Center of Photography (ICP), New York

Solo Exhibitions
2005
Art Cocoon, Tokyo

2006
M.Y. Art Prospects, New York

Group Exhibitions
2003
Graduation show, ICP, New York

Walk on the Web Side, Rencontres Internationales de la Photographie, Arles, France

2004
Digital media exhibition, ICP, New York

IXe exposition de Photographie: Réalité Illusion, Lacanau, France

Photomonth, Starmach Gallery, Krakow, Poland

The Wizard's House: Photography as Alchemy, M.Y. Art Prospects, New York

2005
Gallery Collection: Summer 2005, M.Y. Art Prospects, New York

2006
Auction for Visual Aids, New York

PhotoEspaña 2006, Matados, Madrid (as one of 60 portfolio review finalists)

2007
Auction for White Box, New York

Publications
Gō Sugimoto, "Walk in the Night" [Japanese text], *Studio Voice* (April 2005): 91

Gō Sugimoto, "Darkness of the City" [Japanese text], *Shumi no suibokuga* (November 2005): 1, 16

Allen Frame, "Museo de Papel: Impure Thoughts (Pura Invención, Go Sugimoto)," *Farenheit* (December–January 2007): 37

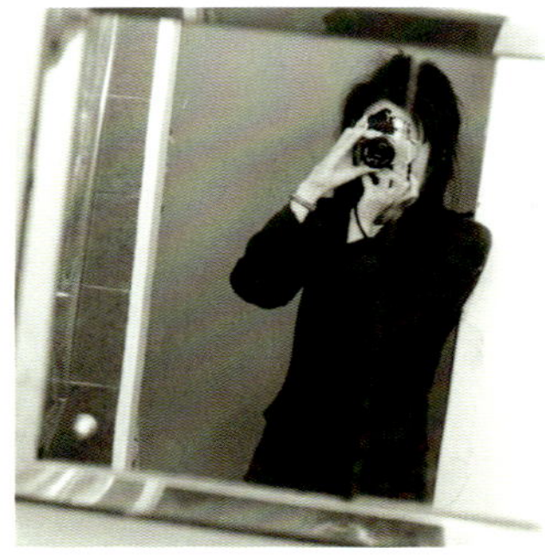

23 KUNIE SUGIURA
杉浦邦恵

Born in Nagoya, Japan; lives and works in Manhattan

1967
BFA in photography, School of the Art Institute of Chicago

Solo Exhibitions
1979
Zeit-Foto, Tokyo (also '86, '89, '93, '95, '96, '98, '02, '04)

1993
Kamakura Gallery, Tokyo (also '95, '97*, '01, '07)

1997
*Leslie Tonkonow Artworks + Projects, New York (also '02, '03)

1998
*Aichi Prefectural Museum of Art, Nagoya

Judy Ann Goldman Fine Art, Boston (also '00, '05)

1999
*Galleria Civica Modena, Italy

2000
*Frances Lehman Loeb Art Center, Vassar College, Poughkeepsie, N.Y.

Nina Freudenheim Gallery, Buffalo

Raffaella Cortese Gallery, Milan

*Sandra and David Bakalar Gallery, Massachusetts College of Art, Boston

2001
*Richard L. Nelson Gallery, University of California, Davis

*University of Maine Museum of Art, The University of Maine, Bangor

Group Exhibitions
1997
New Photography 13, Museum of Modern Art, New York

2000
Gardens of Pleasure, John Michael Kohler Arts Center, Sheboygan, Wis.

Significant Other: The Hand of Man in Animal Imagery, Photographic Resource Center, Boston University

2001
This Is Not a Photograph, University Art Gallery, University of California, San Diego (traveled to Charlottesville, Va., Chicago, and Easton, Pa.)

Wet!, Luise Ross Gallery, New York

2002
PhotoGenesis: Opus 2, Santa Barbara Museum of Art

Retrospectacle: 25 Years of Collecting Modern and Contemporary Art, Photography, Part II, Denver Art Museum

Shadow Play, Roger Smith Gallery, New York

True Blue, Jackson Fine Art, Atlanta

Works on Paper, Weatherspoon Art Museum, The University of North Carolina, Greensboro

2003
How Human: Life in the Post Genome Era, International Center of Photography, New York

Prima Facie, Nina Freudenheim Gallery, Buffalo

2004
Lodz Biennale, Poland

Mask of Japan, Aura Gallery, Shanghai

2004–05
Out of Ordinary/Extraordinary, The Japan Cultural Institute, Cologne (traveled to Barcelona, Canary Islands, Rome, and Berlin)

Subway Series: The New York Mets and Our National Pastime, Queens Museum of Art

2005
Pairs, Groups, and Grids, Leslie Tonkonow Artworks + Projects, New York

The Shadow, Vestsjællands Kunstmuseum, Sorø, Denmark

2006
Math Counts, Contemporary Art Galleries, University of Connecticut, Storrs

Publications
Janet Koplos, "Kunié Sugiura at Zeit-Foto Salon and Kamakura," *Art in America* (December 1995): 102–3

Ken Johnson, "Indoor-Outdoor Relations Along the Hudson," *New York Times*, July 21, 2000

Grace Glueck, "Kunié Sugiura," *New York Times*, January 18, 2002

Janet Koplos, "Shadow Play," *Art in America* (April 2002): 127–31

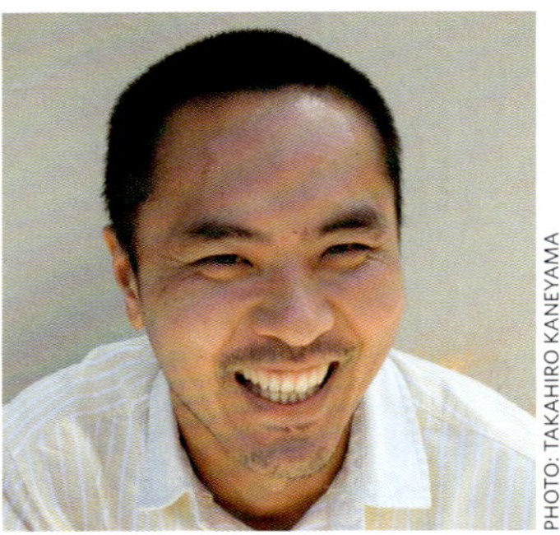

24 HIROSHI SUNAIRI
砂入博史

Born in Hiroshima, Japan, 1972; lives and works in Brooklyn

1992
BFA in visual arts, Purchase College, N.Y.

1996
National Studio Program, P.S. 1, Queens

2001–present
Adjunct professor, NYU Steinhardt, New York

Solo Exhibitions
1999
Andrew Kreps Gallery, New York (also '01)

2000
Galleri Wang, Oslo, Norway

*L.A. Galerie, Frankfurt

2001
Art/32/Basel (Art Unlimited)

2005
*Hiroshima City Museum of Contemporary Art

Group Exhibitions
1997
E Pluribus Nihil, American Fine Arts, New York (also performance)

Hey! You Never Know, Kenny Schachter/Rove, New York (also performance)

2000
Blondies and Brownies, Aktionsforum Parterinsel, Munich

**Desire*, Ursula-Blickle-Stiftung, Kraichtal, Germany and Galleria d'Arte Moderna, Bologna

High Five, Galerie Schedler, Zurich

The Nocturnal Dream Show, Pat Hearn Gallery, New York

**Vertigo*, Voralberger Kunstverein, Bregenz, Austria and Ursula-Blickle-Stiftung, Kraichtal, Germany

2001
Queer Visualities, Staller Center for the Arts, Stony Brook University, N.Y.

**The Americans*, Barbican, London

2002
**Self Exposure*, Kunst en Architectuurgeschiedenis Rijksuniversiteit Groningen, Amsterdam

2004
Connect the Dots, LeRoy Neiman Gallery, Columbia University, New York

2005
Atomika, Lombard-Fried Fine Arts, New York

2006
Crossing the Atlantic ... Uneasy Spaces, Ben Pimlott Building, Goldsmiths College, London

Visual AIDS: Postcards from the Edge, Sikkema Jenkins, New York

Performances
1998
Oriental Nights, Gavin Brown Enterprise, New York

1999
Jack Tilton Gallery, New York

Performance Festival Curated by Tara Delon, P.S.1, Queens

2000
Greene Naftali, New York

Tonic, New York

2001
Arse About Face, Jack Tilton Gallery, New York

Curated Exhibitions/Lectures
2003
University of Girls: T-shirts by Female Artists of NY, United Bamboo, Tokyo

2004
Peace by Piece, Living Museum at Creedmoor Psychiatric Center, Queens and Guild & Greyshkul, New York

2005
Nuclear Disarmament and Arts Symposium, New York University

Peace by Piece, lecture, N.P.T. Conference, U.N., New York

Peace by Piece 2005, former Hiroshima Branch of The Bank of Japan

Publications
Holland Cotter, "Art in Review," *New York Times*, September 24, 1999

Kim Levin, "Voice Choice," *Village Voice*, September 25, 2001

Roberta Smith, "Art in Review," *New York Times*, September 14, 2001

Hiroshi Sunairi, "Buddha Mind in Contemporary Art," *ArtAsiaPacific* (Winter 2007): 126–27

1989
MFA in plastic art and mixed media, University of Tsukuba, Ibaraki Prefecture, Japan

2002–03
Artist in the Marketplace (AIM 23), Bronx Museum of the Arts

2003–04
Japanese Government's Overseas Study Program fellowship (lives in New York)

2006
New York Foundation for the Arts fellowship

Solo Exhibitions
1987
Gallery Natsuka, Tokyo

1989
Heartland Gallery, Tokyo

1991
Gallery K2, Tokyo

2001
Saatchi & Saatchi, Tokyo

2002
White Box, The Annex, New York

2003
Base Gallery, Tokyo (also '05)

2005
White Room Gallery, Los Angeles

Gallery Out of Place, Nara

2006
*Two-person show with Choong Sup Lim, Asian American Arts Centre, New York

2007
*Robert Miller Gallery, New York

Group Exhibitions
1986
Hanging, Tsukashin Hall, Osaka

1987
Icon, Museum of Modern Art, Saitama, Japan

1989
Japanese Artists in New York, Hosomi Gallery, Tokyo

1991
Art of Nerima 1991, Nerima Art Museum, Tokyo

1994
When the Body Becomes Art, Itabashi Art Museum, Tokyo

2001
In Search of Form: Eleven Japanese Artists, Busan Metropolitan Museum, Korea

2002
20th Century: Art Accepted Fiction, Hiratsuka Museum of Art, Kanagawa Prefecture, Japan

2003
The Center for Photography at Woodstock (after fellowship/artist-in-residence)

2004
Monumentum Memo, Gallery 216, New York

2005
Almost, Robert Miller Gallery, New York

2006
Black & Blue, Robert Miller Gallery, New York

**Surrounding Matta-Clark*, Carlos Carvalho Arte Contemporânea, Lisbon

Publications
Shinohara Motoaki, "Cosmos of Ultra-Girls: Mayumi Tarada" [Japanese text], *Bijutsu techō* (August 1986): 31, 66–70

Robert C. Morgan, "Review New York," *Art Press* (October 2002): 82

Jonathan Goodman, "Focus: Suspending Belief," *Contemporary*, no. 49 (2003): 38–43

Mayumi Terada, *In the Bright Room* [Japanese text], photobook (Tokyo: Kyūryūdō, 2003)

Julian Satterthwaite, "Into the Dollhouse," *Daily Yomiuri*, December 22, 2005

Michael Harvery, "Review of Exhibitions," *Art in America* (May 2007): 198–99

Robert C. Morgan, "Artseen," *Brooklyn Rail* (April 2007): 32

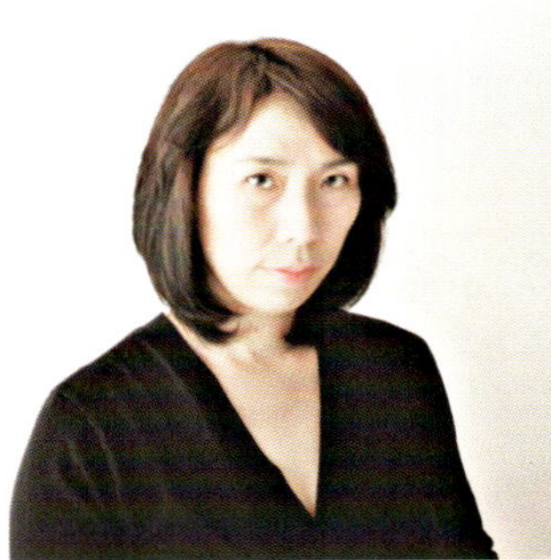

MAYUMI TERADA
寺田真由美

Born in Tokyo, Japan, 1958; lives and works in Manhattan

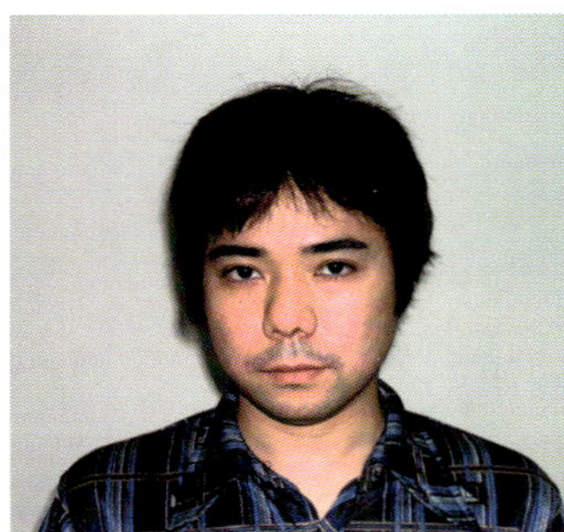

YŪKEN TERUYA
照屋勇賢

Born in Shimajiri-gun, Okinawa Prefecture, Japan, 1973; lives and works in Brooklyn

1996
BFA in painting, Tama Art University, Tokyo

1999
Post BA, Maryland Institute College of Art, Baltimore

2001
Fellowship, The Skowhegan School of Painting and Sculpture, Maine

MFA, School of Visual Arts, New York

2002
Vision of Contemporary Art (VOCA) Prize, Tokyo

2005
Lily Auchincloss Fellowship, New York Foundation for the Arts

Solo Exhibitions
2002
K.S. Art, New York

Shoshana Wayne Gallery, Santa Monica (also '07)

Aldrich Museum of Contemporary Art, Ridgefield, Conn. (award)

2003
Elizabeth Leach Gallery, Portland, Ore.

Murata & Friends, Berlin

2004
Diverse Works Art Space, Houston

Voges + Partner Gallery, Frankfurt

2005
Josée Bienvenu Gallery, New York

*Nassauischer Kunstverein, Wiesbaden, Germany

2006
Hiroshima City Museum of Contemporary Art

*Sumida Riverside Hall Gallery, Tokyo

2007
Asia Society, New York

Group Exhibitions
2002
*Model World, Aldrich Contemporary Art Museum, Ridgefield, Conn.

*VOCA '02, Ueno Royal Museum, Tokyo

2003
*Internal Excess: Selections Fall 2003, Drawing Center, New York

*Slab, University Galleries, Illinois State University, Normal, Ill.

*White Meat & Sunlite 2003, Wiensowski und Habord, Berlin

2004
Dessins et des autres, Galerie Anne de Villepoix, Paris

*Fuchū Biennale, Fuchū Art Museum, Tokyo

*Initial Encounters, Arts Center of the Capital Region, Troy, N.Y.

Newpaper, Cristinerose/Josée Bienvenu Gallery, New York

*Refrain; Korean, Balkan, Okinawa, Total Museum of Contemporary Arts, Seoul

2005
*Anyang Public Art Project, Korea

*Greater New York, P.S.1, Queens

*Lost and Found, Gallery Sowaka, Kyoto

*Material Matters, Herbert F. Johnson Museum of Art, Cornell University, Ithaca, N.Y.

*Views from Abroad, Stadtgalerie Kiel, Germany

*Yokohama Triennale

2006
*5th Asian Pacific Triennial of Contemporary Art, Queensland Art Gallery, Brisbane

*Rapt!, Gertrude Contemporary Art Space, Melbourne and Object Gallery, Sydney

*12th Asian Art Biennale Bangladesh 2006, Dhaka

2007
The Shapes of Space, Guggenheim Museum, New York

Publications
Dave Eggers, "Top Ten," Artforum (April 2000): 58

James Kalm, "RetroFuturePresent at Magnifik," NY Art Magazine (April 2001): 67

Roberta Smith, "Art in Review," New York Times, May 10, 2002

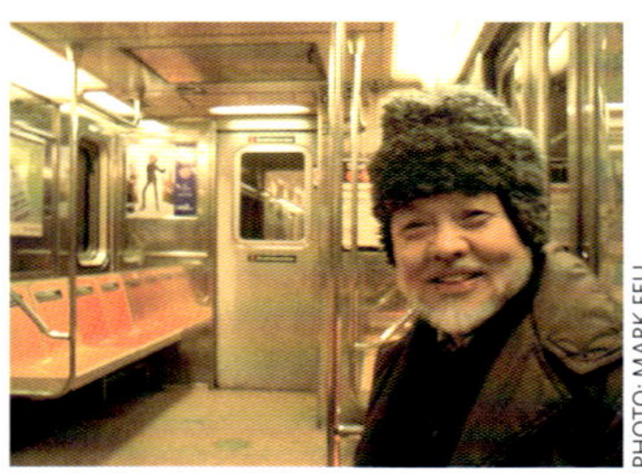

27
YASUNAO TONE
刀根康尚

Born in Tokyo, Japan, 1935; lives and works in Manhattan

1957
BA in Japanese literature, Chiba University, Japan

1960
Co-founder, Group Ongaku, Tokyo

1962
Founding member, Fluxus

1964
Special Award, Nova Consonanza, Rome

1979
Commission, Music for Roadrunners, American Dance Festival (choreography by Merce Cunningham)

1982
Collaboration Fellowship, National Endowment for the Arts

1996–97
Individual Artist Award for Media, NYSCA

2002
Golden Nica Prize in Digital Music, Prix Ars Electronica 2002, Austria

2004
Music grant, Foundation for Contemporary Performance Arts, New York

Group Exhibitions (after 2000)
2001
Bitstreams, Whitney Museum of American Art, New York

*Do It, Museo de Arte Carrillo Gil, Mexico City

*Mutations, TN Probe, Tokyo

*Yokohama Triennale

2003
*I Moderni, The Moderns, Castello di Rivoli Museo d'Arte Contemporanea, Turin, Italy

2004
Off the Record>Sound ARC, ARC/Musée d'Art Moderne de la Ville de Paris

2005
Variation on a Silence, Re-tem Plant, Tokyo

Solo Concerts and Collaborative Performances (after 2000)
2001
*Ashiya City Museum of Art & History, Japan

Tokyo Opera City Art Gallery, Tokyo

Yokohama Triennale, special performance, Yokohama Red Brick Warehouse

2002
Ars Electronica Festival, Brucknerhaus, Linz, Austria

2004
Roulette at Location One, New York

2005
The Media Lab, MIT, Cambridge (collaborative concert with Florian Hecker)

2006
E.I.F., New York

2007
Lovebytes International Festival of Digital Art, Sheffield Central Library, U.K.

Group Performances (after 2000)
2001
Pulse, with Stephen Vitiello, Whitney Museum Midtown, New York

2002
Lovebytes International Festival of Digital Art, Sheffield, U.K.

Sonar 2002, Barcelona Museum of Contemporary Art

Spectacle Vivant, Centre Georges Pompidou, Paris

2003
All Tomorrows Parties Festival, Camber Sands Recreation Center, Sussex, U.K.

Sonic Light 2003, Paradiso, Amsterdam

2004
Launch Festival, New Music Research Centre, University of York, U.K.

2005
All Tomorrows Parties Festival, SeOne, London

Cut and Splice, London Symphony Orchestra St Luke's, London

2006
Dissonanze Festival, Rome

Recordings
1993
Musica Iconologos, Lovely Music CD 3041

1998
Solo for Wounded CD, Tzadik CD 7212

2003
Yasunao Tone, Asphodel CD2011

2004
Palimpsest, with Florina Hecker, Mego CD060

2005
Event: Christian Marclay, Yasunao Tone, Christian Wolff, Asphodel CD2032

Publications
Yasunao Tone, Phase of Contemporary Art: Can Art Be Thought? [Japanese text] (Tokyo: Tabata Shoten, 1970)

Alan Licht, "Random Tone Bursts," Wire (September 2002): 30–33

Yasunao Tone, "John Cage and Recording," Leonardo Music Journal 13 (2003): 11–15

Brandon LaBelle, Background Noise:

Perspective on Sound Art (London: Continuum, 2006), 22–35, 218–29

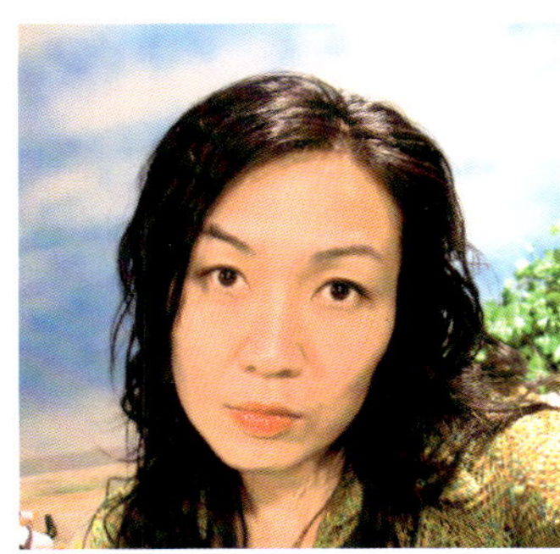

MOMOYO TORIMITSU
鳥光桃代

Born in Tokyo, Japan, 1967; lives in Manhattan and works in Brooklyn

1994
BA in sculpture, Tama Art University, Tokyo

1996–97
International Studio Program, P.S.1, Queens

Solo Exhibitions
1994
Gallery MYU, Tokyo (also '95, '96)

1998
*Momenta Art, Brooklyn

2000
Deitch Projects, New York (also '04)

Galerie Xippas, Paris

2001
*Sumida Riverside Hall Gallery, Tokyo

2004
Fuchū Art Museum, Tokyo

Swiss Institute Contemporary Art, New York

Group Exhibitions
1997
Zones of Disturbances, Steirischer Herbst, Graz, Austria

1998
Attack/Damage, Itabashi Art Museum, Tokyo

Where I Am, Galeria da Mitra, Lisbon

1999
Abracadabra, Tate Modern, London

Videodrome, New Museum of Contemporary Art, New York

2000
Dark Mirrors of Japan, De Appel, Amsterdam

Twilight Sleep, Istituto Giapponese di Cultura, Rome

2001
Biennale di Ceramica nell' Arte Contemporanea, Museo Civico d'Arte Contemporanea, Albissola Marina, Italy

Inoculated Time, Centro Cultural Banco do Brasil, Rio de Janeiro

My Reality: Contemporary Art and the Culture of Japanese Animation, Des Moines Art Center, Iowa (traveled, –'03)

Neo-Tokyo, Museum of Contemporary Art, Sydney

2002
Paris–Brooklyn, Galerie Chez Valentin, Paris

Céramiques d'artistes II, the Musée Ariana, Geneva, Switzerland

Flirt, Smart Project Space, Amsterdam

2004
Akimahen, Collection Lambert Musée d'art contemporain, Lille, France

Democracy Was Fun, White Box, New York

Gwangju Biennale, Korea

2005
Art Parade, Deitch Projects, New York (also '06)

Vanishing Point, Experimenta Media Arts, Melbourne

NY Connection, Hilger Contemporary, Vienna

Out of Place, UBS Art Gallery, New York

Rising Sun, Melting Moon: Contemporary Art in Japan, Israel Museum, Jerusalem

Kunstbanken Hammer, Oslo, Norway

2006
The Garden Party, Deitch Projects, New York

Modern Time, Palazzo Ducale, Genoa, Italy

2007
All About Laughter, Mori Art Museum, Tokyo

Hå Gamle Prestegård, Stavanger, Norway

Thermocline of Art: New Asian Waves, ZKM, Karlsruhe, Germany

Publications
Amei Wallach, "Art/Architecture," *New York Times*, December 22, 2002

Melissa Pearl Friedling, "Momoyo Torimitsu Swiss Institute," *Flash Art* (March/April 2004): 60–61

Paul Laster, "Review of Exhibitions," *Art in America* (May 2004): 154–55

Kay Itoi, "Rejecting Kawaii Culture," *Japan Times*, February 8, 2007

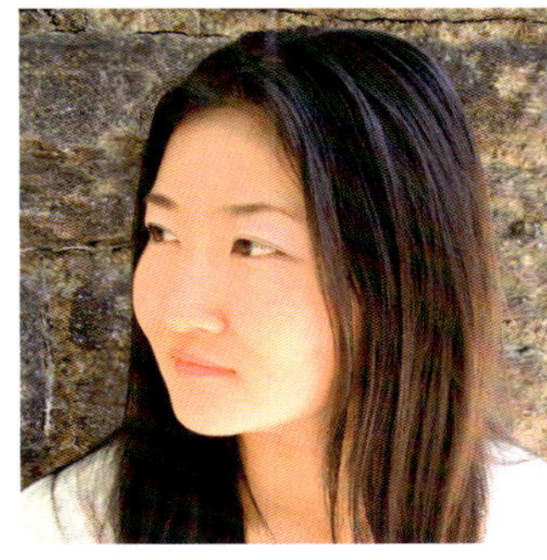

AYA UEKAWA
上川紋

Born in Tokyo, Japan, 1979; lives and works in Manhattan

2004
BFA in painting, Hunter College, New York

Solo Exhibitions
2006
Kravets/Wehby Gallery, New York

2007
Arndt & Partner, Berlin

Group Exhibitions
2005
Drawn, Kravets/Wehby Gallery, New York

Frontier, Roberts & Tilton, Los Angeles

2006
A Certain Likeness, Gallery W 52, New York

Art Basel (Arndt & Partner)

Do Not Stack, Roberts & Tilton, Los Angeles

New Trajectories I: Relocations— Recent Painting, Drawing, and Sculpture from the Ovitz Family Collection in Los Angeles, Douglas F. Cooley Memorial Art Gallery, Reed College, Portland, Ore.

School Days, Tilton Gallery, New York

25 Bold Moves, House of Campari, New York

2007
Japan Inc., Kravets/Wehby Gallery, New York

The Armory Show (Arndt and Partner), New York

The Incomplete, Chelsea Art Museum, New York

Publications
Joseph Gallivan, "Money Makes the Art Go Round: Show Offers Glimpse into the Mind and Eye of Hollywood Mogul," *Portland Tribune*, January 24, 2006

John Motley, "Arts Rodeo," *Portland Mercury*, February 2, 2006

D.K. Row, "Ovitz Collection Takes on Adventurous Dimension," *Oregonian*, February 19, 2006

Oliver Vanzetti, "At the Galleries; New York: Aya Uekawa," *Flash Art* (October 2006): 55

Rebecca Cascade, "Talent Show: Aya Uekawa," *W* (November 2006): 198

Ichikawa Akiko, "New Women: Aya Uekawa" [Japanese text], *Vogue Nippon* (June 2007): 139

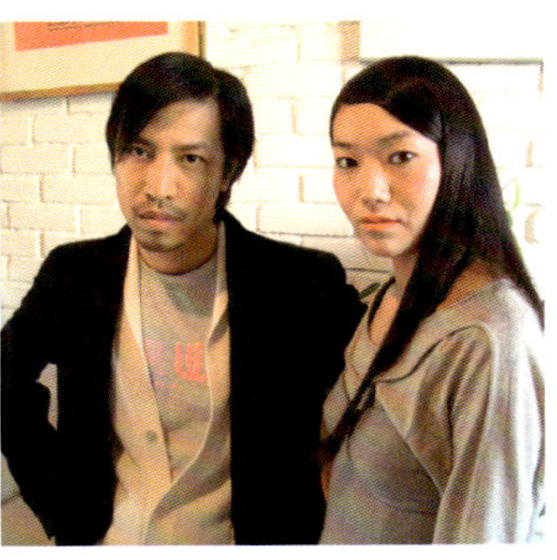

UNITED BAMBOO
ユナイテッド・バンブー

Founded in New York, 1997; based in New York and Tokyo

1974
Miho Aoki born in Ōmiya, Saitama Prefecture, Japan

1991–94
Aoki studies at Stoneleigh-Burnham High School, Greenfield, Mass.

1995
Aoki interns at Bernadette Corporation, New York

1997
United Bamboo founded by Miho Aoki, Siri Kuptamethee, and Sidney Prawatyotin in New York

1998
Thuy Pham joins as a new partner

2003
Only Shop opened at Tokyo's Daikan'yama with architecture by Vito Acconci

2006
Men's Store opened at Tokyo's Omotesandō

Fashion Shows
2004
New York Collection, Spring/Summer 2005

New York Collection, Fall/Winter 2005

2005
New York Collection, Spring/Summer 2006

New York Collection, Fall/Winter 2006

2006
New York Collection, Spring/Summer 2007

New York Collection, Fall/Winter 2007

Publications
Cathy Horyn, "Start in Fashion? Easier to Go Through the Eye of a Needle," *New York Times*, August 29, 2000

Camila Nickerson, "Who's at the Party," *Vogue* (February 2004)

Cathy Horyn, "Suits to Wear on Earth and in the Air," *New York Times*, February 7, 2005

Martin Wise, "Style Wise," *Japan Times*, November 14, 2006

Karl Tracy, "Collection Election," *V Man* (Fall/Winter 2006): 82

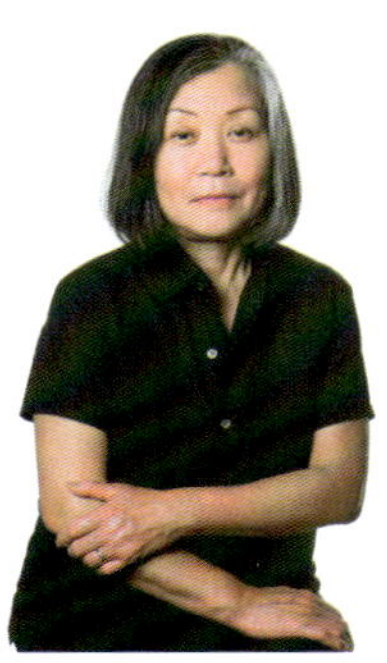

31
JUNKO YODA
依田順子

Born in Miyoshi-gun, Tokushima Prefecture, Japan, 1943; lives and works in Manhattan

1966
BFA in painting, Musashino Art University, Tokyo

1967
Advance course in painting, Musashino Art University, Tokyo

1991
6th Holbein Scholarship, Japan

2005
The Pollock-Krasner Foundation grant

Solo Exhibitions
1968
Miyatake Gallery, Takamatsu, Japan

1979
Middle Space Gallery, Takamatsu, Japan

1980
Zabriskie Gallery, New York (also '87, '04, '06)

1984–85
Galerie Zabriskie, Paris

1985
Hosokawa Gallery, Takamatsu, Japan

1986
NAO, Tokushima, Japan

1989
Muramatsu Gallery, Tokyo (also '91, '94, '99, '06)

1995
Sankokan, Takamatsu, Japan

2002
Two-person show with Winifred Lutz, Zabriskie Gallery

2007
Facial Index, New York

Group Exhibitions
1978
Zabriskie Gallery, New York (also '79, '84, '05)

1985
Roots to Reality: Asian Americans in Transition, Henry Street Settlement, New York

1986
Asian Artists of Brooklyn, Brooklyn Museum Community Gallery

1988
Cultural Currents, San Diego Museum of Art

1995
Collage, Nerima Art Museum, Tokyo

1997
Hung Out to Dry, Steinbaum Krauss Gallery, New York

1998
The World of Collage, Takamatsu City Museum of Art, Japan

2001
Japanese Artists in New York, Takamatsu City Museum of Art, Japan

2002
The AAAC Story, Asian American Arts Centre, New York

2006
Endurance of Seeing/Making: Art of the Late Modernism, Musashino Art University Museum and Library, Tokyo

Publications
Peter Frank, "Art," *Village Voice*, October 2, 1978

Douglas Welch, "Reviews Arts," *Arts Magazine* (September 1980): 27

Michael Brenson, "Art in Review," *New York Times*, August 28, 1987

Susan Freudenheim, "Ethnic Variety Flows in 'Cultural Currents,'" *San Diego Tribune*, July 27, 1988

Cynthia Nadelman, "New York Reviews," *ARTnews* (October 2002): 156

Grace Glueck, "Art in Review," *New York Times*, July 2, 2004

David Ebony, "Junko Yoda at Zabriskie," *Art in America* (June/July 2007): 209–10

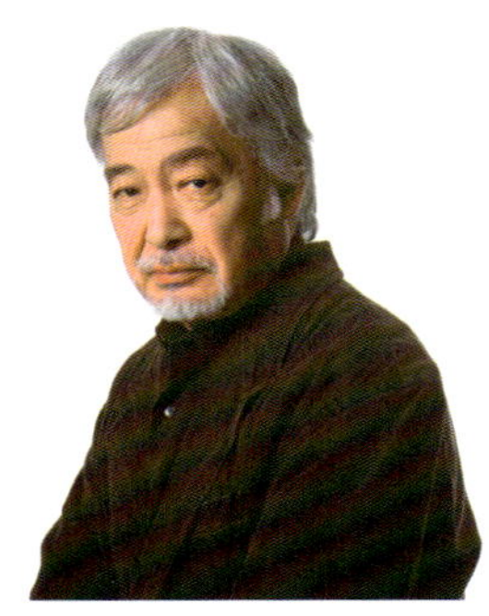

32
TOSHIHISA YODA
依田寿久

Born in Shizuoka, Japan, 1940; lives and works in Manhattan

1965
Completes the special painting course, Musashino Fine Art University, Tokyo

1967–69
Brooklyn Museum Art School

1970
Art Students League of New York

Solo Exhibitions
1975
Lotus Gallery, New York

1979
Two-person show with Stephen Johnson, SoHo Center for Visual Artists, New York

1983
Just Above Midtown/Downtown Gallery, New York

1987
Gallery Okazaki, Kyoto

Community Gallery, Shizuoka Prefectural Museum of Art, Japan

1988
*Nantenshi Gallery, Tokyo (also '98)

1992
*Nantenshi Gallery Soko, Tokyo (also '94)

2006
Facial Index, New York

Group Exhibitions
1972
Contemporary Japanese Art, Union Carbide Building, New York

1976–77
Contemporary Reflections, Aldrich Contemporary Art Museum, Ridgefield, Conn.

1979
Windows on the East: A Survey of Contemporary Japanese Art, World Trade Center, New York

1980
Art Today 80, Seibu Museum of Art, Tokyo

1987
The Tenth Anniversary Exhibition: Painting 1977–87, National Museum of Art, Osaka

1991
90 Fukuyama Art Project, Fukuyama Museum of Art, Hiroshima Prefecture

The 20th Century: Japanese Painting, 3rd Anniversary Exhibition, Fukuyama Museum of Art

1992
NICAF Yokohama '92

Seductive Brush Marks, Kyoto Municipal Museum of Art

1994
Betrayal/Empowerment Part I, 179 Grace Dodge Hall, Columbia University Teachers College, New York

1995
Modern Art of Japan, National Museum of Modern Art, Tokyo

1996
New Acquisitions Show 1993–95, National Museum of Modern Art, Tokyo

1998
Aspects of Line, National Museum of Art, Osaka

2001
Japanese Artists in New York, Takamatsu City Museum of Art, Japan

2002
New Acquisitions + Introduction to Contemporary Art, Hiroshima City Museum of Contemporary Art

2005
Assemblage, Takamatsu City

Museum of Art, Japan

2006
Black & White, Holland Tunnel Gallery, New York

**Endurance of Seeing/Making: Art of Late Modernism*, Musashino Art University Museum and Library, Tokyo

Publications
Fujieda Teruo and Inui Yoshiaki, *Tomorrow's Art* [Japanese text] (Tokyo: Shōgakukan, 1980), 126, 140

Inoue Akihiko and Sumitani Kōichirō, *Chronicle of Art* [Japanese text], vol. 6 (Tokyo: Mainichi Shinbunsha, 1991), 96, 192

Ōtani Shōgo, *The Art Museum of Japan* [Japanese text] (Tokyo: Shōgakukan, 1997), 1124–25

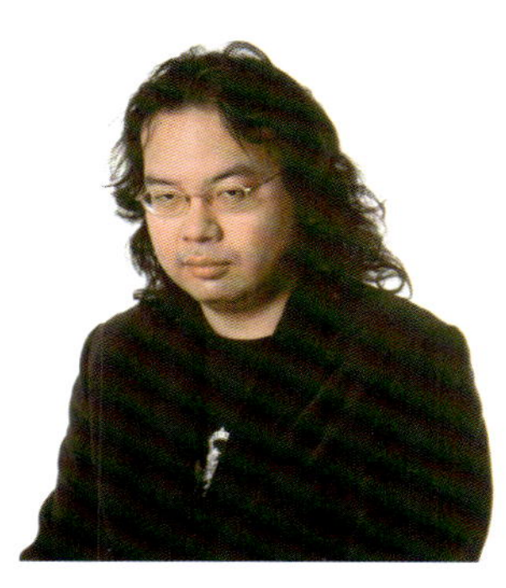

PHOTO: JACQUES DEMELO

∧
33
YŌICHIRŌ YODA
依田洋一朗

Born in Takamatsu, Kagawa Prefecture, Japan, 1972; lives and works in Manhattan

1994
Scenic artist internship, Surflight Theatre, Beach Haven, N.J.

1995
BFA in painting, Tyler School of Art, Elkins Park, Pa.

1998
MFA in painting, Queens College, Queens

2001–04
Art teacher, Center for Unlimited Enrichment Program, Queens College, Queens

2003–04
Video lecturer and artist-in-residence, TIXE Gallery, New York

2004–05
Artist-in-residence, Chashama subsidized space grant, New York (also '06)

2006
Lecturer, New York State Summer School of the Arts, SUNY Brockport

Solo Exhibitions
2000
HEREArt, New York

2001
Gallery Te, Tokyo

2003
TIXE Gallery, New York

2004
Queens Theatre in the Park, Queens

2006
Facial Index, New York

Group Exhibitions
1997
Hold It Now, Hit It, Court Street/ Carroll Gardens, Brooklyn

1998
Autonomous Zones, Art Field, New York

Summer Group Show, Derek Eller Gallery, New York

2000
Night of 1000 Drawings, Artists Space, New York (also '01, '02)

2003
Recession 2003 $99 Show, Cynthia Broan Gallery, New York

The Andrew Jackson Collection, TIXE Gallery, New York

Re: Narrative, Compton-Goethals Gallery, The City College of New York

In the Shadow of 9/11: A Chinatown Memorial Exhibition, Silk Road Place, New York

2004
Butternut Ink, Asian American Arts Centre, New York

2004
Collaboration 1, Creative Art Network, Philadelphia

2006
The Ides of March—2006, ABC No Rio, New York

Publications
Hori Kōsai, "Intricate Perspective: Painting by Yōichirō Yoda" [Japanese text], *Theoria*, no.22 (June 1, 2001): 14–15

Jessica D. K. Park, "Art Review: Butternut Ink," *The New York Art World.com* (November 2004): 17

Bob Daniels, "Last Days of 42nd Street: Yoichiro Yoda," *International Al Jolson Society New York City Newsletter* (Winter 2004–05)

ARTISTS' ACKNOWLEDGEMENTS

Making a Home artists would like to thank the following individuals and organizations for their support and assistance.

ON megumi Akiyoshi
Kawakita family; Ryoko Hatogai; Hitomi Kina; Thomas Lendvai; Simon Lüthi; Mami Rice; Yayoi Nagata; Masami Ueki

Noriko Ambe
Yupo Corporation

Ei Arakawa
Patricia Cazorla; Kimiko Fukuoka; Michiko Hoshi; Miki Ikeda; Mari Mukai; Etsuko Noda; Hisayasu Takashio; Maki Waza; Carol Greene; PoNJA-GenKon

Satoru Eguchi
All my friends, as well as my landlord and roommates, who saw my project in progress and gave me feedback

Ayakoh Furukawa
Tomiko Kusumoto Furukawa; Andrew R. MacBride; Marjorie Lyons; Juan Sanchez, Hunter College; Japanese Artists Association of New York, Inc.

Tōru Hayashi
Alex Keim; John Storey; Kōichi Yanagi; Simon Watson; Sanskriti Kendra Foundation, especially Mr. O. P. Jain

Noritoshi Hirakawa
Thank you to everyone

Yoshiaki Kaihatsu
Masaki Yamaguchi

Takahiro Kaneyama
For all mothers and people who have finished raising children

Emiko Kasahara
All the volunteers who contributed their memories to my work *SHEER*

Misaki Kawai
Ray Otis; Sue Hancock; Clementine Gallery; Jeffrey Deitch; Kathy Grayson; Taylor McKimens; my friends and family

Miwa Koizumi
Jean Barberis; Karin Campbell; Elodie Blanchard; Sebastian Santamaria; Erik Guzman; Marco Scoffier; NGC 224; Dumbo Arts Center; *SuperSpa* guests

Yumi Kōri
Tania Duvergne; Ise Cultural Foundation Gallery; Yasuhiro Sakamoto; Yoshimi Hirota; Matteo Ames; Toshiya Endō

Nobuho Nagasawa
Paul Burnsweig; Marc Nasdor; Andrew Schloss; Dale Stammen; Kazumi Tanimura; Takeshi Koizumi, AROMAC Co., Ltd.

Hiroyuki Nakamura
Kanji & Mariko Nakamura; Kousaku Suzuki; Paul Runyon; people of Akureyri, Iceland; Tomoko Ashikawa; Jackie Battenfield; Lital Mehr; My Friends and YOU

Yoko Ono
I thank our forefathers and mothers who never stopped creating great works of art even in the most dire circumstances.

Hiroki Ōtsuka
Mom, Dad, Love & Peace

Katsuhiro Saiki
Shigeo and Taeko Saiki

Kyōko Sera
Atsuko Kumazawa; Makiko Matake; Aomi Okabe; Jennifer Poole & Eric Vante; Akira Tatehata; Dai-Ichi Life Gallery; Sano Gallery; Shiseido Gallery

Noriko Shinohara
Elizabeth A. Wyckoff; Chūryō Nakabayashi; Takemitsu Ōba; International Print Center, New York; A+D Gallery, Columbia College, Chicago; John B. Van Sickle

Ushio Shinohara
Kōji Iijima; Mitsuko Yamaguchi; Atsushi Yazaki; Noriko Shinohara

Gō Sugimoto
Shizuyo Sugimoto; Mikio Sugimoto; Anna Morgowicz; Brigitte Grignet; Marco Scoffier; Griffin Editions; International Center of Photography; Miyako Yoshinaga; my friends

Hiroshi Sunairi
Diego Cortez; Shida Kuo and Judith Schwartz, Ceramic Department, New York University; Elizabeth Zawada, Greenwich House Pottery; Arnie Zimmerman

Mayumi Terada
Kevin Bartelme

Yasunao Tone
My sincere appreciation for technical advice to Takeshi Kawana and Marco Scoffier

Momoyo Torimitsu
All the people who helped me and supported me to make this project happen

United Bamboo
Miho Aoki thanks her partner Thuy Q Pham and the United Bamboo staff, Shirley Yung, Chie Shikama, and Daisuke Ito

Junko Yoda
Virginia Zabriskie and Alexis Dean, Zabriskie Gallery

Toshihisa Yoda
My great friends, Elena Phipps and Alan Finkel; Nantenshi Gallery, Tokyo

Yōichirō Yoda
Prof. Richard Cramer, Tyler School of Art; Prof. Larry Fane, Queens College; Alison Cayne, Urban Development Corporation

PROFILES OF AUTHORS

Eric C. Shiner is an independent curator and art historian specializing in Japanese contemporary art. He holds two master's degrees in art history, from Yale University and from Osaka University where he studied as a Ministry of Education fellow under the auspices of the Japanese government. His scholarly focus is on the concept of bodily transformation in postwar Japanese photography, painting, and performance art. He was an assistant curator of *Yokohama Triennale 2001*. His curated exhibitions include *Chameleon Dreams: Trans/Forming Identity in Contemporary Japanese Photography* (Julia Friedman Gallery, Chicago, 2002), *Surface to Air* (Ise Cultural Foundation Gallery, New York, 2004), *Triple X: Extended, Exploded, Extracted—Naoto Nakagawa, 1965–1975* (White Box, New York, 2007), and *Bingyi: Dawns Here Are Quiet* (Ethan Cohen Fine Arts, New York, 2007). Shiner will co-curate *Simulasian* at the inaugural Asian Contemporary Art Fair, New York (November 2007). He has also worked with the Andy Warhol Museum in Pittsburgh and the National Museum of Modern Art, Kyoto. He is an active writer and translator, and is a contributing editor for *ArtAsiaPacific*. His most recent article, "The Changing Face of Japanese Contemporary Art," will appear in a forthcoming two-volume anthology on Japanese modern and contemporary art edited by Thomas J. Rimer and published by University of Hawai'i Press. He is Adjunct Professor of Art History at Pace University, New York.

Reiko Tomii is an art historian and curator based in New York, who investigates post-1945 Japanese art in global and local contexts. Her early collaboration with Alexandra Munroe, which resulted in the exhibition *Yayoi Kusama: A Retrospective* (Center for International Contemporary Arts, 1989) and the publication *Japanese Art After 1945: Scream Against the Sky* (Abrams, 1995), convinced her to focus both her scholarly and professional efforts on contemporary Japanese art. She has curated the Japanese sections of *Global Conceptualism* (Queens Museum of Art, 1999) and *Century City* (Tate Modern, 2001). Her publications include "Historicizing 'Contemporary Art': Some Discursive Practices in *Gendai Bijutsu* in Japan," *Positions* 12.3 (Winter 2004) and contributions to *Collectivism After Modernism* (University of Minnesota Press, 2007) and *Art, Anti-Art, Non-Art* (Getty Research Institute, 2007); she has guest-edited "1960s Japan: Art Outside the Box," a special issue of *Review of Japanese Culture and Society* (Jōsai University, Saitama Prefecture), no. 17 (2005). Her past work with Japan Society Gallery as contributor, editor, and translator includes: *Enlightenment Embodied* (1997), *Crosscurrents* (1999), *YES YOKO ONO* (2000), *Transmitting the Forms of Divinity* (2003), *Little Boy* (2005), and *Awakenings* (2007). She is a co-founder of PoNJA-GenKon (Post-1945 Japanese Art Discussion Group/Gendai Bijutsu Kondankai), a listserv group of specialists interested in contemporary Japanese art.

Midori Yamamura is a PhD candidate at the Graduate Center, The City University of New York. Her dissertation title is: "Yayoi Kusama: Biography and Cultural Confrontation, 1945–1969." She is the recipient of the 2006–07 Terra Foundation Predoctoral Fellowship for studies in global aspects of American art at the Smithsonian American Art Museum. In 2007–08, she is an Andrew W. Mellon Dissertation Fellow at the Center for the Humanities, The CUNY Graduate Center, a grant specifically offered for investigating methodologies concerning biography. Since 1990, Yamamura has curated numerous exhibitions that introduced artists from developing countries. She has lectured on Kusama Yayoi at the College Art Association annual conferences in Seattle (2004) and New York (2006), the Smithsonian American Art Museum, The Museum of Modern Art, New York, and the Hammer Museum (2007). Since 2004, Yamamura holds a lectureship at The Museum of Modern Art, New York.

PROFILES OF CONTRIBUTORS

Luis Camnitzer was born in Germany in 1937. He studied sculpture and architecture in Uruguay, where he arrived at the age of one, and has lived in the U.S. since 1964. He represented Uruguay in the Venice Biennale (1988), and participated in the Whitney Biennial (2000) and Documenta XI (2002). He is a two-time recipient of a Guggenheim Fellowship, Viewing Program Curator at The Drawing Center (1999–2006), and professor emeritus in art from the State University of New York College at Old Westbury. His publications include *New Art of Cuba* (1994/2004) and *Conceptualist Art in Latin America: Didactics of Liberation* (2007), both from University of Texas Press. He co-organized *Global Conceptualism* (Queens Museum of Art, 1999).

Kevin Concannon is Associate Professor of Art History at the Myers School of Art at The University of Akron. His publications have focused on 1960s art, including several articles on Yoko Ono. He has curated *Mass Production: Artists' Multiples and the Marketplace* (2006) and *Yoko Ono Imagine Peace Featuring John and Yoko's Year of Peace* (2007), both for University Galleries at The University of Akron. One of the authors of *YES YOKO ONO* (Japan Society, 2000), he also contributed an article on John and Yoko's 1969 Tokyo *War Is Over!* event to "Art Outside the Box," a special issue of *Review of Japanese Culture and Society* (Jōsai University, 2005).

Jonathan Goodman is a writer who specializes in Asian contemporary art. He writes for *Art in America, Sculpture, Yishu*, and *ArtAsiaPacific*. Interested in seeing how artists from classical cultures make sense of the New York art world, he has written at length on Chinese, Japanese, and Korean contemporary artists in an urban context, including Xu Bing, Yumi Kōri, and Nam June Paik. He has won a grant from the Asian Cultural Council to visit Mainland China, where he met with contemporary artists, curators, and gallerists. He currently teaches art criticism and contemporary culture at Pratt Institute and the Parsons School of Design.

Sachiko Hisajima completed her master's degree in art history at the City College of New York in 2006. Her thesis is "Takashi Murakami and Traditional Japanese Art," in which she investigates connections between Edo art and Murakami's production in terms of composition, decorative style, and playfulness. Her thesis adviser was Dr. Reiko Tomii. As an artist, she has shown at Bronx River Art Center & Gallery, Café Loon Loon, and Gallery 128 in New York.

Ryan Holmberg is an art historian and writer. He holds a doctorate in the History of Art from Yale University. His dissertation treats the work of the monthly manga journal *Garo* from 1964 to 1971. Recent writings have appeared in *Art in America*, *Artforum*, *International Journal of Comic Art*, and *Dot dot dot*. He is currently a visiting Assistant Professor in Japanese Art History at the University of Chicago.

Hiroko Ikegami is an art historian who specializes in post-1945 American art and its global impact. She has received a PhD degree from Yale University (May 2007). Her dissertation, "Dislocations: Robert Rauschenberg and the Americanization of Modern Art, Circa 1964," investigates the artist's international activities during the 1960s as a founding element in the Americanization of the global art scene. Her most recent essay, "An American Spectacle: Reconsidering the 1964 Venice Biennale," appears in *Journal of the Japan Art History Society* (March 2007). Her next project concerns postwar reconstruction of Japanese cultural identity and its relationship to the United States.

Yukie Kamiya is an independent curator and critic. She was Associate and Adjunct Curator of the New Museum of Contemporary Art, New York in 2003–06, and a contributing curator for *Thermocline: New Asian Wave* (ZKM, Karlsruhe, 2007). She has curated *Fantasia* (Beijing and Seoul, 2001–02), *Under Construction: New Dimensions of Asian Art* (Japan Foundation Forum+Tokyo Opera City Art Gallery, Tokyo, 2002–03), and *Adaptive Behavior* (New Museum of Contemporary Art , 2004). Her numerous publications include contributions to *Dark Mirrors of Japan* (De Appel, Amsterdam, 2000), *The World Is a Stage* (Mori Art Museum, 2005), and *Taipei Biennial 2006.*

Caleb Kelly is a lecturer in Electronic Arts at the University of Western Sydney and has published papers on 20th-century experimental sound. He has curated and produced numerous sound based exhibitions and events in Sydney. He also produced and directed "impermanent.audio" for six years, and co-directed the experimental sound festival *What Is Music?* Within these practices Japanese artists and musicians have played a predominant role including: Suzuki Akio, Ōtomo Yoshihide, Haco, KK Null, Haino Keiji, Merzbow, Nakamura Toshimaru, Sachiko M, Hiroshige Jojo, and Sugimoto Taku.

Barbara London, curator, founded The Museum of Modern Art's video exhibition program and has guided it over a long pioneering career. She has helped assemble the Museum's premiere media collection. She has written and lectured widely. Exhibitions and projects she has recently undertaken include: *Stir-Fry* (1997), *InterNyet* (1998), and *dot.jp* (1999), a series of Web travelogues in China, Russia, and Japan; *TimeStream*, an online project by Tony Oursler (2001); *Gary Hill: HanD HearD* (2002); *Music and Media*, an interview series including Laurie Anderson/Greil Marcus, Michel Gondry/Ed Halter, and Brian Eno/Todd Haynes; the film series *Anime!!* (2005); *Stillness: Michael Snow/Sam Taylor-Wood* (2005); *River of Crime*, a community on-line project with the Residents (2006); and *Automatic Update* (2007).

Alexandra Munroe, PhD is Senior Curator of Asian Art, the Solomon R. Guggenheim Museum. She served as Vice President of Arts & Culture at Japan Society, New York and Director of Japan Society Gallery in 1998–2005. She is internationally recognized as a pioneer in the field of modern Asian art for her landmark exhibitions and publications including *Yayoi Kusama: A Retrospective* (Center for International Contemporary Arts, 1989); *Japanese Art After 1945: Scream Against the Sky* (Abrams, 1994); *The Art of Mu Xin* (Yale University Press, 2002); and *YES YOKO ONO* (Japan Society, 2000). She is a Trustee of the U.S.-Japan Foundation; Institute of Fine Arts, New York University; the Alliance for the Arts; Longhouse Reserve; and is a member of the Council on Foreign Relations.

Yasufumi Nakamori is an independent curator and PhD candidate in art history at Cornell University specializing in the 20th-century history of architecture and photography in Japan. His dissertation deals with Isozaki Arata's unbuilt architecture and the street photography of the journal *Provoke* from the late 1960s to early 1970s. He assisted in curating *The American Effect* (Whitney Museum of American Art, 2003) and independently organized a dozen exhibitions, including the first U.S. solo exhibition of photographer Hatakeyama Naoya. He is currently working on a book featuring architects including Itō Tōyō and Atelier Bow-Wow (Cornell Architecture Press, forthcoming).

Miwako Tezuka is Assistant Curator at Asia Society, New York. She received her PhD from Columbia University with her dissertation on avant-garde art in 1950s Japan. At Asia Society, she curated *Projected Realities: Video Art from East Asia* (2006), *Condensation: Five Video Works by Chen Chieh-jen*, and *Free Fish: The Art of Yūken Teruya* (2007). Her publications include "Synergy: Takiguchi Shuzo and Experimental Workshop" in *Drifting Objects of Dreams: The Collection of Shūzō Takiguchi* (Setagaya Art Museum, 2005) and "I See Future in Fast Forward: 2006 Asian Contemporary Art Week," *Orientations* (September 2006). She is a co-founder of PoNJA-GenKon.

Shinya Watanabe is an independent curator. He acquired a MA at New York University and has traveled to 34 countries. His main focus has been the relationship of art and nation-states. He has curated *Another Expo—Beyond the Nation-State* (Gallery Level 1, Gallery Soap, Former 130 Bank Gallery, Kitakyūshū, Japan, June 2005; White Box, New York, August 2005) and *Action Painting Battle! Ushio Shinohara vs. Ryōga Katsuma* (Ethan Cohen Fine Arts; co-curated with Ethan Cohen, 2006). He is a so a chair of *Atomic Sunshine: Article 9 and Japan* Exhibition Committee.

Midori Yoshimoto is assistant professor of art history and gallery director at New Jersey City University. Having received her PhD from Rutgers University (2002), she specializes in Japanese avant-garde art of the 1960s. Her publications include: contributions to *YES YOKO ONO* (Japan Society, 2000) and *Japanese Women Artists in Avant-Garde Movements, 1950–1975* (Tochigi Prefectural Museum of Art, 2005); and *Into Performance: Japanese Women Artists in New York* (Rutgers University Press, 2005). Her curated exhibitions include *Do-It-Yourself Fluxus* (Art Interactive, 2003). Currently, she is the Chair of the Committee of Women in the Arts of the College Art Association.

JAPAN SOCIETY

INDEX

Pages on which illustrations and their captions appear are given in bold.